Governance in Sport

Analysis and Application

Bonnie Tiell, EdD
Tiffin University

Editor

Kerri Cebula, JD
Kutztown University of Pennsylvania

HUMAN KINETICS

Library of Congress Cataloging-in-Publication Data

Names: Tiell, Bonnie, editor. | Cebula, Kerri, 1978- author.
Title: Governance in sport : analysis and application / Bonnie Tiell, Editor, Kerri
  Cebula, Author.
Description: Champaign, IL : Human Kinetics, [2021] | Includes
  bibliographical references and index.
Identifiers: LCCN 2019041556 (print) | LCCN 2019041557 (ebook) | ISBN
  9781492589471 (paperback) | ISBN 9781492589495 (epub) | ISBN
  9781492589488 (pdf)
Subjects: LCSH: Sports administration. | Sports and state.
Classification: LCC GV713 .G597 2021 (print) | LCC GV713 (ebook) | DDC
  796.06/9--dc23
LC record available at https://lccn.loc.gov/2019041556
LC ebook record available at https://lccn.loc.gov/2019041557

ISBN: 978-1-4925-8947-1 (print)

The web addresses cited in this text were current as of September 2019, unless otherwise noted.

Acquisitions Editor: Andrew L. Tyler; **Developmental Editor:** Jacqueline Eaton Blakley; **Managing Editors:** Hannah Werner and Anne E. Mrozek; **Copyeditor:** Kevin Campbell; **Indexer:** Nancy Ball; **Permissions Manager:** Dalene Reeder; **Graphic Designers:** Dawn Sills and Joe Buck; **Cover Designer:** Keri Evans; **Cover Design Specialist:** Susan Rothermel Allen; **Photograph (cover):** Christof Stache/AFP via Getty Images; **Photographs (interior):** © Human Kinetics, unless otherwise noted; **Photo Asset Manager:** Laura Fitch; **Photo Production Manager:** Jason Allen; **Senior Art Manager:** Kelly Hendren; **Illustrations:** © Human Kinetics, unless otherwise noted; **Printer:** Sheridan Books

Printed in the United States of America   10 9 8 7 6 5 4 3 2 1

The paper in this book is certified under a sustainable forestry program.

Human Kinetics
1607 N. Market St.
Champaign, IL 61820
Website: www.HumanKinetics.com

In the United States, email info@hkusa.com or call 800-747-4457.
In Canada, email info@hkcanada.com.
In the United Kingdom/Europe, email hk@hkeurope.com.

For information about Human Kinetics' coverage in other areas of the world,
please visit our website: **www.HumanKinetics.com**

E7773

Tell us what you think!
Human Kinetics would love to hear what we
can do to improve the customer experience.
Use this QR code to take our brief survey.

This book is dedicated to my family who supports my passion to read, write, and travel the world for the sake of global sport education. It is for my husband, Greg Tiell, who is my rock and my soul and for our loving daughters, Kimberly and Katie.
—Bonnie Tiell

Contents

Preface

Sport governance, at its simplest, is *power* and *decision making*. Identifying who has the power, and what decisions are being made by those with the power and *why*, is the best way to understand a sport organization's goals, purpose, and structure. Ineffective governance and lackluster leadership in sport organizations have encouraged pervasive corruption in the industry, necessitating an examination of proactive and reactive measures to establish or restore integrity and ethical behavior.

Many textbooks fail to address governance in a way that is interesting and thought-provoking. This textbook delivers by describing a number of recent corruption cases in sport in a way that keeps readers engaged. With rich examples that span the globe, readers will develop an acute sense of how governance works in sport organizations in the United States and around the world.

PURPOSE AND BENEFITS

A critical analysis of governance structures and processes is valuable to every level of sport, be it an international mega-event such as the Olympic Games or a small parks and recreation youth league. This book challenges upperclassmen and graduate students in sport management and related disciplines to critically examine sport governance from three broad perspectives: (1) a legal and managerial overview of practices, processes, and policies in sport organizations; (2) a geographical framework of the regulatory agencies governing local, national, regional (continental), and international sports; and (3) an applied overview of governance and authority in selected sectors of the industry.

Navigating governance in sports organizations is a complex task, but the straightforward organizational style of this text helps to simplify the complexities. Guidelines are discussed for ensuring that sport organizations practice principles of good governance and leaders exercise ethical decision making. The text also addresses the nuances of performance assessment for a sport board, including fiduciary responsibilities, accountability, and stakeholder relationships. Throughout, many examples illustrate conduct by sport leaders that might fall short of the threshold of moral and legal compliance. For example, readers are challenged to critically examine the rationale of the United States Olympic Committee (USOC) in revoking its decision to decertify USA Gymnastics in the wake of the Larry Nassar sexual abuse scandal. Readers are also challenged to address the relationship of leadership and organizational culture by examining the details of the FBI's probe into widespread bribery and fraud among NCAA men's basketball programs as well as athletic departments involved in the Varsity Blues admissions scandal.

On an international level, readers will explore the ethical and legal challenges of gender verification testing by examining the International Association of Athletics Federations' newest eligibility requirements, which mandate that female mid-distance runners with high levels of testosterone use hormonal injections to lower their levels prior to competition. Another global challenge readers will explore is considering the road map for boxing in the Olympics following the International Olympic Committee's decision to suspend the sport's international federation due to an abundance of ethical conduct violations, just 14 months prior to Tokyo 2020.

The benefit of exploring sport governance from both an analytical and applied perspective is that it gives context to how authority, policies, rules, and regulations influence decisions. The benefit for students who study each chapter and engage in the learning activities is a significantly greater appreciation for the nuances that accompany sport governance and authority.

SCOPE AND STRUCTURE

The textbook is divided into three parts that offer a broad-based view of sport governance. The first section provides a foundation to sport governance; the second discusses regulatory agencies in sport according to local, state, national, regional (continental), and global geographical boundaries; and the third section applies governance to eight selected sectors of the industry.

Part I: Foundations of Governance and Authority

Part I begins with chapter 1, a legal primer to sport governance with a focus on basic legal principles, sources of law, and the application of alternative dispute resolution. Chapter 2 examines best practices in decision making, ethical behavior, and leadership to assist sport organizations in creating and sustaining a culture of good governance. For example, professionals must consider the environment in which sports operate when considering the nuances of top-down and bottom-up governance models that affect decision making. Finally, chapter 3 addresses roles and responsibilities in effective board governance and the processes for policy development.

Part II: Framework for Sport Governance

The three chapters in part II provide a geographical framework for examining sport regulatory agencies at the local, state, national, regional (continental), and international levels. In addition to examining various governance challenges and issues, the chapters explore the structures and processes of for-profit, nonprofit, and quasi-public sport organizations at each level. Chapters 4 and 5 include an analysis of the role of municipal, state, and national government in the operation and financing of sport for both the mass public and the elite-athlete community (e.g., Olympic qualifiers). Chapter 6 provides an examination of the roles and processes of the governing entities encompassing the Olympic movement as well as the entities governing international events for non-Olympic sports.

Part III: Governance and Authority in Sport Industry Sectors

The eight chapters in part III apply governance to different sectors of the sport industry including:

- Professional sports
- Amateur sports
- Sport media
- Sporting goods and sport licensing
- Fitness, wellness, and health
- Sport marketing
- Sport wagering
- Esports

Even though the elements or principles of good governance systems are relatively universal, the eclectic nature of the sports industry necessitates an applied understanding of how governance works best in different sectors. Part I's foundational information and part II's framework provide the context for examining governance and authority as they apply to each sport sector featured in the third section.

Part III truly puts governance into action. Readers will explore the recent state-by-state debate of legalizing sport wagering and its impact on professional and college athletics. Readers will also examine the lack of true governance in the esports industry, which is often described as having a Wild West atmosphere with its unprecedented global economic growth. Each chapter provides an interesting and applied perspective on authority, power, decision making, regulations, legal compliance, and ethical behavior in different sectors of the sports industry.

CHAPTER FEATURES

Each chapter begins with learning outcomes and a section called Lead-Off that introduces key chapter concepts. Each chapter ends with a section called Recap that reinforces those key chapter concepts. Features within each chapter include key terms (defined in the glossary at the end of the book), sidebars (Governance in Action) that explore real-world examples of conflicts and conundrums reflecting questions of sport governance, critical thinking questions, and applied activities.

The applied activities are interactive assignments that challenge students' resourcefulness and creativity while reinforcing important governance concepts applied to the sport industry. For example, students may be instructed to design a sport media partnership for a professional league or to outline the blueprint for the governance structure and constitutional elements of a new international organization for esports. Other activities include the creation of a chart to distinguish government funding for municipal recreation available to the masses within three international countries and to research the structure of volunteer recruitment campaigns for multisport competitions.

The Governance in Action sidebars profile a story, case, or example of a governance topic that aligns with the corresponding chapter. For example, the chapter applying governance and authority to professional sports includes one Governance in Action sidebar profiling the disciplinary reign of Roger Goodell, commissioner of the National Football League (NFL), and a second sidebar analyzes the impact of a public battle between two sanctioning bodies in motorsports. Another sidebar in the sport marketing chapter critiques the ethical and legal challenges of advertising campaigns for Beats and Bose headphones in the Olympics, Super Bowl, and other sport events.

SUPPLEMENTARY MATERIALS

Instructor resources included with this text include the following:

◆ An instructor guide with sample syllabus, suggested answers to the activities, and other aids for instruction

◆ A presentation package that guides lectures on each chapter, including the most important figures and tables from the text

◆ A test package covering all the most important content and objectives from each chapter

◆ A multiple-choice quiz for each chapter

For students, purchase of the textbook includes access to an online web resource with case studies that address a wide variety of sport governance topics. These topics range from the reaction of the NFL players' union to a proposed league-wide conduct policy during the national anthem to the influences on sport performance and sport systems in Romania before and after the fall of the communist regime. One of the most fascinating cases provides an exposé of ex-Auburn University assistant basketball coach Chuck Person, who pleaded guilty to conspiracy charges involving illegal payments to influence recruiting decisions. Another case examines the collaboration of Thai government and nongovernment agencies in overcoming challenges to market the World Weightlifting Championships in a city renowned for sex tourism and after eight national athletes were banned by the international federation for using illegal substances. Yet another international case examines the fallout of politically motivated actions profiled in the suspension of a decorated Iranian freestyle wrestler who deliberately lost a match at the U23 World Championships to avoid facing an Israeli wrestler. Students explore these cases in depth and have the opportunity to demonstrate learning through questions for understanding, reflection, and discussion.

Acknowledgments

This book could not have been written without the assistance of countless individuals. In addition to the two-dozen contributing authors of various chapters and case studies, we are deeply appreciative of the individuals who gathered research, reviewed material, created tables, and prepared ancillary items, including Dean "The Sportsman" Greenaway and Tiffin University students Keenan Tarpley, Joshua Jaster, and Austin Usher. We are also grateful to the editorial staff at Human Kinetics for their patience and expert guidance in the publishing process.

Foundations of Governance and Authority

chapter 1

Legal Primer to Governance

Kelley Walton

LEAD-OFF

Who determines whether a college athlete is an amateur or a professional and which people are bound by that decision? Who determines whether a National Basketball Association (NBA) team owner is entitled to keep that ownership and what gives a governing body the authority to make that decision? Who decides whether a player is eligible to compete in the Olympics? Who decides if a player is unable to compete in the Olympics because of contractual obligations?

These types of decisions in the sports industry are typically made by a **governing body**. Governing bodies are the authoritative units responsible for developing, implementing, and enforcing rules for an organization, event, or agency. Governing bodies regularly face legal and ethical challenges in their decision making.

Understanding the formation and structure of governing bodies is important in the field of sport management. Sport managers must also be familiar with the legal system and legal foundations that affect the operation of sport governing bodies. A legal primer to governance in sport provides foundational information for industry practitioners.

This chapter focuses on the legal foundation that governing bodies rely on for their authority to act as a supreme decision maker. The chapter also addresses the legal basics sport managers should be familiar with as a professional. Finally, this chapter describes the alternative dispute resolution measures used throughout sectors of the sport industry to avoid litigation.

Learning Outcomes

- Explain the process by which a sport governing body receives its authority.
- Describe, in general, the structure of sport governing bodies.
- Explain the general function of the United States legal system.
- Define precedent and its importance in the legal system.

AUTHORITY AND GOVERNANCE

Authority is the power to give orders, make decisions, and enforce compliance. A coach or manager is in an authoritative role with the positional power to determine playing time for athletes. However, authority for managing the team may be a function of an entity at a higher level, such as an owner, an athletic director, or a league commissioner. The authority of most governing bodies is derived from legal documents such as a constitution or bylaws.

On occasion, there may be a dispute over which authority or governing body should enforce decisions. For example, in contradiction to the bylaws of the National Collegiate Athletic Association (NCAA), the California legislature passed legislation to permit college student-athletes in the state to receive compensation in relation to their name, image, or likeness and still retain their eligibility. Such disputes are typically settled by referring to a governing body's bylaws or contract, but occasionally, mediation or legal recourse is necessary. Governance in Action 1.1 explains the conflicting authoritative roles of governing bodies that determined whether players in the National Hockey League (NHL) could be excluded from participating in the Olympic Games over the last century.

Governance entails responsibility, rules and policies, communication, transparency, and decision making (Lam, 2014, p. 20). The entities described in Governance in Action 1.1 (NHL, IOC, IIHF, USA Hockey) all have governance or oversight roles in ice hockey.

Sport governance addresses the means by which authority and oversight are managed within a sport enterprise. Often, governance is the responsibility of an elected or appointed official or a group of executives that is tasked with monitoring performance and ensuring that all activities meet compliance standards under the scope of the legal authority for conducting business. Governance may be relegated to a commissioner who serves as the supreme authority for a sport league (e.g., National Football League or Major League Soccer),

or it may be the responsibility of an oversight body such as the board of trustees for the Women's Sports Foundation or the president of an international sport federation.

Governance considers the **stakeholders** of an organization, which includes everyone with a vested interest. In the sports industry, stakeholders represent a wide spectrum of interested parties, including players, coaches, franchise executives, officials, local, national, and international organizations, spectators, the media, commercial (sponsors) and noncommercial interests, and educational and training bodies (Lam, 2014).

Authority is granted to a governing board or commissioner through official documents that outline the scope of power within an organization or enterprise. These documents are generally referred to as constitutions and bylaws.

Constitutions and Bylaws

An organization's **constitution** serves as a foundational document that sets forth the powers and limitations of a governing body and provides important operating principles for the governing body to follow. From recreational leagues to professional leagues to municipal sport commissions to national or international governing bodies for sport, constitutions are commonly created to identify the formal relationships within an organization. The constitution often states the organization's values and core principles.

Bylaws are the organization's written rules for conduct. These rules are more specific and detailed than an organization's constitution. Bylaws may also be called ordinances, statutes, or regulations.

An organization's rights and powers to govern a certain body of persons is derived from the constitution. The constitution determines the fundamental operational aspects of an organization. Its provisions will not be frequently changed over time. For example, Article II of the National Football League's constitution and bylaws (2006, rev) states that the purpose of the NFL is to "promote and foster the primary business of League members, each member being an owner of a professional

GOVERNANCE IN ACTION 1.1

The NHL and Olympic Competition: Examining Governing Authority for Participation

The National Hockey League (NHL) is the governing body for professional hockey players competing on 31 teams in the United States and Canada. Ice hockey has been a part of the Olympics for almost a century since being introduced at the 1924 Games in Paris, France (National Hockey League, 2014). The inclusion and exclusion of NHL players over the years provides insight into the power and presence of competing governing authorities associated with a sport, including the International Olympic Committee (IOC).

Eligibility to compete in the Olympic Games was once reserved purely for amateurs. Rule 26 of the Olympic Charter stated that "professional athletes, semi-professional athletes, and so-called non-amateurs" were not eligible for competition (International Olympic Committee, 1985, p. 21). The International Olympic Committee (1998) reversed its stance on amateurism in 1985 and voted to allow professional athletes (under the age of 23) to compete in the 1988 Olympic Games in ice hockey, tennis, and soccer. While NHL players would have been allowed to compete under the revised IOC rules with the support of the International Ice Hockey Federation (IIHF), the league prevented their participation since the dates conflicted with regular season games (Thomas, 1985).

In 1991, the IOC took extra steps to lift the ban on all professional athletes in the Olympics (International Olympic Committee, 1991). The IIHF, USA Hockey, and other national hockey federations would have gladly placed NHL players on their rosters in 1992 and 1994, but the NHL continued to prohibit participation primarily due to overlapping dates with regular season games.

The NHL agreed to take a 16-day break in the middle of the 1995 season to permit 121 NHL players to represent their respective countries at the 1998 Winter Olympics in Nagano, Japan (Elliott, 1995). Thereafter, NHL players represented their national teams in the 2002, 2006, 2010, and 2014 Winter Olympics ("NHL Players," 2014).

In 2017, however, the NHL reversed its stance (again) and decided not to permit players to participate in the 2018 Winter Olympics in PyeongChang, South Korea, with commissioner Gary Bettman indicating that participation in the 2022 Olympics was unlikely as well (Schad, 2018). Participation would have created a 17-day disruption to the 2018 regular schedule ("USOC, USA Hockey Statements," 2017; Allen, 2018). In addition to the schedule interruption, owners were concerned about medical issues since four players had suffered season-ending injuries in the 2014 Sochi Olympics. Another factor affecting the leagues' decision was the IOC's announcement that travel expenses, insurance, and medical costs for players would no longer be financed (Rosen, 2017). Even though the International Ice Hockey Federation (IIHF) informed the NHL that it would finance the $20 million cost for insurance, the league stood firm in exercising its authority over contracted players, and the 2018 Olympics commenced without NHL professional players.

This case demonstrates that powerful national sport governing bodies are merely bystanders in the fight between the IIHF and the NHL. Clearly, authority over players lies in the hands of the league.

football club located in the United States." Article II also establishes that the league is to be operated as a nonprofit. Article III states that the league shall be limited to 32 teams and that the admission of any new club would require the affirmative vote of three-fourths of the existing member clubs. Article III also provides procedures for the admission of any new member club, transfer of a club's membership, and termination of membership. These procedures provide clear guidance about the fun-

damental operations of initiating, retaining, and terminating membership as a club in the National Football League.

Bylaws are based on an organization's constitution and include more detailed guidelines for how an organization will operate. Bylaws are written in a manner that provides for changes to be made as needed. For example, the NFL bylaws would need to be revised if the league were to add a franchise in the United Kingdom or Canada since currently,

Article II restricts teams to the United States. A constitution, on the other hand, states the fundamental purpose and structure of an organization, which should not change as often. It includes information such as term limits for key positions in the organization.

Constitutions and bylaws may be separate documents, or an organization may choose, like the NFL, to create one document that includes both. Besides the organization's purpose, constitutions and bylaws provide operational guidance for important functions such as membership, commissioner selection and oversight, broadcasting and television rights, eligibility rules, and rules involving player contracts. The content in a sport governing body's operational documents might include such topics as the following:

♦ Name
♦ Purpose and objectives
♦ Terms of membership
♦ Territory definitions and description of rights
♦ Committees, officers, and leadership structure
♦ Meetings
♦ Member conduct
♦ Broadcasting
♦ Rules of play
♦ Eligibility and limitations for players
♦ Schedule
♦ Contracts
♦ Waivers
♦ Season, preseason, and postseason play
♦ Notices
♦ Amendments and bylaws
♦ Resolutions

Constitutions provide for a variety of operational guidelines, such as qualifications for membership in an organization, qualifications for participation in an organization, qualifications to participate in events, rights of participants, rights of members, ownership rights and processes, and termination of ownership rights. It is because of these rules, processes, and regulations that governing bodies have the power to act.

Often constitutions set forth the purpose of an organization. For example, the National Collegiate Athletic Association (NCAA) (2009) states first in its list of purposes, "to initiate, stimulate and improve intercollegiate athletics programs for student-athletes and to promote and develop educational leadership, physical fitness, athletics excel-

lence and athletics participation as a recreational pursuit." The constitution also includes eight other purposes, notably "to uphold the principle of institutional control of, and responsibility for, all intercollegiate sports . . ." The NCAA constitution and bylaws include the following list to outline the association's primary purposes:

1. Establishing standards of scholarship
2. Promoting sportsmanship and amateurism
3. Creating rules of play
4. Preserving records
5. Supervising conduct and eligibility
6. Cooperating with other associations in promoting and conducting national and international athletic events
7. Legislating the administration of intercollegiate athletics
8. Establishing high standards for members to follow

Governance Structure

In order to operate, a sport governing body will define its governance structure, which can be based on either a top-down or a bottom-up leadership model. Top-down organizations are typically corporate business entities with chief executive officers (CEOs) and a leadership team that make decisions. Bottom-up models, on the other hand, may still include a CEO, but they operate through members or associates who have an influence on the strategic direction of the organization and legislate rules and regulations. Figure 1.1 outlines the organizational structure of the headquarters of the National Association of Collegiate Directors of Athletics (NACDA), which is a membership-led organization.

Typically, the constitution of an organization will establish the manner in which the functions and management of the governing body will be carried out. The operating structure varies based on the type of entity creating the structure. It may include a variety of boards with a specified hierarchy to provide guidance and leadership to a large membership, or it may include a single board that has sole authority over operating and management decisions. There is no required structure, but many sport governing bodies, such as a national sport federation or a national Olympic committee (NOC), will have a board of directors, an executive board of directors, a board of governors, or a similar type of unit with authority to oversee the day-to-day operations of the organization.

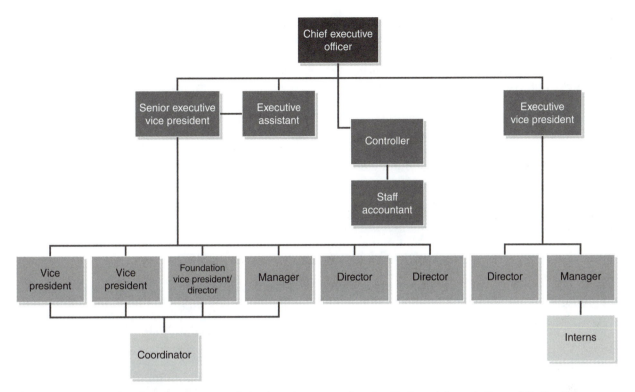

Figure 1.1 Organizational structure of the headquarters for the National Association of Collegiate Directors of Athletics (NACDA) in 2019.

The NCAA has over 1,100 member institutions and is a member-led organization. The NCAA Board of Governors is its highest governing body and is composed of presidents and chancellors from each division. The NCAA also has a board of directors composed of school presidents at each division level (Division I, Division II, Division III). Making a serious commitment to diversity, the NCAA includes a gender and diversity requirement in its constitution. In 2008, the NCAA implemented the policy that the board of directors must include at least one person who is an ethnic minority and at least one person of each gender. The following section from the NCAA (2009) bylaws addresses the diversity requirements for its Leadership Council, Legislative Council, and Championships Cabinet and for the combined membership of the rest of its cabinets. These constitutional requirements set forth clear operating procedures and expectations for the NCAA and member institutions.

> The board of directors membership shall include at least one person who is an ethnic minority and at least one person of each gender, and a single member shall not be considered to meet both minimums. The combined membership of the Leadership Council, Legislative Council and Cham-

pionships/Sports Management Cabinet shall include representatives who comprise at least 20 percent of persons who are ethnic minorities and at least 35 percent of persons of each gender. The combined membership of the Academics Cabinet, Administration Cabinet, Agents and Amateurism Cabinet, Awards, Benefits, Expenses and Financial Aid Cabinet, and Recruiting and Athletics Personnel Issues Cabinet shall include representatives that comprise at least 20 percent of persons who are ethnic minorities and at least 35 percent of persons of each gender (Adopted: 11/1/07, effective: 8/1/08).

Governance structures vary. Many entities have singular authority, such as the NCAA over its member institutions or Major League Soccer (MLS) over its member clubs. However, in other cases there is shared authority over international sport competitions and the athletes who compete across borders. Collaborative leadership is manifested by organizations that create partnerships for the purpose of achieving a primary objective. This model provides a voice for each of the stakeholders in the governance system, even in areas where jurisdiction is clearly articulated. At times, decisions may be changed if better ideas or processes appear that are acceptable to those in authority over a particular area.

Shared governance is an elusive concept to implement, but it can be beneficial when regulatory agencies align their strategic goals or directions. The constitution for the Commonwealth Games Federation (2018, p. 35), for example, clearly identifies the joint responsibility of an organizing committee, host Commonwealth Games associa-

tions (CGA), host governments, and host cities to organize and finance the Games.

When multiple agencies work in concert to share governance of an event or contest such as the World Cup, Commonwealth Games, or Wimbledon Championships (see Governance in Action 1.2), it is important to delineate the specific authority of each entity. Shared governance for a multisport international event such as the Commonwealth Games is facilitated by guidelines that clarify the

GOVERNANCE IN ACTION 1.2

Player Attire at Wimbledon

International federations and various players' associations typically work in concert to address common concerns, such as the safety of competitors or the integrity of the game. Specific measures to address corruption (e.g., match fixing) and player welfare (e.g., on-site medical examinations) are outlined in the bylaws of the Association of Tennis Professionals (ATP) Tour (2018), the governing agency for male players competing in over 60 sanctioned tournaments around the world, and the International Tennis Federation (2018), the agency governing the actual sport. These rules and regulations are important; however, the prevailing authority may be another entity who shares a governance role for an international event.

Chaz Niell/Icon Sportswire

Wimbledon rules penalize players if any of their attire, including undergarments, is not white.

Consider the dress code for players competing in sanctioned international tournaments. The regulations for the ATP include pages of information governing restrictions on styles, logo placements, and designs on attire worn during competition as well as punishment for code violations. The initial rule indicates that "clean and customarily acceptable tennis attire as approved by ATP shall be worn" (Association of Tennis Professionals, 2018, p. 170). The rules also mandate that "no hat or headband, with or without logos, may be worn during the awards ceremony" (Association of Tennis Professionals, 2018, p. 172).

Despite the restrictive guidelines for player attire, the presiding agency for the dress code at Wimbledon, for example, is the All England Lawn Tennis & Croquet Club (AELTC). On championship courts, the club requires all-white attire, including shoes, hats, and visible undergarments (Wimbledon.com, 2018). A breach of the club's dress code was committed by Venus Williams, who changed clothing after a rain delay in a first-round Wimbledon match and had bright pink bra straps partially exposed during play (Sawer and Subar, 2017). Numerous code violations, primarily for visible nonwhite undergarments, have been reported for other lesser-known players, but it is not apparent if penalties have progressed beyond a mandatory apparel change.

Clearly in the case of Wimbledon, the presiding entity over the color of attire is the organization hosting the event, but guidelines governing logos and other apparel issues are the purvey of the players' association for selected tournaments. In that respect, the AELTC and ATP share governance over player attire.

role and authority of each agency for decisions about budget allocations, operations, and various procedures. Games manuals typically are drafted to delineate responsibilities and processes.

In a shared governance system for an international sporting event, a chart may also be drafted to clarify the role of each participating agency as a body that can (1) provide recommendations, (2) engage in consultation, (3) make a final decision, or (4) serve as an appellate organization for a specific area, such as athlete eligibility, volunteer procurement, athlete behavior, or budget approval. Constitutions, bylaws, and event guidelines provide the scope of authority for organizations with oversight responsibilities.

BASIC LEGAL PRINCIPLES

In addition to understanding the legal framework that provides the basis for the authority of a sport governing body, it is also important to understand the legal system and legal foundations that may affect the operation of the governing body. **Basic legal principles** address the means by which laws are made, implemented, and enforced. They also address the area of jurisdiction for the application of laws and ordinances.

Legal Court System in the United States

Courts are the ultimate authority over legal disputes. In the United States, municipal, state, and federal legislatures create laws, and the judicial branch is the ultimate authority for the interpretation of those laws. Courts have **jurisdiction**, which is the authority to hear a case, based on location and subject matter. Figure 1.2 provides an overview of the structure of the court system in the United States from the supreme courts down to state courts.

Supreme Courts

In the United States, the United States Supreme Court is the highest court. The U.S. Supreme Court recently asserted its authority to overturn a federal statute (the 1992 Professional and Amateur Sports Act) that prohibited individual states from legalizing sports betting (Paul et al., 2018). Despite a legal challenge by the National Football League (NFL), National Hockey League (NHL), Major League Baseball (MLB), National Basketball Association (NBA), and the NCAA, the Supreme Court agreed with the state of New Jersey in its ruling that the Professional and Amateur Sports Act was

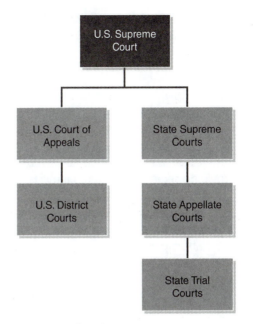

Figure 1.2 U.S. legal system.

unconstitutional (Rodenberg, 2018). Essentially, the Supreme Court ruled that the power to legalize sports betting resides with each individual state, and the federal court system does not have jurisdiction to preempt state legislatures.

The Supreme Court settled a copyright infringement case in 2017 between Varsity Brands and Star Athletica involving cheerleading uniform designs (Mejia, 2017). Conversely, the Supreme Court also exercised its right to decline an appellate hearing in two iconic sport cases in the 21st century, including NFL concussion litigation by retired players and the Ed O'Bannon versus NCAA case over the use of student-athlete images. The refusal to accept a case is an expression of the court's position on appropriate jurisdictions for rendering legal decisions.

Federal Courts

The district courts are the general federal trial courts in the United States. District courts generally have jurisdiction over court cases involving federal laws. Some of the exceptions—lawsuits not related to federal law—include those with parties from different states, those that involve more than $75,000, or those in which there is a dispute as to which state law applies. If a case involves federal law, jurisdiction lies in federal court, such as in the case of parents who brought litigation against a school district in Pennsylvania for prohibiting females from participating on all-male wrestling teams in violation of the Equal Protection Clause of the 14th Amendment (Marquette University Law School, 2014). Governance in Action 1.3 describes

GOVERNANCE IN ACTION 1.3

Varsity Blues and NCAA Basketball Corruption Cases

Two high-profile federal court cases in 2019 involved bribery and corruption tied to intercollegiate athletic programs at NCAA Division I institutions. The first involved the Federal Bureau of Investigation (FBI) announcing a widespread NCAA basketball corruption scandal in 2017 in which coaches, Adidas executives, and aspiring financial advisors were indicted for bribery and fraud. In March 2019, a federal court in New York sentenced two former Adidas representatives and an aspiring sport agent for providing secret payments to families of top athletic prospects in exchange for considering enrolling in a school sponsored by the sportswear manufacturing company (Fischer & Wertheim, 2019; O'Brien, 2019). Several former assistant coaches at prominent NCAA athletic institutions (e.g., University of Arizona and Oklahoma State University) pled guilty to accepting bribes to steer prospects to financial advisers. Shortly after the FBI announcement in 2017, Rick Pitino, former University of Louisville head basketball coach, along with the university's athletic director, were effectively fired for their indirect association with corruption in the program (Schnell, 2017).

Also in 2019, the U.S. Attorney's Office for the District of Massachusetts indicted over 50 individuals, including nine college athletic coaches, for involvement in a $25 million college admissions cheating scam that the FBI dubbed "Varsity Blues." A network of wealthy parents (including several celebrities) paid Rick Singer, owner of Edge College & Career Network, to enhance their children's prospects of acceptance into elite colleges, including Stanford, Yale, Wake Forest University, University of Southern California (USC), University of California–Los Angeles (UCLA), University of Texas, and Georgetown University (Winter et al., 2019). The Yale University case, for example, involved the former women's soccer coach accepting a $400,000 bribe from Singer to recruit an applicant who never played competitively (Steinbach, 2019).

Federal indictments were levied against an athletic administrator and coaches in sailing, crew, soccer, tennis, basketball, and water polo who accepted payments to falsify documents or report roster spots for nonathletes (Cooper, 2019). Singer was charged with racketeering conspiracy, money laundering conspiracy, conspiracy to defraud the United States justice system, and obstruction of justice (Winter et al., 2019).

the basketball corruption case and the Varsity Blues admissions scandal that involved the federal court system handing out indictments in 2019.

State Courts

If a case involves state law, jurisdiction lies in state court. For example, a fan sued the MLB Kansas City Royals in the Supreme Court of Missouri when he was hit in the eye by a hot dog tossed by the team's mascot. Parents sued a local family YMCA for negligence in the state of Georgia when their son collapsed and died after working out on a treadmill (Marquette University Law School, 2014). A recent case that will be settled by a state court of New York if not resolved at a lower level is one involving the use of the Tanner scale to determine if an individual has the physical maturity to play up a level. Four lacrosse players are protesting the New York State Education Department's athletic placement process for scholastic sports after being denied an opportunity to try out for a junior varsity lacrosse team (Doran, 2019). These cases did not involve a federal law or a question of state jurisdiction, so the appropriate state court presided over judgments.

Criminal Versus Civil Law

Courts and laws are further separated by the type of law, criminal or civil. Criminal laws are statutes enacted by municipal, state, or federal legislatures and are enforced by the government. If a person is accused of a crime, the police, prosecutors, and others in the criminal justice system adjudicate the offense. The FBI criminal investigation in college basketball and the Varsity Blues admissions scandal described in Governance in Action 1.3 were both adjudicated in criminal court.

In a civil case, the law is not enforced by the government, but a lawsuit must be brought by one party (**plaintiff**) against another party (**defen-**

dant) describing the legal basis for a claim. The plaintiff must file a legal complaint against a defendant alleging that the defendant has wronged the plaintiff in some way that is supported by the law. An example of a civil lawsuit in sports is that of professional golfer Vijay Singh, who filed a motion in the New York Supreme Court against the Professional Golfers Association Tour (PGA Tour) that was eventually settled out of court in 2019. Singh alleged that the PGA Tour mishandled doping sanctions related to the use of deer antler spray that contained a banned substance (Zoeller, 2016).

ALTERNATIVE DISPUTE RESOLUTION

There are methods of adjudicating a dispute other than filing a lawsuit. This system is referred to as **alternative dispute resolution** (ADR). Mediation and arbitration are the two alternative dispute resolution methods.

Mediation

Mediation can vary in formality depending on the type of dispute. In this situation, both parties hire a mediator who helps the parties to agree on a decision. The mediator does not make any decisions; instead, the mediator serves as a facilitator between two disputing parties to help them to work out a solution together. Therefore, mediation is voluntary, nonbinding, and without prejudice.

Mediation may be the preferred method for contract resolution. In 2012, the NFL and the NFL Players Association used the Federal Mediation and Conciliation Services (FMCS) on three occasions to try to resolve issues in the league's collective bargaining agreement (Bucher, 2011). More recently, FMCS assisted in settling a dispute and negotiating terms of the collective bargaining agreement between Major League Soccer (MLS) and the MLS Players Association (Cohen, 2015).

Mediation is also used for a variety of other situations in which there is a desire to avoid legal action. For example, mediation was used to settle a dispute between top women's soccer players and the Canadian Soccer Association over artificial turf fields for the 2015 World Cup and to resolve issues between the NCAA Big 12 and the Western Athletic Conference over departing member institutions (Sandu, 2015, p. 61).

Mediation might be preferred because it is often relatively quick and inexpensive for the parties involved, and it can ensure confidentiality if either side wishes it. For mediation to succeed, each side must be motivated to negotiate and commit to an agreement.

Arbitration

Arbitration is a form of alternative dispute resolution in which parties hire an arbitrator to hear both sides of a dispute and render a judgment. Often in employment contracts or player contracts, there will be a clause that states that any dispute that arises between the parties will be adjudicated via arbitration. For example, the NBA Uniform Player Contract states that in the event of a dispute, the dispute will be resolved in accordance with the grievance and arbitration procedure set forth in the collective bargaining agreement (CBA). The CBA then states that the grievance arbitrator shall have exclusive jurisdiction to determine any and all disputes involving the contract or any dispute arising under the NBA's policy on domestic violence, sexual assault, and child abuse. This clause means that players who have a dispute based on the player contract must first go through the arbitration procedure set forth in the CBA. If they try to file a lawsuit, the NBA will provide the court with the player contract and collective bargaining agreement, which state that both parties agreed to handle all disputes via arbitration.

Arbitration is often used when athletes appeal an antidoping rule violation, when there are disputes over the selection of national team members, and when athletes appeal disciplinary measures of a sport federation (Sandu, 2015). The NHL and MLB have implemented final-offer salary arbitration processes whereby a decision is rendered to choose between a salary proposed by the team and one proposed by the player or player representative, without any compromise. The NFL and NBA do not use salary arbitration.

A recent case arbitrated on an international level involved a dispute between Caster Semenya of South Africa and the International Association of Athletics Federation (IAAF) over gender eligibility regulations that dictate the level of testosterone permitted in female athletes who race between 400 meters and a mile. Semenya was diagnosed with hyperandrogenism, or elevated testosterone. She and other athletes in a similar condition would be required to undergo hormone treatments in order to compete against women in mid-distance races (Longman, 2018; Wharton, 2019). While the Court of Arbitration for Sport ruled to uphold the IAAF policies in May 2019, a month later the Federal Supreme Court of Switzerland provided temporary protection for Semenya and other female athletes to compete internationally without altering their testosterone levels while awaiting a decision from an appeal (Morgan, 2019).

Major League Baseball and the National Hockey League are the only two professional leagues in North America that use a salary arbitration system. In hockey, salary arbitration is reserved for restricted free agents, is decided by a single arbitrator, and commences during a short window following the Stanley Cup league championship. Only 30 players filed for salary arbitration in 2017, with decisions rendered within 48 hours (Fitzpatrick, 2018).

MLB, on the other hand, uses a three-person arbitration panel that rules for only one of the two proposed salaries. Players are eligible for salary arbitration between their third and sixth seasons, with a filing period of mid-January and decisions rendered in February. Between 1974 and 2015, 522 final-offer salary arbitration cases were settled, with owners winning 301 (57.66%) and players winning 221 (42.34%) (Brown, 2015).

SOURCES OF LAW

Sources of law refer to the unit or entity with the authority to establish and enforce a law. The sources of law addressed in this section as they apply in the sport industry are Constitutional law, statutory law, case law, and executive orders.

Constitutional Law

Just as a constitution serves as a foundational document that sets forth the powers and limita-tions of a sport governing body, a legislative body's constitution does the same. The United States Constitution establishes the basic rules and laws of the U.S. government. State constitutions establish the basic rules and laws of the states. The U.S. and state constitutions provide certain protections to individuals from certain government actions.

Constitutional protections exist only when government action is involved. Private compa-nies and private universities do not face the same constitutional restraints as governments, and therefore individuals do not have the same protec-tions against action from private entities. The U.S. Constitution is most often invoked in sport-related cases involving the First Amendment (religion, speech, assembly), Fourth Amendment (against unreasonable search and seizure), and Fourteenth Amendment (equal protection).

In 2017, an appeals court ruled that a Wash-ington school district was not required to allow a high school coach to pray on the field at the end of each game. The assistant football coach had been put on administrative leave after he refused to stop praying at the end of games. He filed suit, alleging his First Amendment rights of free speech and free expression had been violated. The court heavily relied upon *Santa Fe ISD v. Doe (2000)*, in which the court held that prayer at sports events sponsored by state actors violates the First Amendment. What is known as the Establishment Clause of the First Amendment states, "Congress shall make no law respecting an establishment of religion . . . ." The court made it clear that students may pray at any time they choose and on school property, but that

Damien Poullenot/WSL via Getty Images

The World Surf League, the international governing body for surfing, promotes equal rights under Con-stitutional law in providing equal purses (prize money) to male and female champions.

prayer by state actors such as public-school employees and athletic personnel is prohibited.

Another athletic case involving Constitutional law involved a high school senior who sued the Northern Kentucky Health Department for barring his participation in an interscholastic basketball game when he refused to receive a vaccination against chicken pox. The student's lawyer claimed a violation of the First Amendment, noting the state of Kentucky permits vaccination exemptions based on religious beliefs (Berg, 2019). Similarly, the New Jersey State Interscholastic Athletic Association (NJSIAA) and state Division of Civil Rights investigated an incident in which a wrestler chose to cut his hair on the orders of the referee to be able to compete, even though his lawyer claimed it "fell within regulations regarding length." The wrestler cited unfair treatment, and the referee filed a lawsuit against 12 defendants, including NJSIAA, Buena School district officials, and coaches, claiming defamation and emotional distress (Scott, 2019).

A more high-profile athletic-related case in 2019 involving Constitutional law was the suit against the United States Soccer Federation (USSF) filed in the U.S. District Court of Los Angeles by the U.S. women's soccer team. Noting disparities with their male counterparts, the U.S. women's national team argued gender and wage discrimination as defined by the Equal Pay Act of 1963 and Title VII of the Civil Rights Act of 1964 (Hobson, 2019). Interestingly, while the International Teqball Federation (FITEQ) and the World Surf League offer equal payouts for male and female singles and doubles champions, prize money for the FIFA World Cup was $400 million for the men's 2018 tournament in Russia and only $30 million for the 2019 women's tournament in France (Etchells, 2019; Owen, 2019).

Statutory Law

Statutes are written laws created by municipal, state, or federal legislatures. Statutes may be criminal or civil. A statute provides guidelines for behavior in certain situations and by certain persons. Statutes cover a broad range of activities and may be stated in the form of required conduct, prohibited conduct, or policy declarations.

An example of a statutory law is Title IX. **Title IX** is a federal law that was enacted in 1972. Title IX states that "[n]o person . . . shall on the basis of sex, be excluded from participation in, be denied the benefits of, or be subjected to discrimination under any education program or activity receiving Federal financial assistance" (Title IX, 1972). While Title IX does not specifically state that sport-related activities are covered, this law has afforded protection against discrimination in high school and college athletics in respect to participation, scholarship allocations, and programs offered. The law has also been relied on to provide protections against harassment and assault. However, Title IX applies only to educational institutions that receive federal financial assistance. The Title IX statute isn't a blanket law prohibiting conduct. It is specific to education programs and activities receiving federal assistance.

Another example of statutory law applicable in sports is the **Sherman Antitrust Act**. This statute prohibits behavior that would restrain competition. Section 1 of the Sherman Antitrust Act (1890) states that "every contract, combination in the form of trust or otherwise, or conspiracy, in restraint of trade or commerce among the several States, or with foreign nations, is declared to be illegal."

There is a longstanding belief that too much control by a few powerful entities leads to anticompetitive practices and price controls. These practices are seen as detrimental to the public because of their potential to depress economic growth. Therefore, **antitrust laws** such as the Sherman Antitrust Act have been enacted to prevent concentrations of economic power in the hands of a few, or **monopolies**.

Professional football players Tom Brady (New England Patriots), Peyton Manning (Indianapolis Colts/Denver Broncos), and Drew Brees (New Orleans Saints) orchestrated a class action lawsuit in 2011 against the NFL for antitrust violations during contentious negotiations over the league's CBA (Gorkin, 2014). The league responded with a four-month lockout that eventually resulted in a new collective bargaining agreement before the 2011 season. All professional sport leagues except Major League Baseball are subject to the Sherman Antitrust Act (Farzin, 2015, p. 80).

Case Law

Case law is created by courts when they interpret existing statutes as they apply to certain cases. Previous decisions of courts serve as **precedent** that provide guidance as to how the law has been interpreted in the past and the likelihood of the law being interpreted the same way in the future. The doctrine of **stare decisis** (stair-ee di-sahy-sis), which means to "stand by things decided," is an accepted principle in the practice of law that the decisions of previous courts in similar situations should be followed in future decisions.

In the case of *Cohen v. Brown University*, Brown University announced that it was facing budgetary constraints and would be eliminating four sports:

women's volleyball, women's gymnastics, men's golf, and men's water polo. Brown's student body was 52 percent male and 48 percent female, and its student-athlete population was 63 percent male and 37 percent female. A lawsuit was brought claiming discrimination under Title IX. The court relied upon the Title IX statute and the policy interpretation of the Office of Civil Rights that set forth a three-prong test for determining compliance with Title IX. An institution is in compliance with the three-part or three-prong test if it meets any one of the following parts of the test:

1. The number of male and female athletes is substantially proportionate to their respective enrollments.

2. The institution has a history and continuing practice of expanding participation opportunities responsive to the developing interests and abilities of the underrepresented sex.

3. The institution is fully and effectively accommodating the interests and abilities of the underrepresented sex.

A long procedural battle back and forth between trial courts and appellate courts took place in this case. The case took over five years to litigate from the 1991 announcement that Brown University's athletic department would be cutting sports to the decision by the First Circuit Court of Appeals in 1996. The final ruling by the appellate court was that Brown violated Title IX in the operation of its intercollegiate athletics program. By relying upon the three-prong test, *Cohen v. Brown* became precedent for future cases. The effect of *Cohen v. Brown* was that a set of standards for reviewing Title IX claims was now in place.

In the landmark case of *Flood v. Kuhn*, the antitrust exemption that had been granted to Major League Baseball was upheld by the U.S. Supreme Court. Curt Flood was a professional baseball player for the St. Louis Cardinals. Flood played 12 seasons for St. Louis, including playing in three World Series. In 1969, Flood was traded to the Philadelphia Phillies. Flood wanted to be a free agent but was denied the status due to the reserve clause that gave a team the rights to a player even after the player's contract expired. Flood filed an antitrust suit against Major League Baseball and its commissioner, Bowie K. Kuhn. The trial court granted MLB's motion for **summary judgment** (a request for the court to rule on the case without trial because there are no facts in dispute) based upon precedent from *Federal Baseball Club v. National League* and *Toolson v. New York Yankees*. The courts heavily relied upon precedent to uphold Major League Baseball's antitrust exemption, even noting that Congress could have remedied the exemption by creating statutory law if lawmakers believed that this exemption should not be given to Major League Baseball.

Executive Orders

An **executive order** is a directive issued by the president of the United States that manages the operations of the federal government. An executive order has the same effect as a law. Executive orders are not relied upon as heavily as statutes passed by Congress because they apply only to the operations of the federal government. For example, in 1967, President Lyndon Johnson created Executive Order 11375 to require all entities receiving federal contracts to end discrimination on the basis of sex in hiring and employment. The executive order helped support the movement for civil rights. However, Title VII of the Civil Rights Act of 1964 has much broader application because it applies to all employers with 15 or more employees and includes a wider range of prohibited conduct, prohibiting employers from discriminating against employees on the basis of sex, race, color, national origin, or religion. Title IX, which has had a significant impact on scholastic and higher education athletics, was said to stem from Executive Order 11375.

INTERNATIONAL PERSPECTIVE

Sport is a global phenomenon. It extends far beyond professional sports and college athletics. Internationally, the business of sport and the number of sport governing bodies is significant. Football (aka soccer in the United States), cycling, swimming, golf, tennis, weightlifting, hockey, equestrian, gymnastics, and figure skating are just a small sample of the vast number of sports that exist on the international stage.

The Court of Arbitration for Sport (CAS), located in Lausanne, Switzerland, is the international tribunal that has authority for resolving international legal conflicts in sport, such as the IAAF and Caster Semenya debate over testosterone limits in females. The CAS was created to settle sport-related disputes through arbitration or mediation (Reilly, 2012). The court hears a variety of types of cases ranging from a dispute between the International Olympic Committee and participants challenging a failed drug test, to a dispute between a football club and a football league regarding transfer players or between an individual athlete and the World Anti-Doping Agency.

Francois Nel/Getty Images

The case of Caster Semenya accusing the International Association of Athletics Federation of being unfair in its standards for testosterone levels in middle distance runners is an example of a recent international suit addressed by the Court of Arbitration for Sport and the Swiss Tribunal Federal Court.

The case of apparel guidelines for tennis players at Wimbledon is an example of a nonconsequential shared governance process since there are no conflicting policies. In the event of competing policies and ambiguity in the rank order of presiding authority, however, neutral entities are needed to help mediate or arbitrate decisions. Thus, the Court of Arbitration for Sport was needed to serve as an affiliated but independent regulatory global agency with a specific function distinct from the organizations that govern a sport competition, the sport itself, or the athletes. Otherwise, global sport agencies communicate regularly and practice cooperative and collaborative managerial styles when a shared governance system is apparent for international events or activities.

The CAS serves as an international resource and provides a consistent method of resolving sport-related international disputes. The 2018 PyeongChang Winter Olympics is likely to be remembered for the 169 Russian athletes who competed under a neutral flag. Or it may be remembered for the decision by the CAS hours before the opening ceremony to uphold the IOC ban of 45 additional Russian athletes sanctioned by the IOC for their role in a statewide systemic doping scheme dating back to the 2014 Sochi Games (Butler, 2018). The important role of the CAS in arbitrating decisions with worldwide implications was heightened by the unprecedented media attention before, during, and after the Olympic Games. The governing organization will undeni-

ably play a role in future decisions associated with the ongoing Russian doping controversy as well as with the multitude of disputes in the international sport arena.

RECAP

Whether deciding Olympic sport eligibility or regulating the expansion of a new National Hockey League franchise, a governing body must first have the authority to make and enforce rules and regulations for its members and participants. Once authority is established, then the governing body can act in accordance with those rules and regulations.

With the variety of legal issues that might affect a sport organization, from statutory law to case law to Constitutional law, it is important to be familiar with the U.S. judicial system, international dispute resolution, and general legal concepts that may affect the operation of sport organizations, including national governing bodies.

Mediation and arbitration are two methods used to resolve disputes without involving a court system. Arbitration is commonly used to settle salary grievances in professional baseball (MLB) and hockey (NHL), but it is not available for other sports (Silverwood, 2013). Mediation is a nonbinding means to settle grievances in an industry, and it has been used to assist in collective bargaining negotiations.

There are many examples in the sports industry of legal cases involving Constitutional law, statutory law, case law, and executive orders. It is important for sport professionals to have a general understanding of jurisdiction—that is, which entity has the authority to render a decision over a grievance or legal allegation. The U.S. Supreme Court, for example, has cited issues of jurisdiction in its refusal to hear cases pertaining to profiting from college athlete images.

The Court of Arbitration for Sport is a neutral governing body for settling disputes in international sports. The CAS had a major role in the fate of Russian athletes who were not permitted to compete in the 2018 Winter Olympics.

Critical Thinking Questions

1. What strategies can be used to make sure that shared governance in sports offers an advantage in light of its potential for conflict, role ambiguity, and decision-making delays?

2. Why did the NHL retract its decision to permit players to represent their countries in the 2018 Winter Olympics? Might the NHL reverse its decision again? Why or why not?

3. If the NFL adopted a salary arbitration system, would the better model be the NHL or MLB? Why?

4. What types of criminal and civil cases might an athletic administrator deal with at a university?

Applied Activities

Legal Challenges to Gender Testing

Research the history of gender testing in sports in addition to the ethical and legal challenges. Prepare a timeline with pros and cons and interesting facts about each type of gender test used over the years. Next, address the two opposing viewpoints in Caster Semenya's case against the IAAF; speculate on whether other sports will adopt the ruling or whether the rule will be changed.

Sport Law Journal Review

Perform a cursory review on the Internet and locate two peer-reviewed sport law journals with cases or case abstracts available online. Review each of the websites in depth. Provide general information about each journal, such as the title, editor, URL, most-recent publication date, and frequency of publication. Then, rate the journals using a scale of 1 to 10 (10 = excellent and 1 = extremely poor) on the following criteria while providing comments to rationalize your rating. Finally, identify which journal you prefer and why.

- Currency (up to date)
- Applicability to sport
- Variety of cases
- Navigation of website

Case Study Application

For more information on the legal aspects of sport governance, review *College Basketball Corruption Scandal: Is There a Crime if There Is No Victim?* on the web resource.

Ethics, Decision Making, and Leadership in Sport Organizations

Bonnie Tiell and Kelley Walton

LEAD-OFF

While public scandals in sport are nothing new, significant corruption cases in the last few decades have created an outcry to assess and address ethical behavior, decision making, leadership, and governance in the world of sport. **Corruption** is the abuse of power or position for personal gain. Corruption permeates all sectors of the industry, and people in leadership roles must ensure that systems and processes are in place to deter ethical misconduct.

One of the most prolific corruption cases in the past decade involved over a dozen executives from the Fédération Internationale de Football Association (FIFA) who were indicted for collusion and bribery over the marketing rights to the World Cup and other high-profile tournaments (Panja, 2018; Shevchenko, Ponkin, & Ponkin, 2016). In 2019, the United States Olympic & Paralympic Committee (USOPC) began the process of decertifying the United States of America (USA) Gymnastics federation for its leadership failures in the wake of the Larry Nassar sexual abuse scandal. While USA Gymnastics replaced its board of directors and filed for bankruptcy protection, over 50 former gymnasts filed a lawsuit against the USOPC for its role in failing to protect athletes from prolonged abuse (Diamond, 2019; Hobson & Clarke, 2018).

Also in 2019, Tsunekazu Takeda, president of the Japanese Olympic Committee and former IOC member, was indicted for authorizing bribes to secure the 2020 Tokyo Olympics (Gillen, 2019; Morgan, 2019a). Takeda's indictment is worrisome given that Carlos Nuzman, former IOC member and president of the Brazilian Olympic Committee, was also indicted for a $2 million bribery scheme to secure votes for the 2016 Olympics host site (MacKay, 2019). In May 2019, FIFA's ethics commission imposed a lifetime ban on Afghanistan Football Federation President Keramuudin Karim for his abuse of power in sexually abusing female athletes (O'Kane, 2019).

The National Collegiate Athletic Association (NCAA), the most powerful governing body for college sports in the United States, has an endless record of ethical infraction cases including the recent criminal charges levied against Adidas executives, an aspiring financial advisor, and several assistant coaches in a widespread basketball corruption case (Baskin, Voss, & Meyer, 2018; Nocera, Novy-Williams, & McDonald, 2017).

Ethical behavior is a cornerstone for effective governance in organizations. At the crux of effective governance in an organization is the leadership that influences the behavioral expectations of employees and facilitates an ethical culture that is proactive in deterring all forms of corruption.

This chapter addresses components of ethics and ethical principles. The chapter also addresses decision making, the process for making ethical choices, and the impact of leadership on developing ethical culture in sport organizations.

Learning Outcomes

- Identify examples of corruption associated with a governing sport organization.
- Apply components of the ethical behavior framework to a governing authority for a sport organization.
- Explain the distinctions between the general decision-making process and the process for ethical decision making.
- Identify challenges in the decision-making process.
- Provide examples of why a governing authority for a sport organization may alter his or her style of leadership.
- Distinguish between transactional and transformational leaders in sports.

ETHICS

Ethics are the moral principles that govern behavior. If ethical behavior were truly easy, and if there were no competing interests or reasons to choose unethical behavior, business decisions would be simple. However, when money and power are involved, the lines between what is right and what is wrong can be blurred or, frankly, skipped over if someone was adamant to get to the finish line first regardless of the fallout or consequences from inappropriate behavior.

We understand that most professional sport franchises in America are glorified entertainment businesses with driven values of commercialism, exploitation, and capitalism. Still, it is important that owners promote ethical standards for his or her players and staff. Franchises should operate according to ethical business practices by allowing independent audits, reporting all income, allocating taxes, and accounting accurately for assets and liabilities. Franchise owners should also encourage stadium owners to practice competitive pricing strategies without gouging consumers with exorbitant prices on concessions, souvenirs, and parking.

Ethics are important to leading and managing sports organizations, whether amateur or professional. This section addresses the foundational principles of ethics and components of ethical behavior.

Laura Young/Getty Images

Ethical standards suggest that franchise owners should refrain from price gouging for such things as souvenirs and concessions.

Foundational Principles of Ethics

Two of the foundational concepts in ethics are moral principles and moral reasoning. The expectation that people will act in an appropriate and prudent manner is a guiding principle for examining the ethical nature of behavior as it relates to both moral principles and reasoning.

Moral principles are the foundational principles that determine perceived right and wrong behaviors. When confronted with a question involving ethics, behavior is often guided by **moral reasoning** or a systematic process of determining whether actions are right or wrong. Unfortunately, even with the application of moral reasoning, the answer to whether an action is right or wrong isn't always clear.

Often, laws and rules codify the behavioral expectations of a society, a group, or individuals. A government, for example, publishes laws that codify the expectation that stealing is wrong, and therefore, punishable by law. Similarly, the NCAA publishes bylaws codifying that accepting payment for playing in collegiate sport is wrong and therefore punishable to the extent of forfeiting amateur status and collegiate eligibility ("Amateur Status," 2018, p. 63). In the same realm, sport governing bodies have specific regulations that result in punishment (e.g., suspension) for not following what the organization considers the "right" behavior.

It is clear to members of a society that there is an expectation not to steal, and it is clear to NCAA student-athletes that they must not accept compensation for competing or use performance-enhancing drugs. Rules and regulations are intended to clarify the nature of an offense and establish punishments for behavioral violations such as stealing, accepting payment for play as an amateur student-athlete, or doping. In fact, it is not always clear whether a specific behavior is right or wrong. This ambiguity results in ethical dilemmas.

Another foundational principle in the study of ethical behavior is **autonomy**—respecting the rights of competent persons to behave or make decisions independently in the absence of controlling influences. While some organizations create a culture that permits people to act unethically, it is important to understand that organizations don't "behave" a certain way, people do. The collective decisions and collective actions of individuals at the helm of an organization affect an organization's culture, brand, and reputation. It wasn't FIFA that was considered unethical in the corruption and bribery scandal that shook up the international sports world, it was the individuals who worked for FIFA and made the decisions that tarnished the organization's brand and reputation (see Governance in Action 2.1). When many people in an organization make unscrupulous decisions over an extended period of time, we can deduce that the organization fostered a culture of unethical behavior.

Components of Ethical Behavior

Ethical behavior stems from core values and represents actions that are consistent with societal expectations for what is considered right or moral. Some professional sport franchise owners appear to be nonchalant about encouraging personal ethics in their players when they reward players such as Johnny Manziel, Josh Gordon, Rae Carruth, Bill Laimbeer, Ray Rice, or Michael Vick, who have bad-boy images and police records. The Associated Press wires are full of stories on professional players arrested for kidnapping, substance abuse, domestic violence, assault, sexual harassment, and occasionally, murder convictions.

Owners have been accused of being overzealous in acquiring players who can perennially fill stadiums and win championships regardless of their moral character. The governing leaders of professional teams have a responsibility to set ethical standards for players and to mandate what is and is not appropriate behavior. They must balance personal ethics with a desire to win at all costs.

To promote an ethical culture, team owners may require staff and players to attend educational workshops on ethical conduct and consequences. At a minimum, a sportsmanship code should be visibly posted in locker rooms, codes of ethics should be published in team manuals, "monkey fines" should be administered for code violations, and strict punitive action should be taken for criminal infractions.

Team owners are accountable for making sure that the team's business operations are run ethically. They must also distance the franchise from problematic players or coaches who tarnish the image of a team, and they themselves must demonstrate personal ethics and the expected standards of behavior for players and office personnel.

GOVERNANCE IN ACTION 2.1

Fédération Internationale de Football Association (FIFA) Legal and Ethical Misconduct

The Fédération Internationale de Football Association (FIFA) is the international governing body for soccer (aka football) that comprises 211 member associations ("Associations," n.d.). The governing board for FIFA is a 36-member Leadership Council, which is the decision-making body responsible for selecting host cities for the World Cup tournament and approving changes (e.g., expansion) in the field of competition.

In 2015, dozens of FIFA executives and associates were indicted by U.S. judicial authorities and arrested by Zurich (Switzerland) police for racketeering, wire fraud, money laundering, conspiracy, and tax evasion, among other offenses, in an alleged corruption scheme spanning more than three decades. Within weeks following the arrests, Sepp Blatter, long-reigning president of FIFA, resigned (Sheu, 2016). The case stretched through at least 2019 when a sports marketing firm was fined $1 million for paying a FIFA executive $10 million to secure the rights for the 2016 COPA-American tournament (Associated Press, 2019).

At the core of this scandal was over $150 million in bribes to obtain media and marketing rights to high-profile tournaments, including the 2018 Russia and 2022 Qatar World Cup. According to U.S. Attorney General Loretta Lynch, "the indictment alleges corruption that is rampant and systemic," and it contended that FIFA officials "abused their positions of trust to acquire millions of dollars in bribes and kickbacks" (Gayle, 2015).

FIFA has faced a formidable challenge in restoring its public reputation. Even the new president, Gianni Infantino, faced scrutiny in 2018 after a series of leaked documents suggested he interfered with the organization's supposedly independent Ethics Commission (Morgan, 2019b).

After the election of a new president, FIFA hired independent law firms to conduct an internal evaluation, which resulted in 20,000 pages of evidence submitted to the U.S. Department of Justice and Switzerland's Office of the Attorney General (Maylon & Slater, 2017).

Many reforms were made to FIFA's governance structure. The Leadership Council was directed to embrace the role of gatekeeper for the strategic direction of the organization as opposed to immersing itself in day-to-day management duties. The council also expanded from 24 to 36 members and legislated the inclusion of women. FIFA took concrete measures to restructure its administration and change its internal culture, partially by adopting a zero-tolerance policy for unethical behavior.

One view of the scandal is that the bad seeds who abused their authority were removed, which allowed FIFA to resume its powerful role of governing the sport of soccer around the globe. It is surmised that most of the people associated with the corruption that had permeated FIFA were held accountable. In the wake of one of the most prolific sport scandals in history, FIFA took measures to assess and change its internal structure and processes. What remains today is an organization considered transformed. The forced independent assessment served its purpose to acknowledge and address deficiencies and to become the catalyst for reengineering FIFA's governance structure with a renewed commitment to ethical behavior.

The study of ethical behavior begins with a review of the components or the values and principles that an organization considers important to creating an ethical culture. Recognizing that ethical behavior occurs along a continuum also helps leaders to understand and deal with variances.

Components of Ethical Behavior

Many sport organizations are grounded in core values and guiding principles that describe behavioral expectations of employees at every level. A framework for ethical behavior features an inventory of value-based behaviors that is used to assess individual conduct and how that conduct affects the organization's culture.

In its new model, FIFA identifies transparency, accountability, cooperation, and inclusivity as the four guiding principles in its strategic road map for the future of the sport ("About FIFA", 2016). FIFA had never operated under a vision statement or a set of guiding principles until its restructuring in the wake of its corruption scandal. The four components of ethical behavior are what FIFA deemed important to enable the organization to move forward as the supreme authority around the world for the sport of soccer. Sport organizations routinely publicize core values similar to FIFA's guiding principles. Examples of these are outlined in table 2.1.

The set of core values for Dick's Sporting Goods, Planet Fitness, and the NFL serves as the ethical framework for the behavior in each of these organizations. It is no coincidence that the values of respect, passion, and integrity are common to more than one organization.

Figure 2.1 depicts components of value-based behaviors that are typically apparent in organizations that strive to maintain a strong ethical culture. The eight components in this ethical behavior framework are (1) honesty, (2) integrity, (3) loyalty, (4) equity, (5) fairness, (6) tolerance, (7) respect, and (8) accountability.

Respect and integrity are among the core values publicized by Planet Fitness, Dick's Sporting Goods, and the NFL, while FIFA identifies accountability. Following is the definition and a sport-specific example of each ethical behavioral component.

Honesty **Honesty**, very simply, is defined as truthfulness. In 2017, several members of the basketball staff at the University of Louisville were fired for being involved in bribes to accept recruits. When head coach Rick Pitino was asked about the allegations, he responded that he was shocked by

them. This lack of truthfulness, in the initial acts involving the bribery and the subsequent refusal to admit awareness, affected the University of Louisville's reputation.

Integrity **Integrity** is defined as a behavioral attribute based on high moral principles and truthfulness. Although a difficult construct to measure, integrity is often a desired characteristic in candidate profiles for coaching and sport executive positions such as league commissioners, who are expected to follow rules consistently and to always do things the "right" way.

Loyalty **Loyalty** is the act of demonstrating firm and constant support or allegiance. Occasionally, loyalty can work against an organization, as when employees are so loyal to other team members that their loyalty supersedes the best interests of the organization. For example, the fact that athletic leaders at Penn State University did not report

Figure 2.1 Ethical behavior framework.

Table 2.1 Core Values and Guiding Principles of Selected Sports Organizations

Organization	National Football League (NFL)	Dick's Sporting Goods	Planet Fitness
Core values	Respect Integrity Responsibility to team Resiliency	Passion Commitment Skill Drive	Passion Excellence Respect Transparency Integrity

Data from Mission and Values. (n.d.). National Football League; Who We Are. (n.d.). Dick's Sporting Goods, Inc.; Planet Fitness. (2016, October 19). Code of Ethics.

sexual abuse allegations against former assistant football coach Jerry Sandusky led many to believe that the administration was simply trying to protect the image of the school, the football program, or former head coach Joe Paterno.

Equity Equity is the quality of being fair or impartial. When an organization shows favoritism in its hiring decisions, this is considered inequitable, as opposed to when it promotes a staff member based purely on merit.

Fairness Fairness is action considered impartial in accordance with rules or standards. When Tom Brady, quarterback of the NFL New England Patriots, knowingly used deflated footballs during an American Football Conference (AFC) Championship game in 2015, it was an example of circumventing the rules and creating an unfair competitive advantage.

Tolerance Tolerance is a state of sympathy or indulgence for beliefs or practices that differ or conflict with one's own. The National Basketball Association (NBA) has long been praised for its position on diversity and inclusiveness, with tolerance as an integral component. In 2017, the league moved its All-Star game from the Spectrum Center in Charlotte, North Carolina (Hornets) to the King Smoothie Center in New Orleans, Louisiana (Pelicans) to protest North Carolina's House Bill 2 that required transgender individuals to enter public restrooms based on their biological sex. The bill has since been repealed, and the Hornets were granted the rights to host the 2019 All-Star game, while the NBA and the state of Louisiana were lauded for their tolerance of the lesbian, bisexual, gay, and transgender (LBGT) community (Cacciola, 2016).

Respect Respect represents a state of recognizing the worth of another individual. Coaches and athletic departments promote a culture of respect by expressing and enforcing attitudes, beliefs, and policies against hazing, bullying, and other forms of harassment.

Accountability Accountability is holding others responsible for their actions or a willingness to accept responsibility for one's own actions. The arrest of dozens of executives and sport marketing representatives in the FIFA corruption case is an example where accountability for actions was served.

Spectrum of Ethical Behavior

The study of ethical behavior also addresses the spectrum of ethical behavior. The spectrum of ethical behavior is expressed in the range for which conduct can be assessed. The spectrum varies from high ethical behavior on one end of the continuum to high unethical behavior on the other end. The four conditions of ethical behavior are illustrated in figure 2.2.

The spectrum is ideal for rationalizing how a human resource director at a sport retail business who accepts a $10,000 bribe for agreeing not to disclose a claim of sexual abuse demonstrates a higher degree of unethical behavior than a recreation director who fails to report a staff member who took advantage of an extended lunch period "on the clock." Both directors are likely violating company policy, but the degree of their misbehavior differs.

Historically, the NCAA has categorized infractions as either major or secondary. In a revised system, the NCAA codifies infractions according to four levels based on severity and intentions. Table 2.2 describes an athletic violation in each category.

The recent college basketball corruption scandal initiated by the Federal Bureau of Investigation (FBI) and involving bribery and numerous recruiting and competitive advantage violations will likely result in level I or II NCAA sanctions. At least four universities are involved in the scandal based on the arrests of assistant basketball coaches from four prominent institutions who allegedly accepted cash bribes from Adidas representatives and former agents (Baskin et al., 2018). The Committee on Infractions will determine the level of each infraction based on aggravating and mitigating circumstances, such as an institution's history of major violations, acceptance of responsibility, and cooperative action to expedite a final resolution.

Figure 2.2 Spectrum of ethical behavior.

DECISION MAKING

Decision making is the act of making a choice among two or more courses of action. It has an immeasurable impact on governance because leaders make the choices that affect the livelihood and culture of the organization and its stakeholders. Academic inquiry into decision making includes examining the types of decisions made, the decision-making process, and decision-making biases.

Types of Decisions

Those who lead sport organizations make myriad routine decisions, such as deciding on topics for the monthly board meetings, the timing of posting job announcements, or the structure of a quarterly bonus for ticket associates who exceed their goals. These types of routine and repetitive decisions are often called programmed decisions.

On the other hand, nonroutine decisions, such as how to handle a head tennis professional facing domestic violence charges, or when to kick off a major capital campaign, are those that do not occur regularly. Often labeled as nonprogrammed, these decisions are frequently more complex and may require an extraordinary amount of time and input from multiple constituents.

Decision-Making Process

While the definition of decision making suggests a seemingly simple act of choosing the best alternative, prudent managerial practice favors the process approach to ensure that the best choices are made. The process differs slightly for general decision making versus ethical decision making.

General Decision-Making Process

The general decision-making process is widely accepted in managerial practice. Figure 2.3 outlines each of the phases involved in the process.

For best results, each phase in the process must be considered important, and the phases must be completed in succession. After acknowledging that a choice must be made, the decision maker moves to phase 2, conducting research to provide information for the third phase, which is to identify and evaluate alternatives. The evaluation of each alternative is perhaps the most complex phase since the decision maker must determine

Table 2.2 NCAA Infraction Levels and Examples

Level	Title	Example	Resolution entity
I	Severe breach of conduct	University of North Carolina–Chapel Hill department chair failing to cooperate in NCAA investigation of systematic policy violation that favorably affected student-athlete eligibility (National Collegiate Athletic Association, 2017).	NCAA Committee on Infractions
II	Significant breach of conduct	Four boosters of Brigham Young University men's basketball program providing over $12,000 in impermissible benefits to a student-athlete over a two-year period (National Collegiate Athletic Association, 2018).	NCAA Committee on Infractions
III	Breach of conduct	University of Alabama football staff allowing an impermissible recruiter on-site during an off-campus visit with a prospective student-athlete (Byington, 2017).	NCAA enforcement staff
IV	Minor violation	University of Alabama soccer coach mistakenly sending a text to a prospective student-athlete prior to Sept. 1 of her junior year in high school (Byington, 2017).	Conference office (no NCAA involvement)

Figure 2.3 General decision-making process.

the appropriate assessment criteria, which may reflect a combination of objective and subjective standards. The fourth phase involves the selection of the best alternative, and the fifth and final phase is the behavior or action to implement the decision.

An unfortunate example of a relatively complex decision in intercollegiate athletics is determining which team or teams to eliminate when faced with a financial or legal crisis. Table 2.3 provides the steps of the general decision-making process applied to a case of eliminating athletic teams at Bowling Green State University (BGSU) in Ohio.

The elimination of sport teams is an extreme way to trim budgets and control financial constraints. When a men's athletic program is eliminated, there is a concern that any decision was rendered to satisfy Title IX regulations. The wrestling world has been the most vocal in claiming reverse discrimination created by Title IX, yet, as in gymnastics, the insurance costs to operate wrestling programs and the risks for injury are extremely high. These decisions weigh heavily on administrators, and subsequently, wrestling and gymnastics receive close examination when select-

ing sports to eliminate. By the same token, track and field and tennis are also chosen quite often as programs to eliminate, despite not being subject to high insurance liability or excessive injuries. The only common factor among frequently dropped sports programs is their nonrevenue status.

Ethical Decision-Making Process

The ethical decision-making process is a variation of the general model. The first and the final two phases in each process are identical, but the two middle phases vary slightly. Figure 2.4 illustrates the five steps in the ethical decision-making process, which are (1) choice arises, (2) moral awareness, (3) evaluation, (4) decision, and (5) behavior.

A wide range of ethical issues and dilemmas face sport organizations every day. An **ethical dilemma** is an issue or scenario with two or more moral imperatives or choices. An example of a rather blatant ethical dilemma is whether to follow mandates to entertain multiple bids for a stadium construction project when enticed by a generous donation from one of the contractors who also hap-

Table 2.3 Decision-Making Process Applied to BGSU Elimination of Sport Teams

1. Choice arises

Decision maker acknowledges there is a choice to make.
Paul Krebs, former athletic director (AD) at BGSU, was tasked with deciding which sport teams would be eliminated for the 2003-2004 year primarily to overcome a financial shortfall.

2. Research information

Pertinent information is gathered and analyzed.
The university had already instituted cost-saving measures, such as postponing renovation projects, reducing travel party sizes, busing teams more often, flying commercially instead of contracting chartering planes, increasing the cycle of replacing staff computers by a year, and reexamining cell phone plans. BGSU had already dropped its wrestling and men's lacrosse teams the year before, yet the institution still supported the largest athletic program in the Mid-American Conference with one of the smallest budgets. The university faced a $3.4 million-dollar deficit in the athletic department and $5 million in state funding cuts ("Bowling Green Cuts Four Men's Sports," 2002).

3. Evaluate alternatives

Solutions are generated and evaluated according to appropriate subjective and objective assessment criteria.
Krebs indicated that although economics and competitiveness were the main criteria for the decision, "due to Title IX and equity reasons, once the decision was made to drop sports, we focused exclusively on men's programs" (Bowling Green State University, 2002). Krebs identified and evaluated each of the bottom-tier men's nonrevenue sport teams based on the factors identified.

4. Decision

The best alternative is selected.
A decision was made to eliminate men's track and field, men's swimming and diving, and men's tennis.

5. Behavior

The decision maker acts to implement the decision.
The final step (action or behavior) was communicating the decision to stakeholders (coaches, student-athletes, alumni, the conference office, etc.) and dealing with repercussions such as scholarship obligations, transfer requests, and a heavy backlash from individuals citing the unfairness in targeting only men's programs.

pens to be a personal friend. On the other hand, a minor ethical dilemma is exemplified by a supervisor considering how to handle a student-worker at a recreation desk job who calls in sick when the supervisor knows the person isn't really ill.

It is important to understand the ethical decision-making process that outlines the method for determining behavior in ethical situations. Table 2.4 applies the ethical decision-making process to a scenario in the NFL when a team doctor faces a decision whether to return a potentially concussed player to the field. The scenario is an example of a situation where one sees the benefit of using one's **moral compass**, which embodies the ability to distinguish between ethically right and wrong behavior. Another important tool is one's degree of **moral competence**, or the ability to resolve ethical dilemmas using sound critical reasoning skills.

Challenges in Decision Making

The decision-making process isn't always as easy as it appears. The pressure to win, to generate revenue, to create a strong brand, to protect someone, or to compete at a high level can create pressures that can affect a person's rational decision making. Cognitive dissonance and decision bias present two challenges in the decision-making process.

Cognitive Dissonance

When one experiences a conflict between attitudes and behavior, the resulting state of mental discomfort is labeled **cognitive dissonance**. Before the strict NFL concussion protocol was established, and providing there was no loss of consciousness, many

Figure 2.4 Ethical decision-making process.

Table 2.4 Ethical Decision for NFL Team Physician

1. Choice Arises
Decision maker acknowledges there is a choice to make.   The NFL team doctor is summoned when an incident of on-field helmet-to-helmet contact occurs.

2. Moral Awareness
Decision maker recognizes how the decision affects the interests, welfare, or expectations of others (or themselves) in a manner that may conflict with moral principles.   The NFL team doctor considers whether the football player can return to play after a hard hit to the head. The doctor must have some level of **moral awareness** that the decision could affect the player's physical and mental welfare and that returning him to the field without a complete assessment may not be in the best interests of the player or the team.

3. Evaluation
The potential options are assessed with respect to moral principles and the subsequent impact on the decision maker and others.   The NFL team doctor evaluates whether to follow each step of the league's medical protocol or to send the player back onto the field. While the NFL has a published protocol, the team doctor can still choose whether to follow each or any of the steps.

4. Decision
The best alternative is selected.   The NFL team doctor must determine that either yes, the player can return to the field, or no, the player cannot return to play.

5. Behavior
The decision maker acts to implement the decision.   The team doctor communicates the decision, which results in either a release and return to the field of play or further assessment based on league protocol.

doctors are accused of having sent players back to the field even when they exhibited other subtle signs of a concussion (Mangels, 2012). Cognitive dissonance occurs when team doctors know that sending a player back to the field with a possible concussion is ethically wrong, but they release the player, anyway.

The cognitive dissonance over such a decision may be due to situational factors that are out of the decision maker's control. Moral competence can become clouded by situational factors. For example, what if the NFL doctor in the concussion scenario outlined in table 2.4 was 85 or 90 percent certain the player was concussion free, but other factors were apparent? What if the player who took the hit to the head is the quarterback in the fourth quarter of a championship game? What if the potentially concussed player is the center, it is the first quarter of the season, and the team is already ahead by a score of 10-0? What if the player who was hit in the head is the team's only kicker who just nailed a 50-yard field goal with four minutes remaining in the game to come within two points of the opposing team? Does it matter whether the winning team will advance to the Super Bowl?

Another example of dissonance is apparent in the actions of many leaders who failed to adequately respond to allegations of sexual abuse by Larry Nassar, a former doctor for both USA Gymnastics and Michigan State University (MSU). The number of victims, as well as the number of years that the abuse occurred, was shocking. MSU President Lou Anna K. Simon resigned in 2018, the day Dr. Nassar was sentenced for sexual abuse, following public criticism of her handling of allegations against Dr. Nassar. The university's athletic director resigned days later (Connor & Stelloh, 2018). Although denying the claim, former MSU gymnastics coach Kathie Klages was charged with lying to authorities about whether she knew of allegations of Dr. Nassar's abuse. Other authorities for USA Gymnastics were also arrested for their role in failing to adequately respond to allegations of rampant sexual abuse.

Is the lack of reporting a matter of a lack of moral awareness, or did the individuals involved have moral awareness but choose to behave unethically? In either case, cognitive dissonance likely occurred either initially or after they were implicated in the scandal. One may consider what situations allowed for a person to make the choice to hide evidence or support a person who is being accused of sexual misconduct. Was unethical behavior caused by the people involved being unaware that there were

ethical considerations, or were the ethical considerations evaluated and weighed against other options for action and the individuals specifically chose to act unethically? Did every person involved lack the moral awareness to the extent that the abuser could affect dozens if not hundreds of girls and women, or did they simply choose the route of ignoring the complaints? Or, was the concern over public perception more important than the investigation of a highly esteemed doctor?

It's difficult to know for certain what led to the decisions that resulted in not addressing the abuse to a greater extent. Whatever the answers are to the questions about personal decision making, it is evident that internal challenges can have a significant impact on actions and behavior. In the case of authorities at MSU and USA Gymnastics who consciously or unconsciously failed to adequately address inappropriate behavior, the consequences were severe.

Decision Bias

Decision bias is defined as a cognitive prejudice or predisposition that affects judgment when faced with alternatives. Several biases are intentional, while most are unintentional. **Anchoring** is a common decision-making bias characterized by jumping to conclusions based on limited information. Another common bias is the **availability heuristic**, or basing one's calculation of the probability of occurrence on ready examples. Availability heuristics would be used extensively to predict game outcomes and to decide wagering amounts in states that support legalized sports betting.

Availability heuristics were cited in research that addressed bias in the selection of high-value employees such as NBA draft prospects. Results indicated that players' unexpected positive performance in the NCAA Men's Basketball Tournament (e.g., unexpected scoring and an underdog win) affected future draft decisions by NBA executives (Ichniowski & Preston, 2017). The authors emphasize the importance of executives remaining steadfast in their decision making and committing to the process when faced with exciting or unexpected information. An example of decision bias based on availability heuristics would be considering one exemplary sales performance to be the criterion for hiring a new ticket manager.

Another common decision-making bias is the **halo effect**, which can be explained in relation to virtue ethics as a tendency to only consider a person's positive characteristics. Similarly, **recency** error and **first impression bias** are prejudices in accounting only for people's most recent actions or their very first impression as opposed to an objective appraisal of their general behavior. These biases can also apply to the appraisal of documents if a decision maker considers only partial information.

To effectively serve in a governing role with oversight responsibilities for an organization and its employees, it is vital to remain objective and to recognize and minimize bias, whether intentional or unintentional. In this way, it is more likely that decisions will be rational and will yield optimal results.

LEADERSHIP

Leadership is defined as influence over others due to positional or personal power. Ethical leaders are characterized as "honest, caring, and principled individuals who make fair and balanced decisions" (Brown & Trevino, 2006, p. 597). Leaders, including team owners and others who govern aspects of sport, must contend with results, responsibilities, and relationships (Scott, 2014). As sport organizations continue to develop and improve in governance and ethical behavior, a key component is ensuring that good leaders are in place.

Organizations such as the World Badminton Federation (WBF), the governing body for the sport, operate through effective leaders. WBF leaders quickly and decisively disqualified four pairs of female badminton players from the 2012 London Olympics because they were accused of losing a game at Wembley Stadium on purpose (match fixing) to ensure that a certain team made it past the preliminary rounds. WBF leaders subsequently altered the system of qualifying rounds for the 2016 Rio Olympics and 2020 Tokyo Games to eliminate the incentive for players to willfully throw a match (Caci, 2016).

Sports and athletics by nature are competitive. A primary role of leaders in sports organizations is to help programs to reach their potential through ethical and prudent measures supported by each organization's mission, vision, and core values. Styles of leadership provide a context for decision making and its influence on organizational ethics.

Leadership Styles

Leadership style is the way leaders provide direction and motivate others. The styles proposed by Lewin, Lippet, and White (1939), Chelladurai (1978, 1984), and Goleman (2000) continue to resonate in the study of leadership and its application to the sports industry.

Classic Leadership Styles

Lewin et al. (1939) proposed that leaders demonstrate one of three styles of leadership: authoritarian, participative, or laissez-faire. These styles are generally used to describe the ways individuals lead, but as contingency theories suggest, a leader may select among the different styles for different audiences and situations.

The authoritarian, **authoritative**, or autocratic leader uses strong, directive actions to control the rules, regulations, activities, and relationships in the work environment. An autocratic leader often provides specific instructions or orders for achieving a task and rarely gives followers any authority in the choice of methods. The autocratic style has also been referred to as a militaristic or dictator style of leadership common to many elite Division I football and men's basketball coaches.

The **participative** style is exhibited by leaders who are considered fair and egalitarian and who involve others in decision making. Examples might include the sports professionals who serve as executives for national and global organizations (e.g., IOC, NCAA). The participative leadership style has also been described as a democratic style.

The **laissez-faire** or free-reign leadership style is exhibited by those who have little interaction with subordinates. As contingency leadership theories suggest, it is a style that may be most appropriate if a leader is supported by a competent and experienced staff in routine situations. For example, the executive director of a municipal recreation department with oversight for all summer camps may use a laissez-faire approach to supervise the youth sport director who has successfully organized the camp for the past seven years.

Multidimensional Leadership Style

Chelladurai (1978), a distinguished scholar in sport management, developed a **multidimensional leadership** model based on Lewin et al.'s three traditional styles. The model blends instructional behaviors (training), motivation tendencies, and two of Lewin's decision-making styles. The convergence of factors facilitates the choice of the best authoritative or participative leadership style based on the characteristics of the leader, situational characteristics, and the follower's "preferred" leadership behavior. Similar to the contingency theories on leadership, the result is a behavioral style that is best suited to the context of the situation. The multidimensional model suggests that effective leaders are those who can effectively modify their leadership style to meet the needs of the situation and the audience.

Contemporary Leadership Styles

Dan Goleman (2000), the authority on emotional and social intelligence, expanded on Lewin et al.'s model to develop six types of leadership styles: (1) coercive, (2) authoritative, (3) affiliative, (4) democratic, (5) pacesetting, and (6) coaching.

Goleman's approach to the field of leadership is postmodern and pragmatic. The researcher equates leadership styles with a set of golf clubs. Lower-handicap golfers instinctively know exactly which club to pull out in a given situation and are adept at using more than one (Goleman, 2000). Similarly, effective leaders with a governing role in sports can successfully employ a given style when necessary to obtain the desired results.

Goleman's work suggests the advantage to sport organizations of employing people who are strong in a particular leadership style that can compensate for deficiencies of the owner or other top authority. Table 2.5 provides a definition of each leadership style and an application of each to governing associations in the sport industry.

Leader Types

Contemporary research since the work of Lewin et al. (1939) has added to the field of leadership to define types of leaders by virtue of their roles, responsibilities, behavior, and general interaction with others. Several of the more contemporary leadership types include transformational, transactional, servant, and authentic.

Transformational and Transactional Leaders

The two mutually exclusive types of leaders defined by Burns (1978) are transactional and transformational. The **transactional** leader exchanges rewards such as wages or favors in return for productive effort from employees. Transactional leaders focus attention on identifying and correcting mistakes, provide tangible rewards for performance, express satisfaction when goals are achieved or exceeded, and are considered generally passive leaders.

Transformational leaders, on the other hand, rely on emotional appeal and personal influence to inspire productivity in employees, often beyond the worker's normal capacity. Transformational leaders have been described as visionaries who communicate high expectations and empower others (Bass & Avolio, 1990). They routinely provide opportu-

Table 2.5 Application of Goleman's (2000) Six Leadership Styles to Actions of Sport Governing Bodies

Style	Description	Application
Coercive	Inflicts punitive measures to ensure compliance	The World Badminton Association disqualifies players at the 2012 London Games for match fixing.
Authoritative	Drives others toward a vision or goals with directives	The United States Olympic & Paralympic Committee mandates USA Gymnastics reform its governing board and policies in the wake of the Larry Nassar sexual abuse scandal.
Affiliative	Builds rapport and establishes bonds to influence others	The NCAA teams with the U.S. Department of Defense to establish the Concussion Assessment, Research, and Education consortium (CARE) and to conduct the world's most comprehensive study on the impact of head trauma.
Democratic	Forges consensus through participation	The NFL Players Association holds meetings with players to discuss the owners' new policy governing behavior during the national anthem.
Pacesetting	Employs high standards for achievement to motivate others	The World Anti-Doping Agency (WADA) initiates new regulations in the wake of the Russia statewide doping scandal.
Coaching	Focuses on developing competencies of others as a motivator	The National Federation of High Schools creates seminars to educate coaches and administrators on each state's concussion management requirements.

Based on Goleman (2000).

nities for professional or intellectual growth while demonstrating charisma, confidence, enthusiasm, and selflessness in the context of organizational values (Scott, 2014).

Transformational leadership is apparent in organizations that successfully change their image, reputation, or position in the marketplace. Scott (2014) proposes that when the Harlem Globetrotters acquired a new owner in 1993, his transformational approach resulted in an organization that grew from an average annual attendance of 300,000 to over 2 million and a $1 million-dollar deficit from $9 million in revenue into one that earned $6 million in profits from over $60 million in revenues in 2001 (p. 20). Governance and oversight in sports are best served by transformational leaders. Research concludes that administrators in intercollegiate athletics, for example, are predominantly transformational leaders (Doherty, 1997; Manning, 2012). The roles and responsibilities of such leaders as intercollegiate athletic directors or a secretary general for an international sport federation are varied, and it must be surmised that the transactional leader may still be effective if borrowing upon the traits of the transformational leader and vice versa.

Servant Leaders

A **servant leader** focuses on the needs of followers. This style is based on the premise of serving and putting others' interests, needs, and aspirations before personal interests (Greenleaf, 1977). The servant leader, characterized by trustworthiness and integrity, leads with a mindset conditioned to first and foremost meet the needs of others (stakeholders, customers, employees) before his or her own. The advantage of servant leadership is the potential for greater followership satisfaction as a result of feeling supported and uplifted rather than directed or managed.

Despite their power and authority, governing boards for membership-driven sport organizations are often described as assuming a servant leadership role to protect the interests of the members. Additional characteristics and behaviors of servant leaders include an altruistic calling, emotional healing through a commitment to followers, wisdom, and "persuasive mapping" or the ability to create shared and compelling reasons for actions (Burton, Peachey, & Wells, 2017). Research by Burton et al. (2017) concluded that when sport organizations are led by a servant leader, there is a direct positive influence on the ethical climate partially attributed to the regular practice of procedural justice and a higher level of trust with employees.

Authentic Leaders

The relatively new concept of **authentic leadership**, a type of leadership in which an individual's behavior and actions are grounded in a self-concept of openness and truthfulness, has been widely published in contemporary literature. Authentic leaders build legitimacy by virtue of their personal values and their propensity to develop honest relationships with followers. Two of the general characteristics of authentic leaders, self-awareness and relationship management, are part of Goleman's (1998) concept of **emotional intelligence**, which is the ability to understand and manage one's own emotions while also understanding and managing the emotions of others. Emotional intelligence is a highly valued trait for effective leadership. Authentic leaders also have an internalized moral perspective and practice balanced processing, which requires eliminating bias when dealing with external information (Avolio, Walumbwa, & Weber, 2009).

Research has found that board members who were considered authentic leaders were more apparent in successful nonprofit sport organizations in Australia (Takos, Murray, & O'Boyle, 2018). The successful sport clubs in the study more often included board members who had authentic relationships with the chief executive officer (CEO) and practiced more open and transparent debate. Authentic leadership is a style that leaders with governing authority for sport organizations can develop through diligent attention to value-based behaviors such as integrity and transparency, which are cornerstones of ethical behavior.

RECAP

Ethical behavior is integral to effective governance systems in organizations. It lays the foundation for what is considered normative behavior that is an expectation in every level of an organization from the owner to the lowest tier of employees.

The ethical behavior framework includes eight value-based components apparent in organizations that strive to maintain a strong ethical culture. A systems approach to decision making is prudent for anyone facing an ethical dilemma; cognitive dissonance and decision bias must be avoided.

Sport leaders have a major role in shaping the ethical conduct of organizations. Leadership effectiveness depends in part upon the leader's ability to tailor his or her behavior to the demands of the situation and the maturity level of subordinates.

Leaders exhibit varying styles. The classical styles proposed by Lewin et al. (1939) include authoritative, participative, and laissez-faire. Contemporary research in sports suggests a multidimensional model in which leaders vary their style to account for the followers' preferences and the task significance. Goleman (2000), most noted for his work on emotional intelligence, proposed six leadership styles: pacesetting, affiliative, coercive, democratic, authoritative, and coaching. Most leaders use a variety of leadership styles to motivate employee behavior.

In contemporary research, common types of leaders include transactional, transformational, servant, and authentic. Leaders in these categories are widely apparent in sport leadership studies, especially transformational leaders, who are viewed as visionaries who inspire and influence others.

Critical Thinking Questions

1. Which of the components of the ethical behavior framework are most important for individuals with governing authority in a sport organization? Why?
2. What steps can international organizations like FIFA take to minimize corruption?
3. How can guiding principles and core values be used to help transform an organization with a governing role in sports?
4. Why is emotional intelligence important for leaders in sport organizations?
5. Which leader type is most applicable to those with governing authority in sport organizations?

Applied Activities

Outline Reform Recommendations for USA Gymnastics

Research the available information on the USOPC and USA Gymnastics following the conviction of former team doctor Larry Nassar on sexual abuse charges. Since the conviction, there has been heavy criticism of the role governing entities had in failing to protect victims. The entire USA Gymnastics board resigned shortly after the conviction, and the USOPC began procedures for decertification. After a careful review, outline personal recommendations to potentially reform the structure and operations of USA Gymnastics. Consider research on the transformation of FIFA in response to the rampant corruption that surfaced after the arrest of over a dozen executives and the resignation of long-time leader Sepp Blatter.

Develop a Code of Ethics

Develop a code of ethics for a professional sport team that addresses behavioral expectations.

Case Study Application

For more information on leadership and ethics in sport governance, review *The Many Stakeholders of the NFL Super Bowl "On Location Experience"* in the web resource.

Board Governance and Policy Development in Sport Organizations

Bonnie Tiell

LEAD-OFF

Thomas Bach, president of the International Olympic Committee (IOC), is unquestionably one of the most powerful leaders in sport. In November 2018, he asked Sheikh Ahmad Al-Fahad Al-Sabah of Kuwait to step down as president of the Association of National Olympic Committees (ANOC), the umbrella organization for the 206 member countries. Only days away from the ANOC General Assembly and running unopposed for a second term as president, Sheikh Al-Sabah faced a 2019 trial date for forgery, coup-plotting, and corruption while the IOC Executive Board headed into a two-day session to address the fallout from this event (Morgan, 2018). Kuwait's Olympic Committee remained suspended until July of 2019, and the president of Japan's Olympic Committee was indicted a few months prior for alleged corruption connected with the 2020 Olympic Games (Morgan, 2019a).

While presidents such as Thomas Bach wield a great deal of power to be able to influence an elected leader of a continental federation to step down and to suspend a country's Olympic committee, the true power lies in an organization's executive board, which can trump the power of a president or chief executive officer (CEO).

Not all sport organizations operate through a governing board, especially when they represent a small business such as a local sporting goods store or a privately owned fitness facility. Most sport businesses, however, do operate under board governance, including sport governing bodies (e.g., United States Track and Field Association), collegiate sports (e.g., National Collegiate Athletic Association [NCAA]), professional leagues and tours, commercial sport retail corporations (e.g., Dick's Sporting Goods), sport manufacturers (e.g., Nike and Under Armour), some travel sport clubs, municipal recreation departments, sport commissions, and nonprofit sport associations (e.g., Young Men's Christian Association [YMCA]).

Governing boards are typically tasked with developing, revising, or authorizing policies and procedures for an organization. Policies and procedures are an essential component of the control function in management; they minimize risk and standardize operations to promote efficiency and effectiveness.

This chapter addresses best practices for board governance in sport organizations with a focus on the dimensions of "good" governance. The chapter explores the general structure, purpose, roles and responsibilities, and performance assessment practices of governing boards. Finally, the chapter discusses the strategic role of policies and procedures for guiding sport organizations and the general process used when developing and evaluating the effectiveness of regulations.

Learning Outcomes

- Identify principles of good governance in sport organizations.
- Distinguish between the regulatory and performance-based roles and responsibilities of a governing board.
- Describe the features of a sport organization that promotes an ideal ethical climate.
- Identify appropriate criteria for appointing members to a sport organization's board of directors.
- Explain each stage in the process of developing policies and procedures for a sports league and sport organization.

BEST PRACTICES IN BOARD GOVERNANCE

Board governance applies to the entity that serves as the central decision-making authority for an organization, such as the NCAA Board of Governors. Exemplary models of board governance typically adhere to values of ethical conduct, integrity, transparency, fairness, democratic processes, accountability, and general operational effectiveness. These values align with the principles or best practices for good governance. **Best practices** refer to the processes, procedures, or activities likely to achieve the optimal results. **Good governance** refers to the cultural and operational elements of an organization that lead to effective regulation and compliance. In essence, best practices and good governance are explicitly linked through an organization's culture, leadership, structure, policies, and processes.

Principles of Good Governance

There is an abundance of information available on the components of good governance for the governing boards of sport organizations. A 2018 assessment of good governance practices among the international federations for soccer, swimming, track and field, tennis, and handball included 56 principles that were connected to four similar themes: (1) transparency, (2) democratic processes, (3) internal accountability and control, and (4) societal responsibility (Geeraert, 2018).

Transparency refers to the practice of communicating honestly and openly with public constituents, while **democratic process** refers to an inclusive and representative style of decision making. **Internal accountability and control** refer to the separation of powers and the processes used to ensure that rules and regulations are fol-lowed. Finally, **societal responsibility** addresses an ethical obligation to have a positive impact on stakeholders.

Table 3.1 provides an example of each dimension of good governance applied to the board of directors for a golf and country club and an international sport federation.

The 2018 assessment of international sport federations indicated that the Fédération Internationale de Football Association (FIFA) scored good or very good on 61 percent of the 56 principles of good governance, followed by the International Handball Federation (IHF), which scored similarly well on only 30 percent of the constructs (Geeraert, 2018, p. 24). The results are indicative of a dramatic transformation in the governance structure of FIFA following the 2015 scandal over corruption in the process of selecting host cities for high-profile international events. No other organization scored nearly as high on good governance principles. In fact, all five federations lacked principles related to having independent board members, a dual career policy, and a conflict of interest and risk assessment mechanism. On the other end of the spectrum, all five organizations scored very good for employing a code of conduct and having legal and policy documents (Geeraert, 2018, p. 24).

Another example of good governance practices by the boards of sport organizations has been proposed by the European Union (EU). Many sport federations in the EU have signed a good governance declaration pledge in which they agree to adhere to principles of "integrity, accountability, transparency, democracy, participation and inclusivity" ("A Pledge to Implement Good Governance in Sport," n.d.). The European Commission (2011) of the EU identified four dimensions of good governance similar to the constructs suggested by Geeraert (2018): (1) transparency and public communication, (2) a democratic process, (3) **checks and balances**, and (4) **solidarity** ("Actions for Good Governance in International Sport Organisations," 2013). Checks and balances and the term "solidarity" can respectively be used interchangeably with internal accountability and control and societal responsibilities.

Table 3.2 applies the EU's 10 good governance principles to the board of directors for the United States Olympic & Paralympic Committee (USOPC) during the process of decertifying USA Gymnastics (USAG). Decertification was a response to the

Table 3.1 Principles of Good Governance and Examples of Board Decisions

Principle of good governance	Application to board of directors for a golf and country club	Application to board of an international sport federation
Transparency	The board publishes monthly financial summary reports in the membership newsletter.	The board involves various athletes and members of various committees in developing a strategic plan.
Democratic process	The board permits members to vote on the nature of capital improvement projects.	Quorums are required for boards and general assembly voting.
Internal accountability and control	The board contracts with an independent accounting firm to review quarterly payroll records.	Resignation and eligibility rules are clearly stated for members of the board of directors.
Societal responsibility	The board consults with the head greenskeeper to monitor the weekly quantity of water used for irrigating fairways.	The board develops and implements corruption controls tied to funding requirements.

Table 3.2 The European Union's 10 Principles of Good Governance Applied to the USOPC Board's Involvement With Decertification Decision on USA Gymnastics

Principle 1: Clarity of purpose and objectives	The board consults with the USOPC ethics committee to ensure that standards of ethical conduct and integrity are ever-present in all business matters pertaining to decertification of USA Gymnastics. The board of directors accepts its role as a gatekeeper for national sport federations and publicizes its decision to decertify USA Gymnastics.
Principle 2: Code of ethics	The board consults with the USOPC ethics committee to ensure that standards of ethical conduct and integrity are ever-present in all business matters pertaining to decertification of USA Gymnastics.
Principle 3: Stakeholder identification and roles	The board identifies stakeholders in the process (e.g., members of USA Gymnastics, current and former athletes, athlete's commission, the IOC, SafeSport, the USOPC legal counsel). The board also considers role changes of stakeholders if the organization is decertified, such as what entity will be responsible for managing elite national teams and certifying gymnastic coaches and officials.
Principle 4: Democracy and minimum standards	The board prepares to adhere to minimum standards (majority approval) in the pending vote for decertification.
Principle 5: Delegation and committees	The board appoints a review panel for the fact-finding investigation in the case.
Principle 6: Management	The USOPC board chair sets deadlines and plans the stages of board involvement in the process for decertification.
Principle 7: Judicial and disciplinary procedures	The USOPC board holds judicial powers to revoke USA Gymnastics as a national governing body, but it must follow disciplinary procedures by appointing a review panel and holding a hearing before making a final decision (Park, 2018).
Principle 8: Inclusivity	The board considers the input from all 16 members before voting on decertification.
Principle 9: Statutes, rules, and regulations	The board refers to section 8.1 of the USOPC (2017) bylaws addressing their authority to suspend or terminate the recognition of a national governing body provided notice is given (.30).
Principle 10: Accountability and transparency	The board distributes minutes of meetings and pertinent information to the public regarding the processes and decisions for decertification.

USAG's failure to protect athletes in connection with rampant child pornography and sexual abuse by former team physician Larry Nassar. The USOPC was responsible for demonstrating principles of good governance in dealing with the aftermath, but it ultimately backed off the decertification process after USA Gymnastics filed for bankruptcy protection (Macur, 2018).

The case of the USOPC and USA Gymnastics (USAG) demonstrates the roles and responsibilities of governing boards in sports. The case also demonstrates how governing boards can fail to act in accordance with principles of good governance (see Governance in Action 3.1).

To demonstrate principles of good governance, a sport organization typically begins by clearly articulating the purpose, structure, and role of its board. Thereafter, good governance is facilitated when the organization has developed a culture of ethical behavior along with a process for monitoring and assessing the board's deliverables.

Purpose and Structure of Boards

The purpose and structure of boards are the blueprints for effective operation. While the purpose

---

GOVERNANCE IN ACTION 3.1

The Abuse Scandal That Took Down USA Gymnastics Governing Board

In the wake of the child pornography and sexual abuse scandal resulting in conviction and a 175-year prison sentence for former USAG team physician Larry Nassar, Sarah Hirshland (2018), chief executive officer for the United States Olympic & Paralympic Committee (USOPC), announced that the organization had "taken the first steps to revoke USA Gymnastics' (USAG) recognition as the national governing body (NGB) for gymnastics in the United States." The USOPC board had previously succeeded in revoking the NGB status of USA team handball and taekwondo federations.

In January 2018, a letter from Scott Blackman, then CEO of the USOPC, pressured all current USAG board members to resign to avoid termination of the organization's NGB status. Blackman (2018) characterized USA Gymnastics as a "culture needing fundamental rebuilding." Not only did all USAG board members resign, but according to statements from the Committee to Restore Integrity to USAG, Blackman was also forced to resign following allegations about his role in an alleged cover-up scandal (N. Hogshead-Maker, personal communication, August 20, 2018). Steve Penny, the USAG CEO who resigned in 2017 during the Nassar scandal, was arrested and indicted for tampering with evidence in the case. The first interim CEO to succeed Penny (Kerry Perry) resigned nine months after her appointment, and the second interim CEO (Mary Bono) resigned after only four days on the job (Chavez & Sutton, 2018).

After Bono's departure, Hirshland (2018) announced the decision of the board to begin decertification of USAG, noting that the revocation of the NGB status was "subject to a process clearly outlined in the USOPC bylaws." Hirshland (2018) made it known that

There is a process that must be followed based on the USOPC Bylaws that lay out how we recognize, and revoke recognition, for an NGB. We have filed a complaint. A review panel will be identified, a hearing will be held, a report will be issued, and a recommendation will be made. Then the USOPC board will vote to continue to recognize USAG, or to revoke that status.

Considering the need to follow processes for decertification of USA Gymnastics, the USOPC Executive Board was intentional and deliberate in its actions. However, the executive board also faced scrutiny over its own alleged ethical and managerial lapses before, during, and after the Larry Nassar conviction. The Committee to Restore Integrity to the USOPC, which included Martina Navratilova and Greg Louganis, urged the resignation of members of the organization's board of directors. Several were replaced in 2019. Assertions have been made about the USOPC's governance failures, "even after independent reports demonstrate their culpability in failing to help athletes" (Pavitt, 2019). The larger challenge may be in reforming the USOPC and not just USA Gymnastics.

guides the board's activities, the structure provides the edifice for logistical operations.

Purpose

A governing board is the highest authoritative unit of an organization; its general purpose is to ensure that the organization operates legally and efficiently. The purpose of the governing board is tied to the organizational mission, which helps to define the organization's strategic direction. Governing boards carry out the organization's mission according to applicable laws and regulations.

Governing boards are distinct from advisory boards because of their authoritative status. Advisory boards or councils typically have the purpose of advancing the mission of the organization, but their power and authority are usually limited to providing recommendations as opposed to making binding decisions. An advisory board or council reports to a higher authoritative unit, whether it is the organization's governing board or a single person such as the owner, CEO, or president. For example, according to the bylaws governing the sport advisory board to the Washington Township Parks and Recreation Administration (2014), members report to the city mayor, but responsibilities include establishing and implementing policies, approving hires, and amending legislation. Most of the activities of the sport advisory board, however, require approval from the Washington Township Parks and Recreation Administration.

Some sport organizations, such as the Special Olympics of Florida, operate through both a board of directors and an advisory council, but the level of authority is clear.

Structure

The structure of a board pertains to its general composition and its alignment within the organization as an independent body, an extension of staff, or a combination of the two. Structure also addresses the selection method of board members by either an executive appointment or an election.

The first factor in the composition of a governing body is its size. The size of a governing board is appropriate to its purpose of enabling the organization to carry out its mission. The IOC Executive Board is comprised of 16 members, the NCAA Board of Governors has 20 members, the YMCA National Executive Board has 25 members, and the National Hockey League Executive Board has 31 members in order to represent each team. The Blackswamp Volleyball Club in Tiffin, Ohio, includes six board members, while the Cleveland Metroparks Board of Commissioners includes only three members.

Another factor in the composition of a board is the diversity of its members according to gender, ethnicity, cultural background, age, experience, educational background, and range of knowledge, skills, and abilities. The composition is also reflected by variances in members' terms of office, distinct titles of positions (e.g., CEO, chair, vice president), and the configuration of voting privileges.

Executive boards are typically led by a chair or a president. In addition to general members and depending on the size of the board, other common officer positions include a vice president, secretary, and treasurer. Occasionally, governing boards include one or more ex officio members who may or may not have voting privileges. **Ex officio** is the term for an individual who is a member of a governing board by virtue of his or her position. The executive board for World Archery, for example, includes the chairperson of the Athletes Committee, the secretary general, and chairperson of the Constitution and Rules Committee, who are considered ex officio members who attend meetings but cannot vote ("Executive Board," n.d.). Most ex officio members do not have voting privileges.

An organization's governing documents (articles of incorporation, charter, or bylaws) contain the guidelines for the composition of its board, typically indicating its size, titles of officers, the selection method for members, and term limits. Article 504 in the official rulebook for USA Swimming (2019), for example, stipulates that the board of directors shall be comprised of the elected chairperson, six elected vice-chairs, the secretary general and general counsel, two directors elected from each zone (Eastern, Southern, Central, and Western), and the chair of the National Team Steering Committee (p. 123). Similarly, the bylaws for the City of San Diego's (2018) Parks and Recreation Board stipulates that the board includes 11 members nominated by the city council and appointed by the mayor. Members serve two-year terms (p. 4).

Term limits have recently received more attention from international sport federations. According to a recent report by the Association of Summer Olympics International Federations (ASOIF), the constitutions of 17 of the 33 sponsored sport federations in the 2020 Tokyo Olympics failed to include term limits for their key positions (e.g., secretary general, president). The presidents of 10 of the summer federations had served in their current leadership role for at least a decade. Similarly, the report noted that at least three of the presidents of winter sport federations had served in that role for over 20 years. The 17 federations with no term limits for their president or other key positions also scored on the lower end of the ASOIF governance measuring scale, which assessed the organizations' degree of transparency, integrity, democracy, sport development and solidarity, and control mechanisms (Morgan, 2019b).

In addition to the absence of term limits, diversity is another concern for governing boards of international sport federations as well as most national, continental, and global sport organizations. A strategic initiative to increase diversity has prompted some sport organizations to include gender quotas for boards in their bylaws. **Gender quotas** are the minimum requirement (e.g., expressed as a number or percentage) for representation of the underrepresented gender. Often an organization stipulates a gender quota in order to comply with standards imposed by a higher governing authority.

Governance in Action 3.2 provides a brief overview of gender quota initiatives whose purpose is to increase the number and percentage of females on executive boards of sport organizations.

In addition to composition, the structure of governing boards also refers to the configuration of the board within the organization, which is illustrated by an organizational chart. An **organizational chart** is the diagram that identifies relationships or reporting avenues between departments or positions. Typically, the organizational chart places the governing board at the very top of the diagram to illustrate the reporting relationship from the CEO or president who runs the daily business activities. The governing board may be connected with a dotted line to the side of the organization's CEO or president to denote shared positional power or independence from the organization. Advisory boards are typically configured with a dotted line on an organizational chart.

GOVERNANCE IN ACTION 3.2

Gender Quotas for Governing Boards of Sport Organizations

Historically, women have been underrepresented on governing boards across all industries. The governing boards of sport organizations are no exception. According to the International Sports Report Card on Women in Leadership Roles, females constituted 26.7 percent of IOC Executive Board positions and 37.5 percent of seats on the USOPC Board of Directors in 2015 (Lapchick et al., 2016). In the same report, women respectively comprised 11 percent and 10.3 percent of the Associations for the Summer and Winter International Federations (p. 5).

A handful of organizations and governments are choosing to address the dearth of female leadership by instituting pledges and legislative reforms to achieve gender quotas for boards. In Sweden, gender quotas for sport NGB boards have been required since 1998. France has directed a 40 percent female composition on sport NGB executive boards by the Tokyo 2020 Olympics, and both Germany and the UK have instituted similar mandates (Council of Europe, 2016). Organizations failing to achieve a mandated gender ratio reportedly risk losing funding.

The European Institute for Gender Equality (2015) reported 11 sport federations implemented gender quotas for board representation, including United World Wrestling Europe, European Fencing Confederation, European Handball Federation, European Shooting Confederation, European Weightlifting Federation, Union of European Football Associations, European Hockey Federation, FIBA Europe, European Triathlon Union, European Table Tennis Union, and the European Taekwondo Union.

The lack of female representation on boards is apparent in both amateur and professional sport as well as in the corporate world of sport retail, marketing, and media. In 2018, California became the first state in the United States to pass legislation targeting gender representation on the boards of publicly held companies. Senate Bill 826 mandates that by 2021, corporations with at least six board members must have at least three positions occupied by a female or incur a $100,000 fine for their first offense (Stewart, 2018). When the bill passed, California-based Skechers USA, the third largest footwear maker in the country with almost 12,000 employees, had no women on its nine-member executive board (Ivanova, 2018).

Good governance principles promote the advantages of **independent boards** whose members are not affiliated with the organization as members of its executive team, clients, or contract service providers. There are many cases, however, where members of the governing board are connected to the organization. A travel-based athletic club team or a private indoor soccer facility may have an executive serving on the board of directors, for example. Depending on the organization's bylaws, that person may be a fully participating board member or an ex officio member without voting privileges.

Member-based organizations such as country clubs and national governing bodies for collegiate and scholastic athletics almost always have board representation from members. For example, the board of presidents of the National Association of Intercollegiate Athletics (NAIA) is considered the highest level of authority for the member-based organization and is comprised of presidents elected from member institutions. The NCAA Board of Governors includes a combination of 16 voting and 4 nonvoting members. The voting members are Division I, II, and III chancellors or presidents, and the nonvoting members include the ex officio president of the NCAA and the chairs of the management council for each division ("Board of Governors," 2019).

Roles and Responsibilities of Governing Boards in Sport Organizations

Role refers to the general function(s) of an individual, department, or organization. **Responsibilities** are the specific duties, tasks, and activities under the purview of an individual or unit. Information is abundant on the roles and responsibilities in sport governing boards. Table 3.3 summarizes the general roles for the governing boards of three sport organizations at a local, continental, and international level and demonstrates themes related to strategic planning and policies (or mandates). Many of the roles identified are also relatable to the principles of good governance.

The terms *roles* and *responsibilities* are often used interchangeably, but typically roles are general in nature, while responsibilities are more specific. One means of classification is to ascribe the responsibilities of governing boards to one of two general roles, regulatory or performance-based. Often the responsibilities of a governing board may overlap these two general roles. Table 3.4 outlines 10 responsibilities of sport NGBs as defined by a working group for the United States Olympic Committee (2014) as they align or overlap with regulatory or performance-based roles.

Regulatory Roles and Responsibilities

The regulatory role of a governing board is the control arm of the organization. The term implies the functions of oversight and compliance to ensure that the organization and its employees adhere to applicable laws and regulations as well as to the requirements of ethical behavior. The regulatory role is seemingly acknowledged by Sport New Zealand (2016), which states that boards are essentially "lawyers of ownership" as opposed to "owners of management." Governing boards have a servant leader role as the gatekeepers and protectors of the organization. The board of the USOPC, for example, serves as the gatekeeper for all member governing bodies. In its regulatory role, the USOPC board voted to decertify USA Gymnastics for noncom-

Table 3.3 Summary of Responsibilities for the Governing Board in Selected Sport Organizations

Australian Sport Committee	Illinois Park District	International Olympic Committee
• Strategic planning • Stakeholder involvement • Enhancing the organization's public image • Organizational performance • Reporting • Policy formulation • Management of the CEO • Legal compliance • Management of financial resources • Risk management • Board effectiveness	• Policy formulation • Management of director • Support mission and values • Provide strategic direction • Manage operational and capital finances • Assess and fulfill citizen needs • Long-range planning • Adhere to the organization's code of ethics	• Establish structure for the organization • Regularly review and modify processes • Performance assessments • Facilitate optimum organizational culture

Data from New South Wales Government (n.d.); Boards and Committees (n.d.); Illinois Park District; International Olympic Committee (2001).

Table 3.4 Categories of Roles and Responsibilities for Sport NGBs

Regulatory responsibilities	Performance-based responsibilities	Overlapping responsibilities
• Support and evaluate the chief executive • Protect assets and provide financial oversight • Ensure legal and ethical integrity • Enhance the organization's public standing	• Ensure effective planning • Ensure adequate financial resources • Monitor and strengthen programs and services	• Determine mission and purposes • Select the chief executive • Build a competent board

pliance and its continued pattern of dysfunction before rescinding its decision (see Governance in Action 3.1).

The responsibilities aligning with the regulatory role of a governing board include (1) fiduciary supervision, (2) legal affairs, (3) risk aversion, and (4) succession planning. In one way or another, the four responsibilities are closely related.

Fiduciary Supervision   Fiduciary supervision refers to the legal and ethical obligation to administer, invest, monitor, and distribute tangible and intangible assets of an organization. Tangible assets include land, facilities, investments, cash, and equipment. Intangible assets include an organization's public reputation.

A governing board serves as the fiduciary for an organization according to statutory and common law (Association of Governing Boards for Universities and Colleges, 2015). It is an obligation of the board to protect and optimize an organization's assets and capital investments, which includes public reputation. Fiduciary responsibilities include the duties of obedience, care, and loyalty in a trusted relationship between parties, such as a governing board and the organization it serves. These duties apply to all governing boards, whether associated with a sport or nonsport organization in the private or public domain.

The fiduciary responsibilities outlined for sport organizations may be the same as those of a nonsport organization. A report on guidelines for NGB board members by a working group for the United States Olympic Committee (2014) identified the following eight fiduciary responsibilities that are generic to the extent that they would apply to a large corporation, a small business, or a nonprofit entity:

1. Approving budgets
2. Hiring independent auditors to conduct annual audits
3. Approving any loans, accumulations, and restricted accounts

4. Overseeing bank accounts, investment advisors, and endowments
5. Monitoring sales transactions and checking for any unrelated business income
6. Complying with legal and fiduciary laws and regulations
7. Overseeing compensation, benefits, and liability
8. Approving capital campaigns and fundraising goals

Fiduciary supervision of a governing board for a sport organization, such as an intercollegiate athletic department, sometimes requires unique oversight responsibilities due to the nature of the industry. According to the Association of Governing Boards for Universities and Colleges (2018), fiduciary responsibilities specific to athletics include

1. ensuring that institutional strategy accounts for risks inherent to sport, such as concussions,
2. reviewing and monitoring outcomes related to the institution's plans for gender equity in athletic programs under Title IX,
3. reviewing contract agreements for highly compensated athletics personnel,
4. reviewing financial information concerning athletics,
5. reviewing indicators of the academic progress and well-being of student-athletes,
6. consulting on issues related to conference membership, and
7. reviewing data and certifying compliance with national (e.g., NCAA) and conference regulations.

Legal Affairs   The fiduciary responsibilities of governing boards include a duty and obligation to ensure that the organization operates legally under all applicable laws and regulations. At the

Scott Varley/MediaNews Group/Daily Breeze via Getty Images

Governing boards have fiduciary responsibilities to ensure that organizations can responsibly finance construction ventures such as the building of the SoFi Stadium in Los Angeles, California.

University of Louisville, the board of trustees and the athletic department's board of directors were both involved in a decision to settle a lawsuit for $4.5 million with former athletic director Tom Jurich, who was fired after the institution's basketball program was accused by the Federal Bureau of Investigation (FBI) of being involved in a pay-for-play scandal ("Louisville, Ex-AD Settle Dismissal," 2018). The two respective boards must also navigate through a separate $38.7 million breach of contract lawsuit filed by former Louisville coach Rick Pitino, who was also fired after the FBI probe. The multi-million-dollar decision by the two governing boards in the face of litigation against the University of Louisville exemplifies the magnitude of legal responsibility for all facets of the institution, including athletics.

The responsibilities related to legal affairs are many. A basic legal responsibility under the purview of a governing board is to make sure that organizations pay federal and state taxes or that the appropriate filing fee and applications are in order if claiming tax-exempt status. Additional legal affairs for governing boards include maintaining the proper types and amounts of insurance; making sure that necessary licenses or certifications are current; maintaining diligent document retention practices; and making sure that liability waivers or releases are properly administered. While the tasks associated with any of these broad legal areas

may be delegated to someone in the organization or contracted to a third party, the governing board still has the general fiduciary responsibility for legal affairs.

In intercollegiate and scholastic athletics, the board's legal responsibilities include compliance with antihazing laws and federal Title IX regulations that prohibit discrimination on the basis of gender. For example, a school district's board in suburban Chicago approved a settlement of $199,500 for two football players ($300,000 total) who alleged frequent acts of sexual assault and hazing between teammates (Shields, 2017). This settlement illustrates the ethical and legal responsibilities that boards that oversee coaching have for the safety and well-being of athletes.

Legal and ethical responsibilities of a governing board were apparent during the high-profile sexual abuse cases involving Jerry Sandusky, former assistant football coach at Penn State University, and Larry Nassar, former team doctor for the athletic department at Michigan State University and for USA Gymnastics. In both cases, the governing boards faced repercussions for failing to protect athletes from reported abuse. Similarly, a school board in Polk County, Florida, was found guilty of negligence for failing to protect a football player who alleged repeated physical abuse by his coach. The plaintiff was awarded $125,000 as a result of his claim that administrators and officials failed to remove the coach after disciplinary measures did not stop the abuse (Wolohan & Gau, 2018). Lawsuits over governing boards' duty to protect athletes' safety and welfare are common.

Governing boards are especially vulnerable regarding their duty of care in youth sports, such as a high school athletic department, club team, summer camp, or municipal recreation program. Boards may be guilty of negligence if injury or a fatality occurs because the organization employed a coach or trainer deemed unqualified or out of compliance with certification requirements in first aid, automated external defibrillator (AED) use, or cardiopulmonary resuscitation (CPR). In addition, boards are ultimately responsible for ensuring that anyone involved with youth coaching has undergone required background checks.

In general, governing boards act in the best interests of the organization. On occasion, boards are placed in a precarious position by having to make decisions that are legal in nature, such as filing for bankruptcy protection, opting out of a contract, or seeking judicial action against a third-party vendor. The governing boards of sport organizations must be especially aware of vulnerabilities within the scope of legal affairs.

Risk Avoidance   **Risk avoidance** refers to the tendency to evade or minimize risks. In one respect, the decision by the University of Louisville's board of trustees and board of directors to settle a multi-million-dollar lawsuit in the FBI investigation of basketball corruption was one that avoided the risk of a greater monetary payout if the case were tried in court. Similarly, the decision by the board of directors for the USOPC to begin the decertification process of USA Gymnastics was also a matter of avoiding or minimizing the risk of additional lawsuits being brought upon both organizations for failure to protect athletes from Larry Nassar.

Governing boards are increasingly being held accountable for managing risks and safeguarding their organizations from legal proceedings in addition to any threat of a financial crisis. This responsibility is partially achieved by creating, implementing, and enforcing policies and procedures. For example, in 2016 governing boards for many institutions in higher education discussed or actually implemented policies for changing the status of hourly workers to full-time or limiting total hours of employment for selected athletics personnel when the U.S. Department of Labor announced an increase in the minimum annual salary of exempt employees from $23,660 to $47,476 ("Payment of Coaches and Athletic Trainers," 2016). Although

the mandate was rescinded before the effective date, the governing boards for universities across the United States were addressing the means of compliance as part of their responsibilities for risk aversion.

As part of a proactive compliance strategy to minimize risks, boards may periodically conduct audits to identify or correct any violations. These audits may review reporting protocols or actual occurrences of discrimination, harassment, hazing, safety violations, employee behavior problems, labor complaints, data breaches, contract disputes, erroneous reporting, or any other potential problems. The power of a governing board to impose fines, suspensions, and terminations helps to ensure that the organization is not unnecessarily exposed to liability. Drug testing and education policies are additional measures boards take to minimize risks to their organizations.

Succession Planning   The fourth dimension of regulatory functions is **succession planning**, developing processes and strategies for replacing key employees who leave the organization as a result of death, voluntary departure, or termination. While succession plans are important, they do not guarantee a smooth transition in leadership, as evidenced by USA Gymnastics hiring four CEOs within a two-year span.

Succession planning is essential to the sustainability of an organization; it assures stakeholders that competent leaders will be retained. Effective succession planning can ensure that board processes continue without interruption in the event of a planned or unplanned vacancy. In the case of USA Gymnastics, which lost its entire governing board through forced resignations and which was besieged by turnover in its CEO position, the lack of continuity was an impetus for the USOPC to begin the process of decertification (Hobson & Clarke, 2018). Decertification would have effectively stripped all power from USA Gymnastics.

Succession planning is often equated with personnel development when internal candidates are groomed to fill key positions if vacancies occur. Succession planning may also address the possibility of filling vacancies with external candidates. The key to succession planning is to anticipate vacancies and to establish processes and procedures for filling key positions in the event of a departure or termination. These processes are the partial responsibility of governing boards, which are tasked with identifying key positions, determining skill or experience gaps of potential candidates, and developing a training or hiring strategy for a replacement.

When former National Basketball Association (NBA) Commissioner David Stern announced his retirement, the board already had a process (including a timeline) in place that resulted in the successful hire of Adam Silver as his successor. Planned retirement was also a condition in the case of Herbert Hainer, former CEO of Adidas. Hainer had planned to retire in 2015, but due to the 2016 Olympics in Rio de Janeiro, Brazil, he agreed to a one-year contract extension through 2017. Igor Landou, chair of the Adidas supervisory board, noted that the contract extension had given the group's management team time to groom Hainer's successor and ensure a smooth transition (Thomasson, 2014).

Performance-Based Roles and Responsibilities

The performance of a governing body is the catalyst for organizational effectiveness. A governing board has a vested interest in the vitality of the organization, which helps guide decision making. Governing boards are mainly concerned with the "big picture" performance of the organization, not in micromanaging the daily operations of its employees. The executive board for a municipal parks and recreation department, for example, will not likely involve itself in the hiring of summer camp directors. However, the board would be concerned with ensuring that all of the workers have the skills and certifications necessary for employment.

Primary board responsibilities that are consistent with its performance-based role include (1) strategic planning, (2) operational effectiveness, (3) shareholder or stakeholder relations, and (4) fostering an ethical culture.

Strategic Planning Strategic planning is long-range planning that establishes the direction and priorities of an organization. On occasion, a governing board may assume the entire responsibility for developing a strategic plan.

Strategic plans begin with a review of the organization's mission statement and values. The second step includes an internal and external analysis of the organization's market position and capabilities, examining internal strengths and weaknesses and external opportunities and threats. For example, when the Cleveland Cavaliers instituted Flash Seat technology to become the first NBA organization to use paperless tickets, other NBA teams and professional league franchises viewed the initiative as an opportunity to add to their cadre of client services.

Strategic planning continues by establishing initiatives or goals for an organization to overcome threats and weaknesses or to capitalize on strengths and market opportunities. Key performance indicators (KPIs) are assigned to each goal or initiative as a tool for assessment. The planning then identifies strategies for achieving the KPIs along with the individual or department responsible for implementation, any necessary resources, and timelines for starting and finishing each activity.

Typically, strategic planning addresses intervals of three to five years. Governing board members are generally apprised of progress each year through an executive summary that indicates whether each goal or initiative has been achieved, is ongoing, or has not been activated. Thereafter, further information helps the board to affirm or revise strategies as part of its performance responsibilities.

Operational Effectiveness Governing boards have a responsibility for the organization's operational effectiveness in both the short and the long term. **Operational effectiveness** is the ability of an organization to optimize its business performance in relation to defined standards for areas such as efficiency, growth, profitability, social responsibility, and sustainability. Optimizing performance is an ongoing concern behind governing board decisions. To ensure that an organization is on track to achieve operational effectiveness, boards establish standards and systems to optimize human capital, profitability, market position, or public image. One such board system is regular meetings, which may occur biannually, annually, quarterly, or monthly. Special sessions or meetings are occasionally needed when decisions must be made outside the window of regularly scheduled meetings.

Governing boards accomplish work through committees, councils, or commissions. For example, the 29 directors for the United States Ski and Snowboard NGB are assigned to various committees and councils. In addition to an athlete's council, most committees align with disciplines within the sport, such as freestyle and alpine. The other committees align with functional areas such as nominations and governance, audits, compensation, finance, investments, awards (nominations and purchase), and ethics.

A board member may be assigned to be a committee chair or may serve in an ex officio capacity. Committees may only be required to submit regular reports to the board at specific intervals. In other words, procedures and processes to achieve operational effectiveness may differ from one organization to the next, but the general premise is that a board will have systems in place to produce and monitor desired results.

Examples of board responsibilities for operational effectiveness include assessing key functional areas and business processes, reviewing financial reports, and working with the appropriate staff (or committees) to develop and execute strategies for revenue growth or general improvements. The systems that boards embrace to improve operational effectiveness require a great amount of planning and a strong leadership committed to transparency, accountability, and general principles of good governance in order to sustain desirable results.

Shareholder and Stakeholder Relations **Shareholders** are people with a financial investment in the business as an owner or part owner. Stakeholders are all the parties who have a vested interest in the organization. Boards that practice good governance have an obligation to keep shareholders and stakeholders apprised of performance on a regular basis. Boards should have a communications plan that provides pertinent information (e.g., financial data, business initiatives, and important dates). Communication plans should ensure the flow of two-way conversation, especially in membership-driven organizations where the board represents the interests of its members. Communication calendars, annual state-of-the-business meetings, and periodic newsletters are a few tools used to help maintain regularity.

Governing boards have a direct responsibility to shareholders to protect and manage their interests in the organization. The relationship between the board and shareholders is thus an obligatory affiliation marked by a sense of duty and mutual respect. The Goldclang Group, for example, is a proprietary owner of several baseball clubs in the minor league system, including the St. Paul Saints, the Charleston Riverdogs, the Hudson Valley Renegades, and the Pittsfield Suns. Among the members of the Goldclang group are Mike Veeck, son of revolutionary team owner and promoter Bill Veeck, and actor/comedian Bill Murray, who is credited on baseball staff directories as "Team Psychologist" or "Director of Fun." The board of trustees for Major League Baseball has an obligation to keep the Goldclang Group and all other owners of member franchises apprised of business decisions in the league. Similarly, regular communication is expected to come from ownership groups to the governing board.

The relationship between governing boards and other stakeholder groups (outside of shareholders and owners) may not be as crucial, but it is still a necessity. Among the stakeholders for the Riverdogs and other minor league teams are players, managers, front office personnel, fans and general spectators, community partners, stadium personnel, the city government, agents, Major League Baseball, and the Riverdogs' affiliate team. Managerial practices and good governance encourage linkages and engagement between a board of directors and the stakeholder groups for the organization. Obviously, relationships and the extent of engagement vary for different groups, but planned communication is an important responsibility of governing boards.

Fostering an Ethical Climate **Ethical climate** refers to the degree of ethical conduct or moral behavior apparent in an organization. It is evidenced through policies, practices, and procedures. Shaping the ethical climate of an organization is a matter of setting behavioral standards for employees (and volunteers) and holding them accountable for their actions. On occasion, boards have played a role in the failure of an organization to uphold ethical behavior by employees.

The hypercompetitive nature of sports is often cited as an impetus for corruption and general misbehavior in the industry. Placating shareholders through the mismanagement of team finances or condoning the return of injured athletes to the field before they are physically and mentally ready are examples of unacceptable ethical behaviors. Governing boards are ultimately accountable for inappropriate conduct by an organization or its members. In the case of USA Gymnastics, the entire board was replaced after the Nassar scandal. Similarly, in the wake of the child molestation disgrace involving former Penn State University football coach Jerry Sandusky, the chairman of the Pennsylvania system board of trustees resigned hours after being implicated by the governor for withholding information about direct knowledge of events in the case (Shade, 2012).

An organization's leaders can foster an ethical climate by example and by proactively establishing expectations for standards of conduct. It has been suggested that a servant leadership style, characterized by extreme trustworthiness and integrity, is highly effective in fostering a desirable ethical climate in sport organizations (Burton, Peachy, & Wells, 2017). These types of leaders are driven by an altruistic calling, which is an exemplary characteristic for governing bodies that practice organizational stewardship and foster an ethical climate.

Governing boards must monitor moral or immoral behavior even though they do not directly supervise employees or volunteers. Their attention, coupled with reinforcement of appropriate conduct or condemnation of inappropriate behavior, has a direct effect on the ethical climate.

Performance Assessment of Governing Boards

Among the best practices in board governance, an assessment or audit of performance is necessary to ensure effectiveness and to make sure that people understand their duties. Performance assessment systems include structural components (timing, frequency, method) and the actual evaluative or assessment criteria. In the realm of sports, directors in some organizations are volunteers, while in other organizations they are paid, and it is interesting to explore performance in relation to compensation.

Structure of Assessment Tools

Assessment is a tool to validate whether board members are practicing principles of good governance. If applied correctly, evaluations will identify gaps in core knowledge and expertise and will serve as tools for development. An assessment completed by the board of directors for a private golf facility, for example, may discover a lack of information on costs associated with monthly greens irrigation, or, it may reveal a deficiency in a board member's ability to understand financial reports.

The timing and frequency of assessments refers to when and how often the evaluation occurs. Assessments may occur at regular intervals, such as at the end of every fiscal year. Alternatively, an assessment may be triggered by a specific activity, such as the conclusion of a capital project or the occurrence of a scandal such as the 2015 case involving the Fédération Internationale de Football Association (FIFA), which led to numerous governance reforms for the organization following an independent evaluation of practices and processes.

Annual appraisals are most common for assessing board members, but certainly not the only option. Boards may be evaluated biannually or triennially, depending on the systems created.

The method of evaluation varies. Online surveys are most prevalent due to their ease of administration and ease of data collection. Interviews and written evaluations may also be used. Mixed methods of assessment (e.g., personal interviews and surveys) increase the validity or authenticity of results, while using multiple parties to assess the performance of a governing board increases the reliability or accuracy of the evaluation. Evalua-tions may be done by a third-party independent auditor, members or clients of an organization, or by self-reporting.

Evaluation Criteria

Generally, the evaluation criteria in an assessment of board executives or councils would include measures of skills and competencies (collective and individual) as they relate to good governance principles (e.g., ethical behavior, integrity, and transparency), regulatory functions (e.g. fiduciary responsibilities), and performance factors (e.g., annual profits of the organization). Table 3.5 outlines three general competency areas that can be assessed in board members.

The nature of the organization requires tailored questions to adequately address board performance. In addition to an assessment of general knowledge of basketball rules or skill in prudent decision making, the NBA Board of Governors, for example, may be evaluated on their responsiveness to officiating appeals, an area under their scope of responsibilities.

Sport New Zealand (2016), operating under the umbrella of the Ministry of Sport and Finance, developed an online governance evaluation system to assess board performance for the thousands of recreation and athletic associations in the country. The basis of the assessment tool is a framework of sport governance with four dimensions: (1) clarity and cohesion, (2) people, (3) inside the boardroom, and (4) integrity and accountability. Each dimension of the framework requires documented evidence. To assess the clarity and cohesion of a governing board, for example, the organization would produce documents demonstrating a clear linkage between strategic direction and allocation of resources, an operational plan, and a constitution (or bylaws) that was current for the organization.

Table 3.5 Competency Areas of Governing Sport Boards

Competency area	Examples
Behavioral	Integrity, trustworthiness, adaptability
Knowledge	Understanding of organization's mission, goals, leadership structure, policies, stakeholders, and available services
Skill-based	Decision making, collaboration, financial literacy, communication, analytical expertise

Compensation and Performance

Given the extent of research on the motivating power of pay, it is not surprising that we would see the issue considered for governing boards in sport organizations. However, the sport industry is characterized by a great number of volunteers, especially in nonprofit recreation and youth athletic programs. Many board members are not financially compensated for their services. The same is true for governing boards of traditional country clubs in elite sports such as golf, tennis, polo, and yachting.

Providing remuneration to board members is considered "a rarity" according to benchmark research in 2011 by the American Society of Association Executives. Accordingly, only 13 percent of organizations reported some type of compensation arrangement with the chief elected officer, such as an annual stipend or a per-meeting fee. Compensation for other board positions was less common (Athitakis, 2014).

In the United Kingdom, however, executive remuneration for board members, including those in the sports industry, is considered among the best practices for corporate governance under its 2003 combined compliance code (Wilson, 2011). The question of paying board members in America often comes down to whether the organization is a for-profit corporate entity like the NBA or Dick's Sporting Goods or a nonprofit like the YMCA or a municipal recreation center. Regardless of compensation, governing boards still have a duty to act in the best interests of the organization.

It has been surmised that unpaid, volunteer boards have a higher degree of emotional engagement than paid boards but that they are not always as astute in their commitment to financial performance (Epstein & McFarland, 2011). Often, volunteer board participation evolves into life-long commitments, especially if organizations have former-board-member meetings and honorary board memberships to maintain links to philanthropic and ambassador roles. It is also surmised that the risk of burnout is greater for unpaid board members if, for example, high-level tasks such as chairing a capital campaign for a stadium renovation project or chairing a CEO search committee require significant amounts of time (Epstein & McFarland, 2011).

Linking performance to board compensation is not uncommon when bonus structures are in place for surpassing benchmark standards, such as an athletic department exceeding its fundraising goal or an adventure sport company receiving exemplary safety ratings. Amer Sports, an international sporting goods company based in Helsinki, Finland, for example, provides cash-based annual and long-term incentive programs for its board members. Publicized for adhering to a "pay for performance philosophy," 40 percent of the annual non-incentive-based compensation for board members is derived from company stock shares ("Remuneration," n.d.).

Another example of linking board performance to compensation in the sports industry was apparent at the 2016 Olympic and Paralympic Games in Rio de Janeiro, Brazil. Part of the USOPC executive remuneration package was based on the number of medals Team USA won. According to testimony to the U.S. Senate by Han Xaio (2018), chair of the athlete's commission, when questioned about the practice, a USOPC official noted that staff members were likely to be more responsive to athletes' needs when they had "at-risk compensation" tied to the athletes' performance.

POLICIES AND PROCEDURES IN SPORT ORGANIZATIONS

Governing boards of sport organizations are the gatekeepers of policies and procedures, and they often have a role in the development, review, and enforcement of policies. The responsibilities of sport businesses owners and scholastic and intercollegiate athletic administrators include developing and enforcing policies and procedures. As a preemptive measure in the wake of the Varsity Blues scandal involving prestigious institutions, administrators at the University of South Carolina announced new procedures, including a multilevel review and verification process, for each prospective student-athlete before green-lighting the enrollment office to initiate formal recruitment (Steinbach, 2019).

While the terms are often used interchangeably, policies and procedures differ. A **procedure** refers to the techniques or methods for conducting specific operational functions of an organization or department. A **policy**, on the other hand, represents an adopted course of action that typically includes repercussions for noncompliance. For example, procedures for submitting NCAA recruiting logs require coaches to complete all sections of a standard department form. The policy, on the other hand, is the requirement that logs be submitted on or before the 5th of each month, with the caveat that failure to meet a deadline would result in a warning, fine, or suspension, depending upon the rate of recurrence.

Policies and procedures are often used interchangeably with terms such as guidelines, rules, and regulations. Like policies, rules and regulations are associated with an authoritative directive for expected behaviors or procedures. Routine procedures, such as the systems for opening or closing a fitness facility or for reporting disruptive behavior at an aquatic center, are also referred to as standard operating procedures (SOP). Governing boards may or may not have a role in developing and enforcing SOPs and other operational procedures, but they are almost always responsible for policy development and implementation.

Strategic Role of Policies and Procedures

Policies and procedures have a strategic role in the governance of organizations. They generally serve as tools for monitoring and averting risks and as benchmarks for performance and safety. Most policies and procedures are standard guidelines that note how operations proceed in an organization or that outline the general behavioral expectations for employees and the leadership team. Each, however, is distinct in its general purpose. Policies serve more as guiding principles or authoritative mandates, while procedures explain how operations work.

Policies

Policies serve a strategic informative and advisory role; they clarify expectations and identify the disciplinary consequences for noncompliance. They also serve a regulatory role to ensure that an organization complies with local, state, and federal laws. Policies document the legal and ethical entitlements of employees in areas such as mandatory and discretionary benefits, overtime pay, or the filing of grievances.

Policies also help create the climate and culture of an organization and shape employee behavior. Intentional language in an athletic department employee manual referring to "spousal or same-sex partner benefits," for example, promotes diversity and an inclusive environment.

The punitive aspect of policies, such as fines and suspensions, helps to shape behavior by discouraging risky conduct. In 2016, New England Patriots quarterback Tom Brady served a four-game suspension for his role in the Deflategate scandal that violated NFL ethics policies outlined in the league's collective bargaining agreements.

Eligibility guidelines for athletes and restrictions on the use of performance-enhancing drugs (PEDs) are two examples of policies that are published in manuals, bylaws, and constitutions. Recently, a state judge upheld a ruling denying continuing eligibility outside a six-year window to a basketball player due to policies set forth by the New York State Public High School Athletic Association and the Commissioner of Education in the State of New York (Rodriguez, 2018). The example demonstrates how similar policies are to laws and regulations.

A case example in the retail sports industry involves Badger Sportswear, which supposedly "requires all suppliers to follow its global sourcing policy and has zero tolerance for violations" (Valigra, 2018). Numerous reports noted that shipments in 2018 were routinely being received from an internment camp in western China that employed forced slave labor. In an initial backlash, universities in Maine pulled all Badger items from their stock (Valigra, 2018). Whether Badger Sportswear would penalize itself for violating its own company policy remained to be seen.

Procedures

The strategic role of procedures is to provide efficiency and structure for an organization by making outcomes more predictable and reducing freelance behaviors by employees. Procedures are detailed documents that provide instructions for completing specific operations. Nationwide Arena in Columbus, Ohio, for example, has set procedures and instructions for converting the home ice court of the NHL Blue Jackets to a stage and seating area for a Beyoncé concert.

Procedures are especially necessary in the presence of specific technologies and devices. Increasingly, sport entertainment venues are requiring paperless tickets exclusively, which means spectators must download an app onto their mobile devices and show a barcode to enter the facility. Company procedures for the venue play a vital role in effectively dealing with customer service complaints and generic technological glitches. For example, procedures may permit printing tickets at will-call if someone's phone battery dies.

Systematic processes minimize self-governing behavior by employees and promote operational efficiency. For example, standard procedures in a sport marketing agency may require vetting a digital media campaign through a process to ensure it adheres to brand image specifications and trademark protections. Without a process, digital content specialists working for a sport team may risk copyright infringement if they blindly post material without following publication check-off procedures.

A regular audit of procedures helps to maintain relevance and accuracy following any type of change, such as upgrading to a new software system or deciding to outsource a labor function. An audit typically includes a review of procedure manuals and observation or interviews with personnel to assess adherence to procedures. Misalignment can mean a complete absence of procedures or that procedures are inconsistent with existing practices. Misalignment can also mean a lack of adequate training.

Process for Developing Policies and Procedures

A process model for policy and procedure development can help sport managers to create guidelines that achieve the desired results. The model for developing policies and procedures contains five steps, starting with a needs assessment and followed by research, content creation, review, and adoption (see figure 3.1).

Depending on the size of the organization, it may be necessary to form a policy management team or a task force with representatives from all departments. In other cases, the board of directors, the owner, or the CEO may be tasked with developing policies and procedures. Regardless, all stages of the process must be addressed to increase the likelihood that rules, regulations, guidelines, or instructions are easily interpreted, followed, and enforced. See table 3.8 later in this chapter for an application of the model to develop policies and guidelines for concussion assessment and management among intercollegiate athletics.

Needs Assessment

The first stage of policy and procedure development is to conduct a needs assessment to address the risks or problems that the organization may encounter due to the lack of clear guidelines. It is necessary to define *why* policies and procedures are needed and to address whether new policies or revisions are truly necessary. Considerations include the impact of new or revised policies on the organization and whether the lack of such policies would expose the business to potential legal or ethical risk.

A starting point for determining the need for new or revised policies or procedures is to suggest what rules and regulations or instructional directions should be in place based on a high-level view of what is prudent in the industry sector as well as what will promote the organization's success. The next step is to conduct a gap analysis between these suggested needs and what is (or isn't) currently in place. The needs assessment and gap analysis can be applied to a laundry list of functional areas of the organization, such as human resources, board relations, membership services, and facility maintenance.

Research

The second stage of policy or procedure development is to conduct exploratory research. A review or audit of current policies is a starting point. The research extends to whatever else is needed to provide the pertinent data for developing or revising policies or procedures. Other techniques for gathering research include

- reviewing policy documents created by other organizations on the same topic,
- interviewing external subject matter experts,
- reading industry magazines and journals,
- researching legislation via the Internet,
- consulting with legal advisors,
- reviewing meeting notes or reports, and
- interviewing selected stakeholders (e.g., department directors, clients, customers, or other employees).

Content Creation

Content creation is the third stage of policy or procedure development. If a policy or procedure template is not available through a software system or a standard form, the entity tasked with writing guidelines will develop a uniform system when writing out each policy or procedure. Whatever template is used, it should be a somewhat flexible, modular outline to make the document easy to modify. The goal in writing policies or procedures is to ensure that the language is clear, easily read,

Figure 3.1 Process for developing policies and procedures.

and provides the right information for the intended audience (Cook, 1999).

The initial step in drafting policies or procedures includes outlining broad categories and identifying a laundry list of specific instructions or subsections needed in each category. A written policy includes an informational section denoting what is or isn't permissible and the specific consequences or disciplinary actions for noncompliance.

In terms of format, boldface headings and subheadings are appropriate because they make the document easier to review. Diagrams, graphs, and illustrations are also included whenever appropriate. A numbering system is recommended for ease in reference. A common numbering technique applies a three-digit number to each section of a policy or procedure manual (see table 3.6). Each subsection or subject may be represented by a decimal point and a two-digit number to designate the specific policy or procedure (see table 3.7).

Review

The fourth stage of policy and procedure development is the review process, which is vital before making a rule or regulation official. Draft documents should be circulated to key stakeholders, including a legal advisor to ensure adherence with federal, state, or other laws and compliance with government and industry standards. The review will help to ensure that the language is appropriate for the intended audience. Although a review process is necessary in the initial creation of poli-

cies and procedures, periodic inspections (typically once a year) help to ensure that the information is current and relevant.

Adoption

The fifth and final stage of the process for policy and procedure development is the adoption phase, which usually takes the form of approval by the highest level of the governance structure in an organization, such as a board of directors, general manager, or president. The adoption is typically signified by a date and signature from the authorized entity. After adoption, the policies and procedures need to be institutionalized, which includes publicizing and reinforcing them through meetings and training exercises for the affected personnel.

The systematic process just described has laid the foundation for substantive changes in the NCAA and athletic departments in member institutions regarding the safety and health of student-athletes, especially regarding head trauma (see table 3.8). While the impetus for the NCAA to finally address protocols and best practices for concussion identification and management was a reaction to litigation, the result has been a continuous process for proactively addressing the health and safety of student-athletes.

RECAP

Not all sport organizations operate through a board, but nonprofit agencies and many segments of the industry are governed by a board of directors or council. Governing boards are the decision-making organs of their organizations; hence, their general purpose is oversight. Governing boards also have a legal and ethical responsibility to ensure that organizations operate according to federal, state, and other applicable regulations.

There is a distinction between governance oversight and management oversight. For example, governing boards in higher education are ultimately accountable for policy and oversight of athletics, while the CEO (e.g., the university president) is responsible for implementation and enforcement.

The general roles and responsibilities of governing boards can be classified as either regulatory or performance-based. Regulatory roles include legal affairs, risk aversion, fiduciary supervision, and succession planning. Performance-based roles include strategic planning, operational effectiveness, and shareholder and stakeholder relations. The performance of governing boards is assessed

Table 3.6 Number System for Sections of Athletic Department Policy Manual

100	Athletic training
200	Coaches
300	Equipment
400	Insurance
500	Travel

Table 3.7 Number System for Subsections of Athletic Department Policy Manual

100	Athletic training
100.01	Salaries and benefits
100.02	Supplies
100.03	Certification testing
100.04	Professional development

Table 3.8 Developing Concussion Protocol for Intercollegiate Athletics

Needs assessment	The National Collegiate Athletic Association Student-Athlete Concussion Litigation Case No. 1:13-cv-09116 class action lawsuit was a driving force for the NCAA and member institutions to consider the need for greater attention to protocols addressing concussion prevention and management ("Student-Athlete Concussion Injury Litigation," n.d.). Until 2012, the NCAA had no protocols ("NCAA Concussion Lawsuit," n.d.).
Research	The NCAA-U.S. Department of Defense Grand Alliance was created in 2014 to "conduct the most comprehensive study in the history of concussion research ("Concussion Data and Research," n.d.). The NCAA also formed a concussion safety protocol committee to conduct research, which became the Concussion Assessment, Research and Education Consortium (CARE).
Content creation	The NCAA (CARE) unit created best practices for a concussion management plan and a concussion protocol checklist. A template was drafted for member institutions to modify to draft their own guidelines for concussion protocols ("Concussion Protocol Safety Checklist Template," n.d.).
Review	The NCAA (CARE) group conducts an annual review of its concussion management documents and makes revisions as necessary.
Adoption	To signify adoption of the NCAA concussion protocol checklist template for member institutions, signatures must be obtained by the athletic department head care administrator and whoever is designated per institutional or conference requirement ("Concussion Protocol Safety Checklist Template," n.d.).

by criteria that relate to these regulatory and performance-based roles.

Policies and procedures in an organization, often developed by a governing board, provide the framework for behavior and conduct. The five-step model for creating policies and procedures consists of a needs assessment, research, content creation, review, and adoption.

Critical Thinking Questions

1. Would any entity supersede the authority of a board of governors or a board of directors for a sport organization?
2. Which category of roles for a governing board (regulatory versus performance-based) is more important, and why?
3. Would there be higher expectations for a large city's municipal recreation department board of directors if the directors were paid for their services instead of serving as volunteers?
4. What stakeholders would be important in the review process for creating policies for a golf and country club?

Applied Activity

Research Sanctioning Body

Use the Internet to research the sanctioning body of an individual sport. Identify the members, the governing structure, and the governing documents.

Case Study Application

For more information on board governance and policy development in sport, review *Selecting Olympic Host Cities: Evaluating Alternatives* in the web resource.

PART

II

Framework for Sport Governance

State and Local Sport

Bonnie Tiell

LEAD-OFF

Sport governance at the local and state levels takes many forms and is led by individuals and organizations with varying levels of knowledge and experience. These systems range from recreational sport programs directed completely by parent volunteers to statewide agencies with a paid staff consisting of full-time professionals.

The key distinction between local and state-level governing agencies for sport is their scope of authority. The three basic classification systems for sport organizations, whether a for-profit or nonprofit entity, are private, public, or **quasi-public**. Quasi-public organizations, such as a local YMCA or a municipal sport commission, are those operating through a blended private-public ownership structure, membership base, cadre of service offerings, or financial support system. These organizations, for example, may be owned by private entities who receive government subsidies to serve the public.

A **local sport agency** is a governing body with authority to regulate an aspect of sport in a city, township, territory, district, prefecture, parish, or county. (A prefecture is another term designating an administrative district, common to such countries as Japan and France.) Examples of organizations with a governing role for sports at the local level include the Brevard County Recreation Department in Florida (USA) and the White Rose YMCA in Sheffield, England. If a local sport organization is affiliated with a state or national association, there is additional oversight. For example, a local community sport league may be affiliated with Pop Warner football or Cal Ripken Baseball.

A **state sport agency** is a governing body with authority over sport or sport entities at the state level or one that exerts state-level influence in regulating an aspect of sport. **State** refers to a subregion of a country or nation. In the United States, the primary organizations with a governance role for sport at the state level include sanctioning bodies for competition or participation in sectors such as recreation (e.g., Ohio Parks and Recreation Association), scholastic (e.g., Oregon Schools Activity Association), and disabled (e.g., Special Olympics Alabama, Inc.). Other agencies with a governance role at the state level are those connected to a specific function of sport, such as the New York State Association for Baseball Umpires.

This chapter addresses the structure of groups that organize and supervise sport at the local and state levels. The chapter examines for-profit and nonprofit sport organizations classified as private, public, and quasi-public. Two common challenges for local and state sport organizations are examined including (1) volunteer procurement (and management) and (2) funding, especially where government support is minimal. A more in-depth overview of education-based (interscholastic) sport systems and those affiliated with the fitness, recreation, and wellness sector of sports is provided in part III.

Learning Outcomes

- Identify various types of agencies governing sport at the local and state levels.
- Distinguish between private, public, and quasi-public organizations governing sport at the state and local levels.
- Describe challenges faced by authorities associated with local and state sport governance.

GOVERNANCE AND AUTHORITY IN SPORT ORGANIZATIONS AT THE LOCAL LEVEL

According to market reports, U.S. amateur and adult sport leagues, when combined with local youth sports and travel teams, are expected to generate $41 billion by 2023 (Wintergreen Research, 2017). Authors of a comprehensive study predict a 55 percent growth surge just in the U.S. youth sports segment.

Governance and authority in local sport organizations reside mostly with their ownership or leadership teams, similar in structure to a traditional small business. Local sport agencies can be classified according to whether they operate for profit or as nonprofit entities.

For-Profit Entities

An entity that operates for profit and is open to the public is typically termed a **commercial venture**. In the United States, commercial entities typically must have a name registered and articles of incorporation filed with a state's department of commerce to declare the business a revenue-producing, for-profit entity. Table 4.1 provides a general description and examples of five categories of for-profit sport organizations at the local level.

Private Clubs

Private sport clubs and facilities vary in size and scope. Today, the average-sized private sport club in America has more employees and collects more receipts than three-quarters of other businesses and companies in the country (Club Managers Association of America, 2015).

Traditionally, **private clubs** have been associated with sports considered affluent, such as

Table 4.1 Categories of Local For-Profit Sport Entities

Category	Description	Examples
Private clubs	Organizations with an exclusive membership base, ownership, and funding.	Mohawk Private Golf Club (Tiffin, Ohio); Shakerag Hounds Hunt Club (Hull, Georgia); Boca Lago Tennis Club (Boca Raton, Florida)
Quasi-public organizations	Organizations supported by a mix of private and public funds; typically privately owned businesses that receive a portion of their funding from a public source as a condition for serving a sector of the public.	Lake Erie Crushers (Avon, Ohio); Chickasaw Bricktown Ballpark (Oklahoma City, Oklahoma); Darlington Raceway (South Carolina); Spartan Municipal Stadium (Ohio)
Independent contractors	Self-employed individuals who provide a service without a formal relationship with a company or business. These entities are responsible for filing taxes and personally assuming liability for their business activities.	Personal trainers, nutritionists, dietitians, group exercise leaders, tennis pros, Pilates experts
Commercial independent contractors	Organizations owned by an individual, partnership, or equity group that generate revenue from public consumption and lack a corporate office or chain.	Green Fitness Studio (Brooklyn, New York); Rossford Dome Soccer Center (Rossford, Ohio); Hermes Sports (Cleveland, Ohio)
Commercial franchise facilities	Organizations owned by a parent company that operate independent facilities that generate revenue from public consumption in a local market.	LA Fitness; Planet Hollywood; Top Golf; Dick's Sporting Goods; Warrior Dash; Tough Mudder

hunting (fox), polo, equestrian riding, yachting, tennis, and golf. Modern private clubs are available for a much wider range of sports (e.g., swimming, squash, basketball, volleyball). Private clubs also cater to members who seek exclusivity in fitness, health, and wellness services.

The most common type of private club in the United States, the local country club, offers elaborate social amenities and recreational opportunities, such as a private golf course. The country club is typically associated with the affluent consumer, and its purpose is to generate profits, although a private club may have the opportunity to classify as a nonprofit organization.

Most private sport clubs remain entrenched in antiquated management models based on bylaws created by a privileged few who have grown old or died. Private sport and country clubs typically have deep-rooted legacies, historical traditions, and a service-above-all-else mentality.

Quasi-Public Clubs and Facilities

For-profit sport organizations considered quasi-public are characterized by a mixture of private and government-supported activities. These businesses may or may not include a private membership base. Often they are privately owned but either receive funding from a public source or generate revenue by serving a sector of the public. Privately owned or privately and publicly owned professional or semiprofessional sport teams and stadiums fall under this classification (Diedrich, 2007, p. 24). Governance in Action 4.1 describes some of the challenges of a quasi-public sport enterprise in the case of a privately owned baseball team playing in a leased stadium financed through public taxes.

The premise behind quasi-public sport businesses is that they provide public benefits in the form of comfort, convenience, and general quality of life that the government may supplement. Rules and regulations typically include government stipulations if the organization receives local, state, or federal funding. Governance in these types of organizations is complex to the extent that private team owners must comply with league regulations and private stadium owners must work with multiple governing agencies, ranging from health inspectors for concession operations to league entities governing officiating crews.

GOVERNANCE IN ACTION 4.1

Lake Erie Crushers Exemplify Challenges of Quasi-Public Sport Enterprises

The Lake Erie Crushers baseball team in Avon, Ohio, is a quasi-public sport enterprise. Tom and Jacqueline Kramig, owners of a company named Blue Dog Baseball LLC, purchased the Crushers in 2016. While managing the day-to-day operations of the team and the stadium, the Kramigs do not own the stadium. As a private enterprise employing over 250 seasonal workers, Blue Dog Baseball LLC pays $250,000 in annual leasing fees for the use of Sprenger Stadium as the Crushers' home field and approximately $75,000 in salaries (T. Kramig, personal communication, March 28, 2019). The stadium is partially financed by individuals working in the city of Avon who incur a 15-year, 0.25 percent recreation income tax to pay construction debt exceeding $10 million (Fortney, 2018).

One of the benefits for the city has been free use of the field for the local Avon High School baseball team, but due to an increase in rental contracts with Lorain County Community College, Notre Dame College, and St. Edward High School of Lakewood, city usage has faced significant restrictions. As private owners in the business of maximizing potential profits from public consumption, the Kramigs have the right to lease the field for capital gain, but they must also maintain a sense of corporate social responsibility as members of the community.

When they acquired the Crushers, the Kramigs initially invested in stadium improvements by financing an awning over the third base picnic plaza, adding a new bar down the third base line, and enhancing the Kid's Zone and concession service areas (Shapiro, 2016). The field was also installed with a portable pitcher's mound, making it easier to convert the field for other uses such as concerts, road races, and flag football tournaments. While owner Tom Kramig claims the relationship with the city is a partnership, his status as a landlord who made business decisions that affected the availability of dates for the local high school team illustrates the challenges in governing a quasi-public sport enterprise.

Independent Contractors

Assuming the risks and rewards of their own business, **independent contractors** are self-employed, meaning they are not classified as employees and they do not report to an owner. Professional athletes in individual sports such as tennis, golf, and motorsports are often legally classified as independent contractors, and they assume the liability for their income and expenses. Outside of professional athletes, there are many other examples of independent contractors in commercial sports, such as strength trainers, fitness experts, weight loss specialists, and nutritionists.

Many independent contractors have service agreements with fitness clubs, universities, hospitals, retirement villages, or large local businesses that offer employee wellness programs or on-site fitness facilities, such as Googleplex in California or the Hewlett Packard Company in Texas. Independent trainers and experts may also offer their services to clients individually to provide one-on-one consultation. Independent contractors must practice self-governance to file appropriate taxes, and they often hire an accountant to help them determine legitimate expenses and deductions. They also have an obligation to demonstrate they have the skills and experience to train in the field, prioritize client safety, and operate according to a universal set of ethical standards. However, no state or national regulations exist requiring licensure or certification. Certification, especially from a national or university agency appropriate to their discipline such as such as the International Dance and Exercise Association (IDEA) or the National Strength and Conditioning Association (NSCA), is a means to demonstrate greater credibility in the marketplace.

Commercial Independent Businesses

There is an almost endless supply of independently owned sport enterprises operating as for-profit businesses in local markets. Bowling alleys, aquatic centers, ski resorts, velodromes, health clubs, fitness centers, cross-training facilities, racetracks, equestrian farms, marinas, multipurpose gyms, volleyball academies, soccer academies, batting cages, indoor driving ranges, skeet shooting ranges, water parks, rock climbing facilities, skate parks, archery ranges, adventure courses, ice rinks, and gymnastic facilities are just a sample of businesses using sport as a tool to generate profits.

Commercial independent enterprises include single facilities, such as a yoga studio or gym, that are not connected to a franchise or chain. However, this category also includes independently owned facilities that *may be* attached to a chain of businesses such as a hotel. For example, the Union Club in Cleveland, Ohio, is a fitness facility open to members and "hotel guests from reciprocal clubs" ("Welcome to the Finest Fitness Club," n.d.).

Individual sport businesses in local markets are considered **entrepreneurial enterprises** since they operate under an individual owner, partnership, or ownership group that assumes all related risks and rewards of the business as opposed to being employed by a parent company. Hermes Sports & Social LLC, for example, is a growing sport management company in Cleveland, Ohio, that produces events (primarily road races) on behalf of corporations and businesses. Many businesses like Hermes are set up as limited liability corporations (LLCs) whereby members incur no personal liability for company debt. Identifying as an LLC in the United States involves filing a legal business name, paying the appropriate fee, and submitting the articles of incorporation (corporate charter) to the appropriate secretary of state outlining the purpose and establishment of the organization. A similar process occurs for sole proprietorships and partnership businesses, whose owners assume personal liability if a debt is incurred. The distinction in establishing an individual business as a sole proprietorship, partnership, or LLC is important for state and federal tax filings.

For most small businesses, the owner is the supreme authority for the organization. Independent contractors and owners of commercial independent sport businesses do not work through a board of directors or a shareholder group, which is an important difference from franchise businesses. Owners may develop a senior leadership team that includes a general manager or department heads if the business is large enough, but ultimately, accountability for compliance with legal and financial issues is the responsibility of the owner. Small business owners often hire a third-party accounting agency to oversee payroll and tax filings. An employee manual or operations guide may be drafted by an owner with or without the assistance of a contracted legal source. The manual or guide outlines the rules and regulations for the business and serves as a governing document for operations. The key distinction in the governance model for a commercial independent business is the scope of authority assigned to an owner or owners as opposed to an outside board.

Commercial Franchise Facilities

Commercial franchise fitness, health, and wellness facilities typically offer more amenities than a private local independent club, such as a wider variety of equipment, on-site childcare services, or a smoothie bar. An example of a commercial franchise sport enterprise is the chain of U.S.-based Fitness International LLC (aka LA Fitness), which generates over $2 billion annually and has just under 5 million members in 700 local facilities (Wells & Ellsworth, 2016). A second example of an American-based chain is 24 Hour Fitness, which generates over $1.3 billion annually and has over 4 million members belonging to one of over 400 local facilities (Young, 2014). Many of these American chains have ventured into international locations. Adventure races such as the Spartan Run, Tough Mudder, and Warrior Dash also fall in the category of commercial franchise businesses.

A commercial franchise business owns the rights to trademarks tied to a product or service. Locally operated franchises may be independently owned if a franchise fee was paid for rights. More often, the ownership structure for local commercial franchise clubs is through an outside firm that hires managers to operate facilities.

Governance for private commercial clubs resides with a leadership team at a corporate headquarters and some type of board (of directors). The size and composition of the board varies. The role of the board is generally to contribute to the viability of the business by making appropriate decisions affecting all member clubs. Often, boards are the drivers of acquisitions, such as 24 Hour Fitness and LA Fitness acquiring most of Bally's Fitness centers in recent years (Barr, Bennett, & Bettoncourt, 2014). The decisions of boards affect local clubs, which are governed through corporate policies and procedures in much the same manner as McDonald's or Burger King restaurants, whose processes are standardized in every location.

There has been a great deal of volatility in the private commercial fitness industry due to board decisions and market demands with increased competition. In Canada, for example, VI Fitness, which operated eight facilities in Vancouver, closed its doors through bankruptcy, affecting 9,000 members and 138 employees (Wilson, 2017). The company owed $5.8 million to creditors. Similar stories of acquisitions and closures of commercial fitness centers in the United States are common.

Nonprofit Local Sport Organizations

Nonprofit local sport organizations are available in almost every community. Within cities and territories, recreation departments are subsidized and operate primarily through the support of a municipal government that provides sport oppor-

tunities for public consumption at little or no cost. Models exist for offering sports that may or may not include a cost for participants, but the classification of a sport enterprise as a nonprofit or tax-exempt organization essentially is determined by the IRS.

The IRS will grant 501(c)(3) tax exemption to an amateur sport organization that meets any of the following criteria:

1. The organization is educational (teaches sports to youth or is affiliated with an exempt educational organization).

2. The organization develops, promotes, and regulates a sport for youths in combatting juvenile delinquency or lessening the burdens of government.

3. The organization fosters national or international amateur sports competition, and no part of its activities involve the provision of athletic facilities or equipment.

Local communities receive benefits from national nonprofit organizations such as Play It Forward, which provides sport equipment to underprivileged youth, and the Women's Sport Foundation GoGirlGo program, which encourages programs that promote physical activity for girls. Table 4.2 provides a general description and examples of the four categories of nonprofit sport organizations at the local level.

Municipal Parks and Recreation Systems

For the vast majority of America's youth, their first venture into organized sport was provided by a **municipal parks and recreation agency**. Local governments have long maintained responsibility for providing recreation opportunities for the public. Governance and funding for city and county parks and recreation usually come through state and local governments.

The U.S. Census Bureau (2012) identifies 90,056 independent local governments representing counties (3,031), municipalities (19,519), townships (16,360), special districts (32,266), and school districts (12,880). Most of these local governments support recreational and cultural-scientific facilities for the benefit of residents and visitors. Local government expenditures on parks and recreation and full-time staffing have, however, experienced a significant decline in recent years. Between 2008 and 2014, parks and recreation agency expenditures dropped by over $6.5 billion, 14,000 full-time positions were eliminated, and 18,000 part-time positions were added (Pitas, Barrett, & Mowen, 2017).

Table 4.2 Categories of Nonprofit Local Sport Organizations

Category	Description	Examples
Municipal parks and recreation systems	Government-funded public organizations providing maintained spaces and a range of fitness, health, and wellness programs for the masses	Cleveland Metroparks; Mobile Arlington Park; Cumberland Park; Nashville Parks and Recreation Department; Lancaster Parks and Recreation Department
Affiliate sport leagues	Local nonprofit sport leagues competing under the umbrella of a nonprofit national sport organization	Fairfax County Little League Baseball and Softball; Jasper City Pop Warner Football and Cheer; Sandusky County Cal Ripken Baseball
Quasi-public organizations	Local sport organizations with tax-exempt status that are supported by a mixture of public and private entities	Dayton Young Men's Christian Associations (YMCAs); Detroit Police Athletic League; Boys & Girls Club of Philadelphia
Scholastic sports	Local or district-level athletic programs affiliated with an educational system for primary and secondary grade levels (e.g., junior high and high school)	Roosevelt High School Athletics; Fort Laramie Junior High School Athletics

The United States maintains over 12,000 publicly funded local parks. The largest 100 cities in the United States maintain approximately 13,500 playgrounds, 2,500 recreation centers, 300 skate parks, 10,000 tennis courts, and 1,300 swimming pools (Spengler & Baber, 2015). Many local parks and recreation departments belong to the National Parks and Recreation Association (n.d.), which is governed by a board of between 15 and 30 directors elected from the membership. Park and recreation facilities may include athletic fields and courts, performance and event spaces, fitness and wellness centers, playgrounds and picnic shelters, and, depending on the location, marine and waterfront areas.

Evolution of Local Municipal Parks and Recreation Sport and recreation in local communities evolved significantly shortly before the turn of the 20th century. The concept of organized neighborhood playgrounds in America originated from **sandbox gardens** constructed in school yards and parks in Boston, Massachusetts, in 1885 (Fawver & Spengler, 2014). Over time, the playgrounds progressed from sand piles and pleasure gardens to areas that included equipment (e.g., swings and basketball goals) and sports fields. These places were valued for their role in the development of youth who generally performed better in school, were less disruptive, and were in better physical health than children from neighborhoods that didn't include play areas (Fawver & Spengler, 2014).

As play developed into more formalized recreation, city administrators were tasked with ensuring that public spaces were maintained. The governance of parks and recreation in cities and townships became a function of the municipalities.

Budget lines were created for staffing, programming, and maintaining recreation spaces. Thus, much of the governance for sports and recreation at the local levels was a matter of public oversight as opposed to a private function. Historical research notes that 800 cities had established a public park by 1902, and gymnastics, baths, and fieldhouses were constructed in New York and Chicago by 1905 (Karter, 1959, p. 8).

Structure, Financing, and Governance of Local Municipal Parks and Recreation While the structure, funding, and offerings of local parks and recreation systems vary widely, they generally provide quality opportunities for all through programs that meet the community's need for recreation and learning to benefit health and well-being. Professionals strive to advance people's quality of life by delivering consistent services, maintaining the safety and appearance of city parks and recreation facilities, and instilling community pride. Departments try to be inclusive by providing a range of programming for all ages (infants to senior citizens) and for all abilities, often including activities for people with physical, mental, and emotional challenges.

Funding for local parks and recreation facilities comes from a variety of sources, such as general obligation bonds, park dedication fees, grants, nonprofit partnerships, crowdfunding, federal transportation grants, land and water conservation funds, license plate initiatives, special use permits, specialty taxes, and user fees. In most communities, approximately 75 percent of annual financing for local parks comes from a municipal general fund (Walls, 2009). It is not uncommon for municipalities to offer a referendum asking voters to approve a local bond or tax measure to help finance a local park or recreation system. About 75 percent of referenda for public support of local parks are adopted (Walls, 2009).

The authority to operate local publicly subsidized parks and recreation systems is typically delegated to a board of directors. These boards vary in size, depending on the population served. For example, the Cleveland Metroparks system, spanning over 2,300 acres, employs over 1,500 people during its peak season to service 18 reservations, 300 miles of trails, eight golf courses, five nature trails, and a zoo with over 2,000 animals ("By the Numbers," n.d.). At the helm of the Cleveland Metroparks leadership is a three-person board of commissioners presided over by a president and two vice presidents. A judge is appointed as the authority for the board of commissioners. The second tier of leadership is a 12-member board that includes a chief executive officer, chief financial officer, chief legal and ethics officer, and additional positions titled by function. The leadership holds weekly board meetings to discuss fiscal expenditures, acquisitions, development projects, and activities related to the improvement and maintenance of facilities and programs.

Most local parks and recreation systems operate through an executive team that constitutes a board similar to that described in the Cleveland Metroparks example. The size and responsibilities of these boards differ from place to place, considering the size and nature of the population served and the landmass for parks. The Haywood Area Recreation and Park district in California, for example, operates through an administrative team consisting of a five-person board of directors, a general manager, and four department heads overseeing business, golf, parks, and recreation ("About Us: Administration and Board of Directors," n.d.). Similarly, the city of Oberlin, Ohio, operates a public recreation department through the city government office. The staff includes a superintendent, a recreation coordinator, four site supervisors, and two group leaders ("Program Staff: City of Oberlin," n.d.). A city recreation commission serves in an advisory capacity to the department and meets on a bimonthly schedule (excluding the summer) to discuss ordinances, improvements, and financial issues.

Affiliate Sport Leagues

Affiliate sport leagues are associated with a nonprofit national or international sport organization. While the annual Little League World Series is a globally televised tournament, including eight international and eight domestic teams from the United States, for most, the Little League experience is strictly a local one. The common governance element among local sports that choose to operate under the umbrella of an affiliate, nonprofit organization is the role these entities have in communities where local administrators must ensure that leagues follow the rules and regulations set forth by the national or international office. Examples of affiliate sport leagues in addition to Little League include Babe Ruth League and Pop Warner Little Scholars.

Little League The Little League operational structure begins with the decision of a local community or neighborhood to charter a program at the local level. Local leagues collectively form a district that is managed by a volunteer administrator. The Little League charter establishes its own boundaries to operate, support, and provide children who reside or attend school within a designated territory the opportunity to participate within the league ("Rules, Regulations, and Policies," n.d.).

All league personnel, including the elected board members, officers, team managers, coaches, umpires, and field workers, are volunteers. Every person associated with Little League must pass a national criminal background check. Each league is autonomous and is guided by a board of directors at the district and local levels. Local board members are elected and are responsible for day-to-day operations within the rules, regulations, and policies of Little League. The local league is encouraged to become incorporated, but it is not required. Local Little Leagues are also provided with a suggested structure for organization and elections through the league's constitution.

Although leagues may assess a registration fee to purchase uniforms and equipment and maintain fields, the fee cannot be a prerequisite for playing. Emphasizing the spirit of Little League, rules require that every child play in every game, and no eligible candidate can be excluded from an opportunity to participate. The Little League website includes a series of rules, regulations, and policies covering everything from waiver of rules to accommodate gender identity or disability to the use of Little League in the support of political campaigns ("Positions and Policy Statements," n.d.).

Babe Ruth League Founded in 1951, Babe Ruth League, Inc., is the umbrella organization for Babe Ruth Baseball (ages 13-18), Babe Ruth Softball, Cal Ripken Baseball (ages 4-12), Xtreme fastpitch, and Bambino Buddy Ball. Over one million players and almost two million volunteers participate in over 11,000 leagues in the United States ("History of the Babe Ruth Program," 2019). Similar to the structure of Little League, local organizations wishing to compete under Babe Ruth must submit an application to the national office to register as a charter franchise and must follow the rules of the international organization.

Babe Ruth League (2018, p. 11) requires local leagues to create a constitution and bylaws and to minimally operate through a president, vice president, secretary, and treasurer. The association suggests each local league field appointed and elected officers, among whom are a board of directors, player agent, insurance coordinator, umpire in chief, groundskeeper chairperson, equipment manager, concessions chairperson, chief scorekeeper, publicity director, fundraiser coordinator, team managers, clinic coordinators, website contact, and team administrator (Babe Ruth League, 2018, pp. 13-14).

Pop Warner Little Scholars Pop Warner Little Scholars, Inc., is an umbrella organization for local programs in football, flag football, cheer, and dance. Founded in 1929, the organization serves over 400,000 youth ages 5 to 16 ("History of Pop Warner Little Scholars, Inc.," 2019). The organization's website includes a password-protected online version of its rules and regulations to "prevent tampering and unauthorized use" by unaffiliated organizations ("Official Pop Warner Rules," 2019). In line with the Pop Warner child protection policy, all coaches, staff, and volunteers are required to undergo a national background check, which includes a national criminal background search, a seven-year history search on the national sex offender database, searches of the Boy Scouts of America exclusion list and the Federal Bureau of Investigation Most Wanted List, and a statewide or county courthouse search of an individual's current or longest residence (Dietz, 2018).

Local organizations must submit an application to be granted status as a Pop Warner league. To maintain eligibility, players must not fall below a C average in school, and they must meet a weight requirement for their age before competing in each game (Queen, 2013). Pop Warner does not permit tryouts or "trimming" rosters, and all participants are required to play. Individual awards are only available for academic achievement as opposed to athletic performance.

Quasi-Public Nonprofit Sport Organizations

Supported by a mixture of public and private funds, examples of local quasi-public nonprofit sport organizations include the Young Men's Christian Associations (YMCAs), Young Women's Chris-

tian Associations (YWCAs), Boys & Girls Clubs, Jewish Community Centers, and Salvation Army Kroc Centers. These organizations provide low- to medium-level sport competition and recreation opportunities through a wide mix of funding sources, including private contributions, membership dues, fund-raising events, government grants, facility leasing, certification revenues, sponsorships, and partnerships. These organizations are eligible for tax-exempt status while being free of the political forces associated with public parks and recreation agencies that are staffed and directed through local governments.

In 2013, there were reportedly 4,146 Boys & Girls Club facilities, 2,700 YMCAs, and 350 Jewish Community Centers in the United States (Spengler & Baber, 2015). In 2019, 26 Ray and Joan Kroc Community Centers (n.d.) operated recreation programs in America. Nonprofit facilities such as YMCAs are also required to justify fees in relation to local income levels and provide evidence of adequate subsidies to preserve a 501(c)(3) tax-exempt status under IRS guidelines (Stern, 2011). The local YMCA generally operates through a volunteer board, which assumes a judicial and fiduciary duty to serve in the best interests of local chapters or organizations, in addition to a full-time, paid CEO or manager who oversees full-time, part-time, and volunteer staff for day-to-day operations.

Scholastic Sports

In the United States, the most widely known competitive local sports are found in primary and secondary education systems. Any education system qualifying for federal funding is entitled to tax-exempt status as a nonprofit organization. Only a small percentage of schools in the United States operate as for-profit charter or private institutions.

The governance of scholastic sports aims to ensure compliance with legal areas related to Title IX legislation, disabilities laws, transgender policies, hazing and harassment, among other federal, state, district, and local mandates. To maintain their IRS status as nonprofit entities providing amateur sport opportunities, schools that sponsor scholastic sports must maintain a central mission in tying athletics to educational pursuits while serving the interests of their populations.

Nearly every high school and junior high school in the country provides varsity and junior varsity sport opportunities for students, with many also offering intramural and club sport competition. In 2019, the National Federation of State High School Associations (NFHS) reported that 19,000 high schools in the United States supported interscholastic sports with 7.9 million participants ("Marketing Opportunities," n.d.). According to the 2017-2018 High School Athletics Participation Survey (2018), some of the more obscure sports included outdoor bocce (51 Maryland schools); canoe paddling in Alaska, Hawaii, and Maine; nine-player football in North and South Dakota; rodeo in Arkansas, California, and New Mexico; snowboarding; surfing; riflery; and rhythmic gymnastics.

Local competition for interscholastic sports in the United States is structured through individual schools aligned by divisions based on a combination of school enrollment and the number of schools sponsoring a particular sport. It is common for sports at the same school to compete in different divisions. For example, in 2018-2019, the widely popular sport of football in Ohio included seven divisions, while girls' and boys' swimming with many fewer participants included only two ("Divisional Breakdowns 2018-19 School Year," 2018).

The governance of local school sport programs involves a multilevel hierarchy that moves from school to district to state associations that fall under the umbrella of the NFHS. In addition to following the state association's constitution and bylaws as well as district- and conference-level regulations, schools typically publish their own athletic policy manuals containing information such as disciplinary sanctions, roles and responsibilities of booster organizations, overlapping seasons, attendance policies, dual-sport athletes, transportation policies, tryouts, team awards, reporting and treating injuries, hazing, substance abuse, social media

guidelines, and behavioral expectations for athletes, coaches, and spectators.

The governance structure of each local high school athletic program is bound to differ slightly from others, but all include some involvement of a professional education staff. A director of athletics is typically the highest authority for interscholastic sports at the school level, but his or her power is limited in comparison to the principal, who reigns supreme over all school functions, including athletics. In some cases, schools may lack an athletic director, or the position may be given to a teacher who has a reduced load to compensate for extra duties. Some high school athletic directors may also supervise the junior high school and elementary programs. Independent volunteer-based booster organizations commonly serve as an advisory and fundraiser arm of athletic departments.

While individual sports are categorized by division, the school or athletic department traditionally is affiliated with a conference within the area. Conference offices assign officials, standardize eligibility rules for participation, establish postseason conference championship formats for each sport, design award systems, and publish and enforce athletic policies such as scheduling, forfeits, and penalties for banned substances. There are thousands of high school conferences in the United States operating under an office structure with either an elected president or a commissioner serving as the highest level of authority. Scholastic sports adhere to conference, district, state, and national regulations, which can seem convoluted, especially if

AP Photo/The Huntsville Times, Robin Conn

Girl's wrestling is a growing high school sport, which requires school boards to continue to address safety regulations for both genders.

interpreted differently. Governance in Action 4.2 examines a 2018-2019 local high school wrestling incident that demonstrates the chain of authority for interpreting and enforcing rules and regulations.

GOVERNANCE AND AUTHORITY IN SPORT ORGANIZATIONS AT THE STATE LEVEL

The term *state* is used to describe each subregion or federal geographic landmass for a country, such as the 50 identified in the United States of America, 26 in Brazil, 16 in Germany, and 6 in Australia. A *province* is comparable to a state in countries such as Canada, Peru, and the Philippines. States and provinces are linked to their federal or national government systems, but they are also inclined to exert independent jurisdiction (e.g., through state laws and state taxes) for their geographic territories.

Examples of organizations with a governing role for sports at the state level include the Ohio High School Athletics Association (USA), the California State Games (USA), and the Queensland State Centre Outrigger Canoe Racing Association (Australia). The New York Sport Writers Association, Georgia Athletic Trainers Association, Oregon Masters Swimming, and the Georgia Athletic Directors Association are further examples of state-level entities with a governing role for a functional area of sport. Categories for state sport organizations addressed in this section include state high school athletic associations, state games, state Special Olympics, and state sport commissions.

GOVERNANCE IN ACTION 4.2

High School Sports Authority

In high school wrestling in New Jersey, rules permit a two-pound addition to a weight class as a "growth" allowance, but athletes are not permitted to remove any clothing once they step onto the scale (Niehoff, 2018). Rules also include procedures for addressing hair length, which ignited a social media firestorm when a referee advised an athlete that he had the choice to cut his dreadlocks or forfeit his match since his head cover did not meet specifications. Respecting the official's positional power as the governing authority over the match, the athlete and coaching staff complied, and a video went viral depicting a trainer cutting off the wrestler's locks of hair (Ortiz, 2019). With allegations of racism, the referee in the case was swiftly banned from working in the Bueana district indefinitely pending an investigation by the New Jersey State Interscholastic Athletic Association and state Division of Civil Rights.

The regulations published by the National Federation of State High School Associations (NFHS) stipulate that natural hair must only be contained in a legal hair cover (Niehoff, 2018). Following the episode, an executive council member for the New Jersey state Wrestling Officials Association sent an electronic mail message to official chapter secretaries with several photos accompanied by an interpretation of the types of hair that need to be covered. The director of sports at the NFHS, however, contradicted one of the interpretations, indicating a legal hair covering was not required (Stanmyer, 2019).

In determining which interpretation to follow, the NFHS is the ultimate governing authority and therefore has precedence over interpretations made by the association of wrestling officials in districts. Similarly, although the referee in the incident was suspended indefinitely at the district level, the New Jersey State Interscholastic Athletic Association and the NFHS are higher authorities that can overturn suspension durations. In the interim, the athlete's family was represented by an attorney to consider litigation, while the official filed a lawsuit against 12 defendants, citing defamation of character and emotional distress (Burney, 2019).

The New Jersey wrestling incident suggests a line of authority to follow. At the district level, a governing board for high school sports has authority to "make any rules necessary for its government and the government of its employees, pupils of its schools, and all other persons entering upon its school grounds and premises" (Wann & Kelley, 2007). Therefore, the Bueana district retained the authority to suspend a referee indefinitely. However, the NFHS serves in a higher level of authority and can potentially overturn the district-level decision.

State High School Athletic Associations

Interscholastic sports in the United States are governed at the state level by private athletic associations belonging to the National Federation of State High School Associations (NFHS). The oldest of these associations is believed to be the Wisconsin Interscholastic Athletic Association (WIAA). In May 1895, the University of Wisconsin held a statewide track meet, believed to be the first time a high school state champion was crowned. Administrators met in late 1895 and early 1896 to form the WIAA to promote interscholastic athletic competition (Wisconsin Interscholastic Athletic Association, n.d.). Its oversight responsibilities eventually grew to include rules and rules enforcement.

Governing boards for state athletic associations may consist of a combination of district superintendents, school athletic directors, school principals, and, on occasion, school faculty. A range of titles exists for state associations, such as the California Interscholastic Federation, Colorado High School Activities Association, Maine Principals' Association, and Tennessee Secondary School Athletic Association. Many state associations have opted to use "activities" instead of "athletics" in their titles to denote the inclusion of extracurricular activities such as debate teams, theater groups, or the music department.

While the mission and structure may differ slightly, a state association's purpose is to encourage and direct amateur athletics in member high schools. The general responsibilities include

♦ regulating, supervising, and administering interschool athletic activities as part of the education program;
♦ establishing standards for eligibility, competition, and sportsmanship;
♦ determining qualifications of individual contestants, coaches, and officials; and
♦ conducting statewide championships.

According to Education Law (n.d.), state athletic associations are, for the most part, nonprofit private entities generating revenues though dues structures, tournament events, corporate sponsorships, and limited media rights deals. They are not considered official state agencies or an instrumentality of the state, and this is reflected in their ability to receive state tax allocations. In the state of Alabama, however, lawmakers recently tried to insert government influence by proposing a bill requir-

ing the Alabama Board of Education to review and adopt legislation related to sport participation before it reached the high school state association (Berg, 2019). A legislative council composed of board members from the Alabama High School Athletic Association annually reviews legislative proposals, which begs the question whether jurisdictional interference by state government officials is necessary.

Governance structures for state scholastic athletics vary by size and title, but all operate through a board or council responsible for budgets, regulations (e.g., a constitution), regular operations, and representation of member schools. State associations also operate through numerous committees represented by administrators and coaches belonging to district associations.

State Games

State games provide multisport recreational and competitive events for amateurs. Those states that offer organized competitions on a regular basis typically fall under the governance of the **National Congress of State Games (NCSG)** (n.d.), a membership organization serving as the umbrella organization for 30 summer and 10 winter games.

Examples of state games include the Empire State Games of New York, the Powerade Games of North Carolina, the Nutmeg State Games in Connecticut, the Sunshine State Games in Florida, the Bay State Games of Massachusetts, and the Games of Texas. In addition to Olympic sports, state games select sports with a connection to their regions. For example, the Ohio Games include pickleball and disc golf; the Bluegrass Games of Kentucky include bike polo, ultimate frisbee, and esports; the Georgia Games include Paralympic beep baseball; and the New Mexico Games include arm wrestling.

State games are entitled to 501(c)(3) status as nonprofit organizations, but ownership models vary. The California State Games and Sunflower State Games are their own nonprofit incorporated businesses. The Sunshine State Games and Rocky Mountain State Games, however, are properties of their respective sport commissions (e.g., the Florida Sports Foundation and Colorado Springs Sports Commission). The owner of the Keystone State Games is a private entity, and Premier Amateur Sports LLC is described as a family-owned business. The primary funding for many state games is through fees and corporate sponsorships. As with any nonprofit organization, the games do generate revenues for operational expenses, including payment for their staffs.

While day-to-day operations for state games are handled through a small staff, governance typically stems from an appointed board or sport chairs with varying power to oversee regulations. The Georgia Games, for example, is one of the largest organized multisport state competitions. It was created in 1989 as part of the effort to win the bid to host the 1996 Summer Olympic Games. Over 40 amateur sports competitions comprise the Georgia Games during their summer and winter championships, including many Paralympic events. Officially recognized as a United States Olympic & Paralympic Committee State Games Program Participant, the Georgia Games are part of a nationwide network of state games. A board of commissioners appointed by the state speaker and the state lieutenant governor is responsible for oversight of the Georgia Games. Day-to-day operations are the responsibility of a staff that moves locations throughout the year. Temporary offices and logistical issue point warehouses are erected in different cities based on the location of the games. Championships are staffed by the Georgia Games, the Georgia Sports Foundation, and thousands of volunteers (Georgia Games, n.d.).

The California State Games, headquartered in San Diego, California, is a 501(c)(3) extension of the United States Olympic & Paralympic Committee. The organization hosts amateur sports festivals in both the summer and winter, including a robotics competition. According to the organization's "Rules and Regulations" (n.d.), the National Association of State Games permits non-California residents to participate only if the athlete's resident state does not sponsor competition or his or her sport. Additionally, the California State Games requires all athletes participating in basketball, field hockey, ice hockey, rugby, soccer, or water polo to book accommodations through an approved listing, or else they must pay the association a $100 "deviation" penalty fee ("Rules and Regulations," n.d.).

State Special Olympics

Special Olympics is a nonprofit organization serving the physical needs of individuals with intellectual disabilities through single sport competitions and multisport festivals in the style of the Olympic Summer and Winter Games. Profiled to a greater extent in the chapter addressing regulatory agencies for global sports, approximately 174 countries support the Special Olympics ("2017 Reach Report," 2017). In the United States there are 53 state Special Olympic associations, including the District of Columbia and splitting California into two territories ("Find Special Olympics Near

You," n.d.). While athletics, swimming, basketball, and volleyball are typical sports offered by all 53 associations, additional events vary to reflect the geographic differences between states. In extreme northern states, for example, it is natural to offer alpine skiing and snowboarding, while sailing is available in coastal states.

Governance and authority for Special Olympic state associations stems from a board of directors that is generally responsible for budget approval, policy-making, policy enforcement, and assurance of effective management processes. All state Special Olympic associations make their annual report, audited financial statement, and a copy of the IRS form 990 available on their website, which is a demonstration of good governance through financial transparency.

Each state association is managed by an office staff that can vary in size between states. The staff directory for the Florida Special Olympics, for example, lists 49 employees, while Ohio includes 17 ("Special Olympics Florida," 2019; "Special Olympics Ohio," 2019). The highest authority on staff at each state association is the CEO or president. Several state organizations also operate through an advisory council that reports to the board of directors.

In 2019, the CEO of the Illinois State Special Olympics expressed relief that President Donald Trump reversed a proposed $18 million federal funding cut for the program by Secretary of Edu-

Special Olympics competitions in the United States are administered by 53 state associations serving over 5 million athletes with intellectual disabilities.

Dominika Zarzycka/NurPhoto via Getty Images

cation Betsy DeVos. The state of Illinois receives approximately $300,000 a year from the government, which in 2018 assisted 48,300 volunteers in operating 201 sport competitions for over 23,000 youth and adults with intellectual disabilities (Barlow, 2019).

State Sport Commissions

Many states have a **sport commission**, which is an organization whose mission is to generate economic activity and revenue by attracting visitors to the state for sporting events (e.g., sport tourism). These economic drivers of tourism are referred to as commissions, foundations, partnerships, authorities, or councils. Examples of purely state commissions include the Alabama Sports Council, Delaware Sports Commission, Maine Sports Commission, and Oregon Sports Authority ("Member Roster," n.d.).

Many sport commissions operate through a city or region, such as the Greater Columbus Sports Commission in Ohio, which hosted the NCAA Women's Final Four Basketball Tournament in 2018. The tournament generated $21.7 million in direct visitor spending, which included 32,700 nights in hotel rooms and 23,700 attendees at the Tourney Town interactive fan engagement area ("By the Numbers," 2018). Across the United States, estimated visitor spending associated with sport events in 2016 was $10.47 billion, representing an increase of 10 percent from the year before (National Association of Sports Commissions, 2017). According to the Los Angeles Sports and Entertainment Commission (n.d.), 2018 revenues from the NBA All-Star Game netted $116 million, and the 2015 Special Olympics World Games generated $415 million for the city.

Sport commissions representing states have a wider area of responsibility than those assigned to large cities or regions. Annual responsibilities minimally include involvement with hosting state games and state high school sport championships. Business activity is produced by creating independent sporting events to attract tourists or by submitting applications (and typically fees) to national and global organizations for hosting privileges for an event. The Maine Sports Commission submitted a successful bid to host the 2019 World Snowshoe Wife Carrying Championship while also organizing its own independent sport events, including Pond-a-Palooza (cross-country skiing event), the Lobsterman Triathlon, and the Moose-Dash Snowshoe Race ("Events," n.d.).

In 2011, the Office of Legislative Research noted that sports promotion organizations operated in 12 states, but only six were referred to as state commissions, and of those, two were government agencies, three were quasi-public entities, and the remaining one was classified as nonprofit (Rappa, 2011). Funding sources for the 12 varied. Many received state appropriations and tax income from either hotels or rental cars. The Arizona Sports Marketing and Authority reportedly received tax income generated by the NFL Cardinals, and the Missouri Commission received revenues from racetrack licensing fees. Tax revenue derived from the legislation permitting states to set their own regulations for legalized sport wagering will become another revenue stream.

The National Association of Sports Commissions had 818 members in January 2019, but most of the organizations were private business firms, national organizations, or city-affiliated agencies such as the Atlanta Sport Council and the Bloomington-Normal Area Sport Commission. Several additional state associations included in the membership were the Indiana Sports Corporation and the Florida Sports Foundation ("Member Roster," n.d.).

CHALLENGES FOR SPORT GOVERNANCE AT THE LOCAL AND STATE LEVELS

Participating in sport at the local or state level, whether as a participant or as an organizer, can be enjoyable and rewarding. Two of the biggest challenges in operating sports are funding shortages and overreliance on volunteer labor.

Funding

The threat of an $18 million budget cut to Special Olympics in 2019 was a massively alarming development for state associations that rely on federal funding to support their programming. Every organization, public or private, is challenged to find revenue, and specifically *new* revenue sources. However, community programs for youth are often the first victims of budgetary cuts when cities, towns, and school districts are faced with dwindling resources.

As community professionals are challenged to develop capacity within cities and counties to continue services, they often look to grassroots institutions such as neighborhood associations and similar groups with the ability to engage residents in sustainable community change. Local sports are generally not regarded as a means to anything other than the activity itself, and thus they may be seen as superfluous during tight times (Minzner,

2010). Most services for parks and recreation in the United States are funded by local government tax revenues, which have been under stress for a variety of reasons in recent years. In response, governments have cut spending on local parks and recreation services. According to data from a U.S. Census Bureau local government finances survey (n = 90,056), between 2010 and 2013, parks and recreation expenditures decreased by 21.22 percent, and over a cumulative 11-year period, they suffered significant decreases, ranking seventh among the 10 service sectors receiving the highest budget cuts (Barrett, Pitas, & Mowen, 2017).

Finding creative ways to fund services and practicing careful budget management are required of local sport and recreation leaders. A paper commissioned by the Carnegie Council on Adolescent Development in Washington, D.C., noted that organizations associated with the YMCA, Girls Incorporated, and Boys & Girls Clubs of America received financial support from the 1984 Los Angeles Olympic Torch Relay Event, enabling them to develop new national sports programs. Funding also supported the "Sporting Chance Program" by Girls Incorporated to expand sports opportunities for girls and young women and to introduce team handball and table tennis to members of the Boys & Girls Clubs of America (Seefelt, Ewing, & Walk, 1993, p. 106).

Grant programs for local sports, athletics, and recreation are still available for specific purposes, especially those associated with enhancing community health, wellness, and quality of life for a disadvantaged group such as low-income housing areas, the disabled, or an ethnic population. In time, tax dollars from legalized sport betting, which is gathering momentum in many states, is likely to trickle into local community sports.

A board of directors may choose to pursue sponsorships, fund-raising activities, participation fees, or a combination of options to finance programs and positions in local communities. Regardless of the challenge or the avenue chosen to address the challenge, funding issues are a fundamental aspect of local sport governance.

The United States is not the only country facing challenges in funding state and local sports. Governance in Action 4.3 describes comparable funding challenges for several countries in Europe and Asia.

Volunteers

Amateur community sports in America survive largely due to volunteer commitments. There are two general types of volunteers in the sports industry: those in authoritative roles (e.g., members of a volunteer board of directors) and those who perform hands-on tasks (e.g., collecting tickets for high school football games). A challenge within the U.S. sports industry, especially for local organizations, is an overreliance on volunteer labor.

When overseeing or managing volunteers, an essential concern is mitigating risks. Adequate training and communication mechanisms for volunteers are essential to minimize liability for the organization. While the U.S. Volunteer Protection Act (1997) provides blanket protection to unpaid workers at nonprofit and government entities for ordinary negligence, it does not cover all situations for everyone who serves as a volunteer. The Volunteer Protection Act does not cover gross negligence, reckless misconduct, a conscious behavior affecting individual safety, or numerous other actions.

At the 1996 Olympics, the aquatic venue included 3,000 volunteers and 31 functional managers stationed at Georgia Tech University in downtown Atlanta, Georgia. For two years before the opening ceremonies, 196 volunteer "envoys" (a local liaison assigned to each participating country) engaged in weekly training at area merchant locations (Rogers, 2016). At Frankie Allen Park in a nearby Atlanta suburb, almost every weekend, volunteers are coaching, lining baseball fields, selling concessions, and emptying trash cans. Successful volunteer management is essential to the effective functioning of a sport organization because the organization and its events might not be sustainable without the support of volunteer labor (Cuskelly, McIntyre, & Boag, 1998).

Volunteers routinely serve in authoritative roles for local sport organizations as members of a board of directors for a country club, community soccer league, or high school booster club. Administrators and club pros who oversee day-to-day operations of an organization must learn to work with their volunteer boards to comply with legal and business requirements while also paying attention to individual interests. On occasion, there may be concerns that directives or ideas from the board differ greatly from those of the professionally trained staff. Adherence to shared governance and compliance with established processes can help to ensure that everyone's voice is heard.

Youth sports is inundated with volunteers in authoritative roles. As the #MeToo movement has made its way across America, those with governing authority in youth sport organizations are increasingly requiring mandatory background checks. However, still lacking in many community sport organizations are requirements that coaches be

GOVERNANCE IN ACTION 4.3

The Global Reality of Financing Public Sport at the State and Local Levels

North Rhine Westphalia, the largest of the 16 states, Germany, is home to Landesportbund, the sport governing body serving as the umbrella organization for 122 nonprofit sport organizations at the local and city level. These nonprofits are the parent organizations for over 19,000 sports clubs in which some 500,000 volunteers are involved in coaching and administration. These clubs and programs are largely funded by government allocations. Over 34 million euros (approximately $39 million in U.S. dollars) was allocated to fund nonprofit sport organizations under the Landesportbund between 2013 and 2017 (Jaekel, 2017).

In England, over 1 billion pounds (approximately $1.3 billion in U.S. dollars) was provided by the government for local sports and leisure in 2007. SportEngland, the national governing body for all sport in the country, includes 326 lower-tier agencies administering amateur sport programs for the masses and 152 upper-tier authorities assigned to elite sport. The organization has experienced a steady decline in its labor force from a staff of over 450 in the mid-1990s to its current level of approximately 250 employees (Hull, 2014). One reason for the workforce reduction is England's shift from government-supported sport programming to third-party agencies being contracted to provide sport and recreation for the public.

China, having experienced a surge in sport participation since the 2008 Beijing Summer Olympics and expecting continued increases as host of the upcoming 2022 Winter Games, instituted a lottery system to supplement athletics and local public sport agencies. According to the country's minister of finance, in 2018, statewide legal wagering experienced a 37 percent increase in a single year (Stradbrooke, 2019). The equivalent of almost $7 billion was raised from state lottery sales during the 2018 World Cup, representing four times the amount raised from legal wagering on the 2014 World Cup, the lottery's first year (O'Malley, 2018).

With the advance toward deregulation of sport wagering in the United States, a lottery system such as the one that has benefited sports in China may have a comparable impact on local sports in America. The drastic difference in government financial support for public sports around the world is an area that will continue to be studied to address the current trend of decreasing funds for state and local sport and recreation agencies.

qualified in basic areas such as first aid or proper techniques for teaching skill progression.

Volunteers are essential to helping to coordinate and administer events, yet managing volunteers can also prove frustrating. A professional staff member has no way of ensuring that volunteers will always fulfill their commitments, and thus they might be left having to adjust schedules or finding other ways to meet their goals. For effective volunteer management, authority figures in sport organizations must understand what motivates volunteers and how people may feel about their volunteer activities (Hwang, 2010). In some cases, volunteers may be more interested in the benefits (clothing, tickets, access) of associating with an activity than in providing the services the organization needs.

RECAP

Local and state sport organizations include both public and private entities. In local sports, private and public organizations may function as nonprofits or as for-profit businesses. Classifications of for-profit sport businesses include private, quasi-public, independent contractors, independent commercial enterprises, and commercial franchises.

Nonprofit local sport enterprises include municipal park and recreation systems, affiliate sport leagues, scholastic sports, and quasi-public organizations such as the YMCA. The domain of local sports is so broad that it is almost impossible to address all types of entities. For example, private companies that operate road races, Tough Mudder races, and the entire retail sport sector are not thoroughly addressed in this chapter.

High school associations are prominent entities governing sport at the state level. These groups also oversee extracurricular activities such as theater, band, and drama clubs. Including the District of Columbia, there are 51 state associations in the United States governing interscholastic sports and activities.

State games are amateur multisport festival-style activities that provide competition for elite athletes. Other examples of governing entities for sports at the state level include Special Olympics and state sport commissions, which are economic drivers for sport tourism.

Two major challenges in local sports are inadequate funding and overreliance on volunteer labor. Government support for community and recreation services has dramatically decreased in the past decade. A concern for local sport administrators is to manage volunteers to minimize risks.

Critical Thinking Questions

1. Explain the advantages and disadvantages of ownership and governance of a commercial independent versus a commercial franchise sport organization.

2. What issues must local sport organizations consider when they use independent contractors to provide services?

3. Is it an oxymoron to address a quasi-public sport enterprise as a private domain? Why or why not?

4. Identify ownership models for state games associations, and speculate on the rationale behind the diversity in models.

5. Should responsibility for securing alternative funding for municipal parks and recreation departments be the responsibility of the board of directors or authorized governing unit?

Applied Activities

Sport Tourism and Shared Governance

Select a city and create a multiday sport event that will have a positive economic impact. Consider a sport festival, a street basketball tournament, a road race (triathlon, bike, marathon), demolition derby, charity basketball weekend, golf outing, hall of fame event, extreme sport challenge (e.g., Tough Mudder), or other event. Describe the event in a paragraph. Identify the ownership structure and the coordination of operational duties with various entities in the city. Identify at least three entities with shared governance oversight for the event, and define the responsibilities of each.

Government Funding for Municipal Recreation: A Global Comparison

Identify three countries in three continents other than North America. Research government funding for municipal recreation available to the masses. Create a chart to identify the distinctions.

Case Study Application

For more information on governance and authority in a local high school, review *High School Strength and Conditioning: A Case Study in Caution* in the web resource.

Regional and National Sport

Kerri Cebula and Bonnie Tiell

LEAD-OFF

Sport governance at the regional and national levels takes many forms. Except for the United States and a few other countries, regulation of national sport is often a function of the national government, which designates an official sports authority or a ministry of sport. In addition to these sport ministries, many nongovernmental agencies exist to regulate national and regional sport.

An example of a governing agency at the national level is the National Collegiate Athletic Association (NCAA), the most recognized governing body for intercollegiate sports in the United States. With authority to administer the "death penalty," which effectively banishes athletics programs from athletic competition due to the lack of institutional control, the NCAA recently imposed one of the largest fines in the association's history on The Pennsylvania State University after a former assistant football coach was arrested on child sexual abuse charges and it was discovered that the institution had covered up the allegations. The NCAA levied unprecedented sanctions against the university, including bowl bans, scholarship reductions, vacating all football victories from the previous 14 seasons, and a $60 million fine ("NCAA Decision," 2012; Rapp, 2015). In January 2015, however, the NCAA restored all previously vacated wins to Penn State and announced a stipulation that the $60 million repayment must remain in the state of Pennsylvania as the result of a lawsuit brought by the state treasurer and a state senator (Bonesteel, 2014; Pickel, 2015; Rapp, 2015). Despite the addendum, the Penn State case illustrates the power of the NCAA.

An example of an agency governing sport at a regional level is the Southeast Asian Games Federation (SEAGF) headquartered in Bangkok, Thailand. According to its charter, the SEAGF (n.d.) serves as the governing organization for competition in multiple sports in 11 countries from Cambodia to Singapore. Although operating as an independent or autonomous governing agency, the SEAGF derives its authority from the Olympic Council of Asia (n.d.) under the International Olympic Committee (IOC). At the 2017 Southeast Asian Games in Kuala Lumpur, the SEAGF asserted its governing authority to address schedule changes after a food poisoning scare, disqualified three athletes for failed drug tests, and dealt with the backlash following the arrest of a Malaysian national swim team coach for allegedly raping a diver (Morgan, 2017).

While these examples demonstrate the scope of authority amid somewhat contentious scenarios, there are thousands of governing agencies for sport at the national and regional levels that operate daily without controversy. This chapter addresses the definition and classification of regional and national agencies that have a governing role over an aspect of sport. The chapter also describes the roles, responsibilities, and organizational structures of many of these governing agencies. Finally, this chapter also explores the entwinement of government and sport in many countries.

Learning Outcomes

- Define regional and national sport agencies with a regulatory role over an aspect of sports.
- Recognize how an organization aligns with one of the four classifications of regional and national agencies with a regulatory role over an aspect of sports.
- Identify the differences in governance structure for professional team sports and professional individual sports.
- Describe the two interpretations of regional sport agencies.
- Distinguish between sport ministries and nongovernmental agencies with a regulatory role over an aspect of sport at the national level.

DEFINING AND CLASSIFYING REGIONAL AND NATIONAL GOVERNING SPORT AGENCIES

Other than sport ministries that are under the authority of a country's government, most regional and national sport governing agencies are independent, nonprofit, nongovernment entities. Most sport and business organizations operate under the scope of their **governing documents**. Governing documents are the regulations and policies that define how the organization will be governed. They define the purpose of the organization, the structure of the organization, who is responsible for aspects of operations, and the voting procedures. These documents are usually called a constitution, charter, or bylaws and are an integral component of regional and national organizations that govern sport.

A national or regional sport governing organization may be called a committee, bureau, council, coalition, alliance, union, league, or agency. In addition to geographic jurisdiction, the primary purpose of these governing entities is to serve as the regulatory bodies for some functional aspect of sport.

Defining Geographic Boundaries

While the geographic boundaries for a national organization are straightforward, the struggle to define a regional sport agency comes from the term *regional*. *The American Heritage Dictionary of the English Language* (2016) defines regional as "an often extensive, continuous part of . . . [an] area." In one sense, a regional sport agency is one that governs sport within a section of a single country, such as intercollegiate athletics in the United States, where regional or "super-regional" competition occurs before teams compete for a national championship. A second way to define regional sport agencies is to view them through an international lens, which is the approach taken in this chapter.

National Sport Agencies

A **national sport agency** is a governing body with authority over sport or sport entities at the national level or which exerts national influence in regulating an aspect of sport. Many national governments have an official office dedicated to sport. These government offices are often called ministries, and often the ministry for sport is partnered with a second or third sector of the country's interior such as youth, education, culture, or tourism. **Sport ministries** are government-appointed and controlled offices that regulate all aspects of sport for a single country.

The appointment of a minister of sport is common in countries that operate under a coalition where the highest-ranking government official is a prime minister or premier chancellor. The **sport minister** is a member of the government's cabinet and is defined as the highest-ranking government official with supreme authority for public sport in the country. These government officials are expected to provide direction and policies for the regulation of sport and any other public interest associated with their office. Table 5.1 is a list of selected countries and the titles of their ministers with a functional role in sport.

Apart from ministries, there are many independent, nongovernmental sport agencies that regulate sport, participants, competition, or an associate entity of sport on a national level. Governing many professional sport leagues, such as the National Basketball Association (NBA), is a national league office, which also has jurisdiction for regional franchises.

Table 5.1 Examples of Unique Titles for Ministers of Sport

Country or countries	Title of sport minister
Russia, Brazil	Minister of Sport
British Virgin Islands	Minister of Education, Culture, Youth Affairs & Sports
Thailand, Uruguay	Minister of Tourism and Sport
Sri Lanka	Minister of Telecommunication, Digital Infrastructure facilities, Foreign Employment and Sports
Serbia, Malaysia, Romania, Turkey, Fiji, Australia	Minister of Youth and Sports
France, India	Minister of Youth Affairs and Sport
Bolivia, Myanmar	Minister of Health and Sports
United Kingdom	Minister of Sport, Media and Creative Industries
Tanzania	Minister of Social Affairs and Sport
Vietnam	Minister of Culture, Sport, and Tourism
Cambodia	Minister of Education, Youth, and Sport

At the forefront of national sport agencies are **national governing bodies** (NGBs), which are independent, nongovernmental, autonomous units. NGBs have a regulatory role for sport, competition, and competitors at the national level. In the United States, NGB is reserved exclusively to describe the governing entity of an Olympic, Paralympic, or Pan-American sport organization.

Many national sport associations have a dual role in regulating eligibility and overseeing competitions or championships. For example, the NCAA governs 90 annual national championships in 24 sports while also serving as the regulatory agency for the eligibility of athletes in its 1,100 member institutions ("What is the NCAA?," n.d.). National agencies also serve in a regulatory role for entities or individuals associated with sport (trainers, agents, coaches, lawyers, physical therapists, marketers, etc.) through membership or "trade" organizations such as the National Athletic Trainers Association (NATA) in the United States or the Sports Bar Law Association of Ireland (Cottrell, 2018).

Regional Sport Agencies

From an international perspective, a **regional sport agency** is one that governs sport for multiple countries in a geographic territory or exerts regional influence in regulating an aspect of sport. A region may be defined according to continental boundaries (e.g., Asia and Africa) or according to a grouping of countries or territories (e.g., Pan-America and Oceania). Examples of these types of regional governing sport bodies is the Fédération Internationale de Basketball (FIBA) Europe, the Asia Olympic Committee, PanAm Sports, and the Tarragona 2018 Mediterranean Games Committee, which organizes and hosts competitions involving 26 national Olympic committees.

Classification System

The key distinction between regional and national agencies is obviously their scope of authority, whether a country (national) or a geographic territory (region). Sometimes the geographic distinction pertains to the territorial "influence" of its headquarters. For example, the National Hockey League (NHL) is colloquially considered one of America's professional sport leagues, even though seven of the 31 franchises are based in Canada, and almost 50 percent of the roster spots are filled by international players (Gaines & Nudelman, 2017; Pogroszewski & Smoker, 2011).

A simple classification system for national and regional governing sport agencies is based on their primary purpose in governance over

1. participants (athletes),
2. sport (and disciplines),
3. competition, or
4. sport affiliates (officials, trade associations).

This is not a perfect system for organizing all the agencies that regulate national and regional sport; for instance, many organizations serve as the supreme authority over both participants and the competition. It can be argued that an organization in one category may fit better in another category, and vice versa, but the functional categories used in this chapter help us to organize the myriad agencies that regulate some aspect of sport at the national, regional, or continental level.

REGULATORY AGENCIES FOR NATIONAL AND REGIONAL SPORT PARTICIPANTS (ATHLETES)

Associations with primary governance responsibility over athletes (e.g., the NCAA) typically have a role in organizing and managing competition. Two categories of regulatory agencies with a primary role in governing athletes in national and regional competition are national Olympic committees (NOCs) and players' associations in professional sports.

National Olympic Committees

National Olympic committees (NOCs) are independent, nongovernmental organizations that are instrumental in governing athletic participation in the Olympic Games. The **Association of National Olympic Committees** (ANOC) unifies all NOCs. Each NOC is affiliated with one of the following five **continental associations:**

1. Association of National Olympic Committees of Africa (ANOCA)
2. European Olympic Committees (EOC)
3. Olympic Council of Asia (OCA)
4. Oceania National Olympic Committees (ONOC)
5. PanAm Sports (PAS)

The power of NOCs and their exclusive authority over specific functions is derived from the IOC and defined in the Olympic Charter (Chelladurai & Zintz, 2015). NOCs such as the United States Olympic & Paralympic Committee (USOPC) are nongovernmental agencies, but there are countries with government officials serving in executive roles. Each NOC organizes its respective delegations at the Olympic Games (including Youth Olympics) and at all other regional, continental, and world events that fall under the umbrella of competition recognized by the IOC (2017, p. 64). The person responsible for an NOC's athletes, team administrators, and official entourage at the Olympic Games is the **chef de mission**, who serves as the liaison to the IOC, the international federations, and the host organizing committee.

Government Influence in NOCs

National Olympic committees are required to act autonomously from government or political influence, according to the Olympic Charter. The IOC (2017) mandates that NOCs must "preserve their autonomy and resist all pressures of any kind, including but not limited to political, legal, religious or economic pressures which may prevent them from complying with the Olympic Charter" (p. 60). The model constitution for a national Olympic committee drafted over 50 years ago includes similar language in suggesting a bylaw mandating resistance to "all political, religious or commercial pressures" (International Olympic Committee, 1968, p. 11).

While independence from government pressure is mandated in Rule 6, Article 27 of the Olympic Charter, Rule 4, Article 28 provides authority for NOCs to elect government or public officials as members of the organization (International Olympic Committee, 2017a, p. 62). A 2017 study of 205 NOCs (not including Kuwait) indicated 34 (15 percent) are led by a president or secretary general who has a formal position in that country's national government (Wickstrom & Alvad, 2017, p. 22). Table 5.2 demonstrates that the most concentrated representation of political ties to NOC leadership is in Asia (36.4 percent). Over half (16) of the NOCs with formal government affiliation are from a country in Asia.

Many of the presidents of the NOCs with political positions in their respective countries are the ministers or directors of an area such as internal affairs, security, or tourism. Others are considered princes or part of the royal family. Wickstrom and Alvad (2017) note that several NOC presidents are also the presidents of their countries (e.g., Azerbaijan, Belarus, Tajikistan, Turkmenistan).

Roles and Responsibilities of NOCs

Activities of the NOCs mainly include organizing their Olympic teams, athletes, and officials; facilitating logistics for travel and competition, and enforcing rules such as the amateur principle (Luschen, 1979, p. 13). NOCs are responsible for equipment, apparel, transportation, and accommodations for athletes, coaches, and team officials. They are also responsible for deciding which media will be accredited by the IOC and represented at the Games (Jagodic & Matesa, 2017).

The Olympic Charter states that NOCs are responsible both for developing elite, high-performance sports and for promoting the concept of

PEDRO PARDO/AFP/Getty Images

Many countries that participate in the Summer and Winter Olympics have government officials in executive roles on their national Olympic committees.

Table 5.2 Concentration of Leaders With Government Ties to National Olympic Committees

Continental associations	Number of NOCs	Number of NOCs with government ties	Percentage of NOCs with government ties
Africa (ANOCA)	54	5	7.4%
Asia (OCA)	43	16	36.4%
Americas (PAS)	41	3	7.3%
Europe (EOC)	50	5	10.0%
Oceania (ONOC)	17	2	11.8%

Data from Wickstrom and Alvad (2017).

"sport for all" (International Olympic Committee, 2017a, p. 59). In addition, the Olympic Charter identifies the NOC as the only entity that can select a city in its country as a candidate for organizing or hosting a Summer or Winter Games. NOCs have been accused of being monopolistic organizations because of their sole authority to select athletes for the Games (Jagodic & Matesa, 2017; Somphong, Samahito, & Kutintara, 2015).

The principle of autonomy implies the right of self-regulation through internal governance. NOCs have a degree of self-governance, but the IOC's role is superior. In the late 1960s, the IOC drafted a template for NOCs to use in constructing or revising their constitutions. Areas addressed in the template included Olympic Day, Olympic spirit, cities to stage Olympics, powers and competencies

of the organization, membership, organization, and finance (International Olympic Committee, 1968).

Structure and Funding of NOCs

The organizational structure of each national Olympic committee includes an executive board or committee that resembles those of other nongovernmental, nonprofit agencies governing sports. Typically reporting to the executive committee are numerous commissions, ranging from an elections committee to an athletes' commission. The size of the executive committee and of each commission, plus the scope of responsibilities for each and the terms of office for members, are all detailed in each NOC's constitution. Two NOCs in the mid-1970s reportedly had no office staff, while the average NOC had 24 full-time employees (Luschen, 1979).

Operating budgets and staffing of NOC offices have grown dramatically over the years, primarily due to increased revenues from media and sponsor deals and the creation of the Olympic Solidarity Program (formerly the International Olympic Aid Committee). Research in the mid-1970s noted the discrepancy in operating budgets between NOCs, ranging from zero to over $1 million (Luschen, 1979, p. 11). In 1979, only 20 percent of revenues from media deals were earmarked for national Olympic committees (International Olympic Committee, 2017b, p. 5).

Funding for an NOC comes from multiple sources, including domestic sponsorship and media broadcast rights, licensing royalty income, charitable donations, and assistance from the IOC through the Olympic Solidarity Committee. The Olympic Solidarity budget operates in four-year cycles. Leading up to the 2020 Olympic Games in Tokyo, Japan, the $509 million (USD) in funding was earmarked for athletes, coaches, NOC management, promotion of Olympic values, forums and special projects, and the five continental programs (International Olympic Committee, 2017b, p. 17). In comparison, the United States Olympic & Paralympic Committee reported a gross income of over $340 million for the 2016 calendar year on its annual tax disclosure statement (United States Internal Revenue Service, 2016).

Players' Associations in Professional Sports

Professional **players' associations** have a quasi-governing role for athletes at the national and regional levels, although the presiding authority for players is each athlete's team and league. Players' associations are common in America, Europe, and Australia. Unlike most sport governing organizations, authority is delegated to team representatives who are elected by their peers.

The defunct Brotherhood of American Baseball Players, established in the United States in 1885, was the earliest form of a players' association for Major League Baseball (MLB), followed in 1907 by the European soccer Professional Footballers Association (FIFPro), which still exists (Aydin, 2009; Dabscheck, 2003). Currently, U.S. players' associations exist in the National Football League (NFL), Women's National Basketball Association (WNBA), MLB, NHL, and NBA. Australia and Europe have players' associations for professional football (soccer), rugby, and cricket (Dabscheck, 2003).

Players are employees of the teams and leagues for which they play, but their respective labor unions have a governance role in the case of a work stoppage (e.g., strike by the players or a lockout by league owners). Under the National Labor Relations

Mark Rucker/Transcendental Graphics, Getty Images

In 1885, the Brotherhood of American Baseball Players was known as the earliest form of a union in professional sports.

Act (NLRA) in the United States, players have the right to have a labor organization and the right to collectively bargain with their employers (National Labor Relations Act, 1935). This legislation paved the way for players to collectively bargain for higher salaries, a higher portion of league revenue, and looser restrictions on free agency with the league owners.

While primarily serving in an advisory role representing the players' interests and settling grievances or disputes with a team or league, the union's governing authority over players gives it the power to demand a strike in the face of failed labor negotiations. The Major League Baseball Players Association, for example, had eight work stoppages (strikes or lockouts) from 1972 to 1994 (Fagan, 2018). Across three decades, the MLB actually had some type of work stoppage during every single collective bargaining negotiation prior to 2002 (Birren, 2014).

Players must pay an initiation fee and dues or core fees to their respective players, associations or unions. The players' associations have the authority to mandate a suspension without pay if payment is not received according to the stipulations of the collective bargaining agreement (National Basketball Association and National Basketball Association Players Association, 2017, p. 331).

Within the scope of their governing role, the players' associations act like any workers' union and are responsible for protecting the rights of employees. On behalf of players, the executive director and legal counsel negotiate a collective bargaining agreement with the league owners. The association also serves as the supreme authority for certifying agents and financial advisors. The players control the union, and an executive director runs the day-to-day operations. Players' associations are described to a greater extent in the chapter on professional sports.

REGULATORY AGENCIES FOR NATIONAL AND REGIONAL SPORTS

International sport federations (IFs), described in more detail in chapter 6, are the supreme governing agencies for their sport and its disciplines recognized by the IOC. In addition to the federations that represent Olympic sports, as of 2020, the IOC also recognizes 35 international sport federations that are not part of the official agenda for the Olympics or Paralympics. Among these federations are American football, chess, bridge, bandy, korfball, lifesaving, and tug-o-war ("Recognized Federations," n.d.).

National sport federations, whether representing Olympic or non-Olympic sports, fall under the umbrella of their respective international federations (IFs) but report to a national authority. While national federations are considered independent, nongovernmental entities, in many countries with state-controlled sport policy, the government presides over and funds these federations. Organizations at the regional level are typically identified as continental associations, confederations, or zones. These regional and national entities govern regulations and rules for a single sport (e.g., Russian Basketball Federation, African Cricket Association, USA Football, Paddle Australia), and this authoritative role applies to all disciplines within a sport. For example, a national or regional swimming association is the governing entity for all sanctioned aquatic disciplines, including water polo, open water swimming, diving, and artistic (formerly synchronized) swimming. Similarly, a national or continental gymnastics federation (e.g., Asian Gymnastics Union) regulates tumbling, trampolining, rhythmic gymnastics, and artistic gymnastics in a region.

Sport federations are responsible for promoting interest and participation in their sports, allowing amateur athletes to compete in international competition, encouraging and supporting programs for individuals with disabilities, and, consistent with Title IX of the Education Amendments of 1972 (in the United States), providing equitable support and encouragement for participation by women. The classification system for sport federations include (1) Olympic and Paralympic and (2) non-Olympic.

Olympic and Paralympic Sport Federations

While national sport federations play a role, in cooperation with the NOC, in creating the qualification system for selecting their countries' participants in the Olympics and Paralympics, they do not have authority for policies of the IOC other than serving as a voice to their IFs. Olympic sport federations in many countries fall under the regime of the sport ministry or sport authority, which has a governing role for sport from amateur to elite levels as a function of national policy. Many national governments provide direct subsidies to national sport federations and national Olympic committees. The United States government does not directly fund U.S. sport federations.

In the United States the **Ted Stevens Olympic and Amateur Sports Act** granted the USOPC, not the U.S. government, governing authority over sport federations that are identified as national governing bodies (NGBs). According to this act, an organization can be recognized as a sport NGB if it meets the following conditions:

1. It applies to be the NGB for its sport.
2. It demonstrates that it is a member of an IF that governs its sport.
3. The sport is included in the Olympics, Paralympics, or PanAmerican Games.
4. It is considered autonomous in the governance of the sport.

Under this legislation, sport federations in the United States are given the exclusive ability to select and sponsor athletes for international competition, provided their criteria are not more restrictive than the criteria of the IF (Ted Stevens Olympic and Amateur Sports Act, 2012). As of 2019, the USOPC recognizes 50 sport NGBs, including 37 summer Olympic sport federations, eight winter federations, and five Pan-American sport federations (United States Olympic & Paralympic Committee, 2019). There are also separate NGBs for Paralympic sports if they are not governed by the Olympic NGB in their sport. These are known as Paralympic sport organizations (United States Olympic & Paralympic Committee, 2019).

An example of a sport NGB in the United States is USA Basketball, which is described in Governance in Action 5.1.

Non-Olympic Sport Federations

Many non-Olympic sports other than the 35 recognized by the IOC also have an international federation, regional affiliates, and national associations. Examples of sports with independent, nongovernmental international and regional governing bodies that are not recognized by the IOC are capoeira, sepak takraw, Muay Thai, and buzkashi.

Thailand has over 100 Olympic and non-Olympic governing bodies for regulating sports. Examples of national governing organizations for non-Olympic sports include the Royal Aeronautic Sports Association of Thailand, Woodball Association of Thailand, Thailand Bodybuilding and Physique Sport Association, and the Thailand Powerboat Association (Sport Authority of Thailand,

2017). According to a list of "Sport Associations of Thailand" (n.d.), other examples include the Wushu Federation of Thailand, Xiangqi Association of Thailand, Thailand Squash Rackets Association, Amateur Kabaddi Association of Thailand, Thai Tenpin Bowling Association, and the Royal Automobile Association of Thailand under Royal Patronage.

In the United States, non-Olympic sport associations are not recognized as NGBs since the Ted Stevens Olympic and Amateur Sports Act only recognizes NGBs that compete in the Olympics, the Paralympics, and the Pan American Games. National governing bodies for non-Olympic amateur sports may, however, be recognized by the USOPC under their Multi-Sport Organization Program, whose goal is to increase participation in sports ("Multi-Sport Organizations," n.d.). The national associations recognized by the USOPC under the classification of multisport organizations in 2018 included

USA Football,

U.S. Polo Association,

U.S.A. Ultimate (frisbee),

Underwater Society of America (scuba),

U.S. Orienteering Federation, and

USA Dance.

Following is an overview of several national and continental sport federations for non-Olympic sports.

Lacrosse

US Lacrosse is the national governing body recognized by the Federation of International Lacrosse for all matters relating to American lacrosse on the national, regional, and international levels ("FIL Members," n.d.). While US Lacrosse fields national teams for men and women, the primary focus is on amateur and youth lacrosse ("About US Lacrosse," n.d.).

The governing body for US Lacrosse is the board of directors, which consists of 25 members responsible for defining policies and managing the affairs of the NGB. A second governing body is the executive committee created from members of the board of directors (the officers, plus the chairs of the women's and men's games). The executive committee has the same power as the board of directors except that it cannot alter policies or bylaws (US Lacrosse, n.d.). The day-to-day operations of US Lacrosse are overseen by the president, who

GOVERNANCE IN ACTION 5.1

USA Basketball

USA Basketball was founded in 1974 as the Amateur Basketball Association of the United States of America. The organization changed its name to USA Basketball in 1989, shortly after the Fédération Internationale de Basketball Association (FIBA), the IF for basketball, allowed professional athletes to compete in international competition. USA Basketball is recognized by FIBA and by the USOPC as the governing body for basketball in the United States. The organization is responsible for selecting, training, and fielding teams from the United States in international competition, including the Olympics and the Basketball World Cup, which is the FIBA-run world championship ("About USA Basketball," n.d.).

In order to join USA Basketball, the prospective member must be associated with basketball in the United States and must belong to a recognized association that aligns with one of the five categories defined in the constitution ("Constitution of USA Basketball," 2017). Table 5.3 lists the current membership in each category.

Table 5.3 Categories of USA Basketball Membership

Membership category	Members
Professional	National Basketball Association (NBA) Women's National Basketball Association (WNBA) NBA Development League (G-League)
Collegiate	National Collegiate Athletic Association (NCAA) National Association of Intercollegiate Athletics (NAIA) National Junior College Athletic Association (NJCAA)
Scholastic	National Federation of State High School Associations (NFHS)
Youth	Amateur Athletic Union (AAU)
Associate	National Basketball Players Association National Wheelchair Basketball Association Harlem Globetrotters

The main governing body of USA Basketball is the board of directors. The role of the board is to oversee the management of the association, but not to oversee the day-to-day operations. This mandate is in the constitution of USA Basketball, which is the governing document of the organization. There are 11 voting members of the board of directors who serve four-year terms with no term limits. There are voting members to represent each classification of membership.

Within the professional category, the NBA appoints three directors. The NBA, the WNBA, and the G-League are all run by the NBA, so the board of directors may or may not include individuals from all three leagues.

For the collegiate category, the NCAA appoints three directors. The scholastic category only includes one director from the NFHS. Two active athletes (one male and one female) also serve as directors. An active athlete is one who has represented the United States in Olympic, Pan-American, or World Championship competition in the last 10 years.

Finally, the two remaining board positions are one director elected from the remaining organizations not named and one at-large director who is independent. The board of directors uses weighted voting. The professional, collegiate, and athlete members each receive two votes, while all others receive one vote ("Constitution of USA Basketball," 2017).

At the USA Basketball headquarters in Colorado Springs, Colorado, the day-to-day operations are run by the chief executive officer (CEO). This organizational structure, with a board of directors and a CEO, is common in many governing sport agencies. The CEO is responsible for proposing an annual budget and executing the general managerial and administrative duties assigned by the board ("Constitution of USA Basketball," 2017).

Meg Oliphant/Getty Images

Motorsports is an example of a non-Olympic sport that is still under the authority of governing bodies at the national, continental (regional), and international levels.

is also the chief executive officer. This position is responsible for hiring and supervising the staff, executing legal documents, and overseeing the budget (US Lacrosse, n.d.).

Automobile Competition Committee for the United States

The Automobile Competition Committee for the United States (ACCUS) is the national governing body for motorsports. ACCUS is comprised of the major professional motorsports sanctioning bodies in the United States, including the International Motor Sports Association (IMSA), IndyCar, the National Association for Stock Car Auto Racing (NASCAR), the National Hot Rod Association (NHRA), the Sports Car Club of America (SCCA), and the United States Auto Club (USAC). Amateur motorsports groups are not members.

ACCUS is the national sporting authority for the United States recognized by the Fédération Internationale de l'Automobile (FIA), the IF for motorsports (ACCUS, n.d.). ACCUS is not recognized by the USOPC, however. Many membership organizations under the umbrella of the ACCUS are representative of governing associations for national motorsport competitions in the United States (e.g., NASCAR), demonstrating the shared governance system common in the industry.

European Flying Disc Association

As a branch office of the World Flying Disc Association, the European Flying Disc Association (EFDA) is an example of a regional association for the sport, representing 33 national federations and functioning to promote and advance the sport of flying disc throughout the region. The disciplines of the sport include ultimate frisbee, beach ultimate, guts, disc golf, freestyle, double disc, field events, and discathon (Bernardi, 2015).

Under the German Civil Code, the nonprofit, nongovernmental agency operates through an executive office consisting of a president, vice president, secretary, and treasurer. Four at-large members serve on the extended board of directors, and commissioners serve in advisory roles (About EFDA, n.d.).

Asian Cricket Council

The Asian Cricket Council (ACC) is a non-Olympic continental sport federation formed in New Delhi, India, in 1963. The ACC is one of five continental members of the International Cricket Council and includes 25 member nations. The association has a significant role in managing tournaments throughout Asia. The executive board includes a president, vice president, six board members, five ex officio members, and a convener of finance and operations. The association also operates through a five-member executive committee and a seven-member development committee ("About the ACC," n.d.). Prior to 2003, the headquarters for the Asian Cricket Council (2016) moved every two years to the home country of the newly elected president. In 2003, the permanent location was moved to Kuala Lumpur, Malaysia, until a recent relocation to Sri Lanka ("The Formation of the ACC," n.d.).

REGULATORY AGENCIES GOVERNING NATIONAL AND REGIONAL SPORT COMPETITION

Governance for sport competition at the regional and national levels is through the rights holder, whether it is the IOC working in conjunction with continental and national affiliates, a professional sport league such as the NBA, a private independent entity (e.g., a sport brand) staging a national tournament, or a collegiate, youth, or government organization.

Organizations with a governance role in national and regional competition can be examined according to whether the competition involves a team sport or an individual sport. They can also be examined according to their role in governing multisport or single-sport competition.

Governing Organizations for Team and Individual Sport Competition

Examining sport regulatory agencies through the lens of individual versus team sports focuses on different operating and ownership structures. These structures reflect the complex nature of sport governance for amateur and professional competitions at the national, regional, and continental levels.

Team Sports

Team sports at the regional and national levels often operate through leagues. Examples of league systems at the regional (or continental or confederation) level include the Champions League for association football in Europe and the African Cricket Association. Examples of leagues governing professional team sports at the national level in the United States include the NHL, MLB, NFL, and NBA. In Japan, leagues governing professional team sports at the national level include the Nippon Professional Baseball Organization and the Japanese Professional Football League (Ishigami, 2016). National leagues for netball exist in places like Australia, New Zealand, Singapore, and England, and they can attract considerable television coverage.

While most professional leagues in the United States can be viewed as regional because they often

Justin Tafoya/NCAA Photos via Getty Images

National competition for several intercollegiate team sports are governed by a division of the sport's national sport federation. Two such sports are rowing and rugby, with athletes respectively competing in a USRowing Collegiate Series or a tournament organized by the National Small College Rugby Organization.

include teams from Canada and their finals may be dubbed the World Series or the World Championship, they are still considered national since their headquarters and most of their franchises are located in American cities. The NFL and WNBA do not have any teams in Canadian provinces, unlike the NHL, NBA, MLB, and Major League Soccer (MLS).

The governing document for most professional leagues is a constitution and bylaws, which address rules and regulations for everything from the power of the commissioner to home field advantage for the postseason. Professional leagues in the United States are led by a commissioner, who serves as the supreme authority for policy implementation. Leagues govern competition, and they have a regulatory function in governing players due to their contractual obligations with teams.

Leagues are not the only regulatory agencies for team sport competition. Collegiate rugby and collegiate men's rowing in the United States, for example, are not governed by a league or by any of the national associations that govern college athletics (NCAA, NAIA, NJCAA). Competition and championships are relegated to a division of their respective national sport federations, USA Rugby and USRowing Collegiate Series. The National Small College Rugby Organization (NSCRO) (n.d.) is a division of USA Rugby that organizes the national playoff system for the sport. NSCRO is governed by a board of directors, an executive committee, and four additional committees for education, fund-raising, strategic planning, and leadership development.

Individual Sports

National and regional competition for individual sports typically is organized through a sanctioning body, especially in professional sports. Sport federations may have a shared governance role, especially if the competition is to qualify for a world championship or the Olympics, but the sanctioning body bears great responsibility.

The PGA Tour, the National Association for Stock Car Auto Racing (NASCAR), and the IndyCar Series are examples of individual sport governing bodies, also called **sanctioning bodies**. These nongovernmental agencies are responsible for securing the venue and prize money in addition to managing all aspects of an event.

Individual sport governing bodies are generally owned by a separate group. In the case of motorsports, individual competitors are not a meaningful part of the governing structure since they are considered independent contractors. The governing bodies are the primary regulators of national and regional competition and are considered **close corporations** since shares in the company are held by just a few people, sometimes within a single family (Garner, 1999; "George Is Hulman & Co. Board Chair," 2016; Pockrass & Rovell, 2018).

In the United States, the Association of Tennis Professionals (ATP), the Ladies Professional Golf Association (LPGA), and the American Darters Association are examples of independent sanctioning bodies that govern national and regional competitions for their respective individual sports. Similar sanctioning bodies exist in countries around the world.

Governing Organizations for Multisport and Single-Sport Competition

The definition of multisport implies more than one sport or discipline, while single-sport implies only one sport or discipline. The regulatory agencies for operating national and regional multi- and single-sport competitions are typically the rights holders to the events. The complexity typically escalates for multisport competitions.

Multisport Competitions

Organizations with a governance role for multisport competitions include agencies such as the NCAA (which annually oversees 90 championships in 24 sports) and those that govern a festival-style event commencing over a period of days or weeks in a select city, in the style of the Olympic Games. Both interpretations fall under the category of national and regional agencies governing multisport competitions.

Regional and national festival-style multisport competitions around the world are plentiful, and so are the agencies and associations that organize and regulate championships. From the All-China Games to the Cambodia National Games to the African Continental Games to the Pan American Games, to the Mediterranean Games, the list seems endless. These types of championships may take place annually or on interval years (biannually, quadrennially, etc.). They often serve a special population (e.g., youth, seniors, disabled, military), or they may serve as a qualifier for higher-level competition. The popularity of national and regional festival-style multisport competition has fostered tourism in countries around the world. These types of games typically include a mixture of sanctioned Olympic sports and non-Olympic sports.

Every festival-style multisport competition, whether it is a national or regional event, has an organization tasked with enforcing rules, determining championship formats, and overseeing general logistics for athletes, coaches, team liaisons, volunteers, and spectators. National or regional sport federations may have a shared role in governance, but often another independent agency or organizing committee is tasked with regulating a multisport event.

The National Senior Games Association and the National Association of Collegiate Esports are examples of two national governing entities in the United States. The Indonesia Asian Games Organizing Committee and the 2018 Tarragona Mediterranean Games Committee are examples of independent agencies that govern festival-style multisport competitions at the regional level.

The National Senior Games Association is an independent, nongovernmental organization that conducts a multisport competition in odd years for approximately 10,000 athletes over the age of 55 in 20 sports ranging from triathlon to shuffleboard ("History of the NSGA," n.d.). Governance of the quadrennial Asian Games, which include 40 sports and over 15,000 volunteers, is delegated to an ad hoc host organizing committee formed to regulate all aspects of the games ("About INASGOC," 2018). The Tarragona Mediterranean Games Committee is comprised of a temporary staff of 70 to 80 professionals overseeing a 10-day multisport festival involving 4,000 athletes from Africa, Europe, and Asia, 1,000 judges, 1,000 media representatives, 3,500 volunteers, and 150,000 spectators ("XVII Mediterranean Games," 2018).

The types of organizations that govern multisport events vary with the nature of the competition. Many organizations that regulate national multisport competitions are connected to the governing bodies for participants (e.g., university, military). The USOPC recognizes multisport organizations that sponsor national championships in a minimum of two sports that are included in the official list of Olympic, Pan-American, or Paralympic competition. The USOPC (2018) partners with 38 multisport organizations segmented according to the population served (see table 5.4 for examples in each category).

The structure and leadership of these national multisport organizations vary. Armed forces sport competitions, for example, operate through the Armed Forces Sports Council under the U.S. Department of Defense, which is part of the government. The council is led by an appointed Senior Military Sport Advisor, a position that rotates every four years after the Summer Olympics, and each branch of the military is represented on the council ("About Armed Forces Sports," n.d.).

There are other organizations governing multisport competitions at the national level that are not on the USOPC's official list, such as the National Intramural and Recreational Sports Association (NIRSA), which oversees an annual championship series for college students. In 2018-2019, the number of participants in all NIRSA championships was 16,356 ("NIRSA Championship Series 2018-19 Year in Review," 2019).

The categories in the USOPC's classification system also apply to national organizations in countries around the world that govern championships in multiple sports. National championships in various countries are administered through similar independent organizations. Table 5.5 lists a few of the agencies in Europe and Asia whose

Table 5.4 Categories of Multisport Organizations Recognized by the USOPC

Community-based	Amateur Athletic Union (AAU); Special Olympics, Inc.; Catholic Youth Organization (CYO); Young Men's Christian Association (YMCA); National Congress of State Games; National Senior Games
Disabled	Adaptive Sport USA; USA Deaf Sports Federation
Armed forces	U.S. Army; U.S. Navy; U.S. Air Force; U.S. Marines; U.S. Coast Guard
Educational	NCAA; National Association of Intercollegiate Athletics (NAIA); National Junior College Athletic Association (NJCAA); National Federation of State High School Associations
Precursor for amateur international competition	Underwater Society of America; USA Dance

Table 5.5 National Agencies Governing Collegiate Athletic Championships in Europe and Asia

Country	National collegiate sport association
Great Britain	British University Sports Association
Australia	Australian University Sports
China	Federation of University Sports China
Switzerland	Swiss University Sports Federation
India	Inter-University Sports Board
Hong Kong	Hong Kong Post-Secondary Colleges Athletic Association
Ireland	Council of University Sports Administrators
Philippines	University Athletic Association of the Philippines
Japan	TBD – Japan Collegiate Athletic Association *

*Japan met with NCAA President Mark Emmert to discuss plans for a similar national collegiate athletic association.

Adapted from Li, MacIntosh, and Bravo (2012).

purpose is to govern national collegiate athletic championships.

Single-Sport Competitions

Organizations with a regulatory role in a national or regional single-sport competition can be categorized according to their target populations using the USOPC classifications shown in table 5.4: community-based, disabled, armed forces, educational, and those recognized for advancing amateur national champions to an international level. Sport federations are involved with national and regional or continental sport competitions that serve as qualifiers for Olympic or world championship competitions. The authority to govern competition may otherwise stem from independent agencies (e.g., host organizing committees and sport commissions) and organizations for team and individual sports.

Obstacle course racing is a single-sport competition that is exploding in popularity around the world. Spartan Races, for example, boasts 200 events in 42 countries ("The World's Best Obstacle Races," 2019). Other commercial obstacle race series include The Zombie Run, Roc Race, Tough Mudder, Ninja Warrior, and Warrior Dash. In Kansas City, Missouri, approximately 15,000 people registered for a Warrior Dash race (Keiper, Young, Fried, & Seidler, 2014, p. 89).

USA Obstacle Course Racing (OCR) is the national governing association for the sport, listed along with laser runs and bi- and triathletes as subsports of USA Pentathlon (2019), which is a member of the USOPC. USA Obstacle Course Racing is also part of World OCR, the international governing body for the sport ("Business Structure,"

n.d.). Disciplines of obstacle-style racing include adventure racing (e.g., Eco-Challenge), track OCRs (e.g., Million Dollar Mile), combine OCRs (e.g., Tough Mudder), and Ninja OCRs (e.g., Ultimate Beastmaster) ("Our Disciplines," n.d.). While there is an international federation as well as national and continental confederations for the sport of obstacle course competition, the governance of races and racers is often delegated to an incorporated commercial entity such as Spartan Race, Inc.

The national football collegiate championship in the United States is an example of a single-sport competition with an interesting governance structure. The national championship is governed primarily by the College Football Playoff (CFP) Administration, LLC, a nongovernmental limited liability company that is not affiliated with the NCAA or the United States Federation of American Football. CFP Administration, LLC functions through a board of managers, a management committee, and two additional personnel (executive director and chief operating officer) who run the day-to-day operations. The board of managers and management committee each have 11 appointments representing the 10 NCAA Football Bowl Subdivision conferences and the University of Notre Dame, which is not affiliated with an athletic conference for football ("The Company," n.d.). The championship game is one of approximately 40 bowl games that follow the regular college football season each year. Each bowl operates independently of the others as a nonprofit organization. For example, the Sugar Bowl, sponsored by Allstate Insurance, operates with a staff of 10 people working out of Mercedes-Benz Superdome, home of the NFL New Orleans Saints ("Sugar Bowl Organizational and Financial Information," n.d.).

Obstacle course races are single-sport competitions typically produced by independent corporate or commercial agencies.

REGULATORY AGENCIES FOR NATIONAL AND REGIONAL SPORT AFFILIATES

The final category of agencies with a governing role in some aspect of national and regional sports includes those that serve a specialist function. There is an abundance of independent regulatory agencies for sport affiliates as they pertain to sectors of the industry or functional areas of sport. Functional areas or sectors of sport with a national or regional (continental) governing body include sport education, sporting goods and equipment, fitness certification, officiating licensure, athlete representation, sport medicine, and sport tourism (commissions). National associations operating in countries around the world are available for almost every professional position in the industry (e.g., coaches, officials, judges, trainers, educators, aquatic directors, analytics directors, compliance personnel, development coordinators, marketers, and media).

The National Sporting Goods Association (NSGA) in the United States of America is an example of an independent, nongovernmental advocacy organization serving athletic equipment manufacturers and retailers. One of the divisions of the NSGA is the National Ski and Snowboarders Retailers Association (n.d.), which cooperates with the Snow Sport Industries of America, Professional Ski Instructors of America, and the National Ski Patrol to address and improve retail and manufacturing issues, such as abuses related to Internet pricing and pro form equipment purchases.

Many of the regulatory and governing agencies in the fitness and wellness industry are commercial. For example, there is an abundance of national organizations selling certificates to enable one to be credentialed as a personal (fitness) trainer, life coach, wellness consultant, strength and conditioning specialist, group fitness trainer, Pilates trainer, sport nutrition coach, yoga teacher, aerobics instructor, or functional movement specialist. Examples of national organizations in the United States that offer or sell some type of fitness or training certificate include the National Association for Fitness Certification, the American Sports and Fitness Association, the American Council on Exercise, and the National Federation of Professional Trainers. Examples of certifying agencies on a regional scale include the European Association of Exercise Professionals, the European Fitness Association, the Southern African Underwater and Hyperbaric Medical Association, the Asia Academy for Sport and Fitness Professionals, and the Australian Fitness Network.

CrossFit and other types of fitness competitions have governing bodies at the international, continental, and national levels. USA Functional Fitness, for example, is the governing body that hosts national championships in speed benchmark, team medley, individual medley, and other disciplines of the sport of competitive or "functional" fitness ("Disciplines," n.d.).

Functional areas for all aspects of sport are well represented by national and regional associations, each working to enhance the standing of its specialty. National associations that offer coaching and officiating certifications at different levels are especially plentiful in many countries, even though sport federations have significant authority over officials and coaches. National and regional agencies for certifying coaches and officials, plus a multitude of other organizations with a regulatory role in the many functional areas of sport, are discussed in greater detail in the chapters that focus on specific sectors of the sports industry.

RECAP

Governance of sport at the regional and national levels can be quite complicated. There are national associations for sports that lead to international competition, national associations for sports that lead to national competition, regional sport associations at the international level, and regional sport associations at the national level. It is necessary to understand how the governing agencies for an aspect of sport at regional and national levels are related and how they are different.

The four dimensions for classifying national and regional regulatory organizations in sports are (1) governance of sport, (2) governance of athletes, (3) governance of competition, and (4) governance of sport affiliates. Often, organizations have oversight in more than one category.

Most national governments other than the United States appoint a sport minister to regulate and promote sports from the grassroots to the elite level. Most organizations and agencies with a governing role over sports, athletes, competition, and functional areas of sports are independent, nongovernmental, nonprofit agencies. Organizations range from national and regional Olympic committees to military councils to professional leagues to associations for disabled athletes.

Critical Thinking Questions

1. Review the differences in governance structures between USA Basketball and US Lacrosse. Should US Lacrosse admit organizations that hold lacrosse competitions? Why or why not?

2. What are some of the similarities and differences between professional sport governing bodies for team sports and those for individual sports?

3. Explain the difference between the two interpretations of regional sport governing bodies.

4. In your opinion, is governance at the regional level necessary? Explain your answer.

Applied Activity

Forming an NGB

The International Olympic Committee has decided to admit mixed martial arts (MMA) to the Olympic Games. The USOPC has decided that the United States needs to field an MMA team in future Olympics. You have been tasked with forming an NGB for MMA in the United States: USA Mixed Martial Arts (USAMMA). Using the information given for USA Basketball, determine who should be members of the organization and who should have a vote in the running of the organization.

Case Study Application

For more information on governance and authority in national sports, review *The Influence of Politics in Romanian Sport Before and After the Regime Change From Communism to Democracy* in the web resource.

chapter 6

Global Sports

Bonnie Tiell

Sport on a global stage is governed by people and agencies that have authority, power, and expertise. Arguably the most recognizable agency, the International Olympic Committee (IOC), works with international sport federations (IFs), national Olympic committees (NOCs), the organizing committee for the Olympic Games (OCOG), and an abundance of affiliated entities.

The response to Russia's statewide doping code violations in 2014 exemplifies the complex and often intertwining relationships of global sport organizations. Hours before the 2018 Olympic Opening Ceremony in PyeongChang, South Korea, the Court of Arbitration for Sport (CAS) upheld a decision by the IOC and denied the appeal of almost four dozen Russian athletes who sought restoration of their eligibility to compete in the Winter Games (Axon, 2018). Speculation by the World Anti-Doping Agency (WADA) pointed to the possibility of Russia being banned from the Tokyo 2020 Olympics as well. The saga of Russia's systematic statewide doping incidents provides a framework for examining the distinct roles of regulatory organizations that govern global and transnational sport.

The IOC has supreme power and authority to sanction and penalize athletes and confederations in the realm of the Olympics. The epic case of South Africa's 32-year banishment from the Olympics for apartheid clearly illustrated the IOC's power (Rosner & Low, 2009, p. 63). With respect to punishment levied against Russia for the doping violations, the IOC maintained authority to levy a fine equivalent to $15 million USD against the country's Olympic committee and to banish athletes from competing in the 2016 and 2018 Games (Drake, 2018). The doping code violations linked to Russian athletes between 2014 and 2018 were confirmed by the WADA, another governing body for global sport that assesses compliance but is not authorized to sanction or penalize violations. Finally, CAS, the global sport agency created by the IOC, is an autonomous governing council that played a major role in the 2018 Games as the organization with authority to settle disputes between the Russian athletes and the International Olympic Committee.

The roles and responsibilities of the CAS, IOC, IFs, and WADA often intersect within the international sport arena, but the distinctions between the organizations are apparent when examining each independently, especially within the context of their purposes and strategic capabilities. Cooperation between two or more global sport agencies is essential when staging an international competition like a world championship or the Olympics; however, the organizations operate and exist independently.

This chapter will address the overarching purpose of regulatory agencies for global sports while also examining the similarities and differences in their authority and managerial operations.

Learning Outcomes

- Distinguish between a global and an international sport.
- Explain the practicality of shared governance for an international multisport event.
- Categorize regulatory agencies for global sports according to four functional classifications.
- Identify the distinctive roles and responsibilities of the agencies directly associated with the Olympic movement, including the IOC, national Olympic committees, international federations, and organizing committees for the Olympic Games.
- Identify the role of the World Anti-Doping Agency and the Court of Arbitration for Sport in current events.

DEFINING A GLOBAL SPORT AGENCY

In the context of sport governance, the terms *global* and *international* are used interchangeably to indicate supreme authority over an aspect of sport anywhere in the world. Although the terms may be used interchangeably for governing agencies, there is a fine line between an international sport and a global sport. **Global sport** refers to something that encompasses all five continents, while **international sport** refers to a specific geographic region that spans at least two countries. Swimming and soccer (or football), for example, are two global sports recognized around the world.

Muay Thai and sepak takraw, however, are more commonly called international sports since their roots and competition are primarily confined to Southeast Asia. The supreme governing bodies for these two sports, however, may be labeled as either global or international under the assumption that rules, regulations, and policies would be identical around the world.

A global sport agency operates internationally while serving as the supreme governing organization for an aspect of sport. What these entities have in common is their global context. They obviously all serve sport in some capacity, whether they focus on athletes, competition, training, or rules of play. They also assert their authority and governance across continents.

MOHD RASFAN/AFP/Getty Images

Sepak takraw is popular primarily in Southeast Asia, which distinguishes it as an international as opposed to global sport such as swimming or association-style football (soccer).

General Functions of Global Sport Agencies

The field of sport regulation in a global context is complex (Casini, 2009, p. 426). While there may be some overlap in functions, entities involved in the governance of international sport generally fall into one of the following four categories:

1. Governance of an event considered global or international
2. Governance of athletes
3. Governance of sport
4. Governance of sport affiliates

Additional Functions of Global Sport Agencies

Some of the roles and responsibilities of these organizations are identical or similar, especially with respect to maintaining relationships. Following are eight functions of global sport agencies defined by Forster (2006, p. 73).

1. Creation and maintenance of the laws and rules of a sport and its competitions
2. Global development of a sport at all levels
3. Development and governance of the athletes within a sport
4. Arbitration or resolution of disputes within a sport
5. Hosting of global events, such as world championships, within the sport
6. Maintenance of relationships with affiliated national or continental associations for the sport
7. Maintenance of relationships with governments, regulatory authorities, and sporting bodies outside the sport
8. Maintenance of relationships with commercial entities, such as sponsors

REGULATORY AGENCIES FOR INTERNATIONAL MULTISPORT COMPETITION

While the IOC is the most recognizable global sport agency, there are scores of organizations that serve a similar function for multisport tournaments, festivals, and games geared toward specific markets.

Examples of international multisport competitions include the Paralympics, Youth Games, Special Olympics, Deaflympics, Universiades, Gay Games, World Senior Games, World Transplant Games, and Commonwealth Games. While the Youth Games operate under the direction of the IOC, most of the other entities are governed by an independent, nonprofit, nongovernmental association, federation, or organization that is incorporated in a city and country. An overview of several of the most influential organizations governing multisport competition is presented in this section. Also included as a subset of the IOC is the organizing committee for the Olympic Games (OCOG), which has authority for Games of the Olympiad within the host country.

International Olympic Committee

Based in Lausanne, Switzerland, since 1915, the **International Olympic Committee** (IOC) governs the Olympic Games with "de facto privileges and immunities, no obvious peers, and no market competition (Nelson & Cottrell, 2016, p. 444). A nongovernmental, nonprofit organization with volunteer membership, the IOC is widely considered to be the most recognizable and most powerful agency governing international sport competition. The IOC is directly responsible for the Summer Olympics, Winter Olympics, and Youth Olympics.

The IOC was established as an amateur-based gentlemen's club at the inaugural International Sport Congress in Paris, France, on June 23, 1894, by Pierre de Coubertin, who is credited with resurrecting the modern-day Olympics. It is the supreme authority and governing agency for the celebration, organization, and administration of the Olympic Games. Since the organization's inception, it has evolved into a professionally run global business. The first election of a woman to the IOC occurred in 1981, and the first election of a woman as a vice president occurred in 1997 (International Olympic Committee, 2016).

The Olympic Charter, the governing rules and guidelines of the International Olympic Committee (2017), states that the organization's mission is to "lead the Olympic Movement" (p. 15). The Olympic movement is described as encompassing all activities inspired by "Olympism," a philosophy that blends body, mind, and soul through sport, culture, and education.

Structure and Leadership

The IOC comprises no more than 115 people who are active athletes or who serve in a senior leadership position at an affiliated organization. These individuals are recruited and elected for an initial eight-year term, which is renewable (International Olympic Committee, 2017, p. 33). Members serve until they resign, fail to be reelected, or reach age 70, unless an age extension has been given.

The executive board consists of the president, four vice presidents, and 10 cabinet members (see figure 6.1) (IOC, 2017, p. 45). This board's primary responsibilities include managing IOC finances, preparing annual budget reports, submitting recommendations for IOC membership, establishing the agenda for IOC sessions, maintaining all records, assuring approved organization of the Olympic Games, and managing the bureaucracy of IOC organizational units (Zakkus & Skinner, 2008). The IOC works through commissions to advise the executive board (see Governance in Action 6.1).

The president is elected in a secret ballot by an absolute majority of the IOC members. The initial eight-year term is renewable for four additional years. Thomas Bach, a German lawyer and gold medal fencer at the 1976 Montreal Olympic Games, was elected the ninth IOC president in 2013 to replace Belgium's Jacques Rogge, who served 12 years. American Avery Brundage, who served from 1952 to 1972, is the only non-European to have served as IOC president (Wilson, 2013).

The primary units under the IOC are the national Olympic committees (NOCs) responsible for organizing athletes and official delegates from their countries, the host organizing committees for the Olympic Games (OCOGs) responsible for execution of the Games, and international federations (IFs), which govern the rules of competition for sports. Also under the IOC umbrella is a laundry list of recognized agencies and institutions for athletes, judges and referees, sport technicians, coaches, and affiliates; these are described in Governance in Action 6.1.

The IOC headquarters in Lausanne, Switzerland, includes the executive office of the president, the office of the director general, and the office of the deputy director general. These offices maintain close ties to the various commissions designated by the president to advance the Olympic movement.

Constitution

The IOC operates under the rules and bylaws of the **Olympic Charter**, which includes the official rules, guidelines, and codification of fundamental principles governing the Olympic movement and the Olympic Games. It was initially published in 1908 as a 13-page document. Each revision of the Olympic Charter and its supplemental statutes are

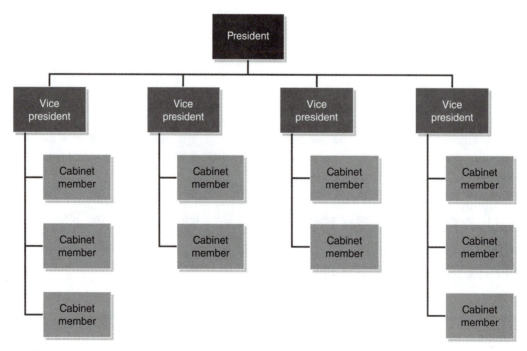

Figure 6.1 Executive board structure: International Olympic Committee.

GOVERNANCE IN ACTION 6.1

Commissions of the International Olympic Committee

The administration of the IOC is the responsibility of the director general, who works with directors of functional business units or with commissions. Under the scope of the president, who has authority to establish both permanent and ad hoc commissions, the vice presidents and cabinet members work in concert to operate the IOC and advise the executive board. The president appoints all members and oversees the dissolution of commissions after they fulfill their mandate. Officially, the Olympic Charter recognizes the following seven commissions:

1. Athletes' Commission
2. Ethics Commission
3. Members' Election Commission
4. Olympic Solidarity Commission
5. Evaluation Commission for Candidate Cities
6. Olympic Games Coordination Commission
7. Scientific and Medical Commission

Among the additional commissions identified on www.Olympic.org, the official IOC website, are the representatives to the World Anti-Doping Agency (WADA) executive committee and foundation board, as well as the following:

Athlete Entourage Commission

Audit Commission

Communications Commission

Culture and Olympic Heritage Commission

Delegate Members

Digital and Technology Commission

Finance

Legal Affairs

Marketing Commission

Olympic Broadcasting Services

Olympic Channel

Olympic Channel Services

Olympic Education Commission

Olympic Programme Commission

Public Affairs and Social Development for Sport

Sport and Active Society

Sustainability and Legacy Commission

Women in Sport Commission

available through the Olympic Studies Center on the www.olympic.org webpage.

The Olympic Charter is a constitution that serves three main purposes: (1) establishing and promoting the fundamental principles and values of Olympism, (2) providing the statutes for operations of the IOC, and (3) defining the rights and obligations of the constituents of the Olympic movement

(IOC, 2016). Approved by the IOC, the Olympic Charter includes six chapters addressing the Olympic movement, the IOC, international federations, national Olympic committees, the Olympic Games, and measures, sanctions, disciplinary procedures, and dispute resolution.

Olympic Congress and Sessions

An **Olympic Congress**, a large gathering of representatives of the constituents of the Olympic movement, convenes at intervals determined by the president (International Olympic Committee 2017, p. 19). This extraordinary session of constituents may also convene upon written request of at least one-third of its members (IOC, 2016, p. 47).

The IOC generally conducts business through annual Olympic Sessions. Several of these are a part of an Olympic Congress, but most are standalone assemblies. The adoption of and modifications to sections of the Olympic Charter occur at these sessions. Among the primary decisions made at ordinary Olympic Sessions are selection of the host cities for the Olympic Games, election of new members, and composition of the sport programs.

International Paralympic Committee

Founded in 1989 and registered in 1991, the nonprofit International Paralympic Committee (IPC) is the global organization for the Paralympic movement. The Paralympic movement is similar in scope to the Olympic movement, but within the context of disabilities. The IPC is responsible for organizing and executing the summer and winter **Paralympic Games**, which is an international multisport competition for qualified athletes with a wide range of disabilities (International Paralympic Committee, 2018b).

The origin of the Paralympics is credited to Dr. (Sir) Ludwig Guttmann, who organized a sport competition for paraplegic patients at the National Spinal Injuries Unit of Stoke Mandeville Hospital in England, the first coinciding with the 1948 London Olympics (Gold & Gold, 2007). Soon, the Games were held in every Olympic year (quadrennially), with participation growing from 400 athletes representing 23 countries in the inaugural 1960 Paralympics in Rome, to over 4,300 athletes from 159 countries who competed in 22 sports at the 2016 Games in Rio de Janeiro, Brazil (International Paralympic Committee, 2016a). By agreement with the IOC, the Paralympic Games have been held in

Atsushi Tomura/Getty Images

The Paralympic Games are separate from the Olympic Games, even though they are held in the same host city. Governed by World ParaVolley, women's sitting volleyball (pictured) was added to the Paralympic agenda in 2004. The World Armwrestling Federation, with headquarters in Bulgaria, is lobbying for its sport to be added to the Paris 2024 agenda.

the same Olympic host city since the 1988 Games in Seoul, South Korea (IPC, 2015).

The first assembly of the IPC (2018b) in 1989 with a Canadian elected as president established the organization as the supreme governing agency both for the Paralympic Games and for the multi-disability World Games and Championships.

Structure and Leadership

Only three presidents have served the IPC, including Canada's Bob Stedward, the founding president, who served from 1989 to 2001. He was credited with completing the first IPC–IOC formal agreement in 2000 that solidified the relationship between the Olympics and Paralympics (International Paralympic Committee, 2018c). The second president, Sir Philip Craven, a wheelchair basketball player, served the association for the next 16 years. The third president, Brazilian Andrew Parsons, was elected in September 2017 to succeed Cravens (International Paralympic Committee, 2017).

With its headquarters in Bonn, Germany, since 1999, the IPC has evolved from a 10-member unit to one that employed more than 80 people in 2019. The IPC formally includes members of the General Assembly, a governing board, a management team, and many federations, standing committees, confederations, and councils. The General Assembly includes 4 international organizations of sport for individuals with disabilities, 17 international federations, 5 regional associations, and 177 national Paralympic associations, which meet every other year (IPC, 2016a). A growing number of national Olympic committees have assumed duties of the national Paralympic committees (Li, MacIntosh, & Bravo, 2012).

The governing board meets at least three times a year and is comprised of 16 members, 12 of whom are elected, including a president, a vice president, and 10 at-large members (International Paralympic Committee, 2015). Elected every four years, a board member can serve only three consecutive terms. The remaining members of the board include the chief executive officer (CEO) for the IPC and two representatives of the athlete's council. The governing board is responsible for executing policies established by the General Assembly.

The IPC management team is comprised of professional staff working under the CEO who are assigned to functional departments. In addition to the executive office, the management team includes people who oversee sports information technology, membership, hospitality and events protocols, finance and corporate services, media and communications, marketing and commercial, and medical and scientific (International Paralympic Committee, 2018a). The management team also works with the various committees advising the IPC (2016a) in the areas of antidoping, development, audit and finance, medical, education, sport science, women in sport, classification, legal and ethics, and the athlete's council.

Also operating in the international headquarters are three divisions, the Atigos Foundation, World Para Sport, and IPC Academy (International Paralympic Committee IPC, 2016a). Launched in 2012, the Atigos Foundation is a global charity dedicated to the development of parasport, while the IPC Academy serves to enhance education in all aspects of parasport.

Constitution

Originally drafted in 1990, the *IPC Handbook* (International Paralympic Committee 2015) provides the governing guidelines for members. The handbook includes two sections, the first addressing the organization's mission, oversight, and membership and the second addressing general rules and regulations. The first section includes the constitution and information on the governing boards, councils, committees, management team, intellectual property, and principles of the Paralympic Games. The logistics of the Paralympic Games are specified in the third chapter, which covers general eligibility for participation, coordination with the host site election process, disciplinary processes and dispute resolution, Games-related legislation, financial obligations, guiding principles of sport programs, and guidelines for the Paralympic brand (International Paralympic Committee, 2015).

The second section of the *IPC Handbook* includes chapters addressing (1) codes, (2) standing orders, (3) policies, (4) position statements, and (5) declarations endorsed by the IPC. The codes section addresses antidoping and IPC classifications for impairments. According to the international standards for eligible impairments, the categories of participation for the Paralympics include impaired muscle power, impaired range of movement, limb deficiency, leg length difference, short stature, hypertonia, ataxia (affecting muscle coordination), athetosis (such as cerebral palsy), vision impairment, and intellectual disability (IPC, 2016b).

Standing orders address conduct and procedures at general assemblies and governing board meetings, while the chapter on policies covers a range of rules related to athletes' nationality, membership fees, confidentiality, diversity and inclusion, suspensions, equipment, and award selections (International Paralympic Committee, 2015). Position statements and declarations in the remaining two sections tie the organization to special-interest groups and ideas, such as human rights, the World Anti-Doping Agency, physical education, women in sports, fair play, and the World Medical Association (International Paralympic Committee, 2015).

Organizing Committee for the Olympic Games

The organizing committee for the Olympic Games (OCOG) is a temporary unit constituted by the IOC and established by a national Olympic committee (NOC) to manage the Olympic and Paralympic

The Asahi Shimbun via Getty Images

The local organizing committee for the Olympic Games represents a cross section of government, educational, corporate, and private agencies in a country acting under the authority of the IOC as specified by the Olympic Charter.

Games in a host location. In addition to planning for funding the Games, the tasks assigned to the organizing committees for each Olympiad include staffing and accreditation of personnel, selection or construction of venues, accommodations, transportation, medical services, and media services (International Olympic Committee, 2018). These responsibilities extend to the conclusion of the Paralympic Games, after which a dissolution process begins.

The Olympic Charter mandates that the executive body of the OCOG include members of the IOC who reside in the host country, the president and secretary general of the NOC, and representatives of the public authorities or other leading figures (International Olympic Committee, 2017). The committee includes both paid and nonpaid personnel. As an example, the staff for the 1976 Montreal Olympics in Canada included over 20,000 employees, of whom 972 were considered permanent (for the duration of the OCOG), 529 temporary, and 18,614 short term (Games of the XXI Olympiad, Montreal 1976: Official Report, 1978, p. 543). The administration consisted of 117 permanent employees from 1972 to 1976. In contrast, the London organizing committee for the Olympic Games (LOCOG) (2012, p. 19) included 3,224 paid staff and over 5,000 additional staff under Lord Deighton, chief of staff. Over 80,000 Games Maker volunteers and ceremony participants added to temporary staffing numbers.

The authority of the OCOG resides in the executive body and the board. For example, the executive board for the London organizing committee for the Olympic Games (LOCOG, 2012) chaired by Lord Sebastian Coe was typical for host locations. The board for the LOCOG included 19 officers and professional advisors, among whom were a chief financial officer and a head of risk assurance. The board was responsible for establishing the nine-member executive body of directors to carry out additional responsibilities related to Games operations. Figure 6.2 provides a plausible organizational structure for the executive board comprising the 2020 Tokyo organizing committee (Executive Board Members, 2019).

Thereafter, the LOCOG operated through four core committees assigned to the (1) Games operations, (2) communications and engagement, (3) organization, and (4) ceremonies. A director's group including key people from each of the core committees and members of the executive body managed the various components of the Games. Figure 6.3 provides an overview of a possible organizational structure for the directors group that would also take into account the Paralympics. A dissolution committee was also created near the end of the 2012 Paralympic Games to close out contracts, dispose of assets, and perform the necessary tasks to dissolve the organization, such as conducting audits and preparing the final report to the IOC.

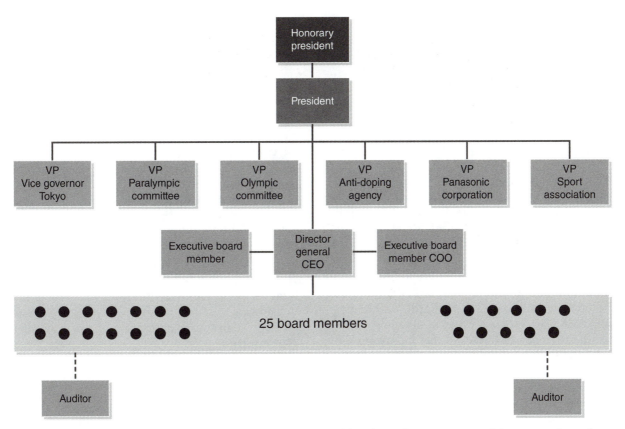

Figure 6.2 Hypothetical structure of the executive board for the Tokyo 2020 organizing committee for the Olympic and Paralympic Games.

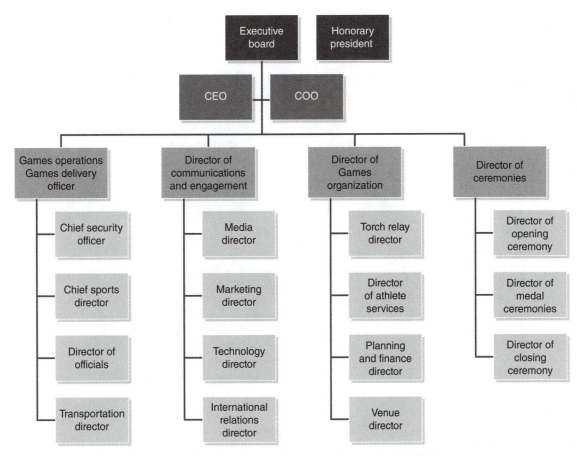

Figure 6.3 Hypothetical structure for the director's group of a typical OCOG.

During its time of operation, the OCOG has the authority to make many decisions that affect the general operations of the Games in a host location. The power of a governing body for Olympic and Paralympic Games operations is only temporary, however.

Special Olympics, Inc.

Special Olympics, Inc., is the international governing body of the Special Olympic movement, similar in scope to the Paralympics, but focused on sport and individuals with intellectual disabilities. A key distinction between the Special Olympics and the Paralympics is the philosophy behind competition. While the Special Olympics strives to be inclusive and to encourage mass participation, the Paralympics includes qualification standards for elite participation. The rules of the Special Olympics (2017) outline the responsibilities of the organization to conduct all world and regional Games.

In 2017, Special Olympics hosted 103,540 athletic competitions associated with 225 national and state programs in 174 countries that included 1,114,697 volunteers serving over 5,169,489 athletes ("2017 Reach Report," 2017). The inaugural **Special Olympic Games** for individuals with intellectual disabilities were held in 1960 in the United States as a joint venture between the Kennedy Foundation and the Chicago Park District

(Special Olympics, 2018b). The Special Olympics World Games alternate between summer and winter and take place every other year. Founder Eunice Kennedy Shriver from the United States served as an original member of the board of directors beginning in 1968. It remains as the world's largest international sport organization for competition among people with intellectual disabilities and is a registered nongovernmental organization of the United Nations, recognized by the IOC (Special Olympics, 2017).

The 1970 Games were the first to include participants from outside of the United States, and the 1993 Games in Schladming, Austria, were the first to be held in a location outside of the Americas. The 2019 Special Olympics World Games in Abu Dhabi of the United Arab Emirates were scheduled to feature seven days of competition in 24 sports for over 70,000 international athletes from over 170 countries.

Special Olympics, Inc. enforces official rules and protocols for the Special Olympics while managing and providing training, technical assistance, and other support to accredited programs throughout the world. The organization ensures that activities are "organized, financed and conducted in accordance with uniform international standards as to best serve the interests of persons with disabilities worldwide" (Special Olympics, 2017, p. 43). On occasion, Special Olympics (2017, p. 17) contracts

Dominika Zarzycka/NurPhoto via Getty Images

The Special Olympics has evolved from a relatively small event held in the United States in 1960 to a global phenomenon providing opportunities for millions of people with intellectual disabilities.

with independent Games organizing committees (GOCs) to finance and organize regional and international competition.

Governance for the Special Olympics World Games is the responsibility of a board that is responsible for all policies that are associated with the Special Olympic movement (Special Olympics 2017, p. 86). The 15-member global leadership team includes a CEO, board of directors chairperson, two senior vice presidents, and 11 additional executive positions (Special Olympics, 2018a). The board works with and through the presidents or managing directors of the regional leadership councils. Over 250 individuals work at the headquarters in Washington, D.C. The organization has the authority to fine, suspend, or permanently ban individuals or agencies, including members of a GOC, for violations of the general rules or uniform standards. Numerous advisory committees are identified by the Special Olympics, including those concerned with sport rules, general rules, and medical issues. The organization also includes a Torch Run Executive Council.

International University Sports Federation

Founded in Luxembourg in 1948, the **International University Sports Federation** (FISU) is the global agency that governs the international university sports movement as well as the Summer and Winter **Universiades** (Games) and World University Championships (Vendien, 2012). Held every other year, the FISU Games are staged during an international multiweek festival combining sport and culture. Only current student-athletes ages 17 to 25 are eligible (International University Sports Federation, 2018a).

There were many precursors to the current cadre of FISU Games, namely the summer and winter World Student Championships organized by the International Confederation of Students. The 1959 Summer Universiade in Torino, Italy, however, is recognized as the inaugural games of the International University Sports Federation (2018b). Twenty-five members were present. FISU drafted statutes during the festival that designated the organization as the entity responsible for organizing future university games at "worldwide levels" (International University Sports Federation, 2018b).

FISU's 174 voting members participate in a General Assembly, held biennially, to approve budgets and establish policies (International University Sports Federation, 2018a). The assembly also serves to elect the Executive Committee, which operates on four-year terms. The Executive Committee consists of a president, a first vice president, four vice presidents, a treasurer, and 15 additional members. Five delegates from the continental associations also serve on the Executive Committee, which meets at least twice per year (International University Sports Federation, 2018a).

Advising the Executive Committee are 14 permanent commissions representing the technical and supervisory operations of each type of game (summer, winter, or world championships) in addition to support services for areas such as student interests, gender equity, international medicine, finance, education, and media (International University Sports Federation, 2018b). A secretary general/CEO is responsible for daily operations. The headquarters are located on the campus of the University of Lausanne in Lausanne, Switzerland, which is also the city address for the IOC and many international federations for sport.

Commonwealth Games Federation

The Commonwealth Games Federation (CGF) (2018a) is the nonprofit, nongovernmental organization that is the supreme authority for staging the Commonwealth Games and Commonwealth Youth Games and for promoting the Commonwealth Sports movement. With headquarters in London, England, the organization operates through 70 nations and territories identified as Commonwealth Games Associations, or CGAs.

Formally known as the British Empire Games, the Commonwealth Games is an 11-day international multisport event staged every four years. The inaugural Commonwealth Games were held in Hamilton, Ontario, in 1930, and the first Commonwealth Youth Games were staged in Edinburgh, Scotland, in 2000 (Commonwealth Games Federation, 2018a, p. 33). Preceding the games is the Queen's Baton Relay beginning at Buckingham Palace, which resembles the Olympic torch relay.

The Commonwealth Games Associations meet at an annual General Assembly and elect a 15-member executive board. The board consists of a president, three vice presidents, several regional vice presidents, an athlete representative, a legal advisor, a medical advisor, the chief executive officer, and an executive from one of the games (Commonwealth Games Federation, 2018b). The constitutional document of the Commonwealth

Games Federation (2018a, p. 11) stipulates that at least 20 percent of the board must represent each gender. In 2015, Louise Martin became the first woman to be elected president of the CGF.

Seven executive board subcommittees assist the federation in decision making. These committees are (1) Athlete Advisory, (2) Sports, (3) Audit and Risk, (4) Development, (5) Governance and Integrity, (6) Performance and Remuneration, and (7) Medical. The management team for the federation includes a chief executive officer, a chief operating officer, a corporate administrator, and seven others serving as managers or directors (Commonwealth Games Federation, 2018c).

Twenty-six games manuals define processes and procedures related to areas such as legal, marketing, knowledge management, Queens Baton Relay, villages, ticketing, brand image, and workforce. Among the areas addressed in the constitutional documents for the Commonwealth Games Federation (2018a) are the composition and responsibilities of committees reporting to the executive board, a quota mandate of a maximum of 3,800 athletes and 300 para-athletes, and the procedure for ensuring gender representation on the executive board when election results fall below the minimum threshold (Commonwealth Games Federation, 2018a). Para-athletes have been competing in the Commonwealth Games since 2002.

REGULATORY AGENCIES FOR ATHLETES IN INTERNATIONAL SPORTS

The landscape of regulatory agencies for coaches and athletes in international sports is complex. Governance may be shared between players' associations and sport federations or with an association that governs a series of tournaments. There are also global sport organizations with a quasi-regulatory or service-oriented role for international athletes and coaches. Global regulatory agencies are typically composed of members from national or continental associations, but some may only be open to people who meet qualification standards and are associated with specific competitions.

Three of the most eclectic governing entities representing international athletes are the Association of National Olympic Committees (ANOC), the World Players Association, and Global Athlete. The section on Additional Associations addresses the context of the many organizations that serve in a governance or advisory capacity for professional and amateur athletes in international sports.

Association of National Olympic Committees

Under the umbrella of the IOC, the Association of National Olympic Committees (ANOC) is viewed primarily as a support system for national Olympic committees that govern athletes, officials, and delegations at the Olympic and Paralympic Games. The inaugural General Assembly of NOCs occurred in 1969, but 1979 is the first "permanent" General Assembly recognized as the origination of the ANOC. Research by a sociologist in the mid-1970s noted that an organization known as the *Federation of National Olympic Committees* existed in Rome, Italy, but further evidence of the presence of a collective entity for NOCs prior to 1979 is scarce (Luschen, 1979, p. 9). ANOC relocated its headquarters in 2010 from Paris, France, to Lausanne, Switzerland, which is the home of the IOC and most IFs.

Authority is granted to ANOC by the IOC and the constitution for the organization. ANOC is governed by an Executive Council elected at the General Assembly to four-year terms. The Executive Council includes a president, 5 vice presidents, 14 members representing the 5 continental affiliates (two or three from each), and a secretary general who oversees the day-to-day operations. Two additional representatives from each continental affiliate (10 total) are appointed to the Executive Council. The constitution of the ANOC (2018) mandates that there be a minimum of one woman from each of the continental associations on the Executive Council in the appointed positions. The chair of the Athlete's Commission, Finance and Audit Commission, and Legal Commission are also appointed positions on the ANOC Executive Council (Association of National Olympic Committees, 2013). Additional commissions and working groups serving ANOC (2019) include the following areas:

- ANOC International Relations Commission
- ANOC Youth Commission
- ANOC Gender Equity Commission
- ANOC Electoral Commission
- ANOC Events Commission
- ANOC Marketing Commission
- ANOC Culture and Education Commission
- ANOC Medical Commission

World Players Association

Established in 2014 and based in Nyon, Switzerland, the **World Players Association** serves and represents the unions and associations for professional players in all continents. The association currently represents over 85,000 professional players from 100 associations in 60 countries (Uni Global Union, 2019). Members include the Major League Baseball Players Association, National Football League Players Association, European Union of Athletes, National Hockey League Players Association, National Basketball Association Players Association, Australian Athlete's Alliance, Federation of International Cricketers' Association, and the federation of International Futbol Professionals.

Concerned primarily with human rights and the positive impact of sports, the World Players Association is governed by a 12-member Executive Committee led by Don Fehr, commissioner of the National Hockey League, and an executive director (Uni Global Union, 2019). The World Players Association's (2017a; 2017b) Declaration of Player Rights obligates international sport organizations to "protect, respect, and guarantee the fundamental rights of players." Topics within the declaration address fair pay, the right to organize and collectively bargain, harassment and violence protection, antidiscrimination, and privacy protection. The World Players Association is also active on the steering committee for the Mega-Sporting Events Platform for Human Rights.

Global Athlete

In 2019, Global Athlete was formed as an advocacy body for elite competitors, primarily Olympians. It is a separate group from the IOC's Athletes' Commission, which serves as a link between competitors and the world's supreme authority for the Games, but it is expected that they will collaborate in the future to strengthen representation of elite athletes. For example, at the 2019 International Athletes' Forum attended by representatives of NOCs and the World Olympians Association (WOA), issues were raised by Germany's independent athlete group, Athleten Deutschland, which has the same focus as Global Athlete. The hot topics at the forum included a push for athletes to receive a greater proportion of IOC revenues and the applicability of Athleten Deutschland's success in Germany to scale back Rule 40 mandating a blackout period for Olympian endorsements (Pavitt, 2019).

Funded by FairSport, an independent nonprofit agency for eradicating cheating in sports, Global Athlete's inaugural director general is Canadian Rob Koehler, former deputy director for WADA. Characterized as a "new movement," Global Athlete seeks to protect and provide a voice for athletes. The creation of Global Athlete was partially motivated by a need to advocate for enhanced rights for athletes following Russia's doping corruption case and USA Gymnastics' sex abuse scandal. The organization will likely address athlete welfare, harassment, distribution of Olympic revenues or prize money, antidoping systems, and better representation on global committees. One of the focal points for Global Athlete is advocating for transparency in the distribution of IOC funds to international federations and NOCs to determine the true percentage that reaches the pockets of athletes (Pavitt, 2019). While Global Athlete has no true governance role in terms of its ability to sanction potential members, its vision and mission affect the governance of international sport organizations by potentially having more athlete representatives in decision-making roles.

Additional Associations

Other organizations that represent athletes competing internationally can be categorized according to their focus on professionals or amateurs.

Regulatory Associations for Professional Athletes in International Sports

Examples of additional global organizations with a governing role for professional athletes include the International Soccer Association (FIFPro), the Federation of International Cricket Associations (FICA), and the International Rugby Players Association (IRPA). FIFPro represents approximately 60,000 professional soccer players belonging to 63 national unions and associations (International Soccer Association, 2013). The IRPA (n.d.) represents over 7,000 professional rugby players from South Africa, England, Australia, Scotland, Wales, New Zealand, Ireland, and France. FICA (n.d.) is representative of professional associations in Sri Lanka, New Zealand, South Africa, Bangladesh, Scotland, Australia, and the United Kingdom.

These nonprofit, nongovernmental associations have memoranda of understanding or agreements with their respective IFs addressing a range of topics, such as financial commitments, load, health and safety requirements, processes for streamlining dispute resolution between players and clubs, transfer right information, and joint participation in special projects. The organizations are typically governed by a president who presides over an executive team, council, or advisory group comprised of member associations.

Examples of associations for professionals competing internationally in tournament or circuit-style sports such as tennis, golf, and esports include the Association of Tennis Professionals (ATP), Women's Tennis Association (WTA), Professional Golf Association (PGA), Ladies' Professional Golf Association (LPGA), and World Esports Association (WESA). Membership in these associations often requires applicants to meet qualification standards to signify their status as professionals or as eligible participants for a sanctioned tournament. The WTA (2018), for example, is described as an "international award competition" (p. 7) and not a players' organization, although its constitution includes age requirements for rankings in the top 10. Similarly, the LPGA (n.d.) identifies as a professional sports organization that evolved from a playing tour, however, the organization maintains authority to fine players up to $1,000 for "plunging necklines" or wearing leggings without a skirt during competition (Chengelis, 2017).

Since professional athletes in sports such as tennis, swimming, golf, motorsports, and boxing compete as independent contractors, the roles and responsibilities of any association are more those of a service organization than a supreme authority for participants. These associations are typically governed by a commissioner or president, a board of directors, and an executive team with oversight responsibilities for each competition, grassroots programs, and player or athlete rankings.

Regulatory Associations for Amateur Athletes in International Sports

In the United States, amateur sports are typically affiliated with recreational, scholastic, and intercollegiate competition, with the NCAA and Amateur Athletic Union serving as examples of regulatory organizations for athletes. There are few regulatory agencies for amateurs competing in international competition beyond representative sport federations addressed later in this chapter. The World Amateur Footgolf Association (n.d.), for example, identifies as a nonprofit organization in 13 countries with the aim of helping to develop amateurs toward a goal of competing for prize money.

REGULATORY AGENCIES GOVERNING INTERNATIONAL AND GLOBAL SPORTS

International federations (IFs) are some of the most commonly recognized regulatory agencies governing sports around the world, especially since the Olympic Charter identifies the IOC, IFs, and NOCs as the three primary units of the Olympic movement. International federations manage and monitor operations of the world's various sports disciplines, including oversight and approval of the technical elements such as rules, rankings, records, and athlete classification.

IFs wield considerable power in the global arena despite their subordination to the IOC. For example, the compliance commission for the International Boxing Association (AIBA) recommended provisional suspension of the executive director of the Kazakhstan Boxing Federation for his association with a group of rogue individuals who aspired to manage the world qualifications for the 2020 Tokyo Olympics (Morgan, 2019a). Prior to the announcement, the IOC had been investigating AIBA for various governance issues, and it eventually stripped the IF's ability to host the 2019 World Championships and 2020 Olympics. One of the key issues was the association's election of a suspected member of Uzbekistan's transnational organized crime network as president (Morgan, 2019b).

Following is an overview of the Global Association of International Sport Federations (GAISF), the umbrella organization for all Olympic and non-Olympic sport federations. Additional information addresses the structure and governance of IFs and several international organizations that govern sports for the disabled.

Global Association of International Sport Federations

The **Global Association of International Sport Federations** (GAISF) (2017), formerly known as SportAccord, is a nonprofit entity encompassing all "international sport federations and international organizations contributing to sport in various fields." In 2020, 114 organizations were listed as members of the GAISF (n.d.). Governed by a council of nine elected members, the GAISF headquarters are located in Lausanne, Switzerland. Member federations are categorized according to five classifications distinguishable by their association with the Olympics and the IOC or as affiliated agencies (see table 6.1).

Since the GAISF is an umbrella organization that encompasses non-Olympic sports, it also serves as an organizer for events, namely the SportAccord Convention and International Federation Forum. GAISF also has a role in developing and organizing multisport competitions, primarily for non-Olympic sports, such as the Urban Games, Mind Games, Combat Games, Beach Games, Artistic Games, and Motor Sport Games (Olympic News, 2017).

The inaugural bureau of international sport federations was formed in 1921, but the first true General Assembly wasn't launched until 2003. The General Assembly, in collaboration with the IFs for the Summer and Winter Olympics, was named the SportAccord Convention and promoted as the World Sport and Business Summit. One of the central issues for the GAISF 2018 General Assembly and SportAccord Convention was central data privacy regulations.

International Federations

International federations for Olympic and non-Olympic sports are similar in structure (comprised of national federations) and function (govern rules and championship formats). The IF serves as the supreme authority for a sport regardless of whether it is recognized by the IOC or considered an independent federation. Since 2017, a feud has existed between the International Canoe Federation (ICF) and the International Surfing Association (ISA) as to the rightful controller of the sport of stand-up paddle boarding (Butler, 2018). Both federations hosted a world championship event in 2019 after initial mediation through the Court of Arbitration for Sport proved unsuccessful.

International Federations for Olympic Sports

The IF for an Olympic sport is comprised of recognized national federations that belong to one of several continental organizations (see Governance in Action 6.2 for a sample structure of the Fédération Internationale de Basketball Association). An example of an IF is the Fédération Internationale de Natation (FINA), established in 1908 as the supreme authority for swimming. FINA (2017a) is comprised of 207 recognized national federations in the disciplines of swimming, open water swimming, diving, high diving, water polo, artistic swimming (formerly synchronized swimming), and Masters. These national federations form five continental organizations recognized by FINA (2017b, p. 9):

Confédération Africaine de Natation (CANA)

Union Americana de Natacion (UANA)

Asia Swimming Federation (AASF)

Ligue Européenne de Natation (LEN)

Oceania Swimming Association (OSA)

International federations for Olympic sports are also categorized as either members of the Association of Summer Olympic International Federations (ASOIF) or the Association of International Olympic Winter Sports Federations (AIOWF). Approximately 75 percent of IFs for Olympic sports are headquartered in Lausanne, Switzerland, dubbed the "Silicon Valley of Sport" with a city population

Table 6.1 Classification of Members of Global Association of International Sport Federations

Classification	Examples
Association of Summer Olympic International Federations (ASOIF)	World Rugby; World Sailing; Union Cyclists International; International Handball Association
Association of International Olympic Winter Sports Federations (AIOWF)	World Curling Federation; International Ice Hockey Federation; International Skating Union
Association of IOC Recognized Sports Federations (ARISF)	World Flying Disc Association; International Cricket Council; Tug-o-War International Federation
Alliance of Independent Recognized Members of Sport (AIMS)	International Federation of Sled Dog Sports; International Association of Body Building and Fitness; International Casting Sport Federation
Associate members	International World Games Association; International Federation of Sport Medicine; European Broadcasting Union

GOVERNANCE IN ACTION 6.2

Fédération Internationale de Basketball Association

The Fédération Internationale de Basketball Association (FIBA) (2017) is the governing body for basketball divided into five autonomous regional governing bodies: Africa, Americas, Asia, Europe, and Oceania (see figure 6.4). USA Basketball is a member of the Americas region.

Under the FIBA General Statutes, the two forms of regional governance include regional offices, considered subsidiaries of FIBA, and zones. A **subsidiary** is a legal entity controlled by another organization, known as the parent organization (Garner, 1999). Regional offices are controlled by an executive director, who is appointed by FIBA to oversee each zone in the region.

Zones are expected to promote basketball worldwide, assist their respective NGBs, and establish events from grassroots to elite levels to grow the sport in their area. In 2017, FIBA Americas appointed Carlos Alves from Brazil as the new executive director for all zones. A former executive with Nike, Alves' experience includes roles as senior brand director for the 2014 Fédération Internationale de Football Association (FIFA) World Cup in Brazil and general manager and senior director for the 2016 Olympic and Paralympic Games in Rio de Janeiro (Etchells, 2017).

Zones are governed by the Zone Assembly, president, board, and committees. The Zone Assembly acts as a legislative body responsible for proposing amendments to governing documents for approval by FIBA's Central Committee. The composition of the Zone Board varies by region, but the members are limited to one per nationality. The board is responsible for the overall governance of the zone, including developing the game of basketball, resolving disputes among members, and handling all finances (FIBA, 2017c).

USA Basketball is a member of the Americas region (FIBA America), which includes 42 NGBs from North, Central, and South America and the Caribbean organized into subzones ("Organization," n.d.) (see figure 6.5). Regions are important because national teams qualify for the Basketball World Cup and for the Olympic Games based on their region.

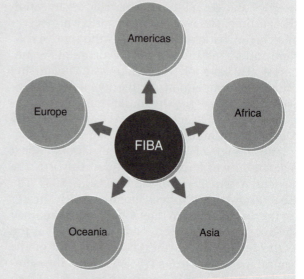
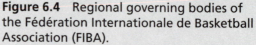

Figure 6.4 Regional governing bodies of the Fédération Internationale de Basketball Association (FIBA).

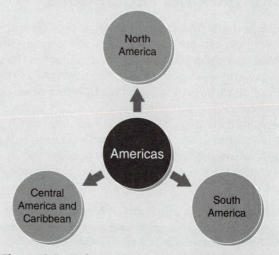

Figure 6.5 Subzones reporting to FIBA's Americas Region.

For the Basketball World Cup, the number of qualifiers from each region is dependent on the number of NGBs in that region. For example, the Americas Region has 42 member NGBs with seven team slots for the World Cup, while Europe has 50 member NGBs with 12 team slots. For the Olympics, qualification is again based on region. Twelve teams qualify for the Olympics: seven regional teams based on their finish in the World Cup, the host nation, and four from Olympic-qualifying tournaments (FIBA, 2017c).

of 140,000 and serving as the home of the IOC headquarters (Ruiz, 2016). The attraction of the city, according to a sports lawyer in Switzerland, is linked to political neutrality, geographic centrality, favorable tax structure, and friendliness to private arbitration (Valloni, 2016, as cited in Ruiz, 2016). Federations that relocate to the Maison du Sport or anywhere in Lausanne, for example, are enticed with two years of free rent, permanent tax exemptions, and assistance in securing work permits and housing (Ruiz, 2016). Governance in Action 6.2 profiles the structure and governance of the IF for the sport of basketball.

It has been surmised that the "scope and influence of IFs varies considerably" due to disparities in the number of national federations and media impact (Chappelet & Kubler-Mabbott, 2008). The Fédération Internationale de Football Association (FIFA) (n.d.), for example, includes 211 national federations belonging to one of six confederations, while the International Bobsleigh and Skeleton Federation (IBSF) includes only 70 national federations.

International Federations for Non-Olympic Sports

Among the international federations for non-Olympic sports, 37 are officially or provisionally recognized by the IOC (as of 2019), and some are considered independent, with no association to the IOC. Sports belonging to the Association of IOC Recognized International Sports Federations (ARISF) (n.d.), established in 1984, may receive funding from the IOC and have connections to IOC commissions.

Many of the federations recognized by the IOC have ambitions to become official Olympic sports. For example, the International Motorcycling Track Federation for the sport of ice racing (112 national members) and the Federation of International Bandy (25 national members) are two IFs recognized by the IOC with aspirations for inclusion in the Winter Games. Their suitability for inclusion in the Winter Games is because bandy and ice racing are considered to rank fairly high in terms of popularity and media appeal, and each federation has a high-functioning formal administrative structure committed to antidoping policies and a business model that accounts for "reasonable" operational expenses (Bliznevskiy et al., 2016).

International federations not recognized by the IOC may also aspire to have their sport on the docket for the Summer or Winter Games. Most of these federations without IOC recognition fall under the scope or authority of the Alliance of Independent Recognized Members of Sport (AIMS). Founded in 2009, AIMS is one of the five categories of the GAISF with a role to support the development of 27 member federations (as of 2019). AIMS independent federations govern sports such as fishing, dog sled racing, sepak takraw, miniature golf, sambo, lacrosse, and dragon boat racing; they are highly organized associations, but they may not have applied for IOC recognition, or their application may have been denied.

International Organizations of Sports for the Disabled

The **International Organizations of Sports for the Disabled** (IOSD) are independent agencies recognized by the International Paralympic Committee (IPC) and the IOC (2015) that serve as the governing bodies and are the sole worldwide representatives for specific impairment sports in the Paralympic Games. Among the four recognized organizations are the Cerebral Palsy International Sports and Recreation Association (CPISRA), the International Blind Sports Federation (IBSA), the International Sports Federation for Persons with Intellectual Disabilities (INAS), and the International Wheelchair and Amputee Sports Federation (IWASF). Examples of sports associated with each international organization are provided in table 6.2.

Table 6.2 IOC and IPC Recognized International Organizations of Sports for the Disabled

International organization	Sport disciplines (examples)
Cerebral Palsy International Sports and Recreation Association (CPISRA)	CP football, frame football, race running
International Blind Sports Federation (IBSA)	Torball, showball
International Sports Federation for Persons with Intellectual Disabilities (INAS)	Para-hockey
International Wheelchair and Amputee Sports Federation (IWASF)	Wheelchair fencing, powerchair hockey

The four organizations oversee adaptive sports and recreation. Each maintains a role in governing and supporting sports in the Paralympics as well as supporting competition for the disability groups that are not part of the Paralympics. Associations for official Paralympic sports include the Boccia International Sport Association, World ParaVolleyball, the International Wheelchair Basketball Association, and International Wheelchair Rugby Association (IPC, 2018b).

REGULATORY AGENCIES IN GLOBAL SPORTS WITH A SPECIALIST FUNCTION

Agencies in global sports with a specialist function are those primarily involved with sports services. Their official title identifies their association with service or with a governing role for a specific target population such as the media, lawyers, or athletic trainers. Examples of organizations with a specialist function connected to global sport include the International Association of Sport Law, the International Sporting Cinema and Television Federation, the International Lifesaving Association, the International Sports Press Association, the International Association of Sport Science and Physical Education, and the International Federation of Sport Medicine. The World Anti-Doping Agency, the Court of Arbitration for Sport, the International Association for Fair Play (CIFP), and the World Olympians Association (WOA) are four affiliated special-function global sport agencies officially recognized by the IOC.

The structure of affiliated special function agencies in global sports share common attributes with organizations and federations that have a governance role for a sport, member athletes, or an international multisport competition such as the Commonwealth Games. These associations include a governing body that operates through a constitution or a list of statutes that address the mission, membership, and other important details.

The service role of these organizations connected to global sports is apparent in the mission or objectives. For example, the primary role of the International Association of Fair Play (n.d.) is to provide education on fair play and preventing adverse behavior.

Two of the most recognizable associations with a specialist function for global sport are the World Anti-Doping Agency (WADA) and the Court of Arbitration for Sport (CAS).

World Anti-Doping Agency

Established in 1999, the **World Anti-Doping Agency** (WADA) is an independent agency funded by the IOC and governments around the world. The mission of WADA (2018a) is to lead a collaborative worldwide movement for doping-free sport. The role of the agency is to coordinate opposition to doping in sport internationally through education, research, advocacy, and monitoring of the World Anti-Doping Code. In 2016, WADA (2017, p. 6) analyzed 193,345 drug-testing samples for Olympic sports and 107,220 samples for non-Olympic sports.

Prior to the creation of WADA, the IOC had played a prominent role in the global fight against doping through a Medical Commission established in 1961. At the 1968 Winter Games in Grenoble, France, and Summer Games in Mexico City, the IOC became the first entity to carry out antidoping and gender testing on a global scale (Chappelet & Kubler-Mabbott, 2008, p. 133).

After three decades of the IOC serving as the entity primarily responsible for global antidoping enforcement, increasing influence from governments in the mid-1990s led to the creation of WADA, partly due to scandals involving the Tour de France and the International Cycling Union (Casini, 2009). The agency had its origins in the World Conference on Doping convened by the IOC in 1998 (World Anti-Doping Agency, 2018b). Over the past several decades, WADA has taken legislative measures to establish and maintain independence from the IOC, although the IOC still has a prominent role as a partner in the organization.

While most of the agencies described in this chapter maintain status as nonprofit, nongovernmental organizations, WADA is distinguished by the central role of national governments in the agency through their representation on the WADA Council and through their primary financial support (Casini, 2009; Handstad, Smith, & Waddington, 2008, p. 242; Toohey & Beaton, 2017). WADA is an example of a hybrid public–private governance body operating in a global domain. While considered a nonprofit organization, both public government entities and the IOC serve as the two key constituents with equal influence.

Intergovernmental cooperation marked the fight against substance abuse, especially that which had occurred in elite sports (Toohey & Beaton, 2017, p. 484). Canada, the United Kingdom, and Australia, for example, orchestrated an International Anti-Doping Agreement that soon attracted other countries who were seemingly displeased with the ineffectiveness of the IOC's previous efforts to curtail doping violations (Hanstad et al., 2008).

WADA's headquarters are in Montreal, Canada, and regional offices are based in Europe (Lausanne, Switzerland), Asia/Oceania (Tokyo, Japan), Africa (Cape Town, South Africa) and Latin America (Montevideo, Uruguay) (World Anti-Doping Agency, 2018c). Governance of WADA is relegated to a 38-member foundation board and 12-member executive board (World Anti-Doping Agency, 2018a). An organizational chart for WADA addresses the role of government agencies, the IOC, IFs, IPC, the Court of Arbitration for Sport, and laboratories that must "achieve and maintain accreditation," according to international specifications identified in the association's technical documents (World Anti-Doping Agency, 2009). WADA's authority partly stems from its power to sanction laboratories that fail to uphold standards. In 2018, the organization administered a six-month suspension to Romania's only statewide drug testing facility in Bucharest (Associated Press, 2018).

Court of Arbitration for Sport

The **Court of Arbitration for Sport** (CAS), headquartered in Lausanne, Switzerland, was established in 1984 as an independent judicial authority for dispute resolution in sport (Court of Arbitration for Sport, n.d.). Sixty members composed the CAS, including 15 members each appointed by the IOC, the IFs, the national Olympic committees, and the IOC president.

One of the primary functions of the CAS is rapid resolution of disputes during the Olympic Games through ad hoc divisions with a 24-hour window for settlement (Chappelet & Kubler-Mabbott, 2008). Settlements are confidential unless both parties agree to public disclosure (Court of Arbitration for Sport, n.d.). In 2003, the CAS was certified as the official appeals body for all international doping disputes.

There have been many reforms to the statutes and bylaws of the CAS, some of which have been necessary to establish independence from the IOC and to create its current structure of two divisions representing (1) ordinary arbitration and (2) appeals. The 1994 reforms were integral in diminishing the role of the IOC, which was responsible for funding and operating the CAS. The International Council of Arbitration for Sport (ICAS) is now the supreme organ governing operations and funding of the CAS with responsibility for safeguarding the association's independence

(Court of Arbitration for Sport, n.d.). The ICAS is a 20-member board that elects its own president, appoints CAS arbitrators, and approves budgets.

A minimum of 150 arbitrators report to the secretary general of the CAS and preside over disputes considered either commercial or disciplinary in nature. Many commercial-related arbitration cases involve contract disputes for issues related to sponsorships, television rights, player transfers, and staging of sporting events. Disputes over relations between coaches or players and clubs also fall into the category of commercial cases. Disciplinary cases, however, primarily address doping violations, and these constitute a majority of CAS appellate division cases. Chappelet and Kubler-Mabbott (2008, p. 129) noted that in 2007, the CAS addressed over 300 disputes, of which 35 percent dealt with antidoping and 40 percent dealt with player transfers, primarily in football. Statistics published by the CAS (2016) indicate the agency addressed only 252 cases in 2007 and 599 in 2016.

In 2019, the International Association for Athletics Federation (IAAF) was challenged in the Court of Arbitration for Sport by South African gold medalist Caster Semenya, who claimed the organization's new ruling over testosterone limits for mid-distance female runners was unfair. The IAAF regulation under appeal in June 2019 requires a female with high testosterone levels to compete in a men's division or take androgen-suppressive drugs to reduce her hormone levels to an acceptable range to compete in the women's competition. Semenya received protection from the Swiss Federal Tribunal court system to race without altering her testosterone levels while an appeal was being considered (Morgan, 2019c). The case was not resolved as of the publication date of this chapter and the two-time Olympian was absent from the 2019 World Championships in Doha, Qatar (Murphy, 2019).

RECAP

There is almost no challenge to the assertion that the Court of Arbitration for Sport and the IOC are two of the most influential agencies governing international sport. The landscape of global sport governance is complex because organizations occasionally have overlapping roles and shared responsibilities.

Regulatory agencies for global sport can be categorized according to their principal purpose, with authority over (1) athletes (and coaches/officials), (2) sports, (3) competition, or (4) a specialist function for international sport. Examples of organizations governing athletes in global sports are the 200-plus national Olympic committees that make up the Association of National Olympic Committees (ANOC). Examples of organizations governing sports include IFs for Olympic and non-Olympic sports. Examples of agencies serving in an oversight capacity for competition include the IOC, the Commonwealth Games Federation, and the International University Sports Federation.

Finally, examples of agencies with a specialist function in global sport are the World Anti-Doping Agency (WADA) and the Court of Arbitration for Sport (CAS).

Most of the regulatory agencies for international or global sport are considered nonprofit, nongovernmental organizations. WADA is in the minority as an example of a global sport organization that depends on governments for financial support and leadership.

Critical Thinking Questions

1. What are some examples of an international sport that is on the cusp of being considered a global sport?

2. Is shared governance a necessity when coordinating a multisport international competition? Why or why not?

3. Besides their affiliation to the IOC, what are some of the similarities and some of the distinct roles and responsibilities of national Olympic committees, international federations, and organizing committees of the Olympic Games?

4. Should the World Anti-Doping Agency revise its policies in response to the Russian statewide doping scandal that affected the 2014 Sochi, 2016 Rio, and 2018 PyeongChang Olympics?

5. Why isn't the Court of Arbitration for Sport used at local and state levels?

Applied Activities

U-18 International Soccer Tournament Responsibility Chart

Assume the role of the executive director for the office of sport tourism in a medium-sized city in the United States with 300,000 residents. Your organization is interested in hosting an international soccer tournament for under-18 soccer teams around the world with the goal of involving a minimum of 30 teams from at least five countries. Create a chart identifying the scope of responsibilities for the various government and nongovernment agencies that would be involved with tournament administration, the athletes, and officiating.

Future Multisport Competitions: Participant and Volunteer Information

Use the Internet to research two upcoming multisport competitions of interest around the world that are not affiliated with the Olympic Games. Identify the name of the competition, the host location, the qualifications for participants, and the qualifications for volunteers. Identify the governing agency responsible for determining the qualifications for participants and the agency responsible for securing volunteers. Elaborate on any additional interesting points about the competition.

Case Study Application

For more information on governance and authority in global sports, review *Taekwondo and Wrestling Tackle International Political Interference* and *Power Limitations in International Sport Federations* in the web resource.

Governance and Authority in Sport Industry Sectors

Professional Sports

Kerri Cebula

LEAD-OFF

The professional sector of the sports industry is often characterized by its association with commercial monetary gains. This association is the primary distinction between amateur and professional sports. Professionalism may have resulted from media coverage and commercialization that fueled entrepreneurial efforts to develop sports into "money-making ventures" (Carvalho, 2010, p. 366). Considering the power and privilege that accompany professional sports, governance and control are essential to achieving organizational goals for profitability and market share gains.

In general, professional sports are divided between team sports, such as basketball and baseball, and individual sports. Individual sports can be further divided between individual performer sports, such as golf, tennis, and boxing, and individual performer team sports, such as motorsports and cycling.

Team sports and individual sports differ in more than just the number of competitors. The governance structure of the professional competitions is also different. In North America, professional team sports are organized as leagues. This type of structure is characterized by a central league office under the control of the member teams. In the United Kingdom, team sports are organized under a club structure. Governance is relegated to a central league office, where the teams have a voice but do not control the organization. Individual sports are structured as tournaments or series of tournaments.

This chapter addresses the governance of professional team sports in the United States with emphasis on the power and authority granted to commissioners. The governance systems of professional leagues in the United Kingdom and Japan will also be explored. Finally, the governance systems for professional individual performer sports will be distinguished from that of individual team sports in the United States.

Learning Outcomes

- Identify the various governance structures in professional sports.
- Explain the differences between the governance structures of team and individual sports.
- Identify the differences between governance structures of professional leagues around the world.
- Explain the central governance issues stemming from current cases in professional sports.

TEAM SPORTS

As firms in the sport-producing sector, individual professional sports teams or **franchises** are responsible for producing games that satisfy the needs and interests of consumers for sport entertainment. Each team usually has an exclusive right to market and operate in a designated area. Gate receipts, sales of premier seats and luxury suites, parking and concessions, corporate sponsorships, and sales of local broadcast rights are examples of the revenue sources the teams have to sustain their operations.

While there are many team sports around the globe, not all have a professional tier. For example, there are currently no professional teams in handball, water polo, or synchronized swimming. Many team sports, however, include a professional sector that operates with a primary business development purpose to entertain and procure a profit.

North America

According to the United States Census Bureau (2017), there were about 840 professional sport teams or clubs affiliated with various leagues at both the major and minor league levels in 2015. Professional team sports in North America are organized in leagues. The leagues are controlled by the teams, or more specifically, by the owners of the teams (see figure 7.1). The teams collectively have the power to hire and fire the league commissioner, to agree to the collective bargaining agreement with players, and to decide on playing rules. The head of the league, generally identified as a commissioner, oversees the day-to-day operations of the league and the league staff and is the public face of the league. Before collective bargaining agreements and player unions were allowed, the power and authority of the commissioner was almost limitless.

The rights and responsibilities of the teams, the league, and the commissioner are set forth in the governing documents. The governing documents

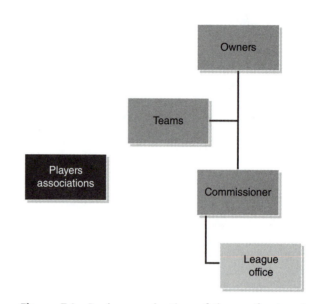

Figure 7.1 Basic organization of the professional sport teams in North America.

are a series of documents that lay out the relationship between the teams and the league. The main governing document is known as the constitution and bylaws. Leagues and the teams that compete within the leagues are considered private entities. This means that neither group is required to make their governing documents, such as the franchise agreement or the league constitution, public.

Under the league structure in North America, teams are separate legal entities, known as franchises, that have a **franchise agreement** with the league office. As a separate legal entity, each team controls all aspects of its operations, within the framework of the franchise agreement and other governing documents of the league. For example, under its franchise agreement, a team in the United States Interregional Soccer League (USISL) agrees to field a team and to comply with all league requirements ("USL Franchise Agreement," n.d.).

The team is also responsible for hiring and firing its employees, including the players. However, the hiring and firing of players must take place according to league rules and agreements. Teams are also responsible for securing local broadcast agreements, securing local sponsorship agreements, paying for their stadiums (either rent or a mortgage), selling tickets, and other things that a business owner would be responsible for in operational terms. The teams pay into the league an amount set forth in the governing documents for running the league office, and teams also receive revenues from the league office as set forth in the governing documents.

The main league offices of Major League Baseball (MLB), the National Basketball Association (NBA), the National Football League (NFL), and the National Hockey League (NHL) are structured as **unincorporated associations**. This means that the league itself is not a separate entity from the teams, which are known legally as "members" of the association (Garner, 1999). Under the governing documents, the league agrees to set the rules, with the teams' input, and to schedule games for the teams. The league office is also generally responsible for negotiating the collective bargaining agreement with players and officials and for disciplinary measures in the event players, team employees, owners, or the teams themselves violate league rules. Finally, the league office is responsible for securing national broadcasting agreements and national sponsorship agreements. The revenues earned by the league flow through the league office to the teams in accordance with the franchise agreement or the leagues' constitution and after paying for the league office expenses (Harwell & Hobson, 2015; "USL Franchise Agreement," n.d.; National Football League, 2006).

Major League Baseball

Professional baseball in the United States began in 1876 with the founding of the National League of Professional Baseball Players, which is today's National League. The American League began in 1894 as the Western League, changing its name in 1901. Major League Baseball began in 1903 when the National League and the American League joined to form the National Commission. Two years after the Black Sox scandal of 1919, in which the World Series was rigged to benefit gamblers, the league hired Judge Kennesaw Mountain Landis to serve as the first professional sports commissioner (Sigman, 2005). One of Landis' stipulations for accepting the role was to be granted judge-like power. The position of commissioner was thereby given broad power to act in the best interests of the league (Sigman, 2005; see Governance in Action 7.1).

The official name of Major League Baseball is The Office of the Commissioner of Baseball. Under the 2005 constitution, there are two levels of governance. The first is assigned to the executive council, and the second denotes the supreme power and authority of the league commissioner.

The executive council includes eight-member clubs comprising four teams from the National League and four from the American League. Club members, each serving a four-year term, are appointed by the commissioner. The Executive Council is responsible for promoting and protecting the interests of the team and "to perpetuate Baseball as the national game of America" (Major League Baseball, 2005). Council members are also responsible for overall budgeting and finance and for representing the interests of the league between league meetings. The entire league meets during the Major League Meetings (also known as the Owners' Meetings) to vote on matters in the collective bargaining agreement. Owners, players, and the umpires vote on items such as playing and scoring rules, expansion rules, and the sale of clubs. All actions taken by the Executive Committee between these meetings are automatically discussed at the meeting and must be approved by the rest of the owners (Major League Baseball, 2005).

The MLB commissioner is considered the most powerful of the four major North American professional sport commissioners. The current MLB commissioner is Rob Manfred, and under the MLB constitution, the commissioner serves as the chief executive officer of the league responsible for labor relations. He has the power to punish teams or individuals and to appoint the presidents of the National and American Leagues. The commissioner also has the authority to resolve on-field disputes and to provide official interpretations of the playing rules (Major League Baseball, 2005). Governance in Action 7.1 details the origins of the decision-making authority granted to the MLB commissioner in the league's constitution.

National Basketball Association

The National Basketball Association (NBA) began in 1949 when rival leagues the Basketball Association of America and the National Basketball League merged and became the NBA. Similar to the MLB, the NBA also has two levels of governance, with a board of governors and the commissioner.

All teams, through a team-appointed governor, are represented on the board of governors responsible for appointing committees and voting on changes in the playing rules (National Basketball

GOVERNANCE IN ACTION 7.1

MLB Commissioners Act in Best Interests of the Game

In 1919, when the heavily favored Chicago White Sox lost the World Series to the Cincinnati Reds, eight White Sox players, who became known as the Black Sox, were accused of fixing the outcome and purposely losing. This scandal, along with other disputes, pushed the owners to hire someone to oversee the integrity of baseball. Judge Kennesaw Mountain Landis accepted the job, provided he had the ability to act in the best interests of the game, which was the mandate of the owners who granted that power and authority to the position (Curtis, 1995; Sigman, 2005). Thus, the concept of the "best interests" of the game through power was established as the authoritative rule for professional baseball.

The Major League constitution in Article II, Section 2(b) grants the commissioner the ability to investigate "any act, transaction or practice charged, alleged or suspected not to be in the best interests of the national game of Baseball . . ." (II.2.b). The commissioners of the NBA and the NFL also have the ability to act in the best interests of the game (see NBA Constitution, Article 24; NFL Constitution, Article 25). When the commissioner uses his best interests of the game power, it is the final decision. There is no opportunity for an appeal.

Several baseball commissioners have used the best interests of the game power. Landis first used the power to ban the eight Black Sox players (Justice, 2013). Bowie Kuhn used the clause to prevent Oakland Athletics owner Charles Finley from selling his best players. Finley sued, but the courts upheld the power and the commissioner's right to use it (*Charles O. Finley & Co., Inc. v. Kuhn*, 569 F.2d 527, *cert. denied* 439 U.S. 876 [1978]). Commissioner Fay Vincent also used the power to suspend George Steinbrenner, then the owner of the New York Yankees, for dealing with an admitted gambler. As it was Steinbrenner's second suspension, there was no appeal to the decision made under the "best interests of the game power" (Chass, 1990). Several other commissioners have also used the power to ban players for acts of gambling and drug use (Justice, 2013).

There have been two times when, to the surprise of many, the commissioner did not use the best interests of the game power. The first instance was when Commissioner Bart Giamatti banned Pete Rose from baseball for life for betting on baseball games while Rose was the manager of the Cincinnati Reds. In a deal made with Rose, Giamatti agreed not to invoke the power, and Rose accepted the ban (Justice, 2013). The second instance was when Commissioner Bud Selig did not invoke the power in suspending Alex Rodriguez for 211 games in 2013 for using performance-enhancing drugs (Ford, 2013; Justice, 2013). No deal was made between Selig and Rodriguez, but Selig understood that using his power would have brought scrutiny from the MLB Players Association.

Association, 2012). The specific duties of the board of governors, other than those just mentioned, are not listed in great detail in the constitution and bylaws.

The second level of governance is the commissioner, appointed by the board of governors by a three-fourths majority vote. The current commissioner is Adam Silver (see Governance in Action 7.2). The commissioner acts as the chief executive officer and is responsible for both the general and day-to-day operations of the league as well as for resolving disputes and scheduling league games. Under Article 24, Section (l), the commissioner has the power to penalize actions when the punishment "in the commissioner's judgment shall be in the best interests of the Association" (NBA, 2012, p. 38).

National Football League

The National Football League began in 1920 as the American Professional Football Association. Jim Thorpe was named the first president. The league changed its name to the National Football League (NFL) in 1922. Under the 2006 NFL constitution and in the same fashion as the NBA and MLB, there are two levels of governance, with an executive committee and commissioner. Each has an important role in the rules and operations of the league.

The NFL's Executive Committee consists of one representative from every team. This representative must be the owner of the team, a holder of an interest in the team, or an officer of the team. The Executive Committee is responsible for financial

GOVERNANCE IN ACTION 7.2

Article 24: NBA Commissioner's Power and Authority

The NBA's longest tenured commissioner was David Stern, who took the helm in 1984 before passing the torch to his deputy, Adam Silver, 30 years later in 2014. Coinciding with Silver's inaugural year at the helm of the NBA, the league published its constitution and bylaws for the first time in history. The constitution includes Article 24, outlining the Authority and Duties of the Commissioner.

Stern used the authority granted by the constitution to issue a $10,000 fine against Cleveland Cavaliers owner Dan Gilbert in 2010 for his disparaging remarks over LeBron James' decision to play for the Miami Heat the following year. In 2011, Stern issued a $250,000 fine against the San Antonio Spurs after head coach Greg Popovich sent four star players, including Tim Duncan and Tony Parker, home before a nationally televised game on the last day of a five-day road trip against the defending world champions, the Miami Heat, so they could "rest" for an upcoming conference matchup against the Memphis Grizzlies (Beck, 2012; Golliver, 2012).

While current NBA Commissioner Adam Silver holds the power to fine teams up to only $100,000 for "resting" healthy players during high-profile games, he has yet to impose the penalty through the 2019-2020 season. Silver also decided not to invoke Article 24 in a 2018 case involving pervasive sexual harassment on the part of several front office employees for the Dallas Mavericks (Wertheim & Luther, 2018). In response to the allegations, owner Mark Cuban pledged a $10 million contribution to women's organizations, which was far more than the team could have been penalized by the commissioner under Article 35A, which limits fines against a team or owner to $1 million ("NBA: Mark Cuban," 2018).

Silver did invoke Article 24 in his inaugural year by issuing a fine of $2.5 million and a lifetime ban of former Los Angeles Clippers owner Donald Sterling following the release of a cell phone audio recording demonstrating that Sterling told his girlfriend not to bring "black people" to the stadium, including L.A. Lakers owner Magic Johnson (Shreffler, Presley, & Schmidt, 2015). The Sterling family eventually sold the team to former Microsoft CEO Steve Ballmer (Berger, 2014; Wood, 2014).

Silver also invoked Article 24 when he pulled the 2017 All-Star Game out of Charlotte due to the state of North Carolina's controversial transgender bathroom law (Garcia, 2018). The law was eventually rescinded, and Charlotte was granted hosting rights to the 2019 All-Star Game.

Both the late David Stern and his successor Adam Silver have been lauded in their role as NBA commissioner. While Silver has seen record attendance and record television ratings during his short reign, during Stern's era, the league expanded from 23 to 30 teams, and player salaries increased from an average of $250,000 to over $5 million (Windhorst, 2012).

---

oversight of the league, including the ability to take out loans in the name of the league and to audit the books and records. The committee can also investigate any matter referred to it by teams or the commissioner, fine anyone associated with a team, or increase or impose additional penalties after the commissioner imposes discipline. The Executive Committee, however, cannot decrease penalties mandated by the commissioner. Finally, the Executive Committee has authority over the commissioner, including the ability to hire and fire. Most of the decisions of the Executive Committee must be approved by a three-fourths majority vote (National Football League, 2006).

The second level of governance is the commissioner; the current commissioner is Roger Goodell.

The commissioner is responsible for running the league office and can bind the league to contracts (e.g., media contracts). The commissioner may also interpret and establish policies and procedures based on the constitution and bylaws. The commissioner has authority to appoint members of all committees, except the Executive Committee, and he serves as an ex officio member of all committees. The commissioner has full, complete, and final jurisdiction over all disputes and is responsible for the enforcement of the constitution and bylaws. Finally, the commissioner has the responsibility to act in the best interests of the game (National Football League, 2006).

In 2006, longtime NFL Commissioner Paul Tagliabue announced his retirement after serving

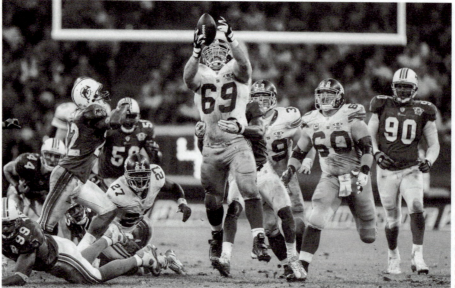

CARL DE SOUZA/AFP/Getty Images

Despite fielding teams exclusively in the United States, the NFL, arguably the most powerful professional league in the world, has routinely staged regular season games in countries around the world. The first international regular season game took place in 2007 at Wembley Stadium in London, England.

as commissioner for 17 years and overseeing the expansion of the league, the introduction of free agency, and explosive financial growth. League owners voted to appoint Roger Goodell, then the NFL's chief operating officer, as the new commissioner. Goodell began his tenure on September 1, 2006, and in 2017, he signed a contract extension through the 2023 season ("NFL Commissioner," 2017). During his time as commissioner, Goodell has overseen the signing of lucrative television contracts and has predicted the NFL will earn $25 billion in revenue by 2027 (Eckstein, 2019). Goodell has also overseen the push toward international expansion with the playing of multiple games overseas and the investment in the Tottenham Hotspurs' new stadium in London, England.

As commissioner, Goodell has exercised his authority granted by the NFL constitution to fine and suspend players and teams for league indiscretions. Governance in Action 7.3 profiles several of the league, player, and owner controversies involving suspensions and fines during Goodell's tenure as commissioner.

National Hockey League

The National Hockey League (NHL) was originally founded in 1917 in Montreal, Quebec, Canada. Over the next several years, teams joined and teams left. By 1942, there were six teams left in the league, forever revered as the "Original Six." Under

the NHL constitution and similar to the other leagues in North America, professional hockey is governed on two levels, including the board of governors and the commissioner.

Each team is represented on the board by a team-appointed governor. In addition, each team must appoint a first and a second alternative governor to act in situations when the designated governor cannot. The board is responsible for hiring the commissioner. Similar to other league governance systems, other duties of the board are described in the constitution (National Hockey League, n.d.).

The second level of governance in the NHL is the commissioner. The commissioner acts as the chief executive officer of the league to oversee general operations. He or she is responsible for scheduling league games and has the full and complete authority to discipline anyone connected to the league and the teams (National Hockey League, n.d.).

The current commissioner of the NHL is Gary Bettman, who added seven expansion teams and has assisted in the league's revenue growth from $732 million in his inaugural season in 1993-1994 to approximately $4.56 billion in 2017-2018. In 1997, Bettman fined the New York Rangers $200,000 for the two days the team attempted to set up its own Internet store broadcasting rights separate from the league (Wyshynski, 2018). Despite his positive influence in the league and North American sport, he has also been criticized

GOVERNANCE IN ACTION 7.3

NFL Commissioner Roger Goodell's Disciplinary Reign

Goodell's tenure as NFL commissioner has been fraught with challenges. One of his first disciplinary actions was suspending Atlanta Falcons' quarterback Michael Vick indefinitely in 2007 for his role in an illegal dog fighting business, only to reinstate Vick two years later on a conditional basis (Payne, 2014). In 2007, Goodell also fined owner Robert Kraft and the New England Patriots $250,000 for stealing signals during the season (Wilner, 2019).

During Goodell's reign, Baltimore Ravens' running back Ray Rice received a two-game, then indefinite, suspension for domestic violence; the Cowboys' running back Ezekiel Elliott received a six-game suspension for domestic violence; and the New England Patriots' quarterback Tom Brady received a four-game suspension for his role in "Deflategate," the name given to the NFL's investigation into footballs being deliberately deflated before a playoff game. The Elliott suspension in 2017 resulted in a lawsuit filed by the National Football League Players Association (NFLPA), which was eventually withdrawn (Goldberg, 2017; Hoffman, 2017). It also occurred during Goodell's new contract negotiations with the NFL's Compensation Committee, which included Dallas Cowboys owner Jerry Jones. Jones was eventually relieved of his duties after threatening to sue the other six owners on the committee for continuing with negotiations (Belson, 2017; Zink, 2018).

Deflategate in 2014 resulted in a $1 million fine against the Patriots and owner Robert Kraft, who is essentially one of Goodell's bosses. Kraft was subject to further discipline by the commissioner due to his 2019 arrest for soliciting prostitution after his team won the Super Bowl.

Goodell had previously levied a $500,000 fine and a six-game suspension in 2014 against Indianapolis Colts owner Jim Irsay for legal and personal issues involving alcohol and prescription drugs. In 2012, he took away draft picks and fined the New Orleans Saints and the team's owner $500,000 for the team's alleged "bounty system," which incentivized players for intentionally injuring opponents. Goodell also suspended and fined former Carolina Panthers owner Jerry Richardson $2.7 million after allegations surfaced of sexual and racial misconduct in the workplace. Richardson thereafter sold the team (Wilner, 2019).

Goodell has been lauded for his decisiveness and professionalism in exercising his fundamental authority granted by the NFL's constitution to impose discipline, although challenges persist. The commissioner received enormous backlash when he implemented a controversial new national anthem policy created in response to former San Francisco 49ers' quarterback Colin Kaepernick's silent protests over police brutality and the oppression of people of color (Kane & Tiell, 2017). In response to his unilateral policy decision, the NFLPA filed a grievance, noting the policy was a matter of the league's CBA, which prompted the NFL to put the policy "on hold" (Maske, 2018). As of the 2019 season, the policy remained in limbo, and the NFL was strategizing to recover from a dip in television ratings that coincided with the season of silent protests. Despite the ongoing league challenges, Commissioner Goodell continues to be regarded as one of the most powerful, respected, and highly paid individuals in sports, earning approximately $40 million per year (Wilner, 2019).

for his role in the cancellation of the entire 2004-2005 season over labor issues.

Major League Soccer

In 1988, the United States Soccer Federation (USSF), the recognized national governing body for soccer in the United States, won the right to host the 1994 FIFA World Cup. As part of its bid, the USSF promised to install a top-flight professional soccer league in the United States. The United States had been without a top-level professional soccer league since 1985 when the North American Soccer League folded, due in part to wide disparities in the financial resources of the teams (Reuter, 2017). In December 1993, the USSF chose between three competing organizations, selecting Major League Professional Soccer, now known as Major League Soccer (MLS), as North America's premier professional level for the sport.

The governance structure of MLS is unlike the structure of the other major professional sport leagues in North America. In 1995, MLS was officially formed as a **limited liability corporation**. This classification means that the league is owned by a number of independent investors, including individuals, partnerships, and corporations who are the shareholders of a nonsport organization (*Fraser v. Major League Soccer, LLC*, 284 F. 3d 47 [2002]; "About Major League Soccer," 2017). The other leagues are not owned by anyone because the teams are considered members.

The major difference between MLS and the other professional leagues in North America is the ownership structure of the teams. Under the MLS structure, the league retains the legal title to the teams. This relationship means that, under the law, the league owns *all* of the teams. The individuals or corporations listed as the team's "owners" are legally considered investor-operators in MLS.

These investors own a share in the league and have the rights to operate a specific MLS club. All investors are represented on the MLS Management Committee, which serves as the league's board of directors (Conrad, 2017). Similar to a team owner in other professional sport leagues, this structure still includes the right to hire front office staff and coaches, the right to license local broadcasts, and the right to sell tickets. The team investor-operators receive a management fee from the league and are responsible for half of their stadium rental fees and all other costs associated with team administration (*Fraser v. Major League Soccer, LLC*, 94 F. Supp. 2d 130 [D. Mass., 2000]; *Fraser v. Major League Soccer, LLC*, 284 F. 3d 47 [1st Cir., 2002]). Teams in the other four professional leagues in North America are separate legal entities, and the owner of each team is the actual owner of the team. The owner of the team in the MLB, NHL, NFL, and NBA retain all of the revenues made, subject to the franchise agreement and other governing documents, but they must also bear all costs of running the team in addition to paying league fees.

Another difference between the MLS and the other professional sport leagues is player contracts. Players are considered employees of MLS, which is responsible for player salaries and benefits (*Fraser v. Major League Soccer, LLC*, 94 F. Supp. 2d 130 [D. Mass., 2000]). In the other four leagues, the players are employees of the teams they play for and are paid by their teams.

Similar to the other major professional leagues, the MLS operates through a central office and a commissioner. Don Graber has been at the helm since 1999, overseeing franchise expansion that will reach 27 teams by 2021 following a low of 10 teams in 2001. League valuations have increased under his tenure from an average of $37 million in 2008 to $240 million in 2019 (Carlisle, 2019).

Women's National Basketball Association

In 1996, the board of governors for the NBA approved the creation of the WNBA, which began play in June 1997 ("History," n.d.). A separate board of governors was established specifically for the new women's league to oversee the collective operations of member teams. The original intentions were to capture a portion of the NBA customer base from the teams that shared cities, and often venues, with their big brothers (Conrad, 2017). During the early stages, the eight teams in the WNBA operated as a pure single-entity league, similar to the structure of MLS. All 29 NBA teams had an equal share in the WNBA, which meant that the big brother incurred all the revenues and expenses of the individual franchises.

Due to fledgling revenues over the first five seasons, the WNBA board of governors made a

Ethan Miller/Getty Images

The WNBA originally operated as a single entity with all NBA teams having an equal share of the league until the board of governors decided to sell franchises to individual owners.

crucial decision to depart from the single-entity model to give NBA teams or third parties the right to purchase franchises. The new structure of the WNBA meant that the profits and losses of each team would belong to the individual owner and would not be pooled as they had been in the past.

One of the first entities to purchase an individual WNBA team was a Native American tribe that owned a casino in Connecticut. The Orlando Miracles team, purchased for $5 million by the Mohegan tribe, was renamed the Suns and relocated to Connecticut (Cavanaugh, 2003). It was the first team to be owned by a non-NBA franchise.

Two of the eight original WNBA teams quickly folded since no individual investors were found, but the league was able to secure owner-investors for expansion franchises, whether NBA teams or third parties. Since the league's inception, teams have folded (only four of the original remain) and others have been permitted to join to create a league of 12, which averaged 7,716 fans per game in 2017 (Bogage, 2017).

The WNBA is governed by a collective bargaining agreement that sets forth rules and regulations for players and owners. In May 2019, Cathy Englebert was hired as the league's first commissioner (Draper & Megdal, 2019). NBA Deputy Commissioner Mark Tatum had served in an interim role while the league was searching for a new leader (Airail, 2019). For 22 seasons, the league operated under the authority of a president and not a commissioner.

Additional Professional Leagues in the United States

The United States is home to several other team-sport leagues considered "professional." The most prominent leagues include Major League Lacrosse (MLL), the National Lacrosse League (NLL), National Pro Fastpitch Softball (NPF), and the National Women's Soccer League (NWSL).

Instituted in 1999, Major League Lacrosse is the premier professional lacrosse league in North America, securing television contracts with ESPN and LAX Sport Network ("About Major League Lacrosse," 2019). National Lacrosse League is the professional league for indoor competition. The two leagues, which operate as separate entities, complement each other due to the playing seasons not overlapping.

National Pro Fastpitch Softball and the National Women's Soccer League offer professional playing opportunities for females in these sports. Teams in the NPF operate as business franchises with owners who can represent an individual, partnership, corporation, or government municipality. The NWSL's structure is as a joint venture of the Canadian and United States Soccer Federations, which pay players' salaries (Pingue, 2018).

There is a long list of professional sport leagues that have failed to thrive in the United States despite relatively sound governance structures. Some of the most notable professional leagues no longer in existence include the United States Football League (USFL), the American Basketball Association (ABA), which folded shortly after the emergence of the WNBA, and the American Football League (AFL), which merged with the NFL in the 1960s.

The XFL, a professional football league that ran for only one season in 2001, re-emerged with eight teams in 2020 as a complementary professional league to the NFL. The XFL comeback is a year after the failed attempt of the Alliance of American Football (AFF), which launched as eight centrally owned and operated teams with an impressive list of players and the backing of a lucrative CBS contract. With two games remaining in the regular season of its inaugural year, the governing board and its chairman Tom Dundon, owner of the NHL Carolina Hurricanes, announced suspension of all operations (Teope, 2019). A statement appearing on the AAF website acknowledged all football operations were suspended and further comments were not available due to "ongoing legal processes" (Alliance of American Football, 2019). The sustainability of the XFL or a re-emergence of the AAF remains questionable given the short-lived history of American-style professional football leagues other than the NFL and the indoor Arena Football League.

Players' Associations

One group that affects the governance of professional team sports in North America without a direct say in the governance of a particular league is the players' associations. Players' associations exist for the four major North American professional leagues (NFL, MLB, NHL, and NBA) in addition to the WNBA and MLS. Players' associations also exist for the National Women's Soccer League and for professional lacrosse athletes.

The National Labor Relations Act (NLRA) applies to private employers, and in Section 7, it grants workers three rights: (1) to join and assist (or not) labor unions, (2) to collectively bargain through representatives of their own choosing, and (3) to engage in concerted activities (e.g., strikes) (National Labor Relations Act, 1935). The **collective bargaining agreement** (CBA) is the contract that results from collective bargaining. This governing document must include the rate and method of pay, the terms and conditions of employment, health and safety, and benefits. These agreements, typically covering a five-year span, also include numerous regulations for areas such as drafts, postseason play, revenue sharing, and personal conduct. The CBA is the controlling document between the players, the league, and the teams. All players play under the CBA; when teams negotiate with individual players, they can generally only negotiate years and money (salary and bonuses). MLB players were the first to organize, forming the Major League Baseball Players Association (MLBPA) in 1952. The other leagues' players quickly followed suit, and now all players in the major team professional sports are represented by a players' association.

The players control the union, and an executive director runs the day-to-day operations. The players' associations act as any workers' unions do, and they are responsible for protecting the rights of the players. When a player has a dispute with a team or the league, the players' association represents the player. For example, when the New England Patriots' Tom Brady and the NFL went to court over his Deflategate suspension after the quarterback was accused of knowingly playing with deflated footballs, the NFLPA was the named party, not Tom Brady. With the players, the association negotiates the collective bargaining agreement. The players' association also is responsible for certifying agents and financial advisors.

Professional Team Sports Around the World

Professional clubs and leagues for sports that are nontraditional in the United States, such as cricket, rugby, and team handball, exist in other countries around the world. Teams sell tickets, pay athletes a salary, and operate under a constitution or set of rules in the same manner as professional sports in the United States. Countries around the world also support professional clubs and leagues for sports considered popular in the United States, such as American-style football, baseball, and basketball. While American-style football is more popular in the United States and Canada than association football (aka, soccer), grassroots efforts by the NFL have paved the way for amateur and professional American-style football leagues in over 60 countries around the world (Johnson, 2014).

While the NFL is colloquially identified as the most profitable professional league in North America, association football, or professional soccer, is by far the most profitable in Europe. Behind the NFL Dallas Cowboys, the next three most valuable professional sport franchises in the world (Manchester United, Real Madrid, and Barcelona) are all association football teams ("Forbes Releases 2018 List," 2018). While the focus is on corporate profitability as in other major professional sports, the general governance of association football is distinctly different than in the United States, especially in terms of ensuring competitive balance among members. Following is an overview of several association football leagues in the United Kingdom and professional baseball in Japan.

Association Football in the United Kingdom

In the United Kingdom, there are four top-flight professional football leagues. Unique to the United Kingdom, football is not organized on a national basis, but is based on the four home countries: England, Scotland, Wales, and Northern Ireland. Each country has its own national governing body and competes separately in international play. This structure has led to each home country offering its own professional leagues.

Professional football in the United Kingdom is organized as a club structure. The club structure today is similar to the league structure, but with key differences. The first key difference is that the governing bodies, which generally use the term "league," are organized as a private limited-by-shares company. Under the Companies Act of 2006, a private company is any company that is not a public company, and a limited company is one in which the liability of the members is limited by the company's constitution. Limited by shares refers to the liability of the members being restricted to the amount unpaid on the shares held by the members (Companies Act 2006, c. 46 [U.K.]).

The second key difference is the system of **promotion and relegation**. Unlike in the United States, teams do not stay at their level forever. Clubs must earn the right to compete at each level. Teams that finish at the bottom of the first division are relegated to the second division. The teams that finish at the top of the second division are promoted to the first division. This process continues through all levels of the league. The number of teams relegated and promoted depends on league rules.

Two examples of professional leagues in the United Kingdom are the Premier League and the

Scottish Professional Football League. Each league shares similar attributes while retaining a slightly different governance structure.

Premier League Professional football began in England in 1888 with the formation of the English Football League. In 1992, the top clubs, known as the first-division clubs, split from the English Football League to form the Football Association Premier League, better known as the Premier League. The Premier League is the top-division football league in England. The remaining three divisions stayed with the English Football League and are connected to the Premier League through the process of promotion and relegation. Promotion and relegation maintain competitive balance within the leagues. Champions of a league are promoted to a higher level, and the teams with the worst record step down to a lower-tier league.

For a club to be eligible to enter the Premier League, a team must qualify for the league through the system of promotion and relegation. The club must also be located in either England or Wales and be promoted through the English Football League. A club is not required to be a member of the Football Association, the national governing body in England, but it must agree to follow its rules. The league is limited to twenty-member clubs (Premier League, 2018).

The Premier League is a limited (by shares) private company. The members of the company are the clubs that are registered as the holders of an ordinary share, and each member can only hold one share. Once a team is relegated, it must forfeit its share and give it to a promoted team. The relegated team no longer has a say or a voice in the governance of the Premier League. The league is governed by the board of directors, which consists of at least two directors but not more than three. One of the directors serves as the chairman and chief executive officer. The board is responsible for the day-to-day operations of the league and for making recommendations to the member clubs. The member clubs can vote on league policy; it is a one-voice, one-vote system (Premier League, 2018).

Scottish Professional Football League Professional football began in Scotland in 1890 with the formation of the Scottish Football League. In 1998, following the formation of the Premier League, the top clubs split from the Scottish Football League and formed the Scottish Premier League. The Scottish Football League and the Scottish Premier League merged in 2013 to form the Scottish Professional Football League (SPFL) (n.d.). The SPFL is home to the top four football divisions in Scotland, including Scottish Premiership, the top division.

For a team to be eligible to enter the SPFL, it must be a member of the Scottish Football Association, the national governing body in Scotland. It does not mean, however, that the club must be Scottish. For example, the Berwick Rangers Football Club is a member of the SPFL and the

Association football, the sport played in the Premier League, is vastly different from American-style football. In addition to association football incorporating promotion and relegation to maintain competitive balance, players are employed by the club instead of the league.

Mike Hewitt/Getty Images

Scottish Football Association, but it is based in Berwick-upon-Tweed, England. Berwick-upon-Tweed is on the Scottish border, and the team is closer to the teams in Scotland than it is to the other teams in England.

Other conditions of membership require a club to support youth football in Scotland and to register its "grounds" or stadium as a home playing field. Most importantly, however, member clubs must qualify athletically for entry into the league through the promotion and relegation system (Scottish Professional Football League, 2018).

The SPFL is also a limited-by-shares private company, and its members are the individual(s) who hold a share in the league. Each member is limited to one share, and the member must be the owner or the operator of a club in the league. The clubs themselves are not members of the league under the Articles of Association; however, the club must be eligible to participate in the SPFL for the owner to have a share (Scottish Professional Football League, n.d.).

The SPFL is managed by the board of directors, which consists of the chairman, the chief executive, and the non-executive director, none of whom may be a director, officeholder, or employee of any member or club. These directors are appointed until they are removed. The clubs are also represented on the board. Three directors are from Premiership clubs, two directors are from Championship (second division) clubs, and one director is from League One and League Two (third and fourth division) combined. These directors are appointed for one year but can be reappointed. The board is responsible for the management of the SPFL and for acting under the rules and regulations of the SPFL, including financial oversight, rules determinations, playoffs, and championships.

Professional Baseball in Japan

The first professional baseball club in Japan, the Great Japan Tokyo Baseball Club, was formed by a newspaper publisher in 1934 following an All-Star game against Americans featuring Babe Ruth and Lou Gehrig. A professional baseball league in Japan was formed two years later, but it disbanded in 1944 during World War II before restructuring in 1950 to become what it is still known as today, Nippon Professional Baseball (NPB) (Metraux, 2016). According to the "Tazawa" rule unilaterally implemented by league owners, players who sign with an MLB team or compete in a professional league in another country must endure a two-year waiting period before becoming eligible to return to the NPB (Piecoro, 2018).

The NPB is a patriarchal organization, relying heavily on tradition and operating through powerful, autocratic owners who unilaterally create regulations such as the Tazawa rule. While a Japanese Professional Baseball Players' Association (JPBPA) formed in 1980 as a union, the organization has little authority in league governance. Unlike MLB, which uses a collective bargaining process, the terms and conditions of employment in the NPB are governed by a unilateral set of guidelines agreed upon solely by the owners (Snyder, 2010).

Salary arbitration and free agency (after eight years of service) are two provisions stipulated in the league rules (Jane, 2012). In 34 seasons between 1974 and 2008, there were six salary arbitration decisions (only one favoring the player) in NPB, compared to 486 decisions in MLB during the same time span (Snyder, 2010). Professional baseball players in Japan have little chance of prevailing in salary arbitration since the system is relegated to a panel consisting of the league commissioner and two presidents who are paid by the owners. In contrast, MLB uses an independent third-party panel of arbitrators.

Part of the disparity in arbitration decisions is due to the governance styles of the two leagues. In MLB, players have a voice in establishing or modifying rules, while in NPB, players are expected to be completely subservient to their owners despite union representation. Although Japanese players prevailed in one of the six salary arbitration cases and were able to organize a brief (multiday) strike in 2004, there has been little momentum for governance reform around these isolated successes. Owners continue to use teams primarily to bolster their public image, yet the league remains profitable, and many NPB players have been signed by MLB franchises.

Most of the franchises in the NPB are owned and named after large corporations. Teams are recognized by the company they represent more than by the cities in which they play. For example, the Yakult Swallows are owned by Yakult Hansha Co. Ltd, a dairy drink company, and the Hiroshima Tōyō Carp are owned by Tōyō Kōgyō Co. Ltd. (Metraux, 2016). Many of the parent companies of NPB teams appear on the Tokyo Stock Price Index (TOPIX), Japan's stock market.

INDIVIDUAL SPORTS

Individual sports are structured very differently than team sports. The Professional Golfers Association (PGA) Tour, the Women's Tennis Association (WTA), the Association of Volleyball Professionals

(AVP), and the National Association for Stock Car Auto Racing (NASCAR) are examples of individual sport governing bodies, also called sanctioning bodies. They are responsible for securing the venues and the prize money and actually putting on the events. The sanctioning bodies are generally owned by a separate, private group, and the competitors are not part of the governing structure in a meaningful way.

Individual sports can be divided into two separate types of sports, individual performer and individual performer team. In **individual performer sports**, the athlete is truly an individual performer. Athletes are responsible for hiring their coaches, deciding their tournament schedules, and signing their own sponsorship agreements. The second type of individual sport is **individual performer team sports**; here the athlete is entered into a competition as an individual athlete, but he or she has teammates. Unlike in true team sports, athletes compete against their teammates, but they may also rely on their teammates for help both on and off the playing surface. The athlete can be considered either an employee or an independent contractor. Athletes cannot decide their own schedules or sign sponsorship agreements in conflict with their teams.

Individual Performer Sports

The sanctioning bodies in individual performer sports have some of the same governance roles and responsibilities as those in professional sports leagues. The bodies are responsible for enforcing rules and codes of conduct, player discipline, and antidoping measures. Some sanctioning bodies run their own antidoping measures, while others rely on the international governing body for their sport to conduct drug testing and to monitor results. Unlike professional sports leagues, sanctioning bodies are responsible for sanctioning tournaments in which their members compete. They are also responsible for player rankings and determining the prize money associated with those rankings. Finally, the sanctioning bodies are responsible for determining eligibility rules for their competitions. (In professional team sports, such rules are typically part of a collective bargaining agreement.)

Legally, the sanctioning bodies for individual performer sports are considered **corporations**. A corporation can issue stock and act under the law as a separate legal entity (Garner, 1999). The sanctioning bodies for individual sports, however, are not public corporations and are not traded on the various stock exchanges. As a rule, these sanc-

NASCAR Cup Series driver Daniel Suarez and Joe Gibbs Racing had a sponsorship with Subway Restaurants cancelled when Suarez handed out Dunkin' Donut brand donuts as part of a television segment with NBC Sports (Spencer, 2017).

Jerry Markland/Getty Images

tioning bodies have more power than their league counterparts. While the leagues are controlled by the owners of the teams, the sanctioning bodies are controlled by their shareholders. Because sanctioning bodies are not public organizations, they are not required to release their governing documents to anyone but the shareholders and members of the organization.

There are many sanctioning bodies with a governance role for individual performer sports in the United States. Examples include the Professional Surfing Association of America, the American Boxing Association, and the United States Pool Players Association. Two additional examples described next are the Women's Tennis Association and the Professional Golfers Association (PGA) Tour.

Women's Tennis Association

The Women's Tennis Association (WTA) is a nonprofit corporation founded in 1973 by professional tennis player Billie Jean King. Her vision was to unite professional women's tennis players under one tour. As a governing body, the WTA is responsible for enacting and enforcing rules, establishing an annual tournament calendar, allocating prize money, and administering rankings for singles and doubles players (Rodenberg & Stone, 2011).

There are two levels of governance in the WTA: the board of directors and the International Tennis Federation (ITF). Members of the board of directors are responsible for long-term planning for the WTA. The board of directors comprises three representatives from a tournament board and three representatives from a players' board. It is unclear how selections are made to the WTA board of directors. It is also unclear who sits on the respective players' and tournament boards and the specific governance role of each.

The International Tennis Federation (ITF), the international governing body of tennis, also has a voice in the governance of the WTA, holding one seat on the board of directors (Women's Tennis Association, 2018b). The day-to-day operations of the WTA are overseen by the chief executive officer. The current chief executive officer of the WTA is Steve Simon.

The members of the WTA include the players, its tournaments, and the ITF. Members of the organization are similar to stockholders of a corporation, only the members of the WTA do not have a direct financial stake in the organization. For players, there are two types of memberships, full and associate. In order to qualify as a full member, a player must have a top-150 ranking in singles or a top-50 ranking in doubles at the end of the tour year, having competed in at least six WTA tournaments in one of the past two years. An associate member must have a singles ranking of at least 750 or a doubles ranking of at least 250 and have participated in at least one WTA tournament in one of the last two years. WTA membership entitles a player to optional medical, dental, and vision insurance while granting full members the opportunity to vote for and serve on the Players' Council (WTA, 2018a). It is unclear what role the Players' Council serves in the governance structure of the WTA.

The governing document for the WTA is an annual rule book addressing areas such as prize money policies, player conduct, and age eligibility requirements. The rule book also addresses commercial benefits for players and regulations for dispute resolution.

PGA Tour

Professional golf in the United States began in 1895 when the first U.S. Open was played in Newport, Rhode Island, by 10 professional players and one amateur player. In the early 1900s, the Professional Golf Association of America (PGA of America) organized tournaments throughout the country. In the 1960s, the tour professionals split from the PGA of America over prize money and formed their own tour (Green, 1968). This tour eventually rejoined the PGA of America as an autonomous group and is now known as the PGA Tour.

There are two levels of governance in the PGA Tour, the PGA Tour Policy Board and the Player Advisory Council. The Policy Board is composed of four current tour players, one tour official, and four public members with a demonstrated interest in the game of golf. Their role is defined in the Articles of Incorporation and Bylaws of the PGA Tour, but that document is not available to the public. The Player Advisory Council is comprised of eight current tour players. Their role is to advise and consult with the Policy Board and the tour commissioner. The day-to-day operations of the tour are overseen by the tour commissioner.

The members of the PGA Tour are the players. To be eligible for membership, a golfer must be 18 years old and must pay the dues associated with his or her membership level. There are several levels of membership, generally based on the golfer's place in the rankings at the end of the season. The ability to vote on tour business is not based on the membership level of the golfer, but on how many sponsored or affiliated tournaments the golfer played in. To qualify as a voting member, the golfer must play in at least 15 sponsored or affiliated tours and must attend at least one mandatory meeting in his or her first year on the tour. Members must also continue to play in at least 15 sponsored and affiliated tours and attend at least one mandatory meeting every tour year. They are then eligible to vote for the Tour Policy Board and the Player Advisory Council (PGA Tour, 2017).

The PGA is governed by a constitution of bylaws and regulations published annually. The constitution stipulates the authority of the board of directors to review governing documents at any time to ensure compliance. Specifically, Article 2 decrees that all interpretations, disputes, or issues with a rule or regulation within the constitution and bylaws shall be resolved by the board of directors, whose decision shall be final (PGA Tour, 2017). The constitution also makes provision for annual and special meetings and contains regulations governing eligibility, rights and classes of membership, and codes of ethics.

Individual Performer Team Sports

The governing role of the sanctioning body in individual performer team sports is similar to those in individual performer sports. Sanctioning bodies for individual performer team sports are responsible for scheduling the tournaments and securing the prize money. The association is also responsible for setting eligibility rules and maintaining an antidoping control program.

Legally, the sanctioning bodies are considered close corporations where shares in the company are held by a few people, sometimes in a single family or corporation (Garner, 1999; "George Is Hulman & Co. Board Chair," 2016; Pockrass & Rovell, 2018). Unlike individual performer sport organizations, the teams and the competitors are not part of the organization and have no legal say in the running of the organization. However, based on their influence in the sport, the sanctioning body will listen to member athletes.

Examples of individual performer team sports are stock car auto racing and professional cycling. These two sports adhere to rules and regulations from their respective sanctioning bodies.

Stock Car Auto Racing

NASCAR is only one governing body for stock car auto racing. They oversee several series, but not all. NASCAR, is responsible for setting the schedule and the technical regulations, securing the prize money, and enforcing the rules ("NASCAR Chairman Brian France," 2018).

While individual drivers are recognized for their performance, there is a complete team behind each racer. Owners or ownership groups (very few racer-owner arrangements exist) assemble teams consisting of a driver, engineer, crew chief, pit crew, and others. In some cases, owners may list multiple drivers. Team Penske, for example, lists 14 drivers, of which five compete on the NASCAR series ("Drivers/Teams," n.d.). They have always had the Owner's Championships.

NASCAR can trace its roots back to the moonshine runners in the southern United States who tried to, and generally succeeded in, outrunning federal agents from the Internal Revenue Service. When they were not trying to outrun the agents, drivers raced against each other. In 1947, a group of 35 men met in Daytona Beach, Florida, to organize NASCAR. Bill France Sr. was voted the first president, and in February 1948, he incorporated NASCAR with himself recognized as the biggest shareholder (Menzer, 2001).

NASCAR is a close corporation; the shares are controlled by members of the France family. It is rumored that the shares are split between only three members of the family. Teams and drivers do not have an official voice in the governance of the sport. Until August 2018, Brian France, the grandson of Bill France Sr., served as chairman and chief executive officer. However, he took an indefinite leave after being arrested for driving while intoxicated and criminal possession of oxycodone. His uncle, Jim France, took over his roles in the interim.

In 2014, team owners formed the Race Team Alliance as an alliance of teams that compete in NASCAR's Cup Series. Their goal is to protect the long-term interests of the racing teams. In 2016, NASCAR and the Race Team Alliance announced they had finalized a Charter Agreement. This system grants 36 charters, which guarantees a starting spot for every point-paying race. This agreement also formed the Team Owner Council, which gives them a formal input into decisions by NASCAR and also gives the teams new revenue opportunities. This agreement, however, does not give the teams an ownership stake in NASCAR, and it limits their ability to join other stock car series (Pockrass & Rovell, 2018).

There is speculation that the Charter Agreement is not working as well as ownership teams had hoped. NASCAR has seen an ongoing drop both in attendance at races and in television ratings, and the team owners are frustrated by the slow response from NASCAR to turn around the numbers. Teams are also concerned about the growing costs of racing, and they are concerned that the attempts by NASCAR to save the teams money has not actually helped. Finally, teams want a greater percentage of NASCAR revenue; they currently receive only 25 percent of broadcasting fees. The Charter Agreement expires in 2020, and it will be interesting to see the future direction of professional stock car racing (Stern, 2018). Governance in Action 7.4 describes an issue in the motorsports industry pertaining to sanctioning entities.

Professional Cycling

Professional cycling is a second example of an individual performer team sport. While there are individual race winners, professional cyclists train and compete in teams of typically 20 or more. Professional cycling teams are also equipped with road managers, mechanics, team doctors, and other

GOVERNANCE IN ACTION 7.4

The Great Open Wheel Split

A classic example of the unrest among a sanctioning body, its athletes, and its tournament hosts is the "Great Open Wheel Split," commonly referred to as The Split. In the early 1990s, open wheel racing, led by the CART IndyCar Series, was the most popular form of auto racing in the United States. The Indianapolis 500, hosted by the Indianapolis Motor Speedway (IMS) and run on the Sunday of Memorial Day weekend, was its most popular event. The chief executive officer of the Indianapolis Motor Speedway Corporation, the owner of IMS, passed away, leaving Tony George, the grandson of the founder, in charge. As CEO of IMS, George was concerned with the rising costs, the reliance on street courses, and the alienation of American drivers. He was a nonvoting member of the CART governing body and was frustrated because he could not make changes in the governing organization. In 1994, George pulled IMS from CART, followed by an announcement of the formation of a new Indy Racing League (IRL) (Zeller, 2004).

Several teams known as the "star power," which included Roger Penske, the Andretti family, and the Vasser family, stayed with CART. George then announced that the Indianapolis 500 would reserve 25 starting spots for the newly formed list of IRL drivers while all remaining drivers would have to compete for the final eight spots (Pruett, 2016).

Controversy over the split ensued as CART quickly organized and announced the running of the US 500 in Michigan on the same day as the Indianapolis 500. The star power went to Michigan. The Indianapolis 500 was won by Buddy Lazier, who had failed to qualify in four of his previous seven attempts. The field also featured 17 rookies.

The battle between CART and the IRL continued amid rising costs and falling television viewership until 2007, when the two merged back together and became the IndyCar Series. The damage to the sport was already done, however. NASCAR's popularity had surpassed open wheel racing, taking both sponsors and viewers. IndyCar has struggled with further bad decisions and driver deaths, which led to George's removal as CEO of Indianapolis Motor Speedway Corporation by his sisters (Pruett, 2016). It is only recently, over a decade after the remerger of the two groups, that IndyCar is beginning to regain some of its popularity and recover from The Split (Errington & Malsher, 2018). The series began a new television agreement in 2019 and has started to focus its marketing efforts on the drivers.

support personnel. During a race, there are often strategic maneuvers to draft teammates or block an opponent's surge by intentionally cycling slowly and allowing a teammate to mount a breakaway from a pack of racers.

The sport is governed by an international federation, the Union Cycliste Internationale (UCI), which oversees amateur, professional, and para-cycling disciplines, including mountain biking, track cycling, cyclo-cross, and BMX. UCI established a Professional Cycling Council comprised of professional riders and race organizers to govern and manage professional racers. In 2005, the UCI Cycling Council instituted the UCI Pro Tour to serve as a super league for professional cyclists. The multistage competition includes events that are separate from grand tour races such as the Tour de France, which are owned and operated by commercial enterprises. The UCI Pro Tour is considered an oligopoly, with the UCI serving a regulatory function in owning the monopoly of the 20 licenses that teams must possess for eligibility to compete (Morrow & Idle, 2008).

The UCI Professional Cycling Council has been the traditional authority and regulatory body for professional cycling in terms of functions such as licensing racers and races, certifying referees and adjudicators, and enforcing disciplinary rules for doping and other violations. In addition to the UCI Professional Cycling Council, three general associations serve as umbrella organizations for the sport. These include (1) the International Association of Professional Cycling Groups (for professional teams), (2) the Association of Professional Cyclists (CPA) (for individual racers), and (3) the International Association of Organizers of Cycling Racers (serving professional race organizers). The overlapping nature of umbrella organizations and the Professional Cycling Council has created a convoluted structure for governance of the sport, especially for race organizers that are not part of the UCI Pro Tour.

All riders under contract with a professional team are automatically members of the CPA, which works through a steering committee and is led by a president, vice president, and secretary general ("The CPA, the Only Association," n.d.). The CPA has a separate division for female professional riders identified as CPA Women. The CPA serves primarily in an advisory role for racers with representation on the commission of the UCI.

RECAP

The governance of professional sports is complicated. It is dependent on the type of sport, whether team or individual, and where the league is located. The major professional team sports in the United States are governed by collective bargaining agreements that are ratified by a vote of players and owners, who contribute equally to the process. In Japan and other countries, professional team sports such as Nippon Professional Baseball are governed by a document that is unilaterally created by powerful, autocratic owners, most of whom are associated with large business corporations. Players in NPB have little say in league governance.

Professional individual sports (e.g., tennis and golf) and individual team sports (e.g., cycling and motorsports) are governed by multiple entities representing the sport, the professionals, and the tours or tournaments. Often the overlapping of associations, whether in a true governance role or an advisory capacity, creates a convoluted structure of authority. The pursuit of profitability drives professional sports as entertainment, enough at times to tarnish the purity of competition.

Critical Thinking Questions

1. Pick a North American sport league not mentioned in the chapter and determine its governance structure.
2. Comparing professional team sports to professional individual sports, what are some of the similarities and some of the differences in their governing bodies?
3. Explain the differences between the two types of individual sports.
4. There is a difference in the governance structures of the Premier League and the Scottish Professional Football League. Which do you think works better? Why?
5. In your opinion, should the athletes have a greater say in the governing of their individual sports? Explain your answer.

Applied Activities

Team Sport Governance

A group of people have decided to start a professional sports league for cricket in the United States. Assume the role of being hired to start the league. Determine whether the best decision would be to adopt a league structure, the Major League Soccer structure, or the United Kingdom structure. Explain your rationale for choosing this structure. Finally, explain how well you expect it to work in the United States as a brand-new league.

Draft Potential Report

Surrounding the central question of "Regardless of the player's athletic ability, would you be reluctant to draft a player based on his personality?" create a draft potential report for five players in a North American professional sport league

(NFL, NBA, MLB, NHL) who were drafted in the most recent draft or are among the top candidates for an upcoming draft. Consider their athletic talent and potential contribution in addition to their personalities both on and off the field before creating your final assessment.

Select one of the four professional leagues in North America (NFL, NBA, MLB, NHL). Start by selecting five players who were drafted in the most recent draft or are among the top candidates for an upcoming draft. After selecting your players, conduct research and collect as much statistical and personal data as possible on each. Research information pertinent to their athletic talent, maturity, and personality. Review any and all statistical information and game summary reports. Search through the mainstream media and review any interviews available. Research the social media pages for each player. Do they have Twitter pages, and are any of their tweets suspect? What about Facebook or Instagram profiles?

Part A: Rate each player on the following:

♦ *Personality Assessment Rating*: Assess your comfort level with each player's personality, and rate each on a scale of 1 to 100, with 1 representing "Major personality problems—do NOT draft" and 100 representing "Perfect personality, absolutely perfect draft pick from personality standpoint."

♦ *Athletic Talent/Potential Contribution Rating*: Assess your comfort level with each player's athletic contribution on a scale of 1 to 100, with 1 representing "Doesn't possess physical athleticism—do NOT draft" and 100 representing "Perfect athletic talent, absolutely perfect draft pick from athletic standpoint."

Part B: Synthesize your information into a one-page, single-spaced Draft Potential Report for each player. Include a picture, name, and position of each player at the top of the page. Note their athletic ability rating score and personality rating score. Prepare three paragraphs for each player to

♦ summarize your opinions of their athletic talent and potential contribution in the league,

♦ summarize your opinions on the viability of the player in terms of personality, and

♦ summarize your opinion of the player as a potential top draft pick.

Include citations in the profile report for each player. Also include a cover page and a reference page. Include the following on each report:

♦ Name

♦ Position

♦ School or other affiliation

♦ Scores: Athleticism and potential contribution _____ / Personality _____

♦ Athletic ability and potential contribution assessment

♦ Personality assessment

♦ Potential draft pick assessment

Case Study Application

For more information on governance and authority in professional sports, review *The Many Stakeholders of the NFL Super Bowl "On Location Experience"* and *The NFL Kneeling Policy* in the web resource.

Amateur Sports

Kerri Cebula and Bonnie Tiell

LEAD-OFF

The term **amateur sport** has been used to define everything from competition at the Olympic level to five-year-old children playing tee ball. A universally agreed upon definition for amateur sport is athletic competition that is void of compensation for participants. Interestingly, a landmark bill (Senate Bill 206) dubbed the "Fair Pay to Play Act" in California that was passed in October 2019 permits college student athletes to retain their eligibility after being compensated for the use of their name, image, or likeness from activities such as providing personal clinics or signing an endorsement deal with a shoe company. Since the law will not go into effect until 2023, the National Collegiate Athletic Association (NCAA), the national governing body for many higher education institutions sponsoring athletics, has time to strategize its response to the bill and its pending impact on the traditional definition of amateurism.

In addition to college athletics, there are countless sport opportunities, both recreational and competitive, available to all populations. Amateur sport encompasses everything from highly organized national multisport festivals to pickup basketball games in a community park. The business of amateur sports is vibrant; note the popularity of amateur road races, adventure challenges, and businesses such as Top Golf and community bowling alleys. Esports is yet another sector of amateur sports evolving at an expeditious rate.

In Canada and the United Kingdom, most amateur sport organizations are private organizations incorporated under their country's system of laws and receive funding from their country's national government to a greater extent than in the United States. Many organizations with a regulatory role for sport in Canada and the United Kingdom include members identified as shareholders. However, the members are not true shareholders because they do not receive a share of the profits if the organization were to produce them.

This chapter breaks down amateur sports into categories of adult participation, youth participation, and intercollegiate participation. While the Olympics are an important sector of amateur athletics, they are not discussed in detail in this chapter because Olympic organizations are profiled elsewhere in this text.

This chapter begins with an initial overview of the Amateur Athletic Union to provide insight into a national governing organization in the United States for amateur sports. Next, the chapter focuses on the structure and governance of amateur school-based and non-school-based youth sport programs in the United States, the United Kingdom, and Canada. Finally, the chapter addresses amateur sport programs for adults and the governance of intercollegiate athletics in the United States, Canada, and the United Kingdom.

Learning Outcomes

- Define amateur sport.
- Classify amateur sport organizations in youth, interscholastic, and intercollegiate athletics.
- Identify different governing structures used in amateur sport.
- Compare the amateur sport governing structures of the United States, Canada, and the United Kingdom.

AMATEUR ATHLETIC UNION

The Amateur Athletic Union of the United States (AAU) was founded in 1888 to establish standards in amateur sport. With over 700,000 youth and adult members and 150,000 volunteers in 2019, the AAU is considered one of the largest nonprofit multisport organizations in the world. Until the formation of the United States Olympic Committee (USOC) in the 1970s, the AAU served as the United States' representative to international federations and helped to train Olympic athletes. After the formation of the USOC, the AAU changed its focus to youth sports, but it still serves all age groups. Today, its eight core programs are baseball, basketball, football, hockey, martial arts, track and field, volleyball, and wrestling. The AAU sponsors a total of 35 sport programs, including strength sports, futsal, target shooting, trampoline, swimming, and baton twirling, among others. It is best known for its basketball program ("About the Amateur Athletic Union," n.d.).

Headquartered in Orlando, Florida, the AAU is divided into 55 districts, each governed by a board of managers and an executive committee. The board of managers is responsible for the business affairs of the district, while the Executive Committee acts on behalf of the board between meetings and is responsible for financial oversight (Amateur Athletic Union, 2018). The Executive Committee is comprised of the officers of the district, the chair of the finance committee, and the director of the district sport committee. District officers include the governor, lieutenant governor, secretary, treasurer, and registrar (Amateur Athletic Union, 2018).

At the national level, the AAU is governed by the Congress, the board of directors, and the officers. The primary powers of the Congress include amending the AAU Code, which serves as the governing document for the organization. Additional duties include the election of officers, establishing districts, and approving budgets.

The national board of directors includes current officers of the AAU, a representative from each zone, the committee chairs, and district representatives. Their role includes acting on behalf of the AAU and the Congress, establishing policies, submitting the budget, and approval of the general counsel. The officers of the AAU are the president, the first vice president, the second vice president, the secretary, and the treasurer (Amateur Athletic Union, 2018).

YOUTH AMATEUR SPORTS

Youth sports include formal and informal athletics for children up until the year of graduation from high school or secondary school. Youth sport has the strongest connection with local communities throughout the world. Many people credit youth sport as an early intervention strategy to promote healthy lifestyles, to help develop valuable life skills (e.g., leadership, sportsmanship, character-building, communication, and teamwork), and to deter counterproductive behavior.

General issues in amateur youth sports, which can be addressed at the appropriate levels of governance, include socioeconomic disparities that affect participation, age-appropriate guidelines for safety, and prerequisite skills for coaches or anyone else (including volunteers) administering athletic programs. There has been a global decline in participation rates in youth sports in countries as widely separated as Sweden, Ethiopia, and the United States (Carlman, Wagnsson, & Patriksson, 2013; Petros, 2017). For example, the Sports & Fitness Industry Association noted a decline in the percentage of U.S. youth who participated in a sport activity from 44.5 percent in 2008 to 40 percent in 2013 (Witt & Dangi, 2018).

The following section provides a basic overview of the structure of amateur youth sports in the United States, United Kingdom, and Canada, grouped by school-based and non-school-based programs.

United States

In 1993, a paper commissioned by the Carnegie Council on Adolescent Development in Washington, D.C., identified six categories of youth sports (see table 8.1). The authors estimated that 35 million youth in America participated in one or more organized sports in the early 1990s, and trends included prolonged sport seasons, pay-for-play models, and year-round competition (Seefelt, Ewing, & Walk, 1993, p. 106). More recent data indicate approximately 45 million American youth participate in organized sport, with a major trend toward increased specialization (Merkel, 2013). The U.S. Sport and Fitness Industry Association noted 69.1 percent of American youth aged 6 to 12 participated in individual or team sports in 2017 ("The State of Play in the U.S. Scoreboard," 2017, p. 13).

School-Based Amateur Youth Sports (U.S.)

School-based amateur youth sports in the United States include intramural and interscholastic sports. **Intramural sports** are athletic competitions staged among students in the same school or school district. **Interscholastic sports** are athletic competitions staged between schools at the secondary level, and they are much more prevalent than intramurals.

In the United States, youth compete in interscholastic sports at the middle school (aka junior high) and high school levels. Middle school generally refers to grades 6 to 8 and high school refers to grades 9 to 12. Some school districts support a competitive sports program at the elementary level, which is generally intramural. Schools choose whether to support both interscholastic and intramural sport programs at all levels, but most concentrate strictly on interscholastic competition.

Since 1920, the National Federation of State High School Associations (NFHS) has led the development of interscholastic sport. From its offices in Indianapolis, Indiana, NFHS serves its members, 50 state high school athletic or activity associations, plus the District of Columbia. The NFHS is divided geographically into eight sections. The 51 state associations operate as nonprofit, unincorporated entities. Each state association is geographically divided into districts, which vary in number based on population. For example, the Ohio High School Athletic Association (2016) has six geographic districts, and the Pennsylvania Interscholastic Athletic Association (2019) has 12. Each district is comprised of conferences and member schools.

The governance structure of the NFHS includes the National Council and the board of directors, whose general responsibilities include managing budgets, establishing standing committees,

Table 8.1 Six Categories of Youth Sports in America

Category	Description	Example of affiliations
Intramural programs	Competition of teams within a school	Local schools
Interscholastic programs	Competition of teams between schools	Local schools
Recreation programs	Programs with a focus on maximum participation and emphasizing social interaction, fun, and physical skill development in lieu of highly competitive activities	Community or municipal parks and recreation departments; local schools; local sport facilities
National youth service organizations	Activities organized primarily to focus on youth development and partially funded by national organizations or outside sources	YMCA; Boy Scouts of America; Girl Scouts of America; Catholic Youth Organization (CYO)
Club sports	Programs typically conducting year-round practices and competitive opportunities with tryouts, a fee-for-service structure, and salaried coaches	Amateur Athletic Union Programs; Local or regional clubs affiliated with USA Volleyball, Wrestling, Gymnastics, Swimming, etc.
Agency-sponsored	Sports sponsored by service clubs	Little League Baseball; Pop Warner Football; Cal Ripken Baseball; American Youth Soccer Organization

Adapted from Seefelt, Ewing, and Walk (1993).

determining sanctions for rule violations, hiring the NFHS executive director, amending the constitution and bylaws, and approving memberships (National Federation of State High School Associations, 2018). Each state has a similar board representation, an executive director, and a relatively small staff. The constitution and bylaws for several state associations mandate that the district committee be represented by at least one representative from junior high or middle schools, school board members, officials, athletic directors, and girls' athletic programs.

Each district association is governed by a district committee composed of a chair, vice-chair, secretary, treasurer (or a secretary-treasurer), and additional elected members filling out the quorum. The district committee is responsible for activities such as administering finances, resolving disputes, and determining the format and eligibility for district postseason tournaments that feed into the state playoffs.

Non-School-Based Amateur Youth Sports (U.S.)

Organized youth sports outside of schools in the United States include (1) community recreation, (2) leagues and tournaments sponsored by national youth service organizations, (3) club sports, and (4) agency-sponsored sports.

Community-based youth recreation programs such as flag football, basketball leagues, or a local holiday road race are often organized by a nonprofit municipal parks and recreation department. However, private community recreation facilities, private groups, and even churches may offer athletic opportunities. There are many models of oversight of youth sports by private and municipal sport and recreation associations. Often a commissioner will be appointed to oversee a community league to resolve disputes, schedule games, and assign officials. Most of the labor for league operations is volunteer.

Leagues and tournaments sponsored by national youth service organizations, such as the YMCA or the Catholic Youth Organization (CYO), appeal to a large youth market. The level of competitiveness is on par with community sport programs, and most are available at little or no cost to participants. These organizations are considered nonprofit agencies, operate through volunteers, and are typically eligible to receive limited government funding.

One of the fastest-growing areas of youth sport is organized travel teams under private club systems.

These are considered to be in the upper echelon of competitiveness in the youth sector, especially since they provide the opportunity to train in a sport year-round. Some club systems are affiliated with national sport federations such as USA Volleyball, and all are considered private entities that operate through a fee structure. Coaches, officials, and administrators are all paid positions. Many clubs operate through a director and advisory board.

Youth programs affiliating with sport agencies such as Pop Warner Football incur membership dues and agree to play according to the rules of the national agency. Seefelt et al. (1993) found that almost all national governing agencies commanded a fee for membership and tournament entries. A local soccer league may be affiliated with the state association under the umbrella of the United States Youth Soccer Association (USYSA). Governance in Action 8.1 examines the United States Youth Soccer Association, the largest youth sport organization in America.

United Kingdom

The United Kingdom is a territory in Europe encompassing four regions, also known as home countries. England, Scotland, and Wales are the three home countries that collectively represent Great Britain. The fourth home country in the U.K. is Northern Ireland. Like the United States, England does not have a minister of sport, while Scotland, Wales, and Northern Ireland have government-appointed ministers of sport who report to the U.K. Department for Digital, Culture, Media and Sport (DCMS).

In contrast with the United States, funding for youth sport in the U.K. primarily stems from the Exchequer (i.e., the government) and a national lottery system that allocates resources to a range of agencies divided among elite and community sport (Keech & Nauright, 2015, p. 13). Youth sports in the U.K. can be categorized as those administered in schools and those administered through non-school programs.

School-Based Amateur Youth Sports (U.K.)

Much of the emphasis on participation in sports through school programs has been a result of initiatives associated with the 2012 London Olympics. In 2015, over 19,000 schools were enrolled in the "School Games" delivered by Sport England,

GOVERNANCE IN ACTION 8.1

The Powerful United States Youth Soccer Association

Founded in 1974, the United States Youth Soccer Association (USYSA) (2017) headquartered in Frisco, Texas, is the nation's largest youth sports organization, including approximately 3 million players, 300,000 coaches, and 600,000 officials (Reid, 2019). The association operates under the umbrella of the United States Soccer Federation (USSF), the national governing body for soccer affiliated with Federation Internationale de Football Association (FIFA). Neither FIFA nor the USSF has a direct governance role in the USYSA, but the USYSA voluntarily chooses to follow both USSF and FIFA rules. Clubs belonging to the USYSA are affiliated with the USSF's Olympic Development Program.

In 2016, a girl's under-18 Olympic development playoff game in Texas ended in a 0-0 tie, guaranteeing that each team would advance to the national championship series. While the USYSA dismissed notions of organized collusion, the national organization levied fines against each team and coach ("US Youth Soccer Statement," 2016). The organization also vowed to review and alter their policies to prevent a similar occurrence.

USYSA is governed on two main levels: state and national. At the national level, the USYSA is governed by a board of directors elected from state associations. The 12-member board is independent; hence, with the exception of the past president, no members can be involved in the governance of soccer, receive compensation from soccer, or hold an ownership interest in soccer within five years of their election date (USYSA, 2017). The national board of directors was tasked with investigating the alleged 2016 match-fixing incident and proposing any revisions to the association's bylaws.

At the state level, there are 55 associations (due to the subdivision of California, New York, and Pennsylvania) organized according to East, Midwest, South, and West regions ("State Associations," n.d.). In line with national office procedures, the state associations use a weighted voting system for approval processes, where the number of votes is dependent upon the number of players in their region. The board is tasked with elections and the approval of members, budgets, and all changes or amendments to the state governing documents (North Carolina Youth Soccer Association, 2017).

Each state association has its own set of bylaws and procedures. For example, the Indiana Youth Soccer Association (n.d.) requires a risk management director in each league or club to conduct background checks for all adults. However, the USYSA parent association has been besieged in litigation for its lack of a nationwide policy on background checks (Reid, 2019).

the government-supported entity for all levels of national sport, and the Youth Sport Trust, a charitable organization under the scope of the DCMS (2015). A national strategy includes assurance that all youth aged 5 through 16 receive a minimum of five hours a week of exposure to sports in schools, primarily through physical education classes (Keech & Nauright, 2015, p. 11). The Youth Sport Trust has earmarked more than 1.23 billion euros through 2019 for improvements to U.K. schools and physical education classes ("Transforming Physical Education," n.d.).

Non-School-Based Amateur Youth Sports (U.K.)

Non-elite youth sports in the U.K. are grounded in communities where governance differs based on whether programs are connected to individual sport (e.g., tennis and golf) or team sports (e.g., basketball and rugby). Individual sports are primarily governed by their national governing body (NGB) for each sport, such as the Lawn Tennis Association (LTA), which operates junior programs and tournaments in addition to "Tennis for Free" clinics in cooperation with commercial partners and local entities. Team sports, however, are governed on two levels, nationally through the NGB and locally through **county** associations.

Amateur youth soccer systems in England operate under the scope of the Football Association (FA) (2018), which is the NGB and sanctioning rules authority for the sport. There are several systems available for youth participation. Academies, which compete for the FA Youth Cup, are the high-performance (elite) youth systems affiliated with professional soccer clubs (e.g., association football clubs from the Premier League such as Liverpool, Arsenal, and Manchester United). Governance in Action 8.2 outlines the training and educational activities for youth within the academy system, in contrast to the systems in the United States, for preparing players for pathways into professional sports.

Beyond the academy system, non-elite amateur youth soccer in England is coordinated through a local league connected to a county association and various league competitions. Local leagues must be affiliated with a county association, and they must appoint a chair, treasurer, and secretary ("Creating a Club," n.d.). Teams compete for the annual FA Youth County Cup, however, there is no system of relegation or promotion in the amateur ranks.

Grassroots programs for non-elite adolescent soccer players may be organized through local youth league competitions, with governance regulated by a management committee. Competitions follow the Standard Code of Rules set forth by the

GOVERNANCE IN ACTION 8.2

Going Pro: USA and European Pathways

The pathway to professional sports in the United States and United Kingdom are vastly different. In the United States, the pathway to professional sports is through the draft process and runs through intercollegiate athletics, while in the U.K., academies affiliated with professional franchises have a stake in future players.

Athletes aspiring to play professionally in the United States will typically attend college to hone their skills. This leads to the NCAA being treated as the minor league or feeder system for professional football and basketball, and it contributes to athlete exploitation, especially in Division I. NCAA rules forbid student-athletes from receiving compensation beyond a full scholarship or a share of profits a university might derive from media exposure, ticket revenues, or bowl game appearances. These limitations have inspired lawsuits and calls for unionization.

To enter the NBA draft, a player must be 19 and one year removed from high school, although the age limit may be lowered to 18 during the 2021 collective bargaining agreement negotiations (Zillgit, 2019). To enter the NFL draft, athletes must be the equivalent of at least three years removed from their high school graduation year. In Major League Baseball (MLB), however, players may be drafted out of high school and enter the minor league system immediately, where professional coaching and salaries are provided. If players choose not to sign with a team and enroll in college, MLB rules stipulate a three-year waiting period before they can be eligible for the draft.

In the U.K., especially in football (soccer), the main pathway to professional sports runs through the academy system. Elite talent is identified at the youth level and given the chance to attend an academy that is owned or sponsored by a professional team. Operating in accordance with the Professional Game Youth Development Rules of the Football Academy (FA), the academy system is overseen by the Premier League and English Football League. The three levels of academy football are Foundation (players U9 to U11), Youth Development (U12 to U16), and Professional Development (U17 to U23).

Academies provide either part-time, hybrid, or full-time training models. Part-time allows players to attend school full time and train during evenings, weekends, and vacation periods. The hybrid model allows students to leave school early for training, but the academy is responsible for a portion of the players' education. Full-time training places the responsibility for education entirely on the academy. Under the full-time training model, the academy cannot terminate or release players until their education is complete (Premier League, 2018).

On average, foundation players train 3 to 8 hours per week; youth development players train 4 to 12 hours per week, and the professional development players receive 12 to 14 hours of weekly training (Premier League, 2018). Under FA rules, an academy player can be registered as a "scholar" at age 14, which means the player is under contract with the professional team and at the age of 17 can be called up to the professional club (The Football Association, 2018).

FA. A management committee is the governing authority for finances, match schedules, and disciplinary action associated with a competition (The Football Association, 2018).

Canada

Canada is the second largest country by land mass in the world following Russia. Approximately 80 percent of its terrain is uninhabited, and most of the population is clustered in cities bordering the United States of America. The country is divided into 10 provinces and three territories. Similar to a U.S. state, a **province** is the designation used for subnational governments.

According to a Canadian youth sports report, 77 percent of youth ages 5 to 19 participated in organized sport or physical activity in 2018 ("Participation," 2018, p. 6). Youth sports in Canada can be categorized as those administered in schools and those administered through non-school programs.

School-Based Amateur Youth Sports (Canada)

In Canada, interscholastic sport competition at the high school level includes grades 9 through 12 except for Quebec, which only supports competition through grade 11. Interscholastic sport is governed in many of the provinces on three levels: national, provincial/territorial, and local. In a few of the provinces, sport is governed on only two levels: national and provincial/territorial. Canada includes approximately 3,200 schools sponsoring interscholastic sports for some 750,000 athletes between the ages of 14 and 18 (Trudel & Camire, 2017). Similar to the European system for soccer, the academy system has been popularized for ice hockey and soccer in Canada, where students attend prep schools and receive specialized training. Some academies are licensed, but none are owned by or affiliated with a professional NHL franchise.

At the national level, interscholastic sport is governed by School Sport Canada (SSC) and its constitution. SSC is comprised of members and the board of directors. The board retains **powers of the corporation**, having the authority to make policies and procedures, to discipline members, and to hire employees of the SSC (School Sport Canada, 2017).

At the provincial/territorial level, interscholastic sport is governed by associations such as the Ontario Federation of School Athletic Associations (OFSAA) or the Alberta Schools' Athletic Association ("Provincial and Territorial Offices," 2017). Members of a provincial or territorial association include the subset of schools in a geographic district. There are generally three governing entities in provincial/territorial associations, (1) the Assembly, (2) the Representative Council, and (3) the Executive Council, which is the highest level of authority. Each sport in a provincial/territorial association may also be governed by a commissioner ("Prince Edward Island Athletic Association Sport Commissioners," 2017). Many provincial territories also have sport advisory committees that report to the Representative Council.

The Assembly includes members of the Representative Council, the Executive Council, the Principals' Council, and the Presidents' Council responsible for approving finances and electing officials (Ontario Federation of School Athletic Associations, 2018). The Representative Council is responsible for transacting the daily business of the association, amending sport playing rules, and approving the championship calendar. The Executive Council is responsible for organizational governance, approval of the budget, and staff appointments.

There are two additional groups with voting privileges at the provincial/territorial level, including a Principals' Council and the Presidents' Council. If a province or territory is large enough, it may be further broken down into additional local associations that operate through conferences. Ontario, for example, has 18 local associations.

Non-School-Based Amateur Youth Sports (Canada)

Non-school-based amateur sports for Canadian youth operate through community clubs, associations, and government-supported programs. Sport Canada is a division of the Canadian government, which is the largest single investor in amateur sport, primarily at the elite level. Within the prime minister's cabinet is the Minister of Science, Sport, and Persons with Disabilities, who oversees amateur sports. A majority of sport infrastructure such as ice rinks and fields are municipally run facilities supported by government assistance and maintained primarily through diverse revenue streams (Javier, 2018).

While hockey has historically reigned as the dominant sport in Canada, youth are gravitating toward swimming and soccer. In 2019, Canadian youth sports were assessed as an $8.7 billion market

Hero Images/Getty Images

Youth ice hockey is one of the most highly organized sports in Canada and is divided into three tiers. Ice hockey is also one of the most expensive sports, considering equipment alone costs approximately $740 per athlete.

according to WinterGreen Research (Westhead, 2019). According to a report by Solutions Research Group Consultants, Inc. (2014), families spend approximately $1,000 annually per child on organized sport, the most per capita in the world. The same report addressing youth ages 3 to 17 noted 531,000 participated in hockey, 767,000 in soccer, and 1,120,000 in swimming (Solutions Research Group Consultants, Inc., 2014). Basketball and baseball were the next most popular sports, partially because of the financial burden of hockey, which averages $740 per participant for equipment alone. In 2018, a report commissioned by a Global News source indicated 40 percent of parents planned on enrolling their child in swimming compared to 15 percent opting for hockey (Javier, 2018).

Boys & Girls Clubs and YMCAs offer free or low-cost recreational opportunities for youth. Most youth sport programs that are non-school-based, however, involve fee structures for participation and training that have traditionally been considered exorbitant when considering the prevalence of travel leagues and tournaments.

Youth sport club systems, typically private enterprises, are highly organized. Minor league hockey includes age brackets for youth ages 7 to 19 divided into three tiers, including Tier III B or BB House recreational leagues with no tryouts required; Tier II A or AA competitive leagues with tryouts; and Tier I AAA highly competitive leagues ("What Do Designations B, A, AA, and AAA Mean?" n.d.). A

majority of club-level individual and team sports require fees for participation and training.

ADULT AMATEUR SPORTS

Amateur sport participation for adults is a popular segment of the recreation and fitness industry, as can be seen from the organized tournaments, races, and leagues available for people age 18 and over. Intercollegiate athletics is considered a segment of adult amateur sports. Figure 8.1 profiles the rate of active participation for U.S. adults in fitness and sport activities in 2019 (Physical Activity Council, 2019).

According to the Physical Activity Council (2019, p. 16), participation rates in adult sport and fitness are classified according to the intensity of calorie-burning activities. There are three levels: (1) low (e.g., windsurfing, bowling, and golf); (2) medium (e.g., aquatics, baseball, volleyball, snowboarding, and kayaking); and (3) high (e.g., adventure racing, basketball, running, and tennis). The highest participation rates were for fitness sports (e.g., running and swimming), outdoor sports (e.g., adventure racing, sailing, and bicycling), and individual sports (e.g., golf and bowling) (p. 15). A 2015 "Sports and Health in America" report noted that adult males are twice as likely as adult females to participate in sport and that those who do participate in sport are more likely to have higher incomes and are more highly educated (Robert Wood Johnson Foundation, 2015, p. 2).

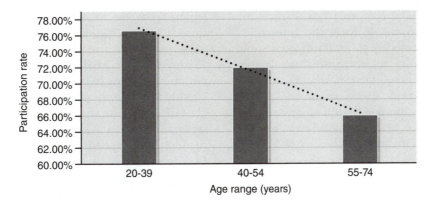

Figure 8.1 2019 Fitness and sport activity participation rates for U.S. adults.

It has been surmised that the "American sporting culture is eroding," as participation numbers decline in sports (Chalip, 2011). While NGBs for Olympic sports offer broad participation opportunities as a condition of the Amateur Sports Act, clubs and leagues often shy away from these entities and select other affiliations that are highly organized and more economical (p. 20).

The availability of non-elite amateur team sport opportunities for adults outside of intercollegiate athletics are abundant, ranging from low-level recreational programs offered at little or no cost by YMCAs, Jewish Community Centers, churches, and municipal parks and recreation departments to highly competitive leagues and tournaments organized through national affiliations such as the United States Adult Soccer Association. The governance structures for amateur team sports are varied, ranging from local private business owners to volunteer boards serving community programs to commissioners and executive boards operating at a national level.

Individual sport opportunities for adults are available through private and public facilities such as golf courses, tennis or racquet clubs, and natatoriums. Independent and franchise owned road races, cycling races, and obstacle course challenges are also abundant. In 2019, 716 marathons were scheduled in the United States, with the Boston Marathon as the largest with 26,632 finishers ("Marathon Statistics," 2019). Models of governance for adult amateur individual sports also vary widely, ranging from a board of directors for a private golf club to high-level executives for commercial brands producing a road race.

Sport commissions are also a provider of both team and individual amateur sports. Sport commissions, profiled in the chapter on local and national governing agencies, organize single-sport events such as the Flying Pig Marathon in Cincinnati and multisport festival-style competition such as the Empire State Games in New York.

INTERCOLLEGIATE ATHLETICS

Intercollegiate athletics are amateur sports competitions between institutions of higher education. There are several similarities between the United States and Canada regarding the structure and governance of intercollegiate athletics, however, intercollegiate athletics in the U.K. are vastly different.

United States

The evolution of varsity intercollegiate athletics grew from informal competition to the highly organized systems operating today, which continue to focus on amateurs. Many colleges in the U.S. (over 1,200) offer intercollegiate athletics in addition to intramurals (recreational activities within the confines of a single institution) and **club sports**, which includes competition against other schools at a level below varsity athletics.

Governance of intercollegiate athletics has experienced tremendous changes since its inception around the turn of the 20th century. The growth and diversification of athletics has become an important component in higher education and a big business for a select number of institutions.

Historical Overview

The first intercollegiate athletic event in the United States was held in 1852 when the Boston, Concord, and Montreal Railroad company sponsored a rowing match between Harvard and Yale on Lake Winnipesaukee in New Hampshire. The first attempt to govern intercollegiate athletics in 1876 came from students at Harvard, Yale, Princeton, and Columbia who met to form the Intercollegiate Football Association to establish consistent playing and eligibility rules. Up until the 1890s, intercollegiate athletics was under the control of the students (Lucas & Smith, 1978). In the mid-1890s, faculty stated their intention to gain greater control over athletics, and in 1895, a handful from several universities formed the Intercollegiate Conference of Faculty Representatives to further establish eligibility rules for student-athletes. This group is now the Big Ten Conference (Lucas & Smith, 1978).

In 1905, college football suffered from a series of deaths on the field, which led President Theodore Roosevelt to decree that university presidents needed to assert their control over college athletics. University presidents formed an alliance to create the Intercollegiate Athletic Association of the United States, which would later become the National Collegiate Athletic Association (NCAA). This group included university presidents conferring on activities to make football safer during a period of escalating catastrophic injuries (Lucas & Smith, 1978). Intercollegiate athletics, also known as college athletics, is now governed on two levels: regionally by an athletic conference and nationally by a national governing body.

Conference Affiliation

Conference affiliations based on similarities between member institutions are apparent in two of the national governing associations for intercollegiate sport, the NCAA and the National Association of Intercollegiate Athletics (NAIA). Conferences are not part of the structure of the National Junior College Athletic Association (NJCAA), which represents two-year institutions.

Most institutions are affiliated with an athletic conference within their division that reflects similar characteristics. An athletic conference operates through an independent commissioner, who serves in a role similar to a corporate executive director: managing office functions, negotiating media deals, processing minor violations, and maintaining relationships with member institutions. His or her staff is typically responsible for conference championships, award recognition programs, grants, education, and officiating.

The highest authority at the conference level is the collective group of presidents or chancellors at member institutions. The president's council (or whatever name the conference assigns) is responsible for conference-wide activities, such as proposing national legislation, hiring a commissioner, or approving revenue disbursements. Additionally, conferences operate and pass legislation through a management or leadership team that includes the director of athletics, senior women's administrator, and faculty athletic representative from each member institution. This group generally meets several times during the year to amend bylaws for the conference or for individual sports and sport championships. Student-athletes from member institutions in the NCAA comprise the Student

The formation of an association to govern intercollegiate athletics was primarily a response to the rash of catastrophic injuries in football.

Northwestern/Collegiate Images via Getty Images

Athlete Advisory Council (SAAC), which confers with the management team and is represented at the national level.

Conferences are permitted to have stricter rules than the NCAA or NAIA and to legislate areas that the national office does not. An example of a rule difference is when a conference places limits on the number of student-athletes in a sport (e.g., football) that can travel to away games when the NCAA does not legislate travel party size for regular season contests. Conferences are not, however, permitted to relax NCAA or NAIA legislation. Conferences are important to their member institutions for representation within their national associations.

National Affiliation

There are five governing bodies in the United States for intercollegiate athletics:

- ◆ National Collegiate Athletic Association (NCAA),
- ◆ National Association of Intercollegiate Athletics (NAIA),
- ◆ National Junior College Athletic Association (NJCAA),
- ◆ United States Collegiate Athletic Association (USCAA), and
- ◆ National Christian College Athletic Association (NCCAA).

Of these five national associations, the NCAA, the NAIA, and the NJCAA are the most well-known. The USCAA and the NCCAA, while conducting their own championships, allow their members to participate in other national governing bodies and recognize that those governing bodies take precedence over theirs (United States College Athletic Association, 2018; "Why the NCCAA?" 2019).

National Collegiate Athletic Association The National Collegiate Athletic Association (NCAA), originally founded as an organization to protect the health and safety of student-athletes, is the largest and most recognizable of the national governing bodies for college athletics. It is a voluntary, unincorporated association serving approximately 450,000 student-athletes at over 1,000 institutions (Bush, 2014, p. 8). Over time, its mandate has grown to include eligibility and rules enforcement in all men's sports. Women's sports were added in 1982.

There are two levels of governance within the NCAA: association-wide and divisional. The divisions are labeled I, II, and III and operate under separate bylaws that delineate the legislation enforceable by the NCAA. Since the NCAA and its governing units are organized as an unincorporated association, the court system is reluctant to interfere with jurisdiction (Bush, 2014). The constitution and bylaws serve as binding documents between the association and members. Both the association-wide and divisional governance structures operate through committees selected from member institutions on a rotating basis.

At the NCAA headquarters in Indianapolis, Indiana, the president is responsible for day-to-day operations and is the public face of the organization. Mark Emmert, appointed in 2010, serves as the current (and fifth overall) president of the NCAA as of 2019 ("NCAA President Mark Emmert." n.d.). Staff members and committees are responsible for conducting national championships (with the exception of the College Football Playoff), determining initial eligibility status for student-athletes, interpreting legislation, and enforcing NCAA rules.

The NCAA Board of Governors is the highest level of administrative authority for the membership. The board of governors includes eight Division I Football Bowl Subdivision members, two Division I Football Championship Subdivision members, two Division I nonfootball members, two Division II members, and two Division III members. These members are all presidents or chancellors of member institutions and are chosen from the Division I Board of Directors and from the President's Councils in Division II and III. This entity is responsible for association-wide issues, such as the NCAA's budget and strategic planning. Association-wide committees, such as the Committee on Competitive Safeguards and Medical Aspects of Sports (which oversees health and safety issues), report to the board of governors (National Collegiate Athletic Association, 2018a).

Member colleges and universities, known as member institutions, are divided among three divisions: I, II, and III. NCAA divisions are self-contained, meaning that Division I institutions do not have a voice in issues pertaining solely to Division II or Division III, and vice versa.

While athletic competition is seen as the dividing line among the divisions, the provision of athletic scholarships is the main distinguishing criterion. For example, Division I institutions, with rare exceptions, must provide a minimum number of athletic scholarships while not exceeding individual sport limits. These scholarships can meet the full cost of attendance for a student-athlete. Scholarships for Division II institutions cannot exceed scholarship limits for each sport, thresholds that are typically lower than the limits in Division I. Division III institutions cannot award athletics scholarships ("Division Differences and the History of Multi-Division Classifications," n.d.).

Membership at the NCAA Division I level is limited to four-year colleges and universities (National Collegiate Athletic Association, 2018a). At the Division II and Division III levels, member institutions must be four-year colleges or universities or two-year upper-level institutions (National Collegiate Athletic Association, 2018b, 2018c). Institutions from Canada and Mexico may belong to the NCAA. For example, in 2012, Simon Fraser University from British Columbia in Canada joined the Division II Great Northwest Athletic Conference ("Early Struggles Not Dissuading SFU," 2017).

NCAA Division I includes approximately 350 member institutions serving 6,000 teams and 170,000 student-athletes ("About NCAA Division I," n.d.). Division I is further divided based on football: Football Bowl Subdivision (FBS; formerly known as I-A), Football Championship Subdivision (FCS; formerly I-AA), and nonfootball schools (formerly I-AAA). FBS member institutions are eligible to compete for the College Football Playoff.

Division I

Conference affiliation is incredibly important at the Division I level in terms of weighted voting privileges and representation on committees. The two oversight committees are the board of directors and the Division I Council. The board of directors consists of 24 members who are presidents or chancellors of their institutions. Ten members represent FBS conference institutions, five represent members of institutions in the FCS, and five are associated with nonfootball conference institutions. One director of athletics, one senior women's administrator, one faculty member, and one student-athlete are also represented on the board of directors, which is responsible for the overall operations of Division I. These include strategic planning, budgets, and the infractions program. As part of its infractions oversight duties, the board is responsible for appointing members to the Committee on Infractions and Infractions Appeals Committee.

The day-to-day operations of the Division are run by the Division I Council, which serves as the primary legislative authority. All conferences are represented on the Council by athletic administrators, but voting privileges are weighted according to conference affiliations. A group known as the **Power 5** are the institutions affiliated with five conferences listed in table 8.2 that are made up of the more powerful FBS schools.

Each conference affiliated with the Power 5 also has a weighted four votes on legislative issues proposed by the Division I Council, while the other FBS conferences not affiliated with the Power 5 only have two votes each. Conferences in the FCS and nonfootball conferences only have one vote apiece. All Division I committees, with the exception of the Committee on Infractions, report to the Division I Council (National Collegiate Athletic Association, 2018a).

One of the unique aspects of Division I is the availability of the Power 5 to propose and pass autonomous legislation that does not affect the entire Division I membership. Under the old system, any legislation passed at the division level affected all Division I members equally, regardless of their ability to afford it. Many times, services provided by athletic departments are attached to operational dollars, and the disparity among finances at different institutions may make these additional mandatory provisions cost prohibitive. For example, the athletic department at Texas A&M University posted a $57 million surplus in 2015-2016 without additional university appropriations. On the other hand, at the University of California at Riverside, an institution whose athletic department had a $306,000 surplus during the same academic

Table 8.2 2017 NCAA Revenue Disbursements to Member Institutions in the Power 5

Conference	Headquarters	Commissioner	Schools	Disbursement**
Atlantic Coast Conference*	Greensboro, NC	John Swofford	15	$25.3-$34.7 million
Big Ten Conference	Chicago, IL	James Delany	14	$37 million
Big 12 Conference	Irving, TX	Bob Bowlsby	10	$34 million
Pac-12 Conference	San Francisco, CA	Larry Scott	12	$30.9 million
Southeastern Conference	Birmingham, AL	Greg Sankey	9	$29.9-$42 million

*Notre Dame University is affiliated with the ACC in all sports other than football, in which it competes as an independent member of the FBS.

**Disbursements based on information tweeted by *USA Today's* Steve Berkowitz in Barnett (2018).

year, 92 percent of its operating budget came from the university (Berkowitz & Schnaars, 2016).

In 2014, a major reform in the Division I governance structure allowed Power 5 institutions to form an alliance to draft and pass legislation affecting members (Tracy, 2014). A controversial legislative area that created the impetus for asserting independence and autonomy for the Power 5 was **cost of attendance stipends**, which are monetary awards added to the maximum amount of scholarship money a student-athlete could receive to cover the full cost of attendance. This legislation would have been difficult for Division I institutions outside of the Power 5 to afford, which ignited fear that the legislation would not pass, even with a weighted voting system favoring the five conferences. In a compromise, the Division I board of directors voted in 2014 to grant these five conferences the ability to pass legislation that would allow them to use their resources to enhance student-athlete well-being without forcing institutions without those resources to follow along (Tracy, 2014; Berkowitz, 2014). Under the autonomy legislation, conferences and their member institutions outside of the Power 5 are allowed to choose whether to adopt regulations (National Collegiate Athletic Association, 2018a). For example, in 2019, the Power 5 conferences unanimously passed legislation requiring schools to make mental health resources available for all student-athletes.

Basketball and football programs in the Power 5 and other Division I conferences have been called feeder programs for the NFL and the NBA. These two leagues lack true minor league systems, although the Gatorade League in the NBA is a fairly recent endeavor providing alternative professional playing opportunities for talented athletes, similar to the Canadian and Arena Football Leagues in football. Most professional players in the NFL and NBA emerge from Division I programs. Governance in Action 8.3 explores the restrictive draft eligibility requirements in the NBA, which some suggest force an athlete to play a year of intercollegiate athletics even if the athlete is physically, mentally, and emotionally ready for the professional ranks.

Division II

Division II has approximately 300 member institutions serving thousands of student-athletes in four geographic regions of the country ("About NCAA Division II," n.d.). Membership on Division II oversight committees is based primarily on proximity in a geographic region as opposed to conference affiliation. The two committees with oversight

of Division II are the President's Council and the Management Council.

Sixteen members make up the President's Council. Selection to the council is based on a formula permitting the inclusion of one president or chancellor per region for every 22 institutions in that region. The President's Council is responsible for budgets and strategic planning.

The day-to-day operations of Division II activities are the responsibility of the Management Council. Representation on the Management Council is based on conferences, and all conferences are represented on the council. All Division II committees report to the Management Council (National Collegiate Athletic Association, 2018b).

Division III

Division III is the largest division, with approximately 450 member institutions serving over 190,000 student-athletes in four geographic regions of the country ("About NCAA Division III," n.d.). The two committees with oversight are also known as the President's Council and the Management Council, with functions similar to those in Division II.

Eighteen members make up the President's Council, the highest level of authority in the division. The 18 members of the council include seven at-large positions and a minimum of two presidents from institutions in each region. They meet on a quarterly basis. There are 21 members of the Management Council which, similar to Division II, conducts day-to-day operations. All Division III committees report to the Management Council (National Collegiate Athletic Association, 2018c).

National Association of Intercollegiate Athletics The National Association of Intercollegiate Athletics (NAIA) was founded in 1937. It had 249 member institutions in 2019, located mostly in the South and Midwest. Headquartered in Kansas City, Missouri, the NAIA conducts day-to-day operations through its president and CEO, who manage the general business of the association. The office staff conducts national championships, determines the eligibility of student-athletes, and interprets and enforces NAIA rules (National Association of Intercollegiate Athletics, 2017).

The NAIA characteristically includes small colleges with an average enrollment of approximately 1,700. The association includes both four-year and two-year institutions, conditional upon a two-year institution awarding at least one bachelor's degree. Divisions are used only in basketball. Member institutions join the NAIA through gender affiliations according to men's, women's, or coeducational sports (National Association of Intercollegiate Athletics, 2017).

The NAIA is considered an unincorporated, membership-driven association. The highest governing authority is the Council of Presidents, with representation from each member conference and two at-large positions. All conference representatives are either a president or a chancellor of a member institution. The council is responsible for fiscal matters and for hiring and supervising the NAIA president and chief executive officer (National Association of Intercollegiate Athletics, 2017).

The Executive Committee is responsible for overseeing the day-to-day operations of the NAIA; it is made up of six members of the Council of Presidents (National Association of Intercollegiate Athletics, 2017; "Council of Presidents," 2019). The Executive Committee is responsible for the business of the NAIA between meetings of the Council of Presidents (National Association of Intercollegiate Athletics, 2017).

GOVERNANCE IN ACTION 8.3

The "One and Done" Saga in NCAA Hoops Prior to the NBA Age Rule Changes

The NCAA, through its member institutions, has vast control over student-athletes. However, the "one and done" phenomenon, in which college basketball players jump to the pros after one season, was never an NCAA rule. It was a provision in the NBA Collective Bargaining Agreement (CBA), which expired at the end of the 2020-2021 season.

Article X, Section 1 stated a draft-eligible player must be at least 19 years old and at least one year must have elapsed since the high school graduation date of his class. An early-entry option existed if an athlete chose to declare an intent to challenge the rule and enter the draft despite not meeting the conditions set forth in NBA guidelines (NBA CBA, 2017, p. 273).

Few high school players can match the athleticism of a LeBron James, Kobe Bryant, Moses Malone, or Kevin Garnett, who jumped from prep to the pros without a day on a college basketball court. A trend of "one and done" rocked the collegiate hard courts as greater numbers of athletes declared for the NBA draft after just one season of college ball.

Approximately 30 early entries are selected each year in the NBA draft (Givony, 2018). A record 236 players declared early entry in 2018 (Goodman, 2018). Most early entries never sign with an agent, and they withdraw their names from the official NBA list by the deadline in order to retain their college eligibility.

The controversy over the NBA's restrictive draft eligibility requirements raises the question of whether college basketball is the de facto minor league system for the NBA as college football is for the NFL. The "one and done" mindset has been cited for influencing a reluctance to attend classes in the spring semester and in escalating the intrusion of shoe companies and agents trying to leverage their association with high-profile collegiate programs. The recent FBI investigation into players being paid by Adidas and NBA agents has placed more than a dozen institutions in the spotlight for their role in the scheme. In October 2018, two officials with Adidas and an NBA player agent were convicted on fraud charges in federal court for giving schools money to give to players (Hobson & Armstrong, 2018). Four college basketball assistant coaches were similarly charged, but pled guilty to lesser charges after the first convictions.

This controversy has led to calls for reform in college basketball, including calls for a repeal of the "one and done" rule. However, the NCAA has no influence since draft eligibility is collectively bargained for by the NBA and its players. NBA Commissioner Adam Silver has stated that the league is ready to do away with the rule, but under the CBA, 2021 would be the earliest changes could be imposed (Amick, 2018; Zillgitt, 2019). A potential change in age restrictions would likely reduce the number of one-and-done collegiate players.

National Junior College Athletic Association Founded in 1938, the National Junior College Athletic Association (NJCAA) is comprised of two-year institutions. Instead of conferences, NJCAA institutions are defined by geographic regions and compete for regional championships. Legislation is also proposed and adopted by regions instead of conferences. Each region includes an elected director and an assistant director for men's sports and for women's sports (National Junior College Athletic Association, 2017).

Similar to the NCAA, the NJCAA includes three divisions based on the awarding of athletics scholarships. Unlike the NCAA, however, NJCAA member institutions are permitted to compete in multiple divisions, meaning one sport can compete in Division II and another in Division I or III. A two-year commitment is mandated before an institution can declare a different division for a sport.

Scholarships are available at the Division I and II levels, but Division II places greater restrictions on the amount, which may not cover the cost of attendance. Each sport has limits on the number of scholarships that a team can award. Division III sports are not permitted to award athletic scholarships ("Divisional Structure," 2018).

At the national level, governance is the responsibility of three entities: elected officers, an executive committee, and a board of directors. The elected officers consist of a president and two vice presidents for men's sports in addition to two vice presidents for women's sports. Officers are elected by the NJCAA member institutions and serve for three years.

The elected officials serve on the executive committee, which also includes two at-large regional directors for men, two at-large regional directors for women, and a president. The executive committee is responsible for the day-to-day operations of the NJCAA between meetings of the board of directors.

The NJCAA Board of Directors is composed of the regional directors and presidential representatives from member institutions. The group is responsible for the overall operation of the association, including adopting legislation and hiring the executive director and his or her office staff (National Junior College Athletic Association, 2017).

At the NJCAA headquarters in Colorado Springs, Colorado, the executive director oversees day-to-day operations. The office staff at the national headquarters is responsible for overseeing national championships and interpreting and enforcing NJCAA rules (National Junior College Athletic Association, 2017).

Canada

Similarities exist in the structure and governance of intercollegiate athletics in the United States and Canada. The main level is **varsity sports**, and universities may also offer a recreational sports program as well. The only governing body for intercollegiate athletics is U Sports.

National

Regulation of sports at the university level in Canada began in 1906 with the formation of the Canadian Interuniversity Athletic Union (CIAU), which was available to universities in the provinces of Quebec and Ontario. The role of the CIAU was to provide common rules and regulations, however, the vast difference among members led to a temporary six-year hiatus of the association from 1955 to 1961 before being reconstituted with the support of the national government. In 1977, women's sports were added. The association also had two name changes in 2001 and 2016. The first change formed the Canadian Interuniversity Sport (CIS) while the second change resulted in its current designation as U Sports ("U Sports History," n.d.).

U Sports is a multisport service organization with headquarters in Richmond Hill, Ontario, for institutions supporting intercollegiate athletics. The association is partially funded by the national government. The organization currently includes 56 universities divided into four regional conferences. U Sports is also incorporated under the **Canada Not-for-profit Corporations Act**, which means the association includes university members but has no share capital or shareholders (Canada Not-for-profit Corporations Act, S.C. 2009 c 23). The role of U Sports is to administer competitive sports conducted between its member universities.

U Sports is governed at the national level by the membership, the board of directors, and standing committees. Members can propose changes to bylaws and to certain policies and procedures, especially if they will have a financial impact on the universities. Members meet annually to vote on admission to membership and to propose changes to articles or bylaws. Each member has one delegate with voting rights (U Sports, 2018a).

The U Sports board of directors, composed of at least two members from each region (one athletic director and one president), is responsible for the general operations of the organization. There are four elected officers—the chair, the treasurer, the secretary, and the chief executive officer, who is considered the highest authority in the organization (U Sports, 2018a, 2018b).

U Sports operates through the Executive Committee, Human Resources Committee, Finance Committee, and Governance Committee, each responsible for their respective functional areas. For example, the Finance Committee is responsible for assisting the board with financial auditing and reporting and matters such as financial policies and strategies (U Sports, 2018b).

Regional

U Sports is divided into four geographic regions, which are similar to conferences in the United States in that they govern athletics in their area of the country. Unlike athletic conferences in the United States, however, universities do not have a choice which region they will join since alignment is based strictly on geography. The regions are incorporated under the Canada Not-for-profit Corporations Act, with universities considered members. The composition and responsibilities of each board of directors varies from region to region.

United Kingdom

University sport began in the United Kingdom in 1918 when university presidents determined there was a need to establish an association to promote the development of sport at the university level. The first competition in May 1919 was a track and field meet involving 10 universities ("Our History," n.d.). University sport in the United Kingdom is different from that in the United States and Canada. There is no varsity program and no traditional athletic department. However, some universities may sponsor **performance sports** geared toward athletes who compete on an international level who wish to train and earn a college degree. Generally, however, intercollegiate sport in the U.K. is administered at the club level through a student union. Some teams may receive support from the university, but it is not a requirement.

National

In 1952, the British Universities Sport Board was founded, which eventually became known as the British Universities Sports Federation (BUSF). The board was formed to manage Britain's general student interest in sport and to represent British universities at the international level. In 1979, the Universities Athletics Union was formed for the same purpose while combining men's and women's

sport. In 1994, these two organizations merged to form the British Universities Sport Association (BUSA) ("Our History," n.d.).

In 1960, the Universities Physical Education Association was formed to represent staff at the universities who were responsible for administering sport. In 1993, it merged with the Association of Polytechnic Physical Education Lecturers to become the British Universities and Colleges Physical Education, which changed names again to University and College Sport (UCS) ("Our History," n.d.).

In June 2008, BUSA and UCS merged and formed the British Universities & Colleges Sport (BUCS), which is incorporated under the **Companies Act 2006** as a limited guaranteed company void of any shared capital (Companies Act 2006, U.K. c.46). Any group that provides higher education services in the U.K. is eligible to become a member of BUCS, which is governed at the national level by its members, the board of directors, and an advisory group. There are currently 189 institutions comprising BUCS across 12 regional groups (BUCS, n.d.).

BUCS members meet at least every 18 months at the **annual general meeting**, where there is a ratification of the board of directors and business is transacted. Each institution appoints two members, each with a vote in legislative activities. One representative must be a student or member of the university's student (or athletic) union (BUCS, n.d.).

The board of directors has a minimum of 4 and a maximum of 10 elected members. At minimum, the board includes the non-executive chair, chair of the Senior Managers Network, and a student. There are currently nine directors on the board, including the BUCS chief executive officer and a company secretary, who serve as nonvoting members. The role of the board is to create the strategic plan, oversee finances, and manage general BUCS business (BUCS, n.d.).

An advisory group is composed of the chief executive officer, four student members, and four staff members who consult with members on policy and important issues. Each region is represented on the national advisory group by its student and staff chairs.

Regional

BUCS is divided into 12 regions based on geographic boundaries. England is divided into nine regions with Scotland, Northern Ireland, and

Wales constituting the remaining regions. Each region supports a staff chair, a student chair, and a secretary.

In Scotland, BUCS is partnered with Scottish Student Sport. All Scottish members of BUCS are members of Scottish Student Sport, but the remaining universities in Scotland are also members. The role of Scottish Student Sport is to improve development, such as best practices and referee training, and competition for Scottish university students (Scottish Student Sport, 2017).

RECAP

There are many ways to govern competitive amateur sport, and the governance model used depends on the type of sport, the level of the sport, and where it is located. Youth and adult amateur sports around the world are generally connected to communities. There are wide variations in the level of financial support governments provide to promote healthy lifestyles, to develop valuable life-long skills, and to deter counterproductive behaviors. A general decline in youth sports has occurred throughout the world, although events such as the London 2012 Olympics have helped to increase participation rates in some places.

Interscholastic sports and intramural sports are widely available in the United States, Canada, and the United Kingdom for youth in secondary schools. Intramural sports are lower-level recreational activities within a school, whereas interscholastic sports are competitive contests between schools. In the United States, the National Federation of State High School Associations (NFHS) is the supreme authority over interscholastic sports. It is comprised of state associations that are divided by districts. Schools are grouped into divisions (generally distinguished by enrollment numbers) and conference affiliations.

The United States has the largest (over 1,000 institutions) and the most sophisticated system of intercollegiate athletics in the world. The most powerful governing organization in intercollegiate athletics in the United States, the NCAA, is often criticized for its labyrinth of rules and regulations and its capitalistic nature, even though it serves as a membership-driven agency. NCAA Division I athletics has been referred to as a feeder system for the NFL and the NBA, whereas the pathway to professional sports in other countries, including the United Kingdom, is the sport academy model. U Sports is the national organization governing intercollegiate competition in Canada with 56 institutions divided into four regional conferences. The national organization governing intercollegiate competition in the United Kingdom is the British Universities & Colleges Sport (BUCS), comprised of 189 institutions across 12 regions in 2019.

Critical Thinking Questions

1. Create a unique definition of amateur sports.
2. Select a youth sport association in the United States and describe its governance structure.
3. Explain the difference between the governance structures for intercollegiate and interscholastic athletics.
4. Select an NCAA athletic conference and describe its governance structure.
5. Should athletes have a greater voice in the governance of amateur sports? Why or why not?

Applied Activities

New Professional Sport Development Model for U.S. Universities

One of the great debates in the United States is the oversized role that college athletics plays both in university life and in professional sports. If the United States were to move to a professional sport development model similar to the one in the United Kingdom while maintaining aspects of the current system, what would it look like? Describe the system for individual and team sports, incorporating both intercollegiate athletics and academy-style programs.

Youth Sports Subsidies in Other Countries

Research youth sports in three countries other than the United States, the United Kingdom, and Canada. Create a chart to address the structure of youth sports in each country, including funding and support from their national government and other entities.

Case Study Application

For more information on governance and authority in intercollegiate sports, review *Best Practices for Financial Accountability of an NCAA Conference Office* in the web resource.

chapter 9

Sport Media

Galen Clavio and Matthew Zimmerman

LEAD-OFF

Representing a third of the world's media market, the United States will reach almost $800 billion in media and entertainment revenues in 2019, according to an estimate by PriceWaterhouseCoopers (United States Department of Commerce, 2018). In this context, sports programming represents a small but significant sector of the total media industry.

A discussion of governance topics in media and sport media reveals a fragmented industry promulgated by increasing costs, increasing competition, mergers, acquisitions, and David-versus-Goliath sagas. Furthermore, ownership and operating regulations in the sports broadcast industry have evolved with the emergence of new media platforms that have produced a greater emphasis on privacy and copyright protection laws.

Media outlets are typically classified as either **traditional** (e.g., print, analog television, satellite television, cable television, radio, film) or **digital** (Internet and mobile). The availability, convenience, and affordability of viewing content on personal computers (PCs), smartphones, and tablets has triggered a shift in consumption patterns that continues to disrupt the traditional media marketplace. According to Nielsen (2018, p. 28) reports, adults over the age of 18, for example, viewed approximately 55 percent more sport programming (79 hours per week) in 2018 than they did in 2002, primarily because of the widespread availability of affordable mobile devices.

Despite digital platforms gaining considerable market share space, live broadcasts on a traditional television screen remain the viewing preference for most sport enthusiasts (Evens, Iosifidis, & Smith, 2013; Smith, Evens, & Iosifidis, 2016). Utilizing electronic and proprietary metering technology to document consumer media behavior, the Nielsen ratings indicate the National Football League (NFL) consistently ranks at the top for television programming in the United States. It is not uncommon for eight or nine of the top-10 most-viewed single telecast programs on television to be NFL game broadcasts. In 2017, an entertainment award show and a game in Major League Baseball (MLB)'s World Series were the only two non-NFL broadcasts among the top 10, with *NFL Sunday Night Football* ranking as the top-rated television series for several years (Nielsen, 2017).

With the rapid growth in online and mobile media devices broadcasting sport content, traditional media outlets have responded by embracing innovative technologies and expanding services to reach a larger consumer base through multichannel platforms. With this expansion and these changes, new challenges to remain relevant have affected business relationships and decisions in the media world, primarily with escalating costs and fewer players controlling more services.

This chapter will address regulatory agencies and governance of both traditional and digital sport media. Further, this chapter will address regulations and issues for sports journalists and broadcasters in the context of sport.

Learning Outcomes

- Identify examples of governance.
- Present an overview of sport media governance.
- Present an overview of media regulation and ownership.
- Present an overview of conglomerates that dominate the media ownership landscape.
- Provide insight into the governance of media relationships by major international sport organizations.
- Explore newer modes of communication, including social media and esports.
- Present the implications of the continued growth of newer media distribution modes.
- Discuss media governance as it pertains to U.S. organizations.

OVERVIEW OF POLITICAL GOVERNANCE IN SPORT MEDIA

Governance of sport media operates somewhat differently than other forms of governance within sport. Whereas most sport entities are directly organized or maintained by a governing body or controlling franchiser (e.g., the NCAA for college athletics, the NFL for professional football), sport media entities have historically been standalone businesses that exist outside of the direct purview of the sports they cover.

Despite this historical business separation, sport media entities in North America exist under a combined system of governance. One of these systems is governmental and involves the control and oversight of the federal government in enforcing agreed-upon standards of broadcast decency (Limburg, 1989). Another system is industrial and is self-imposed by media organizations seeking to maintain certain approaches and standards for how sport is portrayed (Hardin, 2005b). This system works in symbiosis with a commercial system of governance and involves the influence of market forces on sport media coverage and practices. This system includes the governing influence of sport partner organizations upon the coverage that media outlets provide to their respective sports (e.g., Miller & Belson, 2013).

An important aspect of sport media governance involves the changing nature of sport media coverage in the digital era. Since the dawn of social media and the digitization of video and audio, many nontraditional outlets have entered the marketplace. These new entrants include both independently owned media operations and sport organization–owned media operations (Dittmore, Stoldt, & Greenwell, 2008; Grimmer & Kian, 2013).

In the latter case, professional leagues such as the NFL and individual professional franchises such as the New York Yankees have partnered with media organizations to launch their own branded video channels featuring original programming and game broadcasts. In college athletics, conferences such as the Big Ten and SEC have pursued similar partnerships and have crafted multimedia platforms to showcase the games and content of their member schools. These branded and self-controlled media entities have demonstrated governance tendencies that are different in important ways from traditional, independent media.

Due to the fact that the First Amendment to the United States Constitution prohibits government units from regulating the content of the press, mass media in the United States operate primarily through private entities. Such is not the case in countries such as China, Iran, Kazakhstan, and Niger, where television stations, newspaper offices, and Internet sites are considered state-owned enterprises (Djankov, McLiesh, Nenova, & Shleifer, 2003).

Common to sport media and regardless of the individual governance situation, coverage does not end between the lines of the playing venue. For example, societal issues such as sexism have caught the attention of sport media (Fink, Borland, & Fields, 2010). In addition, sport organizations' responsibilities in crisis communication are well documented (Jensen & Sosa, 2008). Also, media coverage has proven to have an impact on how news consumers might view the subjects of that coverage (Fink, Borland, & Fields, 2010). Occasionally, sports coverage in newspapers has even ventured into politics. For instance, in coverage of international events such as World Cup qualifying, newspapers have contextualized global sport performance as it pertained to a country's political situation (Mehler, 2008).

Sport leagues, conference offices, and franchises have negotiated business deals for regional broadcast stations such as the YES Network, owned primarily by the Yankees, and featuring programming for the New York Yankees, the Brooklyn Nets, New York City Football Club (NYCFC), and the Atlantic Coast Conference.

Jim McIsaac/Getty Images

Game broadcasts have also been used by governments for political influence. For example, in Argentina, a program titled *Futbol para Todos*, or *Soccer for All*, became a forum for the Argentine government to become involved in the acquisition of soccer-related television rights (Bar-Ona & De Gaetanob, 2017). This government intervention into broadcast rights policies also occurs in the United States in the form of regulatory organizations (Hoehn & Lancefield, 2003). Pertaining to coverage of international sport such as the Olympics or World Cup, media have been known to equate a level of patriotism with support for a nation's representative athletic teams (Mehler, 2008).

While the government does not own or control the press in the United States, the U.S. Congress has played a significant role in shaping media regulations with the passing of several landmark legislative acts. The Communications Act of 1934 was the initial legislation that established the **Federal Communications Commission (FCC)** as an independent agency with supreme authority for regulating media ownership, policies, and practices. The second significant legislative action was the **Telecommunications Act of 1996**, which relaxed the FCC regulations on media ownership and stimulated deregulation of the communications industry (Zhong, Cao, & Ning, 2008, p. 239).

Federal Communications Commission

Powered by the U.S. Congress, the FCC (2018b) is responsible for implementing and enforcing communication laws and regulations in America, and this applies to all media and sport media outlets. Regulations, for example, limit the number of radio and television stations a company can own, governs public service announcements, and requires licensing for station operations.

The structure of the FCC includes a board of commissioners who operate through seven bureaus and 10 offices. The role of the Media Bureau is to recommend, develop, and administer the policies and licensing programs for electronic media, broadcast, cable, and satellite television (Federal Communications Commission, 2018b). Incorporating analytics from The Nielsen Company, the FCC for example defines 210 **designated market areas (DMAs)** in the United States and essentially governs the media in each (Scherer, 2016). FCC (2018a) rules also prohibit a merger between the four major television networks: (1) the Columbia Broadcasting System (CBS), (2) American Broadcasting Company (ABC), (3) National Broadcasting Company (NBC), and (4) Fox Broadcast Company (FOX).

Media rules and regulations have changed significantly over the years as many FCC rules and regulations have simply become outdated. In 1940, for example, the FCC passed the notorious **duopoly rule**, which restricted individuals and companies from owning more than one broadcast station (Sadler, 2005).

Ownership restrictions have evolved over the years from a single entity being permitted to own a maximum of three national broadcast stations in 1943 (e.g., AM, FM, and TV) to seven in 1953, to more than 20 radio and 12 television stations in the 2000s (Sadler, 2005). The FCC also set limits on the reach of a single broadcast station to no more than 25 percent of the national market, a percentage that has since increased. Another of the antiquated FCC policies was the **blackout rule**, whereby a live sporting event would not be broadcast in the local market if attendance fell below a certain threshold (see Governance in Action 9.1).

The FCC has evolved significantly since the mid-1930s. The primary role of the commission is to promote and expand all communication media, including radio, television, and wireless technol-

---

GOVERNANCE IN ACTION 9.1

Blackouts: A Relic of the Mass Media Era

A blackout refers to a scheduled live event that is not available or transmitted in a designated media market. Blackout rules fall under the jurisdiction of the U.S. Federal Communications Commission (FCC), which regulates all interstate and international communications by television, satellite, radio, wire, or cable. Subscription exclusivity remains as an FCC law protecting local or regional market broadcast rights in the same manner as a blackout.

Professional leagues have also created policies affecting blackouts. Some form of blackout policy is in place for all four U.S. major professional leagues (e.g., MLB, the NFL, the NBA, the NHL), primarily due to local channels or regional sports networks having exclusive broadcasting rights over league subscription services (Gipe, 2019).

In 2014, the FCC (2014, 2016) repealed its original 1975 blackout rule, which had prohibited cable, satellite, and open video system operators from transmitting a sporting event that was blacked out on a local broadcast station. After the FCC repeal, sport leagues were still able to enforce private blackout policies in local markets if a game was not sold out (or reached a minimum quota) within 72 hours of the start. The policy became a regular practice by the NFL until owners voted to repeal the attendance-based blackout rule in 2015. Currently, blackouts in local markets or selected areas still occur, but only as a result of exclusive broadcast deals.

The repeal of the NFL attendance-based blackout rule was partially attributed to the antiquity of the 40-plus-year-old regulation. When the ruling was first enacted by the FCC in the 1970s, 59 percent of NFL games were blacked out due to flagging attendance during a period when ticket sales were the major source of revenue for the league (Plus Media Solutions, 2014; Wise, 2014). Broadcast rights have since replaced ticket sales as the primary revenue source for the league, and thus the percentage of NFL blackouts has declined precipitously over the decades. Blackouts occurred during 40 percent of the NFL games in the 1980s, 31 percent in the 1990s, 8 percent in the 2000s, and less than 5 percent between 2011 and 2014, which included only two games in 2013 and zero in 2014 (ESPN News, 2015). An FCC news release reporting the repeal of the blackout rule called it an "unnecessary and outdated regulation" (Wise, 2014).

The year the NFL agreed to lift the blackout rule (2015) coincided with the first global live streaming of a regular-season game over an Internet-based platform when the Buffalo Bills faced the Jacksonville Jaguars in London, England. Current blackout policies protecting exclusive broadcast rights for professional games have helped marketing efforts for league-wide subscription services (e.g., NBA LEAGUE PASS and MLB.TV) as well as cable and satellite packages tied to a local regional sports network (Gipe, 2019). Major League Baseball provides a lengthy explanation of its policies on blackout restrictions, addressing exclusivities and the availability of a blacked-out game as an archived event streamed approximately 90 minutes after the end of a live broadcast ("MLB-TV Out-of-Market Practices," 2018).

ogy. The FCC also protects the private ownership model for all media entities in the United States. Entrepreneurship and private sector expansion are two key initiatives driving the actions of the commission.

1996 Telecommunications Act

The 1996 Telecommunications Act was one of the most significant laws in the mid-1990s. Through its legislative arm, the U.S. government exerted its power over the independent agency it had created (the FCC) by establishing new regulatory policies for telephone services and equipment manufacturing, Internet and online computer services, cable television, and radio and broadcast television companies. These regulations have also affected the sport media business.

The Telecommunications Act repealed or relaxed almost all previous FCC regulations controlling ownership of the media industry. The new legislation required the FCC to drop a prohibition against a network owning cable stations and repealed or modified ownership limits for radio and broadcast television stations (Sadler, 2005). One of the most significant changes of the Telecommunications Act was that a single television or radio broadcast network was permitted to own an unlimited number of stations, both nationwide and locally.

Since the abolishment of a cap on nationwide station ownership, it has been debated whether the Telecommunications Act increased or decreased competition in the media industry. Many assert that deregulation has resulted in more concentrated markets with fewer producers. While described as a fragmented conglomeration, the media landscape is one of convergence in which deregulation has enabled a smaller number of major corporations to consolidate their power (Zhong, Cao, & Ning, 2008). Examples of this power shift within the sports media landscape include the consolidation of radio station ownership across the country by media conglomerates such as iHeartMedia (formerly ClearChannel), purchases of local television stations by corporations such as Sinclair Broadcast Group, and the purchase of traditional broadcast television network NBC by cable and Internet megacorporation Comcast (Peers, Jannarone, & Linebaugh, 2013). These channels produce and televise sports programming across their multimedia platforms.

The FCC continues to move toward less regulation of ownership and has taken steps in the late 2010s that would have been considered radical a few decades earlier. In late 2017, the FCC eliminated several core components in its traditional stance against multi-outlet ownership within a marketplace. Specifically, the commission removed the rules forbidding the ownership of newspapers and broadcast entities in the same market, as well as rules prohibiting the ownership of radio and television stations in the same market (FCC, n.d.).

Ownership Consolidation

While the intent of the Telecommunications Act was to promote competition in all communication markets, it has been suggested that deregulation has resulted in fewer companies owning more stations, especially in the traditional media marketplace. Initially, there were tight FCC controls on media entities that prohibited ownership of more than one medium. However, deregulation and consolidation have perpetuated the current state of large mass media companies dominating the U.S. system, which includes the landscape of sport media entities. It has been documented that 50 companies were involved in media ownership in the United States in 1983 (Lutz, 2014). However, fast-forwarding through almost 35 years, where mergers and acquisitions have dominated the marketplace, there are significantly fewer players. Table 9.1 is an overview of five of the largest players in the U.S. media marketplace, their CEOs, and selected subsidiary holdings as of 2019.

According to *Fortune* magazine, the media companies among the highest revenue earners in the world are the Walt Disney Company, followed by Comcast, Time Warner (now AT&T Warner Media Co.), and Twenty-First Century Fox ("Fortune Global 500," 2018). These corporations have a reputation for pursuing massive business acquisitions in diverse industries for control of mass media outlets. However, there remain thousands of niche traditional media companies in the United States, providing channels for local and trade industry news.

GLOBAL AND COMMERCIAL GOVERNANCE IN SPORT MEDIA

While government actions had a tremendous impact on sport media through the mass media age, industrial and commercial considerations in sport media governance appear likely to dominate the industry's interactions with sport consumers

Table 9.1 Large Media Companies in the United States (2019)

Company	CEO	Selected holdings
National Amusements, Inc.	Sumner Redstone	CBS, CBS Sports Network; Viacom, Paramount Pictures, Showtime; 247 Sports
Walt Disney Company	Robert Iger	ABC; ESPN; Marvel; SEC Network; Hulu; True Games Interactive; Pixar; Lifetime Entertainment; Twentieth Century Fox Film Corporation; Twentieth Century Fox Television; Lucasfilm
AT&T Warner Media Co. *(formerly Time Warner)*	John Stankey	CNN; Cinemax; HBO; TBS; Turner Sports; adult swim; Time; Time Life
Comcast	Brian L. Roberts	NBC, MLB Network, NHL Network, Golf Channel, Universal, Xfinity
News Corp	Robert Thompson	Fox; Fox Sports; Sun Sports; Big Ten Network; Speed; Harper Collins; *The Wall Street Journal*; Dow Jones & Co.

in the digital media era. Government regulation is most effective when there are relatively few senders of media content; this made the mass media era of the 20th century particularly conducive to the establishment of norms and standards by entities like the FCC. However, in an era when there are a large number of senders of media content and a large number of receivers, the type of governance that the FCC provides becomes much less effective.

Even more important is the truly transnational nature of communication in the 21st century and the resulting implications for sport media governance. With the notable exception of China and its largely firewalled Internet population, the citizens of most advanced and developing nations can interact with each other online and view global sporting events. Governance in Action 9.2 provides an overview of one of the largest media companies in the world, which also happens to be based in China.

Sport enthusiasts in China and across national and cultural borders share the experience of enjoying sporting mega-events such as football's World Cup and the Summer and Winter Olympics due to broadcast privileges with media companies such as InFront Sports. These events and their all-important television and media coverage are not governed by national political entities or the United Nations. Rather, their media rights and access are managed by **supernational entities**, which are organizations or international groups with power and influence that transcend national or continental borders. Two examples of supernational entities are the Fédération Internationale de Football Association (FIFA) and the International Olympic Committee (IOC), who respectively own the rights to the World Cup and the Olympic Games.

FIFA World Cup

The FIFA World Cup is widely recognized as the most popular single sporting event in the world, and the revenues that it garners for its parent organization (FIFA) bear this out. The 2010 World Cup in South Africa, featuring 32 teams from six confederations spread across the same number of continents, was reported to have generated $2.4 billion in broadcast rights worldwide (Associated Press, 2011). Eight years later, the 2018 World Cup reportedly generated more than $3 billion in broadcast rights (Consultancy.uk, 2018).

Controversy has surrounded FIFA in relation to several aspects of its governance of football. A significant scandal engulfed FIFA following the awarding of the 2018 and 2022 World Cups to Russia and Qatar, respectively. In 2015, corruption charges were brought against a number of key figures in FIFA, including sitting Fédération President Sepp Blatter and Union of European Football Association (UEFA) President Michel Platini (BBC News, 2015). The details of these charges indicated how critical sport media rights have become to the financial well-being of FIFA, particularly television rights. Blatter was accused by Swiss prosecutors of "criminal mismanagement or misappropriation over a TV rights deal" (BBC News, 2015, p. 19). A related figure, former general secretary of the Confederation of North, Central American, and Caribbean Association Football (CONCACAF) Charles "Chuck" Blazer, admitted to accepting bribes in connection with the distribution of broadcast rights for that confederation's tournament over multiple years. A related indictment on FIFA-related charges brought by the United States government claimed that "well over $150m" (BBC News, 2015, p. 37)

GOVERNANCE IN ACTION 9.2

Wanda Group: China's Media Company With Powerful Sport Connections

Despite China's government-censored media, the country's Wanda Group is thriving as a worldwide media leader with a substantial sport presence. Wanda Sport Holdings, a subsidiary company of the Wanda Group (2016), became the exclusive global commercial development partner for the Fédération Internationale de Basketball Association (FIBA) in 2016. The Wanda Group (n.d.) has similar arrangements with more than a dozen international sport federations, including badminton, ice hockey, triathlon, and football, owning the naming rights to a renovated state-of-the-art stadium for Spanish power Atletico Madrid that opened in 2017 before selling a 17% stake in the company in 2018 (Zhang & Miller, 2015; Berwick, 2018; Corrigan, 2016).

In addition to sports, the Wanda Group represents the globe's largest chain of cinema operators and was the only non-U.S. company in 2017 to rank among the top 10 Media and Entertainment corporations in the world (United States Department of Commerce, 2018). Among Wanda Group's subsidiary properties is InFront Sports and Media AG, a Swiss marketing company representing more than 40 top-level football enterprises and focusing on distribution of rights, host broadcast services, digital media services, program productions, event operations, brand development, and sponsorship. InFront Sports (n.d.) broadcasts over 41,000 hours of sport content annually, including 20 world championships. The subsidiary was awarded the exclusive media rights to sell broadcast packages in 26 Asian territories for all FIFA events between 2015 and 2022, which includes the 2018 and 2022 FIFA World Cups ("FIFA World Cup – Asian Media Rights," n.d.). While the company headquarters are in Zug, Switzerland, there are 15 satellite offices around the world.

InFront's website notes that groupwide management practices and systems follow the principles outlined in "recent landmark cases and national bribery laws, including the U.K. Bribery Act" of 2010. InFront's (n.d.) managerial board includes the president, chief executive officer (one position), and eight other executives assigned to functional areas (e.g., legal and finance) or sport segments (e.g., football, summer sports). The subsidiary management board for InFront (n.d.) includes 13 executives primarily assigned to geographic territories (e.g., Turkey, Austria, and Germany).

The Wanda Group is also the owner of the World Triathlon Corporation, which organizes Ironman competitions and other endurance events (Zhang & Miller, 2015). The purchase of Ironman from a private equity firm for a reported $650 million in 2015 earmarked Wanda Sport Holdings as the dominant global company in endurance sports (Wahba, 2017).

Also the owner of the world's largest indoor ski resort located in China, the company continues to invest in many projects with a sport focus to position the Wanda Group media conglomerate as a global leader in sports. According to Reuters (2019), the company raised $190.4 million in its U.S. initial public offering (Zhu & Franklin, 2019). The media company has been listed among Fortune's top 500 Global companies, and with a net worth of $22.7 billion, Forbes listed owner Wang Jianlin as the fourth richest man in China (Forbes, 2019).

in bribes and payments were distributed in order to secure television and media rights to broadcast major football events.

The FIFA scandals of this era are an important window into the seedy underworld where global sport media deals are sometimes consummated. Accusations of bribery and corruption in FIFA, particularly in relation to media rights, had dogged the organization for decades before arrests were made (Goldblatt, 2008). The charges levied by sovereign governments were somewhat surprising, inasmuch as many governments had seen fit to stay away from policing such deals in the past. FIFA still appears to be in a strong position with its ability to negotiate for higher levels of media rights compensation because the popularity of football across

Robert Cianflone/Getty Images

Similar to the IOC and Olympic Games, owning the right to authorize media companies to broadcast content of the World Cup or any of its proprietary tournaments generates billions in revenue for FIFA.

the globe has continued to increase. It remains to be seen whether the bribery scandals of the mid-2010s will force FIFA officials to conduct business without resorting to self-enrichment and bribery.

Olympics

While the popularity of football has positively benefited FIFA's coffers, another major international sporting event is struggling with issues of declining popularity in some parts of the globe. The IOC has spent the 2010s fighting off a sense of apathy toward both the summer and winter versions of the Olympic Games, in relation both to bids for hosting the Games and bids to secure media rights. Before the 2020 Summer Olympics in Tokyo, bids for media rights in populous parts of the world had not met the IOC's hopes or expectations. Star India declined its option to televise the 2020 Summer Olympics, and as of mid-2019 no other broadcasters in the country stepped up to match the rights fee of $20 million that was paid for the 2016 Summer Olympics in Rio de Janeiro (Sharma, 2018). Japan-based company Sony finally secured the rights for a reported $12 million (Fry, 2019). Television ratings for the 2016 Olympics in the United States declined considerably from 2012, with traditional television ratings for the opening ceremonies down 28 percent and average daily viewership across all platforms down 9 percent for the length of the Games (Holloway, 2016).

NBC, the longstanding broadcast partner for the Olympics in the United States, is still strongly committed to its relationship with the IOC. However, NBC noted after the 2016 Summer Olympics that achieving continued financial success with the Games would mean NBC will have to incorporate content delivery venues beyond the traditional linear television avenue that defined coverage for decades. The year 2016 saw NBC successfully expand into new areas, including a partnership with online content house Buzzfeed that extended Olympic coverage into the youth-oriented social network Snapchat and promotion of event highlights via social media for the first time (Holloway, 2016). This trend continued during coverage of the 2018 Winter Olympics in PyeongChang, South Korea, with NBC drawing praise for the quality of its online streaming coverage (VanDerWerff, 2018) and the decision to make all events viewable live online (Bucholtz & Fang, 2018).

The future of Olympics coverage is likely to be governed as much by the demands of savvy sport consumers and the changing realities of digital media delivery, as by any governing body. NBC's traditional approach to the Olympics has been to focus on storylines and drama relating almost exclusively to American athletes, at the expense of comprehensive coverage of events and any more than cursory attention paid to non-American participants. NBC's 2018 Olympics coverage appeared to move away from a purely American-focused approach (VanDerWerff, 2018), and it was the availability of digital delivery of Games coverage that helped to make that approach possible. As more consumers choose to eschew linear television and focus their consumption on digital delivery, it will be interesting to see whether NBC's coverage decisions continue to change.

Esports

Competitive video game playing, known colloquially as esports, may be the next frontier of sport media coverage. If so, then it promises to be a frontier unlike any that have existed to this point. The foundation of esports media coverage has been established by the corporate entities that create and promote the games, rather than by traditional or digital sport media entities. Corporations such as Blizzard Entertainment (*Hearthstone*; *Overwatch*; *World of Warcraft*), Riot Games (*League of Legends*), 2K Games (*NBA 2K*), and Electronic Arts (*FIFA*) have taken matters into their own hands, creating their own professional leagues as well as the digital video coverage to go with them.

The approach that Blizzard Entertainment has taken to its *Overwatch* title has been a noteworthy potential future template for the evolution of sport media governance. While the company partnered in 2018 with the ESPN/Disney group to broadcast select *Overwatch* matches (Hume, 2018), Blizzard's primary approach to delivering Overwatch League content is both global and Internet-focused. The company produces its own multicamera broadcasts of each match, streaming them via online services such as Amazon-owned Twitch, and providing native-language broadcasts for the Chinese, French, and Korean markets (Blizzard Entertainment, 2018). Blizzard Entertainment's new centerpiece studio for Overwatch League coverage is the same studio building that NBC used for years as the home of *The Tonight Show with Johnny Carson*. The venue features a 450-seat soundstage redressed into a gaming arena, plus state-of-the-art broadcast equipment, practice rooms for teams, and media rooms for journalists to interview gamers (Dachman, 2018).

There have been previous efforts by sport leagues to form their own content delivery services, such as the NFL forming its own network and broadcasting one live game on the channel each week. However, unlike a cable channel that is generally isolated to an individual country, Blizzard's streaming broadcasts of Overwatch League games can deliver the company's messaging and promotion across multiple audiences in multiple countries. While esports are still in their infancy, the potential global reach of these leagues and the control that their parent companies have thus far been able to maintain over their distribution and messaging could indicate a paradigm shift in terms of sport media governance.

Despite the efforts of governance entities such as the International Esports Federation (IeSF) to establish a global governance structure for esports, the realities of the industry still leave the governance of esports very much within the hands of game publishers. While there are still some questions as to whether esports will gain entry into the Olympic Games as medaled events, the explosive growth of esports poses the question whether the Olympics need esports more than esports need the Olympics. The popularity of esports, particularly in the Asian market, has led to notably large audience numbers for championship events. The 2018 *League of Legends* finals drew a total of 99.6 million global viewers at once, with concurrent viewing numbers rivaling the NFL's Super Bowl broadcast (Goslin, 2018).

PARTNERSHIPS BETWEEN MEDIA AND SPORT ENTITIES

The partnership between media and sport entities continues to evolve with advances in digital and mobile technologies, but television still ranks above all other media as the preferred viewing platform for live sporting events. Live sports accounted for 93 and 89 of the top 100 television shows in America in 2016 and 2018, respectively (Crupi, 2019; Smith, 2016).

Threats to U.S. sport-media partnerships resulting from trust-busting efforts of the early 20th century were intended to forbid industrialists and financiers from operating in anticompetitive ways. However, sport leagues have long been given special privileges by governments across North America and Europe to operate in ways that would likely be considered anticompetitive and monopolistic in other forms of enterprise.

Of the four major sports leagues in North America (i.e., MLB, NFL, NBA, NHL), only Major League Baseball enjoys a broad antitrust exemption, but all four major sports leagues enjoy exemption from antitrust laws in relation to negotiations for television broadcast rights, based on the **Sports Broadcasting Act** (1961). The federal government acknowledged with the passage of this code amendment that there were compelling financial reasons to allow franchises within sport leagues to pool their broadcast inventories, since the franchises were actually in business collaboration with one another, not competition. The act also was used for many years to justify the presence of blackout games, particularly within the NFL.

Broadcast Rights

Most sport organizations generate the majority of their revenues from sales of **broadcast rights**. These rights can take the form of exclusive partnerships with a sole media entity, a tiered or separated series of subpackages that are shared among several media partners, or a system where national media rights are sold separately from local media rights (Puppis, 2008). Table 9.2 provides examples of national and local or regional broadcast partners for various sport entities.

For most collegiate and professional leagues in the United States, local and national rights are sold as separate packages, largely due to the number of games in the league's yearly regular-season inventory. For instance, the 30 MLB teams each play 162 games a year, and most of those games appear only on local or regional television cable channels, called **regional sports networks** (RSNs).

Regional Sports Networks

RSNs are a major part of most professional sports teams' media exposure and revenue production in the United States. Exclusive broadcast rights granted to RSNs result in live game blackouts on national television stations and league-owned subscription-based networks due to FCC syndicated exclusivity rules. The market size of an RSN can often be the determining factor in whether a team is a "big market" or "small market" team. One of the largest U.S. sports franchises in terms of market size in North American sport, the New York Yankees, has reaped considerable financial benefit from its own branded RSN, Yankees Entertainment and Sports (YES) Network. YES has allowed the Yankees to generate revenues that far outpaced nearly every other MLB team, largely due to the nearly 300,000 households that tuned into each game, a number that was nearly double the next closest competitor (Bloom, 2018). In addition to audience numbers from its linear channel, the YES Network also experienced a significant increase in streaming audiences for games in 2018 (Fisher, 2018).

YES was estimated to be worth almost $4 billion in 2012 (Bloom, 2018), and the broadcasting deal that the Yankees struck with YES' then-majority owners FOX Sports guaranteed the team $85 million in broadcast revenue per year, plus a 5 percent increase every year until 2042 (Hoium, 2012). In spring 2019, the Yankees reportedly bought back majority ownership in YES from Disney-Fox for $3.47 billion (Ozanian, 2019).

Most RSNs in North America in the first two decades of the 21st century were controlled by two entities, FOX Sports and NBC Sports. In 2018, FOX Sports' parent company (News Corp) announced that it would be divesting itself of a variety of broadcast assets, including all of the FOX-controlled RSNs. Originally, these RSNs were sold to ESPN owner the Walt Disney Company, but the United States Justice Department forced Disney to sell off the territorial networks to satisfy regulatory and antitrust concerns (Flint & Gottfried, 2019). This governmental decision both highlighted the importance of RSNs to the sport media landscape and left their future ownership, as well as sports teams' revenue streams, in some degree of uncertainty.

National Football League

The NFL is the worldwide leader in revenue generated from broadcast contracts. Since every NFL game played is considered a part of the national

Table 9.2 Broadcast Partners for Selected Sport Entities in the United States

League	National broadcast partner	Local/regional broadcast partner
National Football League	FOX, CBS, NBC, ESPN	N/A
Major League Baseball	FOX, ESPN, Turner	Negotiated by teams
National Basketball Association	ESPN, Turner	Negotiated by teams
National Hockey League	NBC	Negotiated by teams
NCAA (Men's Basketball Tournament)	CBS	N/A
Big Ten Conference	FOX, ESPN, CBS, Big Ten Network	N/A
English Premier League (United States contract)	NBC	N/A

broadcasting contract, the NFL can apply considerable leverage in negotiations with broadcast entities. The NFL is also the only league in the United States that has live game broadcast partnerships with all four major sports broadcasting entities in the country (CBS, ESPN, FOX, and NBC). The league has consistently generated ever-larger deals with broadcast partners and is estimated to earn approximately $5 billion a year in revenue from its combined network contracts (Kaplan, 2018).

The landscape of media rights for NFL games is complex. For example, the Sunday afternoon broadcast rights for an interconference game are mostly dictated by whether the away team represents the American or National Football Conference (AFC or NFC) ("Creating the NFL Schedule," 2019). Adding to the complexity are FCC syndication exclusivity policies affecting blackouts in certain markets, teams sharing the same regional media market (e.g., New York Giants and Jets), and the addition of new media players such as Amazon's coveted space in streaming Thursday night NFL games (at least through 2019). Table 9.3 distinguishes the general broadcast patterns of NFL games based on media rights deals as of 2019.

National Collegiate Athletic Association

The National Collegiate Athletic Association (NCAA) is an interesting case study in the peculiar governance of sport media and revenue. Despite perceptions to the contrary, the NCAA does not control the television contracts of its member schools or conferences in most cases. While the NCAA once executed sole authority for broadcast schedules, a lawsuit that was heard by the United States Supreme Court struck down the NCAA's ability to negotiate contracts for all member schools (*National Collegiate Athletic Association v. Board of Regents of the University of Oklahoma, et al.,* 1984) and allowed schools and conferences to negotiate their own deals with broadcasters. Therefore, the NCAA in actuality makes no money from the most popular collegiate sporting event on the calendar, the College Football Playoff. Instead, the more than $470 million that the playoff generates annually from its contract with ESPN (Bachman, 2012) goes to the group that administers the playoff, a collection of athletic conferences that then distribute the money to their member schools.

The NCAA generates the vast majority of its revenue from one source, which is the broadcast contract and related marketing rights associated with the NCAA Division I Men's Basketball Tournament. The partnership for these rights that exists between CBS/Turner and the NCAA is worth approximately $850 million per year (Sherman, 2016), with an eight-year contract extension worth approximately $1.1 billion per year beginning in 2025 (Brady, 2016). Revenues from the tournament provide 86 percent of the NCAA's yearly operating budget (NCAA.org, n.d.).

Table 9.3 General Broadcast Patterns of NFL Games Based on Media Partnerships

Fox	NFC regional Sunday afternoon games Thursday night games Most NFC postseason games Thanksgiving game Super Bowls 2020, 2023, 2026
CBS	AFC regional Sunday afternoon games Most AFC postseason games Thanksgiving game Super Bowls 2022, 2025, 2028
NBC	National Sunday night game Thursday night games Two postseason games Super Bowls 2021, 2024, 2027
ABC	2019 NFL Draft Pro Bowl games
ESPN	National Monday night games (through 2021) One postseason game Pro Bowl game
Amazon	11 NFL games live streamed (at least through 2019)
NFL Network	NFL London games Thursday night game simulcast

Conflicts of Interest

The issue of conflicts of interest in sport media is a governance issue worthy of consideration. Challenges from the business side of the media rights landscape affect both the journalistic practices and integrity of media outlets. The web of interlocking financial deals for broadcast rights leaves many national newsrooms in a quandary regarding coverage of teams and leagues. Companies such as ESPN are not strictly entertainment channels; they also act as sources of journalism, news gathering, and investigative reporting. ESPN, in particular, built its reputation as the "Worldwide Leader in Sports" in part for its high-quality journalistic coverage of the sports world (Miller & Shales, 2011).

ESPN's investigative journalism has at times negatively affected the corporation's relationships with some of its broadcast partners, most notably the NFL. The partnership between the league and the network deteriorated throughout the 2010s, in part due to ESPN's coverage of issues related to health and safety concerns for players, handling of player protests, and other areas the league deemed sensitive (Ourand, 2018). ESPN and parent company Disney were concerned enough about the relationship that new ESPN president Jimmy Pitaro pledged to reset the interactions between the league and the network (Draper, 2018b). According to sport media observers, ESPN's coverage of the NFL throughout the 2018 season appeared to be driven less by conflict and more by a desire to get along with the league (Simmons, 2018).

Conflict of interest issues in sport media have even extended down to the local level. Given the rocky financial climate in sport media with many newspapers struggling to avoid bankruptcy, advertising and circulation have grown in importance. Many local newspapers rely on sports fans as a key audience demographic due to their consistent interest in their favorite teams. In return, many sports teams are aware of this loyalty and can routinely exercise a level of access control that media members on other beats would find difficult to believe. Public relations departments carefully guard access to collegiate and professional athletes, coaches, and team personnel. Reporters who fail to abide by rules of access are often denied press credentials to cover games in person. Most sports journalists still practice good quality journalism, but they can face pressure from their own business and editorial staffs to maintain cordial relationships with team personnel at the expense of pursuing uncomfortable stories. The situation has been further exacerbated by the emergence of official team media, allowing major college and professional sports entities to bypass local media entirely if they so desire.

DIGITAL AND EMERGING MEDIA IN SPORTS

Sport media operate as a subset of the broader news and entertainment media, and that has been true in both traditional media and in digital and emerging media. As social networks emerged in the early part of the 21st century, sports played varying roles in the development of content and consumers. In some cases, sport media developed their own niches, and occasionally sport media acted as a leading audience attraction on certain media platforms.

The sport media industry is similar to other media sectors that are evolving from a physical domain to a digital economy, where consumers often create and publish their own content. This self-publishing landscape is filled with major challenges for governance issues related to illegal file sharing, piracy, and copyright infringement, whether intentional or accidental.

According to a Bloomberg report, there are over 20 million requests a week on Google web search engines to remove web links to copyright-protected material (Mola & Ovide, 2016). In 2016, a central repository noted complaints of copyright infringement applicable to over 1.5 billion websites (Mola & Ovide, 2016). According to the 1998 **Digital Millennium Copyright Act**, companies are required to remove copyrighted material belonging to the rightful owner. When receiving notices of copyright violations, large Internet companies such as Facebook and YouTube often proceed to remove content without seeking permission from the person who published the material.

Due to the newness of digital and emerging media, traditional governance structures such as those found in broadcast and print ownership rules enforced by governments have not yet developed. Instead, the governance of these new media environments has been dictated by industry trends, audience affinities, and the suitability of certain technologies.

Net Neutrality

Complicating the sport media landscape even further has been the advent of high-speed Internet and mobile connectivity, the accompanying growth of social media, and online consumption of news and entertainment. While the World Wide Web was introduced in 1992, the importance of online sport media was minimal at best for the first 15 or so years following that date. Internet connections were slow, desktop-bound, and lacking infrastructure, since nearly all major aspects of sport media were still focused on traditional media channels such as printed newspapers, magazines, radio, and television.

However, the widespread growth of high-speed Internet in the early 2000s improved the quality and variety of available media content that consumers could access digitally. Instead of dial-up modem speeds restricting stories to words and an occasional photograph, high-speed Internet allowed for the transmission of data-rich media content such as audio and video.

By the end of the first decade of the 2000s, mobile devices had further enhanced the attractiveness of online sport media. The introduction of the iPhone in 2007 (Silver, 2018) created a new world for sport media, one where pictures, sounds, and videos were not only digitally accessible, but portable. As sales of the iPhone and its competitor phones spiked over the next decade, digital sport media in all forms became increasingly important to consumers and media companies alike. Organizations asserted regulations such as blogging policies and social network guidelines to monitor the online behavior of employees (Linke & Zerfass, 2013).

During the 2010s, a policy debate developed concerning the way in which Internet service providers and cellular phone companies should be required to handle the transmission of data. The **net neutrality** conversation has confused a great many people, often because of deliberate misinformation spread by parties to the debate.

In simple terms, the concept of net neutrality is that all data should be treated equally on the Internet by Internet service providers (ISPs) and that companies should not be allowed to favor certain types of content, or content from certain providers, over content provided by others. Supporters of net neutrality argue that this equality of content has been a building block of the success of digital media over its first few decades of development, with consumers able to access data across platforms and content providers with ease. Internet service providers and major content providers, however, have argued that net neutrality stifles innovation and consumer choice (Geller, 2015).

Net neutrality affects sport media in important ways. Access to any digital sport media content is made through an ISP, either via a high-speed Internet subscription or through a mobile phone data plan. The absence of net neutrality creates the possibility that one of these data providers could choose to block or restrict access to another company's content because it rivals the content being provided by that data company or its business partners. Hypothetically, the lack of net neutrality protections could allow a company like Verizon as a mobile data provider to partner with the NFL and allow privileged status to streaming video from that entity, while throttling or restricting access by consumers to streaming video from other professional leagues.

The FCC's position on net neutrality became a highly partisan issue during the last half of the 2010s, with a Barack Obama administration–appointed FCC chairman designating the Internet as a public telecommunications service under Title II of the Communications Act of 1934 (Ruiz, 2015). Two years later, a Donald Trump administration–appointed FCC chairman moved to roll back those protections, with the repeal of those rules taking effect in 2018.

It is uncertain what the future holds for net neutrality, but it is worth noting that sport media entities continue to expand into the digital media space, with large organizations such as ESPN launching subscription streaming services containing access to wide swaths of content (Ha, 2019). As streaming services continue to expand, particular media and entertainment trends have become apparent. These market trends are described in table 9.4.

Social Media

It feels as if **social media** have been around for decades, but in reality, many of the major social networks are still relatively young. Facebook, Instagram, Snapchat, and Twitter have made considerable inroads into popular culture and sport media, but of the four, Facebook is by far the oldest, and it only dates back to 2004 (Bellis, 2019).

As a result, there is very little in the way of official governance or regulation of social media activities beyond general behavior-related policies and guidelines (Linke & Zerfass, 2013). Social networks are used by a variety of sport participants and stakeholders: by sport teams generating their own content, sport media companies looking to connect with younger audiences, athletes leveraging their own brands in conversation with audiences, and corporations designing content to attract

Table 9.4 Market Trends From the Growth of Streaming Sport Services

Trend	Description
The emergence of vMVPDs	Virtual multichannel video programming distributors (vMVPDs) like DirectTV Now, Sling TV, and YouTube TV now hold about 20 percent of the U.S. subscriber market (Engleson, 2018).
The rise of cord-shaving	A million U.S. viewers recently replaced their multichannel subscription services with more streamlined solutions. Nimble media companies will seize the chance to leverage this emerging demand.
The growth of targeted advertising	Pockets of innovation regarding data analytics and personalization are appearing on web landing pages. Look for media and entertainment companies to start augmenting customer information with social media.
Increased attention to virtual and augmented reality	Augmented and virtual reality technologies will gain traction for their ability to enhance storytelling as media companies seek to differentiate their content.

attention and purchase intentions from sport consumers. There is very little distinction between the groups when it comes to the types of messages used. Instead, the content of messages within sport media on social networks is largely dictated by the nature of the networks themselves. For instance, attempts to reach young audiences generally use Snapchat, videos or photos are pushed out on Instagram, and attempts to get the attention of sport media use Twitter.

Facebook, the largest of the social networks with a global audience of more than two billion users, started to come under severe scrutiny by several governments in the late 2010s, including the United States government. These concerns dealt with Facebook's privacy practices and the distribution of so-called "fake news," among other issues (Newcomb, 2018).

Given the popularity and ubiquity of social networks, it would not be surprising to see federal governance of content become a reality. In the interim, policing of social media is the responsibility of multiple entities, not least is the affiliation of the producer. As media platforms become more interconnected, regulations and policies for social media behavior in the sports industry will continue to evolve. Governance in Action 9.3 provides information on policies enacted to regulate social media behavior in intercollegiate athletics and the Olympics.

Official Team Sites and In-House Coverage

Consumers may respond to sport media coverage anywhere on the spectrum from positively to negatively (Linden, 2012). However, the media's influence over public opinion is not as strong as it once was. Previously, the media's profit motive

sometimes led to outlets giving more attention to stories that were out of the ordinary, or had a hint of scandal (Weis, 1986). Additionally, while traditional media previously enjoyed a closer relationship with sport organizations, those organizations' autonomy from standard media norms and coverage has greatly increased (Grimmer & Kian, 2013). Now, sport organizations can create their own media (Dittmore, Stoldt, & Greenwell, 2008), thus causing traditional media organizations to look to change their approach.

Organizational media can take a variety of forms, from the aforementioned full-broadcast approach that Blizzard Entertainment uses for Overwatch League to smaller-scale approaches that involve a combination of Internet and social media outlets. Most major professional teams in the developed world now use in-house writers, social media specialists, broadcasters, and production personnel, with the aim of producing content that directly targets the team's fans, and which takes advantage of access to athletes, coaches, and personnel that is not regularly granted to outside media entities.

Concurrently, sport organizations also have used both traditional media and their own media to promote a positive image outside the playing venue. Professional franchises in particular have sought to increase awareness of their efforts in corporate social responsibility (McGowan & Mahon, 2009). As sport organizations worldwide add more staff in response to such challenges as growing competition and higher expectations of organizational responsibility (Siegfrida, Schlesinger, Baylec, & Giauqued, 2015; Weinberg, 2012), it follows that they will attempt to control their messaging as well. In this vein, for a professional sport franchise seeking a symbiotic relationship with the mainstream media was often a main goal. This was especially true for

Regulating Social Media: The IOC and NCAA

In the current state of digitally networked communication, many issues have arisen related to data security, cyberstalking, and consumer protection. With so many instant and unfiltered platforms available on which to share content, universities, high schools, sport governing bodies, and even the IOC have enacted measures to regulate social media behavior for both pragmatic and ethical reasons.

The IOC publishes social and digital media guidelines for people accredited with the Games. The guidelines restrict the posting of content that intrudes upon the privacy of others, infringes upon intellectual property rights, discloses confidential information, interferes with competition or ceremonies, or violates security (International Olympic Committee, 2017). For any infringement, the IOC (2017) may require removal of content or, depending on the circumstances, it may withdraw accreditation rights, pursue legal action, or impose sanctions "pursuant to the Olympic Charter" (p. 3).

The most controversial application of IOC guidelines is Rule 40 of the Olympic Charter restricting Olympians from using their name or image for advertising purposes during the Games. Violating the endorsement blackout can result in disqualification or stripping an athlete of his or her medal. The IOC (2011) also restricts general social media content that includes swearing, defamatory statements, criminal or immoral behavior, information from an ongoing legal case, or destructive spamming, harassment, or racism.

The NCAA, another private actor exerting its power in the ever-evolving digital media space, has been inundated each year with legislative proposals to amend social media policies published in the association's annual bylaws. NCAA (2018a) rules address content permitted on social media platforms generated by student-athletes, prospective student-athletes, and recruiting or scouting services (e.g., reposting, sharing, endorsing, tagging, retweeting, and following accounts). In 2019, legislation proposed by the NCAA (2018a) Division III membership requested exceptions to rules that restricted accepting a Facebook friend request, liking a post, or inviting a prospective student-athlete to connect on LinkedIn.

The NCAA's objective for regulating social media behavior is primarily to maintain privacy boundaries for prospective student-athletes before they commit to a university. However, per Bylaw 13.4.1.5.1, the NCAA (2018b) does not restrict the use of social media for publicizing camp information, provided the correspondence does not include recruiting language or solicit particular persons to attend a camp or clinic. Rules addressing social media use in recruiting and marketing from the NCAA, a member conference, or a member institution will continue to appear convoluted, begging for continuous scrutinization and modification, especially since self-reporting of infractions is the current system of enforcement.

As private associations with the freedom to manage their own internal affairs, the NCAA and IOC have the legal right to govern social media behavior by member institutions and federations. However, the protectionist nature of the social media rules gives the impression of organizations acting as authoritarian machines rather than as associations promoting education or sporting values (Hernandez, 2013, p. 66).

newer franchises that were trying to become better known and to create a positive image (Jensen & Sosa, 2008).

Until the rise in recent years of in-house media outlets, a major aspect of sport organizations' efforts to control their narratives has been the press conference, during which a leader or someone in authority presents information in the organiza-tions' preferred tone and manner (Kurtz, 2017). For instance, one such press conference took place after the NBA brawl between the Indiana Pacers and Detroit Pistons, later known as the Malice at the Palace (Abrams, 2012). In that press conference, NBA commissioner David Stern tried to counter negative media and fan narratives about NBA athletes by sending a message that strict punishment would be imposed, and the league would commence with a renewed sense of discipline and professionalism (Kurtz, 2017). However, such press conferences have largely disappeared from the media landscape. Concurrent with the rise of in-house media, the increased prominence of social media has diminished the importance of traditional media for sports coverage (Grimmer & Kian, 2013), and organizations can now take their messages directly to interested parties without holding large official press events. With the ongoing rise of online communication technologies, organizations can and will bypass traditional media completely, forging their own connections with the public (Dittmore, Stoldt, & Greenwell, 2008).

Research has indicated that negative coverage may affect not only fan perceptions, but also the psyche of athletes (Kristiansen, Roberts, & Sisjord, 2012). With content created by the organization itself, negative media coverage would likely differ from previous media models, which may have been more critical of individuals in the organization. Such criticism, which can lead athletes to seek coping mechanisms (Kristiansen, Roberts, & Sisjord, 2012), would be much less likely under a model in which the organization produced media content that an athlete might consume. Media attention to sport, including both on- and off-field events and the societal implications of such events as well as sport itself, could include apologetic coverage as well as more critical coverage (Fink, Borland, & Fields, 2010).

The exclusivity of broadcasting contracts and the effect that exclusivity can have on sports consumers' access to events (Hoehn & Lancefield, 2003) also create opportunities for organizations to offer their own in-house media coverage for fans who are otherwise shut out of organizational information. In addition, the use of social media by individual athletes has also affected the continued viability of traditional media (Sanderson, Snyder, Hull, & Gramlich, 2015). However, even in-house social media in sport organizations including by employees or athletes has suggested the need for oversight, as one of the challenges organizations face from social media comes when people in the organization post without oversight (Sanderson et al., 2015).

SPORTS JOURNALISTS

While the mission and responsibility of mainstream news media are understood, sports journalism has at times been dismissed as being less important than regular news coverage (Garrison & Salwen, 1989). However, the stories within sport (e.g., perseverance, hard work, community values) provide a striking example of how media can, through storytelling, make noteworthy points and influence perceptions (Oates & Pauly, 2007).

Organizations for Sport Media Members

Professional organizations provide a context for addressing credibility and journalistic ethics. Most of these organizations have evolved to incorporate the new age of digital media, which are the least restrictive in terms of censorship. Three examples are the Associated Press, the National Association of Broadcasters, and Public Relations Society of America.

Associated Press

Founded in the 19th century, the Associated Press (AP) has thrived for more than a century based on cooperation between media outlets, with this roster having evolved to incorporate social media platforms. Originally, by offering newspapers the advantages of sharing coverage, travel costs were reduced, and news could travel more quickly than before, helped along by the development of the telegraph (Silberstein-Loeb, 2012).

Shortly after forming in the 1970s, the Associated Press Sports Editors (APSE) organization created a code of ethics. This code, enacted in 1975 and revised in 1991, makes clear the professional conditions that sports journalists are expected to abide by. Hardin (2005b) found that often that code is largely ignored as media outlets engage in coverage that is closer to an expression of fandom than to objective journalism. The APSE's directives are often set aside when it comes to sports journalists accepting gifts from a sport organization; however, journalists did report engaging in discussions about journalistic ethics (Hardin, 2005b). In addition, newspaper journalists of all backgrounds have experienced noteworthy levels of job dissatisfaction and burnout (Reinardy, 2011), possibly adding to a reluctance to adhere to a set of codes when individuals are consumed by the day-to-day challenges of the profession.

In 1926, the Associated Press hired its first female reporter, with seven more following by 1931. Sports coverage created by reporters Lorena Hickok and Marguerite Young included boxing, tennis, and swimming (Watts, 2013). More recently, Hardin and Shain (2007) noted that a desire to challenge accepted norms is prevalent among female sports journalists. Research has indicated that the depictions of race and gender in the mainstream sport media have a noteworthy effect on audience perceptions (Kurtz, 2017; van Sterkenberg, Knoppers, & de Leeuw, 2010; van Sterkenberg & Spaaij, 2015). Sports editors have long served as gatekeepers in sports journalism, and with a lack of diversity in that gatekeeping position, women's sports have often received limited coverage (Hardin, 2005a).

Representation of women and minorities among sports journalists has historically been lower than their Caucasian male counterparts (Claringbould, Knoppers, & Elling, 2004). Aware of this, the APSE commissioned a regular study by the Institute for Diversity and Ethics in Sport on AP organizations' hiring practices. The 2014 edition gave a C-plus grade for race-related hiring patterns and a failing (F) mark for gender-related hiring (Lapchick et al., 2014). Four years later, gender-related hiring remained at F, while race-related hiring improved to a B grade (Lapchick et al., 2018). Considering these numbers, the comparative lack of women and minorities in sports journalism has been countered by initiatives such as revised hiring practices and targeted educational programs in an attempt to increase the number of women and minorities in sports media (Claringbould, Knoppers, & Elling, 2004).

National Association of Broadcasters

The National Association of Broadcasters (NAB) represents broadcasting interests in the United States. Similar to the Associated Press, the NAB imposes ethical guidelines on its constituents. Prior to a successful 1979 lawsuit brought by the U.S. Department of Justice, the NAB had instructed television stations to avoid advertisements for items such as hard liquor and weapons, and it also restricted the time allotted for any kind of advertising (Hull, 1990). This code, enacted in 1952, was meant to counter growing concerns about the accessibility of potentially questionable content on the airwaves. The federal government had already banned the airing of ads for smoking and tobacco products in 1970 (Glass, 2018), and it won suspension of the original NAB code restricting airtime (Limberg, 1989).

Television has been a massive driver of decision making in U.S. college sports. Seeking larger television rights deals for conference title games and attractive in-season matchups has been a significant aspect of conference realignment (Weaver, 2013). In 1984, the U.S. Supreme Court ruled in favor of the University of Oklahoma and the University of Georgia, which sought to replace the NCAA's policy of controlling all broadcast rights for Division I teams (Mawson & Bowler, 1989). Having gained control of their television rights, conferences looked to create more enticing games to create viewer—and thus, broadcaster—demand. Broadcast rights for each of the major conferences now garner hundreds of millions of dollars from their respective television broadcast partners (Weaver, 2013).

Similar to the college football power conferences, local television stations also negotiate financial arrangements, called retransmission consent, for their signals to be carried (Smith, 2012). As an example of the type of money involved in sports programming, sports broadcasting giant ESPN helped establish **carriage fees** for connectivity rights to content that is considered proprietary for each cable or satellite network. ESPN continues to charge more than $8 per month per cable subscriber (Wile, 2017).

Public Relations Society of America

As with AP and the NAB, the Public Relations Society of America (PRSA) also has a code of ethics identifying the behaviors in which a practitioner must engage ("Code of Ethics," 2000). The PRSA code of ethics was first enacted in 1950, and it has undergone changes throughout the years, with the latest complete revision (amendments still occur) occurring in 2000 (Fitzpatrick, 2002a). However, even with the research and creation of new guidelines, questions remain. In the wake of the establishment of the current PRSA code of ethics, some scholars have expressed concern about the code's strength considering the difficulty of enforcement (Fitzpatrick, 2002b; Parkinson, 2001).

A specific organization exists for public relations professionals working in American collegiate sport. Under the umbrella of the National Association of Collegiate Directors of Athletics (NACDA), the College Sports Information Directors of America (CoSIDA) provides its members with a code of ethics, yearly conventions for the sharing of work and ideas, and professional development resources ("Our Organization: What Is CoSIDA?" 2019).

While public relations once involved creating messaging and events in order to disseminate information, often through the mass media, public relations practitioners can now go straight to their target audiences through their online presence (Capriatti & Moreno, 2007). Positive messages can be created much more efficiently through online channels, with this mode of communication forming an essential aspect of an organization's overall strategy (Steyn & Niemann, 2014). As media have evolved to incorporate a wider spectrum of digital and mobile platforms, CoSIDA has also evolved its delivery of best practices for streaming and sharing athletics-related content (Syme, 2014).

Another aspect of public relations is **media training**, or the coaching of potential interview subjects to deal with media inquiries and to stay within organizational messaging when dealing with the media. One aspect of training is to keep individuals from sharing anything the organization does not want revealed; notably, interview subjects often do as much preparation as the journalists making the inquiry (Smudde, 2004). Considering this, the need for media training at all levels of the sport industry is significant. For example, prior to the 2019 NFL draft, Turnkey Intelligence, a division of Turnkey Sports, developed an analytical tool for the NFL that profiled the social media behavior of the top 100 draft prospects. The 2019 report indicated that 60 percent of draft picks used derogatory (curse) words, 19 percent had insinuated alcohol and drug use, and one prospect deleted 11,500 social posts (Kahler, 2019). In an effort to minimize or eliminate these types of issues, media training has become routine in high school athletics, intercollegiate athletics, and sport federations.

Emerging Media and Implications for Journalists

Even as print and broadcast media navigate a world in which social media have become a force, the landscape continues to change in unexpected ways. The Athletic, an online venture that started in 2015 behind tens of millions of dollars in venture capital and with the official mantra of "In-depth storytelling that goes beyond game recaps" (TheAthletic.com), has established individualized sites for more than 45 cities, including virtually every major- and minor-league sports town in the United States. The site has hired local reporters away from their previous outlets at a high rate, with most of those hires penning a "Why I'm joining The Athletic" personal essay (Draper, 2018a). In an indicator of ongoing media trends, The Athletic has at times withstood criticism, as one of its founders declared a plan to outlast newspapers and poach their talent (Draper, 2017). In addition, The Athletic's hiring practices have been questioned, primarily because most of its writers are Caucasian men, which advances the practice of white males dominating sectors of the sports industry (Draper, 2018a; Phillips, 2017).

As stated previously, social media can be used by organizations and individuals to bypass traditional media platforms, with fans often visiting team Facebook or Twitter pages rather than more traditional media outlets (Burk, Grimmer, & Pawlowski, 2016). However, as social media outlets have further gained popularity, it has become clear that sports journalists can also have a symbiotic relationship with social media. Reporters can use these media as an essential part of their overall coverage and communication (Nolleke, Grimmer, & Horky, 2017), as well as for live blogging of sporting events (McEnnis, 2016). Journalists' use of social media also may include newsgathering in addition to information distribution (Reed, 2013), utilizing the many-to-many communication aspect of social media outlets.

RECAP

With media and entertainment revenues expected to top $800 billion in 2019, there remains a need for governance as media outlets and technology continue to develop. A shrinking number of conglomerates own most of the major media outlets in the United States, with those outlets in turn controlling most of the sports broadcasting. In addition, some sports entities, including teams and leagues, have created their own television networks, and they engage in their own media production through online distribution methods.

Concurrently, major sport organizations and television networks have entered into partnerships that have resulted in the sports entities exerting control over the coverage provided by those broadcast partners. Further emerging and developing technologies such as esports and social media have added more options for consumers trying to navigate through the various available messages.

The mainstream sport media establishment continues to claim its place in the firmament, with the need for governance stronger than ever before. Organizations including the Associated Press Sports Editors (print and broadcast media), the National Association of Broadcasters, and the Public Relations Society of America serve as these governing bodies. In addition to other support and responsibilities, these organizations create professional codes of ethics for media creators and practitioners.

Critical Thinking Questions

1. Is it important for media companies to have governance? Why or why not?
2. Should it matter to consumers whether broadcasters engage in a partnership with a professional sport league?
3. What are the potential benefits of continued media consolidation under an ever-shrinking number of conglomerates? What are the potential dangers?
4. How often should a media governing body's code of ethics be updated?
5. What are the potential benefits and pitfalls of sport organizations creating their own messages through online media?

Applied Activities

PR Practitioner Critically Examining the PRSA Code of Ethics

Examine the Public Relations Society of America's current code of ethics, established in 2000 and available at https://www.prsa.org/ethics/. Playing the role of a PR and media relations practitioner for a National Hockey League organization, examine and discuss the code with an eye to how it may apply to a sport position. What remains relevant? What should be changed? Should there be a separate code for sports?

Can the Ideal Broadcaster–League Partnership Exist?

Based on media ethics and governance, determine what an ideal sport media partnership with a sport league would look like. Compare and contrast the largest known sport media–sport league partnerships. For instance, ESPN and the College Football Playoff, CBS/NBC/ESPN/Fox/Amazon and the National Football League, ESPN and the NBA, NBC and the Olympics, FOX Sports and FIFA, and ESPN/Fox and Major League Baseball. Does the ideal partnership exist among these? Can it exist in today's media and financial world?

chapter 10

Sporting Goods and Sport Licensing

Daniel A. Rascher and Mark S. Nagel

LEAD-OFF

Governance of the sporting goods and sport licensing industry in an open global marketplace presents challenges for executives in all levels of business. From human rights issues in overseas manufacturing to government-imposed tariffs and the efforts to protect intellectual property, the scope of governance issues facing professionals in the sporting goods and licensing industry is vast. In the sporting goods industry, there are no true oversight organizations like the International Olympic Committee, which is the supreme authority for all entities in the Olympic movement. Only trade organizations advocating prudent business practices operate within the sporting goods and sport licensing industry, and they have little or no authority to enforce their actions.

Notwithstanding economic or political interference, the industry is largely a complex system of designers, manufacturers, intermediaries, merchandisers, and retailers that work in an orchestrated fashion to meet consumer demands. The sporting goods industry is also a global industry, which adds complexity to efforts to address governance issues over legal and ethical threats to consumer protection, intellectual property protection, or employee rights. Regardless of one's place of residence, it should never be assumed that the laws of one jurisdiction apply to another. Even though most governments understand that intellectual property must be protected so that creativity is fostered and rewarded, or that employee and consumer rights must be safeguarded, there continue to be concerns about lax intellectual property and labor laws in some countries.

Accountability, oversight, and engaged executives are critical governance elements for a company or brand. These activities are essential for all players in the sporting goods supply chain, whether domestic or foreign entities. Compliance largely involves either legislative efforts or self-regulation through trade associations and conduct codes. Organizations that regulate themselves must follow processes and procedures to guarantee adherence to legal protections of intellectual property, consumer rights, and general government stipulations, such as ensuring that taxes are collected or products meet federal safety and environmental guidelines.

This chapter examines the size and scope of the sporting goods industry in the United States and around the world. It also examines sport licensing and protection measures for intellectual property. The chapter will also address regulatory measures through legislation (for consumer protection and intellectual property protection) and self-regulation with an overview of codes of conduct and the activities of several national and international trade associations.

Learning Outcomes

- Define the size and scope of the three primary sectors of the sporting goods industry.
- Explain how sporting goods manufacturers deal with lax labor laws in developing countries where many production facilities are located.
- Identify components of intellectual property in the sport licensing industry and ways to protect them from counterfeiters.
- Identify industry practices retailers and manufacturers use to comply with consumer protection regulations in the sporting goods industry.
- Explain self-regulation strategies that go beyond legal compliance in the sporting goods industry.

SIZE AND SCOPE OF THE SPORTING GOODS INDUSTRY

The global sporting goods industry grew by 3.9 percent in 2015 to reach $222 billion (in sales), and it generated a compound annual growth rate (CAGR) of 4.5 percent from 2011 through 2015, with the Asia-Pacific market growing the fastest during the period (Marketline, 2016). The United States accounted for approximately 30 percent of that market share. Similar growth is expected going forward, with global sales estimates for 2020 reaching $281 billion. About two-thirds of sales globally occur through specialty sports retailers (e.g., Dick's Sporting Goods). Nearly 10 percent of global sporting goods sales occur online, and the remaining sales are through general retailers (e.g., Walmart).

An example of a recent lucrative activity in the industry is Nike's 2015 announcement of a lifetime endorsement deal with NBA star LeBron James. Though specifics of the deal were not formally announced, it was believed to easily exceed the 10-year, $300 million contract Nike had signed with Kevin Durant in 2014 (Rovell, 2015). James' representatives insinuated that the overall value of the deal exceeded $1 billion (Connolly, 2016). As one of the industry's leading producers and marketers of athletic shoes and apparel, Nike hoped that LeBron's lifetime deal would help cement its place as the dominant brand not only for total sales but also in cultural relevance. James, regarded as not only the best player but also the most impactful active player-endorser of the last 15 years, has had a significant impact upon the sporting goods industry, though he pales in influence compared to Michael Jordan.

In 2015, the Air Jordan shoe sold eight times more than James' signature shoe, which contributed to a 58 percent market share of the $4.2 billion U.S. basketball shoe market (Badenhausen, 2015). With billions of dollars at stake, companies continue to try to identify the "next" Jordan or James to capture the world's attention and lead to significant sales of shoes that only a small percentage of purchasers actually use to play the sport for which they are designed. These endorsement deals are part of a licensed sporting goods market that is dominated by professional basketball players, in large part because basketball shoes are fashionable to be worn anytime, not just while playing basketball. Baseball players, for instance, can also have signature baseball cleat deals, but the total size of that market is relatively small, and thus those deals are not typically substantial.

Though basketball shoes and other related products often grab the largest headlines, the sporting goods landscape is quite large and diverse in terms of the types of products included. It encompasses not only shoes, but also golf clubs, equipment for fishing, skiing, and ball sports, sports apparel, video games, home décor (logo products), and sport-themed toys, among other items for professional athletes, Olympians, the weekend warrior, the occasional jogger, the yoga mom, and the youth baseball player.

Demand for sporting goods is largely based on consumer interests, but other factors can affect both supply and demand. For example, the Great Depression, a recession, and the U.S. stock market crash in 2008 are economic events that can have a significant impact on sales and production. Governing authorities may decide to significantly decrease production of certain sporting goods during a financial crisis if products are perceived as luxury items, while others may maintain or even increase the production of products perceived to be substitutes for more expensive products on the market.

Another factor driving demand for sporting goods is the changing interests of different demographics, which motivates producers to develop new product lines or increase production. Governance in Action 10.1 explores the enhanced focus on the market for women's sport products, which has contributed to industry growth both online and in stores.

Sporting Goods Industry Sectors

The sporting goods industry is typically divided into three broad categories: (1) footwear, (2)

GOVERNANCE IN ACTION 10.1

Sporting Goods Manufacturers Recognizing Women as a Key Demographic

For most of the first part of the 20th century, formal women's sports programs barely existed in most countries around the world, and a handful of nations such as Saudi Arabia didn't offer females any athletic opportunities. However, women's sports participation began to increase rapidly in the 1970s and 1980s. In the United States, the passage of Title IX in 1972 prohibited gender discrimination in education, including sport. Though its impact in college and high school sports was initially minimal, by the 1980s the legislation was strengthened, additional laws were enacted, and court decisions routinely favored enhancing women's sports. Around the world, countries began to embrace greater athletic opportunities for women. The Olympic Games greatly expanded women's competitions in the 1980s and enacted a rule in 1991 that mandated any new sports applying for Olympic recognition must offer women's events ("Key Dates in the History," n.d.). As the 21st century began, women's sport opportunities increased dramatically. At the 2016 Rio Olympics, 45 percent of the competitors were women (Chitrakorn, 2017).

Today, while it is common to see females compete in amateur and professional sports, the sporting goods manufacturing industry still has not designed enough products to meet the needs of women. Sport industry analyst Matt Powell noted, "In the past, women had to take the hand-me-downs from the men's wardrobe and make them work" (Chitrakorn, 2017, para. 2). That approach appears to be rapidly changing. In 2018, Reebok launched a campaign specifically targeting women and increased its female-targeted offerings across a number of product categories (Mahoney, 2018). According to Erich Joachimsthaler, CEO of branding agency Vivaldi, Nike, long known for being "very male, macho" (Thomas, 2019, para. 7), focused numerous sponsorship and product development initiatives on women's sport. In 2019, the company created and marketed dozens of new styles of sports bras in extended sizes and added a new line of yoga pants. It also launched the "Dream Crazier" campaign using prominent female athletes to spur interest in female participation in sport . . . and Nike sport-related products.

Interest in the female consumer by leading sporting goods manufacturers such as Nike, Reebok, and Under Armour has been spurred, in part, by the success of women-focused activewear brands such as Lululemon, Sweaty Betty, Ultracor, and Outdoor Voices (Chitrakorn, 2017). Those competing brands have been successful in designing products that are both functional and stylish for female consumers. As sporting goods for women continue to evolve and expand, manufacturers are noting the importance of "speaking to" the female consumer as a unique customer base, distinct from men. Amy Montagne, general manager of Global Nike Women's, indicated, "Our women's business is one of the categories that we're supercharging and putting more resources against," while her counterpart at Under Armour noted, "It's an area you'll see us accelerating and evolving into . . ." (Chitrakorn, 2017, para. 6 & 9). Clearly, knowing and understanding the needs and interests of women will be a critical component of the sporting goods manufacturing industry in the future.

apparel, and (3) equipment. Within each sector of the sporting goods industry, different products have varying growth rates.

Footwear

Within the sport shoe or footwear industry, the running and jogging sector exceeded $3 billion in sales in 2017, but it has grown at only a 1 percent rate since 2012, according to the National Sporting Goods Association (Sport Market Analytics, n.d.). On the other hand, over the same time frame, the market for soccer shoes grew about 2.5 percent per year to reach about $235 million. As shown in table 10.1, though many shoe categories increased sales at a high rate, others largely stalled, and some actually declined in overall sales. Since 2005, overall athletic footwear sales in the United States have grown nearly 3.1 percent per year to over $22 billion (Sport Market Analytics, n.d.).

Apparel

According to a company in Germany providing data and statistics for over 600 industries, U.S. sports apparel sales in 2017 were $73.9 billion (Statista, 2018). The global sport marketplace is said to be dominated by a "strong" demand for apparel featuring professional franchises (PRNewswire, 2016a). Teams in the NBA, Premier League, and Major League Baseball (MLB) have grown a worldwide fan base who will purchase logoed apparel (as well as merchandise). A number of other leagues have also increased their licensed merchandise sales both domestically and internationally. The United States, Europe, and the Asia-Pacific region are the geographic territories with the largest consumer base for sport licensed apparel (PRNewswire, 2016a).

Recent sales of selected product types in the U.S. sports apparel market are shown in Table 10.2. Similar to the footwear market, the rates of growth vary by category, with the golf apparel market shrinking, but running and jogging apparel are expanding. Not shown are yoga and cycling apparel, which have grown at 3.85 percent (CAGR) and 2.8 percent (CAGR), respectively.

Equipment

Sports equipment is the third primary area of the sporting goods industry. The changes in consumer interests and tastes are indicated by the sale of various types of equipment over time. For example, in the United States, bicycling and bowling equipment sales have decreased since 2012, exercise equipment and soccer ball sales have increased, and fishing tackle sales have remained essentially stagnant (see table 10.3).

The global sports equipment market is fueled by the increase in international sporting events (e.g., Olympics, World Beach Games, Commonwealth Games), which is expected to increase the demand for sporting goods and apparel. Government reforms in countries such as India and China that encourage sport participation also enhance the demand for sports equipment; however, market growth is expected to be hindered somewhat due to manufacturing quality control issues ("Sporting Goods Market," 2019).

Table 10.1 U.S. Sales of Athletic and Sport Footwear (millions of dollars, selected types)

Item	2005	2007	2009	2011	2013	2015	2017	2012-2017 CAGR	2005-2017 CAGR
Walking shoes	$3,673	$4,197	$4,416	$4,535	$4,846	$5,466	$5,689	4.9%	3.7%
Running/jogging shoes	$2,157	$2,193	$2,363	$2,464	$3,092	$3,215	$3,193	1.0%	3.3%
Basketball shoes	$878	$892	$741	$766	$887	$966	$980	3.6%	0.9%
Tennis shoes	$528	$452	$396	$421	$464	$472	$491	2.4%	−0.6%
Hunting boots	$276	$246	$242	$252	$273	$278	$294	3.5%	0.5%
Soccer shoes	$195	$206	$195	$201	$213	$234	$236	2.5%	1.6%
Football shoes	$99	$105	$92	$108	$119	$128	$128	1.6%	2.2%
Cheerleading shoes	$50	$64	$62	$66	$78	$86	$85	4.9%	4.5%
Bowling shoes	$52	$61	$53	$54	$55	$58	$57	1.1%	0.8%
Total athletic & sport footwear	$15,719	$17,524	$17,068	$18,384	$20,229	$21,634	$22,620	2.9%	3.1%

Adapted from Sport Market Analytics (n.d.), utilizing National Sporting Goods Association data.

Table 10.2 U.S. Sales of Sports Apparel (millions of dollars, selected types)

Apparel type	2012	2013	2014	2015	2016	2017	2012-2017 CAGR
Aerobic exercising	$831	$844	$827	$843	$861	$848	0.4%
Basketball	$303	$317	$308	$323	$329	$323	1.3%
Golf	$1,754	$1,745	$1,675	$1,677	$1,647	$1,628	–1.5%
Running/jogging	$1,035	$1,071	$1,103	$1,159	$1,172	$1,170	2.5%
Soccer	$351	$358	$369	$383	$391	$394	2.3%
Softball	$304	$314	$308	$314	$311	$314	0.6%
Swimming	$1,516	$1,554	$1,617	$1,627	$1,619	$1,644	1.6%
Tennis	$184	$197	$189	$193	$195	$192	0.9%
Total market: 2000-2017	$13,721	$13,867	$14,475	$16,440	$16,560	$16,524	3.8%

The total market definition broadened between 2012 and 2017 to include, among others, cheerleading, ice hockey, and lacrosse apparel; thus the growth rate reflects a broader baseline of product categories.

Adapted from Sport Market Analytics (n.d.).

Table 10.3 U.S. Sales of Sports Equipment (millions of dollars, selected types)

Equipment type	2012	2013	2014	2015	2016	2017	2012-2017 CAGR
Bicycling	$2,378	$2,499	$2,288	$2,393	$2,284	$2,319	–0.5%
Bowling	$183	$182	$171	$175	$174	$170	–1.5%
Exercise	$5,595	$5,815	$6,480	$6,729	$6,963	$6,982	4.5%
Fishing tackle	$1,553	$1,505	$1,548	$1,531	$1,521	$1,554	0.0%
Golf	$3,511	$3,677	$3,408	$3,685	$3,597	$3,571	0.3%
Snowboards	$257	$267	$256	$266	$241	$244	–1.0%
Soccer balls	$84	$88	$93	$104	$107	$110	5.5%
Total athletic & sports equipment	$29,574	$28,018	$28,699	$29,633	$30,126	$30,238	0.4%

Adapted from Sport Market Analytics (n.d.).

Major Players in the Sporting Goods Industry

Sporting goods are produced all over the world by companies such as Nike, Adidas, Under Armour, Decathlon, and more. These companies are truly international operations in that they produce their products in many different countries and sell them in scores of countries worldwide. Thus, the logistics of going from the *supply* side of raw materials to manufacture to retail to the *demand* side of the final sale to the consumer involve many strategic business units in the value chain (see figure 10.1).

There are many variations in how products move from the producer to the end consumer. Table 10.4 presents the three general sectors for the supply chain side with examples in the sporting goods industry and potential governance issues.

The size and market share of companies along each layer of this value chain affect the bargaining that occurs between a seller and buyer, resulting in various prices and profits as the product gets built and shipped along the way to its final sale. With increased concentration (or fewer companies operating at each level) over the past few decades, sales margins have often grown for a number of products (Grullon, Larkin, & Michaely, 2017).

Manufacturers

In the sporting goods industry, most manufacturers have their own regional distribution centers stocking merchandise for retailers. Companies may also have their own online or brick-and-mortar retail stores (e.g., Nike Town), or they may contract with warehouses.

In the fiscal year ending in May 2018, Nike generated about $36.4 billion in revenue worldwide (with about $15 billion in U.S. sales), up from $30.6 billion in 2015 (Yahoo! Finance NKE, n.d.). In the United States, almost two-thirds of Nike's profits are due to footwear sales and one-third from apparel sales. Under Armour, founded in 1996, grew revenues from $4.0 billion in 2015 to $5.2 billion in 2018 (Yahoo! Finance UA, n.d.). French firm Decathlon earned over €11 billion in 2017 (most of it in Europe) from both the retail sector (where it owns over 1,500 stores (van Schaik, 2019) and the manufacture of 20 brands (Decathlon About Us, n.d.). Thus, Decathlon is vertically integrated (meaning that it operates at multiple levels of the value chain).

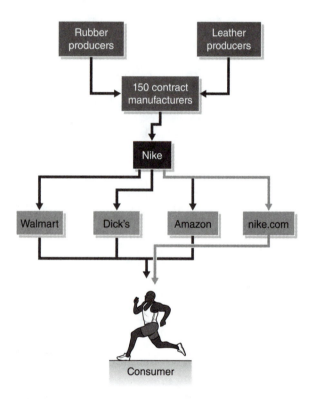

Figure 10.1 Value chain from raw materials to final sale.

Other prominent organizations in the manufacturing of sporting goods include Adidas, The North Face, Champion, Lululemon, Columbia, FILA, Puma, Skechers, New Balance, Callaway, Oakley, Head, Speedo, Salomon, Wilson, Rawlings, Mizuno, and Yonex. For instance, Rawlings, owned by Jarden Corp., makes a variety of equipment for baseball, football, and basketball and is estimated to have annual sales of around $500 million (Hoovers, n.d.). Golf club maker Callaway generated just over $1 billion from the sales of golf and related equipment in 2018. Under the Nike, Jordan, and Converse brands, Nike accounted for about 50 percent of athletic footwear sold in the United States in 2017. The next largest sellers are Adidas, Skechers, New Balance, and Under Armour (Roberts, 2017).

It is an industry standard for sporting goods manufacturers to contract with overseas production facilities. One of the biggest governance issues in manufacturing involves the human rights of employees in third world factories. Problems such as human rights and quality assurance arise when manufacturers seek the cheapest labor sources.

Until the 1950s, most athletic shoes were designed, created, and distributed within a closed economy, either within one country or within one country's colonial system. In the post-World War II era of much greater globalization, the international shoe industry began to expand as many designers from developed nations used cheaper manufacturing options in foreign countries to keep costs low. In the 1960s, most shoe manufacturing occurred in Japan, South Korea, and Taiwan (Clothier, 2005). By the 1970s, those countries' rapidly advancing economies, and the resulting increased labor costs, forced many of the largest shoe companies to use factories in Thailand and other emerging countries. These countries not only produced a large percentage of the world's shoes, but also many products in the burgeoning apparel industry.

By the 1980s, China had opened to limited foreign investment and the Chinese government

Table 10.4 Sporting Goods Supply Chain Players

Sector	Description	Example	Potential governance issues
Manufacturers	Responsible for designing and producing goods	Nike, Inc.; Asics Corporation; Reebok	Human rights and safety issues in factories in third world production facilities
Wholesalers/distributors	Purchase mass quantities of goods from a manufacturer and resell to retailers	Direct Liquidation, LLC; St. Louis Wholesale, LLC	Ethical business relationships with manufacturers; contracts
Retailers	Small, large, and online businesses selling products to consumers	Dick's Sporting Goods; Nike Factory Stores; Amazon.com	Consumer protection laws; counterfeit merchandise

desired to develop industries that would help transition millions of agrarian-based workers to a more industrial-based system. As a result, a large percentage of the world's shoe and apparel manufacturing occurred in cities along the Chinese coastline. China dominated the sector's manufacturing for years, but by the start of the 21st century, rising labor costs forced shoe and apparel makers to move to other Asian countries, most notably Vietnam and Indonesia. Though Indonesia remains a strong exporter of shoes and apparel, its rapidly growing middle class has demanded that more products remain in the country for purchase (Global Business Guide Indonesia, 2017). As domestic demand has increased, the percentage of Indonesian shoe and apparel products that are exported has decreased, with the future of large-scale shoe and apparel manufacturing likely to shift once again to new, less-developed countries.

The use of developing nations for manufacturing has helped those countries' economies to grow and has enabled their workers to develop skills and earn more than they would in most other jobs, but the globalization process has not been without controversy. The cheap labor costs in foreign countries, coupled with efficient and inexpensive transportation systems, enable consumers to enjoy much lower prices than if products were produced domestically. However, although manufacturing workers can make much more than they could elsewhere in their countries, wages are still very low compared to wages in the countries where most products are purchased. These low wages are often accompanied by poor working conditions and lax safety standards. Most sporting goods companies do business in the same countries, and they often use the same factories as their competitors. However, the most prominent companies often bear the brunt of public concern. In the early 21st century, Nike in particular was the target of intense criticism for its use of "sweatshops." In response, the company worked incessantly with manufacturing partners to ensure better working conditions for their employees. Though the controversies of the early 2000s have now largely abated, there is still tremendous concern among some groups that sporting goods manufacturing is among the most exploitative in the world (Nisen, 2013).

Retailers

The retail industry continues to expand its categories and types of stores. Common retail categories carrying sporting goods include specialty stores, department stores, supermarkets, hypermarkets, discount stores, consignment shops, and ecommerce stores. Examples of specialty retailers in the sporting goods space include Eastbay, Foot Locker, Dick's Sporting Goods, Nike Factory Stores, Sport 2000 in Germany, and Sports Direct in the United Kingdom.

Most sport brands and retailers have adapted to the changing behavior patterns of consumers by stretching their point of sales to the online market. Much of the growth in recent U.S. sporting goods sales has been in the online space, nearly doubling since 2012 to over $15 billion in 2016 (Statista, 2018). While in-store sales have only doubled from 1999 until 2016, they have exceeded online sales at over $47 billion.

Governing authorities of purely brick-and-mortar sports retailers have altered strategies to survive in the sporting goods business, often by capitalizing on the explosion of the online marketplace. However, not all retailers who accommodate mobile shopping have been able to sustain their position in the business world. Governance in Action 10.2 examines Dick's Sporting Goods' takeover of Sports Authority, once a thriving sport specialty retailer.

SPORT LICENSING LANDSCAPE

An important component of governance in the sporting goods industry is **licensing**, whereby one person or company contractually grants another person or company the right to use its intellectual property. **Sports properties** is a term used to designate the ownership of intellectual property of a sport entity such as a team, league, facility, organization, or event.

Typically, patents, trademarks, copyrights, and designs are **intellectual property** that can be licensed to another (Sharp, Moorman, & Claussen, 2017, p. 590). Often the owner of the intellectual property may not have the time or resources to maximize its use, and so the owner uses the production, distribution, or marketing systems of other organizations to increase sales.

In an effective **licensing partnership**, both parties benefit: The intellectual property rights holder typically receives a **royalty**, a percentage of sales, which the licensor generates. These royalties often range from 5 percent to 20 percent of either the wholesale or retail price, depending on many factors and the outcome of negotiations (Irwin, Sutton, & McCarthy, 2008; Masteralexis, Barr, & Hums, 2004; Mullin, Hardy, & Sutton, 2007).

There are different ways to define the licensed sport merchandise market, but there is no doubt that it is a vibrant and expanding business. Trans-

GOVERNANCE IN ACTION 10.2

Brick-and-Mortar Sporting Goods Retailers Struggle Against Online Sellers

Sports Authority (SA), a sporting goods retailer, was founded in Florida during the 1980s, but it moved its headquarters to Colorado after its merger with Gart Sports in 2003 (which had purchased Sportmart and Oshman's). In March 2016, SA filed for bankruptcy due to stagnating revenues, a failure to differentiate itself from competitors, and over $1 billion in debt that had accrued.

The SA brand name and other intellectual property, including over 28 million loyalty program members and a list of 114 million customer files, was auctioned, with Dick's Sporting Goods supplying a winning bid of $15 million. Dick's also paid $8 million to assume over 31 SA store leases. Prior to the purchase by Dick's, Sports Authority had failed to find a buyer that would keep it running as a smaller, distinct retailer. The company began liquidating its inventory at 463 stores by putting items on deep discount (Addady, 2016). Dick's claims that there were more than 200 SA stores within five miles of a Dick's business that would be closing, thus decreasing local competition. Dick's profit shares rose 4 percent at the time of the announcement, raising its market capitalization (or company valuation) by $127 million, more than Dick's $23 million combined purchase price.

Despite the continued survival of Dick's, the sporting goods industry has changed dramatically due to changing consumer behavior. Competition with online retailers, notably Amazon, has hurt many store-based (or brick-and-mortar) retailers, including those offering sporting goods. Recently, City Sports Inc. in Boston and Sport Chalet in California have shut down stores. Recognizing the trends, Sports Authority's digital sales increased to over $250 million in 2015, but they were not able to generate enough online sales to offset the losses so many of their brick-and-mortar locations were facing (Hilco Steambank, 2016). Though Dick's has now established itself as the dominant U.S. sporting goods retailer, its future will likely be focused much more on digital sales than on its more than 800 retail locations.

parency Market Research estimates that the market was valued at $27.63 billion (U.S.) in 2015, and it will grow to $48.17 billion (U.S.) by 2024, with a compound annual growth rate of 6.4 percent from 2016 to 2024 (PRNewswire, 2016b). North America has been and will likely continue to be the dominant continent for sales of licensed sport products, although as other nations develop, North America's 54 percent market share in 2015 will likely contract as other areas experience higher growth rates (PRNewswire, 2016b).

The lucrative sport licensing industry is broad based, considering the infinite number of sport properties in the global marketplace. Two of the largest global licensing programs are through the International Olympic Committee (IOC) for all trademarks of the Olympics and through the Fédération Internationale de Football Association (FIFA), which owns all trademarks for the World Cup. FIFA granted permission to the Russian company Megalicense Entertainment to produce and sell World Cup 2018 merchandise and contracted with official fan shops (Furgiuele, 2017). Sport governing bodies such as the United States Olympic

& Paralympic Committee (e.g., USA Swimming; USA Gymnastics) and branded events such as the Commonwealth Games are considered sport properties with local, national, or global licensing programs. Even sport facilities have capitalized on retail licensing arrangements. Trump National Golf Club logo hats manufactured in Pakistan sell for $50 in Trump Towers (Griffin, 2017).

United States

Licensing deals for companies to use the intellectual property of a professional team or league have been a major source of revenue that is likely to continue to grow rapidly. The United States Olympic & Paralympic Committee (USOPC) and U.S. sport federations enter into retail licensing arrangements for the use of the USA insignia with the Olympic rings. In 2019, Nike inked a long-term sponsorship deal with the USOPC and Los Angeles 2028 Olympics (LA28) with a $200 million valuation because of the "wide range of merchandising, licensing, and promotional value" (Lefton & Fischer, 2019, para. 7).

In addition to the USOPC and U.S. sport federations, other highly lucrative licensing deals are in the areas of collegiate and professional sports. Each sector has implemented direct licensing deals or has hired a third party to negotiate contracts.

College Sports Licensing

From key chains to car stickers featuring the University of North Carolina ram mascot or the famous longhorn symbol for the University of Texas, U.S. college sports licensing is a big business. In 2014, it was reported that the college sports licensed merchandise category included $3.88 billion in product, generating about $209 million in royalty payments to universities, representing just over 5 percent of total retail sales (Heitner, 2014).

The American college sport system is unique in a number of ways, most notably in that many schools make significant investments ($100+ million a year) to operate athletic departments that sponsor sports led by multimillionaire coaches with teams playing in highly commercialized facilities and traveling by charter flights. The participants are considered amateurs by the National Collegiate Athletic Association (NCAA), meaning their athletic grants-in-aid are designed to be "education based" and not reflective of the market value that those players may be worth. Big-time college sports, particularly basketball and American football, receive strong consumer interest, and that has generated some unique marketing opportunities and legal challenges.

As the commercialization of big-time college sport increased rapidly in the 1970s, upstart shoe company Nike was approached with an idea from Sonny Vaccaro, an entrepreneur who had been involved in a number of activities, most notably as the organizer of highly popular high school basketball all-star games. Vaccaro pitched Nike on the idea of directly paying the most prominent college basketball coaches to have their players wear Nike shoes. Though the initial compensation to the schools was usually just a few thousand dollars in cash and enough shoes and other gear to help the basketball team defray costs they had typically incurred in previous years, the success from those initial sponsorships spurred greater investments by Nike and other competitors such as Reebok and Adidas. Converse, the long-standing leader in basketball shoe sales in the 1960s and 1970s, found itself falling behind because it did not adequately adapt to the new marketing environment, and by the mid-1980s, Nike had created a dominant market position.

At the same time that the college basketball shoe industry was undergoing tremendous changes, university athletic departments were also beginning to realize that a number of fans were interested in buying and wearing branded apparel. Until the 1970s, most T-shirts, hats, and sweatshirts that bore a school's logo were sold to people interested in wearing them to exercise. By the late 1970s, the idea of having college logos on garments transitioned to a point where it became fashionable to wear school colors to many other social occasions. Sensing an opportunity, in 1981, Bill Battle founded the Collegiate Licensing Company (CLC) (Smith, 2012). CLC offered schools an opportunity to license their intellectual property to a company that could provide expertise in positioning the schools' brand on a number of items that extended beyond just T-shirts and hats. CLC also assured customers that their products were officially licensed by their favorite schools by affixing a hologram to most items that were sold at retail. By the late 1980s, CLC had helped its partner schools to raise revenues significantly by extending licensed product offerings to include items as diverse as beach towels, car tire covers, and toilet seat covers. In 2007, the success of CLC resulted in its being acquired by sport marketing behemoth International Management Group (IMG), which incorporated CLC into its other college marketing activities involving media and sponsorship sales and named the new organization IMG College. IMG continued to expand its presence by merging with its largest competitor, Learfield, in 2018. Interestingly, in the aftermath of the merger, the CLC brand name was reintroduced in 2019 to be an important corporate moniker for Learfield/IMG College.

The college sport industry continued to expand its collegiate marketing activities during the 1990s and into the 21st century. Many NCAA Division I member schools, sometimes via their conferences, began to sell multimedia rights for millions of dollars. College sport programs also became engaged in selling intellectual property to video game manufacturers, which prompted one of the largest class action suits in NCAA history (see Governance in Action 10.3). Even in the wake of the 2018 Adidas college basketball corruption case that involved a number of college basketball coaches, prominent companies continued to use college athletic departments to sell their products (Duffy, 2018). Nike's deals with the University of Texas and the University of Michigan, for example, are reportedly worth nearly $10 million per year per school through 2031 (Leitch, 2018).

GOVERNANCE IN ACTION 10.3

NCAA Forbids Student-Athletes From Profiting From Collegiate Sports Licenses Despite Ed O'Bannon's Legal Victory

While college athletes have been required by the NCAA to have their compensation capped by an athletic scholarship since 1956, the entire college sport industry has expanded rapidly as sales of licensed merchandise have proliferated. One of the most successful products has been college sport–themed video games. When purchasing and playing these games, such as *NCAA Basketball* and *NCAA Football* (developed by EA Sports), consumers expect to see familiar players, coaches, and teams. Yet NCAA rules continued to prevent the "participating" college athletes from being compensated for their names, images, and likenesses (NIL), both while playing college sports and after they left school. Many years after his college and professional basketball playing career had ended, former UCLA star Ed O'Bannon noticed that versions of *NCAA Basketball* had a "historical teams" option in which someone could play his 1995 UCLA team. O'Bannon's image and likeness were clearly visible in the game, which prompted his friend to note that O'Bannon did not receive compensation for his appearance. This initial encounter, combined with other concerns O'Bannon had regarding the treatment of college athletes, eventually led to his class action lawsuit against the NCAA for improper use of NIL.

In *O'Bannon v. NCAA* (2014), the NCAA countered O'Bannon's claim since the NCAA collegiate model does not permit its athletes to be compensated beyond what NCAA rules mandate as part of an athletic scholarship, and that O'Bannon, like all other NCAA athletes, signed away his rights to his NIL as part of his yearly eligibility paperwork.

Judge Claudia Wilken noted the NCAA's actions constituted an illegal and unfair restraint of trade. However, she, and the 9th Circuit Court of Appeals, which upheld part of her ruling, refused to strike down some aspects of the NCAA collegiate model and instead prevented the NCAA from blocking member schools from increasing the value of a full-ride scholarship to also include cost-of-attendance payments as a remedy for their antitrust violations. EA Sports, the actual maker of the video games that were a centerpiece to O'Bannon's claims, and the CLC, both codefendants with the NCAA in the initial lawsuit, settled their part of the litigation by providing $40 million to athletes who appeared in their video games from 2003 to 2013. Former players received as much as $4,000 as part of the settlement (Farrey, 2014).

Though EA Sports discontinued its NCAA-related video games in 2013, and a number of colleges and universities have discontinued the sale of football and basketball jerseys with individual numbers that could denote specific players, there is still a concern among many that the massive commercialization of college sport—and the refusal by the NCAA to permit players to fully partake financially in the open market—may not only be unethical, but also illegal. Certainly, EA Sports, Nike, Reebok, and other potential licensors would be happy to allocate licensing fees to college athletes, though the NCAA rules currently prohibit it. There continue to be efforts on a number of fronts to change the rules.

Professional Sports Licensing

All four major professional sport leagues in America have created properties groups to serve as licensing agents for the sale of their trademarks on a variety of licensed products. For example, formed in 1963, National Football League (NFL) Properties LLC has exclusive rights to negotiate merchandising and license deals for most NFL marks (logos). Currently, according to the NFL "Licensing Pre-Qualification Terms and Conditions," (n.d.), manufacturers wishing to obtain authorization to use any NFL mark must ensure the ability to pay a minimum royalty guarantee of approximately $100,000 per year, and they must carry a commercial insurance policy valued at a minimum of $6 million. In 2018, NFL Properties had licensing deals with approximately 180 companies (Kaminsky, 2018). Though it has long generated millions of dollars on hats, shirts, and a number of other traditional products, one of the newest NFL trends is expanding its line of homegating products that offer fans the chance to celebrate their favorite team with authentic team cookware, drinkware, and home décor.

In 2017, MLB Properties garnered $54.2 million in licensing revenue, which included merchandising agreements with a variety of companies, including Topps, a trading card company, and Sony Interactive Entertainment, the manufacturing company for the *MLB, The Show* video game (Fisher & Mullen, 2018). The National Hockey League (NHL) reportedly had 211 licensing deals in 2012 ("List of NHL Sports Licenses," 2012).

Retail licensing deals involving other professional teams and leagues (e.g., Major League Soccer [MLS] or Women's National Basketball Association [WNBA]) or individual sports (e.g., Professional Golfers Association [PGA] Tour or Association of Tennis Professionals [ATP]) in North America are subject to arrangements with the sport properties owning the official rights to trademarks. The map of the United States and flag serving as the official logo of the Masters golf tournament is the officially registered trademark of Augusta National, Inc., not the PGA Tour ("Official Site of the 2019 Masters Tournament," 2019). The National Association of Stock Car Auto Racing (NASCAR) has its own official registered trademark, but the trademark for its individual races may be retained by the track hosting that race.

Global and International Sport Licensing

Though the United States has dominated the sporting goods licensing industry from a consumption standpoint, other areas have extensive programs in place. Sophisticated markets such as the United Kingdom and France have capitalized on sport licensing agreements, albeit at a slightly slower rate than the United States. In 2017, the highly valuable Manchester United professional football club in the English Premier League generated $136.76 million (U.S.) in retail, merchandising, apparel, and product licensing ("Commercial Revenue by Segment," 2012). The club is a highly effective producer of soccer (football) talent, but it is not necessarily effective in manufacturing and distributing products around the world. However, through a series of licensing partners, most notably Adidas, the club is positioned to receive a percentage of all sales of products produced with its logo.

Much like other clubs in Great Britain's Premier League, Manchester United's licensing revenue has been increasing rapidly over the past few years. The

Phil Walter/Getty Images

Sport licensing deals with professional leagues and teams have been a lucrative business, especially in Europe and Australia.

aforementioned $136.76 million was an increase of nearly $100 million from the $41.56 million it generated in that category in 2015 (Statista, 2018). Interestingly, Nike was recently fined $14.14 million by the European Commission (competition authority in much of Europe) because it blocked the cross-border sale of Manchester United and other soccer club products, for which it was the manufacturer. Nike's contracts contained clauses to prevent sales outside of certain geographic areas, in the face of a push to increase online trade and growth by European authorities (Reuters, 2019).

In 2011, the Nippon Professional Baseball League in Japan earned the equivalent of approximately $50 million from licensing deals (Rosner & Shapiro, 2011). Other popular professional leagues and teams around the world such as the Turkish Airlines EuroLeague (basketball) also have historical licensing deals with companies to increase the sale of logoed merchandise, jerseys, and other apparel. The NBA, NHL, MLB, and NFL all have global licensing programs to expand their territorial markets and capitalize on royalties.

Formula One professional racing also has an interesting licensing arrangement with a third party. While the Fédération Internationale de l'Automobile is one of the dominant governing bodies for worldwide motorsports, including Formula One racing, a completely separate entity named Formula One Group owns, controls, promotes, and exploits the sport's commercial rights (Zakrzewski & Smith, 2018). In 2019, German-based Puma signed a long-term deal as Formula One's exclusive merchandise retail partner ("Formula One Signs Merchandise Partnership," 2019). A year earlier, Formula One reportedly signed an exclusive merchandising retail deal with Fanatics, one of the global leaders in licensed sport merchandise (Dhyani, 2018).

Other entities with governing authority over professional individual sports around the world also have a rich history of licensing deals. The Professional Golfers Association (PGA) Tour had 120 licensing deals generating $1.6 billion in gross sales in 2016 (Smith, 2016). A 20-year relationship with International Marketing Group (IMG) ended in 2016 when Fermata Partners, a subsidiary of Creative Artists Association (CAA), was retained as their trademark licensing agency. Since then, the company has increased its global footprint in licensing deals around the world, selling rights to its tournament trademarks, such as the Presidents Cup.

Even with the number of highly lucrative licensing deals that already exist around the world, some emerging marketplaces are expected to grow their market share at a high rate in the near future. In particular, the Asian marketplace is expected to experience tremendous growth in the sport licensing industry as sport popularity—as well as disposable time and money—increase in countries such as China, Indonesia, and Vietnam. While the ever-expanding global marketplace offers tremendous opportunities to increase the sales of licensed products, the disparate intellectual property laws between countries may dampen companies' ability to maximize sales. Substantial amounts of time and money may be needed to maintain control of protected products, processes, trademarks, and slogans upon entering a new market.

REGULATING AND POLICING THE INDUSTRY

Regulations are typically needed within the sporting goods and licensing industry to ensure legal and ethical compliance for general business operations, to protect intellectual property, and to protect consumers. Two broad categories of regulating and policing the industry are legislative regulation and self-regulation.

Legislative Regulation

There is no direct regulation of the quality of sporting goods; it is quite unlike the restaurant industry, for example, where multiple government inspections are the norm. There are entities, however, that help to ensure certain protections, which, on occasion, will call upon federal, district, state, or municipal court action. In the United States, much of the regulation of sporting goods is through intellectual property laws or through the application of various consumer laws when something goes wrong.

Consumer Protection

Typically, complaints against sporting goods companies would occur through the **Federal Trade Commission (FTC)**, state or local authorities, or entities like the Better Business Bureau. Settlements or restitution may or may not involve the formal legal system. The FTC is the independent agency of the U.S. government that regulates deceptive or unethical business practices. In addition to the FTC, individual states have consumer protection divisions. There are countless examples of filings and decisions involving the FTC and complaints about sporting goods. For example, in an address to the Sport and Fitness Industry Association, the director for the Bureau of Consumer Protection said that the FTC filed a lawsuit against athletic apparel company Tommie Copper for making unsubstantiated claims that its copper-infused compression clothing relieved inflammation and chronic pain "caused by arthritis and other diseases" (Rich, 2016). Similarly, in 2012, the Georgia Department of Law Consumer Protection Division proved Dick's Sporting Goods used deceptive advertising when it inflated original prices to create perceptions of greater discounts for its "sale" prices ("Dick's Sporting Goods Settles," 2012).

Founded in 1912, the **Better Business Bureau** is a nonprofit, nongovernmental organization in the United States that monitors unethical business practices and helps consumers and businesses to settle complaints. In 2018, the Better Business Bureau noted Big Baller Brand, Inc., the 2016 sports apparel start-up company founded by LaVar Ball, had a string of poor customer service complaints and delivery issues. In 2019, amid allegations of

Neil Johnson/fotolia.com

While many people focus attention upon football helmets, equestrian sports are among many others that also have helmet safety laws for participants.

embezzlement and the firing of its cofounder, the online store and website stopped functioning (Joseph, 2019).

In some cases, consumers may take formal legal action and file civil lawsuits against companies. For instance, in *Alea v. Wilson Sporting Goods Company, Inc.*, the purchaser of a baseball bat filed suit under state consumer fraud and deceptive business practices laws, complaining that the bat rotated slightly after a brief period of use, severely diminishing the quality of the product by making the ball not come off the bat as expected (*Alea v. Wilson Sporting Goods Company Inc.*, 2017).

Independent organizations also have played a role in contributing to consumer protections in the sporting goods industry. As an example, head injuries and concussions are common in equestrian sports, with thousands of annual emergency room visits. Certifications for the quality of equestrian helmets exist from the American Society for Testing and Materials and the Safety Equipment Institute (Fershtman, 2017). A few states and municipalities have equestrian helmet laws, while about half of the states have bicycle helmet laws. In New York, minors under age 18 riding horses must wear a helmet, while in Florida the requirement is for those under 16. The international governing body Fédération Equestre Internationale requires headgear as of 2013 for all of its riders (with some exceptions).

Similarly, independent or third-party testing labs have been used to document cases of faulty equipment, helping to provide the burden of proof in legal cases. For example, NBA player Francisco Garcia sued Ledraplastic, an exercise ball company, for lost future earnings when the ball he was balancing on while lifting free weights allegedly burst and injured him (Lu, 2012). Garcia claimed false advertising and breach of the manufacturer's warranty because the product was marketed as being able to handle 600 pounds. Lab testing, however, demonstrated the ball burst at 400 pounds. Garcia settled the lawsuit for an undisclosed amount. This is an example of governance by lawsuit—that is, the application of general consumer protection laws to sporting goods.

Underwriters Laboratories, Inc. and National Technical Systems, Inc. (NTS) are two companies involved in sport product safety testing. Underwriters Laboratories, Inc., accredited in the United States by the federal government's Occupational Safety & Health Administration (OSHA), publishes a litany of safety standards, such as electrical code requirements for electrically powered hobby and sports equipment rated for 250 volts or less, and intended only for home entertainment by adults. Similarly, NTS is a private company that tests sports equipment and certifies safety standards.

GOVERNANCE IN ACTION 10.4

The Golf Club Industry Experiences Problems With Counterfeits and Knockoffs

The golf club industry has been one of the most competitive in the sport world over the past 30 years. New club designs and lighter and more effective materials have spurred sales in an industry where participants often have substantial disposable income and will pay for top-of-the-line clubs, sometimes as much as hundreds of American dollars for the best driver or putter. While club design has incorporated many technological innovations, the production of most clubs has occurred in foreign countries.

Though for many years much of the world's golf club manufacturing was done in Taiwan, the country's advanced economy and increased wages have shifted a tremendous amount of production to China, where golf club companies can save considerable money compared to producing equipment in the United States or most European countries. Unfortunately, the Chinese marketplace now accounts for nearly 90 percent of worldwide counterfeit golf club production (Stachura, 2016).

For some Chinese workers, stealing and selling golf club secrets can be considerably more lucrative than working for an entire year. Even with some production centers conducting daily employee body searches at the end of a work shift, the allure of stealing and selling trade secrets often results in new designs quickly becoming "available" to counterfeit producers (MyGolfSpy, 2009). In addition, the Chinese government often turns a blind eye toward counterfeiters and the various storefronts that often openly peddle counterfeit golf clubs and other goods. The opportunity to sell directly to consumers through the Internet has also created problems because policing of Internet storefronts is often a low priority for many foreign governments.

Though most top golf club companies are reluctant to move their production from China, where the labor costs are low and the intellectual property laws are often lax, there have been more calls for consumers to pay close attention to the products they buy. Even if governments cannot or will not enforce intellectual property laws, consumers can use a number of techniques to better protect themselves from purchasing counterfeit golf clubs, which often perform poorly in comparison with genuine products (Stachura, 2016). In addition to closely examining the paint and other markings on golf clubs for irregularities, one of the most important things a buyer can do is request a club's serial number. If a seller refuses to provide this information, the clubs are probably fake. Also, titanium clubs, among the most popular on the market today, will not adhere to a magnet, so if a magnet will attach to a club that is supposed to be titanium, it is a counterfeit product (MyGolfSpy, 2009).

Ultimately, consumers must protect themselves from the fake golf club industry that continues to expand in places like China, where intellectual property laws are not enforced with the same rigor as in many other countries. Once a counterfeit claim is proved, legal remedies for reimbursement in the global market are challenging, but it is even more challenging to try to shut down companies that engage in counterfeit production and deceptive sales practices.

Intellectual Property Protection

One of the most important governance issues in the sporting goods and sport licensing industry is protecting intellectual property. According to the USOPC, "Federal law gives the USOPC extensive rights to control the use of USOPC IP in the United States and allows the USOPC to file a lawsuit against any entity using such intellectual property" ("How Does the USOPC Protect?" 2019, para. 1).

Sport leagues and teams create intellectual property via logos, for instance. It is then their responsibility to defend those forms of intellectual property by policing counterfeit products, but consumers also have a responsibility to detect fake products, as Governance in Action 10.4 explains.

To put sports product counterfeiting into context, it is estimated that the size of the global counterfeit sporting goods market (not including apparel) was over $23 billion in 2012 and nearly

$27 billion for sports apparel. Based on data from U.S. Customs and Border Protection in 2010, athletic shoes accounted for 24 percent of the value of seized goods, topping the list, with sports apparel third on the list. An estimate from a decade earlier noted an approximate 11.5 percent drop in a company's revenues due to counterfeiting of branded sporting goods (Weisheng, Kwang-yong, & Doyeon, 2014).

Moreover, not only are revenues lost when counterfeit products are purchased instead of the real thing, the quality of those products can often be lower, thus harming the company's brand if consumers are unaware that they bought a fake product. Diluting a brand's image with low-quality knockoffs can lead to future financial losses due to perceptions of lower quality.

As the size of the licensed sport merchandise industry has expanded, the need for both large and small sport organizations to protect their intellectual property has increased. In the NFL, where some player replica jerseys sell at retail for over $200, it is not difficult to envision dozens, hundreds, or even thousands of fake jerseys and other products being sold. During a one-year period from January 2018 to January 2019, over 285,000 fake NFL items worth over $24 million were seized (Kass, 2019). Though it is easy to see why franchises in the NFL, the NBA, and the Barclays Premier League must investigate potential sales of pirated merchandise, efforts by unscrupulous actors to try to sell nonlicensed sport-oriented apparel also occurs at a lower level of competition. In the 1990s, the University of Northern Colorado doctoral program investigated local retail outlets and discovered that despite their NCAA Division II status, a number of pirated University of Northern Colorado Athletics–related products were being sold outside of the schools' official licensing program (D. Stotlar, personal communication, June 3, 2019).

Unfortunately, the growth of the Internet has made it much more difficult for some organizations to successfully protect their marks, necessitating greater governance measures. A key aspect of stopping pirated merchandise sales is to identify those trying to fool the public with fake merchandise. In the United States, once pirating is identified, a **cease and desist** letter can be sent, with additional legal actions then taken if the products continue to be sold. A cease and desist order places an injunction on the culprit to prohibit an activity identified as illegal. It is not always binding if the letter comes from an organization or company as opposed to state action.

Although counterfeit retailers may offer **disclaimers** on products in an effort to avoid trademark infringement, these defensive measures do not exempt the seller from legal recourse in America. A disclaimer is merely a statement to delimit, specify, or shift the scope of responsibility or obligations for actions or intentions. The focus for the court system becomes the intent of the merchandiser who is using protected marks without consent (Adams, 2013). Similarly, counterfeiters in the United States have generally been unsuccessful in asserting a defense against infringement through the **doctrine of expressive use**, which considers the alteration of a trademark such as adding words or phrases to accompany the registered mark in a creative source such as a book.

With so much business now being conducted on the Internet, often by nearly anonymous vendors, it is difficult for law enforcement to do much about the sale of fake merchandise. Sometimes fake merchandise will function acceptably, but far too often it will break, fade, or shrink well before the officially licensed version would. In the worst cases, an Internet vendor pockets the money and fails to deliver anything. It is for these reasons that most sport organizations have continued to warn customers about only buying officially licensed products.

Patents   A **patent** is typically used to protect inventions so that non-patent holders cannot unfairly profit from intellectual property they did not create. The patent could be for the functional aspects of the invention, known as a utility patent, or for the appearance of the invention, known as a design patent. Patent-protected inventions are important in the sporting goods industry, particularly for equipment. One of the most famous patents in the sporting goods industry was the Nike "waffle trainer," so named because in 1972 Bill Bowerman used a waffle iron to create its cushioned sole, which ". . . has short multi-sided polygon shaped studs . . . which provide gripping edges that give greatly improved traction" ("Nike Waffle Trainer," n.d., para. 1). The industry has certainly expanded since the early 1970s; since 1976, there have been over 22,000 golf patents in the United States alone, with thousands more granted in other countries (Schupak, 2018). Recently, wearable smart devices have offered an amazing array of patented technology. Fitbit, Inc., one of the industry leaders, was granted 45 patents in 2018 and has been assigned hundreds of other patents since its founding in 2007 ("Patents Assigned to Fitbit, Inc.," n.d.).

Successfully securing a patent in most cases is an arduous process. Most inventors secure legal assistance when filing for patent protections. In the United States, utility patents are typically granted for 20 years and design patents are granted for 14 years. Over the last 30 years, creating uniform patent and other intellectual property laws has been a goal of the international business community, especially as more and more nations have developed advanced economies. Any country, but particularly those in emerging markets, that does not have adequate patent protections will find it difficult to encourage its citizens to develop new products and to attract international investments. The World Trade Organization (WTO) passed the Agreement on Trade-Related Aspects of Intellectual Property Rights (TRIPS) in 1990. TRIPS mandates a number of key requirements, most notably that patents should be recognized for at least 20 years. Despite the near universal public acceptance of the World Trade Organization throughout the world, a number of nations, or organizations located within their borders, have not always closely adhered to patent and other intellectual property laws.

Trademarks   A **trademark** (or servicemark) is a symbol, design, logo, word, or words legally registered as representing a company or product (Friedman, 1995). A trademark identifies the specific source of a good or service. In most cases, successfully securing trademark protection is a much simpler and more inexpensive legal process than securing a patent. It is important that the trademark be distinctive and not likely to cause confusion in the marketplace. In some cases, multiple companies may use a similar trademark as long as their products and services are not related.

Within the sporting goods industry, Nike's distinctive swoosh and its famous slogan, "Just Do It," are among the most recognizable and valuable trademarks next to the Olympic rings. Nike's Jordan Brand also has the distinctive Jumpman logo. However, Nike's top competitors also have distinctive and widely recognizable trademarks: Adidas' Trefoil, Under Armour's logo of a U layered with an A as well as their slogan, "I will . . . protect this house," and Puma's cat logo and formstrip are all well-known in many nations around the world. Interestingly, Under Armour sued Nike in 2013 for using variants of the phrase "I Will" in a number of advertisements that Under Armour claimed diluted the distinctiveness of its mark (Mihoces, 2013). Though the case was settled out of court, it indicated the importance companies place on their trademarks (Harwell, 2015).

Though the aforementioned companies are worth billions of dollars, smaller sporting goods companies also work to establish their trademarks and enhance their brand identities. Former NFL player Marshawn Lynch was known for his style of play, popularly known as "Beast Mode." Later in his career he established an apparel company, Beast Mode, which offers a variety of T-shirts, sweatshirts, leggings, and other products. Lynch has expanded his affiliation to include other types of products, such as a specialty line of BMX bicycles. Even nonprofit organizations work to protect their trademarks. For example, Ducks Unlimited, a nonprofit company dedicated to the preservation of the wetlands needed to sustain the future of waterfowl hunting, has specific and extensive language on its website that indicates it will protect its trademarks and investigate any company that infringes upon its intellectual property (Marrone, n.d.).

The **Lanham Act**, also known as the Federal Trademark Act of 1946 (and amended in 1996), is the U.S. federal law governing the use of trademarks (Turner & Miloch, 2017). The Lanham Act constitutes a small portion of the federal legislation governing unfair competition since **trademark infringement**, or the misuse of a trademark without the expressed consent or authorization of the rights holder, is a form of deception (Kahn, 2004). While a trademark must demonstrate distinctiveness, exclusive rights are awarded to the entity that first uses it in commerce. Therefore, infringement, regardless of whether a trademark is registered, may result in legal action where a civil court would render a decision after considering factors such as the strength and similarity of marks, evidence of confusion, and the defendant's intent when selecting the mark.

In *Boston Pro. Hockey Ass'n, Inc. v. Dallas Cap & Emblem Manufacturing* (1973), NHL teams won a federal judgment for their logos being reproduced on merchandise without an authorized licensing or distribution deal (Kahn, 2004). Before Super Bowl LII in Minneapolis in 2018, NFL Properties LLC along with the Philadelphia Eagles and New England Patriots brought litigation against "large-scale professional counterfeiters" to curtail the production and sale of unlicensed merchandise (Kaminsky, 2018).

Copyright Protection   A **copyright** grants protection for original works of authorship, typically for items such as books and other written works, music, photographs, paintings, drawings, films, dances, and a number of other materials. The creator of a work automatically creates a copyright, but to receive formal protection from the United States government, two copies of the work must be registered with the Copyright Office in Washington, D.C. In general, copyrights last for the life of the author plus 70 years (Spoo, 2012). After that, the work becomes part of the public domain and can be commercially utilized, though not owned, by anyone. Just like the Federal Trademark Act of 1946, the **Copyright Act of 1976** protects owners of original work from having their work reproduced, derived, distributed, or publicly displayed without the consent and authorization of the original author of the work. Even while protected by a copyright, some works, however, can be used in a limited fashion as long as it is not for profit. For example, educators can typically use some elements of copyrighted works to improve student learning.

The use of copyrights in sport is extensive, though not necessarily in sporting goods, where patents and trademarks are more common. The production of a sport broadcast can be protected by a copyright. A media outlet cannot stop someone from describing what happened in a game, but it is usually prohibited for someone else to rebroadcast its game coverage. For example, if ABC broadcasts an NBA game, that broadcast cannot be shown in its entirety by other media companies. However, in the case of limited sport highlights, many media outlets permit other entities to rebroadcast those small segments of the complete broadcast. This willingness to permit others to use some broadcast elements has been heightened in the age of YouTube and other online viewing services, where policing illegal use is difficult (though not always impossible).

Even though copyrights are not usually involved in the sporting goods industry, a recent court case demonstrated that they do sometimes apply. The famous Jumpman logo, which has long been trademarked and used as one of the world's most well-recognized brands, was in dispute in a case filed by photojournalist Jacobus Rentmeester. While still an amateur basketball player training for the 1984 Olympics, Michael Jordan was photographed by Rentmeester in his famous "legs-outstretched-and-one-hand nearing-a-dunk" pose on an outside basketball court. Though Rentmeester retains copyright of his photograph, he claimed that the Jumpman logo was created unfairly from another Nike photograph that closely mimicked his original version. After a district court failed to support Rentmeester's claim, the 9th Circuit Court of Appeals determined in 2018 that the pose itself could not be copyrighted, and the United States Supreme Court declined to hear the case in 2019 (McCann, 2019).

Self-Regulation

In business and industry, **self-regulation** refers to the use of internal processes and systems, independent of government or other external influences, to ensure compliance with a minimum threshold of legal, ethical, or safety standards. Self-regulation requires a commitment from the top levels of an organization. Effective self-regulation stems from operational oversight, generally from an independent board that calculates risks to protect shareholder interests while minimizing the likelihood of employee or company negligence. Creating an internal compliance program, for example, is a form of self-regulation. Figure 10.2 outlines a six-step process for the creation of an internal compliance program.

Self-regulation goes beyond legal compliance, especially when used to demonstrate ethical behavior and foster an impression of responsible business operations and **corporate social responsibility** (CSR). Corporate social responsibility, similar to corporate citizenship, refers to an organization's obligation to maintain a socially moral image within its community with respect to environmental, safety, health, and public welfare concerns. For example, Amer Sports (2019) donating over 30,000 Wilson volleyballs, basketballs, and soccer balls to children in Tanzanian schools is a demonstration of the company's CSR. Outdoor apparel company Patagonia also demonstrated CSR by pledging the company's $10 million in tax savings in 2018 to environmental groups instead of reinvesting the funds back into the company (Roggie, 2019). Another example involved the decision by Dick's Sporting Goods to voluntarily stop selling assault-style weapons from their Field & Stream stores after learning the culprit in a mass shooting in Parkland, Florida, purchased a shotgun and ammunition in their stores (Meyersohn, 2019). Research has demonstrated that perceived philanthropic gestures do increase favorable attitudes toward retailers, especially when sports organizations engage in social causes in distant locations (Kulczycki, Mikas, & Koenigstorfer, 2017).

Corporate social responsibility also includes accountability for consumer safety, compliance with lean or acceptable manufacturing processes that contribute to environmental safety, and health protocols that meet or exceed waste and clean air standards. Self-policing is critical for organizations

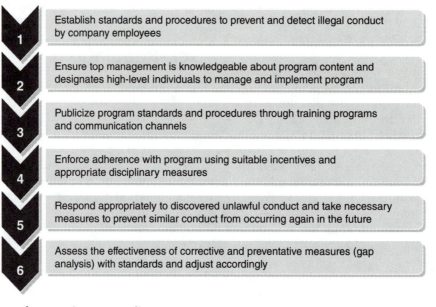

Figure 10.2 Steps for creating a compliance program.

Based on Peterson (2012).

enforcing compliance programs and using self-regulation to promote CSR. It requires a proactive approach to prevent code or ordinance violations and a reactive approach to report infractions and impose sanctions or corrective measures in a timely manner.

Voluntary product recalls are an example of self-policing. Dick's Sporting Goods' (2018) website publishes a fairly lengthy list of product recalls, many of which are voluntarily recalled as opposed to being mandated by an external entity such as the U.S. Consumer Product Safety Commission. Ocean Reef (2019), a brand of diving and snorkeling equipment, issued a voluntary recall of nine models of their Neptune space integrated diving masks and offered a replacement or refund.

Codes of Conduct

Codes of conduct also contribute to an organization's self-regulation efforts. Many codes of conduct stem from recommendations by industry trade associations. Given the complexity of the supply chain in the sporting goods industry, various parts of the chain have created codes of conduct to maintain certain ethical standards. A code of conduct or code of ethics outlines behavioral expectations (e.g., social norms) applicable to employees or partners of an organization, industry, or industry sector.

Dick's Sporting Goods, for instance, has a vendor code of conduct that calls on its suppliers to comply with all laws, including those that pertain to imports, exports, antitrust, fair competition, bribery and kickbacks, labor and age regulations for workers, rights to organize, discrimination, harassment, safety, and environmental responsibility. They also expect their suppliers to adapt to technological changes, innovate and improve their products, and report any violations (Dick's Sporting Goods Vendor Code of Conduct, 2016).

Nike has perhaps one of the most in-depth codes of conduct among sports retailers. This came about following the backlash against the company that occurred in the 1980s and 1990s, when its reliance on manufacturers in countries with lax environmental and safety standards came under fire from critics. Nike has also been criticized for relying on internal auditors instead of independent auditors to visit and assess working conditions in its suppliers' factories.

A 2006 report on Nike and other brands (e.g., Rawlings) criticized companies for partnering with manufacturing sites, sometimes referred to as sweatshops, with substandard working conditions compared to those in the United States and other developed nations (Powell & Skarbek, 2006). The company's current conduct codes for its manufacturers describe how workers should be respected, treated fairly, and provided a safe work environment, while also using sustainable business practices (Nike Code of Conduct, 2017).

For many sporting goods brands and companies with a high reliance on overseas labor, environmentally sustainable business practices are the latest additions to their upstream and downstream codes of conduct. The Sustainability Accounting Standards Board (2015) has created standards and metrics for reporting on sustainability efforts, and it notes that publicly traded companies have a legal duty to be accurate with their information. These standards include treating workers fairly, providing safe labor conditions, ensuring suppliers are in compliance with regulations, and providing a social code of conduct addressing (at minimum) the items identified in figure 10.3.

Scholars and activists have challenged the effectiveness of voluntary conduct codes that sport brands and companies mandate for their global network of manufacturers and suppliers. This is why the Sustainability Accounting Standards Board (2015) calls for **audits** to be conducted, preferably by an independent party. An audit is an assessment or inspection of standards for a department or organization.

Over time, there have been improvements in factories that manufacture sports apparel and shoes in emerging markets. The basic improvements, noted by Barrientos and Smith (2007), have primarily been realized in the standards of worker outcomes (better health, shorter working hours). However, many places do not yet have some of the protec-

tions that have been established in more developed countries, such as union organization, freedom of association, and antidiscrimination. Despite the improvements that still may need to be made, the present conditions in many manufacturing centers are far better than they were before, and they often remain far better than other employment options in those countries.

The Fair Play Foundation, a Dutch-based nongovernment, nonprofit organization, has conducted audits on many factories in the garment industry to assess compliance with standards of conduct using an independent three-person team considered local experts in either worker interviews, health and safety, or document inspection (Egels-Zanden & Lindholm, 2015). The experts are trained to detect problem areas such as factory managers falsifying records or instructing workers how to respond to questions in an audit. Having conducted over 40 rigorous audits of factories, including those contracted by Nike, results noted moderate improvement in worker conditions and an inability to identify process rights violations (such as freedom of association or discrimination or harassment violations), concluding that "auditing is thus more fundamentally flawed than assumed in previous research" (Egels-Zanden & Lindholm, 2015, p. 2). Just because an audit does not report

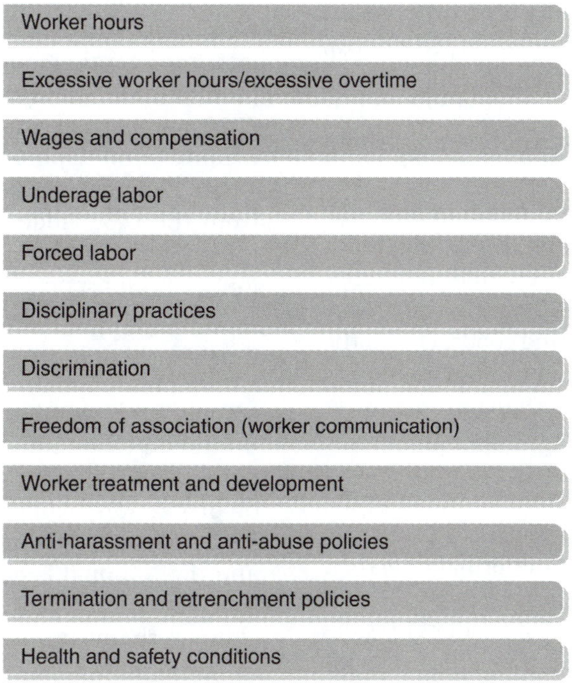

Worker hours

Excessive worker hours/excessive overtime

Wages and compensation

Underage labor

Forced labor

Disciplinary practices

Discrimination

Freedom of association (worker communication)

Worker treatment and development

Anti-harassment and anti-abuse policies

Termination and retrenchment policies

Health and safety conditions

Figure 10.3 Components of a social code of conduct for manufacturing companies and suppliers.

Adapted from Sustainability Accounting Standards Board (2015).

profound cases of concern, it does not mean that there are no occurrences. There may be an unfortunate incentive for some entities to cover up or hide corrupt practices.

Sporting Goods and Sport Licensing Trade Associations

An important form of self-regulation occurs when organizations and businesses active in the same industry collaborate to establish a self-regulatory regime in the form of a professional industry association. Trade associations or industry trade groups are typically nonprofit associations comprised of members within the same industry or with similar goals and issues. Besides enabling members to share ideas and best practices, some of these associations exercise a governance role by recommending policies and research and even promoting congressional lobbying on their members' behalf.

In sporting goods, there are many trade associations and committees, especially at the level of each product type or sport. However, in a macro sense, two national organizations and one international organization are prominent in promoting research, education, networking, and advocacy in the sporting goods industry: the National Sporting Goods Association, the Sports & Fitness Industry Association, and the World Federation of the Sporting Goods Industry. These organizations work closely with the **National Operating Committee on Standards for Athletic Equipment** (NOCSAE), a nonprofit, nongovernment organization established in 1970 that provides U.S. safety standards and certification for sports equipment ("About NOCSAE," n.d.).

National Sporting Goods Association In operation since 1927, the National Sporting Goods Association (NSGA) provides research, resources, networking, business solutions, and advocacy generally for retailers of sporting goods. One of the advocacy areas the NSGA is pursuing is promoting federal legislation for sales tax fairness for brick-and-mortar retailers who compete with online marketers. Another is objecting to the Youth Sports Concussion Act introduced by the U.S. Senate, which would make manufacturers of protective sports equipment liable for the performance of their products ("Government Advocacy," 2019).

The NSGA publishes a code of conduct for sales agents, which includes concepts such as responsibility to conduct business in a manner that reflects credit upon the "manufacturer, customer, association . . . and the entire industry" as well as to "respect the contractual relationships (written or otherwise) between manufacturers and other agents and to refrain from solicitation of manufacturers already represented" ("Division for Sales Agents," 2019, para. 2). The NSGA also publishes a code of conduct for participants in its annual Management Conference & Team Dealer Summit, noting that violators will be subject to appropriate enforcement, which may include expulsion from the conference "without warning or refund and prohibition of attendance from any future event" ("NSGA Management Conference," n.d., para. 2).

Information published by NSGA helps manufacturers and retailers to know and comply with any new regulations affecting the industry, such as the new NOCSAE standards for lacrosse goalie chest protectors and USA Swimming's restriction on tech-suits worn by swimmers age 12 and under ("Rules Changes," 2018). The NGSA therefore supports the self-regulation efforts of industry players who use the information, for example, to retire chest protectors that do not meet specifications and tech-suits too small to be worn by teenagers and adults.

Sports & Fitness Industry Association Formerly known as the Sporting Goods Manufacturers Association, the Sports & Fitness Industry Association (SFIA) is a nongovernment, nonprofit membership organization providing services mostly for brands and manufacturers in the sporting goods industry. SFIA promotes itself as the "premier trade association" of sporting goods and fitness brands, manufacturers, retailers, and marketers in the sports products and fitness industry ("SFIA Overview," 2019, para. 1). Serving as the industry voice in the media and on Capitol Hill, SFIA launched a China Tariff Exemption Plan in 2019 to provide relief from the U.S. Trade Representative's 25 percent tax collected on all imports from China, including footwear and sport and fitness equipment.

SFIA's organizational structure includes committees such as the Head Protections Working Group, which assists manufacturers' efforts to comply with standards from the U.S. Consumer Product Safety Commission regarding proof of performance that products meet minimum levels of protection. Another committee, the Sports Rules Task Force, works jointly with the NCAA and the National Federation of State High School Associations to share timely information about rule changes so inventories can be managed by manufacturers and retailers. Thus, these committees foster industry self-regulation by helping retailers and manufacturers to make informed decisions that improve safety for consumers.

World Federation of the Sporting Goods Industry Established in 1978 with offices in Switzerland and Hong Kong, the World Federation of the Sporting Goods Industry (WFSGI) is a global organization officially recognized by the IOC that provides information, networking, a job market, and webinars for members, which include brands, retailers, manufacturers, sport federations, and other trade associations (such as the SFIA) ("About WFSGI," 2017). The association promotes responsible and sustainable practices in the sporting goods industry and helps to improve quality standards for all sporting goods produced. For instance, the organization publishes a database of product labeling requirements that manufacturers use to ensure compliance with the consumer protection laws that differ by country.

The WFSGI has been called as an expert witness in dispute cases and mediation involving product engineering. Its manufacturing committee continuously addresses labor practices in the digital age and worker empowerment in the supply chain, while its trade committee monitors proposed tariffs that may have a particular impact on the sports apparel and footwear industry (e.g., trade disputes between the United States and China). Occasionally the committee engages in bilateral free trade agreement negotiations, such as the European Union–Vietnam 2019 deal that was affected by the threat of the United Kingdom's Brexit ("Activity Report," 2019). The legal committee is pursuing improved legislation against third-generation Asian counterfeiters that do not display legitimate trademarks.

Of great importance to supporting industry self-regulation is the WFSGI's extensive code of conduct, which outlines internationally recognized labor standards. FIFA, for example, requires all of its licensees and manufacturers of certified FIFA products (e.g., footballs, equipment, and artificial turf) to provide an audit report issued by an independent, internationally recognized auditing agency demonstrating compliance with each of the standards published in the WFSGI code of conduct ("FIFA Quality Programme," 2017). The code of conduct includes such provisions as prohibiting prison, indentured, or bonded labor; treating foreign or domestic migrant labor equal to local employees; providing employees excess pay for working beyond their normal requirements at a rate exceeding their regular hourly compensation rate; ensuring that no employees work over 60 hours a week; and ensuring at least a consecutive 24 hours of rest within a seven-day week ("Working Conditions," 2016).

FUTURE OF THE INDUSTRY

With advances in the industry and a focus on technology, consumer protection concerns have expanded to include data breaches. Much of the innovation currently occurring in sporting goods, and likely to continue into the future, involves wearable technology, such as watches and even wearable clothing to track biometric information. Companies such as Athos, Sensoria Fitness, OMsignal, and Carre Technologies are developing shirts and pants that track information about muscle exertion, heart rate, breathing patterns and volume, calories burned, steps taken, skin temperature, blood pressure, and oxygenation (Pai, 2014). Similarly, ProFLEX Heavy Duty and ThermaCELL are toying with Bluetooth technology and remote-controlled heating devices in socks. While many aspects of wearable technology are in their infant stages, FitBit has shown that there is a market for these products that provide performance feedback; the company reached $1.5 billion in sales in 2018. Across the entire industry, it was estimated that 780 million wearable devices would be used by the end of 2018 (Draper, 2018a).

Of course, collecting and analyzing data is not without potential concerns. As data is measured and stored, consumers can use it to note changes and to make health- and performance-related decisions. However, that data could potentially be misused by the company that designed the device, or, more likely, the data storage system could be breached by outside hackers. The Center for Digital Democracy at American University noted that consumer protection laws regarding misplaced or stolen health data have not been adequately addressed in the United States (Draper, 2018a). A number of data breaches have already occurred. Perhaps most concerning was the data breach that revealed the location of soldiers on active duty. In 2018, the United States Department of Defense issued a memorandum banning soldiers from carrying cell phones or wearable devices after it was learned that many of the devices could be identified and the person tracked while in the field (Draper, 2018b). American soldiers in war zones or stationed on overseas bases must adhere to the order.

Even when data is properly collected and stored, there is a concern about misapplication and indiscriminate release. In competitive sports, concerns have already arisen about the ownership of biometric data collected by teams and leagues. For professional athletes (and even college athletes), knowing how much stronger or faster one has become can be a valuable part of successful training. It can also be an excellent way to engage fans as people often find information about player performance enhances their understanding and their overall consumer experience. However, the data could also be used by a team or league to counter player salary demands. When the National Basketball Players Association (NBPA) learned that some teams were incorporating player biometric data into their contract negotiations, a clause was inserted in the most recent collective bargaining agreement to limit the use of such data to player health and team on-court tactical and strategic purposes (Leung, 2017). Despite this contractual language governing the NBA and other leagues with similar clauses, there is concern that such private player data may unofficially become part of a team's evaluation process. Interestingly, at the college level, Nike's most recent apparel deal with the University of Michigan's athletic department is worth about $170 million to the university in cash and equipment and apparel (Tracy, 2016). The deal can allow Nike to gather some of the data from the wearable technology that will be created for use by Michigan's college athletes.

In addition to concerns about player data privacy among employers, there are also concerns that hacked player data could be used by unscrupulous gamblers. Access to biometric player data that was to remain private could provide gamblers with inside information that could provide an unfair edge in betting decisions. As legalized and illegal gambling activities in the United States and other countries increase, it will become even more important that biometric data be protected much like other private information that bettors are not allowed to access.

The increased focus on safety in sports (e.g., concussions in many different sports) will continue to spur innovation in training and rules within sports, but also in the equipment used, including improved helmet technology. All participants want to feel that the enjoyment of sports is worth the potential physical risks, but parents in particular want to have a safe environment for their children. As more and more sports are scrutinized for their safety records, better-designed products will be needed to make sports safer.

Perhaps most importantly for the future of the sporting goods industry is the continued incorporation of sports into areas that for years were not a mainstream industry focus. The number of shoes and other athletic apparel items sold for nonsport purposes increased greatly in the 1980s, and sales have continued to expand. Many sporting goods are never used for sports. As much as the safety and functionality of sporting goods will continue to be important, the ability of products to be sold to a wide array of consumers will be a key to profitability. Basketball is a popular sport, but there are only so many basketball players who need shoes for competition. The number of consumers who buy basketball shoes for other reasons is far greater. Whether it is yoga pants, sweatshirts, fishing jackets, hats, or any other sporting good, if there is a demand for that product from mainstream culture, the company producing that product can expand sales tremendously. Though the sporting goods industry has and will continue to be about sports, it is likely to maintain its current level of importance only if many nonsport participants continue to purchase the myriad sporting goods available.

RECAP

The size of the sporting goods industry, measured in economic terms, is growing both in the United States and internationally. The three broad categories of the industry are apparel, shoes, and equipment. The industry supply chain includes manufacturers, distributors or wholesalers, and retailers who all work in concert to meet customer demand. The retail sporting goods business is shifting to put a greater focus on online purchasing options, with brick-and-mortar retailers feeling the repercussions of a downsized market for in-store purchases. Dick's Sporting Goods' 2016 acquisition of Sports Authority created a robust online store to complement their retail branches. This type of activity exemplifies the company's business-minded approach to adapting and thriving in the changing marketplace.

For manufacturers, governance issues include ensuring human rights and fair labor practices in the low-wage, third-world factories they use to produce their products. Other governance issues in manufacturing include compliance with product safety specifications for consumer protection. A challenge for manufacturers is dealing with different countries that vacillate between strict and lax consumer protection and labor laws.

Connected to the sporting goods industry is sport licensing, where one person or company contractually grants another person or company the right to use its intellectual property, such as in the production of logo merchandise or apparel. Protecting intellectual property such as trademarks, copyrights, and patents is a governance concern for all entities in the industry, but particularly for rights holders. Counterfeit merchandise, especially in Asia, is a growing issue.

One way to regulate the industry is through the prosecution of companies and individuals who produce counterfeit goods or use trademarks and intellectual property without proper authorization. Other government entities, such as the Federal Trade Commission, also can be involved in potential enforcement. In the absence of specific state and federal laws governing sporting goods, self-regulation is important to demonstrate responsible business practices and to create a favorable impression of corporate social responsibility (CSR) for stakeholders, including customers. Creating internal compliance programs and establishing codes of conduct is another means of self-regulation. Codes of conduct are often proposed by trade associations in the industry.

Critical Thinking Questions

1. What are the main issues sporting goods companies must consider as they contemplate their supply chain?
2. Identify ways to minimize and defend against counterfeiting in the sporting goods industry.
3. What are the main forms of intellectual property protection available in the sporting goods industry? Is each enforced uniformly around the world?
4. Describe how the pursuit of personal fitness will be different 10 years from now.
5. Describe the issues surrounding head safety and sports equipment.

Applied Activity

Product Design to Market

Describe a new sports equipment product and include a sketch. Next, outline how the new product addresses the following questions:

1. What sector of the sporting goods industry is it in, and what market share would be ideal in its product category?
2. How will the design differ for versions of the new product if intended for females and youth?
3. What will be the preferred distribution channels to get the product from the manufacturer to the end user?
4. What sorts of regulation will it fall under?
5. Explain the licensing arrangements that will be created and how counterfeiting will be addressed.

Case Study Application

For more information about protecting intellectual property rights in the sporting goods industry, review *Ink, You Are Infringing* in the web resource.

chapter 11

Fitness, Wellness, and Health

Scott R. Jedlicka

LEAD-OFF

Although sport governing bodies tend to receive the most attention from those who study sport governance, the sector of the sport industry catering to fitness, wellness, and health promotion allows for an examination of both regulated and unregulated businesses and business practices. On one hand, promoting public health has long been a governmental function. Local, state, and national government agencies are responsible for everything from establishing minimum healthy standards for nutrition and exercise to combating the spread of chronic and infectious diseases. On the other hand, personal wellness is increasingly viewed as something that should be shaped by a person's choices and preferences, and an array of private actors have emerged to meet consumer demand.

The fragmentation of authority in the fitness industry sometimes creates gaps in governance. For instance, while many private agencies offer national certifications for personal fitness trainers, the landscape is an unregulated field of legitimate and questionable entities. At present, there is not even a legal requirement that a personal fitness trainer be certified to practice the trade.

The health sector also has many unaddressed regulatory issues. For example, the United States Food and Drug Administration (FDA), the federal agency responsible for ensuring the safety of food and medications in America, does not require nutritional supplements to be proven safe or effective before they can be marketed to consumers. Yet a recent report indicated 76 percent of American adults regularly consume dietary supplements, ranging from general vitamins and minerals to more specific substances targeted at weight loss and sport performance (Council for Responsible Nutrition, 2017). Almost 90 percent of adults surveyed by the Council for Responsible Nutrition (2017) expressed "confidence in the safety, quality and effectiveness of dietary supplements," but the lack of regulatory oversight can have far-reaching implications. First, there are obvious concerns about any substance that has not been rigorously proven safe for consumption; second, there is a potential for a "natural" supplement to contain an ingredient that is also a banned performance-enhancing substance, which can result in an unexpected doping violation.

This chapter examines the governance and structures of private gyms, commercial franchises, and public health facilities. The chapter also explores the business aspects of producing and selling nutritional supplements.

Learning Outcomes

- Identify the range of public and private authorities in the fitness, wellness, and health sector of the sport industry.
- Describe the governance and functions of private fitness and health clubs.
- Assess the current regulatory approach to personal training.
- Explain how sport governance intersects with public health governance.
- Identify regulatory issues in the nutritional supplement industry.
- Describe the governance and operation of commercial fitness facilities.

PRIVATE FITNESS AND HEALTH CLUBS

At the end of the 19th century, **voluntary sport clubs** emerged as an outlet for Americans' pent-up energies. In addition to clearing timber, digging wells, and planting crops, Americans were forming organizations that provided them with opportunities to socialize, discuss community issues, and exercise their bodies. The sport clubs of the 19th century were especially shaped by the growth of ethnic and status-based subcommunities (e.g., gentlemen's clubs) in urban areas (Rader, 1977). Immigrants turned to ethnic sport clubs to assimilate new citizens and celebrate old traditions. The sport clubs of the middle and upper classes excluded working-class people, and membership was a status symbol.

Some sport clubs, particularly baseball clubs, would eventually become professional teams. Other clubs, such as the prestigious New York Athletic Club (founded in 1868), exist today in largely the same form as they did when they were created. What early American sport clubs had in common, though, was that they were primarily social organizations. While members got together to play sports and games, the clubs played a much broader role in building communities across the country.

Twenty-first-century private fitness and health clubs, the descendants of the voluntary sport clubs of yesteryear, appear vastly different than their 19th-century predecessors. For one, the term "sport clubs" as it is used today often refers specifically to organizations that field competitive teams and athletes. Also, clubs based on members' ethnicity are much rarer than they were a century ago. More generally, fitness and health clubs are not the vibrant social organizations that they once were. Nevertheless, these organizations have retained many of their core governance features.

Clubs

Clubs are a type of **membership organization** that offers members the opportunity to pursue shared interests and develop interpersonal relationships. There is no single standard or correct approach to governing a club. The governance of the largest clubs may be similar to the hierarchical governance of a multinational corporation, while small, informal clubs might not have much formal governance at all.

Because of their rather intimate nature, fitness and health clubs are typically located in a single municipality, often at a single location. In some cases, local clubs (or chapters) may be part of a larger organizational structure that operates regionally, nationally, or internationally. Due to their size, clubs usually rely on member dues and donations as their main revenue source and are often established as **nonprofit organizations**, even though they may still generate a revenue surplus (see Governance in Action 11.1).

Whether a private club's status is classified as profit or nonprofit, most operate through a constitution or handbook outlining the restrictions, dues structures, and general benefits for members as well as defining the responsibilities and electoral process for serving on the board of directors. Private sport clubs and facilities operate under their own rules and regulations. Typically, the constitution outlines the process for electing board members, who are considered the authorities in a private club.

Often at private sport clubs, the pro or general manager reports to the board, which serves as the entity empowered to make all decisions affecting the direction and operation of the club. The size and scope of activities of a board are determined by the number of active members, the amenities, and revenue generated. Among private fitness and health clubs, a classification system distinguishes between athletic clubs, located primarily in urban

GOVERNANCE IN ACTION 11.1

Private Clubs: Profit Versus Nonprofit Status

One of the distinctive features of the private sport club, regardless of its ability to generate revenue, is the option to operate as a nonprofit organization. The mention of nonprofit organizations typically conjures up entities such as the Salvation Army, Red Cross, or Girl Scouts. In the same classification as these social service organizations are private country clubs that serve the affluent and generate millions of dollars in revenue through high-priced membership fees, tournament fees, greens fees, and cart rentals. The U.S. Internal Revenue Service (IRS) identifies country clubs and amateur "hunting, fishing, tennis, swimming, and other sport clubs" among examples of tax-exempt social and recreational organizations, contingent upon meeting certain criteria ("Examples of Tax-Exempt Social and Recreational Clubs," 2019).

Not all private sport clubs are considered nonprofit organizations. Private clubs that do not limit the amount of nontraditional public funding sources, for example, do not qualify for an IRS tax exemption. An example of a private club without tax exemption status is the Augusta National Golf Club in Georgia (see Governance in Action 11.2), which generates over $100 million from hosting the annual Masters Tournament (Jolly-Ryan, 2006; Sirak, 2015).

Tax-exempt social clubs are classified as 501(c)(7) nonprofit organizations if they meet the conditions defined by the IRS. A primary condition is ensuring that the club is financially supported by membership dues, fees, and assessments. The IRS also stipulates that a "substantial" amount of the activities of a 501(c)(7) social club must be for the primary purpose of recreation or pleasure, which includes "legal or illegal gambling" ("Exempt Organizations Determinations Manual," n.d.). The premise behind the tax exemption for social and recreational clubs is to avoid penalizing members who choose to pool their resources for the purpose of recreation or leisure.

Another IRS stipulation is that only 15 percent of gross revenues generated by a nonprofit private club may be derived from nonmember use of club facilities. Augusta National is considered a for-profit private club because more than 15 percent of its gross revenue is derived from income generated through the Masters.

The IRS also stipulates that goods and services available at private nonprofit social clubs cannot be afforded to the general public. Interestingly, a provision specifies that a private sport club for stock car racing may conduct races and be considered a nonprofit organization, but the proceeds from public admission cannot be distributed to members participating in competition ("Exempt Organizations Determinations Manual," n.d.).

areas, and country clubs, which are found primarily in suburban or exurban locations.

Private Athletic Clubs

An **athletic club** is likely to be found in any major city in the United States. These clubs are probably the closest relatives to the voluntary sport clubs of 19th-century America, although today many of them more closely resemble commercial fitness facilities. According to the Club Managers Association of America (2015), there were 2,600 private sport and athletic clubs in 2013 that generated $21 billion in revenue and served 2 million members.

The governance structures of private athletic clubs are similar to the governance structures of national and international sport federations in that dues-paying members often elect a smaller group of people (a board, executive committee, or management team, along with officers) to oversee and direct the strategic direction of the club. This small group of people has a responsibility to the club's membership in that it must make decisions and enact policies that align with members' interests.

While athletic clubs' main function is to provide exercise and recreational services to their members, some of these clubs offer other amenities to members as an incentive to join. For instance, many athletic clubs have a members-only restaurant, spa, and a social or bar area. Older, more established athletic clubs typically promote social status as a perk of membership. Belonging to the club provides members with an opportunity to demonstrate their affluence as well as to network with other prominent community members.

Country Clubs

Whereas athletic clubs are found mostly in urban areas, **country clubs** are mostly located in suburban or exurban areas. This distinction is because country clubs typically focus on a more limited range of activities, especially golf. Almost 80 percent of private clubs belonging to the Club Managers Association of America (2015) in 2013 were golf courses that hosted over 17,000 cause-related charity tournaments that generated in excess of $150 million in charitable contributions. In 2017, over 11,000 private golf courses and country clubs generated $24 billion in revenue (IBIS World, 2018). Two years later, the number of businesses had decreased slightly to 10,910 while still generating $24 billion and employing 316,044 people (IBIS World, 2019).

Country clubs make up an estimated 30 percent of all golf facilities in the United States (National Club Association, 2010). In addition to a golf course, country clubs will often feature a swimming pool, tennis courts, and a fitness facility, as well as the nonfitness amenities typically offered at athletic clubs. Country clubs also are accustomed to offering dining facilities, private locker rooms (some with steam rooms and hot tubs), and a pro shop to schedule lessons, to book tee or court times, and to sell apparel and equipment. Like athletic clubs, country clubs usually adopt a membership model of governance in which members are responsible for participating in the governance of the organization by electing club leaders.

Historically, country clubs have been criticized for membership policies that have excluded women and people of color. In 2002, the Augusta National Golf Club, one of the most famous country clubs in the world and home to the Masters Tournament, came under fire for its all-male membership policy (the club, open since 1932, did not even admit its first black member until 1990). Although the issue attracted a great deal of media attention when it was first raised (see Governance in Action 11.2), it was not until a decade later, in 2012, that the first female members were admitted to Augusta National (Associated Press, 2012). Country clubs and golf courses in general have also been criticized for their intensive use of natural resources and their negative impact on the environment (Adler, 2007; Salgot & Tapias, 2006; Wheeler & Nauright, 2006).

Private Nonprofit Fitness and Health Organizations

While most private fitness clubs are constituted as nonprofit organizations, there are other types of nonprofit entities focused on fitness and health that are not quite so exclusive. Nonprofit organizations generally exist to support or advance a particular social cause. In the case of private clubs, that cause is essentially the interests of a club's membership. Other nonprofit fitness organizations exist to serve broader social and community interests. While these organizations might adopt a membership model similar to that of a private club, their facilities and services are generally available to everyone.

Two prominent examples of nonprofit fitness and health organizations are the Young Men's Christian Association (YMCA) and the World Young Women's Christian Association (World YWCA). Both of these organizations are headquartered in Switzerland and are international in scope. Largely because of their global reach, both the YMCA and the World YWCA use a **federation model** of governance. This means that while all YMCA and World YWCA chapters share a common purpose and vision, individual chapters are allowed to adapt their programming and services to their locales. Depending on the size of the community that the chapter serves, a YMCA or World YWCA staff might be quite large and complex (with a governing board and functional committees) or consist of only a few full-time employees led by a CEO or general manager.

Especially in the United States, YMCAs and World YWCAs have traditionally housed fitness facilities and offered various types of health and fitness programs, especially for young people. To generate operating revenue, many chapters offer memberships, though the membership fees at YMCAs are typically not as expensive as private club memberships. Further, YMCAs and World YWCAs will typically subsidize membership for low-income people, which is why the organizations may also be referred to as quasi-public entities, as described in chapter 4 on sport governing agencies in local and state sports.

There are YMCA facilities in 119 countries around the world. There are 2,700 chapters in the United States employing approximately 20,000 full-time staff and 600,000 volunteers in 10,000 communities ("Organizational Profile Facts and Figures," n.d.). Nationally, the YMCA is governed by 25 council members charged with ensuring compliance with all regulatory requirements to retain a nonprofit status. The YMCA advises local governing boards to review corporate documents (e.g., charter and articles of incorporation) every three to five years to ensure compliance with state and federal nonprofit laws. According to a document outlining best practices for board leadership

GOVERNANCE IN ACTION 11.2

Augusta National Golf Club: Changes in Attitude

On April 11, 2002, journalist Christine Brennan's column in *USA Today* read:

In golf, there are two kinds of discrimination: There is acceptable discrimination, and then there is unacceptable discrimination. In the Age of Tiger [Woods], it's obviously no longer acceptable to discriminate against African-Americans on the golf course. It's entirely fine, however, to discriminate against women.

Brennan went on to argue that Augusta National, a private golf club located in Augusta, Georgia, best known for hosting the Masters Tournament, should admit women as members. Her column sparked women's rights activist Martha Burk, leader of the National Council of Women's Organizations, to ask club chairman William "Hootie" Johnson to consider the idea of allowing women to become members (Weinreb, 2018). Johnson immediately went on the defensive, issuing a lengthy and incendiary press release that characterized the club and its members as victims of a feminist plot. Johnson asserted that the club's membership would not be "bullied, threatened, or intimidated," and that while Augusta National might one day admit women, "that timetable will be ours, and not at the point of a bayonet" ("Statement by Hootie Johnson," 2002). So began a lengthy debate lasting years that focused on inclusion, representation, and the rights of private organizations.

Although Augusta National is much more lucrative than the average private club, anyone who holds a governance position in this type of organization will be confronted with the question of how to balance public and private interests. Johnson, as the club's leader and spokesman, believed his first duty was to serve the club's members and more importantly, to retain its autonomy as a private organization to make its own decisions instead of succumbing to public pressure. Johnson ultimately decided to cancel commercial agreements with many top sponsors to protect them from potential public backlash; as a result, the 2003 and 2004 Masters Tournaments were aired commercial-free (Associated Press, 2003).

Meanwhile, critics of Augusta National said that if the organization did not change its stance on admitting women, it would risk tarnishing the reputation that made it such an attractive and exclusive club in the first place. While Augusta National is structured like most private clubs (a voting membership, an executive board, and executive officers), it has traditionally allowed the chairman (Johnson) a great deal of authority over the decision-making process (Weinreb, 2018). Johnson, however, resigned his chairmanship in 2006.

The public spotlight on Augusta National's exclusion policy surfaced again in 2012 when Ginni Rometty, IBM's first female CEO, was not extended the same membership privileges as all previous CEOs of the company. In response, Billy Payne, Johnson's successor as chairman, decided to admit the club's first two female members: former Secretary of State Condoleezza Rice and prominent financier Darla Moore (Ginni Rometty would become a club member in 2014). In 2019, gender barriers were broken again when Augusta National hosted its first women's championship event (McDonald, 2019).

and governance, the YMCA (2011) identifies seven areas of responsibility for overseeing a facility:

1. Legal and ethical integrity
2. Rules and regulations (e.g., developing whistleblower policies)
3. Fiduciary oversight, board development
4. CEO selection and supervision
5. Philanthropic leadership
6. Cause-driven strategies
7. Community standing

Nonprofit sport and fitness organizations that rely on membership revenue as their primary source of income are often forced to compete for members with commercial gyms and specialized private for-profit training facilities. This competitiveness presents a distinct governance challenge. Unlike commercial or for-profit fitness centers and businesses, YMCAs and similar private nonprofit agencies are charitable organizations, which means that they must adhere to certain criteria in order to be exempt from paying income taxes. This has created tension with private for-profit orga-

Tom Williams/CQ Roll Call

YMCAs are examples of private membership organizations that receive government subsidies to serve the greater public need for affordable fitness opportunities for low-income families.

nizations, which have complained that YMCAs, because they do not have to pay the same taxes as do commercial facilities, have an unfair advantage in competing for customers. In fact, during the 1980s, there was a brief but intense movement to challenge the YMCA's tax-exempt status, leading some chapters to undertake significant reform efforts (Stern, 2011).

COMMERCIAL FITNESS AND HEALTH (FOR PROFIT)

For a variety of reasons, most American adults do not exercise regularly. The U.S. Department of Health and Human Services (2017) reports that "less than 5% of adults participate in 30 minutes of physical activity each day" and "only one in three adults receive the recommended amount of physical activity each week." Every year, many people turn to membership organizations to motivate (or perhaps coerce) themselves to improve their fitness routines. There is a longstanding adage that the busiest month of the year for private fitness facilities is January, when people are still trying to stick to their New Year's resolutions. While not everyone can develop a regular exercise routine (and many who can do not frequent private facilities), there remains a relatively stable market for commercial fitness and health facilities that can satisfy a diverse mix of consumer needs. However, these organiza-

tions can vary significantly in terms of how they are structured, operated, and regulated.

Commercial fitness facilities are typically operated as for-profit organizations, or as part of such an organization. Like many businesses, commercial fitness organizations often have a governing hierarchy. At the top, there is usually a governing board (e.g., a board of directors) and a small group of chief executives such as a CEO, a chief operating officer (COO), a chief financial officer (CFO), and so forth. While commercial facilities may adopt a membership model similar to that of a private club, their goal is to generate profits for their shareholders, which means that a member of a commercial fitness organization is more like a customer purchasing a good than a person joining a closed social group.

Examples of major commercial fitness organizations include LA Fitness, CrossFit, Anytime Fitness, Snap Fitness, Life Time Fitness, Gold's Gym, and Planet Fitness (see Governance in Action 11.3). LA Fitness is owned by Seidler Equity Partners ("Partner Companies," n.d.). Similarly, 24 Hour Fitness is owned by three partners: AEA Investors, Ontario Teachers' Pension Plan, and Fitness Capital Partners ("Chris Rousses Named CEO," 2017). Planet Fitness is a franchise corporation with multiple equity companies owning individual locations or groups of facilities. In addition to these national enterprises, commercial fitness facilities can also operate at the regional and local levels.

Large commercial fitness organizations often adopt a **franchise business model**. While franchises are probably best known in relation to the fast food industry (think McDonald's), they are also common in the fitness industry. Franchising allows an organization to grow quickly—rather than an organization (the franchiser) having to purchase and set up new facilities in new markets, it can simply sell the branding and operational model to local operators (franchisees) in exchange for a set of agreed-upon fees. The main risk involved in franchising is associated with brand equity and quality control—the franchiser often cannot directly regulate the actions of franchisees on a daily or even weekly basis.

Big or small, commercial fitness providers are fundamentally businesses and are regulated as such. While they must comply with applicable employment laws and other regulations (e.g., guidelines pertaining to construction and renovation of a facility), they are not subject to any oversight with regard to the types of services and products they sell. As noted previously, this lack of regulation is an example of a governance gap in the fitness and health industry. While physical activity guidelines are developed by public sector agencies, those agencies lack the authority to ensure that private sector entities (like commercial gyms) are adhering to those guidelines.

GOVERNANCE IN ACTION 11.3

Planet Fitness, Inc.

"We're going after the 80% of the population that doesn't have a gym membership" is the mantra of Chris Rondeau, Planet Fitness, Inc. CEO since 2013 (Rondeau, 2019). Founded in 1992, Planet Fitness began franchising in 2003, issued its initial public offering (IPO) in 2015, and has seen its stock price more than triple (from a $16/share IPO to over $50/share) as of December 2018. The chain markets itself and its gyms as "judgement free zones," a place where people can exercise without having to confront the high-energy, high-performance expectations often associated (rightly or wrongly) with traditional gym settings.

With more than 95 percent of its stores operated by franchisees, the governance of Planet Fitness is primarily concerned not with the day-to-day management of fitness facilities, but with "big picture" corporate strategy. Because Planet Fitness is a for-profit, publicly traded company, the overarching goal of its leaders is to increase the company's stock price. Planet Fitness is governed by a board of directors, which is responsible for exercising the company's business affairs. Membership on Planet Fitness' board of directors is determined first by the board itself (which nominates potential candidates) and finally by the shareholders, who are responsible for electing new members of the board.

Most of the board's specific functions involve approving and monitoring the organization's strategic plans. For instance, if Planet Fitness' management wanted to pursue a different marketing strategy, open new locations, change hiring practices and policies, or require equipment upgrades at all of its franchises, the board would have to consider whether these moves would be consistent with the company's overall direction as well as whether they would be profitable.

In addition to strategic considerations, the board is also responsible for "selecting, evaluating and compensating" the company's CEO and providing "advice and oversight" in the selection of senior-level managers.

Planet Fitness' corporate governance structure is not uncommon in the commercial fitness world. In some cases, the board of directors may take a very active role in governance decisions, while in other cases, the board might be content to defer to the CEO and upper-level management to make the important decisions. Even within a simple structure, therefore, there is still room for flexibility and political maneuvering. Ultimately, however, the performance of corporate governors is often judged in terms of the bottom line. In this respect, at least, Planet Fitness' corporate governance seems to be up to the task.

The preceding information is sourced from Planet Fitness, Inc.'s Corporate Governance Guidelines, available at http://investor.planetfitness.com/investors/corporate-governance/governance-documents/default.aspx

TRAINERS: CERTIFICATION AND LICENSURE

According to the U.S. Department of Labor, there were around 300,000 people working as fitness trainers and instructors in the United States as of 2016 (Bureau of Labor Statistics, 2018). **Personal trainers** usually work with clients individually to help them achieve their fitness goals, while **fitness instructors** typically teach group classes in activities like indoor cycling, yoga, and aerobic dance. Although the number of trainers and fitness instructors is projected to steadily increase over the next decade, there is not much regulation or oversight of this labor market sector.

If a fitness trainer isn't employed directly by a fitness center or facility, he or she may operate independently as an individual contractor, typically as a sole proprietor or a limited liability corporation (LLC). This type of personal trainer or fitness expert may still be hired by clubs and facilities to conduct classes and private training, but the arrangement as a third-party service provider presents a different relationship than a part-time or full-time employee with respect to tax filing and liability protections. Instead of having the protection of the employer's liability insurance policy in the event of negligent acts, independent contractors are personally liable or culpable for their own actions. In both the United States and Canada, independent contractors are not covered by workers' compensation, which provides monetary benefits if one is injured in the workplace. There is, however, the potential to achieve higher earnings when self-employed than when working for an employer, particularly if the self-employed person has an incorporated company (Findlay, Corbett, & Lech, 2003).

It is assumed that personal trainers and fitness specialists have the requisite experience, special knowledge, and professional expertise to operate in their field, which is another matter of self-governance. Currently, there are no state or federal laws requiring people who work as trainers or fitness instructors to be certified or licensed. While many people will have at least some training or experience in the field before beginning to work as a personal trainer or fitness instructor, there are no legal standards in place to ensure a minimum competency level. This lack of top-down regulation has both benefits and drawbacks. For many trainers and instructors, a lack of licensing requirements makes it easier to earn a living because such requirements (which typically involve administrative fees and continuing education courses) can sometimes be rather costly. On the other hand, a lack of standardization increases the likelihood that consumers could be harmed by trainers who, due to a lack of knowledge or experience, recommend inappropriate or dangerous exercise regimens.

Despite a lack of direct governmental regulation, many trainers and fitness instructors will voluntarily seek out certification in order to improve their skills and to legitimize their practice to potential clients. Also, trainers and instructors who use or are employed by commercial fitness facilities or private athletic clubs may be required by the facility to obtain some sort of certification. Table 11.1 provides a partial list of private organizations that have developed programs and courses to meet this demand for certification and licensure.

Table 11.1 Selected Organizations Offering Certification and Licensure in Personal Training and Fitness Instruction

Association	2019 Exam price
American College of Sports Medicine (ACSM)	$349
American Council on Exercise (ACE)	$399
American Fitness Professionals & Associates (AFPA)	$149+
Athletics & Fitness Association of America (AFAA)	$499
International Sports Sciences Association (ISSA)	$499
National Academy of Sports Medicine (NASM)	$599
National Council on Strength & Fitness (NCSF)	$299
National Exercise Trainers Association (NETA)	$399

Adapted from American College of Sports Medicine. (n.d.). Personal Trainer Comparison Chart. www.acsm.org/get-stay-certified/get-certified/comparing-personal-trainer-certifications; American Fitness Professionals & Associates. (n.d.). Personal Fitness Trainer Certification. www.afaa.com/courses/personal-fitness-trainer; National Council on Strength & Fitness. (n.d.). Choose Your Program. www.ncsf.org/personal-trainer/

The associations listed in table 11.1 represent just a select few of the more prominent certifying organizations. Again, even for trainers and instructors who are seeking certification, the lack of a standard, centralized certification and licensure program presents benefits and drawbacks. On one hand, trainers can seek out the licensing program that best fits their needs and constraints, and similarly, licensing organizations can carve out specialized niches catering to particular types of fitness professionals. On the other hand, because licensing organizations have to compete for customers, they may have an incentive to make certification relatively easy to obtain. This relative ease of obtaining a license can in turn diminish the authenticity of all certifications—while some certified trainers may have undergone rigorous testing, others may have been subject to much lower standards.

As the importance of physical activity and exercise to basic health becomes more widely acknowledged, it is likely that the demand for personal trainers and fitness instructors—that is, for people with the expertise to help others achieve fitness goals and health outcomes—will also increase. As a result, it is likely that local and state governments, and perhaps even the federal government, will consider adopting certification and licensure standards for fitness professionals (Werner, 2017). However, under the current governance model (or lack thereof), it is largely up to the consumer to determine (1) whether trainers are certified and (2) if they are, the quality of that certification.

PUBLIC HEALTH

Physical fitness has always figured prominently in the American imagination. In 1956, President Dwight D. Eisenhower established the President's Council on Youth Fitness (today known as the **President's Council on Sports, Fitness & Nutrition**) to reinvigorate and reshape physical education programs across the country (Bowers & Hunt, 2011). Anyone enrolled in a physical education class between the 1960s and the 2010s might remember (perhaps not very fondly!) taking the fitness tests that made up the President's Challenge, a program designed to motivate youth to get and stay physically fit. While this program was phased out during President Barack Obama's second term, it is just one illustration of the efforts undertaken by the federal government to promote good health among American citizens.

Today, public health is still largely the responsibility of federal, state, and local governments. The logic behind the government's interest in public health is simple. When people are sick or injured, they often cannot work or otherwise lead productive lives. This creates a two-fold cost for society and, by extension, for a government. First, there is the direct cost of providing people with care and treatment. In the United States, many people's health care is provided through the private sector, but elderly and low-income Americans (who tend to get sick and injured more often than wealthier people) rely on government programs in order to

Up until the Obama era, the Presidential Fitness Challenge motivated youth to stay physically active by completing age- and gender-appropriate standards through sit-ups, push-ups, and other activities.

access the care that they need (Marmot, 2002; Pickett, James, & Wilkinson, 2006; Woolf et al., 2015). Second, there is the opportunity cost created when someone is too sick or hurt to work. The time a person spends recovering from an illness or injury is time that could have been spent working, volunteering, or taking part in recreational activities. Due to these costs, governments in particular have an incentive to ensure that people are leading healthy lifestyles and can get health care when they need it.

When it comes to public health, the updated edition of physical activity guidelines for the United States indicates youths ages 6 through 17 should have at least 60 minutes of moderate to vigorous aerobic physical activity daily (p. 48), and adults should have a minimum of 150 minutes per week (U.S. Department of Health and Human Services, 2018, p. 56). Setting guidelines and standards is one of the governance functions of governmental agencies assigned to public health. The other two functions are conducting research and providing funding and other support for health programs. Before exploring each of these functions, it is important to first have a basic understanding of the governmental bodies involved in public health.

Governmental Public Health Administration

There are a number of federal entities involved in public health, most of which are housed within the **U.S. Department of Health and Human Services (IHS)**, which is the agency that publishes the federal guidelines on physical activity. HHS is part of the president's cabinet in the executive branch of the federal government. The top official in this department holds the title of secretary, is nominated by the president, and must be confirmed by the Senate. However, it is the assistant secretary for health who actually oversees most of the government's work in public health. Of the 11 operating divisions in HHS, eight comprise the United States Public Health Service (USPHS), which is specifically concerned with public health and is directed by the Assistant Secretary for Health:

- Agency for Healthcare Research & Quality (AHRQ)
- Food and Drug Administration (FDA)
- Centers for Disease Control and Prevention (CDC)
- Agency for Toxic Substances and Disease Registry (ATSDR)

- Health Resources & Services Administration (HRSA)
- Indian Health Service (IHS)
- National Institutes of Health (NIH)
- Substance Abuse and Mental Health Services Administration (SAMHSA)

In addition to the divisions comprising the Public Health Service, the assistant secretary for health oversees other agencies involved in public health, such as the Office of the Surgeon General, the Office of Disease Prevention and Health Promotion, and the President's Council on Sports, Fitness & Nutrition.

Governing public health is a large and complex undertaking. The divisions and agencies listed (which is far from an exhaustive list) all have their own staffs and organizational structures. Each state government also has some form of public health authority that, like the federal government, is responsible for communicating information about how to live a healthy lifestyle. Additionally, state health departments are typically responsible for credentialing medical professionals and facilities (doctors, nurses, and hospitals) as well as issuing birth, death, and marriage certificates.

While the number and scope of government agencies in the health sector are vast, there are a few entities that deal specifically with issues connected to exercise and nutrition as opposed to communicable disease, substance abuse, and the health of specific populations. Nevertheless, there is a much closer relationship between sport-related activities and health than is often acknowledged, and the role sport can play in improving public health programs cannot be dismissed.

Research

The **National Institutes of Health (NIH)** is an umbrella agency consisting of 27 specialized institutes that conduct and fund medical and public health research. The NIH receives funding from the U.S. Congress, most of which is redistributed to researchers in the form of **research grants**. The NIH's budget in 2018 was around $37 billion (Kaiser, 2018). The other federal agency that plays a significant role in public health research is the **Centers for Disease Control and Prevention (CDC)** housed in Atlanta, Georgia. While NIH tends to focus its research efforts on formal academic studies, the CDC tends to focus more on problem-oriented research projects and programs. For example, an NIH research project might seek to understand the biological factors that increase a person's risk of developing diabetes, while a CDC research project might explore which methods work best for preventing diabetes, especially within specific demographic groups.

Standards and Guidelines

Perhaps the most important function of public health governance is setting standards and guidelines for healthy living, among which are the new 2018 physical activity guidelines for youth and adults. The standards and guidelines help the public to know what foods and food groups make up a balanced diet and how much as well as which types of exercise help to maintain a healthy weight and reduce the risk of chronic disease. It is partially the responsibility of health agencies in America, funded by the government, to make sure that people know the risks of abusing alcohol, tobacco, and other drugs or know how to spot warning signs in someone who might be mentally unwell.

While discussions and debates about health and what constitutes good health are always evolving, the consensus at this point is that being healthy means much more than simply being "not sick." Definitions of health today vary; the World Health Organization (WHO) defines health as "a state of complete physical, mental and social well-being and not merely the absence of disease or infirmity" (International Health Conference, 1946). A more recent definition proposes that health is "the experience of physical and psychological well-being" and that good and poor health do not occur as a dichotomy, but as a continuum (Card, 2017, p. 131). Regardless of the definition to which one subscribes, the general consensus is that exercise

and physical activity play an important role in promoting and maintaining good health.

HHS is usually considered the authoritative source on health guidelines, including the appropriate amount of exercise for specific age groups. The department's information is based on data gathered through a number of different agencies, including the CDC and the NIH. These exercise guidelines are typically published in a government document and disseminated by traditional public relations methods (press releases, social media, websites, etc.). Key physical activity guidelines, published in the second edition of *Physical Activity Guidelines for Americans* (U.S. Department of Health and Human Services, 2018), are listed in table 11.2.

While the minimum standards for physical activity may be considered relatively low (e.g., even a recreational endurance athlete might engage in single training sessions of two hours or more at times), the most recent survey data indicate that "only 26 percent of men, 19 percent of women, and 20 percent of adolescents report sufficient activity to meet the relevant aerobic and muscle-strengthening guidelines" (U.S. Department of Health and Human Services, 2018, p. 15).

In addition to physical activity guidelines, government agencies also develop standards for healthy eating. In addition to HHS, another government agency traditionally involved in developing these standards is the **U.S. Department of Agriculture (USDA)**. Nutrition is an important factor in public health, especially given the fact that so many Americans do not get the recommended amount of exercise. In the past, nutritional standards have been rather specific, recommending precise numbers of servings from different food groups as well as overall calorie consumption

Table 11.2 HHS Key Physical Activity Guidelines

Group	Age range	Physical activity recommendation
Preschool-aged children	3–5 years	Daily with varied types of activity
Children and adolescents	6–17 years	60+ minutes daily; primarily aerobic, combined with muscle- and bone-strengthening activities
Adults	18–64 years	2.5 to 5 hours of moderate activity OR 1.25 to 2.5 hours of vigorous activity weekly; primarily aerobic with at least two days of muscle-strengthening activity
		Adults with chronic health conditions or disabilities should seek guidance from a health care provider about appropriate types and amounts of physical activity
Older adults	65+ years	Approximately 2.5 hours of moderate activity weekly as health allows; equal emphasis on balance, aerobic fitness, and muscle strength
Pregnant and postpartum women	n/a	2.5 hours of moderate aerobic activity weekly

limits. With rates of obesity and chronic disease on the rise, these specific, targeted guidelines have been replaced by more general recommendations designed to promote sustainable healthy eating habits. The *2015-2020 Dietary Guidelines for Americans* (U.S. Department of Health and Human Services & U.S. Department of Agriculture, 2015, p. xii) lists five general dietary guidelines:

1. Follow a healthy eating pattern across the lifespan.
2. Focus on variety, nutrient density, and amount.
3. Limit calories from added sugars and saturated fats and reduce sodium intake.
4. Shift to healthier food and beverage choices.
5. Support healthy eating patterns for all.

The shift to a more general, holistic approach to diet reflects a growing acknowledgment of how economic and cultural differences affect people's eating habits. In other words, a one-size-fits-all approach to healthy eating might not be useful or feasible for many Americans.

The power of governmental agencies to set standards and guidelines for (among other things) exercise and nutrition is an important aspect of public health governance. These standards and guidelines are used to shape the content of sport and physical education programs as well as to evaluate the effectiveness of those programs. Because these agencies

are a part of government, they are sometimes criticized for basing their decisions on short-term political considerations rather than on the best interests of the public. For instance, early in 2017, the CDC hastily canceled a scientific conference dealing with the relationship between health and climate change out of concern that the event might antagonize the incoming Trump administration (Mole, 2017). At the same time, these agencies are often more transparent, accessible, and accountable to the public than private organizations.

Funding and Support for Programs

In addition to setting standards and guidelines, government agencies also provide support and funding for the implementation of public health programs. Support typically means providing public health program managers with training and educational materials to administer programs at a local level. Funding, as with public health research, is usually in the form of competitive grants. Two programs that fall under the purview of support for public health programs are the Office of Disease Prevention and Health Promotion (ODPHP) and the President's Council on Sports, Fitness & Nutrition (PCSFN).

The ODPHP, as its name suggests, is the agency connected to HHS that is largely responsible for transforming information about public health

iStockphoto/Catherine Yeulet

Promotional campaigns, whether funded and administered by private or government agencies, have targeted exercise and nutrition to improve overall public health.

into action. One way this is done is through promotional campaigns, such as the Move Your Way campaign designed to educate people about recommended healthy levels of physical activity and to provide resources for public health officials at the state and local levels. The campaign website includes fact sheets, posters, videos, and other tools for increasing and sustaining physical activity. These resources are useful not only for those who are interested in becoming healthier, but also for those who work with people on a broader scale to improve their fitness, such as recreation center directors, physical educators, personal trainers, and medical professionals, to name a few. Through these types of campaigns, ODPHP takes a very broad and vague problem (getting people to be more active) and provides the support and direction necessary for people to start finding and implementing solutions.

The PCSFN has a much more targeted goal: getting young people to become involved in sports and physical activity. Like the ODPHP, the PCSFN provides information about physical activity guidelines and ways to become more active. However, the PCSFN is more directly involved in program administration as well as financial support for youth fitness. The Presidential Youth Fitness Program provides physical educators with fitness assessment tools and benchmarks and encourages them to be involved in the program by nationally recognizing schools, students, and teachers who demonstrate commitment to an active lifestyle and the achievement of fitness goals. Additionally, educators who are involved in the program can apply for financial support from the National Fitness Foundation, which awards small (up to $1,000) grants to schools that are implementing or plan to implement the Presidential Youth Fitness Program.

These two examples, in addition to illustrating how governmental agencies are involved in public health programming, also demonstrate two distinct approaches to governance. The ODPHP, through the Move Your Way campaign, takes a relatively decentralized governance approach. While everyone has access to the same set of resources, individuals and program managers are free to adapt those resources to their needs and populations. On the other hand, the PCSFN's Presidential Youth Fitness Program adopts a more centralized approach. The program components are determined at the federal level, and while teachers have some flexibility in implementation, the assessment tools and overall program goals are relatively similar for all schools involved in the program.

Sport Programs and Public Health

Since public health governance is a broad topic—exercise and nutrition programs are just a small part—it is occasionally difficult to make a direct connection to sports. The reasons are complex. As elite sport has become more commercialized and socially significant, many countries have adopted a trickle-down approach to sport development, reasoning that successful elite sport programs will result in increased mass participation. However, there is not much (if any) strong evidence to suggest that this causal relationship exists (De Bosscher, Sotiriadou, & van Bottenburg, 2013; Hanstad & Skille, 2010). Further, there are often significant social and economic barriers to sport participation for women, people of color, and poor people (Gillard & Witt, 2008; Kay, 2000; Koivula, 1999). There is also growing concern that an overemphasis on winning in youth sports leads many children to develop negative feelings about sport. This, in turn, makes sport seem less appealing as a form of physical activity for many adults (Coakley, 1992; Wall & Côté, 2007).

Can sport be used to accomplish public health objectives? Perhaps. Some researchers believe that systemic changes are needed for sport to be an effective public health tool (Arai & Pedlar, 2003). In addition to (or instead of) focusing on the development of talented athletes, sport programs should target activities and concepts to enhance basic skill or motor development, social inclusion, and enjoyment (Blodgett et al., 2008; Kirk, 2005; Morgan, 2001). Likewise, in addition to traditional physical activity recommendations such as walking, swimming, and cycling, public health agencies might consider promoting sport participation as a way to achieve basic fitness and physical activity standards. In either case, if governing organizations are to use sport for public health purposes, they will probably need to reassess the ways in which sport programming is currently delivered.

International and Nongovernmental Public Health Agencies

International and nongovernmental organizations (NGOs) also play an important role in public health. The **World Health Organization** (WHO), a subsidiary agency of the United Nations (UN), is an international organization that seeks to coordinate and support public health efforts around the world. Similar to the responsibilities of U.S. government agencies, the WHO is responsible for monitoring public health through data collection efforts, developing health standards and guidelines, and providing financial and technical support to local public health initiatives. All UN member states are eligible to join the WHO. Similar to other UN divisions, the WHO has a plenary body (the World Health Assembly) as well as an executive board comprised of public health experts.

There are also a number of international and national NGOs that participate in public health governance. These organizations are typically organized as nonprofits and are dedicated to addressing specific, acute problems (e.g., curing a specific disease, refugee health, providing health care in combat zones). Unlike the WHO, public health NGOs are not made up of governmental delegations, but instead are staffed by private citizens and volunteers.

NUTRITIONAL SUPPLEMENTS

As indicated in the chapter lead-off, the manufacturing, sale, and use of nutritional supplements is widespread and lightly regulated. Legally, **dietary supplements** are defined as "products taken by mouth that contain a dietary ingredient." Examples of dietary ingredients include "vitamins, minerals, amino acids, and herbs or botanicals" (U.S. Food and Drug Administration, 2017). People use supplements for a variety of reasons, from enhancing athletic performance to improving general health. Given the prevalence of nutritional supplements in the daily lives of Americans, it is important to understand the governance structures and processes that shape the supplement industry in the United States.

Production

Currently, manufacturers do not need to obtain FDA approval before producing a nutritional supplement. Neither do they need to prove that the supplement is safe or effective, or that it is produced in a clean, uncontaminated facility. According to the **Dietary Supplement Health and Education Act** (DSHEA) of 1994 Pub. L. 103-417, 108 Stat. 4325, a supplement producer is only required to notify the FDA at least 75 days before bringing the product to market and to provide "information, including any citation to published articles" that has led the producer to determine that its product is safe. While supplement manufacturers are required to comply with all applicable local,

state, and federal laws governing the operation of a business enterprise, the quality and safety of the supplement(s) they produce are not subject to much oversight at all.

The lack of direct regulation in the supplement industry is often defended from a free market perspective. If supplement manufacturers do not produce a safe and effective product, so the reasoning goes, they will soon be out of business. Consumers will not want to buy a product that does not work or has negative side effects, and perhaps more importantly, a company that produces a low-quality product will harm its brand, potentially affecting sales of its other products.

Are market forces an effective regulation mechanism? In an (in)famous scene from the 2008 documentary *Bigger, Stronger, Faster*, director Chris Bell hires a few day laborers to help him produce a legal nutritional supplement designed to promote muscle growth. The catch? The "supplement" is actually gel capsules filled with little more than rice flour. Bell claims that a bottle of this product, which costs him about $1.40 to produce, can be sold for $60, equating to a markup of almost 4,200 percent! At this rate, profit can be generated quickly, even if sales are relatively poor. While reputable manufacturers may be able to resist the "get rich quick" temptation, as this example demonstrates, the profit motive might not always lead to improved product quality when it comes to nutritional supplements.

Marketing

Like their production, the marketing and advertising of nutritional supplements are loosely regulated. The FDA is responsible for monitoring product labeling, while the Federal Trade Commission (FTC) regulates other marketing communication, including print, broadcast, and online advertising. The DSHEA requires manufacturers to include two disclaimers on product labels: first, that any claims to effectiveness and safety have not been evaluated by the FDA, and second, that the product is not intended to "diagnose, treat, cure or prevent any disease" (U.S. Federal Trade Commission, 2001, p. 23). However, aside from these two statements, when it comes to assertions about a product's effects, producers are not required "to prove to FDA's satisfaction that the claim is accurate or truthful before it appears on the product" (U.S. Food and Drug Administration, 2017).

The FTC requires supplement advertisements to comply with basic truth-in-advertising standards. This means that advertisements cannot overstate (or outright fabricate) the effects of a supplement, and they must disclose information about the known risks and potential side effects of taking the supplement. Further, manufacturers must be able to substantiate all claims made in any marketing materials, though the standards for adequate substantiation are somewhat flexible (U.S. Federal Trade Commission, 2001).

Usage

While there are guidelines in place governing how nutritional supplements are produced and marketed, consumers are also expected to play a role in regulation. As the FDA (2017) itself notes, its "role with a dietary supplement product begins only *'after the product enters the marketplace'*." Especially given their limited resources, regulatory agencies only learn of deceptive or unsafe practices after a problem has occurred. Consumers thus bear most of the burden for (1) ensuring that a supplement is safe and (2) triggering the enforcement systems that are in place by making a complaint, either to the product manufacturer or to the FDA.

Athletes who are subject to antidoping protocols have an additional incentive to pay close attention to the supplements they put into their bodies. The rules enforced by antidoping organizations—most notably the World Anti-Doping Code—do not provide exceptions to athletes who mistakenly take supplements that may have been tainted with banned performance-enhancing substances.

Due to the lax regulation of the supplement industry, it is often difficult to know whether a product's label is accurate or if the product was produced in a clean facility. These questions are a clear example of inconsistent governance in sport. Relatively limited regulation in the supplement industry, combined with very rigid regulation of performance-enhancing substance use in sport, leaves athletes (some of whom might rely on nutritional supplements to support their training and general health) in a very precarious situation.

RECAP

The fitness, wellness, and health sector of the sport industry is home to a diverse group of organizations and governance systems. This chapter has examined the governance and regulatory environments surrounding private fitness and health clubs, personal trainers and fitness instructors, public health, nutritional supplements, and commercial fitness organizations. Each of these areas is distinct in terms of its relevant actors and approach to regulation.

For the most part, the governance of fitness providers—whether they be private clubs, commercial facilities, or individual trainers and instructors—is characterized by a lack of central authority. While these entities must conform to basic laws and regulations that govern all organizations, there is no definitive hierarchical structure within which these actors operate. Instead, their actions are constrained and directed primarily by their members (in the case of private clubs), their shareholders and corporate leaders (in the case of commercial organizations), or basic supply and demand (in the case of trainers and instructors). Indeed, the lack of clear governance authority is evident in the emerging market for personal training certifications, in which a number of competing licensing organizations vie for the chance to sell certification courses to trainers and fitness instructors.

The same lack of regulation is evident in the production and sale of nutritional supplements. While manufacturers are subject to some basic rules and guidelines, these expectations are far more lax than those applied to the manufacture of food and pharmaceuticals. This oversight can have potentially catastrophic consequences for elite athletes, who could ingest products tainted with performance-enhancing substances. Additionally, lax standards can be problematic for the average person who could have an adverse reaction to an ambiguously labeled supplement.

One area that does feature a more defined (though also more complicated) governance system is public health. National governments have typically taken a leading role in governing public health due to the government's interest in keeping health care costs low and economic productivity high. In the United States, governmental agencies are primarily responsible for developing standards and guidelines for healthy living, including establishing appropriate recommendations for physical activity levels and diet. Sport has not traditionally featured prominently in the public health conversation. However, the growing acknowledgment of exercise's role in maintaining good health presents the opportunity for sport to become a more widely used public health tool.

Although sport governance often is aligned with competitive sport, it is important to maintain an awareness of sport's relationship to the broader areas of fitness and health and to understand the ways in which these areas are governed. As this chapter has demonstrated, there are points at which these two worlds clearly intersect. This intersection creates possibilities for new approaches to sport governance as well as new ways for sport to enrich people's lives.

Critical Thinking Questions

1. What societal purpose did voluntary sport clubs serve at the beginning of the 20th century, and do they serve that same role in the 21st century? Why or why not?

2. Should there be stricter laws and regulations governing the certification of personal trainers and fitness instructors? Why or why not?

3. Could sport participation be an effective way of getting adults to exercise? Or should we continue to emphasize various forms of physical activity?

4. After reading this chapter, should someone who takes nutritional supplements be more concerned about the lack of oversight in this industry?

5. Suppose Planet Fitness' board of directors decides to raise membership rates, based on data that clearly indicate that this move will be profitable for the company. However, this will mean that some franchises in low-income areas (where Planet Fitness is the only nearby affordable facility) will have to shut down. Assuming the CEO is deeply committed to the organization's mission of inclusiveness, should he or she challenge the board's decision? Why or why not?

Applied Activity

Pros and Cons of Governance Roles

This chapter has surveyed various organizations involved in the governance of fitness and health. In general, public sector (i.e., governmental) organizations are responsible for developing guidelines and recommendations for physical activity, while private sector organizations (i.e., private clubs, commercial facilities) are largely relied upon to provide the resources necessary for people to engage in physical activity. As obesity rates among Americans remain high, the need for people to become more physically active has taken on increased importance and has in turn raised questions about current governance approaches.

Using information from the chapter, develop lists of pros and cons for two different scenarios: one in which public sector governing agencies take a more direct role in implementing fitness programs, and one in which public sector governing agencies do not play any role in fitness and health.

Case Study Application

For more information about governance and politics in the fitness industry, review *High School Strength and Conditioning: A Case Study in Caution* in the web resource.

chapter 12

Sport Marketing

Justin B. Kozubal, David W. Walsh, and Michael A. Odio

LEAD-OFF

Sport has become one of the fastest growing and most effective media for brands and companies to market their products and services, with approximately $65 billion spent globally from marketing budgets each year (Handley, 2018). Whether it's advertising to consumers through commercials during the Super Bowl each February, soliciting potential consumers through social media outlets during March Madness, or borrowing equity from a top athlete to endorse a product, the sport manager is faced with myriad governance and legal issues related to the marketing environment.

The money exchanged in the sport advertising, endorsement, and promotion business in America alone demonstrates the influence of marketing. For example, the $11.5 million in tennis tournament prize money Roger Federer earned between June 2017 and June 2018 didn't compare to his $65 million in earnings during the same period from endorsement deals with Wilson, Credit Suisse, Jura, Lindt, Rolex, Mercedes-Benz, and NetJets (SI Staff, 2018). In the media world, ESPN paid $1.9 billion for the rights to televise Monday Night Football through 2021, while Amazon paid $50 million for the rights to stream Thursday Night Football during the 2018 National Football League (NFL) season (Jackson, 2017). The Mercedes-Benz auto giant contracted to pay $324 million over 24 years to own the naming rights to Atlanta's newest stadium (White, 2017).

Sport marketing specialists are in the business of generating revenue and brand recognition for clients who may be athletes, university athletic departments, cities, organizations, or events (e.g., marathons). The marketing executive for a professional sports team may be tasked with the promotion of the organization's brand name, players, tickets, and advertising, while the marketing executive for a public recreation center may be tasked with increasing annual membership and promoting community service.

The governance of sport marketing focuses on the ethical and legal responsibilities of industry professionals with decision-making authority. Regulating the sport marketing industry is a function of legal and moral compliance with laws and industry standards. These compliance areas extend to federal product advertising regulations, contract laws, consumer protection laws, and government codes or public ordinances associated with marketing activities in venues and within specified locations. A prudent managerial approach is necessary for professionals to comply with the myriad governance areas associated with sport marketing activities.

This chapter examines the governance of sport marketing by looking at relationships and processes. The chapter also addresses the governance and legal issues the sport professional will face while managing the marketing function, ranging from ambush marketing and Rule 40 of the Olympic Charter to consumer laws affecting social media.

Learning Outcomes

- Critique common issues associated with athlete endorsements and the relationship between marketing agencies, sport governing bodies, athletes, and sponsors.
- Critically assess the multiple elements of sporting events and how these may be managed appropriately.
- Discuss the influence of local, state, and national governments in marketing sport.
- Understand the impact of ambush marketing and anti-ambush tactics related to sport events.

MARKETING THE SPORT PRODUCT

Marketing is one of the oldest functions of business, and brands and companies have been leveraging sport to promote their goods and services for over 90 years. Coca-Cola became an official sponsor of the Olympic Games in Amsterdam in 1928, a partnership that still exists today (Hepburn, n.d.). In 1934, New York Yankees great Lou Gehrig became the first professional athlete to appear on a Wheaties cereal box (Shannon, 2010). NBA megastar Michael Jordan became a regular pitchman for Gatorade and Nike through the 1980s and 1990s, while major companies paid top dollar in the 1990s and 2000s to own the naming rights of the newest stadiums. In 2019, Duke University basketball player Zion Williamson's size 15 Nike PG 2.5 shoe exploded on the court during a game against North Carolina, causing the company's stock to drop 1.73 percent, or $1.12 billion in market value (Curtis, 2019). Moreover, Nike's ancillary departments such as marketing, sales, product, legal, and research and development collaborated with intermediaries such as agencies and outside legal counsel to devise a recovery plan for their image and for the relationship between Nike and Duke University.

By definition, **marketing** is the process by which companies engage customers through authentic relationships in order to provide value to the customer while capturing value from the customer in return (Armstrong & Kotler, 2017). The American Marketing Association (AMA) further defines marketing as "the activity, set of institutions, and processes for creating, communicating, delivering, and exchanging offerings that have value for customers, clients, partners, and society at large" (Fetchko, Roy, & Clow, 2018).

People generally associate marketing with television advertising. Moreover, the term **sport marketing** is perceived as the act of sponsor-

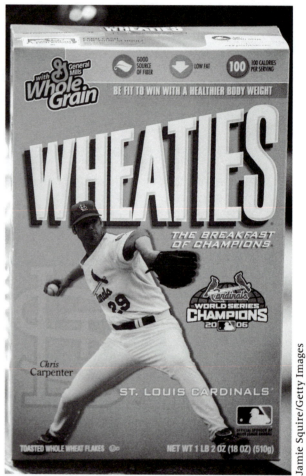

Dating back to 1934, Wheaties has a long history of using sport as a marketing tool by featuring Olympians and celebrity athletes on their cereal boxes.

Jamie Squire/Getty Images

ing sporting events, or selling goods and services related to sport. However, sport marketing should be understood as a managerial process in which sport executives and their organizations build profitable relationships by providing products or services that satisfy a customer's or client's needs.

To better understand sport marketing, one needs to look no further than the National Collegiate Athletic Association (NCAA) Men's Basketball Tournament, which transforms intercollegiate basketball into a global social phenomenon resulting in an annual average of 70 million tournament brackets completed, an estimated $10 billion in wagering, and close to $869 million in revenue for the NCAA (Purdum, 2017). Pitts and Stotlar (2007) define sport marketing as "the process of defining and implementing activities for the production, pricing, promotion, and distribution of a sport product or sport business product to satisfy the needs or desires of consumers and to achieve the company's objectives" (p. 69).

In many ways sport, such as a Major League Baseball (MLB) game, is considered a product itself with unique characteristics outlined in table 12.1. While the product is the game, auxiliary items include concessions, merchandise, parking, and entertainment features such as the carousel rides inside Comerica Park, home of the MLB Detroit Tigers. The **sportscape** is the extended environment within and around the event facility that helps the sport manager to sell an entertainment experience rather than just a game ticket. It permits a sport manager to create a tangible product from an intangible event. Table 12.1 lists the unique characteristics of the sport product that dictate how to engage in marketing activities as well as the governance considerations each area presents.

SPORT MARKETING ORGANIZATIONS

Whether marketing through sport or marketing sport products and services, there is a real need to understand the bigger picture of who is involved making or controlling decisions at all levels. While there is no entity serving as a supreme authority for governing the sport marketing profession or professional, there are many organizations with functional roles in the industry. These organizations are categorized according to the following three central functions of sport marketing and sponsorship:

♦ organizations that make, market, and manage sport (sports commissions and event producers);

♦ organizations that facilitate sport marketing transactions (sport agencies); and

♦ organizations that support the sport marketing industry (professional associations).

Table 12.1 Characteristics of Sport and Associated Governance Considerations

Characteristic	Application	Governance consideration for sport managers
Consumption	Sporting events are consumed live, in a captive audience setting either in a sport facility or through one's television or mobile device.	Sport managers must be aware of advertising laws, such as what can and cannot be advertised to minors.
Affinity	Consumers love their favorite sports teams, which make consumers more open to being marketed to by a team or league's advertisers or the team or league itself. Further, sport can be highly emotional, and today's sport consumers prefer to create a connection to their favorite teams and athletes.	Legal considerations include copyright and trademark protection practices for logos and insignias.
Intangibility	A sporting event is not a product purchased off a shelf or online and immediately used. Aside from a ticket stub, hot dog, or item from the merchandise shop, a sporting event is intangible, making it more complex to sell.	Governance areas include contract provisions, leases, revenue sharing deals, risk management, and staffing as part of the overall plan to market a sport event.
Unpredictability	Most sporting events are not predetermined. Other traditional products and services may offer consistent functions and results, whereas weather, injuries, time, playing surface, crowd, and the abilities of the participants can all affect the outcome of a sport event.	Governance areas include risk assessment and emergency response or risk management plans.
Expiration	Where a traditional product may offer an extended or infinite shelf life for use in a home, the live sport product has a definite expiration date, sometimes only lasting a few hours.	Governance areas may include contract fulfilment and truth in advertising laws.

Sports Commissions and Event Producers

For large and small events alike, there is usually a team of people behind the scenes coordinating the planning and execution of the event. These entities are critical to setting, negotiating, implementing, and managing the sport marketing and sponsorship process. The role of sports commissions, leagues and governing bodies, and others that produce events is rarely straightforward, but understanding these complexities is necessary for understanding governance and authority in the world of sport marketing and sponsorship. Following is an overview of various types of nonprofit, for-profit, and governmental sport organizations involved in producing and managing sport events.

Sports Commissions

Sports commissions act at a local, regional, or state level to attract, create, produce, and manage sport events in their communities. These organizations can take the form of an independent, nonprofit organization, an extension of a visitor's bureau, or as a formal part of a local government. For example, the St. Louis Sports Commission in Missouri is an independent and privately funded nonprofit organization, the Kissimmee Sports Commission in Florida is a nongovernmental extension of the Osceola County Tourism, Sales, and Marketing Authority, and the Harris County-Houston Sports Authority in Texas is an actual government agency. In any case, sports commissions usually work very closely with local and state governments in addition to local sports and recreation entities. A primary responsibility of sports commissions is to bid for and host events in their communities to spur economic growth and improve the quality of life for residents.

In terms of structure, the National Association of Sports Commissions (NASC) (n.d.), formed in 1992, states that most sports commissions are independent, nonprofit organizations managed by a board of about 15 to 30 community stakeholders. Regardless of their organizational structure, sports commissions typically produce their own events, such as marathons and festivals, or bid to host existing events and tournaments, such as the NCAA Final Four or Super Bowl. Selling sponsorships to local and national brands is a major source of revenue. With more than 100 sports commissions in the United States, each owning or operating dozens of events—including recreational, youth, high school, college, and professional tournaments, races, and more—there are countless marketing and sponsorship activities involved. Additional revenue sources include membership sales, donations, grants, tax revenue, and various income related to events (registration fees, etc.). Although the goal of any sports commission is to help the economic and image-related needs of a community, revenue is needed to support staff salaries and continued efforts to bid and host events.

Sport Leagues and Governing Bodies

Perhaps the most well-known sport event producers are leagues and governing bodies. Sport leagues and governing bodies are often nonprofit associations, such as the Professional Golfers Association (PGA) Tour or the United States of America (USA) Gymnastics, but many are also privately owned companies such as Formula One, or publicly traded companies such as International Speedway Corporation and Speedway Motorsports, who own the tracks sponsoring National Association of Stock Car Auto Racing (NASCAR) races. These differing business models are apparent all over sports, and they can affect how events are managed and how sponsorships and marketing rights are determined.

Most sport governing bodies own and host a premiere tournament, championship, or series of events. The International Olympic Committee (IOC) owns the rights to the Summer and Winter Olympics, soccer's FIFA owns the Men's and Women's World Cup, and the NFL hosts the annual Super Bowl. However, most leagues and governing bodies, especially the larger ones, own other initiatives and events that add to their portfolio of assets and create opportunities for additional marketing and sponsorship activities. For example, the NFL also owns the Pro Bowl, and FIFA also is the rights holder for the FIFA Club World Cup.

Despite the size and scope of these entities, few events are exclusively owned and operated by one organization. Although some events are held in the same location every time, such as the NCAA's College World Series in Omaha, Nebraska, other events are bid on by host communities or countries who take on a large portion of the event's operations. These bids typically include a series of marketing requirements. On the other hand, rather than seeking bids, many leagues and governing bodies continually collaborate with other entities to produce some of the largest events in sport.

The College Football Playoff (CFP), a tournament used to crown an NCAA Division I Football Bowl Subdivision (FBS) champion, is owned by a private corporation called CFP Administration (College Football Playoff, n.d.). This for-profit entity is led by a board of managers that includes university presidents, conference commissioners, and the University of Notre Dame athletic director, thanks to Notre Dame's lack of a conference affiliation (College Football Playoff, n.d.). The CFP tournament consists of three games each year that rotate between the following six major bowl games: The Orange Bowl, Rose Bowl, Sugar Bowl, Cotton Bowl, Peach Bowl, and Fiesta Bowl. These bowl games are properties independently owned by other entities. For example, the Capital One Orange Bowl is owned by the Orange Bowl Host Committee, a nonprofit entity that also owns a basketball tournament and a series of youth sports and community events (Orange Bowl, n.d.).

The events associated with sport leagues and governing bodies are some of the most culturally and financially significant in the world. The organizations that own, bid on, operate, and manage sporting events can be very complex, and they can have different ownership structures that determine how they work with and relate to other entities with a shared regulatory function.

Other Event Producers

Many private companies create their own events. Some independent event producers collaborate very closely with other leagues, such as the previously mentioned Orange Bowl Host Committee. Another example of a classification of private independent event producers are talent agencies such as International Marketing Group (IMG), which owns and operates the Miami Open tennis tournament that is played at the Hard Rock Stadium and is part of the Association of Tennis Professionals (ATP) World Tour. However, some private companies have created strong independent events, such as Tough Mudder, which owns a series of obstacle courses and reported over 3.5 million participants in 2020 (Tough Mudder, n.d.).

Interestingly, nonsport companies have expanded into event production as a means of extending their brands, including Red Bull, perhaps one of the most well-known examples. As a heavy investor in sport sponsorship globally, the Austrian energy drink company moved from aggressively sponsoring events and signing athletes as product endorsers to owning and operating

Joe Kohen/WireImage/Getty Images

Red Bull has invested heavily in sport. The company produces its own sport events, owns several international sport teams, and uses celebrity athletes such as Olympic snowboarder Shaun White to market and promote the brand.

events in cliff diving, auto racing, and airplane competitions. Red Bull has also extended its sport affinity by becoming an owner of professional international esports, soccer, and racing teams.

The power of sport to attract interest and connect with an audience has led to many innovative approaches from companies in and out of sport to find new ways to increase awareness of their brands or achieve other marketing objectives. Governance in Action 12.1 demonstrates the innovation of a governing board for a small village suburb of Chicago to invest and connect with a sport property in efforts to stimulate economic growth.

Sports Agencies

A second component critical within the marketing function is governance over agency relationships.

Sport **agencies** may represent athletes, or they may represent sport companies, brands, and organizations. There are many considerations given to differing types of agencies. First, it is important to understand the law of agency defined by Sharp, Moorman, and Claussen (2014) as "a relationship between two parties in which one party (the agent) agrees to act as a representative of the other party (the principal)" (p. 244). Agency law exists to further define the rights and responsibilities of each party within the differing types of agency relationships. Table 12.2 profiles examples of three types of agency relationships advanced by Sharp, Moorman, and Claussen (2014).

GOVERNANCE IN ACTION 12.1

Village Naming Rights to the Bahamas Bowl Is a Profitable Decision

While many brands invest in team ownership, leagues, and event rights, the overall success of such a sponsorship can be tied to the brand's commitment to spend incremental revenue on activating the event sponsorship. One notable example changing the landscape of naming rights valuation is Elk Grove Village's sponsorship of the Bahamas Bowl. Elk Grove Village is a small suburban village located near Chicago's O'Hare International Airport. To entice businesses to consider Elk Grove Village as a distribution or headquarters hub, the village invested $300,000 to own the naming rights to the 2018 Bahamas Bowl, one of the NCAA's Division I football bowl games broadcast on ESPN and via streaming platforms (Placek, 2019). The investment decision was delegated to the village mayor and his board of directors.

The village board chose its business slogan "Makers Wanted" for the naming deal, therefore branding the bowl game as the "Makers Wanted Bahama Bowl." The Elk Grove Village board of trustees also invested an additional $10,000 to create a "Makers Wanted" advertising campaign, which was promoted through the bowl sponsorship platform.

Through qualitative and quantitative measurement, the partnership was determined to have generated over $12 million in media equivalency, with statistically significant increases in awareness, impression, and consideration of Elk Grove Village (Placek, 2019). Media hits extended as far as India. During the televised broadcast, the Elk Grove Village website received 20,000 visits, including 1,000 hits within a five-minute span during the airing of its first commercial in the first quarter. An additional benefit of the naming rights deal was a reduction from 7 percent to 3 percent in industrial park vacancy rates in the village as a result of new businesses securing available lease space (Placek, 2019). The economic benefits prompted the Elk Grove Village board of trustees to renew the sponsorship deal for 2019.

There is relevance to the way sponsorship is measured and economic impact studied. The Bahamas Bowl is considered a mid- to lower-tier bowl game, pairing teams from NCAA mid-major conferences. Attendance for the game averages just about 13,000, and it draws close to 882,000 television viewers. Compared to higher-profile bowl games, those numbers are small, but compared to other weekday afternoon programming, the numbers are good. ESPN, which is owned by the Walt Disney Company and owns and operates the Bahamas Bowl, leverages its portfolio of networks to promote the game. The result has been a win-win for the Elk Grove Village and bowl game producers.

Table 12.2 Agency-Client Relationships

Relationship	Example
Employee-to-employer relationship	NHL San Jose Sharks and their front office staff
Principal-to-agent or agency relationship	Creative Artists Agency and athlete client list
Principal-to-contractor relationship	Creative Artist Agency Ventures and Drone Racing League

The roles and responsibilities of sport agencies have evolved over time from a single person who assisted in negotiating a player contract to Shawn "Jay Z" Carter's Roc Nation sport marketing agency that brokers professional player contracts, negotiates sponsorship deals, drafts endorsement and equity agreements, and handles financial portfolios as well as social media profiles. Today, thousands of sport agencies operate across the United States.

Agency types are typically driven by their niche or functionality. Pedersen and Thibault (2014) label agencies as full service (see table 12.3), general, or

Table 12.3 Full-Service Sport Agencies: 2018 Commissions and Clients

Agency	Commission (in million $)	Headquarters	Athlete clients	Properties/services
Boras Corp.	$105.2 M	Newport Beach, California	Prince Fielder, Max Scherzer, Jacoby Ellsbury	Full-service agency for baseball
Creative Artists Agency	$348.8 M	Los Angeles, California	Matthew Stafford, Matt Ryan, Eli Manning, Carmelo Anthony, Sidney Crosby	Madison Square Garden, Formula One, Riot Games *League of Legends*, consulting, naming rights, sales and sponsorships
Excel Sports Management	$168.2 M	New York, New York	Tiger Woods, Clayton Kershaw, Blake Griffin, Andre Drummond	NBA jersey patch deals (Hornets, Rockets, Bulls). FYG U Music + Tech Festival, brand strategies, consulting, sales and sponsorships
Independent Sports & Entertainment	$90.2 M	Beverly Hills, California	Miguel Cabrera, Leonard Williams, Demarcus Cousins, Justin Verlander	Contract negotiations, endorsements, personal brand development, media relations, social media strategy
Lagardère Sports	$50.6 M	New York, New York	Phil Mickelson, Caroline Wozniacki, Trumaine Johnson	Live show productions: "Salut les copains, le spectacle musical," "Disco, le spectacle musical"
Newport Sports Management	$79.4 M	Mississauga, Ontario, CA	Zach Parise, P.K. Subban, Phil Kessel	Contract negotiations, financial management, tax and estate planning, brand/product endorsement
Octagon Sports & Entertainment	$142.4 M	New York, New York	Steph Curry, Aly Raisman, Simone Biles, Michael Phelps	Walmart NW Arkansas LPGA Championship presented by P&G, Delta NCAA partnership
Priority Sports & Entertainment	$44.7 M	Chicago, Illinois	Kirk Cousins, Bradley Beal, Gordon Hayward	Player services
Roc Nation Sports	$28.9 M	New York, New York	Todd Gurley, Saquon Barkley, Robinson Cano, CC Sabathia	Marketing and endorsement deals, brand strategy
Unique Sports Management	$57.3 M	Kings Langley, UK	Harry Kane, Wilfred Zaha, Ryan Sessegnon	Player services
Wasserman Media Group	$174.9 M	Los Angeles, California	Draymond Green, Klay Thompson, Russell Westbrook, Andrew Luck, Marshawn Lynch	USOPC Road to Rio Tour, Barclays ATP World Tour, Barclays Premier League Live Mumbai, brand sponsorships
WME-IMG	$47.7 M	New York, New York	Serena Williams, Novak Djokovic, Jordan Spieth	Event management, marketing and licensing, content creation, sports properties
YouFirst Sports	$41.8 M	Madrid, Spain	Luis Alberto, Mariano Diaz, Serge Ibaka	Brand consultancy, activation, events and public relations, business development, digital media

Data from Forbes, *Sport Agencies* (2018). www.forbes.com/sports-agencies/list/#tab:overall

specialty. The scope of agency functions is the key differentiator. For example, talent agencies are typically categorized as specialty agencies since their sole purpose is to represent athletes and celebrities. Other specialty agencies may focus specifically on insights and research (e.g., turnkey intelligence subdivision of Turnkey Sports & Entertainment) or solely on event management (e.g., Columbus Arena Management). Additionally, some agencies may focus on niche areas such as social media, creative design, or advertising campaign management.

A general agency offers a wider scope of functions (e.g., business intelligence solutions and social media services), whereas a full-service agency would serve as a one-stop-shop managing an inclusive menu of marketing and business functions. Full-service agencies such as Wasserman Media Group work with brands, companies, and athletes to provide best practice consultation in strategic and tactical marketing, contract negotiation, event planning and execution, sponsorship services and activation, portfolio management, digital and social content creation, and consumer research and insights.

The benefit of using an agency is leveraging expertise. The agency is paid to represent the best interests of a company, brand, or athlete and is held accountable for producing the results for which they have been hired. Sport professionals working with agencies must govern the stipulations of contracts and manage relationships with staff assigned to enhance their brand image or complete the scope of work agreed upon by the two parties.

National Organizations and Associations

While agencies, sports commissions, leagues, governing bodies, and other entities are directly involved in the sport marketing process, there are other important organizations in the industry. These associations connect people working in a specific sector of business (e.g., sport marketing) for the purpose of advancing the profession and addressing big issues facing the industry. Additionally, these associations help establish professional norms and ethics and assist in the recruitment of new employees. Two national organizations that work to advance the sport marketing profession include the National Sport Marketing Network (NSMN) and the Sport Marketing Association (SMA).

National Sport Marketing Network

The National Sport Marketing Network (NSMN) is a board-governed, membership-based trade association founded in 1998 that serves the interests of sport business professionals ("About Us," 2019). With over 12,000 individual and corporate members, NSMN operates through an executive director, a 15-member executive board, over 40 board members representing chapters in select cities, and an advisory circle ("Board Members," n.d.). Executive members hold leadership roles in organizations such as the National Basketball Association (NBA), NASCAR, and PGA America, and they promote educational and charitable initiatives on a national level.

Sport Marketing Association

Founded in 2002, the Sport Marketing Association (SMA) is a private, independent, nonprofit, membership-based organization promoting service to advance the sport marketing industry through networking, scholarly activities, and career development opportunities ("Mission," n.d.). Operating through a constitution and bylaws, the SMA is led by a 13-member executive board, which includes a president, president-elect, past president, three vice presidents, two at-large positions, and five people whose title is manager or director ("Article 1, Officers," n.d.). The organization includes both professional and student members and is known for its *Sports Marketing Quarterly* scholarly journal in addition to its annual national conference featuring a student case competition.

MARKETING THROUGH SPORT

Sports as a vehicle for marketing and advertising products can be a productive way to connect with consumers during a passion point. The advertising is a generally a form of sponsorship marketing.

In the 1970s film, *The Bad News Bears*, Chico's Bail Bonds served as the official sponsor of the youth baseball team. A very large patch featuring the company logo appeared on the back of each jersey. Sponsorship marketing has come a long way from serving to generate revenue for youth sports to its current function as a multi-billion-dollar sector of the sport business. In 2018, global sport spending was $62 billion, with North American brands spending $24 billion to associate with rights

Jon Durr/Four Seam Images via AP

The growth of sponsorship deals and revenue has skyrocketed over the decades, but local sponsorship for youth sports has continued to help communities to fund athletic uniforms and other team needs.

holders such as professional teams (e.g., the New York Giants), leagues (the NFL), or properties (the Super Bowl) (Ukman, 2015).

The regulatory functions of marketing through sport include selecting a sponsorship, developing a budget, choosing the assets, and final activation. Those with authority for marketing decisions, whether employed by a brand or a sport organization, must recognize the nuances of buying versus selling sport sponsorships.

Buying Versus Selling Sports Sponsorship

There are two very distinct perspectives to evaluating sports sponsorship: the buyer's perspective and the seller's perspective. The rights holders (teams, league, properties) selling sponsorships have a responsibility to connect corporate partners with their consumers (e.g., fan base) using sport as the medium while achieving revenue goals set by the organization. The buyers (companies and brands) have a responsibility to evaluate and select sponsorship platforms that uniquely and authentically integrate their brand's overall strategy into the fabric of an event, and then to activate the sponsorship to amplify the rest of their marketing campaigns. The buyer must consider how aligning with a sport team, league, or property will help the company

to achieve its marketing goals, whether the objective is brand awareness, incremental product sales, shopper marketing programs, consumer data generation, product sampling, client hospitality, or a new product launch.

The sponsorship contract is the best way for both the buyer and seller to manage expectations and agree on the assets the buyer will receive and the fees the buyer will pay. From a seller's perspective, the sponsorship proposal should clearly articulate deliverables and the provisions for protecting the organization in case of a breach of contract. From a buyer's perspective, the company or brand should evaluate how the sponsorship assets will be measured and the extent of its return on investment.

Sponsorship Platform Decisions: Client Fit

The initial regulatory function of sponsorship marketing is deciding on the appropriate sponsorship platform—that is, finding the right team, league, or property to sponsor. This decision is based on the sponsorship's ability to target the brand's consumer base, its ability to help connect the brand to new users, the scalability, seasonality, and retail potential of the sponsorship, and how compatible the sponsorship is with the brand. The seller must analyze the fit of the client with its personal brand.

For example, to connect with Generation Z and Millennials, the National Basketball Association (NBA) has negotiated sponsorship deals with EA Sports video games, YouTube TV streaming services, and Beats by Dre audio headphones (Smith, 2018).

An example of another client fit involves The Scotts Company, LLC, the world's leading lawn and garden business. Scotts has served as the official lawn care provider of Major League Baseball since 2010 and renewed its commitment in 2019 ("Scotts Extends Partnership," 2019). The grass outfield and springtime schedule make the MLB a natural sponsorship platform for Scotts. Consider the same sponsorship opportunity between the Scotts Company and a National Hockey League (NHL) team; the lack of congruence is obvious. While one could argue that an NHL audience may have homeowners in need of lawn care products, consider that hockey is a cold weather sport, played indoors, on ice, during winter months when no one is thinking about the lawn. Moreover, sponsorship with one team, while often lucrative, is not as scalable as a sponsorship deal with an entire league.

Budgeting for Sponsorship

Those with authority to negotiate sponsorship deals must contend with budgets. Currently, North American brands budget about 19 percent of their marketing on sports and entertainment (Ukman, 2015). The success of the sponsorship is tied to what assets are chosen in the sponsorship and how well the sponsorship deal is woven into all other aspects of the company's marketing plan. The marketing executive evaluating sponsorship must collaborate with and consider all areas of the marketing communications team, including media, public relations, digital and social, ecommerce, creative, packaging, and brands before signing a deal with a rights holder. Without collaboration, aspects of a sponsorship deal may end up underutilized.

Choosing the Assets

When considering the assets to include in a sponsorship, both the buyer and seller have agendas. The seller needs to sell certain aspects of a stadium or event inventory (signs, announcements, naming rights), while a buyer seeks the best opportunity to connect with its consumer segment. The most typical assets packaged into a North American sponsorship deal include in-stadium or event signage, such as dasher boards in hockey, outfield wall signs and scoreboard signs in baseball and football,

signage around the pitch in soccer, and LED video signage throughout an arena or stadium. Media assets such as social media posts, radio spots, television broadcast sponsorship, and online streaming assets can also be packaged into a deal. Additional assets, such as owning the naming rights to certain areas of a facility—restaurants, concession stands, kid zones, team stores, family sections, and so on—create different ways for a buyer's brand to be more prominent than other company signs. Further, video board announcements, in-stadium entrance and exit product sampling, and sponsorship of promotional nights such as bobbleheads and firework nights, are also unique ways buyers position their brands as providing benefits to fans.

It is incumbent on both the buyer and the seller to work together to craft a sponsorship that satisfies both agendas. A good seller and rights holder will assign governing authority to an account representative to work with the buyer to ensure that all contracted sponsorship deliverables are met and are exceeding expectations. This makes the contract more likely to be renewed.

Activation

Activation, the final functional phase of sponsorship marketing, is simply the mechanism by which companies and brands take the sponsorship rights purchased and transform them into meaningful and positive associations for their consumers. This typically requires spending advertising dollars in addition to the fees paid to the rights holder. Most companies spend $2.18 to activate for every $1 in sponsorship (Ukman, 2015).

An example of successful activation is the "Official Confectionery Partner" sponsorship deal between Reese's, owned by Hershey's, and CBS Sports, Turner Sports, and the NCAA. The sponsorship goes beyond receiving the rights to use the NCAA Final Four logo in their advertising. Reese's also produced in-store sweepstakes and displays, title sponsorship of the Reese's College All-Star Game during NCAA Final Four Weekend, and captivating social media content. During the 2019 NCAA Tournament, Reese's sent a pallet of three-cup packages of peanut butter cups to every third-seeded school in the NCAA tournament and promoted the events through their social handles (Wilson, 2019).

People with authority to decide how to spend incremental dollars on activation are driven by a combination of budgetary restrictions and the need to satisfy sponsorship objectives. Governance in Action 12.2 profiles the strategic decisions of

GOVERNANCE IN ACTION 12.2

Bose Versus Beats and the NFL: Sponsorship Activation Decisions and Brand Exposure

In March 2014, Massachusetts-based audio equipment maker Bose Corporation replaced Motorola as the Official Sound of the National Football League (Cushnan, 2014). The partnership makes Bose just one of four brands (Nike, Gatorade, Microsoft) with access to on-field branding during NFL games, which is considered the highest premium advertising in all professional sports (Cushnan, 2014). While numbers have not been disclosed, the partnership fee is estimated to be far greater than the $40 million per year Motorola previously paid (Cushnan, 2014). However, partnership fees and on-field access are not the biggest story. The storyline is the battle between Bose and Beats by Dre and how individuals with governing authority for brand activation strategize to enhance brand exposure.

Both Bose and Beats do an exceptional job of communicating their brand position to their respective demographics. Beats by Dre is focused on Gen Z and Millennials who value expression and resonate with ESPN, hip hop culture, sports, and music (Crimson Hexagon, 2014). Beats' brand identity focuses on who uses the headphones, so celebrity **endorsements** are extremely important to their marketing strategy, which requires top decision makers to carefully consider product endorsers who are emulated by Gen Z and Millennials. Bose consumers, however, are more mature people who have affinities for health, travel, soccer, and technology (Crimson Hexagon, 2014). While Beats executives focus on endorsement deals, decision makers for Bose focus on strategies to accentuate sound quality and superiority claims to build consumer support (Crimson Hexagon, 2014).

Today, Beats owns about a 70 percent share of the premium headphone business, while Bose registers below 25 percent (Helm, 2019). Executives for both companies use sports platforms to gain brand equity and create brand advocates. Beats has clearly captured the younger Gen Z/Millennial audience by leveraging creative advertising that features athletes like Colin Kaepernick and Sherman Edwards (Paquette, 2015). At one point, LeBron James was trending on social media for purchasing new custom Beats for all his teammates for the 2008 U.S. national basketball team (Helm, 2019).

The new Bose–NFL partnership is serving two very important purposes for the company. First, due to the strategic decisions of its executives, the company is staying true to its demographic and brand identity by having every middle-aged wealthy coach on an NFL sideline wear a headphone set with the Bose insignia, which is broadcast to millions of viewers by ESPN, CBS, and NBC. The second strategic initiative cleverly implemented by Bose executives is the competitive block created by negotiating language in its agreement preventing NFL players or other team personnel from wearing Beats by Dre on camera (SI Wire, 2014). This shrewd maneuver initiated by Bose executives has served to combat the number of media impressions Beats was generating by having so many NFL players seen stepping off a bus or walking into a stadium wearing headphones with the Beats by Dre insignia. It may not be Coke versus Pepsi, but the battle for sound has never been more interesting.

marketing executives for two prominent audio equipment companies who regularly use sport as the medium to promote their brands.

MARKETING THROUGH SPORT MEGA-EVENTS

Mega-events routinely require a minimum of $10 billion in capital investment while typically occupying several hundred acres of land and requiring massive infrastructure to accommodate, transport, and keep secure hundreds of thousands of visitors and tens of thousands of athletes, officials, and media personnel (Muller, 2015). Mega-events are intended to be economic drivers with the infusion of foreign exchange earnings. The appeal of mega-events from a marketing perspective is their massive scope and visibility that are easily identifiable to the general public. A mega-event is "the most complicated event to execute, requiring years of planning to implement, (and) a bid process to gain the rights to host the event" (Paule-Koba, 2015, p. 94).

Navigating the amorphous landscape of marketing mega-events presents many challenges. Organizers tend to approach these events with ambitious goals because of the intense pressures of trying to deliver on the expectations of various stakeholder groups. This can produce myopic planning habits and misguided outcome evaluations that make governing difficult (Muller, 2015; O'Brien & Chalip, 2007). Mega-events can be transformative ventures for host cities and can serve as a catalyst for urban development, so the governing authorities responsible for marketing them face arduous challenges beyond the relatively routine decisions required in traditional sport marketing endeavors. Two of these challenges from a governance perspective are bidding for mega-events and image management.

Bidding for Mega-Events

For a city that hosts a mega-event, the process from idea formation to actual event execution takes years. For example, seven years is the common timeline that begins *after* the IOC awards the rights for a city to host an Olympics. Generating the idea, formulating the bid, and creating alliances around common missions and goals may take three to seven years before the rights are even awarded (Hums & MacLean, 2009). One of the essential elements of the bid is to demonstrate local support, not only in committing resources, but also in showing that all stakeholders converge philosophically around the common ideals, values, and purposes of the event. Thus, the **bid** acts as a comprehensive application that showcases how the city will plan, produce, and execute the event using the city's resources.

Bid Proposal

Bids are announced through an RFP, or a request for proposal, in order to maximize competition. The RFP ensures quality, delivers minimum requirements to apply, sets clear guidelines and event expectations, provides detailed revenue and expense projections, and tests the applicants' ability to garner local, state, regional, and national support from city officials, sponsors, media, and the local community (Supovitz, 2005). According to Supovitz (2005, p. 92) the main components of the RFP are

1. introduction,
2. event description (including history and impacts),
3. event schedule,
4. role of the event organizer,
5. role of the host city,
6. definition of the ideal event site,
7. benefits of the host city,
8. sponsors and marketing rights, and
9. response format.

The bid is typically developed and submitted by the local organizing committee, and most of the bid is concentrated on the host city section. In addition, the sponsor and marketing rights section outlines specific requirements concerning potential sponsors of the event and the details of marketing rights associated with the event. Once the bid is finalized by the organizing committee, it is submitted to the host country's national governing body of the sport or to the national organizing committee to obtain approval. Once approved, the bid is sent to the event rights holder (e.g., the IOC for the Olympic Games, the NCAA for the Final Four, and FIFA for the World Cup). Finally, the bid is selected and awarded to the host committee, and planning begins by the local organizing committee of the city that initiated and designed the bid.

Bid Specifications for Marketing Requirements

Effective marketing and promotional campaigns are among the most challenging parts of the bid to develop. Clear and unambiguous marketing policies are crucial for both planning and control purposes.

Because each stakeholder will have his or her own objectives, it is imperative for the event's right holders to understand that potential stakeholders should align their marketing messages to generate mass appeal (Jago, Chalip, Brown, Mules, & Ali, 2003; O'Brien & Chalip, 2007). For a mega-event, marketing and promotions involve multiple levels of branding: for the city, for the sport organizations, for the sport itself, for the sponsors, and for many grassroots initiatives that may range from youth sport to community engagement to corporate social responsibility. Marketing messages should outline the main characteristics, traits, and meanings of the event's brand to facilitate the planning for an integrated marketing and promotion campaign that maximizes resources. Otherwise, conflicting messages are bound to confuse the audience. Further, detailing the marketing requirements allows the host committee to prepare inventory such as signage or branded merchandise to be sold for the purposes of enhancing value propositions in sponsorship campaigns.

Marketing requirements that appear in bids must specify the obligations of those who buy television rights, advertising rights, merchandising and licensing rights, and sponsor rights. Marketing policies in the bid help the host committee to drive value as high as possible while respecting the interests and intellectual property of the event rights holder. The event rights holder typically provides detailed guidelines for advertising and promotions that support its values and outlines exclusions that do not assimilate with its interests, particularly third parties who are not officially associated with the event. For example, the NCAA issues advertising and promotional guidelines for the Final Four Championships that specifically align with the ideals of higher education and student-athletes (National Collegiate Athletic Association, 2016). Some of the principles stated in this guide include promoting the NCAA's attributes (e.g., fair play, character, learning), championing the student-athlete, supporting specific ideals (e.g., diversity, gender equity, nondiscrimination, ethical conduct, health and safety), enhancing the value of higher education, and projecting a consistent brand image with the NCAA (2016).

Not only do marketing guidelines help the event rights holder to control the messages and preserve their ideals, they are also designed to increase the value of associating with their brand. Brand association for sponsors and other entities (e.g., media, fans, event organizers) with mega-events has become a multi-billion-dollar licensing business. The brand of the event itself is an extremely valuable and leverageable resource. Due to this level of interest in brand association, intellectual property rights need to be controlled and formally authorized to prevent third parties from devaluing this asset and using the brand without authorization and without following the guidelines of the host committee or event. Typically, mega-events will issue promotional and advertising guidelines that specify intellectual property regulations that protect their copyright and trademark rights extending to the use of trademarks, logos, designs, event terminology, exclusivity rights, and ticket usage, just to name a few. The capital outlay to associate with mega-events has increased exponentially over time, making marketing deals too cost prohibitive for many corporations and third-party entities to justify the expense. For the 2013 NCAA Men's Basketball Championship, some spent nearly $35 million for rights (Horowitz, 2013). This cost escalation has produced an unparalleled fervor to associate with the event *unofficially*, as in the tactic of ambush marketing, which is covered in more detail later in this chapter.

Image Management

In hosting mega-events where competing interests are inevitable, local and global public perception of the city and the rights holder create challenges that marketers must address in their long-term and short-term planning. Mega-events can create both a positive and a negative impression, requiring a collaborative and intentional approach by decision makers representing various stakeholders to shape perceptions.

Positive impressions are created when legacy moments endure in the minds of viewers, spectators, and participants. Symbols and imagery are important to the mega-event marketer. For example, the look and feel of the Olympics is represented by the Olympic interlocked rings, highlighting not only the five continents of the Olympic participants, but also the six colors (including the white background) of all the flags of the world. These rings, originally designed by contemporary Olympics founder Pierre de Coubertin in 1912, symbolize the world coming together and sharing in the ideal and values of Olympism (International Olympic Committee, 2015).

A negative perception of a mega-event, however, can be just as instantaneously generated from incremental building blocks of unfavorable impressions. A negative perception often results from broken promises when significant gaps occur between forecast and actual outcomes or between economic and noneconomic rewards of a mega-event, which is too often the case. There is a huge risk of losing potential interest if there is a perception that the mega-event is a burden to the city as was the case when Boston, Massachusetts, rescinded its bid proposal for the 2024 Olympic and Paralympic Games (Seelye, 2015).

Managing tangible and intangible images is important to the success of mega-events for all stakeholders. First, governing authorities must address the role and importance of mega-events as a destination magnet, and secondly, they must strategize to manage the media.

Rick Friedman/Corbis via Getty Images

After significant investment in both capital outlay and time, Boston, Massachusetts, rescinded its bid for the 2024 Olympic and Paralympic Games due to public discourse over the potential financial burden.

Host Cities as Destination Magnets

Host committees seek to leverage mega-events as entrepreneurial tools to promote their cities as tourism destinations. Marketing goals generally aspire to reinforce or change the image of a host destination, and they become a catalyst to increase tourism both during and after the event by creating an international profile that will help to attract visitors in the longer term. Managing the impression of a host city's safety (e.g., terrorism and street crime) and health risks is a major marketing concern.

Marketing efforts to change perceptions require a joint commitment by a host committee and the local, regional, and national governments, especially if there is a need to tackle stereotypes and preconceptions. Rio de Janeiro, Brazil, faced these perceptions before the 2014 World Cup and the 2016 Summer Olympics due to the city's reputation as a heavy crime district, its water contamination issues, and the threat of the Zika virus (Tiell & Ying, 2016). Marketing professionals were also challenged by the socio-spatial polarization of residents who either embraced the potential for vast improvements in infrastructure and urban development or chastised the governing authorities who displaced tens of thousands of Brazilians from their homes and diverted scarce state resources otherwise intended for health, education, and general public welfare (Muller, 2015). Months of violent demonstrations by disgruntled residents before both the 2014 World Cup and the 2016 Olympics challenged marketers who wished to showcase

the magnificent topography of Brazilian beaches sparked by the allure of Copacabana and South America's vibrant culture.

Similarly, mega-event organizers in Beijing, China, had to address the preconceptions of poor air quality, traffic congestion, and the country's deplorable track record of human rights violations fueled by communism when marketing their city to host the 2008 and 2022 Summer Olympics. Countertactics to create a favorable impression focused on images of the city's traditional and postmodern architecture. Organizers of the 2014 Sochi Olympics also faced a public relations nightmare following Russian President Vladimir Putin's signing of a law prohibiting propaganda materials about nontraditional sexual relations around minors just months before the opening ceremonies (Stanglin, 2014). Similar public relations battles ensued for marketing PyeongChang, South Korea, for the 2018 Winter Olympics; it became a geopolitical backdrop to showcase the improvement in the strained relations between neighboring North Korea and the United States.

Role of the Media in Image Management

The media play a vast role in shaping public perception, and mega-event organizers are keenly aware of their role in managing media coverage. The Centennial Park bombing at the 1996 Atlanta Olympics and the death of the father-in-law of a USA Volleyball assistant coach after he was stabbed while visiting the Drum Tower during the 2008 Beijing Olympics were two unavoidably negative stories sensationalized by the media, with the event organizers seemingly having little control. However, organizers can shape the perception of their handling of critical incidents by following what are hopefully well-defined crisis management plans that include providing accurate, timely, and honest information to the media. Governing authorities for the marketing of mega-events have a responsibility to reduce the chances of the media communicating incorrect information and further exacerbating an already difficult situation.

Additionally, knowing that bad news sells, governing authorities must navigate the appetites of journalists who seek out negative stories, which is why the plight of disadvantaged groups within the host community often receive ample media attention. Displacing some residents has been a long-standing practice in the effort to prepare for mega-events. Therefore, it is vital for the host destination to have a large supply of well-developed stories for media distribution that focus on the positive attributes of the destination that the host wishes to promote.

Governing authorities for mega-events can manage the media from the top down through credentialing and policy restrictions, or from the bottom up by feeding the media positive stories. Calculated maneuvers to shape public perception are vital to increase favorable international coverage of the destination generated by the mega-event. For example, the tourism arm for Australia initiated the Visiting Journalist Program to enhance the image of Sydney prior to the 2000 Summer Olympics (Jago, Dwyer, Lipman, van Lill, & Voyster, 2010). Months before the opening ceremonies, invited journalists traveled to the host city, where they received exclusive tours and were provided with stories and video images to promote the assets of the area with permission for usage before, during, and after the event. Using both top-down and bottom-up methods to manage media relationships is essential for governing authorities if a destination is to derive maximum benefit from the media exposure generated by hosting a mega-event.

LEGAL ISSUES IN THE MARKETING ENVIRONMENT

In order to properly execute the sport marketing function, the sport manager should be aware of legal and governance issues in the marketing environment. Sport marketing requires the coordination of relationships between many different entities. These relationships, managed either through an intermediary (i.e., agency) or directly, can be very complex and even volatile. Fortunately, legal protections provide some guidance for these relationships and common sport marketing practices. Among the legal issues in the marketing environment are those involving contracts, waivers, intellectual property law, consumer laws and social media, and sweepstakes and contests.

Contracts

A contract is a legally binding agreement by two or more parties for which the law provides remedy when breached (Pedersen & Thibault, 2014). The sport manager will create or execute contracts for different purposes; personal services agreements when using athletes for endorsements, sponsorship agreements, agency agreements, event agreements, and sweepstakes are just a few examples. It is critical that sport managers collaborate with their organization's legal counsel when developing or reviewing potential contracts, particularly around the topic of indemnification, which is the act of compensating one party due to loss or anticipated loss. For instance, what happens when a stadium naming rights sponsor suddenly files bankruptcy and ceases operation? To a lesser degree, how are team sponsors like Skyline Chili, Scotts Lawn, Kroger, and PNC Bank compensated when the Cincinnati Reds experience 10 rainouts? The contract will require language protecting both parties from harm. The basic elements of a contract include an offer by one party, typically in the form of a proposal; terms of the contract, which include what each party receives, the fees that will be paid, and recourse for breach of contract; and an acceptance from at least one other party once the negotiation of terms has been finalized.

Waivers

Sport managers working for a rights holder or a brand may also use waivers and releases. These are examples of exculpatory agreements used to transfer risk from one party to another. Waivers or releases are commonly used in such sport activities as participating in a local race or obstacle competition such as Tough Mudder, participating in a between-innings promotion on the field of a minor league baseball game, or entering a kids' zone at a sports stadium. The intent of the waiver or release is to inform the participant of the inherent risk of engaging in the activity and to release the team or brand from liability for any harm the participant may experience from the activity. Marketers also have a duty of care to the participants, to ensure the provision of a safe environment for participation; otherwise, the law states that individuals or organizations can be held liable for negligence. Providing proper staffing and staff training, on-site medical resources, signage, and safety and emergency protocols are examples of proactive measures the sport manager can take to reduce risk at the marketing event.

Intellectual Property Law

One of the reasons companies and brands spend so much money on sponsorships is for the rights to use a team, league, organization, or athlete's likeness, trademarks, or logos in their advertising. Intellectual property as it applies to patents, copyrights, and trademarks is addressed in greater depth in chapter 10. A product itself, its labeling, package design, and taglines may all be considered intellectual property of a brand or company. Further, an athlete's intellectual property could be his or her personal brand, likeness, and image. Partnering with a team, league, or athlete gives a brand access to a rights holder's intellectual property. Consider that every year in late January and early February, companies and brands will begin to talk about "the big game." Of course, the big game they are referring to is the Super Bowl. However, the NFL owns the term "Super Bowl," and therefore no one is permitted to use the term unless they are an official sponsor of the NFL, paying for the rights to use the NFL marks, logos, and registered trademarks.

Athletes use their intellectual property to promote and endorse products and companies. Although Roger Federer won just one Grand Slam tennis tournament in 2018, he still earned over $65 million in endorsements. According to *Sports Illustrated*, LeBron James brought in over $50 million in endorsement revenue, while eight other athletes, including Tiger Woods, Kevin Durant, and Stephen Curry, brought in over $30 million for pitching products (SI Staff, 2018).

Trademarks

The sport manager responsible for using or leading a brand's image should be aware of trademark law and trademark infringement practices. Trademark infringement is simply the use, or misuse, of a trademark without the expressed consent or authorization of the rights holder. More common misuse of trademarks in sport include high schools using professional team mascots and colors without permission, companies using an athlete's or team's likeness in their advertising without permission, and use of team or league marks in print or video without permission. One of the earliest cases involving professional sport team logos was a case won by the Dallas Cowboy Cheerleaders against Pussycat Cinema, LTD, who, without an authorized licensed deal, replicated the NFL team's trademark logo on uniforms worn by actresses in the movie *Debbie Does Dallas* (Friedman, 1995, p. 694).

Too often companies and brands will make attempts to ambush the intellectual property of athletes, teams, or major events to create a buzz for themselves without paying the required partnership fees. During the famous Super Bowl blackout of 2013 in New Orleans, Nabisco's Oreo brand was quick to leverage the 34-minute delay by posting to social media and letting fans know "you can still dunk in the dark" (Pathak, 2017). While Oreo's clever response was technically considered ambush marketing by definition, it was an example of a brand borrowing the equity of the major sporting event and rights holder without paying to be a sponsor. The post was declared to have "won the Internet" by garnering millions of views.

Copyright

Another aspect of intellectual property is copyright law—protecting one's original ideas and creative written works. In 2019, Peloton, makers of at-home exercise bikes, was required to remove tunes from its streaming workout library after a lawsuit claimed the company was using more than 1,000 songs without the permission of the artists (Osborn, 2019).

Within the context of intercollegiate sport, the use of student-athlete images in marketing to promote the university and generate revenue is highly debated. As a common practice, colleges and universities require students to sign waivers giving up the rights to their images, which has prompted a firestorm of controversy for denying compensation for use of a player's name or likeness in marketing materials.

An area often at risk in copyright controversies is reuse or redistribution of sport broadcasts. Leagues such as the NHL, MLB, NBA, and NFL own their rights to broadcast games, and they sell those rights to networks such as ESPN, FOX, or TBS. Once the game is produced, the broadcast is then protected under the Copyright Act of 1976 (Horner, 2014). Today, more fans stream live games and content than ever before. The Digital Millennium Copyright Act of 1996 was enacted to preserve copyright protections on the Internet, while providing immunity from copyright infringement to passive service providers (Horner, 2014). This protection extends to team websites, social media accounts, and streaming of competition.

Consumer Laws and Social Media

It is estimated that consumers spend 2 hours and 22 minutes per day on social networks and messaging and that over 42 percent of the population (3.2 billion) uses social media daily (Mohsin, 2019). Facebook, YouTube, Instagram, and Snapchat continue to be the social media platforms most used by Generation Z, Millennials, Gen X, and Baby Boomers.

With the advancement of technology and social media, today's sport consumer relies less on marketer-supplied information than ever before, creating both opportunities and challenges (Armstrong & Kotler, 2017). Teams, leagues, and sport properties now consider websites and social media platforms when crafting marketing plans to engage consumers in the digital space. It is extremely important that marketers understand and comply with legal issues such as the appropriate use of intellectual property and ensuring privacy protections when creating and executing such plans.

It is a common practice for brands to capitalize on the digital space by employing athletes to serve as social influencers since approximately 49 percent of consumers depend on influencer recommendations on social media when making purchasing decisions (Mohsin, 2019). However, the Federal Trade Commission (FTC), the independent agency of the U.S. government that regulates deceptive or unethical business practices, requires hashtags to read "#ad or #sponsor" to ensure that consumers know that a social media post is an advertisement and an individual (e.g., celebrity or athlete) is being paid (Pedersen & Thibault, 2014). The policy is based on the mandate that athletes have a duty to disclose their relationships as paid influencers when making endorsements in social media (Sharp, Moorman, & Clausen, 2014).

Sweepstakes and Contests

There are several legal issues sport marketers must contend with when considering the use of sweepstakes and contests, which are typically used to drive sales, collect consumer data, and increase brand awareness or brand affinity for sponsors. Most of these issues apply to state laws for taxation and federal compliance with consumer privacy and intellectual property rights as well as compliance with antifraud rules. Several states mandate official sweepstakes registration, cash equivalencies options in lieu of prizes, and bonding requirements if the aggregate value of prizes exceeds $5,000 ("Sweepstakes as a Marketing Tool," n.d.).

One of the biggest misunderstandings about consumer contests and sweepstakes is the form of entry. Brands will often use the wording "purchase and be automatically entered," when in fact by law, no purchase is required. The FTC notes that it is illegal in the United States "to pay or buy something to enter or increase your odds of winning" in sweepstakes-type promotions ("Prize Scams," 2014).

By definition, a **contest** is a game or competition requiring a skill or task where a winner is determined by judges, score, or other method of accomplishment. For instance, it is a common marketing tactic to select one lucky fan to shoot a half-court shot or kick a field goal for a prize opportunity. A **sweepstakes**, on the other hand, is simply a game of chance, free to enter, whereby winners are selected at random. Lotteries, which are becoming legal in states passing new sport wagering legislation, are similar to sweepstakes due to the random odds of winning, but the form of entry requires a purchase. Raffle lotteries have been popular fundraisers for youth, high school, and small college sport teams.

When devising a sweepstakes or consumer contest, best practices recommend working with legal counsel or a credible agency to ensure all appropriate legal considerations have been met in the official rules to reduce or eliminate risk. It is also advisable to use an unaffiliated third party to select a winner or to conduct the actual drawing to minimize the assumption of fraudulent activity and to maintain a list of winners. Examples of sweepstakes and consumer contests affiliated with sports or sport properties are outlined in table 12.4 (Grauschopf, 2019).

AMBUSH MARKETING

Ambush marketing, defined by Chadwick and Burton (2011), describes the efforts of individuals or brands to "capitalize on the awareness, attention, goodwill, and other benefits, generated by having an association with an event or property, without

Table 12.4 Sport-Affiliated Sweepstakes and Consumer Contests

Name	Type	Description
MLB Clean Up and Win	Sweepstakes	Win tickets to the MLB All Star Game
PGA Tour Must See Moments	Sweepstakes	Win tickets to select PGA event
ESPN Streak for Cash	Contest	Accumulate longest winning streak in a month by correctly selecting winning team or player to win prizes
Capital One NCAA March Madness Bracket Challenge	Contest	Players can compare brackets with millions of users including celebrities such as Charles Barkley
Doritos "Crash the Super Bowl" ad	Contest	Entrants submitting a commercial had opportunity to air their product during the Super Bowl and win $1 million (ended in 2016)
Nationwide VIP Sweepstakes	Sweepstakes	Winner receives Zamboni ride and four lounge tickets for an NHL Columbus Blue Jackets game
Sun & Ski Sports National Bike Month	Sweepstakes	Weekly winners win a free bike
DrinkNOS Get Sideways on Snow and Ice	Sweepstakes	Grand prize: European Ice Driving Adventure for two

the organization having an official or direct connection to that event or property" (p. 714). Ambush marketing circumvents the high costs of an official designation with an event by attempting to piggyback on the hype and creating a connection with the event in the minds of the consumer. Payne (1998) notes that ambush tactics are immoral and unethical, describing their practices as "parasitic" in nature. This form of deceitful advertising specifically targets the cognitive processes of the consumer, such as recall, recognition, and association with a brand, with a deliberate attempt to mislead. Although trademark infringement, copyright violations, or false advertising are against the law, third parties will creatively avoid the legal traps to obtain the perception of their association and accentuate their brand value.

Ambush by Intrusion

Ambush by intrusion occurs when trademarks or other company branding are strategically placed in event spaces that will be captured on media outlets or by event attendees when no rights fees have been paid (Bartlett, 2007). An example of ambush by intrusion would be Pepsi handing out new beverages to sample on egress in an unprotected area (e.g., across the street from a mega-event venue) during an Olympic event when Coca-Cola is an official TOP (the Olympic Program) sponsor of the Games. Another example of ambush by intrusion is brands supplying athletes with apparel to wear during competition, as in the case of Beats by Dre supplying Michael Phelps and other athletes with special edition headphones during the 2012 London Olympics while Panasonic served as a TOP sponsor.

Official sponsors often face ambush intrusion when staging activation elements and by immersive experiences during the lead-up to games and events or during the extended time period between competitions. Impressions made through these types of experiential marketing activities are more resistant to change in the minds of consumers (Pritchard, Havitz, & Howard, 1999). The Coca-Cola Torch Relay before the Olympics, branded inflatables during the Reese's Senior Bowl Tailgate Party, and autograph sessions during the Capital One Fan Fest at the NCAA Final Four Championship are several examples of interactive experiences that official sponsors stage in relatively large and open spaces that are susceptible to ambush by intrusion.

Ambush by Association

Ambush by association is an intentional or unintentional tactic of creating confusion in public perception of links between brands and an event or property. Ambush by association tactics are effective with consumers only if the consumers are unaware of the official sponsors of the event (Meenaghan, 1998; Shani & Sandler, 1998). Brands may defend their actions by claiming the general public has no preconception of whether its company has or hasn't paid associative rights fees as an official sponsor of an event or property. Brand recall and recognition outcomes are notoriously unreliable and volatile, making it fairly easy for marketers to confuse the minds of consumers (Crompton, 2004; Romaniuk & Sharp, 2004).

Examples of ambush by association are plentiful. At the 1984 Los Angeles Olympics when the IOC first initiated exclusivity agreements within brand sponsorship categories, Fuji inked a deal as the official camera company of the Games. Kodak, however, retained as an official sponsor of the U.S. broadcast, unknowingly created a mistaken public perception of its brand being recognized among the list of official Olympic sponsors (Dumais, 2014). Similarly, Nike has a storied history of the public mistaking the company as an official World Cup sponsor as opposed to Adidas, FIFA's official sponsor. Nike's product commercials during World Cups often feature action footage of their celebrity soccer clients, and the company has strategically launched mobile soccer applications during the World Cup that create confusion in the minds of consumers. Nike's defense, however, is their constitutional right to associate with the sport of soccer even though they do not have a direct relationship with the World Cup.

Curtailing Ambush Marketing

During the men's basketball gold medal ceremony at the 1992 Barcelona Olympics, Michael Jordan and Charles Barkley, two spokesmen for Nike and members of the United States Dream Team, draped the U.S. flag over their shoulders to seemingly hide the Olympic official sponsor Reebok's logo on their warm-up jackets. At the 2012 London Olympics, the local organizing committee trained and deployed 270 Olympic Delivery Authorities (ODA) volunteers to spot ambush culprits up to 200 meters outside and above Olympic venues (Hill, 2016). A bakery and a butcher shop owner were ordered to remove five bagels and five sausages arranged in rings from their window displays (Sharp, Moorman, & Claussen, 2017, p. 614).

To mitigate the effects of misleading advertising by ambush marketing tactics, research supports the use of **corrective advertising**, disseminating accurate messages to replace erroneous consumer beliefs (Dyer & Kuehl, 1978; Mazodier, Quester, & Chandon, 2012). However, while corrective advertising can change public opinion, it does little to actually curtail ambush marketing.

Anti-ambush measures are very difficult to implement. However, effective sponsorship management can lessen the impact of ambush marketing and third-party association with the event. Sponsorship management involves creating specific guidelines, defining clear sponsorship categories, and maintaining realistic expectations for sponsors. By developing sponsorship categories that organize businesses according to common characteristics, host committees can identify the needs and wants of sponsors within and across groups

more easily, and they can match value with available assets to sell to "like" sponsors. This practice allows host committees to establish exclusivity clauses as valuable commodities. **Exclusivity** is when sponsorship categories, like quick service restaurants, are established and can only be sold to one company in that category, effectively eliminating its competition. Exclusivity enhances the value of a sponsorship package and clearly identifies potential third-party ambushers. In addition, exclusivity may increase the power a sponsor accrues, potentially decreasing the event's ability to control its own activities or outcomes, leading to the rise of more effective ambush marketing activities by the brand marketing managers.

In addition to sponsorship management, other measures to curtail ambush marketing include litigation, policies such as the Olympics' Rule 40 and Rule 45, and the establishment of clean zones.

Litigation

Historically, savvy ambush marketing efforts have been extremely difficult to prosecute in court, leaving events holders trying other means to protect their brand value such as cease and desist orders, which may or may not be binding. The inability of event organizers to successfully hinder or block ambushers in the courtroom has resulted in a vociferous debate whether ambush activities are a moral or ethical dilemma (e.g., O'Sullivan & Murphy, 1998; Payne, 1998; Welsh, 2002).

Sport event organizers such as the IOC and FIFA have successfully influenced national governments in Russia, Canada, Australia, South Africa, and other countries to legislate the prohibition of ambush marketing as a condition of having their host city bids considered (Scassa, 2011, p. 354). The London Organizing Committee for the Olympic Games (LOCOG) successfully passed regulations for the protection of authorized Games Marks, which included trademarks listed in a statutory register maintained by authorities (Hill, 2016, p. 212).

There are few examples of successful legal attempts to block ambush marketing tactics. More plentiful are examples of failed litigation. In conjunction with the 2003 Women's World Cup, for example, FIFA sued Nike for using the phrase "USA 2003" on its apparel since the brand was not an official sponsor. However, judgment favored Nike since the phrase seemingly "did not cause confusion to the public" (*FIFA v. Nike, Inc.*, 285 F. Supp. 2d 64 / D.C. Cir. 2003). More recently, the Australian Olympic Committee (AOC) lost a legal battle against Telstra, an official technology sponsor of a broadcast station in the country. Telstra was accused of deceiving the public into believing they were actually an official sponsor of the AOC when they launched their "I Go to Rio" advertising campaign during the 2016 Rio Olympics ("AOC Loses Full Federal Court Appeal," 2017).

The legal means to stop ambush marketing is typically through a cease and desist order. Under Armour recently sent a cease and desist order to a local retail business named Cascade Armory due to "brand confusion" (Miller, 2018). Often, a company, organization, or brand will issue its own version of a cease and desist order without going through a legal authority, which may render the order nonbinding. The United States Olympic & Paralympic Committee (USOPC) has been criticized for its "heavy-handed" policing of its trademarks through cease and desist orders (Sharp, Moorman, & Claussen, 2017, p. 614).

Olympic Rule 40 and Rule 45

The IOC efforts to minimize ambush marketing from brands associated with athlete endorsements and to protect the value of the Olympic sponsors are Rules 45 and 40. Rule 45 prohibits athletes from making commercial appearances during the Olympic Games in order to prevent nonsponsors from gaining access to the athletes for commercial exploitation. Rule 40 prevents third parties from using participant images or likenesses that make a connection to the Games and the third parties. This rule takes effect from approximately nine days before until three days after the Olympics. Rule 40, from the IOC's Olympic Charter (2015), states "except as permitted by the IOC Executive Board, no competitor, coach, trainer or official who participates in the Olympic Games may allow his person, name, picture or sport performances to be used for advertising purposes during the Olympic Games" (p. 79).

Further, according to the World Federation Sporting Goods Industry's (2016) guidelines used in preparation for the Rio 2016 Summer Olympic Games, the overarching goal of Rule 40 is to protect the Olympic Games and brand from "over-commercialization" and to provide value to its partners (p. 19). Prior to the 2016 Rio Olympics, the IOC considered amending Rule 40 by allowing athletes to give credit to their sponsors through their Olympic story, particularly through the use of social media (Hill, 2016). As of 2019, the only IOC action was President Bach's encouragement for athletes to negotiate with their respective national Olympic committees (NOCs) over restrictions placed upon them in their own countries. That encourage-

ment occurred after the Federal Association of the German Sport Goods Industry, the German athletes' group Athleten Deutschland, and two athletes won a lawsuit in the country's Federal Cartel Office that "scaled back" Rule 40. Specifically, the court ruled to uphold a scaled-back list of banned Olympic terminology applying to advertising and social media platforms in Germany (Pavitt, 2019).

Clean Zones

Clean zones (also referred to as safety zones) are established by the event organizer as part of the bid that requires the host committee and the local government to coordinate efforts that prohibit unauthorized advertising in areas in and around the mega-event and its subsidiary activities. Areas identified as clean zones are authorized by city ordinance, special legislation enacted specifically for the mega-event during the bid process.

Clean zones can be many square miles around certain city property deemed necessary for the events to occur. For example, Sliffman (2011) explicitly showed what the NFL Super Bowl bid required for clean zones, including temporary structures, temporary sales permits, temporary signage, inflatables, building wraps, and contingency funds devoted to ambush marketing prevention. Host committees are responsible for executing the plan to enforce clean zones as well, working with local law enforcement, volunteer groups, official sponsorship staff, local businesses, and event organizers. In addition to the city ordinance legislation, host committees may send nonthreatening letters, as a preemptive measure, encouraging clean zone participation from the local community and to outline specific do's and don'ts during the timeline of the event. Effectively, the goal is to gain a commitment from the local community to avoid ambush tactics.

McKelvey and Grady (2008) point out that the primary mission of clean zones is to protect event organizers and their official sponsors from ambush marketing, despite their claims to create safe areas for the public and prevent excess commercialization. This practice, however, can be viewed as disingenuous. Sliffman (2011) argues that establishing and authorizing clean zones are unconstitutional, violating the First Amendment. McKelvey and Grady (2008) further discuss how clean zones may infringe upon property rights, entrepreneurship, free commerce, and freedom of expression. These are just some of the unintended consequences that arise and must be accounted for by sport managers. Governance in Action 12.3 profiles the use of clean zones at the 2017 Super Bowl in Houston, Texas.

GOVERNANCE IN ACTION 12.3

Houston NFL Super Bowl's Clean Zones

In 2016 and 2017, Houston, Texas, was the host of the NCAA Men's Final Four and the NFL's Super Bowl, respectively. Up until this time, Houston was the only city to host both of these mega-events within a 10-month time frame. Historically, Houston is a sport mecca, regularly showcasing domestic and international sporting events. The city set a new NFL record for food and beverage sales as part of the $347 million the Super Bowl brought to Houston in 2017.

Houston is a world-class sporting event city with highly distinguished sport managers. One of the key organizations that help ensure Houston's sporting success is the Harris County-Houston Sports Authority (HCHSA). Doug Hall, vice president of special projects for the HCHSA, was president and CEO of the 2016 Final Four Local Organizing Committee and part of the 2017 Super Bowl Committee. Doug provided his insights into effective management of ambush marketing.

We are lucky here in Houston because the clean zone city ordinance is well established and very effective. The city and its municipalities strongly support, facilitate, and help enforce clean zones, but they also are experienced to understand the difference between the unscrupulous, illegal actors and the companies that may, sometimes unknowingly, just try to be a part of the exciting festivities. One unusual circumstance we had to deal with was during the Super Bowl and one of its main sponsors, Verizon. Verizon is the official wireless sponsor of the NFL and wanted to bring in support and service infrastructure at the different sites of the Super Bowl activities around the city. They were entitled to do this as the official sponsor, filling out the proper permits for operation and activation in the clean zones. Yet, other wireless and communication services like Sprint, AT&T, and T-Mobile, according to the letter of the clean zone law, would be banned from obtaining a permit to operate. This policy may cause major problems for the fans, media, operational staff, and others who will be in the clean zones that do not have Verizon wireless service. So, it's a balance to use common sense to understand the needs of both sponsors and fans. As a compromise, the other wireless companies were allowed to be issued a permit with certain conditions to bring in equipment for service only, but (they) could not set up branded types of marketing/promotional elements in the clean zones, whereas Verizon was allowed. This compromise helps to limit the focus on more of the obvious, but still challenging, ambush marketing tactics, like Sprint's use of street teams and grassroots marketing leaflets (Doug Hall, personal communication, May 12, 2019).

The important takeaway is that sport governance pertaining to an array of different marketing issues, from sponsorship activation to ambush marketing, is not always a clear black and white issue. One must clearly understand the needs of all parties involved in order to plan and coordinate efforts effectively.

RECAP

The sport marketing environment consists of a variety of organizations and systems. Marketing and sponsorship arrangements can be made directly between two parties, through the use of intermediaries (i.e., agents), or as part of a multifaceted relationship involving many parties, contracts, and agreements. It can involve private, for-profit and nonprofit, or governmental organizations. This chapter examines issues relating to endorsements, agents, governing bodies, athletes, and sponsors, and offers insight into important processes that take place between these entities.

Whether marketing sport products or marketing through sport, by studying the organizations, relationships, and issues involved, sport managers can envision the bigger picture and learn to navigate these issues effectively. Fans and spectators usually see the advertisements and signage at the events, but in order to make those exciting and innovative things possible, careful coordination and planning between many different entities is needed.

Critical Thinking Questions

1. What are two distinctive definitions of marketing, and how do these definitions apply to sport marketing?

2. What are the five unique characteristics of sport as defined in the chapter, and how do these affect the job of marketing a sporting contest such as an NFL game? What are potential governance issues?

3. What are the unique differences between the buyer and seller in sport sponsorship with respect to their governing role when entering into contract negotiations?

4. What is a contract, and how are contracts employed in the sport marketing industry?

5. What are waivers used for in sport marketing, and what best practices should be followed when executing a waiver?

6. What is ambush marketing, and what appears to be the attitude of the IOC and local organizing committees for the Olympic Games in policing especially small businesses in a host city to minimize confusion with the official sponsors of the Olympics?

7. What is Rule 40, and should the rule be amended? If so, should the IOC or NOCs be responsible for interpretations and changes?

Applied Activity

Identifying Sponsors and Partners

Part A: Select a major sport event to analyze for this activity other than the Olympics or World Cup. Once you select an event, conduct research to identify the sponsors. Next, identify the different organizations involved in producing the event from the local community, sports commission, state and local government, host committee or sport governing bodies or league(s), etc. Through research into each organization, identify and record the sponsors or partners for each organization.

Part B: Identify examples of complementary and conflicting sponsors and partners with the main event sponsors. Finally, considering both ambush by intrusion and ambush by association scenarios, describe the potential for ambush marketing and include the potential tactics that can be used to minimize the effects in advance of the event, during the event, and after the event.

Case Study Application

For more information on marketing and sport governance, review *Overcoming Challenges in Thailand Adventure Tourism* and *The Many Stakeholders of the NFL Super Bowl "On Location Experience"* in the web resource.

Sport Wagering

Bonnie Tiell and Kerri Cebula

The sport wagering industry has developed rapidly into one of the most dynamic industries in the world, and the United States is one of the latest entrants in the legal global marketplace. There are countless debates over the advantages of legalizing wagering. Sport gambling has long elicited polarized views, with proponents contending that the increased taxable income can benefit social causes, and naysayers citing compromises to the integrity of athletic competition. Many opinions have been publicly rendered by commissioners and executives throughout the global sport community. Current National Basketball Association (NBA) Commissioner Adam Silver (2014) noted that "gambling has increasingly become a popular and accepted form of entertainment in the United States."

In May 2018, the U.S. Supreme Court ruled that a federal ban prohibiting lotteries, sweepstakes, and all other types of betting schemes on competition involving amateur or professional athletes was unconstitutional (Professional and Amateur Sports Protection Act, 28 U.S.C. § 3701, et seq.). Overturning the Professional and Amateur Sports Protection Act (PASPA), which had been in place since 1992, essentially shifted the regulation of sport betting on professional and amateur competition to individual states as opposed to the federal government. The landmark decision resulted in eight states fully legalizing sport gambling in 2018 and over 20 introducing similar legislation in 2019. In the first year after PASPA was overturned, it was estimated that $150 billion was wagered illegally on sports in the United States compared to $4.5 billion bet in the legal, yet unregulated market (Glanz, 2018; U.S. Sports Integrity, 2018).

This chapter provides a brief history of sport gambling in the United States, including the status of individual states as of July 2019 and reaction from sport entities (e.g., professional leagues and the NCAA) to the Supreme Court's decision to overturn PASPA. Information will also address the scope of sport betting around the world, including an overview of national, continental, and global regulatory agencies in the industry.

Learning Outcomes

- Trace the history of sport wagering in the United States.
- Explain the scope of the Professional and Amateur Sports Protection Act of 1992 and the legal ramifications of the 2018 Supreme Court decision overturning the federal restrictions.
- Evaluate the impact of legal sport wagering on the National Collegiate Athletic Association and major professional sport leagues.
- Explain the scope of legal sport wagering internationally.
- Recognize and identify the general purpose of national, continental, and global agencies involved in regulating the sport wagering industry.

HISTORY OF SPORT WAGERING IN THE UNITED STATES

The evolution of gambling in the United States has been a complex affair. Sport wagering was a part of early America during the colonial era, especially in the sport of **lottery** systems and betting on horse racing. Since that time an abundance of federal laws and policies, featuring many loophole provisions, have been passed to regulate the sport gambling industry.

Evolution of Sport Wagering Through the 19th Century

Public lotteries were introduced in the United States during the colonial period in the early-to-mid-1600s (Barker & Britz, 2000, p. 232; Vacek, 2011, p. 90). The first commercial racetrack in the United States was built in New York in 1665, where early forms of sport wagering were permitted (Smiley, 2017). Lotteries continuing during the 1700s and 1800s supported the Revolutionary War as well as the development of Ivy League universities such as Yale, Harvard, Princeton, and Columbia (Gray, 2018).

Plagued by its association with corruption, almost every form of gambling was banned by local, state, and federal governments in 1860 except for horse racing. The Preakness Stakes, Belmont Stakes, and Kentucky Derby were established in 1867, 1873, and 1875, respectively, and by the turn of the 19th century, over two dozen tracks were legally operating (Gray, 2018). Illegal gambling operations by organized crime flourished during this era.

Amy Nichole Harris - Fotolia

Despite early bans on gambling activities by government entities, horse racing in the United States thrived with the Preakness Stakes, Belmont Stakes, and Kentucky Derby established in 1867, 1873, and 1875, respectively.

Twentieth Century

At the turn of the 20th century, organized crime continued to be associated with all forms of gambling, including sport betting. The most notorious case involving mob activity was the Black Sox scandal of 1919, when a handful of Chicago White Sox players were accused of being paid $10,000 each to intentionally lose the Major League Baseball (MLB) World Series to the Cincinnati Reds (Gray, 2018; Ostertag, 1992).

In 1931, gambling was legalized in the state of Nevada, primarily to finance the Hoover Dam project. In 1949, Nevada officially legalized betting on professional sports to further invigorate the tourism industry. Almost immediately, the federal government yielded its supremacy and imposed a 10 percent fee that was eventually reduced to 2 percent in 1974 and .05 percent in 1984 (Smiley, 2017).

Sport gambling in Nevada was restricted to **bookmakers** or **sportsbooks**, the term for the entity legally permitted to accept wagers on the outcome of competition such as horse races and professional games in the National Basketball Association (NBA), National Hockey League (NHL), NFL, and MLB. The Nevada sportsbooks initially operated in **turf clubs** known as such because they were located outside the casinos. Those turf clubs became obsolete when sport betting was assimilated into regular casino operations (Gray, 2019).

Various laws passed during the 20th century served primarily to curb the mass infiltration of organized crime that plagued the gambling industry. Regulation was also deemed necessary to protect the integrity of sports by deterring athletes, officials, and managers from compromising their ethics and altering the natural outcome of games as a result of bribery temptations. Scars from the 1919 Black Sox World Series bribery case and a string of NCAA basketball point-shaving scandals involving seven universities in the early 1950s provided impetus for legislators to enact federal laws to regulate sport wagering in the United States (Humphreys, 2017).

In 1961, President John F. Kennedy signed the **Wire Act of 1961** into law, making it illegal for those engaged in betting or wagering to knowingly use a wire communication facility for the transmission in interstate or foreign commerce of bets or wagers. It also made it illegal to use wire communication to share information for the purpose of placing bets (18 U.S.C. §1084). Three years later, the **Sports Bribery Act of 1964** made it illegal to conspire to intentionally influence the outcome of a sport contest; the act carried penalties of fines and imprisonment for up to five years (18 U.S.C. § 224). These two laws are still enforced today.

In sections of the country, forms of gambling were considered legal if they occurred on location at horse tracks, greyhound dog racing tracks, and jai alai arenas in Florida. During the 1970s and 1980s, commercial casinos in Las Vegas experienced significant growth, and only in Nevada could people legally place off-track bets on horse races via simulcast broadcasts from tracks around the country. In 1976, New Jersey approved an amendment to permit casinos to open in Atlantic City, which provided a monopoly for gambling on the East Coast in the image of Las Vegas, but sport betting was prohibited. Casinos in both Atlantic City and Las Vegas were notorious for sponsoring high-profile boxing matches as well as commercialized wrestling for entertainment, but not for gambling. In 1979, the Seminole tribe opened and operated the first Native American casino in Florida. Quickly, Native American–owned casinos on federally recognized reservations expanded their operations throughout the country, but sport betting was largely prohibited.

Despite the Sports Bribery Act, moderate corruption in collegiate and professional sports remained entwined with the gambling industry. NCAA point-shaving scandals erupted at Boston College in the late 1970s and Tulane University in the mid-1980s. In 1989, MLB placed a lifetime ban on Cincinnati Reds player and manager Pete Rose for his incessant gambling (Ostertag, 1992).

Three years after the lifetime ban of Pete Rose, PASPA was signed into federal law by President Bill Clinton, rendering almost all forms of sport wagering illegal in America by prohibiting any person or governmental entity from directly or indirectly "sponsoring, operating, advertising, or promoting" betting schemes, lotteries, or sweepstakes on one or more competitive games in which professional or amateur athletes participate (Professional and Amateur Sports Protection Act 28 U.S.C. § 3701, et seq.). Limited exemptions were permitted in the states of Nevada, Montana, Oregon, Delaware, and New Jersey due to their history of operating some form of legal sport betting schemes prior to the introduction of PASPA (Moorman, 2010).

Exempt from PASPA, Las Vegas became the destination location in America to legally bet on sports. The other three states grandfathered into the PASPA exemption operated more restrictive forms of sport wagering activities, which involved parlay betting. A **parlay bet** is a series of interconnected wagers whereby the only payout is to someone who guessed the correct outcomes on all individual bets in the series. For example, someone would win only if he or she correctly guessed the NFL game winner, whether the point spread was covered, and whether the final game score was over or under a predicted number. Delaware, for instance, only permitted NFL parlay bets for one season in the mid-1970s, which was enough to earn its exemption from federal PASPA legislation (Johnson, 2018). Oregon had passed legislation to permit NFL parlay betting three years before the passage of PASPA. Meanwhile, Montana sponsored both a state lottery system permitting fantasy bets on stock car racing and NFL player performance and a sport pool law allowing the sale of squares representing potential game scores throughout (e.g., after one quarter or at halftime) or at the end of competition (Humphreys, 2017). A final exemption was written into PASPA to allow a state that offered a betting, gambling, or wagering scheme, other than a lottery, conducted exclusively in casinos to offer sport wagering, but only if that state passed legislation allowing it within one year of the implementation of PASPA (28 U.S.C. 3704). New Jersey was the only state that allowed such a scheme at the time, but it did not pass legislation allowing sport wagering within the one-year period.

Another NCAA institution, Arizona State University, was named in a point-shaving scandal in 1994 as PASPA took hold in the United States. Throughout the latter portion of the 20th century, Las Vegas remained at the forefront of legal sport betting in addition to widespread pari-mutuel gambling on horse racing and greyhound racing throughout the country. The estimated volume of legal sport betting in Nevada in 1999 was $2.5 billion (Humphreys, 2017). The Internet age resulted in online gambling filtering into American households and social organizations, and this posed additional challenges for regulating the sport wagering industry.

New Millennium

In the new millennium, legislation served to usher the sport wagering industry's entrance into cyber space. An amendment in 2000 to the Interstate Horse Racing Act of 1978 expanded the virtual sport gambling market by making pari-mutuel betting on simulcast races permissible (Gray, 2019). In 2006, the federal government passed the Unlawful Internet Gambling Enforcement Act to block individuals or entities from accepting restricted transactions for wagers, such as credit or funds from an illegal online money transmission business.

A notable corruption scandal during the era resulted in federal conspiracy charges against former NBA referee Tim Donaghy in 2007 for providing insider tips to members of the mob while also placing wagers on games, many of which he was actively officiating (Johnson, 2018). Toledo University (2009), and the University of San Diego (2011) were also cited in point-shaving scandals (Humphreys, 2017).

In 2012, 48 states sponsored some type of legal gaming action in casinos or through lottery systems (Repetti & Jung, 2014). Native American casinos generated over $30 billion in revenues in 2017, with 242 tribes operating 494 casinos in 28 states (Meister, 2017). Commercial casinos in Las Vegas thrived, while the hundreds of Native American casinos throughout the country experienced relative success in the new millennium. Casinos in Atlantic City, New Jersey, however, experienced a decline during the period, with a handful shutting their doors by 2010. Restaurant traffic and hotel bookings in the area also declined precipitously.

In 2009, the first serious legal challenge to PASPA occurred. Delaware's state legislature passed the Sports Lottery Act, which would have allowed the state to implement full-scale sport wagering, similar to the offerings in Las Vegas. Delaware was permitted to implement sport wagering under PASPA because Delaware had offered parlay betting on NFL games prior to the passage of PASPA. The NCAA and the four major professional sport leagues filed for an **injunction** to prevent Delaware from implementing full-scale sport wagering, stating that it was a violation of PASPA. The Third Circuit Court of Appeals ruled that PASPA was constitutional, and that under PASPA, Delaware was not permitted to offer full-scale sport wagering because the state had not offered it prior to the passage of PASPA. The court ruled that PASPA allowed Delaware to offer parlay betting on NFL games only and granted the injunction (*Ofc. Comm Baseball v. Markell*, 579 F.3d 293 [2009]). Delaware began offering parlay betting on NFL games in September 2009.

To reinvigorate the casino industry in Atlantic City, in 2010, New Jersey state legislators proposed a referendum to appear on the 2011 ballot to permit sport betting in the state (Schoenfeld, 2019). Under PASPA, New Jersey had been given a year from the implementation of PASPA to pass legislation to allow sport wagering, but the state failed to do so. The referendum passed, and in 2012, the New Jersey state legislature amended its Casino Control Act, allowing the Casino Control Commission, the state agency overseeing gambling, to begin offering licenses to casinos and racetracks to take sports bets. In response, the NCAA and the four major professional sport leagues filed for an injunction to prevent New Jersey from implementing sport wagering. Again, the Third Circuit Court of Appeals ruled that PASPA was constitutional and that under PASPA, New Jersey was not permitted to offer sport wagering (*NCAA v. Governor of New Jersey*, 730 F. 3d 208 [2013]). New Jersey again passed legislation to permit sport wagering in 2014 and, again, the four major professional sport leagues filed for an injunction. The injunction was again granted by the Third Circuit Court of Appeals (*NCAA v. Governor of New Jersey*, 832 F. 3d 389 [2016]). This time, however, the United States Supreme Court granted **certiorari**, or an order for the higher court to review the case of the lower court. In May 2018, the Supreme Court declared that PASPA violated the **Tenth Amendment** and was therefore unconstitutional (*Murphy v. NCAA*, 138 S. Ct. 1461 [2018]). The Tenth Amendment generally relegates powers to the states that are not asserted at the federal level through the United States Constitution. Justice Samuel Alito, writing for the majority, noted "Congress can regulate sports gambling directly, but if it elects not to do so, each state is free to act on its own" (*Murphy v. NCAA*, 138 S. Ct. at 1484 – 1485). This decision meant that it was up to the states to determine if they would offer sport gambling, and it opened the floodgates for all 50 states to pass legislation to legalize sport gambling if citizens approved it.

STATUS OF SPORT WAGERING IN THE UNITED STATES

Estimates vary on the amount of money wagered (legally and illegally) on sports in America each year. Levinson (2006) speculated that Americans annually wager between $80 and $380 billion illegally on sporting events, while more current estimates range from $150 to $400 billion (Glanz, 2018; Humphreys, 2017; Lapointe, 2019; Silver, 2014). The estimated volume of legal sport betting in Nevada in 2018 was almost $5 billion ("Sport Betting Revenue by State," 2019).

As the federal restrictions on sport gambling disappeared in 2018, the landscape for sport betting evolved rapidly, with each state having the ability to create forms of legal sport wagering. Many states quickly integrated sportsbooks into existing casinos, according to the American Gaming Association, which monitors casino action. In the United States, $5.9 billion was wagered in the eight states where sport betting was legal during the first 10 months after PASPA was overturned ("Americans Will Wager," 2019).

The American Gaming Association estimates 47 million people in the United States wagered approximately $8.5 billion on the 2019 NCAA Division I Men's Basketball Tournament, which represented a 40 percent increase from bets placed on the Super Bowl ("Americans Will Wager," 2019). Eilers & Krejcik Gaming, a company that tracks sport gambling legislation, estimates $15.2 billion would be made on the NCAA tournament alone if sport wagering were legalized across the country and not in a few select states (Perry & Swanson, 2019).

When profiling the status of sport wagering in the United States, it is imperative to address the scope of state legislation and the impact on organizations such as the NCAA and major professional leagues, which have a vested interest in ensuring competitive integrity is maintained. While individual states have an interest in the integrity of athletics when gambling is added into the equation, other entities represent a wider-based societal perspective on sport wagering and have therefore amended or enacted policies to minimize cheating.

Scope of State Legislation

A year after PASPA was overturned, many states had introduced or passed legislation permitting forms of legal wagering on sport competition (see table 13.1). As of July 2019, sport betting was legal and operational in 10 states, while seven states were pending. Eilers & Krejcik Gaming estimates that sport betting will be legal in 39 states by 2023 (Perry & Swanson, 2019).

Each state has the discretion to pass legislation to permit or restrict activities related to sport gambling. Some states, for example, set age limits and prohibit certain types of online gambling for single sport bets while allowing on-location (e.g., casino) betting. Other states have almost completely legalized the industry.

Nevada was the first state to legalize sport wagering in 1949. It was not until Delaware in 2009 that another state legalized full-scale sport wagering. New Jersey followed in 2012 with its attempt to legalize sport wagering. Pennsylvania and West Virginia passed legislation to allow sport wagering and Mississippi repealed legislation banning sport wagering while *Murphy v. NCAA* was being decided by the U.S. Supreme Court ("Mississippi Sports Betting," 2019; "Pennsylvania Sports Betting," 2019; "West Virginia Sports Betting," 2019).

Table 13.1 Status of Legal Sport Gambling Bills as of July 2019

Legal and active sport betting	Close or passed legal sport betting (pending)	Pending sport betting legislation	No pending sport betting legislation
Arkansas	District of Columbia	Alabama	Alaska
Delaware	Illinois	Arizona	Florida
Mississippi	Indiana	Colorado	Idaho
Nevada	Iowa	Connecticut	Nebraska
New Jersey	Montana	Georgia	Utah
New Mexico	New Hampshire	Hawaii	Wisconsin
New York	North Carolina	Kansas	Wyoming
Pennsylvania	Tennessee	Kentucky	
Rhode Island		Louisiana	
West Virginia		Maine	
		Maryland	
		Michigan	
		Minnesota	
		Missouri	
		North Carolina	
		North Dakota	
		Ohio	
		Oklahoma	
		Oregon	
		South Carolina	
		South Dakota	
		Texas	
		Vermont	
		Virginia	
		Washington	

A state listed as "No pending sport betting legislation" has not yet had legislation authorizing sport betting introduced in its state legislature.

Based on Rodenberg (2019).

All states with active sport wagering have similar legislation and regulation for sport wagering (see table 13.1). All states allow gambling at their casinos and **raceinos** (horse racing facilities that are combined with casinos). All states but Mississippi permit online wagering, but because of the Wire Act of 1961, online wagering is only permissible if the individual making a bet is physically located in the state. A person must be 21 to wager in all states where sport betting is legal, except in Rhode Island, where the legal age is 18 ("Delaware Sports Betting," 2019; "Mississippi Sports Betting," 2019; "Nevada Sports Betting," 2019; "Pennsylvania Sports Betting," 2019; "Rhode Island Sports Betting," 2019; "West Virginia Sports Betting," 2019). All states permitting wagering on professional and college sports exclude wagering on high school and other amateur sports where a majority of the participants are under 18. Additionally, all states with legal sport betting prohibit wagering by participants (e.g., athletes) and by those with influence over competition.

Several states have additional stipulations to sport wagering. In Delaware, there is no wagering permitted on a Delaware college or university contest or on any amateur or professional sport involving a Delaware team (Del. Code Ann. tit. 29, § 4801 [2019]). Nevada will ban wagering on a team from Nevada at the request of that team's governing body (Nev. Admin. Code § 22.120 [2018]). So far, no governing body has made that request ("Nevada Sports Betting," 2019). New Jersey bans wagering on a college sporting event that takes place in New Jersey or involves a college from New Jersey (N.J. Admin. Code § C.5:12A-10 [2018]). Mississippi and Pennsylvania do not have additional restrictions (see Miss. Code Ann. §75-76-301 [2018]; 53 Pa. Code § 1401.6 [2019]).

New Mexico is a curious case. The state legislature has not passed legislation that would allow sport wagering in the state. However, Native American casinos in the state are permitted to offer sport wagering because of a gaming compact with the state that expressly allows sport wagering. It is believed that wagering on events involving the University of New Mexico and New Mexico State University is prohibited (Rodenberg, 2019).

Impact of Legislation on U.S. Sport Organizations

Prior to the overturning of PASPA, the NCAA and the four major professional sport leagues in the United States voiced their opposition to legalized gambling under the fear of violating the integrity of athletic competition, and not without reason. Their long-standing opposition to sport wagering stems from multiple cases where players and coaches were or could have been compromised and could influence the outcome of games. The first occurred in 1919 when several members of the favored Chicago White Sox were accused of intentionally losing the 1919 World Series to the Cincinnati Reds at the behest of members of organized crime. This led to baseball team owners hiring Judge Kennesaw Mountain Landis, a former federal judge, as the first commissioner in professional sports. The accused members of the White Sox were acquitted of crimes, but Landis banned them from baseball in 1921, a ban still in force today (Davies, 2017).

In 1951, the New York City district attorney announced the arrest of seven men, including three players on the City College of New York (CCNY) team, on charges of conspiring to fix college basketball games. Overall, 32 players from seven universities admitted to taking bribes to fix 86 games in 17 states. The University of Kentucky was forced to cancel its 1952-1953 season for its involvement in the scandal, while CCNY de-emphasized its athletic department and Long Island University shut down its athletic program for a six-year period (Goldstein, 2003).

In 1963, NFL Commissioner Pete Rozelle had his own gambling scandal. He suspended Paul Hornung of the Green Bay Packers and Alex Karras of the Detroit Lions for betting on league games and for associating with known gamblers. In addition, Rozelle fined five additional Detroit Lions for placing bets on the 1962 Championship Game. None of the accused players bet on their own team, and Hornung and Karras' suspensions were lifted a year later (Schwartz, 2003; Maule, 2015).

MLB had a second betting scandal in 1989 when reports surfaced that Cincinnati Reds manager Pete Rose bet on baseball. He denied the allegations, but a subsequent investigation alleged that Rose placed bets on 52 Reds games during the 1987 season, games which he managed and could influence the outcome of. In a deal with Commissioner Bart Giamatti, Rose accepted his placement on MLB's ineligible list and Giamatti agreed to make

Diamond Images/Getty Images

Commissioner Pete Rozelle exerted his authority to suspend Paul Hornung of the Green Bay Packers and Alex Karras of the Detroit Lions for gambling on NFL games and associating with known gamblers.

no formal finding on the gambling allegations. In his book, *My Prison Without Bars*, Rose admitted to betting on baseball, and specifically Reds games (Davies, 2017; Rose & Hill, 2000).

Five major governing bodies in the United States, the NCAA, NBA, NFL, MLB, and NHL, were proponents of PASPA and fought all attempts to legalize sport wagering. When Delaware passed legislation to allow full-scale sport wagering in 2009, they were the five that filed for the injunction to stop it from happening. They were the same five that sued to stop New Jersey from implementing full-scale sport wagering.

Since states began adopting legislation for legal sport wagering, however, colleges and professional leagues have been forced to embrace the reality of the new marketplace. One of the realities has been capitalizing on means to monetize their stake in the new landscape. Several of the professional leagues, for example, have entered into sponsorship arrangements with gaming operators and data providers. The five governing bodies are also seeking **integrity fees** to effectively police their athletes, although efforts have been unsuccessful thus far. Integrity fees are monetary installments requested by professional sport leagues to assist in providing better monitoring of the "integrity of the game" due to legal sport betting becoming more widespread in the United States. The following section describes the activities and positions of the NCAA and major professional leagues before and after the federal ban on sport wagering in America was lifted.

NCAA

The NCAA has been aggressive in protecting the integrity of amateur competition; however, gambling has been pervasive in college sports, evidenced by the amount legally wagered in Las Vegas each year on the NCAA Division I Men's Basketball Tournament.

Prior to the overturning of PASPA, NCAA policy was to not hold any NCAA championship games in a state that allowed sport gambling. When Delaware introduced legislation in 2009 to allow sport wagering, the NCAA stated it would not place championships in the state, a particular concern to the University of Delaware, which often hosted Football Championship Subdivision playoff games, and Wilmington University, which often hosted Division III playoff games. When the Third Circuit Court of Appeals granted the injunction, the NCAA continued to host championship events in Delaware.

In 2012, the NCAA did remove six championship rounds from the state of New Jersey because an injunction had not yet been granted ("Sports Wagering Law Forces NCAA," 2012). In the wake of the Supreme Court decision in *Murphy v. NCAA*, the NCAA Board of Governors suspended this policy and allowed states with sport wagering to host NCAA championship events ("NCAA Examining Impact," 2018).

Both before and after the overturning of PASPA, the NCAA worked with state gaming commissions and private firms to monitor wagering on college athletics to determine if there were irregularities in games, such as fan interference and late game official calls that might have affected wagers. The procedures were for member institutions and conferences involved, plus regulatory agencies and law enforcement organizations, to be notified when irregularities were suspected ("NCAA Uses Technology Services," 2018).

The NCAA has supported a federal model to oversee sport wagering with President Mark Emmert stating, "strong federal standards are necessary to safeguard the integrity of college sports and the athletes who play these games at all levels" (James, 2018). At the state level, university officials are addressing legislators as they consider or draft laws concerning sport wagering. Eric Barron, president of The Pennsylvania State University, contended that the state's sport wagering legislation should include an integrity fee, while University of Pittsburgh Athletic Director Heather Lyke expressed her concerns about the obligation to disseminate information about a student-athlete's injury or playing status. In Arkansas, the University of Arkansas and three other state institutions recommended regulations to prohibit "in-game proposition bets on the performance or non-performance of a team or an individual participant during a college sporting event" (Rodenberg, 2019).

For the student-athletes, staff members, conferences, and officials, NCAA legislation prohibits anyone involved in college athletics from participating in sport wagering activities on intercollegiate, amateur, or professional athletics in a sport the NCAA sponsors. This restriction means that a student-athlete cannot place a bet on an intercollegiate football game or on an NFL game. Legislation also prohibits those involved in college athletics from sharing information with anyone involved with or associated with sport wagering activities (Bylaw 10.3). Shortly before PASPA was overturned, member institutions voted to remove legislated sanctions for student-athletes and to instead address individual incidents on a case-by-case basis through the Committee on Student-Athlete Reinstatement (Proposal 2017-15).

Major Professional Sport Leagues

In line with the stance taken by the NCAA, the four major professional sport leagues have been aggressive in protecting the integrity of their competitions. However, much like betting on the NCAA tournament, sport wagering is pervasive in professional sports. A survey by the American Gaming Association in January 2019 indicated that 22.7 million Americans planned to bet $6 billion on Super Bowl LIII, with almost 2 million Americans planning to bet illegally through a bookmaker or bookie ("Super Bowl LIII Wagering Estimates," 2019). Table 13.2 summarizes the results of a study conducted by The Nielsen Company and commissioned by the American Gaming Association to project the annual revenues from gambling services

Table 13.2 2018 Gaming-Related Revenue Projections for Major Professional Sport Leagues (in millions)

	NBA	MLB	NFL	NHL
TV advertising revenue from gambling services	$57 M	$64 M	$451 M	$24 M
Sponsorship revenue from gaming operators	$78 M	$62 M	$92 M	$35 M
Data and product revenues for gambling services	$25 M	$28 M	$30 M	$6 M

Based on The Nielsen Company (2018).

for the four major professional sport leagues. The income sources reflect a growth in advertising deals with gambling services that appear during league games, sponsorship revenues for gambling services, and payments received to release official league data.

Despite the NFL's antigambling stance, in 1976, CBS realized that the NFL had become a favorite of gamblers and added *Las Vegas Sun* columnist Jimmy "The Greek" Snyder to its *NFL Today* pregame show. Snyder wrote a weekly sport betting column for the *Sun* and also had his own sports handicapping business. Snyder's role on *NFL Today* was to predict that afternoon's games. Despite their antigambling stance, the NFL was okay with Snyder's appearance on the show, and both the NFL and CBS denied that his presence encouraged people to bet on games. However, bookmakers monitored his appearance and adjusted their betting lines accordingly (Davies, 2017).

In 2009, the NFL approved the use of team names and logos for state lottery tickets, with prizes including league-licensed merchandise and special event tickets (Moorman, 2010). The New England Patriots, for example, negotiated a deal in 2009 with the Massachusetts State Lottery to feature the team's logo on a scratch-off lottery ticket. Agreements were immediately considered by other NFL teams, such as the Detroit Lions, Tennessee Titans, Buffalo Bills, and New York Jets and Giants, who were all interested in negotiating similar deals (Abelson, 2009).

Adam Silver succeeded David Stern as the NBA's commissioner in 2014 and immediately softened the stance of the league with regard to sport wagering while noting the need to legislate strict regulations and technological safeguards (Silver, 2014). MLB Commissioner Rob Manfred, who took office in 2015, joined Silver's call for federal regulation (Rodenberg, 2015). In 2016, the NHL became the first professional league to place a team in Las Vegas.

Since the overturning of PASPA, MLB, the NBA, and the NHL have been proactive in acknowledging the potential of widespread legal gambling, with the NBA leading the way. Three months after the decision, the league became the first to establish MGM Resorts International as the official gaming partner of the NBA. As the exclusive gambling partner, MGM has rights to use NBA and WNBA logos as well as all team logos for marketing purposes. MGM also retains the right to use official real-time NBA data on its betting platform. The deal includes a provision to create a collaborative arrangement with the NBA to detect and prevent fraud and potential game fixing (Draper, 2018). Shortly after establishing the gaming partnership, the league was also the first in the United States to create a multipartnership deal with two companies to track real-time NBA betting activity by licensed gaming operators in each state where sport wagering is legal ("NBA Announces First Betting-Data Partnership," 2018). The first partner, Sportradar, is a global data-distribution and technology company based in Switzerland, while the second partner, Genius Sports, is the official NBA data provider in the United States.

In the wake of legal sport wagering, Gary Bettman, commissioner of the National Hockey League, has suggested that gambling on hockey games can potentially create more fans in the league ("Betting on Hockey," 2019). In 2018, the league established a partnership with MGM Resorts as the official gaming partner and resort destination of the NHL (Rosen, 2018), while the Las Vegas Golden Knights and New Jersey Devils partnered with William Hill to bring tote boards into their arenas; the Devils made a second partnership with Caesars to create a gambling-themed lounge inside their building. Even NFL team owners have suggested revenues can be derived and entertainment value enhanced if spectators could bet on game situations through apps on their phones in the way Premier League teams in the United Kingdom have been able to capitalize on legal wagering (Breer, 2018).

Generally, professional sport leagues are widely in support of laws mandating the use of official data such as starting lineups and the assignment of officials. For example, a new policy for the 2019 MLB season requires teams to submit their starting lineup to the official data operations department at least 15 minutes prior to public disclosure to reduce the value of inside information, which can compromise the integrity of the game for legal oddsmakers and gamblers ("Betting and Baseball," 2019).

As in the NCAA, the players, staff members, and owners of teams in the major professional sports are not permitted to place bets on league games. In the NBA, a player who wagers money or anything of value on an NBA game is subject to discipline by the commissioner (NBA Collective Bargaining Agreement, 2017). An NFL player is subject to discipline by the commissioner if he accepts a bribe or agrees to fix an NFL game, if he bets on an NFL game, or if he knowingly associates with gamblers or gambling activity (NFL Collective Bargaining Agreement, 2011). The MLB collective bargaining agreement does not outright ban sport wagering, but it does state that a player who engages in conduct that is detrimental to the best interests of baseball or is in violation of state law can be disciplined by the commissioner (Pacifici, 2014). In the NFL, owners can have their ownership rights terminated if they try to influence the outcome of a game (National Football League, 2006). NBA owners can have their ownership rights terminated if they place a bet on any game an NBA team participates in or allow their employees to do so (NBA Collective Bargaining Agreement, 2017).

STATUS OF SPORT WAGERING INTERNATIONALLY

In 1991, legal sport lotteries and pools were active in 37 countries such as Australia, the United Kingdom, and Germany (Smith, 1992). According to the World Casino Directory (2019), over 150 countries offer legal sport wagering operating over 550 sportsbooks around the world (see table 13.3). Legal sport gambling continues to grow and expand around the world at a rapid pace, but it remains fairly unregulated, especially in the online market. This section provides a brief overview of sport wagering around the world.

North America

Sport wagering is legal in all forms in Mexico and legal in some forms in Canada. In Mexico, the sport wagering industry is licensed through the Ministry of Interior, but it is widely unregulated

Table 13.3 2019 Scope of Sportsbooks Around the World

Continental region	Countries with legal gambling	Sportsbooks
North America	3	383
South America	10	3
Caribbean	22	24
Central America	7	10
Europe	44	142
Asia	20	12
Africa	34	8
Middle East	4	0
Oceania	7	5

Based on World Casino Directory (2019).

as unlicensed sportsbooks are still a popular way to bet on sports. The most popular sport to bet on is football (soccer), with basketball, baseball, and boxing also being popular. Local sports, such as charreada, bull fighting, and Basque pelota, are also popular with sports gamblers ("Mexico Sports Betting," n.d.).

Governance in Action 13.1 profiles the ownership of a professional sport team by a powerful figure tied to casino operations, which exacerbates a common situation in Mexico, a nation plagued by corruption.

In Canada, sport wagering is legal in some forms. Under Canada's Criminal Code, wagering on a single game is illegal, but provinces are permitted to offer sport wagering provided it is not on a single game. For example, Ontario permits wagering on the outcome of three to six games (Pro-Line, n.d.). In Quebec, bettors can make between one and eight predictions ("Mise-Au-Jeu," n.d.). With 90 percent of the Canadian population living within 100 miles of the U.S. border, in March 2019, Ontario's Finance Minister advocated for an amendment to the country's Criminal Code to allow **single-game betting** (Holden, 2019).

Central and South America and the Caribbean

Legal sport wagering is permissible in many counties in Central America, South America, and the Caribbean. The wide variances in regulations and restrictions demonstrate the overall convoluted nature of the industry.

GOVERNANCE IN ACTION 13.1

Conflict of Interest: Team Ownership in Mexico

Club Tijuana Xoloitzcuintles de Caliente (Xolos or Club Tijuana) is a professional soccer franchise founded in 2007. In 2012, Xolos became the youngest club to win Mexico's Apertura championship ("History," n.d.). In 2018 and 2019, Club Tijuana continued to rank among the top six teams in the Liga MX, the top level of soccer in Mexico belonging to the Mexican Football Federation.

Club Tijuana is managed by two young front office executives, one of whom is also president of Club Dorados, a professional franchise in Ascenso MX, the country's second-tier division. Dorados is located in Sinaloa, Mexico, a state best known as home to jailed drug lord Joaquin "El Chapo" Guzman (Miselem, 2018).

Grupo Caliente, an empire of hotels, casinos, dog tracks, and jockey clubs, has a 60 percent ownership stake in Club Dorados and 100 percent ownership of Club Tijuana ("Bienvenido [Welcome]," 2019). The owner of Grupo Caliente is Jorge Hank Rhon, father of Jorgealberto Hank Inzunza, who serves as president and chairman of the two soccer clubs.

Tijuana's mayor from 2004 to 2007, Rhon has 19 children and has faced numerous accusations of felonious activity, including extensive involvement in organized crime. In 1988, two of Rhon's bodyguards were convicted in the murder of a newspaper journalist who was investigating potential criminal activities by the tycoon. Rhon was questioned a decade later about potential involvement in another murder case and was arrested in 2011 for having 80 guns and thousands of rounds of ammunition in his mansion. More recently, Rhon was accused of trafficking endangered tigers and chimpanzees (Miselem, 2018).

A professional franchise being owned by an entity associated with a gaming casino is not unique. Currently, the Native American Mohegan tribe owns three casinos in addition to a professional team in the National Lacrosse League and a professional team (Connecticut Suns) in the Women's National Basketball Association (WNBA) (Bustillos, 2018). Tilman Fertitta, owner of the Golden Nugget Casinos and Hotels in Las Vegas, paid $2.2 billion in 2017 for ownership rights to the National Basketball Association's (NBA) Houston Rockets (Melzer, 2018). Betting on the Rockets was immediately banned in Golden Nugget casinos.

The conflict of interest in the association of a professional sport team with casino ownership is an ethical conundrum. Regulatory agencies that monitor sport gambling are aware of the potential for misuse of information and other questionable activities.

It is predicted that Brazil will soon reign as the world's second-largest regulated market for online gambling, after the United Kingdom ("An Unlimited Number of Licenses," 2019). This prediction followed the passage of Law 13,756/2018 in 2018, which authorized land-based and online sport betting in Brazil. However, the legislature continued in 2019 to debate the implementation plan to determine licensure and authorization models for sportsbooks.

Sport wagering in Trinidad and Tobago is legal under the Gambling and Betting Act, but it is unregulated by the government ("Trinidad and Tobago," n.d.) Legislation known as the Gambling (Gaming and Betting) Control Bill was introduced in Parliament to try to provide a framework for controlling the industry. The bill failed in 2013 and 2015 and was reintroduced in 2016. It is still under consideration by the House of Representatives ("The Gambling [Gaming and Betting] Control Act," 2016).

Argentineans began wagering on horses in the 1880s, and in 1971, the country permitted betting on soccer through a lottery system ("Argentina Sport Betting," 2019). In 2018, the country voted to ban the ability to bet on soccer. Prior to the ban, the Argentina Ministry of Sport and professional leagues respectively received 13.5 percent and 25 percent of lottery revenues until the system was banned by the government ("Which Countries Allow," 2018).

Antigua, Costa Rica, and Curacao in the Caribbean each offer online sportsbook licenses. One of the first countries to legalize sport wagering in

1994, Antigua provides a healthy regulated market. Similarly, Curacao is among the most regulated countries in the region for sport betting, with a licensure fee for sportsbooks of $6,000 per year following an initial investment of $21,000. Although the fee is exorbitant, the benefit is that individuals only pay a 2 percent tax on profits, which is miniscule compared to countries around the world that command 20 to 30 percent or more from a total of gross revenues. Unlike their Caribbean neighbors, in Costa Rica, there is no governing body such as a gaming commission to oversee online sportsbooks, which therefore makes the country more free from regulation than any other location in the world ("The Jewels of Caribbean Archipelago," 2019).

Europe

Sport wagering is legal throughout most of Europe, but if sport wagering had a home, the United Kingdom would be the number one location. Sport wagering in Europe was made legal with the passage of the Gaming Act 1845, which legalized betting on horse races. The first known sportsbook began in the U.K. in 1886 and is still in operation today. The Betting and Gaming Act 1960 legalized betting on all other sports ("UK Sports Betting," n.d.).

As of 2019, the U.K. had approximately 8,500 licensed sport betting parlors in operation, including every major stadium ("UK Sports Betting," 2019). To put that in perspective, Domino's Pizza operates 5,500 franchises in the United States (Schoenfeld, 2019). Individuals in the U.K. can bet on sports at a betting parlor, at the stadium via kiosks, online, on their mobile phones, or even with their television remote control (Silver, 2014). In 2017, 17 percent of U.K. residents claimed to have placed a sports wager, worth over $40 billion ("A Look Inside," 2018).

Overall, Europe has been lauded for its mobile-centric approach to sport wagering, but the market is a Wild West landscape of regulated and unregulated online sites. The NBA, for example, supposedly blacklisted 2,480 betting websites in Cyprus in 2017 ("Gambling Laws in Europe," 2017).

Poland operates 14 sportsbooks issued by the Ministry of Finance after the country amended legislation for online wagers in 2017 (Stradbrooke, 2019). In the Netherlands, 2017 legislation permitted an unlimited number of five-year licenses for sportsbooks, who pay 29 percent in taxes on gross revenues in addition to 2 percent for the Dutch Gaming Authority and an addictions fund ("Gambling Laws in Europe," 2017).

Asia and Oceania

Many countries in Asia have banned gambling, including sport gambling. Some countries do allow limited sport wagering. In Japan, the Criminal Code generally bans gambling, but there are a few exceptions. One of those exceptions is limited sport wagering on horse races, motorboat races, and motorcycle races.

In China, gambling is technically illegal. However, there are two state-run lotteries that are not considered to be gambling: (1) the China Welfare Lottery Distribution Center, founded in 1987, and (2) the China Sports Lottery Administration Center, founded in 1994 (Li, Zhang, Mao, & Min, 2012). The sports lottery allows wagering on football (soccer) matches from around the world, including the English Premier League, Spain's La Liga, and the J.League in Japan. Sport gambling has become a major segment of China's sport industry, although the gambling market is still not considered mature. Through 2019, China supported lotto, sport betting, numbers games, and Internet gaming, while it was suggested that the national sports lottery provided nearly 300,000 jobs on the mainland. In 2011, an official in the China Sports Lottery Administration Center claimed that the sports lottery provided $176.5 million, $205.9 million, and $235.3 million in tax revenue for the years 2006, 2007, and 2008, respectively (China Sports Lottery Administration Center, 2011). The sports lottery is the main source of revenue for the Olympic Supporting Program.

In Australia, betting on track horse racing was legalized in the early 1800s, and sport betting (including online) was permitted in 1980 with rugby and Aussie football representing the most popular wagering pools, followed by cricket. Individuals typically can bet on the outcome of a contest up to about a half hour before the start of a competition or through to approximately five minutes remaining in a game. The Australian government promotes a code of practice for gambling agencies, primarily to protect youth from exposure. Extra restrictions for media advertising, for example, exist between the hours of 5:00 a.m. and 8:30 p.m. ("Australian Communications and Media Authority," 2018).

Africa

Sport wagering is legal throughout most of Africa. There are still exceptions, such as in Sudan where Islamic religious laws forbid gambling, with viola-

GLYN KIRK/AFP/Getty Images

In Australia, the most popular sports for legal wagering include Aussie football, professional rugby, and cricket.

tions for betting on sports being subject to public lashing ("Gambling Laws in Africa," 2019).

Sport wagering became legal in Ghana in 1960, and it is legal to bet both online and in person ("Which Countries Allow," 2018). People in Ghana can bet on sports like European football (soccer), the NBA, and the NFL, as well as domestic sports. One of the more interesting effects of sport wagering is the decline in the popularity of Ghana's domestic football leagues. This decline is attributed to the overall popularity of European football leagues such as the English Premier League and Spain's La Liga, and because of their popularity, bettors are more excited about those leagues ("The State of Sports Betting in Ghana," 2018).

A recent study reported over 60 million residents in Nigeria spend an average of the equivalent of $15 per day on sport betting ("Popularity of Sports Betting in Africa," 2019). It is speculated that the high unemployment rate of youth, the zealous attitude toward sport, and lenient sport betting laws contribute to the high rate of sport wagering throughout the African continent (PricewaterhouseCoopers, 2014). Only South Africa is considered a regulated market ("Popularity of Sports Betting in Africa," 2019).

REGULATORY AGENCIES FOR SPORT WAGERING

Beyond national and state or provincial governments, attempts to regulate the sport wagering industry and promote responsible gambling occur through associations that track and monitor betting activity or that provide licensure to operate gaming systems. Regulatory agencies investigate corruption, including match fixing, and promote responsible gambling through measures such as age verifications, capping maximum betting amounts, prohibiting the use of credit to enter wagers, limiting gaming hours, and establishing a licensing protocol.

Collaboration among agencies has become increasingly important due to the widespread ease of online consumer gambling. Various countries and states employ gaming authorities, which may grant licensure for sportsbooks and at the very least, work in conjunction with law enforcement agencies to regulate the industry. Following is an overview of selected agencies and organizations with a role in governing or regulating the sport wagering industry in the United States and internationally.

National and State Agencies

The regulation of gambling, including sport wagering, around the world is typically a function of the government as opposed to an independent agency. It may be the responsibility of individual states or provinces. To provide a perspective on regulatory practices around the world, profiled in this section are national and state agencies regulating sport wagering in the United States, South Africa, the United Kingdom, and Japan.

United States

NBA Commissioner Adam Silver (2014) stated several years ago that sport gambling was "a thriving underground business that operates free from regulation or oversight." Historically, both federal and local law enforcement were the most reliable regulatory agencies for sport wagering; sport wagering was illegal in 49 states, and bookmaking was illegal in all 50 states. Notably, the U.S. Department of Justice and the Federal Bureau of Investigation (FBI) have been the enforcement agencies for illegal sport betting operations in the country. The primary agencies involved in regulating gaming in the United States are the gaming commissions and lotteries in states where gaming is legal. With the overturning of PASPA, the gaming commissions and lotteries in states with legalized sport wagering have added the oversight of sport wagering to their duties.

Federal Regulation The Department of Justice, through various U.S. attorneys' offices and the FBI, is charged with enforcing both the Wire Act of 1961 and the Sports Bribery Act of 1964. The Wire Act, in conjunction with other legislation, is used to prosecute illegal bookmaking, and the Sports Bribery Act is used to prosecute those accused of bribing athletes and officials to throw games.

Approximately six months following the Supreme Court's decision to overturn PASPA, the federal government again demonstrated its broad interest by proposing Senate Bill S.3793, the **Sports Wagering Market Integrity Act of 2018**.

S.3793 was introduced to "maintain a distinct federal interest in the integrity and character of professional and amateur sporting contests." If passed as a law, the bill would essentially grant district courts the power to create an independent national sport wagering clearinghouse and initiate civil action against individuals who wagered on sports in states that had not yet opted to legalize sport betting. The penalty proposed for an initial offense would either be $10,000 or up to three times the amount wagered (U.S. Congress, 2018). As of July 2019, the bill was dormant, without a date scheduled to reappear in another congressional session.

State Regulation In the states that have active sport wagering, a **state agency** is responsible for regulating sport wagering activities in each state. These activities can include creating the rules and regulations for sport wagering and licensing sport wagering operations. Three such agencies are the Delaware Lottery, the Nevada Gaming Commission, and the Pennsylvania Gaming Control Board.

Regulation of sport wagering in Delaware is through two separate agencies: the Delaware State Lottery Office, known as the Delaware Lottery, and the Division of Gaming Enforcement. The Delaware Lottery is responsible for promulgating the rules and regulations for sport wagering in Delaware and for issuing licenses to casinos wishing to run a sportsbook. The Division of Gaming Enforcement (DGE) has exclusive jurisdiction over criminal offenses that relate to gaming in a licensed video lottery facility and that relate to the Delaware Lottery, both of which include sport wagering. In Delaware, bribing an official or a participant in a sporting event to fix the outcome of the event and accepting such a bribe are criminal actions, so the DGE would be the group responsible for investigating such actions. The DGE is also responsible for completing background checks on those who have applied for licenses through the Delaware Lottery.

In Nevada, regulation of sport wagering is also done by two separate agencies: the Nevada Gaming Commission and the Nevada Gaming Control Board. The Gaming Control Board is responsible for the day-to-day operations of gaming in Nevada, including licensing sport wagering operations and ensuring the collection of taxes and fees related to gaming. The Enforcement Division of the Gaming Control Board is responsible for conducting criminal investigations (Enforcement Division, n.d.). Bribery to influence sporting events is a felony in Nevada, and it appears that the Enforcement Division has the responsibility for those investigations. The Gaming Commission acts on the recommendations of the board in licensing matters and has the final authority. The commission is also responsible for promulgating the rules and regulations for gaming and for acting as the disciplinary authority over license holders.

The Pennsylvania Gaming Control Board (PGCB) is a government agency of the Commonwealth of Pennsylvania and is responsible for overseeing slot machines and casino games. When sport wagering became legal in 2018, the PGCB added the oversight of sport wagering to its duties. The board's main role is to issue rules and regulations for sport wagering and to license those wishing to operate sportsbooks. The board, through its Bureau of Investigations and Enforcement, is responsible for enforcing gaming legislation. As of July 2019, it appears that there is no section of the Pennsylvania Crimes Code that makes bribery to influence sporting events illegal.

South Africa

The National Gambling Board is the entity responsible for oversight of sport wagering and all gaming in South Africa. The board was established through the National Gambling Act (NGA) No. 7 of 2004, and it oversees nine provincial gambling and racing boards that are authorized to issue licenses to sportsbooks ("Sports Betting Law in South Africa," 2019). South Africa's National Gambling Board works with the county's Financial Intelligence Service to conduct audits, inspect licenses, and formulate guidance notifications for compliance with legislation. The national board also conducts evaluations of the processes and activities of each provincial board.

United Kingdom

Regulation of sport wagering in the United Kingdom is a function of the national and regional governments. The United Kingdom Gambling Commission was established in accordance with the Gambling Act of 2005 and retains oversight responsibility for the national lottery while also regulating all commercial gambling in cooperation with licensing authorities ("What We Do," n.d.). The Gambling Commission (2019) publishes conditions and codes for licensure with regulations addressing pool betting for football, horse racing, and dog racing. The commission also uses a sport betting intelligence unit to help curtail **match fixing**, money laundering, fraud, or additional gambling violations. The unit traditionally defers to Crown Prosecution Services, the United Kingdom's law enforcement, to wield punitive actions against individuals or organizations that fail to comply with regulations.

Japan

The Japanese Ministry of Education, Culture, Sports, Science and Technology serves as the regulatory agency for monitoring sport wagering in Japan. There is no gambling commission since Japan has no casinos. The 1998 Sports Promotion Voting Act permits legal betting on soccer toto or football lottery pools for the Japanese professional J.League. Sport wagering is restricted exclusively to football, horse racing, cycling, motorcycling, and boat racing. The Ministry of Education, Culture, Sports, Science and Technology works with other agencies to regulate wagering in each sport. For example, the Japan Sports Council operates the toto football lottery, the Ministry of Agriculture, Forestry and Fisheries supervises horse racing, and the Foundation of Japan Motorboat Racing Association through the Ministry of Land, Infrastructure, Transport and Tourism operates betting on boat races (Hanamizu, 2016).

One means to regulate wagering has been for the government to place limits on the maximum amount a player can wager and to remove automated bank teller machines (ATMs) from permissible betting areas ("Sports Betting in Japan," 2019). Additionally, Japan's penal code stipulates that habitual gamblers may be subject to a prison term of up to three years, which is enforced by the National Police Agency (Hanamizu, 2016).

Regional Agencies

Regional (e.g., continental) agencies involved in regulating sport wagering activity have oversight responsibilities for the entire gaming industry within their geographic borders. Examples of regional agencies profiled in this section are the North American Association of State and Provincial Lotteries and European Lotteries.

North American Association of State and Provincial Lotteries

Founded in 1971, the North American Association of State and Provincial Lotteries (NASPL) represents 52 lottery systems in the United States, Canada, and Mexico ("Welcome to NASPL," n.d.). The association operates through an executive board and committee structures, including a sport committee.

The organization primarily serves as an educational, information-based resource center. It has lobbied legislators to ensure the sovereignty and to protect the rights of lotteries in the face of federal and state antilottery laws while also generating sales data reports, which are available through a password-protected domain ("The History of NASPL," n.d.).

European Lotteries

With headquarters in Lausanne, Switzerland, and Brussels, Belgium, European Lotteries (EL) is the European association for state-owned and state-licensed lotteries. It provides approximately 2 billion euros per year for grassroots and amateur sport (The European Lotteries Sports Integrity Plan, 2013). Established in 1983, EL added a sport betting operator's division in 2007. As of 2014, the sport betting division included 80 members operating in 46 countries (The European Lotteries Code of Conduct on Sport Betting, 2014, p. 12). EL also adopted a Sport Charter in 2012 and created a seven-point Sports Integrity Action Plan in 2013. The Sport Charter recognizes new forms of sport betting and the applicability of regulatory policies, which promote responsible betting and high ethical principles. The charter also recognizes the role of sport wagering as a means of funding and contributing to the promotion of safe and healthy sport while maintaining an agency to monitor patterns and potential problems in sport betting ("The European Lotteries Charter 2012," 2012). Table 13.4 provides an overview of the seven points of the EL Sports Integrity Action Plan (2013).

In 2009, EL was credited as the first organization to officially provide surveillance of sport wagering activity through the European Lotteries Monitoring System (ELMS). The monitoring of soccer matches commenced in 2005 in cooperation with the Union of European Football Associations (UEFA).

The EL Code of Conduct on Sport Betting (2014) requires members identified as signatories to guarantee law enforcement intervention against illegal gaming operators and stresses verification of player identification, protection of minors, availability of problem gambling treatment services, responsible advertising practices, and a promise to alert the appropriate authorities in the event of suspicious sport betting activity.

The European Convention on the Manipulation of Sports Competitions

Also known as the **Macolin Convention**, the European Convention on the Manipulation of Sports Competitions represents a legal framework that can be applied by individual countries to regulate sport wagering. The treaty, set forth by the Council of Europe, is designed to protect the integrity of sports by combatting the manipulation of sport competitions (Explanatory Report to the Council of Europe Convention on the Manipulation of Sports Competitions, 2014). The Macolin Convention defines manipulation of sport competitions as

> an intellectual arrangement, act or omission aimed at an improper alteration of the result or the course of a sports competition in order to remove all or part of the unpredictable nature of the aforementioned sports competition with a view to obtaining an undue advantage for oneself or for others (Council of European Convention on the Manipulation of Sports Competitions, C.E.T.S. No. 215).

The purpose of the Macolin Convention is to create a legal framework for countries to strengthen cooperation among governments, law enforcement agencies, sport organizations, and sport wagering organizations (Panorama Convention on the

Table 13.4 Seven Points of the 2013 European Lotteries Sports Integrity Action Plan

Action item	Description
Fight against illegal operations	Urges actions against operators without a license and law enforcement measures to protect consumers (e.g., banning illegal advertising and publishing blacklists)
Strong legal framework and sanctions	Urges standardization of definitions, stronger penal sanctions, and classification of corruption and criminal activities involving manipulation of sporting events
Education and prevention	Urges education materials and programs targeting athletes, officials, managers, prosecutors, and sport administrators to raise awareness of illegal betting and match fixing
Corporate governance	Urges adoption of standards to prevent conflict of interest and separation of individuals employed at a lottery or gambling operation and in the sport world
Monitoring against betting irregularities and match fixing	Urges the development of globally coordinated monitoring of sport wagering, including real-time betting odds and macroeconomic data
Sport betting regulation	Urges regulators to be vigilant in identifying risks of gambling systems and to create a group of experts to further analyze risks (e.g., exposure to money-laundering schemes)
International coordination and cooperation	Urges national and international measures to fight match fixing and illegal betting operations in sport

Manipulation of Sports Competitions, 2018). As of July 2019, 31 countries in the Council of Europe had signed the treaty, but only four had ratified it.

Global Agencies

Global agencies that monitor sport wagering activity generally have the broader purpose of overseeing the entire worldwide gaming industry, of which sport betting is one segment. These agencies serve mainly to identify irregular gambling activity and to collaborate with other entities authorized to impose sanctions. Two global agencies with a regulatory role in sport wagering are the World Lottery Association and the Global Lottery Monitoring System. Also included in this section are international sport governing bodies, the IOC and FIFA.

World Lottery Association

Formed in 1999 and with offices in Montreal, Canada, and Basel, Switzerland, the World Lottery Association (WLA) is a member-driven organization with the mission to "advance the interests of state-authorized lotteries" ("About the WLA," 2019). The WLA serves five regions, including Africa, Asia/Pacific, Europe, North America, and South America. Members must be licensed or authorized to operate lottery and betting games in a country or state recognized by the United Nations as a territory free of "strategic deficiencies" ascribed by the Financial Action Task Force on Money Laundering (World Lottery Association Bylaws, 2018, p. 4).

Governance is asserted over members through bylaws and an enforceable code of conduct. Members may be expelled by the executive committee for failure to pay dues or for supplying goods or services to entities that do not adhere to the association's code of conduct. Areas of the WLA Code of Conduct (2018) include standards of good practice, security and consumer protection requirements, licensing requirements, provisions for the prevention of underage gambling, compulsive gambling, and privacy breaches. Several of the standards of good practice or good governance include provisions for verifying that players are residents of the gambling agency's jurisdiction, limits on spending, rules for subscription services, reliable methods to ensure data protection, and transmission of currency.

The power to enforce the code of conduct is granted to the executive committee, which is comprised of an executive director and members from 13 different countries who vote on whether to expel members who violate provisions of the code.

Global Lottery Monitoring System

The **Global Lottery Monitoring System** (**GLMS**) is an international surveillance organization that detects irregularities in the sport gaming industry. Originating in Europe and operating globally since 2015, the GLMS requires extensive coordination among gaming regulators, law enforcement authorities, and sports organizations to monitor suspicious activity ("What Is GLMS," 2019).

The GLMS operates through an eight-member executive committee abiding by the organization's statutes and code of conduct (2018), which describe its role in safeguarding the "integrity and credibility" of sport betting (p. 4). Similar to the WLA, the GLMS Code of Conduct (2018) on sport betting addresses the protection of age limits, proper jurisdiction for clients and gaming organizations, the necessity of player identification, periodic audits, and safeguarding the moral integrity of sport participants.

Members include lotteries and associations belonging to the WLA or other recognized lottery regulators such as the NASPL. As a relatively new agency, GLMS is developing strategic partnerships and using a monitoring platform powered by TXODDS, an analytics company delivering sport betting odds and reliable data ("About TXODDS," 2019). The organization facilitates the sharing of sport betting information.

According to a GLMS Mid-Term Monitoring Report (2018), 264 of 355 alerts about irregularities detected in the sport gaming industry were associated with association-rule football (soccer) and reported to FIFA and the Union of European Football Associations (UEFA). In addition to notifying local gaming authorities, additional irregularities were reported to the International Olympic Committee (IOC) and the Tennis Integrity Unit.

Six continental groups and one international territory are represented in the GLMS report. In the first half of 2018, North America was cited for issues with esports and basketball gambling, while Europe was connected to betting irregularities in 10 separate sport disciplines ("GLMS Mid-Term Monitoring Report," 2018). Alerts range from minor adjustments in odds to rumors of match fixing by a source.

International Sport Governing Bodies

International sport governing bodies also have considerable authority in the regulation of sport wagering, especially with regard to match manipulation. In Australia, the National Rugby League banned Ryan Tandy for life in 2010 for match fixing, and in 2014, the league banned additional players for placing multiple bets on their own teams (Bricknell, 2015). Players have also been banned and fined in tennis for match fixing and in Aussie football for sharing insider information ("Which Countries Allow," 2018). The IOC and FIFA wield considerable enforcement power and have extensive monitoring systems.

International Olympic Committee Through its power and authority granted by the Olympic Charter, the IOC serves as a regulatory agency for monitoring sport wagering in international competitions around the world. The IOC monitoring system for improprieties in the sport gaming industry incorporates the Integrity Betting Intelligence System (IBIS), launched in 2013. The system relies on collaboration and information exchange among law enforcement, sports organizations, betting operators, and sport betting regulating entities. It also facilitates communication between all partners on the sports side and the different sport betting entities, including GLMS and lottery systems.

The International Olympic Committee's (2016) Ethics and Compliance Office collaborated with the International Criminal Police Organization's (INTERPOL) Integrity in Sports Anti-Corruption and Financial Crimes Unit to create a handbook on protecting sport from manipulation. The handbook noted there were media reports of competition manipulation (e.g., match fixing) in 52 countries in 2015, primarily in badminton, basketball, cricket, cycling, football, handball, horse racing, snooker, tennis, volleyball, and wrestling (p. 20). It also noted that the IOC has the authority to oversee competition integrity during the Olympic Games, while acknowledging the role of international federations between Games (p. 41).

To strengthen its commitment to preventing manipulation of competitions, the IOC Executive Board passed the Olympic Movement Code on the Prevention of the Manipulation of Competitions in 2015 and first implemented it at the Rio Games in 2016. The code itself complies with the Macolin Convention. All international federations within the Olympic movement must adopt the code, and during the Olympic Games, everyone must comply with the code ("Olympic Movement Code," n.d.). Finally, the IOC adopted an integrity and compliance hotline where reports on suspicious activities could be reported confidentially and anonymously.

Fédération Internationale de Football Association FIFA takes an active role in monitoring sport integrity and wagering by partnering with Sportradar, a company that detects manipulation in athletic competition by identifying and analyzing any suspicious betting behavior and patterns. Before partnering with Sportradar, FIFA used its own detection system, the Early Warning System ("FIFA Strengthens Global Football Integrity," 2017). In addition to monitoring, FIFA also has a system in place where reports about match manipulation can be submitted. Finally, FIFA has a disciplinary role in punishing match manipulation.

FIFA's role in preventing match manipulation is also an educational one. It holds workshops for referees and member associations ahead of international competitions. At both the men's and women's World Cups, FIFA met with the teams and the referees before the final competition to discuss potential integrity issues. Finally, FIFA supports its member associations in their educational efforts ("FIFA Integrity," n.d.).

THE FUTURE OF SPORT WAGERING

Advances in technology have affected sport viewership and will likewise drive the future of sport wagering. Digital technology in the 21st century has been transformative in the industry. Live streaming on mobile devices has significantly influenced sport consumption patterns, while digital technology has made it easier to wager on live sports by simply touching or swiping a screen.

In the future, teams might employ sport gambling data analysts. Data collected through technological advances will create greater opportunities for engaged real-time betting on activities other than a game outcome or point spread. However, at least for the major professional sports in the United States and Major League Soccer (MLS), the leagues will need to engage in collective bargaining to require athletes to wear data tracking devices, which was addressed in the 2017 NBA CBA (Booton, 2019). The production of official data will explode to include unimaginable categories of arguably "useless" information that might be interesting to oddsmakers and fans. For instance, analytics already calculates pitch speeds, how hard baseballs are hit, the distance they travel when hit, the speed of a puck entering a goal, and how many miles a soccer player runs during a game. The future might have bets available on how many times NBA player Steph Curry wipes his forehead in a quarter or how many times a football coach removes his headphones.

The potential to drive fan interest by permitting betting opportunities on obscure facts and live action outcomes is one of the positives of legalizing sport wagering. A gambling-centric concept for staging athletic contests will soon become a reality, just as the Battle of the Sexes showcasing Billie Jean King and the aging Bobby Riggs in one of the first made-for-television tennis matches garnered a Super Bowl–size audience. America may soon experience a "made-for-gambling" athletic event with a stadium of spectators making wagers that dictate actions on a field or court or screen.

RECAP

Gambling in the United States originated with lotteries and horse racing in the colonial era. Throughout the 19th and 20th centuries, gambling's reputed association with organized crime was the impetus for federal restrictions.

To help control corruption, the U.S. government legislated the Wire Act of 1961, making it illegal for those engaged in betting or wagering to knowingly use a wire communication facility in interstate or foreign commerce, and the Sports Bribery Act of 1964, which prohibited conspiracy to intentionally influence the outcome of a sport contest. A series of point-shaving scandals in collegiate basketball and the lifetime ban of Cincinnati Reds player and manager Pete Rose in 1989 prompted the passage of the Professional and Amateur Sports Protection Act in 1992, placing a federal ban on sport wagering in the United States. Limited exemptions were permitted in the states of Nevada, Montana, Oregon, Delaware, and New Jersey due to their history of operating some form of legal sport betting scheme prior to the law's passage. The state of New Jersey brought numerous challenges to PASPA, receiving criticism from the NCAA, NFL, MLB, NBA, and NHL. Eventually, in May 2018, the U.S. Supreme Court overturned PASPA; this landmark decision shifted power to individual states to determine their own laws and policies for sport wagering. Since then the growth of legal sport wagering has been staggering, with at least 20 states preparing to consider legislation to legalize sport betting by 2020.

Legal sport wagering is popular around the world. There are many national, regional, and global organizations with a regulatory role in overseeing legal sport wagering. Most of the authority to regulate illegal sport betting comes from national governments and licensure programs, but international sport governing bodies have also played a part. The future of legal sport gambling will likely merge data analytics and technology to further assist with monitoring a seemingly unregulated industry or to provide a multitude of interesting real-time wagering opportunities to engage the sport consumer.

Critical Thinking Questions

1. How has the landscape of legalized sport wagering in the United States continued to evolve since the publication of this textbook?

2. Are regulations governing sport wagering in the United States more or less stringent than regulations around the world? Why or why not?

3. Speculate on the extent to which one of the major professional sport leagues in America will further embrace legal sport wagering as a tool to increase fan engagement and enhance the spectator experience during games.

4. Speculate on efforts by major professional sport leagues and the NCAA in seeking integrity fees for games and competition.

5. Explain the general purpose of national, continental, and global agencies involved in regulating the sport wagering industry.

Applied Activity

Fantasy Basketball Scoring System

Part A: Select an NBA team and a week of regular-season competition. Complete the fantasy scoring system chart for the last three games played during the selected week in the regular season using official NBA data available at https://stats.nba.com/schedule and follow these instructions:

- Turn off "hide previous dates," select the week under the "calendar," and select the team.
- Note the location of the game (home or away), opponent, and scores.
- Click on the Box Score to locate the attendance for home games only.
- Attendance: <12,000 = −2, 12,000-14,000 = −1, 14,000-16,000 = +1, 16,000-18,000 = +2, >18,000 = +3

Date of game	Home or away	Opponent	Team score	Opponent score	Win-loss points earned (+3 per win)	Attendance (home games only)	Attendance points earned/lost (see above)
1.							
2.							
3.							

Part B: Next, review national and local media sources (television, print, digital) for the team and calculate a score for player media attention.

1. Player featured in a national advertisement (+2 each) _____
2. Player reprimanded/fined/suspended (−2 each) _____
3. Player draws negative attention to team in media (−2 each) _____
4. *Total points for player media attention (add the three categories)* = _____

Part C: Record the scores for each category to calculate the total fantasy basketball score.

1. Win-loss points earned _____
2. Attendance points _____
3. Player media attention points _____
4. *Total* = _____

Part D: Finally, add a paragraph to describe how the scoring system can be monetized to create wagering opportunities for a sportsbook.

chapter 14

Esports

Steve Borawski, Michael Kidd, and Bonnie Tiell

LEAD-OFF

The growing sector of the esports industry has been described as a "new wild west frontier" due to the lack of universal regulations and governance for amateur and professional play (Chao, 2017). Esports is ever evolving, which makes it difficult to pin down a universally accepted definition or even a consistent spelling.

Esports, or electronic sports, is commonly understood as competitive video gaming. Hamari and Sjöblom (2017) defined esports as "a form of sports where the primary aspects are facilitated by electronic systems, which includes the input of players and teams and the output of a system mediated by human-computer interfaces." Wagner (2006) defined esports as "an area of sport activities whereby people develop and train mental or physical abilities using information and communication technologies." A different perspective suggested by the American Bar Association (2016) is that esports is an umbrella term for the inclusion of a multitude of electronic or digital games, just as sports is a general word that encompasses a variety of physical games. Figure 14.1 shows several commonly used spellings.

Esports can take place on any number of devices, from personal computers (PCs) to consoles such as the Xbox and PlayStation, to mobile smartphones and tablets. Gamers can embody first-person shooters, racers, participants in multiplayer online battle arenas (MOBAs), and many other formats.

Figure 14.1 Common spelling options for esports.

Unlike many conventional sports, esports isn't a single game, nor does it follow a common set of rules and regulations. Esports is characterized by players, developers, tournament organizers, and the interconnection of multiple gaming platforms. Esports is breaking onto the world stage with a fury, but unified governance over the industry is lagging despite efforts to create a universal ethics oversight agency and to establish national and international governing bodies to regulate competitive gaming.

A major challenge for esports governance is the inability to simply copy the infrastructure and ecosystem that have been built around traditional professional sports as entertainment. Esports lacks the universal regulations associated with competitive integrity (e.g., match fixing and doping policies are absent) to address the duty of care toward game players, many whom have been classified as professionals. Organizations such as the International Esports Federation (IeSF) and the World Esports Association (WESA) have made valid attempts to regulate the industry, but the reality is that without radical changes, governance will continue to lag behind the developers and tournament holders.

Emphasized throughout the chapter are the enormous challenges facing governance of esports as an industry. After distinguishing esports from traditional sports, the chapter describes the evolution of video gaming. The chapter then addresses organizational efforts to provide governance at the global, continental, and national levels and finally, it considers enforceable areas in need of regulation throughout the esports industry.

Learning Outcomes

- Analyze whether esports fits the traditional definition of a sport.
- Identify the types of entities who primarily create rules and regulations for esports.
- Explain the reason for the lack of governance of esports as an industry.
- Explain the benefits of the franchise league system in esports.
- Identify organizations with regulatory roles for esports in North American high schools.

ESPORTS COMPARED TO TRADITIONAL SPORT

An international federation is the supreme authority or governing body for a sport. When disputes arise involving global competitions or competitors, the Court of Arbitration for Sport (CAS) serves as the legal decision-making body, often drawing upon statutes from international sport federations. Despite the emergence of esport federations, at present, the International Olympic Committee (IOC) and the Global Association of Sport Federations does not include an international federation for esports among the 102 listed in 2018 ("Members," n.d.). Additionally, the CAS has yet to recognize esports as a sport, let alone arbitrate any disputes (Ptascynski, 2018).

As esports gains in popularity, revenue, and viewership, it's more difficult to ignore its impact on society and culture regardless of whether it fits a traditional view of sport. In 2014, ESPN President John Skipper downgraded the connection of esports as a mainstream sport noting, "It's not a sport . . . it's a competition. Chess is a competition. Checkers is a competition" (Chmielewski, 2014). Four years later, esports were televised on ESPN in a primetime slot (Roberts, 2018). In a similar manner, researchers have debated whether esports should be classified as competition or recreation (Hallmen & Geil, 2018).

The argument about whether esports is genuinely a sport (see table 14.1) may be mere semantics, but the designation has vital importance for establishing an international federation, and it has significance for countries that provide government grants, subsidies, and tax relief to traditional sports (American Bar Association, 2016). Proponents note how esports is beginning to take on the general characteristics of an individual professional sport like tennis, golf, and motorsports with similarities due to the inclusion of prize money, player salaries,

Sponsorships have increasingly become available for esports players and competitions.

Chesnot/Getty Images

and sponsorships. In addition, professional esports "athletes" can receive P-1A visas from the U.S. government, which were reserved exclusively for traditional athletes until 2013 (U.S. Citizenship and Immigration Services, n.d.). Finally, universities are providing esports gamers with athletic scholarships, and high schools are fielding teams.

On the other hand, there are many who question whether esports fits the definition of traditional sports such as football, tennis, and rodeo. Traditional football, baseball, or basketball players who have spent years practicing and bringing their bodies to peak fitness may be more than a little incredulous that video gaming would be called a sport and players would be called athletes. It is also difficult to grasp the concept that unlike traditional sports, esports can field competitors who may or may not be in the same room or even on the same continent; digital gameplay, along with the Internet, allows players to compete with one another across the world.

According to the most widely accepted definition offered by sociologist Jay Coakley (2006), to be classified as a traditional sport, an activity must include the following characteristics:

♦ An aspect of competition
♦ A degree of physical exertion or physical skill
♦ Institutionalized rules or regulations

Coakley (2006) defines sport as an "institutionalized competitive activity that involves vigorous physical exertion or the use of relatively complex physical skills by individuals whose participation is motivated by a combination of intrinsic (e.g., self-satisfaction that comes with competition) and extrinsic (e.g., money and public adoration) factors." Similarly, the National Collegiate Athletic Association (NCAA) defines sport as an activity involving physical exertion with competition against teams or individuals under standardized

rules with rating or scoring systems that have been ratified by a regulatory agency or governing body ("Definition of Terms," n.d., pp. 1-2).

There are common arguments as to why esports may or may not be classified as a traditional sport (see table 14.1). While esports generally meets the criteria for a sport in terms of being competitive, it is more difficult to validate whether it meets the second and third qualifying conditions (a degree of physical exertion and institutionalized rules). There are some sports (e.g., basketball or pole vaulting) where strenuous physical activity and a level of skill are obvious. However, with games such as chess or golf, it is more challenging to demonstrate physical exertion, which has prompted debate as to whether these activities, too, should be classified as sport or leisure activities ("Is Golf a Sport?" 2017; Strege, 2012).

In terms of the physical prowess and skill required for esports, studies have indicated that during training and competitions, high-level gamers do exhibit signs of physical exertion (Li, 2016; Green & Bavelier, 2015; Rodriguez et al., 2016; Stroud, Amonette, & Dupler, 2010). Stroud et al. (2010) noted evidence that video game playing stimulates increases in oxygen usage and basal metabolic rates. In terms of skill, as early as 2007, researchers documented video game playing as an effective means to train surgeons (Rosser et al., 2007). The question whether to justify esports as a traditional sport then becomes, how much physical effort or skill is needed for an activity to be considered a sport? At this point, it's impossible to offer a definitive answer as to whether esports could make the cut regarding the need for physical exertion, leaving it up to society to make its own judgment call.

In terms of institutionalized rules, esports is gaining ground, but it still lags behind traditional sports. The industry is rapidly moving toward institutionalization with the establishment of national

Table 14.1 Common Arguments to Validate Why Esports May or May Not Be Classified as a Traditional Sport

Why esports IS a sport	• Skill is required. • Prize money is available. • Competitions, tournaments, and players may be sponsored. • Professional players may receive salaries. • Collegiate athletic scholarships are available. • International competitors may receive P-1A visas, traditionally reserved for athletes.
Why esports IS NOT a sport	• Arguably, esports lack true physical prowess. • Like chess and checkers, esports is a competition, not a sport. • Players do not need to be in the same location. • Gaming is considered a compulsion or a form of entertainment.

and international governing bodies (Funk, Pizzo, & Baker, 2018). However, the governing organizations are mainly the companies that make the games and stage tournaments, as opposed to independent confederations or entities with authority to establish uniform guidelines.

HISTORY OF COMPETITIVE VIDEO GAMING

Competitive video gaming has become one of the quickest-growing segments of the entertainment industry (Holden, Kaburakis, & Rodenberg, 2017). In 2015, only a few hundred players in the United States were reportedly on salary, but 6.1 million American players were participating in esports (Hollist, 2015). Those numbers have increased.

It has been suggested that society is witnessing the creation of a whole new sport or sport category that is redefining what it means to be an athlete. To provide some context, consider the early years of American football. Before Walter Camp, also known as the father of gridiron football, there was no line of scrimmage, no down and distance rules, and no rules defining pass interference calls or offsides. At this stage, participants were still sorting out what the game would encompass, even to the point of not knowing yet how players would dress to play (e.g., whether helmets and shoulder pads would be a good idea). In a similar way, this newly developing area of esports is undergoing a massive amount of transition, and much of what is written could quickly change in the future.

Origins

In the early and mid-1970s, video games were being played by home audiences with the aid of a Magnavox Odyssey, the first home video game console. Soon households were purchasing Atari's smash hit, *Pong*, known to many as the first commercially successful coin arcade game.

Pong was not the first video game, however. That distinction can be traced back to 1947 when computers still filled a room and the cathode-ray tube amusement device required turning a knob to bounce a ball around a screen resembling a World War II radar display (Good, 2012). It should be noted that there is still room for debate as to what was the first video game and it really depends on how the term video game is defined.

The earliest known video game competition was held at Stanford University on October 19, 1972, for the game *Spacewar!* (McGlaun, 2011). Students were invited to participate in an Intergalactic Spacewar! Olympics with a grand prize of a one year's subscription to a magazine. Atari's 1980 Space Invaders Championship was the earliest large-scale video game competition, with thousands of participants across the United States ("Space Invaders Revel," 2015).

Early Industry Growth

As video games started to enter the home and youth filled their local arcades, the general public and the media began to take notice of this new form of competition. During the 1970s and 1980s, video game players and tournaments began to be featured in popular magazines such as *Life* and *Time*. To promote themselves, arcades started to host unstructured competitions and high score tournaments. **Twin Galaxies** (n.d.), established in 1981, became known as the "Official Scoreboard for Electronic Entertainment." At a time before the arrival of the Internet, players could send in photographic proof of their high scores, which could be shared with the wider gaming community.

Video games started to make appearances on television screens and at the movies, with top players receiving endorsements by major corporations. The spotlight on this new gaming culture, however, was not always positive; U.S. Surgeon General C. Everett Koop declared in 1982 that video games were creating "aberrations in childhood behavior" and had an addictive quality (Poole, 2000; Sheff, 2011). Parents, too, demonstrated concern with the violence inherent in some video games as well as with the delinquency that periodically cropped up in arcades. As the 1980s wore on, arcades began to falter as home video gaming systems grew in popularity.

Competitive video game playing advanced when home video game consoles were able to match the graphics and interactivity of the arcade experience. Over the decades, consoles, PCs, and video games continued to develop a more immersive experience for players. The stage was set for esports, but there was one key ingredient missing: the ability to connect with players from remote locations.

For decades, gamers who wanted to compete against other players had to go where the equipment was located, meaning traveling to an arcade or to someone's house who happened to have the latest edition of a highly sought-after game release. There were limits to a gamer's competitive circle due to the need for compatible equipment and proximity.

A shift in competitive gaming took place in 1987 with the release of *Street Fighter*, which was credited with temporarily reinvigorating the slowing arcade industry. Up to this point, most of the competition that occurred between players in video game competitions was to achieve the highest score possible. With *Street Fighter*, however, gamers were able to pit their skills directly against each other as opposed to a scoreboard (Carle, 2010).

Rise in Competitions and Gaming Communities

Early video game competitions were organized by either groups of game fans, arcade promoters, or the game makers themselves. These early tournaments had minimal rules and often were disconnected from one another. Most of these early tournaments and competitions were one-offs made up of amateur gamers since there were no real professionals at this stage. Walter Day, an arcade owner, began keeping and releasing a verifiable record of high scores on his Twin Galaxies system, which eventually became relied upon by the *Guinness Book of World Records*.

Throughout the 1980s, this pattern of tournaments and one-off events continued, but as the arcade industry faltered, the burden fell more and more onto game makers and fans. There was still no overarching body that controlled or regulated video game competitions besides some rules put in place by game makers.

In the mid-to-late 1990s, the true foundations of what we would consider the modern-day esports and gaming culture started to coalesce. Two key gameplay styles began to emerge, the first-person shooter (FPS) and the real-time strategy (RTS) games. The third most popular genre of video games are sport games. **First-person shooters** are video games that are designed to allow players to view the action through the eyes of the character; they involved shooting enemies and other targets. **Real-time strategy games** often have an aerial view of the gameplay map where players try to secure resources and destroy opponents' assets. These three genres of gameplay allowed for more team-based play and were considered more engaging for spectators.

All three genres had extensive online followings where people would discuss strategic play and share tips to improve performance. Video game communities and their player organizations would often rise and fall with the popularity of one particular game. For example, when a new blockbuster video game was released, an active community for that game would often be developed with the assistance of the game producer. Tournaments and player organizations would emerge around the new video game; however, many were short-lived as the game aged and new games were introduced. These transitions made for a tremendous amount of instability and prevented the creation of a governing body for esports.

Revolutionary Advancements

A revolution in the industry occurred in 1989 with a game called **Netrek**, which allowed 16 players to connect PCs over the Internet to compete (Anon, n.d.). While this game was not the first Internet game to enable competition, it was the first team-based game and the first that had persistent user information. Even though *Netrek* was a breakthrough and gave players the ability to compete with others regardless of where they were located, Internet gaming would still take time to develop mass appeal. Connectivity was still limited to PCs, and there were few online games at the time that could compete with the quality of video game consoles. While there were some early attempts to integrate connectivity into gaming consoles, Xbox Live in 2000 was the first truly successful online gaming platform that was an alternative to a PC.

Players began forming communities around their favorite games. Soon there were message boards and websites dedicated to video gaming that reached an almost cult-like status with fervent fan bases that were eager for the next iteration of a game. PC gaming also began to create richer content. Massive multiplayer online (MMO) games emerged in which hundreds and thousands of players could interact, compete, and generally live a virtual life within an online fantasy world.

Early attempts to establish players organizations, primarily for specific games such as *Quake*, occurred in the late 1990s. Then, new professional organizations promoted cross-platform tournaments on a global scale, which formed the backbone of the current esports market. The Cyberathlete Professional League (CPL), for example, considered a pioneering organization for the industry, was established in 1997. While organizing their own world tournaments, rival competitor organizations, primarily owned by game makers, quickly burst onto the esports scene. In 2000, two large-scale, international, nongame-specific tournaments were organized: (1) the World Cyber Games (WCG) and (2) the Electronic Sports World Cup (ESWC). At its peak, the WCG attracted one million participants in over 78 countries.

In 2002, Major League Gaming (MLG), one of the most influential organizing bodies for esports tournaments and competitions, was created. MLG developed a pro points ranking system that continues to serve as a benchmark for determining a competitive player's global ranking. MLG hosts both in-person and online tournaments with a bracketing system that allows players of different skill levels to compete. With the rise of organized tournament holders such as MLG came a more structured format for competition, and people aspiring to host their own tournaments had nationally accepted rules and standards for game competitions.

Modern Era

The popularity of esports, or electronic gaming, can be seen from the interest shown in the 2018 World Championship organized by Riot Games in South Korea, which surpassed 200 million simultaneous viewers ("About Worlds 2018," 2018). This exceeded the 2018 Super Bowl, which attracted 118.2 million viewers across all platforms (Lafayette, 2018). With large followings in North America, South Korea, China, Germany, and the United Kingdom, the esports market was predicted to become at least a $1.9 billion-dollar industry in 2019 (American Bar Association, 2016; Gaudiosi, 2015; Holden, Kaburakis, & Rodenberg, 2017; Steinbach, 2017; Wang, 2018).

The explosion of esports in its current state is far advanced from the revolution period when virtual gaming communities and competitions erupted onto the scene. With the popularity of digitally mediated video game competitions, mass media outlets took notice, and networks such as G4 TV were created to focus exclusively on the gaming culture. Even though gaming was gaining more and more popularity, television coverage in the United States was still sporadic, even though in some countries like South Korea, competitions were a mainstay of prime-time television.

When Twitch.tv, a livestreaming video platform, burst onto the scene in 2011, gamers no longer needed to rely on television broadcasts to showcase their gaming skills. Video game players not only could upload their best gameplay and tips and tricks, but they were also able to livestream their gameplay to other fans and viewers. All the fervor around livestreaming came to a crescendo when Twitch was purchased by Amazon in August 2014

for almost $1 billion, giving the ecommerce giant direct access to the esports market (Kim, 2014). During this period, Twitch rated behind Netflix, Google, and Apple as the fourth-largest Internet traffic producer in the United States (Hollist, 2015).

Team owners in the National Basketball Association (NBA) and celebrities such as Jennifer Lopez have recently entered the esports space, and companies such as Mercedes Benz and Coca-Cola are major sponsors in the industry (see Governance in Action 14.1). Over 600 brand sponsorships were associated with esports alone in 2017 (Deloitte Insights, 2018). The exponential growth is partially credited to the emergence of developer-sponsored leagues in which the game developer and league owner are the same entity (Hollist, 2015). These leagues are in a comfortable position to finance general tournament operations and to broadcast championship rounds, while providing salaries for commentators and players.

As a multibillion-dollar global industry, research indicates that more people worldwide play electronic games than participate in physical sports (Steinbach, 2017). When compared to 2017 statistics, the reported 380.2 million esports global audience size in 2018 included a 15.6 percent increase in "enthusiasts" (e.g., competitive players) and a 14 percent increase in occasional viewers (New Zoo, 2018). Mobile esports was the largest sector of the industry in 2018. The staggering esports growth trends include an influx of diverse and increasing revenue streams in addition to rising audience numbers. Figure 14.2 provides an overview of cur-

Figure 14.2 Categories of revenue streams for esports according to New Zoo (2018).

rent revenue streams for esports (New Zoo, 2018).

The future of esports is likely to include increased competition over media rights, more partnerships with professional leagues and tournaments, and possibly status as a recognized sport in a forthcoming Olympics given its inclusion as a medal sport in the 2022 Asian Games (Lanier, 2018). Governance in Action 14.1 profiles the trend for esports integration with professional North American sport leagues.

ESPORTS GOVERNING AGENCIES AND AUTHORITIES

The current regulatory landscape for esports is fragmented and ambiguous. In general, multiple entities are trying to regulate an industry where the legal boundaries are still being determined both globally and nationally. One of the primary

---

GOVERNANCE IN ACTION 14.1

North American Professional Sports and Their Association With Esports

The NBA 2K League was launched in 2018 with 17 franchises, each requiring an initiation fee of $20 million (Deloitte Insights, 2018). NBA Commissioner Adam Silver announced the league's inaugural draft picks—all professional esports gamers, not basketball players, who signed lucrative contracts that included a guaranteed salary, insurance benefits, housing, relocation fees, and a retirement fund. In 2019, the first female player was drafted by the Golden State Warriors (Associated Press, 2019).

Silver recognized NBA 2K as the "4th league," which referred to the NBA's role in also establishing the WNBA and G-League in addition to its main product, 30 mainstream NBA franchises. The NBA is the first American professional sport league to invest in an esports franchise, although individual teams and team owners have dabbled in the esports business space for the past few years. In the three years between 2015 and 2018, 13 NBA, 6 Major League Baseball (MLB), and 3 National Football League (NFL) team ownership groups had "invested or acquired" an esports business (Youngmisuk & Wolf, 2018). For example, Robert Kraft, owner of the NFL New England Patriots, invested $20 million for a spot in the popular esports Overwatch League, and the co-owner of the NBA Memphis Grizzlies purchased an Immortals team for esports' *League of Legends* in 2015 (Deloitte Insights, 2018). The NBA Philadelphia 76ers owns Team Dignitas and Team Apex, who play in the *League of Legends* tournaments, and NBA Dallas Mavericks owner Mark Cuban is part of a group that invested $38 million in an esports betting start-up in Seattle, Washington, called Unikrn (Youngmisuk & Wolf, 2018).

The National Hockey League (NHL) recently entered the esports arena by hosting a World Gaming Championship involving its 31 franchises (Andrews, 2018). Despite hosting an international esports hockey competition, neither the NHL nor any of the league owners have yet to significantly invest in an esports franchise.

The franchise model is one of the reasons the NBA 2K League is projected to yet again revolutionize the esports industry through a structure that facilitates sustainability. Major sports leagues in the United States operate in a franchised system (NBA, NFL, MLB, and NHL) that is recognizable to corporate and private entities. The franchise structure fosters longer-term investments from content owners, sponsors, buyers, and marketing agencies and therefore fuels the accelerated growth of the league as a whole (New Zoo, 2018).

The franchise structure of NBA 2K necessitates a league governance system, evidenced by the draft arrangement, minimum salaries, and competition rules. However, it is further evidence that game developers are the ultimate drivers of esports governance without authority for the industry as a whole. The NBA has a limited role in the governance of the NBA 2K League as part of its joint venture with Take-Two Interactive, an American video game holding company.

problems is that there are too many shareholders determining the rules and standards for esports. National agencies, international bodies, and commercial businesses (the game developers and tournament organizers) are each creating their own rules and regulations with little crossover.

The current fracturing of governance between national governments, content developers, and tournament organizers creates inconsistent rules, regulations, and guidelines. Following is an overview of agencies and associations that have entered the playing field for regulating an aspect of esports, either globally or on a national level.

Global Esports Governing Agencies and Authorities

While cyber-technology has facilitated a global playing field for esports, there is currently no international entity recognized as the single supreme authority for the industry. Even though an International Esports Federation (IeSF) exists, it is not yet recognized by the Global Association of International Sport Federations (GAISF), and the IOC maintains that "no organization currently exists that represents esports globally or aligns with the Olympic values, rules and regulations set forth in the Olympic Charter" (*IOC News*, 2018).

The IeSF is not the only organization striving to provide governance of esports on a global level. Organizations such as the World Esports Association (WESA) and the Esports Integrity Commission (ESIC) also seek to maintain their authority on a global stage as governing organizations for esports.

International Esports Federation

Based in Busan, Republic of Korea, the International Esports Federation (IeSF) was founded in 2011 by nine national esports associations (Horvath, 2013). In 2019, the federation included 51 members primarily from Europe and Asia as well as the Americas (Argentina, Mexico, and Costa Rica), Africa, and Oceania ("Member Nations," n.d.). Notably absent is any type of esports association from the United States (Hollist, 2015).

The IeSF establishes standards for referees, players, certifications, titles, and competition. The organization is governed by statutes that establish the general meeting as the legislative body, outline the process for membership application, and define the policies for areas such as antidiscrimination, doping, and arbitration (International Esports Federation, 2017). The board includes eight elected officials identified as the president, secretary general, vice president, chair of the Player's Committee (Athlete's Commission), and four additional members.

In striving to become the world's first international sports organization for esports, the IeSF faces many challenges. For one, esports is not yet recognized as a sport by the IOC, and the IeSF is not among the 100-plus organizations listed as members of the GAISF (see Governance in Action 14.2). Secondly, the IeSF statutes indicate that disagreements not resolved at the organizational level will be decided by the Court of Arbitration for Sport (CAS), but there is no evidence of litigation reaching the supreme authority for international sport disputes. The CAS has yet to recognize esports as a sport and has not arbitrated any cases (Ptascynski, 2018).

World Esports Association

WESA was founded in May 2016 by the Electronic Sports League and several industry-leading esports teams ("WESA Founded," 2016). The organization seeks to professionalize esports through player representation and revenue sharing policies. The executive board consists of five elected individuals, two of whom are representatives from the Electronic Sports League (ESL) and one of whom serves as commissioner ("WESA Structure," n.d.).

WESA's (2016) code of conduct and compliance for teams and players is a 10-page document outlining the jurisdiction of the executive board, duties of neutrality, and policies addressing forgeries, falsification, conflicts of interest, bribery and corruption, discrimination, integrity of matches, doping, and failure to respect decisions. The code of conduct and compliance refers to the World Anti-Doping Agency (WADA) for determination of prohibited substances and stipulates that drug testing is only at the request of an executive board member or commissioner, whether by target testing or lots (WESA, 2016, p. 9).

The organization is the first to reportedly create an operative player council ("WESA Founded," 2016). It also established and operates the Arbitrator Court for Esports (ACES), an independent three-person judicial mechanism to settle disputes such as contract disputes, prize money distribution, financial misconduct, and player representation (Stubbs, 2016).

While WESA has seemingly worked through the complexities of creating a governing body for

GOVERNANCE IN ACTION 14.2

Esports and the Olympic Games

An international federation is the cornerstone of global governance for traditional sports ranging from cycling, ice hockey, and softball to more obscure sports such as samba, lifesaving, and chess. The Global Association of International Sport Federations (GAISF) includes over 100 Olympic and non-Olympic sport federations, but entering 2020, there was no recognition of a federation for esports.

According to the Olympic Charter, without a universally recognized independent, nongovernmental international federation, esports is not eligible for consideration as an Olympic event. The IOC concluded that there was currently no organization representing esports globally that aligned with the Olympic movement, with officials citing fragmented governance, licensing issues, and inherent violence that were problematic (*IOC News*, 2018; Segerra, 2019). Despite the rhetoric precluding esports from becoming an Olympic sport in its current context, steps have been taken to set the stage for future inclusion.

For one, the International Esports Federation (IeSF), which works with 54 national esports federations around the world, has made formal applications and appeals with both the IOC and the GAISF for official recognition. In 2016, the federation received correspondence from the IOC outlining the evaluation process and next steps for esports to be considered as a recognized Olympic sport in the same manner as surfing, rock climbing, and other recent additions to the cadre of events (Polacek, 2016).

Despite the setback with the IeSF not being officially recognized, esports has been a topic at major international meetings, including the 2017 Olympic Summit (*IOC News*, 2017). The IOC and GAISF co-hosted an esports forum involving over 150 industry representatives, which led to the formation of an esports liaison group with a platform at the GAISF International Federations forum, the Associations of the National Olympic Committees General Assembly, and future IOC Olympic Summits (*IOC News*, 2018).

Possibly the greatest support for esports as a possible future Olympic event is its inclusion as a medal sport at the 2022 Asian Games in Jakarta, Indonesia. The Asian Games are a continental event recognized by the IOC. The Asian Electronic Sports Federation (AESF) is recognized by the Olympic Council of Asia, which governs the Asian Games.

While continental Games typically include nonmainstream sports that are germane to a geographic region (e.g., canoe polo and esports were a demonstration sport at the 2018 Asian Games), it is problematic to identify competitive gaming as a potential Olympic sport ("AESF Confirms," 2018). However, discussions are emerging for inclusion of esports as an exhibition event, either at the 2024 Paris Olympics, likely in a restricted format, or through "virtual and connected" events preceding the Games and resembling online versions of existing sport such as sailing (Chao, 2017; Lanier, 2018; Morgan, 2019).

There is moderate anticipation that esports may one day be governed by a recognized international federation, whether it is the IeSF or another organization. In the meantime, there appear to be insurmountable hurdles to clear before esports would be considered a potential true Olympic sport.

esports, it is not without its drawbacks. WESA is recognized as a voluntary organization with "aspirational motivations," but there is skepticism about its ability to enforce rules beyond the scope of its membership (Ifrah Law, 2018).

Esports Integrity Commission

Established in 2016, the Esports Integrity Commission (ESIC) is a nonprofit members' association operating through a set of principles that align with good governance practices ("Principles," n.d.):

♦ Integrity and respect

♦ Fair processes

♦ Implementation and enforcement of codes

♦ Mutual recognition of sanctions

♦ Sharing of information

♦ Confidentiality

ESIC is responsible for "prevention, investigation, and prosecution of all forms of cheating in esports" ("What We Do," n.d.). The board and staff consist of a commissioner and two individuals responsible for esports and antidoping. Eight people constitute the organization's disciplinary panel.

ESIC uses an independent panel of judges to prosecute cases, and it contracts with **Sportradar's Fraud Detection System**, a service that tracks odd changes and liquidity across markets to detect irregular betting patterns in real time (Higgins, 2016). ESIC also maintains a centralized database of sanctioned violations, which includes a tracking system to ensure that individuals who transfer to another game or team will retain a record of discretion.

The organization publishes codes for ethics, conduct, antidoping, and anticorruption for its 14 member organizations representing game developers, leagues, media platforms, tournament organizers, and a national governing body from the Middle East (Higgins, 2016). ESIC partners with various gambling authorities and international gaming regulators, including the Global Lottery Monitoring System and the U.K. Gambling Commission.

Continental and National Esports Governing Agencies and Authorities

Countries, and even continents around the world, with varying degrees of success, have recognized the need for oversight in the esports industry and have taken affirmative steps to address regulatory gaps. The continental landscape currently is represented by the Asia Electronic Sports Federation and the Oceania Esports Council (New Zealand and Australia). North America does have an Esports Federation, but only for scholastic competition. Europe only supports a Gaming League. Many countries with national esports federations are members of the IeSF, the international association that is not yet accepted as a global federation by the IOC.

The largest continental association for esports is the Asia Electronic Sports Federation (AESF), established in 2013 and recognized by the Olympic Council of Asia as the sole authority for esports in the continental region. AESF currently serves as the governing entity for 19 national esports organizations under the former vice president of Hong Kong's Sport Federation and Olympic Committee (Garren, 2017). The AESF is the reason esports will become a medal sport in the 2022 Asian Games.

Government support is a necessity to ensure the success of a national esports governing body (Chao, 2017). South Korea, the United Kingdom, and Russia all have government backing. In fact, seven years after its inception, the Russian eSports Federation became the first esports organization in the world to achieve state (national) recognition when the Ministry of Sport officially recognized esports as a sport discipline (Chao, 2017; "Member Nations," n.d.). Germany, on the other hand, lacks the same support as Russia, although its esports federation is listed among member nations by the IeSF. Germany's Berlin House of Representatives and the Olympic Sport Confederation both resolved that esports should not be reclassified as a sport (American Bar Association, 2016; "DOSB Closes Before Esports," 2018).

Following is information about esports associations and regulations in Korea, the United Kingdom, France, and the United States of America.

Korea

The Ministry of Culture, Sports and Tourism established the Korea e-Sports Association (KeSPA) in 2000 as a nongovernmental organization (Chao, 2017). KeSPA is also a member of the Korean Olympic Committee and has long been recognized as one of the "strongest and most advanced governing bod[ies] within eSport in comparison with national associations within modern sport" (Thiborg, 2009).

With the support of the South Korean government, the association built the world's first dedicated esports stadium. KeSPA also officiates and organizes tournaments, manages player registration, coordinates licensing deals and media broadcast rights, regulates sponsorships, and enforces professionalism and ethical conduct. Korea is also one of the first countries to offer minimum salaries (comparable to domestic professional sport leagues) and contracts for esports athletes (Chalk, 2014).

Despite regulatory measures including fines and banishment, pervasive corruption continues to plague esports in South Korea and other parts of the world. Reportedly, government officials are routinely bribed to delay the regulation of microtransactions for digital games and apps. In 2010, 11 Korean players were arrested for throwing matches, followed by nine players in 2015, five in 2016, and another in 2017 (Nordmark, 2018). Players have been fined, imprisoned, and banned by KeSPA. In one of the most notorious corruption cases, the Korea e-Sports Association shut down the popular *StarCraft* game due to the proliferation of players throwing matches to profit from illegal gambling entities. In 2017, a former KeSPA president and three employees were arrested on embezzlement, bribery, and money-laundering charges (Wolmarans, 2017). In 2018, the Seoul National Police Agency Cyber Security Department arrested 13 South Korean esports players for violating the Game Industry Promotion Act for making cheat programs and fixing matches (Pugatschew, 2018). That law essentially asserts government authority over all aspects of the gaming industry from developing standards to policing illegal activity.

United Kingdom

The United Kingdom eSports Association (UKeSA) was the country's official esports governing body until filing for bankruptcy protection in 2009. The national governing body for esports is currently the British Esports Association (BEA), founded in 2016 as an independent organization under the authority of the United Kingdom government in conjunction with the Department for Digital, Culture, Media and Sport (Chao, 2017).

The BEA produces its own content, works with schools for the promotion of positive gaming, handles contracts and visas for professional players, and addresses online harassment. The three primary goals of the organization are the promotion of esports, improved standards, and inspiring future talent.

Having partnered with the Association of Colleges Sport, BEA is also a member of the Sport and Recreation Alliance and the Welsh Sports Association ("About the British Esports Association," 2018). The association launched a scholastic esports competition in 2018 while continuing to promote esports as a field of education in universities.

France

French gambling laws classified esports as a "lottery" scheme until 2016 when the **Digital Republic Bill** went into effect (O'Brien, 2016). The bill recognizes esports as its own distinct entity, which facilitates tax and social benefit systems for eligible players while also requiring parental consent for minors (under the age of 16) to participate in tournaments (American Bar Association, 2016). The French Senate essentially legalized video game competitions, leading to minimum standards for professional player contracts and regulations to curb exploitative entry fees (Chao, 2017). The

law bans players 12 and under from participating in competitions that include prize money while limiting professional contracts to five-year terms (Ionica, 2017).

Another outcome of the Digital Republic Bill was the establishment of the country's first national esports federation. The Association France Esports is a nonprofit law organization founded in 2016 with the official support of the Ministry of Economy and Finance (Vansyngel, Velpry, & Besombes, 2018).

Unlike Russia and Korea, the French Ministry of Sports does not recognize esports as a sport. Despite the absence of formal recognition, the new governing body for esports in France is committed to adhering to the "values and fundamental principles of Olympism" but articulates that "the association does not seek to have esports recognized as a sport" ("Presentation of the France Esports Association, n.d.). A new governance model in 2017 structured the association into three "colleges" for players, promoter representatives, and creator-publishers. It operates through a charter, a list of statutes, and rules of procedure that will likely, if permitted, help to stage esports build-up events based on Olympic sports (e.g., sailing and basketball) prior to or during the 2024 Paris Olympics (Morgan, 2019).

United States of America

Computer and video game companies in the United States employed over 220,000 people in 2017 (Wang, 2018). Esports is a huge business in America, but there are no established governmental regulations for esports players beyond recently relaxed visa requirements for professionals (Ionica, 2017). The evolving landscape of esports governance in the United States includes professional, collegiate, and scholastic sectors.

Professional Governance of professional gamers in the United States primarily remains tied to league and tournament organizers. Previously, the NBA 2K League was profiled as an example of effective oversight and authority for professional gamers. However, the league exists primarily to promote the NBA brand through a manufactured electronic video game and does not have authority over any other esports games.

A relatively new esports association in the United States claims to provide a voice for players beyond the extent of most leagues and organizations with a governance role in the industry. In 2016, seven North American esports teams formed the Professional Esports Association (PEA) to emulate the governance structure of traditional professional team sports in a league system (Chao, 2017). The association has since grown to nine teams that share in the decision-making process and equally split profits from the league between owners and players ("Professional Esports Association Launches," 2016). The PEA has a commissioner, investments from NBA team owners, a rules committee, and a grievances committee (Vincent, 2016).

Collegiate Because esports has only recently been recognized as varsity competition at higher education institutions, governing bodies such as the NCAA and the National Association of Intercollegiate Athletics (NAIA) have not been able to address governance of esports at the college level. This is not to suggest these organizations are shying away from developing governance guidelines. In fall 2018, the NCAA Board of Governors, the association's highest-ranking committee, explored reasons why it should sponsor esports and whether programs were better suited to be housed in athletics or student affairs. The outcome, however, was "considerable opposition to involvement from the governing body and its amateur model" (Fisher, 2018).

There are many issues to address if the NCAA were to accept esports as a traditional sport. For one, the board of governors could not determine if the championship season should be classified as a fall, winter, or spring sport (Fisher, 2018). Additionally, the Title IX equal opportunity requirement would also prove problematic in a sport dominated by males. Finally, the NCAA limits practices to no more than 20 hours a week, which is well below the proclaimed 60-plus hours per week necessary to stay competitive under the current esports model (Hollist, 2015).

The NAIA has been a huge proponent in the creation of the National Association of Collegiate eSports (NACE), which serves as a "governing body for institutions that have given out millions in esports scholarships" (Blum, 2017). According to the articles of organization in the esports constitution and bylaws (2016), the 10-member elected board can only be approved and removed by the NAIA Council of Presidents. Regulations and rules address financial aid, postseason competition requirements, policies and qualification plans for championship events, athlete eligibility, and transfer rules. As defined in the association's

bylaws, for esports to stage a national collegiate championship, 32 or more institutions must sponsor intercollegiate esports and declare their intent to participate in a championship.

Game developers have also addressed rules and regulations for collegiate players. For example, according to the Collegiate Star League (CSL), teams at the college level must meet specific player rankings for varsity or junior varsity teams. This rule ensures that the teams are more evenly matched and allows for different rankings for smaller schools. However, colleges with fewer than 5,000 students or online colleges are not allowed to participate in tournaments for the CSL ("Season Guide to Fall 2018–Spring 2019," 2018).

Scholastic It is no surprise that the governance of esports for scholastic teen players is fragmented, with multiple entities vying to capture the youth market by serving as regulatory agencies. Basic rules for scholastic competitors typically include a minimum grade point average, a minimum age standard of 13, proof of enrollment, and a stipulation that a high school player cannot appear on the roster of a professional team or league. Due to the nature of esports, it is very possible that a 13-year-old student could have a professional ranking and be part of a roster for a professional team, but that person would not be permitted to compete on a scholastic team.

In 2019, three entities were trying to regulate high school esports in the United States (see table 14.2). All three have a commercial subscription-based pay-to-play gaming competition. One of the organizations is the National Federation of State High School Associations (NFHS), which serves as the governing authority for all high school sports and activities. The second organization is a scholastic federation associated with a university in California, and the third organization is the High School Esports League.

The NFHS, which governs eligibility, championships, and officials for mainstream sports and extracurricular activities (e.g., band and debate clubs), just added esports to the list. Officially, the NFHS authorizes esports among its "other sports." The governance model of esports under the NFHS is a partnership with PlayVS, an infrastructure that operates Internet and mobile gaming specifically for high school students. The NFHS website hosts the equivalent of a rule book titled an "esports playbook" and requires a $16 per month student player fee ("Esports in High School," 2018).

Table 14.2 High School Esports Regulation Entities in the United States

National Federation of State High School Associations	• Association governs mainstream scholastic sports • Partner is PlayVS, a mobile and Internet gaming platform • Student subscription rate: $16 per month
North America Scholastic Esports Federation	• Based at the University of California, Irvine • Membership includes almost 200 scholastic clubs • Clubs are required to participate in NASEF tournaments
High School Esports League	• Membership includes over 1,500 high schools • Student subscription rate: $6.07 to $8.67 • Boasts largest prizing in high school esports history

Founded in 2018, the North America Scholastic Esports Federation (NASEF) is the second association with a stake in governing high school esports. Currently, the federation identifies eight partners, including three associated with the University of California, Irvine (UCI). A code of conduct serves as a governing document for the organization, which includes a 10-member general advisory committee and five technical advisors. The NASEF staff, led by a commissioner who is also an employee of UCI, includes a chief executive officer, chief technology officer, chief operation officer, communications director, esports specialist, and coordinators for social media, league operations, esports ambassadors, and coaching ("Federation Office," 2018). Almost 200 clubs are recognized as members, and players are required to have a minimum 2.0 GPA ("Student Eligibility," n.d.).

The High School Esports League, which claims to be "the leader in high school esports," is the third association targeting the youth market at a price of $6.07 to $8.67 per player per month based on the number of registrations ("2018 Fall Registration Packages," 2018). While having no direct affiliation with the NASEF or the NFHS, the league included 15,000 students from 800 high schools in 2017 (Schwartz, 2018). In 2019, the league included 1,500 member high schools and the largest prizing pool in high school esports history (Fogel, 2019). The 79-page general rule book prohibits cheating, doping, substance abuse, betting, match fixing, spamming, intentional delays, tainted accounts, and use of a name associated with a gang affiliation, drugs, politically charged symbols, and sexual or offensive material. It also includes the "fair connection rule" mandating that the difference between each team's average pings can be no greater than 40 milliseconds (High School Esports,

2018, p. 28). Disputes are initiated by the complainant submitting an online form.

AREAS OF ESPORTS GOVERNANCE AND LEGISLATION

Governance and legislation in sport are needed to standardize playing rules and regulations, protect players, and ensure its viability. Some of these areas include child protection, age ratings, and consumer affairs. Since the structure and rules of esports are the privy of the individual game developers that dictate playing rules, there is little connectivity among all stakeholders to establish an independent form of governance for the esports industry. Rules and regulations involving scoring, standings, player transfers, and other areas are typically established by corporate game developers motivated by company sales and profits. The other primary decision-making body in esports is the tournament organizers who are also generally motivated by profits from media rights, sponsorships, ticket sales, and other revenue streams.

A law review articulated the governing authority of Riot Games, producer of one of the most profitable games in the industry (*League of Legends*) and owner of a professional esports league. As a game developer, Riot has the authority to issue bans on players in its own league and on players in other, third-party *League of Legends* leagues. As a league owner, Riot can also impose fines and ban its league players for failure to follow the rules that Riot (as the developer) has created. The conundrum is that unlike most traditional professional sports leagues, players and teams cannot appeal these rulings (Hollist, 2015).

There is a current trend toward league and broadcaster regulation, with companies such as Twitch, FACEIT, and ESL all becoming involved in the rollout of rules and regulations for particular games and tournaments. Twitch, a subsidiary of Amazon, is a livestreaming video gaming platform. FACEIT is a gaming platform originating in London, and ESL is a gaming network.

Regulatory deficiencies plague the industry on multiple levels, primarily in the inability to create or enforce universal standards for competitive integrity and player welfare. The esports industry lacks universal regulated elements that are common to mainstream traditional professional sports, such as policies governing entry drafts, standardized contract terms, and league oversight of player behavior (Funk, Pizzo, & Baker, 2018). These elements typically are apparent in the rules governing an individual esports league such as NBA 2K or for a specific competition. Game developers, tournament organizers, and leagues typically mandate that players must have a game account that has not been banned for inappropriate behavior or cheating. This policy pairs with the rules prohibiting cheating, betting, using performance-enhancing software, hardware, or drugs such as ADHD medications.

Governance in the esports space needs to be transparent, and regulation is needed to avoid player exploitation and contract abuse. Enforceable sanctions for policy violations are often where associations fail to become true governing agencies since so many are voluntary organizations with authority only over their membership. Several of the areas of esports governance and legislation addressed next include intellectual property rights, player welfare, competitive integrity, and dispute resolution.

Intellectual Property and Publicity Rights

Intellectual property rights is the general term for ownership of property, typically through patents, copyrights, or trademarks. **Publicity rights** are the protectable property interest of an individual's name, identity, or persona (likeness). The esports landscape involves very controversial views on both intellectual property rights and publicity rights.

Intellectual property rights in esports are still in their infancy, with licensing and contract deals heavily favoring game developers and tournament organizers while limiting players' rights. In some cases, individuals registering for a tournament or participating on a team roster sign a contract that stipulates that there is no appeals process or grievance procedure in the event of a dispute.

It should be noted that individual games used in esports competitions are considered audiovisual literary works owned by the companies that have developed them (Coogan, 2018). This relationship means that game publishers, as original authors, maintain original copyright privileges over their property and can decide their own rules of play. However, during competitions, the interactive component of a game precludes outright copyrightability, and games therefore can be classified as derivative works (Coogan, 2018, p. 419). The ownership conundrum leads to licensing issues when professional esports leagues and tournament organizers use the game at a public event.

One of the specific intellectual property rights issues associated with esports is ownership of avatars, which serve as the in-game representations of the players. One position is that game publishers grant implied permission for players to create derivative works since the design of an avatar depends on the tools provided in the gaming system (McTee, 2014). Preexisting avatar characters are copyrighted products of the game publisher, but if alterations can be made, there could be a claim of at least joint ownership of the copyright, and both the player and the game creator could gain commercial value. There is also a concern about intellectual property protection violations if an avatar bears a player's likeness without his or her authorization. This was the premise of the widely publicized class action lawsuit filed by Ed O'Bannon against the NCAA and EA Sports.

Contracts between game publishers and a tournament or league organizer are becoming more common to address legal areas such as the licensing and use of the game intellectual property in esports events. These contracts may extend to include stipulations on how the events are operated and marketed. Governance in Action 14.3 describes an esports intellectual property case between a national governing body and a game developer with a license agreement.

Player Welfare

An area of legal and regulatory concern in the esports industry is athlete exploitation, especially because the market is filled with young players. Since many professional esports athletes are minors, a person in high school could be recognized as a professional, which leads to questions

GOVERNANCE IN ACTION 14.3

Korea e-Sports Association
Versus Blizzard Entertainment

A dispute over intellectual property rights occurred in 2010 between South Korea's esports governing body (KeSPA) and the American game publisher Blizzard Entertainment (Blizzard), currently incorporated as Activision Blizzard. The dispute focused on KeSPA unilaterally negotiating broadcast agreements for tournaments of a popular Blizzard game (*StarCraft*) without consulting the entertainment company.

Through a licensing fee with Blizzard, KeSPA had exclusive rights for operating the *StarCraft* league. The deal included ownership rights over all sponsorships, broadcast programs, and program videos (Chao, 2018). Therefore, KeSPA believed they had sole authority to negotiate media rights for their *StarCraft* league. On the other hand, as creator and owner of the *Starcraft* game, Blizzard maintained that the license agreement with KeSPA did not include negotiating broadcasting deals for *StarCraft* or any game without its authorization (Burk, 2013, p. 1543).

The dispute ended with Blizzard breaking all ties with KeSPA and securing its own media rights deal with an alternative licensee for broadcasting *StarCraft* tournaments.

KeSPA filed a lawsuit maintaining it was a league organizer as opposed to a governing organization, while Blizzard was identified as a private corporation. Blizzard's legal team argued that as a tournament organizer, KeSPA did not have authority over the game developer, even though a license deal was valid. Blizzard also contended that as a private company, it retained the right to select who it wants to negotiate with in contract agreements. It was therefore the privy of Blizzard to choose to discontinue contracting with KeSPA and end its relationship with Korea's esports authority.

Lars Ronbog/FrontZoneSport

Potential exploitation is a reality for esports due to the popularity of video games with the younger generation.

such as whether teens need proper representation or if they are subject to child labor laws if they receive salaries from a team owner. Players are also often placed under restrictions that limit their ability to transfer between leagues or even games due to contract agreements.

There are also concerns about the health and social risks associated with extreme commitments to player training. In 2014, a 26-year-old professional gamer died in the middle of a livestreamed tournament, a 22-year-old player logged five hours of play while in the hospital for a collapsed lung, and a 17-year-old player attempted suicide by jumping off a 12-story building after turning in his team for alleged match fixing (Hollist, 2015). There are also many examples of teens who turned professional and dropped out of high school.

Athlete welfare is a tremendously contentious area that currently lacks universal regulations in the esports industry. Published reports of team owners refusing to pay roster players after victories may result in team bans from competition, fines, or imprisonment for criminal offenses. Other managers may subject players to brutal working conditions, such as a 16-hour nonstop training regime. There are no uniform regulations defining sanctions for exploiting athletes.

Competitive Integrity

Competitive integrity is essentially the ethical conduct and behavior expected when competing. It encompasses a respect for rules and regulations, both implicit and explicit. The opposite of competitive integrity is corruption. Because of the lack of governance in the industry in addition to the availability of substantial monetary rewards, esports is plagued with examples of corruption and scandalous behavior to gain a competitive advantage. Players, tournament organizers, managers, coaches, and game developers have all been guilty of corrupt behavior.

There are many ways to cheat in a virtual environment; it can be difficult to detect and prove violations and difficult to punish them. Ensuring compliance and enforcing rules against cheating and corruption in esports is complicated by the lack of universal governance of the industry (Holden, Rodenberg, & Kaburakis, 2017).

Rules and regulations to promote competitive integrity in esports are created by various organizations connected to the industry, such as commercial game developers, tournament organizers, and groups aspiring to governance. Regulations and sanctions for the same infraction may differ from game to game or from league to league. Threats to competitive integrity include e-doping and illegal gambling (primarily match fixing).

E-Doping

E-doping is a term for using performance enhancement substances while playing electronic games. In competitive gaming, Adderall, a stimulant used to treat attention deficit hyperactivity disorder (ADHD), has been said by many players to improve their play. Adderall is rarely detected by drug testing, which for the most part is absent in the unregulated esports industry.

The ESL is cited as the first major league in esports to implement a drug testing policy (Mueller, 2015). Other leagues and competitions, such as the NBA 2K League, are adding drug testing policies and sanctions in their regulations. There is a concern, however, that when players are banned for violating a league substance abuse policy in esports, they can simply join another league or change their screen name to assume a new identity.

Organizations such as the World Esports Association refer to the WADA to determine the list of prohibited substances for members, but there is no uniformity from organization to organization about what is considered a banned substance. There are also no uniform sanctions, demonstrating yet again the fragmented state of esports governance.

Gambling

Gambling, legal or illegal, is a second huge threat to competitive integrity. The U.S. Supreme Court decision overturning the Professional and Amateur Sports Protection Act (PASPA), a decision that now permits individual states to legalize gambling, will likely change the landscape of betting on esports. For one, states will need to determine if esports falls under the definition of traditional sports such as football or if it is classified in the same category as the World Series of Poker, which is labeled under "other events." New Jersey, for example, excluded esports in the legislation that legalized sport wagering in the state due to the young demographic profile of a majority of esports participants (Sperdlow & Tangle, 2018).

Demonstrating the proliferation of youth gamers was a 2016 federal class action lawsuit filed in the state of Washington alleging esports losses by minors who were gambling virtual weapons (Needleman, 2016; Holden & Echrich, 2017). Four class action lawsuits were filed across the United States in the same year alleging Valve Corporation (Valve), a game developer, facilitated gambling by minors. However, the court determination was that the virtual "skin" pieces being wagered were essentially prizes. Allegations of operating an illegal gambling business and violating the federal Racketeer Influenced and Corrupt Organizations (RICO) statutes were all dismissed, but the Washington State Gambling Commission ordered Valve to cease facilitating gambling via virtual gun and knife skins (Holden, Kaburakis, & Rodenberg, 2017).

Match fixing is perhaps the most documented corruption area in esports. Forbes cited match fixing as the "biggest threat" to the industry with the proliferation of younger players who may be more susceptible to bribes in exchange for influencing game results (Heitner, 2018). A second reason cited for the proliferation of match fixing is the hyperdigital nature of esports, which facilitates an integrated virtual communication system, making it relatively easy for collusion and for online betting to occur given recent relaxed gambling restrictions in the United States. In addition to the cases of

Korean players being charged with match fixing over the years, an Internet search reveals many examples from the United States and countries around the world of similar corrupt activities.

Dispute Resolution

One final area of esports governance is **dispute resolution**, which is the process for resolving a grievance between two or more parties. In most cases, disputes between players or players and tournament operators are settled by interpreting rules established by the game developer or the league. In some cases, there are no systems in place to file a grievance beyond a court of law, which poses a challenge for parties in two countries. Some league contracts may simply stipulate that a player forfeits his or her right to appeal any decision or ruling. The esports industry is such an unregulated industry that dispute resolution may not exist in a league with its own rules that does not have a process for a grievance.

An independent judicial entity is needed to resolve most esports disputes that occur across the vast international landscape of virtual gaming. Most cases are resolved by an arbitrator or arbitration council that is empowered to make binding decisions. Arbitration is described as a much more efficient method of decision making than traditional court litigation, which is typically a much slower process.

While the CAS has yet to rule in any esports case, there are two organizations that currently serve the industry. The first organization, the Esports Integrity Commission (ESIC), has been called "the CAS for esports" (Ptascynski, 2018). Established in 2015, the coalition includes a disciplinary panel that resolves disputes for its members ("Members and Supporters," n.d.). The second organization, the Arbitration Court for ESports (ACES), is a subsidiary of WESA. Unique to the dispute resolution process is that each party in the grievance may select one of the three tribunal members (World Esports Association, 2016, p. 5).

The most notable concern about ESIC and ACES is that neither of these has sanctioning authority beyond the scope of their membership. Secondly, the fact that two organizations exist to legislate esports disputes can be problematic to an industry without a universal governance system. With the momentum the industry is gaining toward acceptance as a recognized sport, however, it may just be a matter of time before the first esports case is referred to the CAS.

RECAP

The classification of esports as a true sport is one of the most controversial issues to challenge sport practitioners, administrators, and legal professionals. Esports has many of the characteristics of traditional professional sports in terms of viewing hours, long-term engagement, and monetization (prize money). In fact, the NBA cofounded the NBA 2K League. However, the International Olympic Committee, the National Federation of State High School Associations in the United States, and the Court of Arbitration for Sport currently do not recognize esports as a sport.

The primary stakeholders in the landscape of esports include players, game developers, and league or tournament operators. Sponsors, media entities, advertisers, and affiliated esports associations enter the equation, but any form of governing rules is most often relegated to the corporation that created and manufactured a game or to the business entities that organize major competitions and tournaments. Esports players are typically absent from decision-making processes.

Many entities on the global stage are trying to serve as regulatory bodies for esports, including the World Esports Association and the International Esports Federation. Neither entity is listed with the Global Association of International Sport Federations, and the IOC has publicly declared that no international esports federation exists that exemplifies the Olympic values. Therefore, esports, despite its inclusion in the 2022 Asian Games, cannot be considered as a potential Olympic sport in its current state.

The numerous organizations trying to serve as esports regulatory bodies have had varying government support and varying success. The current structure of competing entities for high school esports players in the United States is an example of the complexity of an unregulated industry.

Regulations and rules for games, tournaments, and leagues vary significantly in a fragmented, relatively young industry that continues to evolve and mature in a digital world. Some of the areas needing regulation include intellectual property and publicity rights, player welfare, competitive integrity, and dispute resolution. Esports governance faces an interesting yet complicated future.

Critical Thinking Questions

1. Take a stance and defend whether esports fits the traditional definition of a sport.

2. Explain why esports is often cited as an unregulated or fragmented industry.

3. What are the similarities and differences between the NBA 2K League and a traditional North American sport league?

4. Distinguish among the most important industry regulations for esports scholastic and professional players.

5. Describe the state of the esports industry in 2050.

Applied Activity

Creating a New International Federation

The task is to create a completely new international esports federation responsible for governance of the upcoming esports world championships. Consider areas such as powers of the president; player representation; processes for the election of officials and length of their terms; the nature, duties, and power of the organization and any representatives; the relationships and the allocation of resources between member countries; the process for determining the host sites for world championships; regulations for financial disclosures; and any other measures of good governance. Outline the blueprints for the new organization.

Case Study Application

For more information on governance issues in esports, review *Poaching Problematic in Esports Industry* in the web resource.

Case Study Abstracts

Best Practices for Financial Accountability of an NCAA Conference Office

Shonna Brown

Shonna Brown is the associate commissioner for business/chief financial officer at Conference USA. Brown has worked in four conference offices and the NCAA. She has served on several NCAA governance committees. Brown has participated on numerous panels during national conventions.

Abstract

The National Collegiate Athletic Association (NCAA) directory lists 143 conferences, 23 of which are labeled I-FCS, denoting member institutions that compete in the football championship series (e.g., the Big Ten, Atlantic Coast Conference). A conference office is charged with organizing, administering, and promoting intercollegiate athletics at nationally competitive levels on behalf of its members and their student-athletes.

To operate at optimum levels, a conference must maintain financial integrity in its managerial accounting practices while constantly exploring new opportunities for revenue generation and cost savings. Conference commissioners work closely with the conference chief financial officer (CFO) to create the annual budget, which incorporates assistance funds provided by the NCAA. In addition to these NCAA funds, conferences are responsible for generating revenue primarily through sport championships, marketing activities, and television deals. The NCAA has varying levels of expectations for fund generation based upon factors such as division and sport.

To assist members in sustaining long-term financial stability, the NCAA distributes four different categories of funds to conference offices. These categories are the (1) Academic Enhancement Fund, (2) Equal Conference Fund, (3) Basketball Performance Fund, and (4) Student Assistance Fund. Conference offices have discretion in determining how to distribute NCAA funds to member institutions. This case study explores various models that conferences use for fund distribution and revenue sharing. It also details methods of accounting for income and expenses incorporating NCAA funding, championships, bowl games, media contracts, and marketing and sponsorship deals.

College Basketball Corruption Scandal: Is There a Crime if There Is No Victim?

Stephen L. Butler

Stephen L. Butler is the director of the Language Training Detachment at the United States Air Force (USAF) Special Operations School and the former dean of academic affairs at the United States Sports Academy. Full disclosure: Dr. Butler is also a friend of Chuck Person.

Abstract

The college basketball world was rocked in November 2017 when it was announced that several prominent assistant coaches, executives from Adidas, and sports agents had been indicted by a federal grand jury in New York on federal corruption and bribery charges. One of those indicted was Auburn University's associate head coach, Chuck Person.

Person is still the leading scorer in Auburn history and is regarded by most as the second-best player ever at Auburn, behind only Charles Barkley. After his illustrious college career, where he was a two-time All-American and three-time All-Southeastern Conference (SEC) selection, Person was the fourth player chosen in the 1986 NBA draft. Person played 14 years in the NBA for five different teams. He was chosen as NBA Rookie of the Year in 1987.

After his playing days, Person became an assistant coach and worked for some of the greatest coaches in NBA history, including Phil Jackson, Gregg Popovich, and Dr. Jack Ramsey. Person joined Bruce Pearl's Auburn staff in 2014 and was named associate head coach in 2015.

Chuck Person, along with several others, was taken into custody by the FBI on September 26, 2017, and released on $100,000 bail. The former assistant faced up to 80 years in prison after pleading guilty to six bribery and fraud charges. However, in July 2019, he avoided jail time and was sentenced to 200 hours of community service.

High School Strength and Conditioning: A Case Study in Caution

Cory Schierberl

Cory Schierberl is a certified strength and conditioning specialist (CSCS) and tactical strength and conditioning facilitator (TSAC-F). He is the head strength and conditioning coach for the Red Storm women's basketball and softball teams and former athletic performance director at Force 10 Performance, the official training center of the Women's National Basketball Association's Seattle Storm.

Abstract

This case study reviews the circumstances of Broadview Heights High School in Ohio and how the use of noncertified personnel in its strength and conditioning program led to the career-ending injury of one of its student-athletes. The case examines the course of action that led directly to the transition of a closet-sized weight room run by an unqualified history teacher to a professionally staffed, state-of-the-art training center capable of providing athletic performance and injury prevention through a partnership with one of the state's largest hospital systems.

The case highlights the need for quality comprehensive athletic performance training and injury prevention programs at the amateur sports level. This case also demonstrates how governance in strength and conditioning may not always work with the authoritative structure of a high school and how grassroots-level efforts can play a major role in changing the status quo.

Stakeholders in the case were eventually persuaded that the addition of a strength and conditioning coach was essential for the school's student-athletes. Unfortunately, funding was not available to accomplish what they had hoped, and initial fund-raising efforts proved to be ineffective.

Ink, You Are Infringing: A Case Study

Chloe Goodlive and Jacob M. Ward

Jake Ward is a registered patent attorney for Jake Ward Law Office, in Tiffin, Ohio. He is also registered as a patent agent, nonresident, in Canada and is the founder of the Anticipate This! Patent and Trademark Law Blog. *Chloe Goodlive is an associate attorney at Jake Ward Law Office and formerly worked in the editorial operations department for CAS, an information technology and services firm in Columbus, Ohio.*

Abstract

A current intellectual property case pending before the Southern District of New York, *Solid Oak Sketches, LLC v. Visual Concepts, LLC*, analyzes whether or not the company responsible for producing the *NBA 2K* video game franchise, Take-Two, infringed upon the copyright of a tattoo holding company, Solid Oak. In its video games, Take-Two included replicas of tattoos on LeBron James, Eric Bledsoe, and Kenyon Martin, in which Solid Oak claims copyright ownership. Solid Oak has sued Take-Two for the alleged infringement. Take-Two believes the replication of the tattoos falls into two defenses against copyright infringement, namely, fair use and *de minimis* use. The fair use arguments, however, are noteworthy and have widespread implications for athletes, tattoo artists, and video game designers. An ultimate decision in favor of Solid Oak could have a chilling effect on authentic video game re-creations. The copyright owners of every tattoo on every athlete could flood the courts with lawsuits alleging copyright infringement in the absence of a licensing agreement. The outcome of this case could have broad implications in the sporting goods and licensing industry for athletes, video game producers, and even tattoo artists.

Overcoming Challenges in Thailand Adventure Tourism

Sinsupa Wannasuth and Bonnie Tiell

Sinsupa Wannasuth is a professor of customer service and management at Suan Dusit University, a consultant for the Thailand Triathlon Federation, and a former member of the Thai national sailing team.

Abstract

The 2019 World Weightlifting Championships were held in Pattaya, Thailand. The International Weightlifting Federation (IWF) voted to keep the event in Thailand despite two reigning Olympic champions and six additional Thai lifters testing positive for banned substances at the 2018 World Championships (Nair, 2019). The decision was somewhat unprecedented since bylaw 12.3.1 of the IWF Anti-Doping Policy (2017) states that three or more violations in a calendar year result in suspension of a member federation from "any IWF activity" for up to four years (p. 39).

The 2019 championships contributed to the Thai sport tourism industry, which is an important economic driver for the country. The highest percentage increase in Thailand's gross domestic product has been derived from sport tourism for the past several years. This increase supports the Sports Authority for Thailand and Ministry of Sport and Tourism's focus on "encouraging Thailand as a quality adventurous sport tourism destination for high value tourists for sustainable competitive advantages" (Wichasin & Wannasuth, 2018).

It would have been a devastating blow to Thailand's economy if the country had been prohibited from hosting the 2019 World Weightlifting Championships. This case focuses on efforts by multiple stakeholders to assist in Thailand retaining the IWF World Championships and overcoming a unique challenge in marketing the city of Pattaya as a sport tourism destination given the city's notorious reputation for employing thousands of sex workers (Bragg, 2018).

Poaching Problematic in Esports Industry

Michael Kidd

Michael Kidd is the Information Technology Program Director at Baker College and former assistant professor at Tiffin University. After beginning his career as a network specialist in the U.S. Army, Kidd spent 15 years in network administration and cyber security, focusing on enterprise intrusion defense and counter-hacking.

Abstract

With the rise of esports as a reputable career path for young, eager video game enthusiasts and the multitude of professional and semiprofessional teams popping up throughout the world, players and teams alike are finding that a lack of governance within the sport creates many challenges. Player poaching, or enticing an individual to switch teams without consent from the current team, is just one of the many governance problems facing esports. There are countless examples of player poaching, but few cases are tried in court. Poaching typically falls under the jurisdiction of rules governing esports tournaments.

Roster shuffles are expected when a team disbands and players become "free agents," but poaching players who are under contract obligations and enticing them to switch allegiances is both immoral and illegal. Few lawsuits seeking financial remuneration for poaching are filed, primarily because of the burden of proof falling upon the accuser. Individuals typically file a formal complaint with a game producer having the authority to impose penalties for blatant acts of poaching.

One of the most recent poaching cases involved G2 Esports, a popular team in Europe. G2 Esports was accused of entering negotiations with several younger players from another team before their contract terms expired. In lieu of taking judicial action, multiple teams filed a formal complaint with Riot Games, the American video game developer for *League of Legends*. This case explores the problem of poaching players, including a 2016 incident involving an esports player nicknamed Flamboozle.

Power Limitations in International Sport Federations

Morgan Fuller Kolsrud

Morgan Fuller Kolsrud is a sports event management professional and a member of the 2012 U.S. Olympic Synchronized Swimming Training Squad. Morgan serves as the USOPC Athletes' Advisory Council Representative for Synchronized Swimming and is on the USA Synchro Board of Directors.

Abstract

International sport federations (IFs) recognized by the IOC wield considerable power. However, the IOC is the prevailing authority, with power to suspend federations or to overturn rules approved by a federation's executive board. This case examines recent events involving the Fédération Internationale de Natation Association (FINA) and the Association Internationale de Boxe Amateur (AIBA) demonstrating the complexities of international sport organizations with respect to their governing power, authority, and ethical climate.

During its General Congress session in July 2017, FINA, the governing body for swimming and diving, voted to change the name of synchronized swimming to artistic swimming. The international synchronized swimming community immediately voiced its disappointment over social media, lamenting that the name change undid years of work by athletes to gain acceptance and respect by reminding them of the days when the sport was referred to as "water ballet." A Change.org petition calling on FINA to reverse the name change received over 11,000 signatures (Harley-Jesson, 2017).

In May 2019, the IOC suspended AIBA and stripped the association's rights to operate events for the World Championships and 2020 Tokyo Olympics. The suspension followed a six-month investigation into the AIBA's governance, finances, and refereeing practices, which included electing a president listed by the U.S. Treasury Department as "one of Uzbekistan's leading criminals" (Morgan, 2019a). The IOC assumes the responsibility for the sport in the wake of the suspension, including consideration of proposals by other boxing entities interested in replacing AIBA as the supreme authority for the sport.

Selecting Olympic Host Cities: Evaluating Alternatives

Jonathan Rosenberg

Jonathan Rosenberg is a professor of business and economics at the College of Mount Saint Vincent in Riverdale, New York. Rosenberg also served as chair of the 2018 Sport and Society: Exploration and Discovery in the 21st Century Conference.

Abstract

The governing authority of the International Olympic Committee (IOC) supersedes politics and global regimes of power. In recent years, there has been a renewed discussion as to whether a policy change is needed in the IOC's method for selecting Olympic host cities. The primary reason given for reform is the current situation whereby the IOC profits greatly from the Games while the host cities often face financial difficulties (Baade & Matheson, 2016).

Proponents of the policy change also contend that the IOC has often ignored nations' human rights violations, as long as they could make the necessary financial commitment and put on a wonderful spectacle (Hyde, 2016). Beijing (2008, 2022) and Sochi (2014) are offered as examples of reputedly corrupt locations granted host status. Reforms to IOC policies may minimize the selection of cities deemed inappropriate.

One solution offered for selecting a host city is to revert to the practice of the ancient Games, whereby one city stands as permanent host (Friedman, 2016; Worstall, 2016). Others have offered a hybrid solution, whereby selected cities representing different continents rotate on a consistent basis (Aspen Institute, 2016; Patrick, 2017). The IOC is the only entity that can modify the selection process through a policy amendment within the Olympic Charter. This case explores the pros and cons of alternatives for selecting Olympic host cities for future Games.

Taekwondo and Wrestling Tackle International Political Interference

Scott R. Jedlicka

Scott R. Jedlicka is an assistant professor of sport management at Washington State University.

Abstract

Because competitors in international sporting events are typically identified by the nation-states they represent, international sport maintains a very visible and persistent connection to international politics. This connection can often place sport governing bodies in difficult situations. Although it is tempting to believe that sport transcends politics, the reality is that political conflict often influences where events are held, the security at those events, who is able to attend and participate, and even the outcome of the competitions themselves. In 2018, the long-standing political, ethnic, and religious conflict between Israel and Palestine directly affected the United World Wrestling U23 World Championships as well as the World Taekwondo World Junior Championships. In one case, a youth wrestler from Iran was ordered to intentionally lose a match to avoid facing an Israeli opponent. Shortly thereafter, four Israeli taekwondo athletes were banned from entering the country of Tunisia for the World Junior Championships.

In both instances, the international federations staging the events were forced to confront their (limited) capacity to prevent politics from "interfering" in sport. These two examples of interference demonstrate the ways in which international sport governing bodies navigate the fallout from politically motivated actions. More generally, these cases also reveal the extent to which the choices of sport governing bodies are themselves shaped by political considerations.

The Influence of Politics in Romanian Sport Before and After the Regime Change From Communism to Democracy

Noemi Zaharia and Valentin Cristian Zaharia

Noemi Zaharia is a two-time Olympic medalist swimmer and two-time Olympian, in 1988 and 1992, who represented Romania at all world competitions. She is also a multiple NCAA title winner. Noemi is a director of the Aquatic and Fitness Center at Miami Dade College and an adjunct professor of sport management and exercise science at Florida International University (FIU). Noemi is a doctoral candidate in education in sport management and leadership with a specialization in coaching, and she holds a master's degree in sport management from FIU. Valentin Cristian Zaharia is a 1992 Olympian and World Championship bronze medalist in team handball, and he was national champion and MVP as a professional player in Romania, Sweden, France, and Germany. As the head coach of the U.S. men's national team, he won the bronze medal at the Pan Am Games in 2003. Valentin is an adjunct professor at FIU teaching business courses as part of the sport management degree and at Miami Dade College teaching various business courses in the School of Business. Valentin holds an MBA from Western Governor's University and a baccalaureate degree in business from Miami Dade College.

Abstract

Sport has been and continues to be at the center of society, not only as a recreational activity, but also as a propaganda vehicle to promote a country and its national government's interests. Sport is not only beneficial to the health and wellness of a country's population, but it also serves as a global ambassadorship by showcasing elite national athletes who compete on the world stage.

During the communist era, the ruling Romanian Communist Party used its athletes and their success to promote the country's political ideas worldwide. The government was dictating, organizing, and subsidizing all aspects of sports from recreational to Olympic levels. After the fall of communism, in Romania, sport lost its appeal as a propaganda machine, resulting in drastic changes. The mismanagement of limited available funds, coupled with a lack of adaptability to the changing political and economic landscape in Europe and around the world, led to a dramatic decline in Romania's Olympic Games ranking and an almost complete halt to construction projects for sporting facilities.

Through new sponsorship laws over time, Romania was able to achieve a slow turnaround to eventually begin securing financial contributions from private businesses. These revisions in turn created new jobs and new revenue sources for sport. Most notably, Romania was able to capitalize on lucrative hosting opportunities for international sporting events. This case explores the evolution of sport in Romania from the totalitarian communist era to the current age of democracy.

The Many Stakeholders of the NFL Super Bowl "On Location Experience"

David W. Walsh, Michael A. Odio, and Dexter Davis

David W. Walsh is a clinical assistant professor and internship coordinator at the University of Houston Sport Administration program within the Health and Human Performance Department. Michael A. Odio is an assistant professor at the University of Cincinnati Sport Administration program within the School of Human Services. Dexter Davis is an associate professor of sport management at University of Tennessee at Martin within the school of business and global affairs. All three authors are involved annually in supervising student volunteers during the Super Bowl.

Abstract

Just the words "Super Bowl Sunday" conjure up images of a party, a de facto national holiday, a time to celebrate arguably the most successful sport league in the world, the National Football League (NFL). Governing mega-events such as the Super Bowl is challenging due, in part, to the multiple stakeholders involved in decision making. One stakeholder is the local organizing committee (LOC), which is challenged to balance community support with professional staffing. LOCs recruit thousands of volunteers and contract with corporate entities to produce and manage the NFL "on location experience" (OLE), which has been described as a theme park-style fan-fest.

Starting with Super Bowl XLVII hosted by New Orleans in 2013, LOCs began forming partnerships with area colleges and universities with sport management and hospitality management programs. Colleges supplied eager volunteers who were rewarded with professional development opportunities. This case examines the tensions that arose between stakeholders when enthusiastic college students were asked to manage elements of an OLE Touchdown Tour event that displaced volunteers from the local organizing committee.

The case introduces Jessica O'Hara, a liaison for the 2017 Houston Super Bowl Host Committee (HSHC). O'Hara has a long history of navigating complex relationships between people in different organizations. As an industry veteran, the LOC executive put her leadership skills to the test in defusing a political conflict stemming from impressionable college students who were unintentionally denied a prominent role they were promised in executing a Touchdown Tour event for Super Bowl LI.

The NFL Kneeling Policy

Daniel Kane

Daniel Kane is an adjunct lecturer at CUNY Kingsborough Community College and CUNY School of Professional Studies. He is also a doctoral student at the United States Sports Academy.

Abstract

On August 14, 2016, during the team's first preseason football game, Colin Kaepernick, a backup quarterback for the San Francisco 49ers, sat during the playing of the national anthem. Eventually, he started kneeling, and when his actions were noticed, he asserted that he was protesting the oppression of people of color and police brutality. Other players in the NFL also started to kneel during the national anthem, which ignited a wave of copycat protests throughout the league that spilled into college, high school, and other professional athletics. An intense debate ensued over whether players had the right to kneel or if they had to stand at attention during the national anthem.

The 2011-2020 NFL collective bargaining agreement does not discuss player protocol during the national anthem. The NFL responded to the wave of silent protests by creating a policy for what players are to do during the national anthem, approved by the team owners, but without input from the players. The National Football League Players Association (NFLPA) filed a grievance against the new policy since they were not consulted about the decision. Currently, the policy is suspended and awaiting changes. This case study explores the NFL's new "kneeling" policy, which was approved without collaboration with the players' association. Debate over the policy could be a point of contention in the next NFL collective bargaining agreement. If a new agreement is not signed, the NFL could experience a lockout.

Glossary

CHAPTER 1

alternative dispute resolution—A method of resolving legal disputes outside of the court system through mediation or arbitration.

antitrust law—A body of law that prevents trusts or monopolies from forming that would restrict competition in business.

arbitration—A process of settling a dispute outside of the legal system through a third party who has the authority to render a judgment for either side.

authority—The power to give orders, make decisions, and enforce compliance.

basic legal principles—The means by which laws are constructed, implemented, and enforced.

bylaws—The written rules defining the conduct of an organization.

constitution—A foundational document that sets forth the powers and limitations of a governing body and provides important operating principles for the governing body to follow.

defendant—The party against whom a civil legal action is brought.

executive order—A directive issued by the president of the United States that manages the operations of the federal government.

governance—Pertaining to responsibility, rules and policies, communication, transparency, and the central component of decision making.

governing body—The authoritative unit responsible for developing, implementing, and enforcing rules for an organization, event, or agency.

jurisdiction—Authority to hear a case.

mediation—A voluntary, nonbinding means of settling a dispute through a third party who assists both sides in forming an agreement outside of the legal system.

monopolies—Concentrations of economic power in the hands of a few businesses.

plaintiff—The party who brings a civil legal action.

precedent—A legal principle that a court will rely upon past court decisions when faced with interpreting the law in a legal case.

shared governance—Governance by more than one entity.

Sherman Antitrust Act—A federal law enacted in 1890 that prohibits monopolistic behavior that would restrain trade.

sport governance—The means by which authority, oversight responsibilities, and decision making are managed within a sport enterprise.

stakeholders—The composite of all individuals with a vested interest in a business.

stare decisis—Latin for "stand by things decided," which means to rely on precedent.

statutes—Written laws created by municipal, state, or federal legislatures.

summary judgment—A request for the court to rule on the case without trial because there are no facts in dispute.

Title IX—A federal law enacted in 1972 that prohibits gender discrimination in education programs or activities receiving federal assistance.

CHAPTER 2

accountability—Holding others responsible for their actions or a willingness to accept responsibility for one's own actions.

anchoring—A decision-making bias characterized by an individual jumping to conclusions based on limited information.

authentic leadership—A type of leadership in which an individual's behavior and actions are grounded in a self-concept of openness and truthfulness.

authoritative—A leadership style exhibited by individuals who are direct and make decisions independently (synonymous with autocratic).

autonomy—Respecting the rights of competent individuals to behave or make decisions independently in the absence of controlling influences.

availability heuristics—The calculation of the probability of occurrence based on ready examples.

cognitive dissonance—When an individual experiences conflict between attitudes and behavior.

corruption—The abuse of power or position for personal gain.

decision bias—A cognitive prejudice or predisposition that affects judgment when faced with alternatives.

emotional intelligence—The ability to understand and manage one's own emotions while also understanding and managing the emotions of others.

equity—The quality of being fair or impartial.

ethical behavior—Actions and activity that are consistent with societal expectations for what is considered right or moral.

ethical dilemma—An issue or scenario with two or more moral imperatives or choices.

ethics—Moral principles that govern behavior.

fairness—Acting impartially in accordance with rules or standards.

first impression bias—Prejudices in accounting only for an individual's very first impression.

halo effect—A tendency to only consider a person's positive characteristics.

honesty—The act of being truthful.

integrity—A behavioral attribute based on high moral principles and truthfulness.

laissez-faire—A leadership style exhibited by leaders who have little interaction with subordinates (also known as free-reign).

leadership—Influence over others due to positional or personal power.

leadership style—The way leaders provide direction and motivate others.

loyalty—Providing or demonstrating firm and constant support or allegiance.

moral awareness—The realization that a decision or action could affect the interests, welfare, or expectations of others or of themselves in a manner that may conflict with moral principles.

moral compass—The ability to judge what is right and wrong and then act accordingly.

moral competence—The cognitive ability of a person to resolve ethical dilemmas using sound critical reasoning skills.

moral principles—Foundational guidelines that govern right and wrong behavior as accepted by a certain individual or group.

moral reasoning—A systematic approach to deciding whether actions and behaviors are right or wrong.

multidimensional leadership—A leadership style based on intuitively selecting an optimal authoritative or participative leadership style based on a congruence between a leader's activities and the follower's preferred leadership behavior.

participative—A style of leadership exhibited by leaders who are considered fair, egalitarian, and willing to involve others in decisions.

recency error—Prejudices in accounting only for an individual's most recent actions or behavior.

respect—A condition of recognizing the worth of other people.

servant leader—A type of leader who focuses on the needs of the follower and who puts others' interests, needs, and aspirations before personal interests.

tolerance—A state of sympathy or indulgence for beliefs or practices differing from or conflicting with one's own.

transactional—A leader type characterized by individuals who exchange rewards such as wages or favors in return for productive effort from employees.

transformational—A leader type characterized by individuals who rely on emotional appeal and personal influence to inspire productivity in employees, often beyond the worker's normal capacity.

CHAPTER 3

best practices—The processes, methods, or activities likely to achieve optimal results.

board governance—Pertaining to the entity serving as the central component of decision making and authority for an organization.

checks and balances—The processes for accountability to ensure that rules and regulations are followed (used interchangeably with internal accountability and control).

democratic process—The presence of representative, inclusive, active decision making.

ethical climate—Referring to the degree of ethical conduct or moral behavior apparent in organizations evidenced through policies, practices, and procedures.

ex officio—The term for an individual who is a member of a governing board by virtue of his or her position. For example, the commissioner serves ex officio on the competition committee because he or she is commissioner. Participation and voting rights are determined in the organization's governing documents.

fiduciary supervision—The legal and ethical obligation to administer, invest, monitor, and distribute tangible and intangible assets of an organization.

gender quota—A measurement standard establishing the minimum requirement for the number or percent of an underrepresented gender to be represented on a roster (e.g., committee, employee list, board, etc.).

good governance—The cultural and operational elements or an organization that lead to effective regulation and compliance.

independent boards—A board where members are not affiliated with the organization as a member of the executive team or client list.

internal accountability and control—The separation of powers and the processes used to ensure that rules and regulations are followed (used interchangeably with checks and balances).

operational effectiveness—The capability of an organization to optimize its business performance in relation to defined standards for areas such as efficiency, growth, profitability, or sustainability.

organizational chart—The diagram that illustrates the structure of the organization by identifying the relationships or reporting avenues for various departments or positions.

policy—An adopted course of action for an organization.

procedure—The techniques or methods for conducting specific operational functions of an organization.

responsibilities—The specific duties, tasks, or activities under the purview of an individual or unit.

risk avoidance—The tendency to evade or minimize risk.

role—The general function of an individual or unit within an organization.

shareholder—An individual with a financial investment in the business as an owner or part-owner.

societal responsibility—An ethical obligation to have a positive impact on stakeholders.

solidarity—The commitment and efforts of an organization in demonstrating ethically and environmentally responsible behavior.

succession planning—Developing processes and strategies to replace key employees who leave the organization as a result of death, voluntarily departure, or termination.

transparency—The descriptive term for communicating honestly and openly to public constituents.

CHAPTER 4

commercial independent enterprise—Independently or individually owned enterprise operating as a for-profit business in local markets.

commercial venture—An entity with a legal name registered and articles of incorporation filed with a state's department of commerce that declares the business as a revenue producing, for-profit unit.

entrepreneurial enterprise—A start-up business operating under an individual owner, partnership, or ownership group who assumes all related risks and rewards of the business as opposed to being employed by a parent company.

independent contractor—Self-employed individuals assuming the risks and rewards of their own business.

local sport agency—A governing body with authority to regulate an aspect of sport in a city, township, territory, district, prefecture, parish, or county.

municipal parks and recreation agency—A government-funded local public organization providing a range of services and programs for residents.

National Congress of State Games (NCSG)—A membership organization in the United States serving as the umbrella organization for the state associations that organize amateur statewide sport competitions, typically in the form of an Olympic-style multisport festival.

private club—An entity (group or facility) void of public support or public membership.

quasi-public—Organizations that operate with a blended private-public ownership structure, membership base, service component, or combined source of capital or operational funding while maintaining a tax exemption.

sandbox gardens—The earliest forms of organized neighborhood playgrounds in America constructed in schoolyards and parks.

Special Olympics—A nonprofit, nongovernmental organization serving the physical needs of individuals with intellectual disabilities through sport competitions that include multisport festivals.

sport commission—An organization whose role (and mission) is to serve as an economic driver to generate revenue by attracting visitors to the area for sporting events.

state—A subregion or federal geographic landmass for a country.

state sport agency—A governing body with authority over sport or sport entities at the state level or with state-level influence in regulating an aspect of sport.

CHAPTER 5

Association of National Olympic Committees—A nongovernmental, nonprofit organization that promotes and protects the common and collective interests of the national Olympic committee members.

chef de mission—The person designated as the lead contact for a national delegation, especially at an international event.

close corporation—A corporation in which shares in the company are held by a few people, sometimes in a single family. These are generally private corporations and are not traded on any of the stock exchanges.

continental associations—Independent, nongovernmental associations regulating an Olympic or Paralympic sport at the regional level. (Occasionally referred to as *confederations*.)

governing documents—The documents that define how the organization will be governed. They define the purpose of the organization, the structure of the organization, who is responsible for what, and the voting procedures.

national governing bodies—Any independent, nongovernmental, autonomous authority regulating an aspect of sport at the national level. In the United States, the term is reserved for the regulatory agencies for an Olympic, Paralympic, or Pan-American sport.

national Olympic committees—The independent, nongovernmental organizations under the umbrella of the International Olympic Committee responsible for organizing the athletes and official delegation from their country.

national sport agency—A governing body with authority over sport or sport entities at the national level or which exerts national influence in regulating an aspect of sport.

players' association—A union for professional athletes in North America.

regional sport agency—A governing body that governs sport at the regional level (within one country or internationally based on territorial grouping) or which exerts regional influence in regulating an aspect of sport.

sanctioning body—The governing body of individual professional sports with a role in the organization of competition.

sport minister—The highest-ranking government official with supreme authority for all sport in a country.

sport ministry—A government-controlled office regulating all aspects of sport for a single country.

Ted Stevens Olympic and Amateur Sports Act—The U.S. law that created the United States Olympic Committee and national governing bodies for Olympic sports.

CHAPTER 6

Court of Arbitration for Sport—The independent judiciary authority for dispute resolution in international sport.

Global Association of International Sport Federations—The umbrella organization representing international sport federations (Olympic and non-Olympic) and international organizations contributing to sport in various fields.

global sport—Sport that is recognized or played on all five continents.

international federations—The supreme bodies that manage and monitor operations of the world's various sport disciplines, including oversight and approval of the technical elements such as rules, rankings, records, and athlete classification.

International Olympic Committee—The supreme authority and governing agency for the celebration, organization, and administration of the Olympic Games.

International Organizations of Sports for the Disabled—Independent agencies recognized by the International Paralympic Committee (IPC) and the International Olympic Committee (IOC) that serve as the governing bodies and sole worldwide

representatives for specific impairment sports in the Paralympic Games.

international sport—Sport confined to a specific geographic region or when competition includes participants from at least two countries.

International University Sports Federation—The global agency governing the international university sports movement as well as the Summer and Winter Universiades (Games) and World University Championships.

Olympic Charter—The official rules, guidelines, and codification of fundamental principles governing the Olympic movement and the Olympic Games.

Olympic Congress—A large gathering of representatives of the constituents of the Olympic movement, which convene at intervals determined by the president.

Paralympic Games—An international multisport competition involving only athletes with a variety of disabilities.

Special Olympic Games—A multisport competition involving only athletes with specific intellectual disabilities.

subsidiary—A legal entity controlled by another organization, known as a parent organization.

Universiades—Also identified as *Games*, the name designated for multisport competition involving only athletes attending or recently graduated from a university.

World Anti-Doping Agency—The independent, nonprofit global organization supported by governments and the IOC that coordinates opposition to doping in sport internationally.

World Players Association—A collective organization comprised of associations or unions for professional players.

CHAPTER 7

collective bargaining agreement—An employment contract between a league and its players or officials. The CBA is negotiated by the league and the players association and all players play under this contract. It includes work rules, benefits, and health and safety provisions.

corporation—A legal entity, such as a company, that is authorized to act as a single entity. The company must be incorporated under the laws of the state of incorporation before it can use the term.

franchise—Another name for a team competing within a North American professional sports league responsible for producing games to satisfy the needs and interests of consumers for sport entertainment.

franchise agreement—The agreement between a team and a professional league that sets out the duties of both sides.

individual performer sport—A sport such as tennis or golf where athletes compete solely as independent persons representing themselves.

individual performer team sport—A sport such as motorsports or cycling where athletes compete individually while also having teammates.

limited liability corporation—A corporation in which the members (stockholders) of the company are not personally liable for the corporation's debts or liabilities.

promotion and relegation—A system in European association football whereby the champions of a league are promoted to a higher level and the teams with the worst record step down to a lower-tier league.

unincorporated association—A legal entity created by a group of unrelated businesses, called members.

CHAPTER 8

amateur sport—A sport where participants do not receive compensation.

annual general meeting—A meeting of the general members of a corporation where the members hear information about the corporation and vote on current issues. The annual general meeting should be held each year, but in some cases it can be held every 18 months.

Canada Not-for-profit Corporations Act—The law governing the formation of not-for-profit companies in Canada.

club sports—The term used in the United States to signify that an interscholastic or intercollegiate sport is not sponsored by the university. It is used in the United Kingdom to differentiate between intercollegiate athletics and elite performance athletics.

Companies Act 2006—The law governing the formation of companies in the United Kingdom.

cost of attendance stipends—Monetary awards added to the maximum amount of scholarship money a college student-athlete could receive to cover the full cost of attendance.

county—The designation used in England for a political division that forms the largest unit of local government.

intercollegiate athletics—Sport competition staged between institutions of higher education.

interscholastic sports—Athletic competition staged between schools at the secondary level.

intramural sports—Athletic competition staged among students in the same school or school district.

performance sports—A classification of sport in the United Kingdom generally reserved for international-level athletes who wish to train and earn a college degree.

Power 5—The coalition of institutions in the five most influential conferences in the NCAA Football Bowl Subdivision.

powers of the corporation—Powers granted to a corporation through legislative statute and through the articles of association.

province—The designation used for subnational governments in Canada. It is a political division similar to a state in the United States.

U Sports—The multisport service organization in Canada for institutions supporting intercollegiate athletics.

varsity sports—The term used in the United States to signify that an interscholastic or intercollegiate sport is competed at the highest level and that the sport is sponsored by the school or university.

youth sports—Informal and formal athletics for children up until graduation from high school or secondary school.

CHAPTER 9

blackout rule—A former Federal Communications Commission (FCC) mandate prohibiting a live sporting event from being broadcast in the local market if attendance fell below a certain threshold.

broadcast rights—The right of a media entity (or entities) to broadcast a sporting event. The rights can be an exclusive partnership with a sole media entity, a tiered or separated series of subpackages that are shared among several media partners, or a system where national media rights are sold separately from local media rights.

carriage fees—Associated payments for connectivity rights to content that is considered proprietary for each cable or satellite network.

designated market areas (DMAs)—The geographic areas in which the FCC permits people to receive the same (or similar) media coverage regardless of the outlet (e.g., television, newspaper, or Internet).

digital media outlet—A relatively new form of media distribution channel that includes Internet and mobile devices.

Digital Millennium Copyright Act—Legislation requiring the removal of copyrighted material belonging to the rightful owner.

duopoly rule—A former FCC regulation restricting individuals and companies from owning more than one broadcast station.

Federal Communications Commission (FCC)—The independent agency with supreme authority for regulating media ownership, policies, and practices.

media outlet—The distribution channel for dissemination of news, stories, or images to an audience.

media training—The coaching of potential interview subjects to deal with media inquiries and to stay within organization messaging when conversing with the media.

net neutrality—The concept that all data should be treated equally on the Internet by Internet service providers (ISPs).

regional sports networks—A network of exclusive sport programming designated by a geographic territory defined by its market size.

social media—The digital and electronic communication platforms or applications enabling the creation of communities or social networks.

Sports Broadcasting Act—The 1961 federal government code amendment that allowed professional sport franchises within their respective sports leagues to pool their broadcast inventories.

supernational entities—Organizations or international groups headquartered in a particular country but having power and influence that transcend national or continental borders.

Telecommunications Act of 1996—Legislation that relaxed the FCC regulations on media ownership and stimulated deregulation of the communications industry.

traditional media outlet—Distribution channels for media that have been entrenched over time, including print, analog television, satellite television, cable television, radio, and film.

CHAPTER 10

audit—An assessment or inspection, preferably by an independent party, of standards for a process, report system (e.g., budget), department, or organization.

Better Business Bureau—A nonprofit, nongovernmental organization in the United States that monitors unethical business practices and provides information to develop trust between businesses and consumers.

cease and desist—A formal request, which may be supported by government action, demanding an identified activity to stop. Activities such as replicating a protected trademark without authorization or paying a rights fee may be met with cease and desist requests.

codes of conduct—A document outlining social norms of expected behavior within an organization or industry sector.

copyright—Legal protection for original works of authorship, typically for items such as books and other written works, music, photographs, paintings, drawings, films, dances, and a number of other materials.

Copyright Act of 1976—A federal law protecting owners of original work from having their work reproduced, derived, distributed, or publicly displayed without the consent and authorization of the original author of the work.

corporate social responsibility—An organization's obligation in maintaining a socially moral image within its community in respect to environmental, safety, health, and public welfare concerns.

disclaimer—A statement to delimit, specify, or shift a scope of responsibility or obligations for actions or intentions.

doctrine of expressive use—A defense for counterfeiting or intellectual property infringement that considers the alteration of a trademark such as adding words or phrases to accompany the registered mark in a creative source, such as a book.

Federal Trade Commission (FTC)—An independent agency of the U.S. government that regulates deceptive or unethical business practices.

intellectual property—The rights associated with patents, copyrights, trademarks, and trade secrets.

Lanham Act—Officially known as the Federal Trademark Act of 1946, it is the primary federal law governing the use of trademarks.

licensing—The action of one person or company contractually granting another person or company the right to use their intellectual property.

licensing partnership—An agreement between two parties for one entity to be able to use the intellectual property of another in exchange for compensation or something of value to the owner.

National Operating Committee on Standards for Athletic Equipment—A nonprofit, nongovernment organization established in 1970 that provides U.S. safety standards and certification for sports equipment.

patent—Legal protection granted by the United States Patent and Trademark Office to inventors to prevent others from using their invention for a period of time.

royalty—The fee paid to the owner of intellectual property based on the percentage of sales generated by the licensor.

self-regulation—A business, organization, or industry's use of internal processes and systems, independent of government or external influences, to ensure compliance with a minimum threshold of standards.

sports properties—A term designating ownership of intellectual property as it pertains to a sport entity such as a team, league, facility, organization, or event.

trademark—Any word, name, symbol, or device, or any combination thereof, adopted or used by a manufacturer or merchant to identify its goods and distinguish them from those manufactured or sold by others.

trademark infringement—The use, or misuse, of a trademark without the expressed consent or authorization of the rights holder.

CHAPTER 11

athletic club—A private fitness club usually located in an urban area that provides members with opportunities to exercise and to play intramural and extramural sports.

Centers for Disease Control and Prevention (CDC)—The federal agency concerned with promoting public health, especially by conducting research and providing the public with information and programs supporting healthy living.

country club—A private fitness club usually located in a suburban or exurban area that provides members with a limited range of exercise and recreation opportunities, especially golf.

dietary supplement—Products taken by mouth that contain a dietary ingredient such as vitamins, minerals, amino acids, and herbs or botanicals.

Dietary Supplement Health and Education Act—Federal law regulating the production and sale of nutritional supplements.

federation model—A system of governance in which autonomous entities (often called *chapters* or simply *member organizations*) are organized under a central governing body.

fitness instructor—A fitness provider who typically teaches classes in a variety of activities, such as indoor cycling, yoga, dance, or aerobics.

franchise business model—System in which a central organization (franchiser) licenses rights to the franchiser's brand and operational procedures to a separate business entity (franchisee) in exchange for a fee.

membership organization—An organization that derives its revenue from people who pay a flat fee (usually referred to as *dues*) to belong to the organization and obtain the benefits it offers.

National Institutes of Health (NIH)—An umbrella agency in the U.S. Public Health Service consisting of 27 specialized institutes that conduct and fund medical and public health research.

nonprofit organization—A business entity that exists to support or advance a particular social cause. Nonprofit organizations are exempt from paying income taxes and, unlike for-profit organizations, spend their surplus revenues on operational expenses.

personal trainer—A fitness provider who typically works with clients individually to develop an exercise regimen and pursue the client's fitness goals.

President's Council on Sports, Fitness & Nutrition—A government agency under the Department of Health and Human Services dedicated to promoting physical activity and sports participation for young people.

research grant—A competitive financial award given to researchers to gather data, conduct experiments, develop technology, and test solutions to problems.

U.S. Department of Agriculture (USDA)—The government agency with primary responsibility for governing farming, food safety, and nutrition.

U.S. Department of Health and Human Services (HHS)—The government agency with primary responsibility for managing public health in the United States.

voluntary sport clubs—Social organizations that were formed around sport and other recreational activities in the 19th century.

World Health Organization—A United Nations agency responsible for international public health governance, including the collection of health data, establishing standards and best practices, and providing support to national governments.

CHAPTER 12

agency—A group of industry experts serving as intermediaries between their client and a business function. Agencies are paid to represent the best interests of a company, brand, or athlete and are held accountable for the results of the task for which they have been hired.

ambush by association—Creating confusion in public perception of linkages between brands and events or property.

ambush by intrusion—Deliberate acts of capitalizing on exposure opportunities with an event or property.

ambush marketing—The process by which an entity tries to steal equity from a person or organization's intellectual property without authorization or payment of fees for the purpose of creating buzz and awareness of their own brand or person.

bid—The comprehensive application that showcases how a city will plan, produce, and execute an event using various resources.

clean zone—Area in and around an event and its subsidiary activity locations where unauthorized advertising is prohibited.

contest—A game or competition requiring skill or a task where a winner is determined by judges, scoring, or other method.

corrective advertising—The practice of disseminating accurate messages to replace erroneous consumer beliefs.

endorsement—The act of publicly approving a person, place, product, service, or organization.

exclusivity—Sponsorships only to be sold to one company in set categories, effectively eliminating its competition.

marketing—The process by which companies engage customers through authentic relationships in order to provide value to the customer while capturing value from the customer in return.

sports commissions—Organizations that act at a local, regional, or state level to attract, create, produce, and manage sports events in communities.

sport marketing—A managerial process by which sport executives and their organizations build profitable relationships by providing products or services that satisfy a customer's or client's needs.

sportscape—The extended environment within and around the event facility that assists in selling an entertainment experience rather than just a game ticket and transforming an intangible event into a tangible product.

sweepstakes—A game of chance whereby winners are selected at random.

CHAPTER 13

bookmaker—The entity that accepts wagers (synonymous with *bookie*).

certiorari—An order issued by an appellate court directing a lower court to deliver a case for review by the appellate court.

Global Lottery Monitoring System (GLMS)—An international surveillance organization that detects irregularities in the sport gaming industry.

injunction—A judicial order prohibiting an individual from engaging in actions that would invade or violate the legal rights of another.

integrity fees—A fee requested by professional sport leagues to assist in providing better monitoring of the integrity of the game due to legal sports betting becoming more widespread in the United States.

lottery—A form of wagering or betting that involves drawing a lot with the chance of winning a prize.

Macolin Convention—The European Convention on the Manipulation of Sports Competitions, representing a legal framework that can be applied by individual countries to regulate sport wagering.

match fixing—Competition manipulation.

parlay betting—A type of bet whereby to win, a person must succeed in a series of interconnected wagers, such as correctly identifying the winner and also whether the final game score is over or under a predicted number.

raceino—A horse racing facility that is combined with a casino.

single-game betting—Wagering that involves a money line, point spread, or over–under score wager on one competition.

sportsbook—The sports entity that accepts wagers.

Sports Bribery Act of 1964—The law making it illegal in the United States to conspire to intentionally influence the outcome of a sport contest (18 U.S.C. § 224).

Sports Wagering Market Integrity Act of 2018—A proposed bill to grant district courts the power to create an independent national sport wagering clearinghouse in the United States and to levy civil action against individuals who wager on sports in states that had not yet opted to legalize sport betting.

state agency—The entity responsible for regulating sport wagering activities in a state, such as the Nevada Gaming Commission.

Tenth Amendment—The amendment to the United States Constitution that relegates powers to the state level that are not asserted at the federal level.

turf clubs—The term used in the 1950s and 1960s to describe independent legal bookmaker operations, many of which later appeared in Las Vegas casinos.

Wire Act of 1961—The law making it illegal in the United States for those engaged in betting or wagering to knowingly use a wire communication facility for the transmission in interstate or foreign commerce of bets or wagers or to share information for the purpose of placing bets (18 U.S.C. §1084).

CHAPTER 14

competitive integrity—The ethical conduct and behavior expected when competing.

Digital Republic Bill—A law passed in France in 2016 that redefined esports outside of the scope of a lottery scheme, banned players 12 and under from participating in competitions that included prize money, and placed limits on professional player contracts.

dispute resolution—The process for resolving a grievance between two or more parties.

e-doping—The use of performance enhancement substances while playing electronic games.

esports—Electronic gaming.

first-person shooters—A genre of video games that are designed to allow players to view the action through the eyes of the character and that often involve shooting enemies and other targets.

intellectual property rights—The ownership of property, typically through patents, copyrights, or trademarks.

Netrek—The first system that allowed multiple video game players to connect personal computers.

publicity rights—The protectable property interest of an individual's name, identity, or persona (likeness).

real-time strategy game—A genre of video games often having an aerial view of the gameplay map where players try to secure resources and destroy opponents' assets.

Sportradar's Fraud Detection System—A complex virtual system that tracks odd changes and liquidity across markets to detect irregular betting patterns in real time.

Twin Galaxies—A system that permitted the posting of verifiable individual player game scores.

References

Chapter 1

Allen, K. (2018, February 16). Wondering why NHL players are not at the 2018 Winter Olympics? Here's why. *USA Today*. Retrieved from www.usatoday.com/story/sports/winter-olympics-2018/2018/02/16/wondering-why-nhl-players-not-2018-winter-olympics-heres-why/344314002

Association of Tennis Professionals Tour. (2018). *The 2018 Official ATP Rule Book*. VIII. The code. Onsite medical examinations.

Berg, A. (2019, March). Unvaccinated student sues over basketball ban. *Athletic Business*. Retrieved from www.athleticbusiness.com/safety-security/unvaccinated-student-sues-over-basketball-ban.html?eid=616217836bid=2398282

Brown, M. (2015, February 23). Who's winning the MLB salary arbitration game? Here's data from 1974 to 2015. *Forbes*. Retrieved from www.forbes.com/sites/maurybrown/2015/02/23/whos-winning-the-mlb-salary-arbitration-game-heres-data-from-1974-to-2015/2/#3b482cf0391c

Bucher, T. (2011). Inside the huddle: Analyzing the mediation efforts in the NFL's Brady settlement and its effectiveness for future professional sports disputes. *Marquette University Sports Law Review, 22*(1), 211-234.

Butler, N. (2018, May 3). IOC to appeal CAS decision to overturn sanctions against 28 Russian athletes. *Inside the Games*. Retrieved from www.insidethegames.biz/articles/1064656/ioc-to-appeal-cas-decision-to-overturn-sanctions-against-28-russian-athletes

Civil Rights Act of 1964 § 7, 42 U.S.C. § 2000e et seq. (1964).

Cohen, J. (2015, March 27). MLS's CBA negotiations: Federal mediation, salary cap and steps toward free agency. *Law in Sports*. Retrieved from www.lawinsport.com/topics/articles/item/major-league-soccer-s-collective-bargaining-negotiations-federal-mediation-salary-cap-and-steps-toward-free-agency

Cohen v. Brown University, 809 F.Supp. 978 (D.R.I. 1992).

Cohen v. Brown University, 101 F.3d 155 (1st Cir. 1996).

Commonwealth Games Federation. (2018). Constitutional documents of the Commonwealth Games Federation. Retrieved from https://thecgf.com/sites/default/files/2018-03/constitution.pdf

Cooper, S. (2019, March 19). How 9 college coaches made millions in FBI fraud case headlined by Felicity Huffman, Lori Loughlin. Retrieved from https://sports.yahoo.com/here-is-what-all-of-the-coaches-charged-in-the-college-bribery-scandal-are-accused-of-193710803.html

Doran, E. (2019, March 25). CNY students, parents say school sports physicals biased against girls, inadequate. *Central New York News*. Retrieved from www.syracuse.com/news/2019/03/cny-students-parents-say-school-sports-physicals-biased-against-girls-inadequate.html?__vfz=rtw_top_pages%3D6366100017234

Elliott, H. (1995, September 30). NHL stars will compete in 1998 Winter Olympics. *The Los Angeles Times*. Retrieved from http://articles.latimes.com/1995-09-30/sports/sp-51793_1_nhl-players

Etchells, M. (2019, March 21). International Teqball Federation announces commitment to maintaining mixed gender status. Retrieved from www.insidethegames.biz/articles/1077063/international-teqball-federation-announces-commitment-to-maintaining-mixed-gender-status

Farzin, L. (2015, January 1). On the antitrust exemption for professional sports in the United States and Europe. *Jeffrey S. Moorad Sports Law Journal, 22*(1), 75-108.

Federal Baseball Club v. National League, 259 U.S. 200 (1922).

Fischer, J., & Wertheim, L. (2019, June 4). Shadow of doubts: Could a rogue FBI agent derail the NCAA corruption probe? *Sports Illustrated, 128*(12), 15-18.

Fitzpatrick, J. (2018, June 12). Your guide to understanding salary arbitration. *Thought Co*. Retrieved from www.thoughtco.com/nhl-salary-arbitration-explained-2778981

Flood v. Kuhn, 407 U.S. 258 (1972).

Gorkin, R. (2014). Sports-league player restraints, section 1 of the Sherman Act, and federal labor law in the context of the National Football League. *Harvard University Law School Journal of Sports and Entertainment Law, 5*, 2-90.

Hobson, W. (2019, March 9). U.S. women's soccer players file suit citing gender bias. *The Washington Post*, A-18.

International Olympic Committee. (1985). *Olympic Charter 1985*. Lausanne, Switzerland: Author.

International Olympic Committee. (1991). *Olympic Charter 1991*. Lausanne, Switzerland: Author.

International Olympic Committee. (1998). Ice hockey men. Retrieved from www.olympic.org/nagano-1998/ice-hockey/ice-hockey-men

International Tennis Federation. (2018). *Memorandum, articles of association, and bylaws of ITF Limited trading as the International Tennis Federation*. The Constitution of the ITF Limited.

Lam, E. (2014). The roles of governance in sports organizations. *Journal of Power, Politics & Governance, 2*(2), 1931.

Longman, J. (2018, June 19). Caster Semenya will challenge testosterone rule in court. *The New York Times.* Retrieved from https://www.nytimes.com/2018/06/18/sports/caster-semenya-iaaf-lawsuit.html

Marquette University Law School. (2014). 2014 annual survey: Recent developments in sports law. *Marquette Sport Law Review, 25*(2), 617-659.

Mejia, Z. (2017, March 27). The Supreme Court says the iconic American cheerleading uniform design is protected by copyright law. *Quartz Media.* Retrieved from https://qz.com/939637/the-supreme-court-ruled-that-varsity-brands-cheerleading-uniform-designs-are-protected-by-copyright-law/

Morgan, L. (2019, June 4). Semenya given huge boost as Federal Supreme Court of Switzerland suspends IAAF regulations. *Inside the Games.* Retrieved from www.insidethegames.biz/articles/1080083/semenya-given-huge-boost-as-federal-supreme-court-of-switzerland-suspends-iaaf-regulations

National Collegiate Athletic Association. (2009). Constitution and bylaws. NCAA.org. www.ncaa.org.

National Football League. (2006, Rev). Constitution and bylaws effective February 1, 1970. Retrieved May 15, 2018 from www.nfl.com/static/content/public/static/html/careers/pdf/co_.pdf

National Hockey League. (2014, February 7). NHL players in 2010, 2006, 2002, 1998 Olympics. Retrieved from www.nhl.com/news/nhl-players-in-2010-2006-2002-1998-olympics/c-704710

O'Brien, R. (2019, March 6). Ex-adidas executive gets 9-month sentence in basketball bribery case. *The Wall Street Journal*, online, 1, accession 135101764.

Owen, D. (2019, March 1). Women's World Cup winners to get $4 million prize money. Retrieved from www.insidethegames.biz/articles/1077064/womens-world-cup-winners-to-get-4-million-prize-money

Paul, R., Weiss, L., Rifkind, S., Wharton, J., Garrison, L., Nobel, M., & Pollack, M. (2018, May 18). Murphy v. NCAA: Supreme Court permits states to legalize sports gambling based on the anticommandeering doctrine. Client referendum. Paul, Weiss, Rifkind, Wharton, & Garrison, LLC. Authors.

Reilly, L. (2012). Introduction to the Court of Arbitration for Sport (CAS) & the role of national courts in international sports disputes. *Journal of Dispute Resolution, 1,* 63.

Rodenberg, R. (2018, July 11). State by state sport betting tracker. *ESPN.* Retrieved from www.espn.com/chalk/story/_/id/19740480/gambling-sports-betting-bill-tracker-all-50-states

Rosen, D. (2017, April 3). NHL will not participate in 2018 Olympics. National Hockey League. Retrieved from www.nhl.com/news/nhl-will-not-participate-in-2018-winter-olympics/c-288385598

Sandu, C. (2015, April). ADR in sport disputes: Should mediation be used over arbitration? *Conflict Studies Quarterly, 11,* 57-68.

Santa Fe ISD v. Doe, 530 U.S. 290 (2000).

Sawer, P., & Subar, R. (2017, July 3). Venus Williams changes bright pink bra mid-match after breaching Wimbledon's 'all white' rule. *The Telegraph.* Retrieved from www.telegraph.co.uk/news/2017/07/03/venus-williams-shocking-pink-bra-courts-controversy-wimbledon/

Schad, T. (2018, February 23). Gary Bettman doesn't believe NHL players will go to 2022 Beijing Games. *USA Today.* Retrieved from www.olympic.org/nagano-1998/ice-hockey/ice-hockey-men

Schnell, L. (2017, September 17). Scandal finally, correctly, finishes Rick Pitino at Louisville, but his legacy is set. *USA Today.* Retrieved from https://www.usatoday.com/story/sports/ncaab/columnist/2017/09/27/rick-pitino-louisville-legacy-great-coach-too-many-scandals/709384001/

Scott, J. (2019, March). Wrestling ref readies suit following dreadlocks controversy. Retrieved from www.athleticbusiness.com/high-school/wrestling-ref-readies-suit-following-dreadlocks-controversy.html

Sherman Act. (1890). 15 U.S.C. §§ 1-7.

Silverwood, E. (2013, March 15). Dick Woodson's revenge. The evolution of salary arbitration in Major League Baseball. *Pepperdine Law Review, 1,* 21-38.

Steinbach, P. (2019, March). Six coaches plead not guilty in admissions scandal. *Athletic Business.* Retrieved from www.athleticbusiness.com/law-policy/six-coaches-plead-not-guilty-in-admissions-scandal.html?eid=616217838&bid=2404023

Thomas, R. (1985, March 1). Olympics to allow pros in 3 sports. *The New York Times.* Retrieved from www.nytimes.com/1985/03/01/sports/olympics-to-allow-pros-in-3-sports.html

Title IX of the Educational Amendments of 1972. (1972). 20 U.S.C. §§ 1681.

Toolson v. New York Yankees, 346 U.S. 356 (1953).

USOC, USA Hockey statements on NHL decision not to participate in 2018 Olympics. (2017, April 3). United States Olympic Committee. Retrieved from www.teamusa.org/News/2017/April/03/USOC-USA-Hockey-Statements-On-NHL-Decision-Not-To-Participate-In-2018-Olympics

Wharton, D. (2019, March 17). Uncertainty chases after star South African runner; Does Caster Semenya have an unfair advantage? *Los Angeles Times*, A-1.

Wimbledon.com. (2018). Clothing and equipment. Retrieved from www.wimbledon.com/en_GB/about-wimbledon/clothing_and_equipment.html

Winter, T., Williams, P., Ainsley, J., & Schapiro, R. (2019, March 12). Lori Loughlin, Felicity Huffman among 50 charged in college admissions scheme. *NBC News.* Retrieved from www.nbcnews.com/news/us-news/feds-uncover-massive-college-entrance-exam-cheating-plot-n982136

Zoeller, A. (2016, April 1). Singh v. PGA Tour: A David vs Goliath battle. *Jeffrey S. Moorad Sports Law Journal, 23*(1), 337-362.

Chapter 2

About FIFA. (2016, October 13.). Our strategy. FIFA.com. Retrieved from www.fifa.com/about-fifa/who-we-are/explore-fifa.html?intcmp=fifacom_hp_module_corporate

Amateur status. (2018, August 1). *2018-19 NCAA Division I Manual.*

Associated Press. (2019). Marketing group fined $1 million in corruption case. APnews.com. Retrieved from www.apnews.com/d661f2e-b09e24724a444601682035e48

Associations. (n.d.). Fédération Internationale de Football Association. FIFA.com. Retrieved from www.fifa.com/associations/index.html

Avolio, B., Walumbwa, F., & Weber, T. (2009). Leadership: Current theories, research, and future directions. *Annual Review of Psychology, 60,* 421-449.

Baskin, J., Voss, J., & Meyer, W. (2018, September 5). DOJ and FBI take a closer look into collegiate athletics: Necessary policies and compliance safeguards in a pay-to-play culture. *The Anti-Corruption Report.* Acuris Company.

Bass, B., & Avolio, B. (1990). *Transformational leadership development: Manual for the Multifactor Leadership Questionnaire.* Palo Alto, CA: Consulting Psychologists Press.

Bowling Green cuts four men's sports: Athletics facing $3.6 million deficit. (2002, May 22). *The Beacon Journal.* Retrieved from www.ohio.com/mld/ohio/sports/2912282.htm

Bowling Green State University. (2002, March 21). Comments from Paul Krebs. BGSU Athletic Website News Archives. Retrieved from http://bgsufalcons.ocsn.com/genrel/032102aab.html

Brown, M.E., & Trevino, L.K. (2006). Ethical leadership: A review and future directions. *The Leadership Quarterly, 17*(6), 595–561.

Burns, J.M. (1978). *Leadership.* New York: Harper & Row.

Burton, L.J., Peachey, J.W., & Wells, J.E. (2017). The role of servant leadership in developing an ethical climate in sport organizations. *Journal of Sport Management, 31*(3), 229-240.

Byington, A. (2017, June 30). Saban cited among 22 minor rules violations Alabama self-reported to NCAA. *Montgomery Advertiser.* Retrieved from www.montgomeryadvertiser.com/story/sports/college/alabama/2017/07/01/alabama-reports-22-minor-ncaa-violations-nine-which-involve-football-program/445154001/

Cacciola, S. (2016, July 22). NBA moves all-star game in protest over bathroom bill. *The New York Times,* pp. A1-A3.

Caci, N. (2016, July 31). Olympic badminton rules shift for Rio after cheating scandal in 2012. *Sports Illustrated.* Retrieved from www.si.com/olympics/2016/07/31/olympic-badminton-preview-rio-2016

Chelladurai, P. (1978). A contingency model of leadership in athletics. Unpublished doctoral dissertation, Department of Management Sciences, University of Waterloo, Waterloo, ON, Canada.

Chelladurai, P. (1984). Discrepancy between preferences and perceptions of leadership behavior and satisfaction of athletes in varying sports. *Journal of Sport Psychology, 6,* 27-41.

Connor, T., & Stelloh, T. (2018, January 28). Larry Nassar scandal: MSU athletic Director Mark Hollis resigns. *NBC News.* Retrieved from www.nbcnews.com/news/us-news/larry-nassar-scandal-msu-athletic-director-mark-hollis-resigns-n841391

Diamond, J. (2019, March 16). More than 50 women suing United States Olympic Committee over Nassar abuse. Retrieved from www.insidethegames.biz/articles/1076864/more-than-50-women-suing-united-states-olympic-committee-over-nassar-abuse

Doherty, A. (1997, July 1). The effect of leader characteristics on the perceived transformational/transactional leadership and impact of interuniversity athletic administrators. *Journal of Sport Management, 11*(3), 275-286.

Gayle, D. (2015, May 27). US indicts FIFA officials with 'rampant, systemic and deep-rooted' corruption. *The Guardian.* Retrieved from www.theguardian.com/football/2015/may/27/us-indicts-fifa-officials-rampant-systemic-deep-rooted-corruption

Gillen, N. (2019, January 10). Twenty-eight professional tennis players arrested by Spanish police for match-fixing. *Inside the Games.* Retrieved from www.insidethegames.biz/articles/1074047/twenty-eight-professional-tennis-players-arrested-by-spanish-police-for-alleged-match-fixing

Goleman, D. (1998, December). What makes a leader? *Harvard Business Review,* 93-102.

Goleman, D. (2000, March-April). Leadership that gets results. *Harvard Business Review,* 79-90.

Greenleaf, R. (1977). *Servant leadership: A journey into the nature of legitimate power and greatness.* New York: Paulist Press.

Hobson, W., & Clarke, L. (2018, November 5). USOC seeks to revoke USA Gymnastics' status as sport's national governing body. *The Washington Post.* Retrieved from https://www.washingtonpost.com/sports/olympics/usoc-seeks-to-revoke-usa-gymnastics-status-as-sports-national-governing-body/2018/11/05/82fe07c0-e14a-11e8-b759-3d88a5ce9e19_story.html

Ichniowski, C., & Preston, A. (2017, October). Does March Madness lead to irrational exuberance in the NBA draft? High-value employee selection decisions and decision-making bias. *Journal of Economic Behavior and Organization, 142,* 105-119.

Lewin, K., Lippit, R., & White, R. (1939). Patterns of aggressive behavior in experimentally created social climates. *Journal of Social Psychology, 10,* 271-301.

Mangels, J. (2012, May 27). NFL could face thousands of lawsuits from ex-players over brain damage from concussions. *Cleveland Plain Dealer*. Available at www.cleveland.com/science/index.ssf/2012/05/thousands_of_ex-player_lawsuit.html

Manning, L. (2012, May). NCAA athletic directors' self-perspective of transformational / transactional leadership. Doctoral dissertation. East Carolina University. Department of Educational Leadership.

MacKay, D. (2019, March 23). All roads lead to Senegal in IOC corruption scandals. *Inside the Games*. Retrieved from https://www.insidethegames.biz/articles/1077149/duncan-mackay-all-roads-lead-to-senegal-in-ioc-corruption-scandals

Maylon, E., & Slater, M. (2017, March 31). FIFA hand over 20,000 pages of evidence to authorities after two-year corruption investigation. *The New York Times*. Retrieved from www.independent.co.uk/sport/football/international/fifa-corruption-investigation-hand-over-evidence-sepp-blatter-michel-platini-a7659761.html

Mission and Values. (n.d.). National Football League. Retrieved from www.nfl.com/careers/values

Morgan, L. (2019a, January 11). Japanese Olympic Committee president indicted on corruption charges in France. *Inside the Games*. Retrieved from www.insidethegames.biz/articles/1074077/japanese-olympic-committee-president-indicted-on-corruption-charges-in-france

Morgan, L. (2019b, March 4). Liam Morgan: Exemplary governance standards a pipe dream for some international federations amid recent scandals. Retrieved from www.insidethegames.biz/articles/1076375/liam-morgan-exemplary-governance-standards-a-pipe-dream-for-some-international-federations-amid-recent-scandals

National Collegiate Athletic Association. (2017, October 13).

National Collegiate Athletic Association. (2018, November 9). Brigham Young University public infractions decision. Retrieved from https://ncaaorg.s3.amazonaws.com/enforcement/infractions/decisions/Nov2018INF_BYUPublicInfractionsDecision.pdf

Nocera, J., Novy-Williams, E., & McDonald, M. (December 13, 2017 corrected December 15, 2017 4:26 PM EST). College basketball made Louisville, then broke it. *Bloomberg News*. Retrieved from www.bloomberg.com/news/features/2017-12-13/college-basketball-made-louisville-then-broke-it

O'Kane, P. (2019 June 8). Afghanistan Football Federation President banned for life after being found guilty of sexually abusing female footballers. *Inside the Games*. Retrieved from https://www.insidethegames.biz/articles/1080315/afghanistan-football-federation-president-banned-for-life-after-being-found-guilty-of-sexually-abusing-female-footballers

Panja, T. (2018, July 13). For FIFA executives, World Cup perks survive a scandal. *The New York Times*, p. 167, B-19.

Planet Fitness. (2016, October 19). Code of Ethics.

Scott, D. (2014). *Contemporary leadership in sport organizations*. Champaign, IL: Human Kinetics.

Sheu, V. (2016, September 1). Corrupt passions: An analysis of the FIFA indictments. *Texas Review of Sport Entertainment and Law, 18*(1), 65-84.

Shevchenko, O., Ponkin, I., & Ponkin, A. (2016). Limits of interventions and immunities of international sports. Case study of FIFA issue in 2015. *International Sports Law Review, 11*, 3-14, 336-344.

Takos, N., Murray, D., & O'Boyle, I. (2018). Authentic leadership in non-profit sport organization boards. *Journal of Sport Management, 32*, 109-122.

University of North Carolina at Chapel Hill public infractions decision. (2017). National Collegiate Athletic Association. Retrieved from http://www.ncaa.org/sites/default/files/Oct2017_University-of-North-Carolina-at-Chapel-Hill_InfractionsDecision_20171013.pdf

Who We Are. (n.d.). Dick's Sporting Goods. Retrieved from www.dickssportinggoods.jobs/about-us

Chapter 3

Actions for good governance in international sport organisations. Play the game. (2013, April). Danish Institute for Sports Studies. Copenhagen, Denmark.

A pledge to implement good governance in European Sport. (n.d.). Annex 6. Retrieved from https://www.ido-dance.com/ceis/ido/rules/idoStatues/A-PLEDGE-TO-IMPLEMENT-GOOD-GOVERNANCE-IN-EUROPEAN-SPORT.pdf

Association of Governing Boards for Universities and Colleges. (2015). AGB board of directors' statement on the fiduciary duties of governing board members. Reports and Statements. Retrieved from https://agb.org/reports-and-statements/agb-board-of-directors-statement-on-the-fiduciary-duties-of-governing-board-members/

Association of Governing Boards for Universities and Colleges. (2018). Governing board responsibilities for intercollegiate athletics. Retrieved from https://agb.org/reports-and-statements/agb-board-of-directors-statement-on-governing-boards-responsibilities-for-intercollegiate-athletics/

Athitakis, M. (2014). Should board members be paid? American Society of Association Executives. Retrieved from https://www.asaecenter.org/resources/articles/an_magazine/2014/january-february/should-board-members-be-paid

Blackman, S. (2018, January 25). Open letter to the USA Gymnastics Board of Directors. Colorado Springs, CO: United States Olympic Committee. Retrieved from https://usagym.org/PDFs/Home/usoc_012518.pdf

Board of Governors. (2019). National Collegiate Athletic Association. Retrieved from http://web1.ncaa.org/committees/committees_roster.jsp?CommitteeName=EXEC

Burton, L., Peachy, J., & Wells, J. (2017). The role of servant leadership in developing an ethical climate in sport organizations. *Journal of Sport Management, 31*, 229-240.

Chavez, N., & Sutton, J. (2018, October 19). Former USA Gymnastics president arrested on charge of evidence tampering in Larry Nassar case. *CNN*. Retrieved from www.cnn.com/2018/10/18/us/usa-gymnastics-former-president-steve-penny-arrest/index.html

City of San Diego. (2018). San Diego Park and Recreation Board bylaws. Retrieved from https://www.sandiego.gov/sites/default/files/prbbylaws.pdf

Concussion data and research. (n.d.). National Collegiate Athletic Association. Retrieved from www.ncaa.org/sport-science-institute/topics/concussion-data-and-research

Concussion protocol safety checklist template. (n.d.). National Collegiate Athletic Association. Retrieved from www.ncaa.org/sport-science-institute/topics/concussion-safety-protocol-template

Cook, J. (1999, August). Writing standard operating procedures and guidelines. *Fire Engineering, 152*(8), 107-112.

Council of Europe. (2016). Developing gender equality indicators in sports. Vilnius, Lithuania: European Institute for Gender Equity. Retrieved from https://rm.coe.int/168064b436

Epstein, M., & McFarland, W. (2011, March). Non-profit vs. for-profit boards: Critical differences. *Strategic Finance*, 28-35.

European Commission. (2011, January 18). Developing the European dimension in sport. Brussels. Communication from the Commission to the European Parliament, the Council, the European Economic and Social Committee, and Committee of the Regions.

European Institute for Gender Equality. (2015). Gender equality in power and decision-making: Report – Review of the implementation of the Beijing platform for action in the EU member states. Retrieved from https://eige.europa.eu/publications/gender-equality-power-and-decision-making-report

Executive Board. (n.d.). World Archery. Retrieved from https://worldarchery.org/Executive_Board

Flickinger, T. (n.d.). So you want to serve on the park district board? What does that mean? Brochure. Illinois Park District.

Geeraert, A. (2018). Sports governance observer 2018. An assessment of good governance in five international sports federations. Aarhus: Play the Game/Danish Institute for Sports Studies.

Hirshland, S. (2018, November 5). Open letter to the gymnastics community in the United States. USOC statement regarding action to revoke USA Gymnastics' recognition as member National Governing Body. Colorado Springs, CO: United States Olympic Committee. Retrieved from https://www.teamusa.org/News/2018/November/05/USOC-Statement-Revoke-USA-Gymnastics-Recognition-As-Member-National-Governing-Body

Hobson, W., & Clarke, L. (2018, November 6). USOC seeks to decertify USA Gymnastics as sports national governing body. *The Washington Post*.

Ivanova, I. (2018, October 1). Nearly 100 California companies have no women on their board of directors. *CBS Money Watch*. Retrieved from www.cbsnews.com/news/nearly-100-california-companies-have-no-women-on-board-of-directors/

Lapchick, R., Davidson, E., Grant, C., & Quirarte, R. (2016, August 3). Gender report card. International Sports Report Card on Women in Leadership Role. Orlando, FL: The Institute of Diversity and Ethics in Sport.

Louisville, ex-AD settle dismissal. (2018, May 19). *The Florida Times-Union*, p. C-9.

Macur, J. (2018, December 6). USA Gymnastics files for bankruptcy. *The New York Times*, p. B-10.

Morgan, L. (2018, November 25). Exclusive: Sheikh Ahmad set to step aside as ANOC president before election after Bach plea. *Inside the Games*. Retrieved from www.insidethegames.biz/articles/1072663/exclusive-sheikh-ahmad-set-to-step-aside-as-anoc-president-before-election-after-bach-plea

Morgan, L. (2019a, January 11). Japanese Olympic Committee president indicted on corruption charges in France. *Inside the Games*. Retrieved from www.insidethegames.biz/articles/1074077/japanese-olympic-committee-president-indicted-on-corruption-charges-in-france

Morgan, L. (2019b, March 4). Liam Morgan: Exemplary governance standards a pipe dream for some international federations amid recent scandals. Retrieved from www.insidethegames.biz/articles/1076375/liam-morgan-exemplary-governance-standards-a-pipe-dream-for-some-international-federations-amid-recent-scandals

NCAA Concussion Lawsuit. (n.d.). Raizner Slania LLC. Retrieved from www.raiznerlaw.com/ncaa-class-action-lawsuit-concussions/

New South Wales Government. (n.d.). Boards and committees. Role of the board. Office of Sport. Retrieved from https://sport.nsw.gov.au/clubs/ryc/governance/boards

Park, A. (2018, October 29). 'Enough is enough.' It's time to decertify USA Gymnastics or start all over again, gymnasts say. *Time Magazine*. Retrieved from http://time.com/5431333/usa-gymnastics-decertify-aly-raisman

Pavitt, M. (2019, January 5). Group of Olympians calls for near complete resignation of USOC board. *The Guardian*. Retrieved from www.insidethegames.biz/articles/1073877/group-of-olympians-call-for-near-complete-resignation-of-usoc-board

Payment of coaches and athletic trainers under federal law. (2016). [White paper.] The College and University Professional Association of Human Resources and the National Collegiate Athletic Association. Retrieved from https://www.ncaa.org/sites/default/files/AWFIN_White-Paper-Exempt-Status-of-Coaches-and-Trainers_20160520.pdf

Remuneration. (n.d.). Amer Sports. Retrieved from www.amersports.com/investors/governance/remuneration/

Rodriguez, M. (2018, December 11). What you need to know about Justin Johnson eligibility case. *Buffalo News*. Retrieved from https://buffalonews.com/2018/12/11/west-seneca-west-basketball-juston-johnson-eligibility-case-information-news-2018/

Shade, M. (2012, July 19). Ex-Penn State board chair becomes first trustee to quit after scandal.

Shields, T. (2017, December 22). Lake Zurich school district will pay out $399k in football hazing lawsuit. *Pioneer Press Newspapers*. Chicago.

Sport New Zealand. (2016). Governance in the New Zealand sport and recreation sector. Retrieved from https://sportnz.org.nz/assets/Uploads/SportNZ-GovernanceDocument.pdf

Steinbach, P. (2019, April). USC announces student-athlete admission protocol. *Athletic Business*. Retrieved from www.athleticbusiness.com/college/usc-announces-new-student-athlete-admissions-protocol.html?eid=616217836bid=2429770

Stewart, E. (2018, October 3). California just passed a law requiring more women on boards. It matters, even if it fails. Retrieved from www.vox.com/2018/10/3/17924014/california-women-corporate-boards-jerry-brown

Student-athlete concussion injury litigation. (n.d.). National Collegiate Athletic Association. Retrieved from www.ncaa.org/sport-science-institute/topics/student-athlete-concussion-injury-litigation

Thomasson, E. (2014, March 4). Adidas extends CEO contract as starts succession plan. *Business News*. Retrieved from www.reuters.com/article/us-adidas-ceo-contract/adidas-extends-ceo-contract-as-starts-succession-plan-idUSBREA2313720140304?feedType=RSS

United States Olympic Committee. (2014, October). NGB board member guidelines. Proposal by National Governing Body and Athlete's Advisory Council Working Group.

United States Olympic Committee. (2017, March 9). Section 8.1. Board Authority. United States Olympic Committee Bylaws. Retrieved from https://www.teamusa.org/Footer/Legal/Governance-Documents.aspx

USA Swimming. (2019). *Rulebook*. Retrieved from https://www.usaswimming.org/docs/default-source/rules-regulations/2019-rulebook.pdf

Valigra, L. (2018, December 18). Maine colleges pull sportswear from shelves over supplier's alleged ties to slave labor. *Bangor Daily News*. Accession number 2W63088779743.

Washington Township Parks and Recreation. (2014, January). Sport advisory board. Bylaws. Retrieved from https://www.twp.washington.nj.us/SAB%20bylaws.pdf

Wilson, R. (2011). *Managing sport finance*. New York: Routledge.

Wolohan, J., & Gau, F. (2018, November/December). School board found negligent in coaches abuse. *Athletic Business*, p. 22-24.

Xaio, H. (2018, July 24). Testimony of Han Xaio, chair of the USOC athlete advisory committee, before the U.S. Senate Commerce Committee subcommittee on consumer protection, product safety, insurance, and data security. Russell Senate Office Building Room 253. Retrieved from https://insurancenews-net.com/oarticle/senate-commerce-subcommittee-issues-testimony-from-athletes-advisory-council#.XZP8SOhKjyQ

Chapter 4

About us: Administration and board of directors. (n.d.). Haywood Area Recreation and Park District. Retrieved from www.haywardrec.org/138/Administration-Board-of-Directors

Babe Ruth League. (2018). *Presidents Handbook*.

Barlow, K. (2019, March 29). Normal based Special Olympics Illinois relieved funding cut short lived. *The (Bloomington, Illinois) Pantagraph*. Accession number 2W61929212654.

Barr, R., Bennett, R., & Bettoncourt, W. (2014, November). Investment activity report. L.A. Fitness.

Barrett, A., Pitas, N., & Mowen, A. (2017). First in our hearts, but not in our pocketbooks: Trends in local government financing for parks and recreation 2004-2014. *Journal of Parks and Recreation, 35*(3), 1-19.

Berg, A. (2019, February). Alabama lawmaker poses student-athlete eligibility bill. *Athletic Business*. Retrieved from www.athleticbusiness.com/law-policy/alabama-lawmaker-poses-student-athlete-eligibility-bill.html?eid=616217836bid=2361269

Burney, M. (2019, March 19). Referee in Buena wrestler dreadlocks controversy alleges 'emotional distress' and character defamation. Retrieved from www.philly.com/news/new-jersey/andrew-johnson-wrestler-hair-dreadlocks-cut-buena-new-jersey-civil-rights-probes-20190319.html

By the numbers. (n.d.). Cleveland Metroparks. Retrieved from www.clevelandmetroparks.com/about/cleveland-metroparks-organization/by-the-numbers

By the numbers. (2018). Event Report. 2018 NCAA Women's final four. Greater Columbus Sports Commission. Retrieved from https://assets.simpleviewinc.com/simpleview/image/upload/v1/clients/columbus/WFF_Event_Report_Digital_370ce71b-6926-4da3-9006-16acfbdc3474.pdf

Club Managers Association of America. (2015). Club management: Path to a rewarding future. Alexandria, Virginia.

Cuskelly, G., McIntyre, M., & Boag, A. (1998). A longitudinal study of the development of organizational commitment amongst volunteer sport administrators. *Journal of Sport Management, 12*(3), 181-202.

Diedrich, C. (2007). Homefield economics. The public financing of stadiums. *Policy Matters, 4*(2), 22-27.

Dietz, J. (2018, June). 2018 background check procedures memo: Pop Warner Little Scholars.

Divisional breakdowns 2018-19 school year. (2018). Football. Ohio High School Athletic Association. Retrieved from https://ohsaa.org/School-Resources/Divisional-Breakdowns-2018-19-School-Year

Education Law. (n.d.). High school athletic associations. Retrieved from https://usedulaw.com/332-high-school-athletic-associations.html

Events. (n.d.). Maine Sports Commission. Retrieved from http://mainesportscommission.com/events

Fawver, B., & Spengler, J. (2014, March). Funding for youth sport: Learning from the past and aligning resources for the future. The Aspen Institute Project Play. [Research brief.] University of Florida Sport Policy and Research Collaborative.

Find Special Olympics Near You. (n.d.). Special Olympics. Retrieved from https://staging.specialolympics.org/north-america/

Fortney, L. (2018, February 3). Lake Erie Crushers owners defend booking decisions. *The Chronicle.* Retrieved from www.chroniclet.com/Local-News/2018/02/03/Lake-Erie-Crushers-owners-defend-booking-decisions.html

Georgia Games. (n.d.). Retrieved from http://georgiagames.org/About%20Us.html

High school athletics participation survey. (2018). National Federation of State High School Associations. Retrieved from https://members.nfhs.org/participation_statistics

History of Pop Warner Little Scholars, Inc. (2019). Pop Warner Little Scholars. Retrieved from https://tshq.bluesombrero.com/Default.aspx?tabid=1579750

History of the Babe Ruth Program. (2019). Babe Ruth League. Retrieved from www.baberuthleague.org/about-babe-ruth-league.aspx

Hull, D. (2014). Governance models for sport across the UK and Ireland. Research and information service research paper, Northern Ireland Assembly. In Jaekel, T. (2017). Modern sports for all policy: An international comparison of policy goals and models of service delivery. [Working paper.] National Research University Higher School of Economics.

Hwang, J. (2010). Does sport really matter to volunteers? Implications from an empirical comparison between sport volunteers and non-sport volunteers. Florida State University. Dissertation. Retrieved from https://fsu.digital.flvc.org/islandora/object/fsu%3A181685

Jaekel, T. (2017). Modern sports for all policy: An international comparison of policy goals and models of service delivery. Working paper. National Research University Higher School of Economics. Retrieved from https://ideas.repec.org/p/hig/wpaper/04-psp-2017.html

Karter, T. (1959, May). The development of organized recreation in the United States. *Social Security Bulletin* 8-15.

Los Angeles Sports and Entertainment Commission. (n.d.). About Lasec. Retrieved from http://lasec.net/about-lasec

Marketing opportunities. (n.d.). National Federation of High School Athletic Associations. Retrieved from https://www.nfhs.org/marketing-and-media/marketing

Member roster. (n.d.). National Association of Sports Commissions. Retrieved from www.sportscommissions.org/membership/member-roster

Minzner, E. (2010, October 8). Youth sport in community development. Tufts University. Unpublished master's thesis. Retrieved from https://search.proquest.com/openview/5369593ea8def7208ffdfa3149792694/1?pq-origsite=gscholar&cbl=18750&diss=y

National Association of Sports Commissions. (2017, April). Sport tourism. State of the industry report. In collaboration with Ohio University.

National Congress of State Games. (n.d.). About. Retrieved from www.stategames.org/about

National Parks and Recreation Association. (n.d.). Leadership and governance. Retrieved from https://www.nrpa.org/About-National-Recreation-and-Park-Association/leadership/

Niehoff, K. (2018, October 22). NFHS wrestling rules interpretations. 2018-19. National Federation of High School Associations. Retrieved from https://www.nfhs.org/sports-resource-content/wrestling-rules-interpretations-2018-19/

Official Pop Warner rules. (2019). Pop Warner Little Scholars. Retrieved from https://tshq.bluesombrero.com/Default.aspx?tabid=1579496

O'Malley, A. (2018, July 23). Nearly 7 billion raised through China's sports lottery during 2018 World Cup. Retrieved from www.vegasslotsonline.com/news/2018/07/23/nearly-7bn-raised-through-chinas-sports-lottery-during-world-cup/

Ortiz, E. (2019, November 10). N.J. wrestler forced to cut dreadlocks still targeted over hair, lawyer says. NBC News. Retrieved from https://www.nbcnews.com/news/nbcblk/n-j-wrestler-forced-cut-dreadlocks-still-targeted-over-hair-n957116

Pitas, N., Barrett, A., & Mowen, A. (2017). Trends in local park and recreation department finances and staffing in the early twenty-first century. *Journal of Park and Recreation Administration, 35*(2), 20-34.

Positions and policy statements. (n.d.). Little League. Playing Rules. Retrieved from www.littleleague.org/playing-rules/position-policy-statements/

Program staff: City of Oberlin. (n.d.). City of Oberlin Recreation Department. Retrieved from www.cityofoberlin.com/city-government/departments/recreation/contact-recreation-department/staff/

Queen, J. (2013). Pop Warner to launch in county. *The Dispatch*. Retrieved from www.the-dispatch.com/sports/20130418/pop-warner-to-launch-league-in-county

Rappa, J. (2011, September 9). Sport commissions and other similar entities. Office of Legislative Research. Retrieved from www.cga.ct.gov/2011/rpt/2011-R-0305.htm

Ray and Joan Kroc Community Centers. (n.d.) Retrieved from www.kroccenter.org

Rogers, V. (2016, July 18). 20th anniversary of the Atlanta Games. Retrieved from www.news.gatech.edu/features/20th-anniversary-atlanta-games

Rules and regulations. (n.d.). California State Games. Retrieved from www.calstategames.org/rules

Rules, regulations, and policies. (n.d.). Little League. Resources for parents. Retrieved from www.little-league.org/playing-rules/rules-regulations-policies/

Seefelt, V., Ewing, M., & Walk, S. (1993). Overview of youth sports programs in the United States. Youth Sports Institute, Michigan State University, East Lansing, Michigan 48823. Paper commissioned for Carnegie Council on Adolescent Development for its Task Force on Youth Development and Community Programs.

Shapiro, T. (2016, March 3). Lake Erie Crushers under new ownership. *The Chronicle*. Retrieved from www.chroniclet.com/lake-erie-crushers/2016/03/03/Lake-Erie-Crushers-under-new-ownership.html

Special Olympics Florida. (2019). Special Olympics Florida staff. Retrieved from https://specialolympicsflorida.org/who-we-are/staff/

Special Olympics Ohio. (2019). Contact us. Retrieved from https://sooh.org/contact-us/

Spengler, J., & Baber, O. (2015). Where's the money? Research on innovation in financing of sport and recreation spaces. The Aspen Project. Project Play. Retrieved from www.nrpa.org/uploadedFiles/nrpaorg/Professional_Development/Innovation_Labs/Wheres%20The%20Money%20Pres.pdf

Stanmyer, M. (2019, January 9). Attempt to clarify wrestling dreadlock-covering rules foiled by contradictions. New Jersey High School Sports. Retrieved from http://highschoolsports.nj.com/news/article/5605258339317335022/clarification-and-alleged-contradictions-fuel-wrestling-hair-rule-debate/

Stern, M. (2011). Real or rogue charity? Private health clubs vs the YMCA: 1970-2010. *Business and Economic History, 9*, 1-16.

Stradbrooke, S. (2019, January 25). China's 2018 lottery sales up one-fifth on sports lottery strength. Business. Retrieved from https://calvinayre.com/2019/01/25/business/chinas-lottery-sales-rise-one-fifth-2018-sports-lottery-strength/

2017 Reach Report. (2017). Special Olympics. Retrieved from https://soar.brightspotcdn.com/c8/3f/6a2961e044508191ac0ed828c141/2017-special-olympics-reach-report-four-pager.pdf

U.S. Census Bureau. (2012). Local governments in individual county areas 2012. Retrieved from https://factfinder.census.gov/faces/tableservices/jsf/pages/productview.xhtml?src=CF

U.S. Volunteer Protection Act. (1997). Pub. L. No. 105-19. Codified at 42 U.S.C. §§ 14501.

Walls, M. (2009, June). Parks and recreation in the United States. Local park systems.

Wann, H., & Kelley, J. (2007, January 8). Interscholastic athletics in Ohio. *Members Only* [information brief for members of the Ohio General Assembly], *127*(1).

Welcome to the finest fitness club in Cleveland, Ohio. (n.d.). The Union Club. Retrieved from www.theunionclub.org/Fitness-Center

Wells, J., & Ellsworth, G. (2016, October). The quiet ascension of LA Fitness (No. 9-717-424). Boston, MA: Harvard Business School Publishing, 1-19.

Wilson, C. (2017, August 25). Members, staff of bankrupt VI fitness centres won't get any money. *Times* [Victoria, British Columbia]. Business, p. B-1.

Wintergreen Research. (2017). Youth, team, league, and tournament sports. Market shares, strategies, and forecasts, worldwide: 2017-2023. Retrieved from www.wintergreenresearch.com/youth-sports

Wisconsin Interscholastic Athletic Association (WIAA). (n.d.). About WIAA - WIAA history. Retrieved from https://www.wiaawi.org/About-WIAA

Young, E. (2014, May 30). 24 hour fitness sold to private equity, pension fund investors. *San Francisco Business Times*. Retrieved from https://www.bizjournals.com/sanfrancisco/news/2014/05/30/24-hour-fitness-sold-to-private-equity-pension.html

Chapter 5

About Armed Forces Sports. (n.d.). *U.S. Department of Defense*. Retrieved from https://armedforcessports.defense.gov/About.aspx

About EFDA. (n.d.). European Flying Disc Association. Retrieved from www.efdf.org/about/what-is-the-efdf

About INASGOC. (2018). Indonesia Asian Games Organizing Committee. Asian Games 2018. Retrieved from https://asiangames2018.id/about/inasgoc

About the ACC. (n.d.). Asian Cricket Council. Retrieved from www.asiancricket.org/index.php/the-acc/47

About USA Basketball. (n.d.). USA Basketball. Retrieved from www.usab.com/about/about-usa-basketball.aspx

About US Lacrosse. (n.d.). US Lacrosse. Retrieved from www.uslacrosse.org/about-us-lacrosse

ACCUS. (n.d.). Automobile Competition Committee for the United States. Retrieved from www.accusfia.us

The American Heritage dictionary of the English language. (2016). Boston, MA: Houghton Mifflin Harcourt Publishing.

Asian Cricket Council. (2016). Annual report & accounts. Retrieved from www.asiancricket.org/downloads/2016/Annual%20Report%202016%20Web%20use.pdf

Aydin, U. (2009). *Player associations in the professional sports sector and the situation in Turkey.* Poster Presented at the 15th World Congress. International Labor and Employment Relations Committee.

Bernardi, V. (2015, August 3). International Olympic Committee grants full recognition to disc sports. Professional Disc Golf Association. Retrieved from www.pdga.com/international-olympic-committee-grants-full-recognition-disc-sports

Birren, G. (2014). A brief history of sports labor stoppages: The issues, the labor stoppages and their effectiveness (or lack thereof). *DePaul Journal of Sport Law and Contemporary Problems, 10*(1), 1-30.

Bonesteel, M. (2014, November 5). In e-mails, NCAA admitted it bluffed Penn State into accepting Jerry Sandusky sanctions. *The Washington Post.* Retrieved from www.washingtonpost.com/news/early-lead/wp/2014/11/05/in-e-mails-ncaa-admitted-it-bluffed-penn-state-into-accepting-jerry-sandusky-sanctions/?noredirect=on&utm_term=.b2800f4be5a1

Business Structure. (n.d.). United States Obstacle Course Racing. Retrieved from https://usaocr.org/organization

Chelladurai, P., & Zintz, T. (2015). Functions of national sport governing bodies: A network perspective. *Public Policy and Administration, 14*(4), 529-544.

The company. (n.d.). College football playoff governance. Retrieved from https://collegefootballplayoff.com/sports/2016/10/11/_131504729614425311.aspx

Constitution of USA Basketball. (2017). USA Basketball. Retrieved from www.usab.com/about/about-usa-basketball/constitution.aspx

Cottrell, S. (2018, March 2). Sports Law Bar Association of Ireland - Tim O'Connor and Robert McTernaghan - Episode 61. [Video file]. Retrieved from www.lawinsport.com/topics/features/podcast/item/sports-law-bar-association-of-ireland-tim-o-connor-and-robert-mcternaghan-episode-61

Dabscheck, B. (2003). Paying for professionalism: Industrial relations in Australian rugby union. *Sport Management Review, 6,* 105-125.

Disciplines. (n.d.). USA Functional Fitness Federation. Retrieved from https://usafunctionalfitness.org

Fagan, R. (2018, February 5). Baseball strikes and lockouts: A history of MLB work stoppages. *Sporting News.* Retrieved from https://www.sportingnews.com/us/mlb/news/mlb-free-agents-labor-dispute-history-1994-1981-strike-1990-lockout-marvin-miller-mlbpa/lhl6crvxn0ya1xrc5n9m915xf

FIL members. (n.d.). Federation of International Lacrosse. Retrieved from https://filacrosse.com/fil-members

The formation of the ACC. (n.d.). Asian Cricket Council. Retrieved from www.asiancricket.org/report0607/images/020a.jpg

Gaines, C., & Nudelman, M. (2017, November 17). The NHL is on pace to have more American players than Canadian players in 11 years. *Business Insider.* Retrieved from www.businessinsider.com/nhl-american-canadian-players-2028-2017-11

Garner, B., ed. (1999). *Black's Law Dictionary* (7th ed). St. Paul, MN: West Group.

George is Hulman & Co. board chairman. (2016, July 25). *Performance Racing Industry.* Retrieved from www.performanceracing.com/news/george-hulman-co-board-chairman

History of the NSGA. (n.d.). About. Retrieved from http://nsga.com/about

International Olympic Committee. (1968). *Model constitution for a National Olympic Committee.* Lausanne, Switzerland: IOC.

International Olympic Committee. (2017a). *Olympic Charter 2017.* Lausanne, Switzerland: Author.

International Olympic Committee. (2017b). *Olympic Solidarity Plan 2017-2020.* Lausanne, Switzerland: Author.

Ishigami, H. (2016). Relative age and birthplace effect in Japanese professional sports: A quantitative evaluation using a Bayesian hierarchical Poisson model. *Journal of Sport Science, 34*(2), 143-154.

Jagodic, T., & Matesa, Z. (2017, February). The autonomy of the national Olympic Committee and the relation with different legal subjects and athletes. *Collected Papers of the Faculty of Law, Zagreb School of Economics and Management, 54,* 373-396.

Keiper, M., Young, S., Fried, G., & Seidler, T. (2014). The legal aspects of obstacle racing. *Journal of Legal Aspects in Sport, 24,* 78-94.

Li, M., MacIntosh, E., & Bravo, G. (2012). *International sport management.* Champaign, IL: Human Kinetics.

Luschen, G. (1979). Organization and policies of National Olympic Committee — Problems of methodology, access and the results of a pilot study. *International Review for the Sociology of Sport, 14*(2), 5-31.

Morgan, L. (2017, October 4). Southeast Asian Games gold medallist from Malaysia fails drugs test as diving coach arrested following rape claim. *Inside the Games.* Retrieved from www.insidethegames.biz/articles/1056138/southeast-asian-games-gold-medallist-from-malaysia-fails-drugs-test-as-diving-coach-arrested-following-rape-claim

Multi-sport organizations. (n.d.). United States Olympic Committee. Retrieved from www.teamusa.org/about-the-usoc/in-the-community/partner-programs/multi-sport-organizations

National Basketball Association and National Basketball Association Players Association. (2017). Collective bargaining agreement. Retrieved from https://cosmic-s3.imgix.net/3c7a0a50-8e11-11e9-875d-3d44e94ae33f-2017-NBA-NBPA-Collective-Bargaining-Agreement.pdf

National Labor Relations Act, 29 U.S.C. §§ 151-169 (2012).

National Ski and Snowboarders Retailers Association. (n.d.). History. Retrieved from www.nssra.com/history

National Small College Rugby Organization. (n.d.). Governance. Retrieved from www.nscro.org/governance

NCAA decision on Penn State: All wins gone 1998-2011, $60 million fine. (2012, July 23). *Penn Live*. Retrieved from www.pennlive.com/midstate/index.ssf/2012/07/ncaa_decision_on_penn_state.html

NIRSA Championship Series 2018-19 year in review. (2019). National Intramural and Recreational Sports Association. [Video]. Retrieved from www.youtube.com/watch?v=arqsVys-jYo

Olympic Council of Asia. (n.d.). South East Asia Games. Retrieved from www.ocasia.org/Game/GamesL1.aspx?SYCXGjC0df+J2ChZBk5tvA==

Our Disciplines. (n.d.). World Obstacle Course Racing. Retrieved from https://worldocr.org/ocr-disciplines

Pickel, J. (2015, July 23). Penn State football sanctioned by NCAA over Sandusky: Then and now. *Penn Live*. Retrieved from www.pennlive.com/sports/index.ssf/2015/07/penn_state_football_sanctioned.html

Pockrass, B., & Rovell, D. (2018, May 10). France family exploring potential sale of NASCAR. *ESPN*. Retrieved from www.espn.com/auto/story/_/id/23435578/france-family-exploring-sale-nascar

Pogroszewski, A., & Smoker, K. (2011). Cross-checking: An overview of international tax issues for professional hockey players. *Marquette Sports Law Review, 22*(1), 187-209.

Rapp, G. (2015, October). Institutional control and corporate governance. *Brigham Young University Law Review, 4*(6), 984-1049.

Recognized federations. (n.d.). Sports governed by international federations recognized by the International Olympic Committee. Retrieved from www.olympic.org/recognised-federations.

Somphong, S., Samahito, S., & Kutintara, I. (2015) Corporate governance on the National Olympic Committee of Thailand. *Open Journal of Social Sciences, 3*, 124-133.

Southeast Asian Games Federation. (n.d.). *SEAGF Office*. Retrieved from www.seagfoffice.org/contact.php

Sport Associations of Thailand. (n.d.). Sport Authority of Thailand. Retrieved from www5.sat.or.th/th/sport-for-excellence/sport-association-of-thailand.aspx?lang=en

Sport Authority of Thailand. (2017). Participant list. 2017 international certification in sport management program.

Sugar Bowl organizational and financial information. (n.d.). Retrieved from https://allstatesugarbowl.org/allstate-sugar-bowl/about-us/

Ted Stevens Olympic and Amateur Sports Act, 36 U.S.C. §§ 220501 - 220543 (2012).

United States Internal Revenue Service. (2016). Department of Treasury. Form 990 for the United States Olympic Committee.

United States Olympic & Paralympic Committee. (2019). National governing bodies. Retrieved from www.teamusa.org/About-the-USOPC/Structure

USA Pentathlon. (2019). Subsports. Obstacle course. Retrieved from www.teamusa.org/usa-modern-pentathlon/sub-sports/obstacle-course-racing

US Lacrosse. (2016). Amended and restated by-laws of US Lacrosse, Inc. Retrieved from www.uslacrosse.org/sites/default/files/public/documents/about-us-lacrosse/us-lacrosse-bylaws.pdf

What is the NCAA? (n.d.). NCAA.org. Retrieved from http://www.ncaa.org/about/resources/media-center/ncaa-101/what-ncaa

Wickstrom, M., & Alvad, S. (2017, June). *Autonomy in National Olympic Committees: An autonomy index*. Copenhagen, Denmark: Play the Game (Danish Institute for Sport Studies). Retrieved from https://playthegame.org/knowledge-bank/downloads/autonomy-in-national-olympic-committees-2017-/e3cb0290-dadf-4ed0-940b-a78b00b46398

The World's Best Obstacle Races. (2019). Spartan Race. Retrieved from www.spartan.com/en/the-race

XVII Mediterranean Games. (2018). Tarragona 2018. Retrieved from www.tarragona2018.cat/en/que-son/

Chapter 6

Associated Press. (2018, February 16). World anti-doping agency suspends Romanian laboratory. *Sports News*. Montreal.

Association of IOC Recognized International Sport Federations. (n.d.). About. Retrieved from www.arisf.org/who-we-are.aspx

Association of National Olympic Committees. (2013, June). *Constitution of the Association of National Olympic Committees*.

Association of National Olympic Committees. (2016, November 16). *Constitution of the Association of National Olympic Committees*. Adopted at the General Assembly in Doha, Qatar.

Association of National Olympic Committees. (2018). About ANOC: Organization - structure. Retrieved from www.anocolympic.org/structure/

Association of National Olympic Committees. (2019). ANOC commissions and working groups 2019. Retrieved from https://www.anocolympic.org/downloads/list-anoc-commissions-and-working-groups-2019-engl.pdf

Axon, R. (2018, February 8). 2018 Winter Olympics: Court dismisses appeals of 45 Russians excluded from competition. *USA Today*. Retrieved from www.usatoday.com/story/sports/winter-olympics-

2018/2018/02/08/2018-winter-olympics-court-dismisses-appeals-45-russians-excluded-competition/322278002

Bliznevskiy, A., Porteous, B., Kvale, H., Briznevskaya, V., Nemec, M., Ermakov, S., & Kudryavtsev, N. (2017). Comparative analysis of new sport types—potential candidates for inclusion in the Winter Olympic games. *Journal of Physical Education and Sport, 16*(4), 1334-1339.

Butler, N. (2018, April 15). Stand-Up Paddle dispute continuing after ICF and ISA refuse to compromise. *Inside the Games.* Retrieved from https://www.insidethegames.biz/articles/1063968/stand-up-paddle-dispute-continuing-after-icf-and-isa-refuse-to-compromise

Casini, L. (2009). Global hybrid public-private bodies: The World Anti-Doping Agency (WADA). *International Organizations Law Review, 6,* 421-446.

Chappelet, J., & Kubler-Mabbott, B. (2008). *The International Olympic Committee and the Olympic system.* New York: Routledge, Taylor & Francis Group.

Chengelis, A. (2017). Our players not sweating new clothes code; recently approved do's and don'ts go into effect this week. *The Detroit News,* p. C1.

Commonwealth Games Federation. (2018a). Constitutional documents of the Commonwealth Games Federation. Retrieved from https://thecgf.com/sites/default/files/2018-03/constitution.pdf

Commonwealth Games Federation. (2018b). Executive committee. Retrieved from https://thecgf.com/about/executive-board

Commonwealth Games Federation. (2018c). Management team. Retrieved from https://thecgf.com/about/management-team

Court of Arbitration for Sport. (n.d.). Origins. Retrieved from www.tas-cas.org/en/general-information/history-of-the-cas.html

Court of Arbitration for Sport. (2016). CAS statistics 1986-2016. Retrieved from www.tas-cas.org/fileadmin/user_upload/CAS_statistics_2016_.pdf

Drake, J. (2018, February 22). Russia pays $15 million doping fine to Olympic committee to lift suspension. *Bloomberg News; Moscow Times.* Retrieved from https://themoscowtimes.com/news/russia-pays-15-million-doping-fine-to-olympic-committee-lift-suspension-60595

Etchells, D. (2017, July 6). FIBA Americas appoints new executive director. *Inside the Games.* Retrieved from www.insidethegames.biz/articles/1052381/fiba-americas-appoints-new-executive-director

Executive Board Members. (2019, September 20). Tokyo 2020. Retrieved from https://tokyo2020.org/en/organising-committee/structure/officer

Fédération Internationale de Basketball. (2017). *FIBA internal regulations - governing the zones - book 5.* Mies, Switzerland: Author.

Fédération Internationale de Football Association. (n.d.). FIFA Associations. Retrieved from www.fifa.com/associations/index.html

Fédération Internationale de Natation (FINA). (2017a, June 7). Bhutan Swimming Federation joins FINA as 208th National Member Federation. *Federation News.* Retrieved from www.fina.org/news/bhutan-swimming-federation-joins-fina-208th-national-member-federation

Fédération Internationale de Natation (FINA). (2017b, July 22). *FINA constitution.* Retrieved from https://www.fina.org/sites/default/files/1._fina_constitution_approved_by_the_fina_congress_on_22.07.2017_final.pdf

Federation of International Cricket Associations. (n.d.). Members and affiliations. Retrieved from www.thefica.com/

Forster, D. (2006). Global sports organizations and their governance. *Corporate Governance, 6*(1), 72-83.

Games of the XXI Olympiad, Montreal 1976: Official Report, v.1. (1978). Retrieved from https://digital.la84.org/digital/collection/p17103coll8/id/28455

Garner, B., ed. (1999). *Black's Law Dictionary* (7th ed). St. Paul, MN: West Group.

Global Association of International Sport Federations. (n.d.). Members. Retrieved from https://gaisf.org/members/#

Global Association of International Sport Federations. (2017, April 7). Statutes. Retrieved from https://gaisf.sport/wp-content/uploads/gaisf-statutes-2019-eng.pdf

Gold, J., & Gold, M. (2007). Access to all: Rise of the Paralympic Games. *The Journal of The Royal Society for the Promotion of Health, 127*(3), 133-141.

Handstad, D., Smith, A., & Waddington, I. (2008). Establishment of the World Anti-Doping Agency. A study of the management of organizational change and unplanned outcomes. *International Review for the Sociology of Sport, 43*(3), 227-249.

International Association of Fair Play. (n.d.). Mission. Retrieved from www.fairplayinternational.org/mission-1

International Olympic Committee. (2016). IOC annual report 2016. Credibility, sustainability, and youth. Retrieved from https://stillmed.olympic.org/media/Document%20Library/OlympicOrg/Documents/IOC-Annual-Report/IOC-Annual-Report-2016.pdf

International Olympic Committee. (2017, September 15). *Olympic charter.* Retrieved from https://stillmed.olympic.org/media/Document%20Library/OlympicOrg/General/EN-Olympic-Charter.pdf

International Olympic Committee. (2018). Organizing Committee for the Olympic Games. Main tasks. Retrieved from www.olympic.org/ioc-governance-organising-committees

International Paralympic Committee. (2015, January). IPC handbook. Bylaws, governance and organizational structure. Retrieved from https://www.paralympic.org/ipc-handbook

International Paralympic Committee. (2016a). Annual report 2016. Retrieved from https://www.paralympic.org/sites/default/files/document/170824082342043_IPC+Annual+Report+2016_Accessible.pdf

International Paralympic Committee. (2016b, September). International standards for eligible impairments. Retrieved from www.paralympic.org/sites/default/files/document/161007092455456_Sec+ii+chapter+1_3_2_subchapter+1_International+Standard+for+Eligible+Impairments.pdf

International Paralympic Committee. (2017, September 8). Andrew Parsons elected new IPC president. Retrieved from www.paralympic.org/news/andrew-parsons-elected-new-ipc-president

International Paralympic Committee. (2018a). The IPC – Management team. Retrieved from www.paralympic.org/the-ipc/management-team

International Paralympic Committee. (2018b). The IPC – Who we are: About us. Retrieved from www.paralympic.org/the-ipc/about-us

International Paralympic Committee. (2018c). 25-year anniversary of the IPC. Retrieved from www.paralympic.org/ipc-25-year-anniversary/history

International Rugby Players Association. (n.d.). Members. Available at http://irpa-rugby.com/

International Soccer Association. (2013). About FIFPro. Retrieved from www.fifpro.org/en/about-fifpro/about-fifpro

International University Sports Federation. (2018a). Current structure. Retrieved from www.fisu.net/about-fisu/current-structure

International University Sports Federation. (2018b). History. Retrieved from www.fisu.net/about-fisu/history

Ladies' Professional Golf Association. (n.d.). About LPGA. Retrieved from www.lpga.com/about-lpga

Li, M., MacIntosh, E., & Bravo, G. (2012). *International sport management*. Champaign, IL: Human Kinetics.

London Organizing Committee of the Olympic Games. (2012, September). Reports and accounts for the 18 month period ending September 30, 2012. Retrieved from https://stillmed.olympic.org/media/Document%20Library/OlympicOrg/Games/Summer-Games/Games-London-2012-Olympic-Games/Facts-and-Figures/LOCOG-Report-and-Accounts-for-the-18-Month-Period-Ended-30-September-2012-London-2012.pdf

Luschen, G. (1979). Organization and policies of National Olympic Committee — Problems of methodology, access and the results of a pilot study. *International Review for the Sociology of Sport, 14*(2), 5-31.

Morgan, L. (2019a, April 27). Kazakhstan official claims AIBA has gone against democracy after provisional suspension recommendation. Retrieved from www.insidethegames.biz/articles/1078491/kazakhstan-official-claims-aiba-has-gone-against-democracy-after-provisional-suspension-recommendation

Morgan, L. (2019b, May 23). IOC taskforce to oversee organisation of boxing at Tokyo 2020 after AIBA suspended. *Inside the Games*. Retrieved from www.insidethegames.biz/articles/1079552/ioc-taskforce-to-oversee-organisation-of-boxing-at-tokyo-2020-after-aiba-suspended

Morgan, L. (2019c, June 4). Semenya given huge boost as Federal Supreme Court of Switzerland suspends IAAF regulations. *Inside the Games*. Retrieved from www.insidethegames.biz/articles/1080083/semenya-given-huge-boost-as-federal-supreme-court-of-switzerland-suspends-iaaf-regulations

Murphy, M. (2019, September 29). Defending champion Caster Semenya sidelined at worlds. *Associated Press*. Retrieved from https://apnews.com/bd6559b788ee-45bfb96db168cfe426b1

Nelson, T., & Cottrell, M. (2016). Sport without referees? The power of the International Olympic Committee and the social politics of accountability. *European Journal of International Relations, 222*(2), 437-458.

Olympic News. (2017, November 8). IOC and Global Association of International Sport Federations (GAISF) sign ground-breaking MOU. Retrieved from www.olympic.org/news/ioc-and-global-association-of-international-sports-federations-gaisf-sign-ground-breaking-mou

Organization - FIBA Americas. (n.d.). Fédération Internationale de Basketball. Retrieved from www.fiba.basketball/americas/organisation

Pavitt, M. (2019, April 12). International athletes' forum to take place amid calls for improved representation and greater share of Olympic revenue. Retrieved from www.insidethegames.biz/articles/1077876/international-athletes-forum-to-take-place-amid-calls-for-improved-representation-and-greater-share-of-olympic-revenues

Rosner, S., & Low, D. (2009, September 1). The efficacy of Olympic bans and boycotts on effectuating international political and economic change. *Texas Review of Entertainment and Sports Law, 11*(1), 27-80.

Ruiz, R. (2016, April 23). Swiss city is Silicon Valley of sport. *The New York Times*, p. D1.

Special Olympics. (2017). Official general rules. Retrieved from https://media.specialolympics.org/resources/leading-a-program/general-rules/Special-Olympics-General-Rules-Amended-2015-8-17.pdf

Special Olympics. (2018a). Global leadership team. Retrieved from www.specialolympics.org/leaders.aspx?src=navwho

Special Olympics. (2018b). History. Retrieved from www.specialolympics.org/Sections/What_We_Do/History/History.aspx

Toohey, K., & Beaton, A. (2017). International cross-sector social partnerships between sport and governments: The World Anti-Doping Agency. *Sport Management Review, 20,* 483-496.

2017 reach report. (2017). Special Olympics. Retrieved from https://soar.brightspotcdn.com/c8/3f/6a2961e044508191ac0ed828c141/2017-special-olympics-reach-report-four-pager.pdf

Uni Global Union. (2019). World Players Association. Retrieved from www.uniglobalunion.org/sectors/world-players/about

Vendien, L. (2012, August 12). FISU (Fédération Internationale du Sports Universitaire) and the World University Games. *Quest, 22*(1), 74-78.

Wilson, S. (2013, September 10). Thomas Bach of Germany new IOC president; Former fencing gold medallist defeats five rival candidates to succeed Jacques Rogge. *The Toronto Star,* p. S2.

Women's Tennis Association. (2018). 2018 WTA official rulebook. Retrieved from http://wtafiles.wtatennis.com/pdf/publications/2018WTARulebook.pdf

World Amateur Footgolf Association. (n.d.). Home page. Retrieved from www.wafga.com/contact

World Anti-Doping Agency. (2009). Global anti-doping organizational chart. Retrieved from https://www.wada-ama.org/sites/default/files/resources/files/WADA_PK_Global_ADO_Chart_200901_EN.pdf

World Anti-Doping Agency. (2017). Total samples analyzed (all sports). 2017 Anti-Doping Testing Figures. Retrieved from https://www.wada-ama.org/sites/default/files/resources/files/2017_anti-doping_testing_figures_en_0.pdf

World Anti-Doping Agency. (2018a). Governance. Retrieved from www.wada-ama.org/en/governance

World Anti-Doping Agency. (2018b). Mission. Retrieved from www.wada-ama.org/en/who-we-are.

World Anti-Doping Agency. (2018c). Regional offices. Retrieved from www.wada-ama.org/en/regional-offices

World Players Association. (2017a, December 17). World Players Association launches universal declaration of player rights. Uni Global Union. [Press release].

World Players Association. (2017b). World players rights policy. Uni Global Union.

Zakkus, D., & Skinner, J. (2008, December). Modelling organizational change in the International Olympic Committee. *European Sport Management Quarterly, 8*(4), 421-442.

Chapter 7

About Major League Lacrosse. (2019, February 25). *Major League Lacrosse.* Retrieved from https://majorleaguelacrosse.com/news/2019/2/25/about-mll.aspx?path=mlax

About Major League Soccer. (2017, January 1). *MLS Soccer.* Retrieved from www.mlssoccer.com/post/2017/01/01/about-major-league-soccer

Airail, C. (2019, March 29). Too bad a WNBA president isn't in place to attend this year's NCAA Women's Basketball Tournament. Retrieved from www.swishappeal.com/2019/3/22/18272507/ncaa-womens-march-madness-wnba-president-search

Alliance of American Football. (2019). Retrieved from https://aaf.com/

Beck, H. (2012, November 30). Spurs fined $250,000 for resting 4 regulars. *The New York Times.* Retrieved from www.nytimes.com/2012/12/01/sports/basketball/nba-fines-spurs-250000-for-sending-home-four-starters-ahead-of-game-in-miami.html

Belson, K. (2017, November 8). Jerry Jones threatens to sue N.F.L. to block Roger Goodell's contract. *The New York Times.* Retrieved from www.nytimes.com/2017/11/08/sports/jerry-jones-nfl-roger-goodell-david-boies.html?_r=0

Berger, K. (2014, August 12). Sale of Clippers to Steve Ballmer closes; Donald Sterling out. *CBS Sports.* Retrieved from www.cbssports.com/nba/news/sale-of-clippers-to-steve-ballmer-closes-donald-sterling-out

Bogage, J. (2017, December 6). For the WNBA, business isn't as bad as it looks. *The Washington Post.* Retrieved from www.washingtonpost.com/news/early-lead/wp/2017/12/06/for-the-wnba-business-isnt-as-bad-as-it-looks/?noredirect=on&utm_term=.61a6b53b5943

Carlisle, J. (2019, February 14). Don Garber signs five-year deal to remain MLS commissioner. Retrieved from www.espn.com/soccer/major-league-soccer/story/3775174/don-garber-signs-new-five-year-deal-to-remain-mls-commissioner

Carvalho, M. (2010). Professional sport in Portugal: An overview of its framework law. *International Sport Law Review, 8*(3-4), 361-374.

Cavanaugh, J. (2003, January 28). Mohegan Tribe to own W.N.B.A. team in Connecticut. *The New York Times.* Retrieved from www.nytimes.com/2003/01/28/sports/pro-basketball-mohegan-tribe-to-own-wnba-team-in-connecticut.html

Charles O. Finley & Co., Inc. v. Kuhn, 569 F.2d 527 (7th Cir.), *cert. denied,* 439 U.S. 876 (1978).

Chass, M. (1990, August 1). Faced with suspension, Steinbrenner sought an alternative. *The New York Times.* Retrieved from www.nytimes.com/1990/08/01/sports/baseball-faced-with-suspension-steinbrenner-sought-an-alternative.html

Companies Act 2006, c. 46 (U.K.), www.legislation.gov.uk/ukpga/2006/46/pdfs/ukpga_20060046_en.pdf

Conrad, M. (2017). *The business of sports: A primer for journalists* (3rd ed.). New York: Routledge.

The CPA, the only association for riders recognized by the UCI. (n.d.). Cyclistes Professionnels Associés. Retrieved from www.cpacycling.com/en/Default.asp

Curtis, T. (1995). In the best interests of the game: The authority of the commissioner of Major League Baseball. *Seton Hall Journal of Sports Law, 5,* 5.

Draper, M., & Megdal, H. (2019, May 15). W.N.B.A. selects Cathy Engelbert as commissioner. *The New York Times.* Retrieved from www.nytimes.com/2019/05/15/sports/wnba-cathy-engelbert-president.html

Drivers/teams. (n.d.). Team Penske. Retrieved from www.teampenske.com/drivers

Eckstein, J. (2019, September 24). How the NFL makes money. *Investopedia.* Retrieved from https://www.investopedia.com/articles/personal-finance/062515/how-nfl-makes-money.asp

Errington, T., & Malsher, D. (2018, April 5). Vasser: IndyCar has recovered from "The Split." *Motorsport.* Retrieved from www.motorsport.com/indycar/news/vasser-indycar-has-recovered-from-the-split-1022042/1399931

Forbes releases 2018 list of most valuable teams. (2018, July 18). *Forbes.* Retrieved from www.forbes.com/sites/forbespr/2018/07/18/forbes-releases-2018-list-of-the-worlds-most-valuable-sports-teams/#3ba680c075ff

Ford, B. (2013, August 6). Selig drops the ball on A-Rod. *The Philadelphia Inquirer.* Retrieved from www.philly.com/philly/sports/phillies/20130806_Selig_drops_the_ball_on_A-Rod.html

Fraser v. Major League Soccer, LLC, 94 F. Supp. 2d 130 (D. Mass., 2000).

Fraser v. Major League Soccer, LLC, 284 F. 3d 47 (1st Cir., 2002).

Garcia, A. (2018, February 20). NBA's Adam Silver: Two decisions that have defined my tenure. *CNN Business.* Retrieved from https://money.cnn.com/2018/02/20/news/companies/adam-silver-nba-commissioner/index.html

Garner, B., ed. (1999). *Black's Law Dictionary* (7th ed). St. Paul, MN: West Group.

George is Hulman & Co. board chairman. (2016, July 25). *Performance Racing Industry.* Retrieved from www.performanceracing.com/news/george-hulman-co-board-chairman

Goldberg, R. (2017, August 11). Ezekiel Elliott suspended 6 games after domestic violence investigation. *Bleacher Report.* Retrieved from https://bleacherreport.com/articles/2720233-ezekiel-elliott-reportedly-suspended-6-games-for-domestic-violence

Golliver, B. (2012, November 30). Spurs fined $250K for resting players. *Sports Illustrated.* Retrieved from www.si.com/nba/point-forward/2012/11/30/gregg-popovich-david-stern-spurs-fined-nba

Green, B. (1968, August 20). Rebel golfers number 205. *Eugene Register-Guard.* Retrieved from https://news.google.com/newspapers?id=Y6hVAAAAIBAJ&sjid=6OADAAAAIBAJ&pg=5464%2C4294626

Harwell, D., & Hobson, W. (2015, April 28). The NFL is dropping its tax-exempt status. Why that ends up helping them out. *The Washington Post.* Retrieved from www.washingtonpost.com/news/business/wp/2015/04/28/the-nfl-is-dropping-its-tax-exempt-status-why-that-ends-up-helping-them-out/?noredirect=on&utm_term=.56819f1bff1d

History. (n.d.). Women's National Basketball League. Available at www.wnba.com/history

Hoffman, B. (2017, October 12). Ezekiel Elliott's 6-game NFL suspension reinstated by court. *The New York Times.* Retrieved from www.nytimes.com/2017/10/12/sports/football/ezekiel-elliott-suspension-nfl.html

Jane, W. (2012). Overpayment and reservation salary in the Nippon Professional Baseball League: A stochastic frontier analysis. *Journal of Sport Economics, 14*(6), 463-483.

Johnson, J. (2014, December 26). (Inter)national football leagues: American football around the globe. Retrieved from www.fromthegrapevine.com/lifestyle/international-football-leagues-american-football-around-globe

Justice, R. (2013, August 1). "Best interests of baseball" a wide-ranging power. Major League Baseball. Retrieved from https://www.mlb.com/news/richard-justice-best-interests-of-baseball-a-wide-ranging-power-of-commissioner/c-55523182

Kane, D., & Tiell, B. (2017, July). Application of normative ethics to explain Colin Kaepernick's silent protest in the NFL. *The Sport Journal.* Retrieved from https://thesportjournal.org/article/application-of-normative-ethics-to-explain-colin-kaepernicks-silent-protest-in-the-nfl/

Major League Baseball. (2005). *Major League Baseball constitution.* Retrieved from http://thesportsesquires.com/wp-content/uploads/2014/05/MLB-Constitution-2005.pdf

Maske, M. (2018, July 19). NFL puts national anthem policy on hold under agreement with NFLPA. *The Washington Post.* Retrieved from www.washingtonpost.com/news/sports/wp/2018/07/19/nfl-puts-national-anthem-policy-on-hold-under-agreement-with-nflpa/?noredirect=on&utm_term=.d090cea48041

Menzer, J. (2001). *The wildest ride: A history of NASCAR (or how a bunch of good ol' boys built a billion-dollar industry out of wrecking cars).* New York: Simon & Schuster.

Metraux, D. (1934). Baseball in Japan and the U.S.: History, culture and future prospects. *Education About Asia, 21*(2), 41-47.

Morrow, S., & Idle, C. (2008, December). Understanding change in professional road cycling. *European Sport Management Quarterly, 8*(4), 315-335.

NASCAR chairman Brian France takes leave of absence after arrest for DWI and oxycodone possession. (2018, August 6). *Chicago Tribune.* Retrieved from www.chicagotribune.com/sports/breaking/ct-spt-nascar-ceo-brian-france-arrest-20180806-story.html

National Basketball Association. (2012). *Constitution and by-laws of the National Basketball Association.* Retrieved from http://thesportsesquires.com/wp-content/uploads/2014/01/NBA-Constitution-and-By-Laws.pdf

National Football League. (2006). *Constitution and bylaws of the National Football League.* Retrieved from http://static.nfl.com/static/content//public/static/html/careers/pdf/co_.pdf

National Hockey League. (n.d.). *Constitution of the National Hockey League.* Retrieved from www.lakelawgroup.com/wp-content/uploads/2017/02/constitution-NHL-.pdf

NBA: Mark Cuban didn't pay enough attention to Mavericks' business culture. (2018, September 19). *ESPN.* Retrieved from www.espn.com/nba/story/_/id/24732020/dallas-mavericks-owner-mark-cuban-not-face-penalty-allegations-harassment-violence-organization

NFL commissioner Roger Goodell signs five-year extension. (2017, December 6). *ESPN.* Retrieved from www.espn.com/nfl/story/_/id/21691975/nfl-commissioner-roger-goodell-signs-contract-extension

Payne, E. (2014, September 16). NFL Commissioner Roger Goodell isn't a newcomer to controversy. *CNN.* Retrieved from www.cnn.com/2014/09/12/us/godell-tenure-controversy/index.html

PGA Tour. (2017). *2017-2018 Player handbook and tournament regulations.* Retrieved from https://qualifying.pgatourhq.com/static-assets/uploads/2017-18_pga_tour_handbookregs_final.pdf

Piecoro, N. (2018, August 29). Diamondbacks' deal with Shumpei Yoshikawa raises questions about signing top Japanese talent. *USA Today.* Retrieved from www.usatoday.com/story/sports/mlb/diamondbacks/2018/08/29/diamondbacks-deal-raises-questions-signing-japanese-talent/1131523002

Pingue, F. (2018, March 22). Women's soccer league gaining foothold in the U.S. *Reuters.* Retrieved from www.reuters.com/article/us-soccer-women-usa/womens-soccer-league-gaining-foothold-in-u-s-idUSKBN1GY2OE

Pockrass, B., & Rovell, D. (2018, May 10). France family exploring potential sale of NASCAR. *ESPN.* Retrieved from www.espn.com/auto/story/_/id/23435578/france-family-exploring-sale-nascar

Premier League. (2018). *Premier League handbook 2018/19.* Retrieved from www.premierleague.com/publications

Pruett, M. (2016, May 27). The oral history of The Split, the event that transformed American motorsports. *Road and Track.* Retrieved from www.roadandtrack.com/motorsports/a29328/the-oral-history-of-the-split

Reuter, J. (2017, November 10). From Raúl to ruin: The rise and fall of the NASL, once MLS's challenger. *The Guardian.* Retrieved from https://www.theguardian.com/football/blog/2017/nov/10/from-raul-to-ruin-the-rise-and-fall-of-the-nasl-once-mlss-challenger

Rodenberg, R., & Stone, D. (2011, June 1). The short and long-run labor market effects of age eligibility rules: Evidence from women's professional tennis. *Journal of Labor Research, 32*(2), 181-198.

Scottish Professional Football League. (n.d.). *Articles of association of the Scottish Professional Football League.* Retrieved from https://spfl.co.uk/admin/filemanager/images/shares/pdfs/067_324__articlesofassociationofthescottishprofessionalfootballleaguelimitedasat20july2016_1470742749.pdf

Scottish Professional Football League. (2018). *The rules and regulations of the Scottish Professional Football League.* Retrieved from https://spfl.co.uk/admin/filemanager/images/shares/pdfs/067_324__rulesofthespflasat19_january_2018_1518083042.pdf

Shreffler, M., Presley, G., & Schmidt, S. (2015, January). Getting clipped: An evaluation of crisis management and the NBA's response to the actions of Donald Sterling. Case study 5. *Case Studies in Sport Management, 4*(1), 28-37.

Sigman, S. (2005). The jurisprudence of Judge Kennesaw Mountain Landis. *Marquette Sports Law Review, 15*(2), 277-330.

Snyder, D. (2010, January 6). Automatic outs. Salary arbitration in Nippon Professional Baseball. *Marquette Sports Law Review, 20*(1), 79-93.

Spencer, L. (2017, September 3). Did the "Donuts with Daniel Suarez" segment on NBC get the Joe Gibbs Racing rookie in hot water with sponsor Subway? *Motorsports.* Retrieved from www.motorsport.com/us/nascar-cup/news/nascar-subway-terminates-suarez-sponsorship-949133/3044469/s

Stern, A. (2018, May 14). Owners to NASCAR: pick up the pace. *Sports Business Journal.* Retrieved from www.sportsbusinessdaily.com/Journal/Issues/2018/05/14/Leagues-and-Governing-Bodies/NASCAR.aspx

Teope, H. (2019, April 2). AAF suspending operations, canceling season. Retrieved from www.nfl.com/news/story/0ap3000001025120/article/aaf-suspending-operations-canceling-end-of-season

USL Franchise Agreement. (n.d.). Exhibit 10.2. Retrieved from https://www.sec.gov/Archives/edgar/data/1054311/000091205700044461/a2027504zex-10_2.txt

Wertheim, J., & Luther, J. (2018, February 20). Exclusive: Inside the corrosive workplace culture of the Dallas Mavericks. *Sports Illustrated.* Retrieved from www.si.com/nba/2018/02/20/dallas-mavericks-sexual-misconduct-investigation-mark-cuban-response

Wilner, B. (2019, February 23). How Roger Goodell and the NFL could discipline Roger Kraft. *Boston Globe*. Retrieved from www.boston.com/sports/new-england-patriots/2019/02/23/nfl-roger-goodell-patriots-robert-kraft-discipline

Windhorst, B. (2012, October 25). David Stern has date for retirement. *ESPN*. Retrieved from https://www.espn.com/nba/story/_/id/8550645/david-stern-retire-nba-commissioner-2014

Women's Tennis Association. (2018a). *2018 official rulebook*. Retrieved from http://wtafiles.wtatennis.com/pdf/publications/2018WTARulebook.pdf

Women's Tennis Association. (2018b). *2018 WTA media guide*. Retrieved from http://wtafiles.wtatennis.com/pdf/publications/2018WTAGuide_lowres.pdf

Wood, R. (2014, June 4). Donald Sterling's last laugh: Tax-free $2 billion Clippers sale. *Forbes*. Retrieved from www.woodllp.com/Publications/Articles/pdf/Donald_Sterling.pdf

Wyshynski, G. (2018, January 31). Bettman's legacy. The good, the bad, and the ugly of Gary's Bettman's 25-year NHL tenure. *ESPN*. Retrieved from https://www.espn.com/nhl/story/_/id/22273439/good-bad-ugly-gary-bettman-25-year-nhl-tenure

Zeller, B. (2004, February). CART vs. IRL: Who won the war? *Car and Driver*. Retrieved from www.caranddriver.com/features/cart-vs-irl-who-won-the-war-mario-andretti-aj-foyt-weigh-in-page-3

Zink, A. (2018). The suspensions are killing me: Why the NFL's approach to off-field conduct needs rehab. *Journal of Legal Aspects of Sport, 28,* 222-248.

Chapter 8

About NCAA Division I. (n.d.). National Collegiate Athletic Association. Retrieved from www.ncaa.org/about?division=d1

About NCAA Division II. (n.d.). National Collegiate Athletic Association. Retrieved from www.ncaa.org/about?division=d2

About NCAA Division III. (n.d.). National Collegiate Athletic Association. Retrieved from www.ncaa.org/about?division=d3

About NIRSA. (n.d.). Who we are. National Intramural and Recreational Sports Association. Retrieved from https://nirsa.net/nirsa/about/

Amateur Athletic Union. (n.d.). About the Amateur Athletic Union. Retrieved from https://aausports.org/page.php?page_id=99844

Amateur Athletic Union. (2018). *2019 AAU code book*. Retrieved from https://aausports.org/Governance-Policies/AAU-Codebook

Amick, S. (2018, July 10). Move to eliminate NBA one-and-done rule gaining momentum, commissioner Adam Silver says. *USA Today*. Retrieved from www.usatoday.com/story/sports/nba/2018/07/10/adam-silver-nba-one-and-done/773991002

Barnett, Z. (2018, May 25). Here's how much each Power 5 conference paid its members in 2017. *Football Scoop*. Retrieved from http://footballscoop.com/news/heres-much-power-5-conference-paid-members-2017/

Berkowitz, S. (2014, August 8). Judge releases ruling on O'Bannon case: NCAA loses. *USA Today*. Retrieved from www.usatoday.com/story/sports/college/2014/08/08/ed-obannon-antitrust-lawsuit-vs-ncaa/13801277

Berkowitz, S., & Schnaars, C. (2016). NCAA Finances. *USA Today*. Retrieved from http://sports.usatoday.com/ncaa/finances

BUCS. (n.d.). *British Universities & Colleges Sport*. Retrieved from www.bucs.org.uk/athlete.asp?section=18695&sectionTitle=BUCS+Regions

Bush, C. (2014, September 1). The legal shift of the NCAA's big 5 member conferences to independent athletic associations: Combining NFL and conference governance principles to maintain the unique product of the NFL. *University of Denver University Sport and Entertainment Law Journal, 5*-48.

Canada Not for Profit Corporations Act, S.C. 2009 c 23 (Can.).

Carlman, P., Wagnsson, S., & Patriksson, G. (2013). Causes and consequences of dropping out from organized youth sports. *Swedish Journal of Sport Research, 1,* 26-54.

Chalip, E. (2011). The future past of the Amateur Sports Act: Developing American sport. *Journal of Coaching Education, 4*(2), 4-29.

Companies Act 2006, c. 46 (U.K.).

Council of Presidents. (2019). National Association of Intercollegiate Athletics. (NAIA). Retrieved from https://www.naia.org/council-of-presidents/index

Creating a Club. (n.d.). Football Association. Retrieved from http://www.thefa.com/get-involved/player/clubs-leagues/fa-charter-standard-programme/creating-a-club

Divisional Structure. (2018). National Junior College Athletic Association. Retrieved from www.njcaa.org/member_colleges/Divisional_Structure Department for Culture, Media and Sport

Division differences and the history of multi-division classification. (n.d.). National Collegiate Athletic Association. Retrieved from http://www.ncaa.org/about/who-we-are/membership/divisional-differences-and-history-multidivision-classification

Early struggles not dissuading SFU from its NCAA experiment. (2017, September 2). *CBC News*. Retrieved from www.cbc.ca/news/canada/british-columbia/sfu-ncaa-2017-1.4267951

Football Association. (2018). *The FA handbook*. Retrieved from http://handbook.fapublications.com/#!/book/26 www.usyouthsoccer.org/state-associations

Givony, J. (2018, March 22). Testing the NBA draft waters? More complicated than it sounds. *ESPN.* Retrieved from www.espn.com/nba/story/_/id/22854438/testing-nba-draft-waters-more-complicated-sounds

Goodman, J. (2018, April 24). NBA's early-entry list breaks record with 236 players. *ESPN.* Retrieved from www.espn.com/nba/story/_/id/23307754/nba-official-early-entry-list-sets-new-record-236-players

Hobson, W., & Armstrong, K. (2018, October 24). All three defendants found guilty of wire fraud in college basketball corruption trial. *The Washington Post.* Retrieved from www.washingtonpost.com/sports/colleges/all-three-defendants-found-guilty-of-wire-fraud-in-college-basketball-corruption-trial/2018/10/24/fba5b866-d7be-11e8-a10f-b51546b10756_story.html?noredirect=on&utm_term=.fa9ad18bae01

Indiana Youth Soccer Association. (n.d.). Risk management suggested guidelines. Indiana Youth Soccer Association Risk Management Committee. Retrieved from https://www.soccerindiana.org/assets/58/6/riskmanagementfinal_(2).pdf

Javier, C. (2018, February 19). Among may factors, cost could be the biggest player in Canada's evolving sport culture. Retrieved from www.capilanocourier.com/2018/02/19/changing-game-cost-sports-culture-canada/

Keech, M., & Nauright, J. (2015). Sports industry and policy in the United Kingdom. Unpublished manuscript. University of Brighton. Centre of Sport, Tourism and Leisure Studies. Paper prepared for collection on Sport Industry Around the World to be published in China later than 2015.

Lucas, J., & Smith, R. (1978). *Saga of American sport.* Philadelphia: Lea & Febiger.

Marathon Statistics. (2019). Find my marathon. Retrieved from http://findmymarathon.com/statistics.php

Merkel, J. (2013, May 31). Youth sport: Positive and negative impact on young athletes. *Open Access Journal of Medicine, 4,* 151-160.

National Association of Intercollegiate Athletics. (2017). *2017-2018 official & policy handbook.* Kansas City, MO: Author.

National Collegiate Athletic Association. (2018a). *2018-19 NCAA Division I manual.* Indianapolis, IN: Author.

National Collegiate Athletic Association. (2018b). *2018-19 NCAA Division II manual.* Indianapolis, IN: Author.

National Collegiate Athletic Association. (2018c). *2018-19 NCAA Division III manual.* Indianapolis, IN: Author.

National Federation of State High School Associations. (2018). *NFHS handbook 2018-2019.* Indianapolis, IN: Author.

National Junior College Athletic Association (2017). *2017-2018 handbook & casebook.* Colorado Springs, CO: Author.

NBA and NBA Players Association. (2017). Collective bargaining agreement. (2017). *National Basketball Players Association.* Retrieved from https://nbpa.com/cba

NCAA President Mark Emmert. (n.d.). National Collegiate Athletic Association. Retrieved from www.ncaa.org/about/who-we-are/office-president/ncaa-president-mark-emmert

North Carolina Youth Soccer Association. (2017). *Bylaws of the North Carolina Youth Soccer Association.* Retrieved from https://cdn4.sportngin.com/attachments/document/0118/2784/ncysabylawscurrent.pdf?_ga=2.11047152.559215225.1547584840-2085280933.1547584840

Ohio High School Athletic Association. (2016). OHSAA structure and governance. Athletic director update. *OHSAA Fall Magazine, 20.*

Ontario Federation of School Athletic Associations. (2018). *Constitution and bylaws.* Retrieved from www.ofsaa.on.ca/about/constitution-and-bylaws

Our History. (n.d.). *British Universities & Colleges Sport.* Retrieved from www.bucs.org.uk/page.asp?section=17396&sectionTitle=Our+History

Participation. (2018). The participation report card on 2018 physical activity for children and youth. 2018 report card.

Pennsylvania Interscholastic Athletic Association. (2019). *PIAA handbook.* Retrieved from www.piaa.org/resources/handbook/default.aspx

Petros, L. (2017). Reasons for youth sport dropout from organized sport: The case of Ethiopian youth sport academy athlete Tirunesh Dibaba sport training center. In Gaudin, B., *Kenyan and Ethiopian athletics—Towards an alternative scientific approach.* Addis Ababa: OSSREA-IRD Editions.

Physical Activity Council. (2019). 2019 physical fitness council overview report on U.S. participation. Retrieved from http://www.physicalactivitycouncil.com/pdfs/current.pdf

Power 5 Conferences vote to provide mental health services. (2019, January 25). *ESPN.* Retrieved from http://athleticops.com/power-5-conferences-vote-to-provide-mental-health-services-espn-com/

Premier League. (2018). *Youth development rules 2018/19.* Retrieved from www.premierleague.com/publications

Prince Edward Island School Athletic Association sport commissioners. (2017). 2017-18. PEISAA. Retrieved from http://peisaa.pe.ca/page.php?page_id=109417

Provincial and territorial offices. (2017). *School Sport Canada.* Retrieved from www.schoolsport.ca/board-of-directors/

Reid, S. (2019, April 19). U.S. Youth Soccer facing legal challenge over background checks. Excerpts from the *Orange County Register.* Retrieved from https://gp1.com/u-s-youth-soccer-facing-legal-challenge-over-background-checks/

Robert Wood Johnson Foundation. (2015). Sports and health in America. Harvard T.H. Chan School of Public Health.

School Sport Canada. (2017). *Constitution*. Retrieved from www.schoolsport.ca/wp-content/uploads/2010/09/2017-SSC-new-bylaws-and-appendices.pdf

Scottish Student Sport. (2017). Membership pack 2017-2018. Retrieved from www.scottishstudentsport.com/wp-content/uploads/2016/06/Scottish-Student-Sport-Membership-Pack-1718.pdf

Seefelt, V., Ewing, M., & Walk, S. (1993). Overview of youth sports programs in the United States. Youth Sports Institute, Michigan State University East Lansing, Michigan 48823. Paper commissioned for Carnegie Council on Adolescent Development for its Task Force on Youth Development and Community Programs.

Solutions Research Group Consultants, Inc., (2014, June 10). Massive competition in pursuit of the $5.7 billion Canada youth sports market. Retrieved from https://www.srgnet.com/2014/06/10/massive-competition-in-pursuit-of-the-5-7-billion-canadian-youth-sports-market/

State associations. (n.d.). U.S. Youth Soccer East, Midwest, South, West. Retrieved from www.usyouthsoccer.org/state-associations/

The state of play in the U.S. scoreboard. (2018). State of play 2018: Trends and developments. The Aspen Institute. Project Play.

Tracy, M. (2014, August 7). N.C.A.A. votes to give richest conferences more autonomy. *The New York Times*. Retrieved from www.nytimes.com/2014/08/08/sports/ncaafootball/ncaa-votes-to-give-greater-autonomy-to-richest-conferences.html

Transforming physical education. (n.d.). Youth Sport Trust. Retrieved from http://strategy.youthsporttrust.org/transforming-physical-education/

Trudel, P., & Camire, M. (2017, July 8). *High school sport. The Canadian perspective*. Presentation at the International Council for Coach Excellence and International Association for Physical Education in Higher Education Symposium. Retrieved from www.icce.ws/_assets/files/trudel-camire.pdf

United States Youth Soccer Association. (2017). *Bylaws of the United States Youth Soccer Association, Inc.* Retrieved from www.usyouthsoccer.org/file.aspx?DocumentId=64

U Sports. (2018a). *U Sports by-laws*. Retrieved from https://usports.ca/uploads/hq/By_Laws-Policies-Procedures/2018/By-Laws_-_June_2018.pdf

U Sports. (2018b). U Sports governance policy. Retrieved from https://usports.ca/uploads/hq/By_Laws-Policies-Procedures/2018/EN/Governance_Policy_August_2018.pdf

U Sports history. (n.d.). *U Sports*. Retrieved from https://usports.ca/en/about/history

US Youth Soccer statement on under-18 girls Ambassadors vs. Carlsbad game. (2016, July 30). US Youth Soccer Association. Retrieved from www.usyouthsoccer.org/us_youth_soccer_statement_on_under-18_girls_ambassadors_vs_carlsbad_game/

Westhead, R. (2019, March 1). Canadian youth sports industry worth $8.7 billion, company says. *Canadian Television W5*. Retrieved from www.ctvnews.ca/w5/canadian-youth-sports-industry-worth-8-7-billion-company-says-1.4316678

What do designations B, A, AA, and AAA mean? (n.d.). Retrieved from http://assets.ngin.com/attachments/document/0021/5473/Designations.pdf

Why the NCCAA? (2019). National Christian College Athletic Association. Retrieved from https://thenccaa.org/documents/2017/8/25/Why_the_NCCAA.pdf

Witt, P., & Dangi, T. (2018). Why youth/children drop out of sport. *Journal of Park and Recreation Administration*, *36*, 191-199.

Zillgitt, J. (2019, February 21). NBA proposes lowering draft age from 19 to 18. *USA Today*. Retrieved from www.usatoday.com/story/sports/nba/2019/02/21/nba-draft-eligible-age-limit-proposal-18-years-old/2942228002

Chapter 9

Abrams, J. (2012, March 20). The malice at the Palace. *Grantland*. Retrieved from http://grantland.com/features/an-oral-history-malice-palace

Associated Press. (2011, October 27). FIFA raises 1.85bn in broadcast deals for 2018 and 2022 World Cups. *The Guardian*. Retrieved from www.theguardian.com/football/2011/oct/27/fifa-broadcast-2018-2022-world-cups

Bachman, R. (2012, November 21). ESPN strikes deal for College Football Playoff. *The Wall Street Journal*. Retrieved from www.wsj.com/articles/SB10001424127887324851704578133223970790516

Bar-Ona, T., & De Gaetenob, A.M. (2017). Futbol para todos (Soccer for all): Democratization, populist legitimization or quasi-authoritarianism? *The International Journal of the History of Sport, 34*(11), 1061-1087.

BBC News. (2015, December 21). FIFA corruption crisis: Key questions answered. *BBC.com*. Retrieved from www.bbc.com/news/world-europe-32897066

Bellis, M. (2019, August 22). The history of Facebook and how it was invented. Thought Co. Retrieved from https://www.thoughtco.com/who-invented-facebook-1991791

Berwick, A. (2018, February 14). China's Dalian Wanda sells 17 percent stake in Spain's Atletico Madrid. *Reuters*. Retrieved from https://www.reuters.com/article/us-atletico-dalian-wanda/chinas-dalian-wanda-sells-17-percent-stake-in-spains-atletico-madrid-idUSKCN1FY0XJ

Blizzard Entertainment. (2018, January 9). Where to watch the Overwatch League. *OverwatchLeague.com.* Retrieved from https://overwatchleague.com/en-us/news/21349827/where-to-watch-the-overwatch-league

Bloom, B.M. (2018, August 28). Yankees intent to buy back YES Network in sale of Fox to Disney. *Forbes.* Retrieved from www.forbes.com/sites/barrymbloom/2018/08/28/yankees-intend-to-buy-back-yes-network-after-fox-sale-to-disney/#2b826d14161d

Brady, E. (2016, April 12). NCAA extends tournament deal with CBS, Turner through 2032 for $8.8 billion. *USA Today.* Retrieved from https://www.usatoday.com/story/sports/ncaab/2016/04/12/ncaa-contract-extension-cbs-turner-ncaa-tournament-march-madness/82939124

Bucholtz, A., & Fang, K. (2018, February 26). The good, bad and ugly of NBC's coverage of the 2018 PyeongChang Olympics. *Awful Announcing.* Retrieved from https://awfulannouncing.com/nbc/good-bad-ugly-nbc-coverage-pyeongchang-olympics.html

Burk, V., Grimmer, C.G., and Pawlowski, T. (2016). "Same, same, but different!" On consumers' use of corporate PR media in sports. *Journal of Sport Management, 30,* 353-368.

Capriatti, P., & Moreno, A. (2007). Corporate citizenship and public relations: The importance and interactivity of social responsibility issues on corporate websites. *Public Relations Review, 33,* 84-91.

Claringbould, I., Knoppers, A., & Elling, A. (2004). Exclusionary practices in sport journalism. *Sex Roles, 51*(11/12), 709-718.

Code of ethics. (2000). Public Relations Society of America. Retrieved from www.prsa.org/ethics/code-of-ethics

Consultancy.uk. (2018, June 22). Broadcast haul of FIFA World Cup 2018 in Russia leaps to $3 billion. *Consultancy.uk.* Retrieved from www.consultancy.uk/news/17637/broadcast-haul-of-fifa-world-cup-2018-in-russia-leaps-to-3-billion

Corrigan, D. (2016, December 9). Atletico Madrid's new stadium to be named 'Wanda Metropolitano'. *ESPN.com.* Retrieved from https://www.espn.com/soccer/atletico-madrid/story/3015424/atletico-madrids-new-stadium-to-be-named-wanda-metropolitano

Creating the NFL schedule. (2019). *NFL.com.* Retrieved from https://operations.nfl.com/the-game/creating-the-nfl-schedule

Crupi, A. (2019, January 3). Network TV can't survive without the NFL: Live sports accounted for 89 of the year's 100 most-watched broadcasts. *Adage.* Retrieved from https://adage.com/article/media/top-50-u-s-broadcasts-2018/316102/

Dachman, J. (2018, March 7). Behind the scenes at Blizzard Arena: Inside the home of Overwatch League, the hottest property in esports. *Sports Video Group.* Retrieved from www.sportsvideo.org/2018/03/07/behind-the-scenes-at-blizzard-arena-inside-the-home-of-overwatch-league-the-hottest-property-in-esports

Dittmore, S.W., Stoldt, G.C., & Greenwell, T.C. (2008). Use of an organizational weblog in relationship building: The case of a Major League Baseball team. *International Journal of Sport Communication, 1*(3), 384-397.

Djankov, S., McLiesh, C., Nenova, T., & Shleifer, A. (2003, October). Who owns the media. *Journal of Law and Economics, 46,* 341-381.

Draper, K. (2017, October 23). Why the Athletic wants to pillage newspapers. *The New York Times.* Retrieved from www.nytimes.com/2017/10/23/sports/the-athletic-newspapers.html

Draper, K. (2018a, August 24). At the Athletic, a hiring spree becomes a story in itself. *The New York Times.* Retrieved from www.nytimes.com/2018/08/24/sports/the-athletic-netflix.html

Draper, K. (2018b, September 10). ESPN's new boss changes course, in step with the NFL. *The New York Times.* Retrieved from www.nytimes.com/2018/09/10/sports/espn-nfl-jimmy-pitaro.html

Engleson, S. (2018, August 14). When linear TV and digital collide: The rise of the virtual MVPD. Retrieved from www.comscore.com/Insights/Blog/When-Linear-TV-and-Digital-Collide-The-Rise-of-the-Virtual-MVPD

ESPN News. (2015, March 24). NFL to suspend blackout policy. *ESPN.* Retrieved from www.espn.com/nfl/story/_/id/12545081/nfl-suspend-tv-blackout-policy-2015-owners-vote

Evens, T., Iosifidis, P., & Smith, P. (2013). *The political economy of television sports rights.* Basingstoke: Palgrave Macmillan.

Federal Communications Commission. (2014, September 30). FCC eliminates sports blackout rule. Order removes unnecessary and outdated regulations. Washington, D.C. [news release].

Federal Communications Commission. (2016). Consumer guide. Sport blackouts. Retrieved from https://www.fcc.gov/consumers/guides/sports-blackouts

Federal Communications Commission. (2018a). Ownership rules. Retrieved from www.fcc.gov/consumers/guides/fccs-review-broadcast-ownership-rules

Federal Communications Commission. (2018b). Strategic plan 2018-2022. Retrieved from https://www.fcc.gov/document/strategic-plan-2018-2022

FIFA World Cup—Asian media rights. (n.d.). *InFront.* Retrieved from www.infrontsports.com/properties/fifa/fifa-world-cup-tm-asian-media-rights

Fink, J.S., Borland, J.F., & Fields, S.K. (2010). Sexist acts in sports: Media reactions and forms of apologia. *International Journal of Sport Communication, 3,* 198-216.

Fisher, E. (2018, May 16). YES Network putting up big streaming numbers for Yankees. *New York Business Journal*. Retrieved from www.bizjournals.com/newyork/news/2018/05/16/yes-network-putting-up-big-streaming-numbers-for.html

Fitzpatrick, K.R. (2002a). Evolving standards in public relations: A historical examination of PRSA's code of ethics. *Journal of Mass Media Ethics, 17*(2), 89-110.

Fitzpatrick, K.R. (2002b). From enforcement to education: The development of PRSA's member code of ethics 2000. *Journal of Mass Media Ethics, 17*(2), 111-135.

Flint, J., & Gottfried, M. (2019, January 11). Fox won't bid to reacquire its regional sports networks from Disney. *The Wall Street Journal*. Retrieved from www.wsj.com/articles/21st-century-fox-says-it-wont-pursue-fox-regional-sports-networks-11547219030

Forbes. (2019). #36 Wang Jianlin. Retrieved from https://www.forbes.com/profile/wang-jianlin/#747e77573142

Fortune Global 500. (2018). Most profitable companies. Retrieved from http://fortune.com/global500/

Fry, A. (2019, March 15). Sony replaces Star as IOC's India Olympic partner. *Digital TV Europe*. Retrieved from https://www.digitaltveurope.com/2019/03/15/sony-replaces-star-as-iocs-india-olympic-partner/

Garrison, B., & Salwen, M.B. (1989). Professional orientation of sports journalists: A study of Associated Press sports editors. *Newspaper Research Journal, 10*(4), 77-84.

Geller, E. (2015, February 4). Supporters and opponents of the FCC's net neutrality plan, in their own words. *The Daily Dot*. Retrieved from www.dailydot.com/layer8/fcc-net-neutrality-title-ii-plan-supporters-opponents

Gipe, K. (2019, January 20). NHL TV and blackouts: Why they happen. Retrieved from https://thehockeywriters.com/nhl-blackouts-why-they-happen

Glass, A. (2018, April 1). Congress bans airing cigarette ads, April 1, 2018. *Politico*. Retrieved from www.politico.com/story/2018/04/01/congress-bans-airing-cigarette-ads-april-1-1970-489882

Goldblatt, D. (2008). *The ball is round: A global history of soccer*. London, UK: Penguin.

Goslin, A. (2018, December 11). The 2018 League of Legends World Finals had nearly 100 million viewers. *Rift Herald*. Retrieved from www.riftherald.com/2018/12/11/18136237/riot-2018-league-of-legends-world-finals-viewers-prize-pool

Grimmer, C.G., & Kian, E.M. (2013). Reflections of German football journalists on their relationships with Bundesliga club public relations practitioners. *International Journal of Sport Communication, 6*(4), 446-463.

Ha, A. (2019, April 12). ESPN launches its streaming service ESPN+. *TechCrunch*. Retrieved from https://techcrunch.com/2018/04/12/espn-plus-launch

Hardin, M. (2005a). Stopped at the gate: Women's sports, 'reader interest,' and decision making by editors. *Journalism & Mass Communication Quarterly, 82*(1), 62-77.

Hardin, M. (2005b). Survey finds boosterism, freebies remain problem for newspaper sports departments. *Newspaper Research Journal, 26*(1), 66-73.

Hardin, M., & Shain, S. (2006). "Feeling much smaller than you know you are": The fragmented professional identity of female sports journalists. *Critical Studies in Media Communication, 23*(4), 322-338.

Hernandez, A. (2013, September 1). All quiet on the digital front: The NCAA's wide discretion in regulating social media. *Texas Review of Entertainment and Sport Law, 15*(1), 53-66.

Hoehn, T., & Lancefield, D. (2003). Broadcasting and sport. *Oxford Review of Economic Policy, 19*(4), 552-568.

Hoium, T. (2012, November 21). The Yankees score big with a $1.5 billion TV deal. *AOL.com*. Retrieved from www.aol.com/2012/11/21/yankees-score-big-with-billion-dollar-tv-deal

Holloway, D. (2016, August 23). How Rio ratings surprised NBC and will impact future Olympics. *Variety*. Retrieved from https://variety.com/2016/tv/news/2016-olympics-ratings-rio-nbc-1201843200/

Hull, B.B. (1990). An economics perspective ten years after the NAB case. *Journal of Media Economics, 3*(1), 19-35.

Hume, M. (2018, July 11). ESPN secures Overwatch League broadcast rights, continuing esports' mainstream surge. *The Washington Post*. Retrieved from www.washingtonpost.com/news/early-lead/wp/2018/07/11/espn-secures-overwatch-league-broadcast-rights-continuing-esports-mainstream-surge/?utm_term=.d2cefa9d10c5

InFront Sports. (n.d.). About InFront. Retrieved from www.infrontsports.com/about-infront/

International Olympic Committee. (2011, May 23). Moderation guidelines for social media. Retrieved from https://stillmed.olympic.org/Documents/Various/MODERATION-GUIDELINES-FOR-SOCIAL-FINAL.pdf

International Olympic Committee. (2017, September 1). IOC social and digital media guidelines for persons accredited to the XXIII Olympic Winter Games PyeongChang 2018. Retrieved from https://stillmed.olympic.org/media/Document%20Library/OlympicOrg/Games/Winter-Games/Games-PyeongChang-2018-Winter-Olympic-Games/IOC-Social-and-Digital-Media-Guidelines/PyeongChang-2018-Social-Media-Guidelines-eng.pdf

Jensen, R., & Sosa, J. (2008). The importance of building positive relationships between Hispanic audiences and Major League Soccer franchises: A case study of the public relations challenges facing Houston 1836. *Soccer & Society, 9*(4), 477-490.

Kahler, K. (2019, April 24). How NFL draft prospects are learning to protect themselves from social media snafus. *Sports Illustrated.* Retrieved from www.si.com/nfl/2019/04/24/nfl-draft-social-media-kyler-murray-nick-bosa-josh-allen-old-tweets-cleanup

Kaplan, D. (2018, October 29). NFL's TV deals hedge against work stoppage. *Sports Business Journal.* Retrieved from www.sportsbusinessdaily.com/Journal/Issues/2018/10/29/Leagues-and-Governing-Bodies/NFL-TV-deals.aspx

Kristiansen, K., Roberts, G.C., & Sisjord, M.K. (2012). Coping with negative media content: The experiences of professional footballers. *International Journal of Sport and Exercise Psychology, 9*(4), 295-307.

Kurtz, J.B. (2017). With malice towards all? Moral authority, violence, and the (affective) discipline of basketball (bodies). *Communication and Sport,* 1-19. doi: 10.1177/2167479517747870

Lapchick, R., Bloom, A., Balasundaram, B., Bello-Malabu, A., Cotta, T., Morrison, E., et al. (2018, May 2). *Associated Press sports editors racial and gender report card.* The Institute for Diversity and Ethics in Sport, University of Central Florida, Orlando, FL.

Lapchick, R., Guiao, A., Salas, D., Sanders, D., Howell, E., Robinson, L., et al. (2014). *Associated Press sports editors racial and gender report card.* The Institute for Diversity and Ethics in Sport, University of Central Florida, Orlando, FL.

Limburg, V.E. (1989). The decline of broadcast ethics: US v. NAB. *Journal of Mass Media Ethics, 4*(2), 214-231.

Linden, A.D. (2012). Looking at losing: Presentations of the media's narrative of the Cleveland Browns' relocation. *The International Journal of the History of Sport, 29*(12), 2575-2598.

Linke, A., & Zerfass, A. (2013). Social media governance: Regulatory frameworks for successful online communications. *Journal of Communication Management, 17*(3), 270-286.

Lutz, A. (2014). These six companies own 90% of the media in America. *Business Insider.* Retrieved from www.businessinsider.com/these-6-corporations-control-90-of-the-media-in-america-2012-6

Mawson, L.M., & Bowler III, W.T. (1989). Effects of the 1984 Supreme Court ruling on the television revenues of NCAA Division I football programs. *Journal of Sport Management, 3*(2), 79-89.

McEnnis, S. (2016). Following the action: How live bloggers are reimagining the professional ideology of sports journalism. *Journalism Practice, 10*(8), 967-982.

McGowan, R.A., & Mahon, J.F. (2009). Corporate social responsibility in professional sports: An analysis of the NBA, NFL, and MLB. *Academy of Business Disciplines Journal, 1*(1), 45-82.

Mehler, A. (2008). Political discourse in football coverage—the cases of Cote d'Ivoire and Ghana. *Soccer & Society, 9*(1), 96-110.

Miller, J.A., & Belson, K. (2013, August 23). NFL pressure said to lead ESPN to quit film project. *The New York Times.* Retrieved from www.nytimes.com/2013/08/24/sports /football/nfl-pressure-said-to-prompt-espn-to-quit-film-project.html?pagewanted=all&_r=0

Miller, J.A., & Shales, T. (2011). *Those guys have all the fun.* Boston: Little, Brown & Company.

MLB.TV out-of-market practices. (2018, May 24). *MLB.TV.* Retrieved from www.mlb.com/live-stream-games/subscribe#blackout

Mola, R., & Ovide, S. (2016, March 23). The war on Internet piracy. Big tech companies like Google clash with media companies over copyrighted materials. *Bloomberg.* Retrieved from www.bloomberg.com/gadfly/articles/2016-03-23/google-and-media-titans-clash-in-a-war-on-internet-piracy

National Collegiate Athletic Association. (2018a, November 15). 2019 NCAA convention Division III legislative proposals question and answer guide. Retrieved from https://ncaaorg.s3.amazonaws.com/governance/d3/legislation/2019DIIIGov_LegPropQA.pdf

National Collegiate Athletic Association. (2018b, August). *NCAA Division I 2018-2019 manual.*

National Collegiate Athletic Association v. Board of Regents of the University of Oklahoma, et al. (468 U.S. 85, 1984).

NCAA.org. (n.d.). Where does the money go? *NCAA.org.* Retrieved from www.ncaa.org/about/where-does-money-go

Newcomb, A. (2018, March 24). A timeline of Facebook's privacy issues – And its responses. Retrieved from https://www.nbcnews.com/tech/social-media/timeline-facebook-s-privacy-issues-its-responses-n859651

Nielsen. (2017). *Tops in 2017: Television and social media.* Retrieved from www.nielsen.com/us/en/insights/news/2017/tops-of-2017-television-and-social-media.html?afflt=ntrt15340001&afflt_uid=E08xMNP8a70.QIqgj5Y8UbFZIBcGPI_uHX__RQWt60TY&afflt_uid_2=AFFLT_ID_2

Nielsen. (2018). *Year in sports media report. U.S. 2017.* The Nielsen Company.

Nölleke, D., Grimmer, C.G., & Horky, T. (2017). News sources and follow-up communication: Facets of complementarity between sports journalism and social media. *Journalism Practice, 11*(4), 509-526.

Oates, T.P., & Pauly, J. (2007). Sports journalism as moral and ethical discourse. *Journal of Mass Media Ethics, 22*(4), 332-347.

Ourand, J. (2018, March 12). ESPN's tricky NFL problem. *Sports Business Journal*. Retrieved from www.sportsbusinessdaily.com/Journal/Issues/2018/03/12/Media/Pitaro.aspx

Our Organization: What is CoSIDA? (2019). College sports information directors of America. Retrieved from https://cosida.com/sports/2013/7/25/general.aspx

Ozanian, M. (2019, March 8). New York Yankees buy back YES network for $3.47 billion. *Forbes*. Retrieved from www.forbes.com/sites/mikeozanian/2019/03/08/new-york-yankees-buy-back-yes-network-for-3-47-billion/#834d342483c1

Parkinson, M. (2001). The PRSA code of professional standards and member code of ethics: why they are neither professional nor ethical. *Public Relations Quarterly, 46*(3), 27.

Peers, M., Jannarone, J., & Linebaugh, K. (2013, February 13). Comcast buys rest of NBC's parent. *The Wall Street Journal*. Retrieved from www.wsj.com/articles/SB10001424127887324880504578300432831438770

Phillips, C.J. (2017, August 24). Unfortunately, new website The Athletic reflects old diversity problem in sports media. *New York Daily News*. Retrieved from www.nydailynews.com/sports/new-site-athletic-reflects-old-sports-media-diversity-problem-article-1.3458067

Plus Media Solutions. (2014, September 14). Sports blackout rules. Final ruling. U.S. Office of the Official Registry. Retrieved from https://www.federalregister.gov/documents/2014/10/24/2014-24612/sports-blackout-rules

Puppis, M. (2008). National media regulation in the era of free trade: The role of global media governance. *European Journal of Communication, 23*(4), 405-424.

Reed, S. (2013). American sports writers' social media use and its influence on professionalism. *Journalism Practice, 7*(5), 555-571.

Reinardy, S. (2011). Newspaper journalism in crisis: Burnout on the rise, eroding young journalists' career commitment. *Journalism, 12*(1), 33-50.

Reuters. (2019, January 11). China's Wanda files for U.S. IPO of sports unit to raise up to $500 million. *The New York Times*. Retrieved from www.nytimes.com/reuters/2019/01/11/business/11reuters-wanda-sports-ipo.html

Ruiz, R.R. (2015, March 12). F.C.C. sets net neutrality rules. *The New York Times*. Retrieved from www.nytimes.com/2015/03/13/technology/fcc-releases-net-neutrality-rules.html

Sadler, R. (2005). *Electronic media law*. Thousand Oaks, CA: Sage Publications.

Sanderson, J., Snyder, E., Hull, D., & Gramlich, K. (2015). Social media policies within NCAA member institutions: Evolving technology and its impact on policy. *Journal of Issues in Intercollegiate Athletics, 8*, 50-73.

Scherer, D. (2016, December 16). The FCC's rules and policies regarding media ownership, attribution, and ownership diversity. Congressional Research Services. Retrieved from https://fas.org/sgp/crs/misc/R43936.pdf

Sharma, R. (2018, August 28). IOC media rights: No takers for 2020 Tokyo Olympics in India. *Inside Sport*. Retrieved from https://www.insidesport.co/ioc-media-rights-no-takers-for-2020-tokyo-olympics-in-india/

Sherman, R. (2016, April 12). The NCAA's new March Madness TV deal with make them a billion dollars a year. *SB Nation*. Retrieved from www.sbnation.com/college-basketball/2016/4/12/11415764/ncaa-tournament-tv-broadcast-rights-money-payout-cbs-turner

Siegfrieda, N., Schlesinger, T., Baylec, E., & Giauqued, D. (2015). Professionalisation of sport federations – a multi-level framework for analyzing forms, causes and consequences. *European Sport Management Quarterly, 15*(4), 407-433.

Silberstein-Loeb, J. (2012). Exclusivity and cooperation in the supply of news: The example of the Associated Press, 1893–1945. *Journal of Policy History, 24*(3), 466-498.

Silver, S. (2018, June 29). The story of the original iPhone, that nobody thought was possible. *Apple Insider*. Retrieved from https://appleinsider.com/articles/18/06/29/the-story-of-the-original-iphone-that-nobody-thought-was-possible

Simmons, B. (2018, December 26). The year-end edition: Sports gambling, player podcasts, awards shows, and more. *The Ringer*. Retrieved from www.theringer.com/the-bill-simmons-podcast/2018/12/26/18156429/the-sports-repodders-year-end-edition

Smith, C. (2016, June 24). The relationship between television and sport. *Global Media and Sports*. Retrieved from https://www.globalmediasports.com/docs/GMS-OTT-presentation-24Jun16.pdf

Smith, G.H. (2012). Statement of Gordon H. Smith, president and CEO, National Association of Broadcasters. Hearing on "The Cable Act at 20." *Journal of Current Issues in Media and Telecommunications, 5*(2), 143-146.

Smith, P., Evens, T., & Iosifidis, P. (2016). The next big match: Convergence, competition and sports media rights. *European Journal of Communication, 31*(5), 536-550.

Smudde, P.M. (2004). The five --P's for media interviews: Fundamentals for newbies, veterans and everyone in between. *Public Relations Quarterly, 49*(2), 29.

Sports Broadcasting Act of 1961, 15 U.S.C. §§ 1291-95 (1961).

Steyn, B., & Niemann, L. (2014). Strategic role of public relations in enterprise strategy, governance and sustainability—A normative framework. *Public Relations Review, 40*(2), 171-183.

Syme, C. (2014, June 20). Social media best practices: What students need to know. CoSIDA. Retrieved from https://cosida.com/news/2014/6/20/GEN_0620143053.aspx?path=general

Telecommunications Act of 1996. (1996). Pub. L. No. 104-104, 110 Stat. 56.

United States Department of Commerce. (2018). 2017 Top markets report: Media and entertainment—Sector snapshot. Retrieved from www.trade.gov/topmarkets/pdf/Top%20Markets%20Media%20and%20Entertainment%202017.pdf

VanDerWerff, T. (2018, February 25). NBC's Winter Olympics coverage was the best it's been in years. *Vox.com*. Retrieved from www.vox.com/culture/2018/2/25/17046048/nbc-winter-olympics-2018-review

van Sterkenburg, J., Knoppers, A., & De Leeuw, S. (2010). Race, ethnicity, and content analysis of the sports media: A critical reflection. *Media, Culture & Society, 32*(5), 819-839.

van Sterkenburg, J., & Spaaij, R. (2015). Mediated football: Representations and audience receptions of race/ethnicity, gender and nation. *Soccer & Society, 16*(5-6), 593-603.

Wahba, P. (2017, September 26). Inside China's endurance empire. *Fortune*. Retrieved from http://fortune.com/2017/09/26/dalian-wanda-china-marathon/

Wanda Group. (n.d.). Sport holdings. Retrieved from www.wanda-group.com/sports_holdings/

Wanda Group. (2016, December). History. Retrieved from www.wanda-group.com/history/

Watts, L. (2013). AP's first female reporters. *Journalism History, 39*(1).

Weaver, K. (2013). Media deals, college football, and governance: Who's in charge? *Change: The Magazine of Higher Learning, 45*(4), 15-23.

Weinberg, B. (2012). The future is Asia? The role of the Asian football confederation in the governance and development of football in Asia. *The International Journal of the History of Sport, 29*(4), 535-552.

Weis, K. (1986). How the print media affect sports and violence: The problems of sport journalism. *International Review for the Sociology of Sport, 21*(2-3), 239-252.

Wile, R. (2017, March 14). The most popular TV channels are the ones you can watch for free. *Time*. Retrieved from http://time.com/money/4700663/cable-prices-most-popular-tv-channels-espn-abc-discovery-hbo

Wise, J. (2014, September 30). FCC eliminates sports blackout rules. Federal Communications Commission. Washington, D.C. [news release].

Zhang, S., & Miller, C. (2015, August 25). China's Wanda buys Ironman Triathlon owner for $650 million. *Reuters*. Retrieved from https://www.reuters.com/article/us-world-triathlon-m-a-dalian-wanda/chinas-wanda-buys-ironman-triathlon-owner-for-650-million-idUSKCN0QW04X20150827

Zhong, K., Cao, Y., & Ning, Y. (2008). The deregulatory effects of the Telecommunications Act of 1996 on the broadcasting industry: Expectations vs. reality. *Journal of Accounting and Public Policy, 27*(3), 238-261.

Zhu, J., & Franklin, J. (2019, July 26). China's Wanda Sports raises $190.4 million in downsized IPO. *Reuters*. Retrieved from https://es.reuters.com/article/americasIpoNews/idUKL4N24R3QQ

Chapter 10

About NOCSAE. (n.d.). National Operating Committee on Standards for Athletic Equipment. Retrieved from https://nocsae.org/about-nocsae/history/

About WFSGI. (2017). World Federation of the Sporting Goods Industry. Retrieved from www.wfsgi.org/about-wfsgi

Activity report. (2019). *Trade Committee Magazine*, official publication of the World Federation of the Sporting Goods Industry, 72-73.

Adams, J. (2013). Flag on the play: Professional sports teams calling trademark infringement on their superfans. *Villanova University Charles Widger School of Law Digital Repository, 20*(2), 631-662.

Addady, M. (2016, June 30). Dick's just paid $15 million for Sports Authority's name. *Fortune*. Retrieved from http://fortune.com/2016/06/30/dicks-sports-authority

Alea v. Wilson Sporting Goods Company et al., No. 1:17-cv-00498 (7th Cir., 2017).

Amer Sports. (2019). Citizenship and community. Retrieved from www.amersports.com/responsibility/social/citizenship-and-community

Badenhausen, K. (2015, March 11). How Michael Jordan still makes $100 million a year. *Forbes*. Retrieved from www.forbes.com/sites/kurtbadenhausen/2015/03/11/how-new-billionaire-michael-jordan-earned-100-million-in-2014/#4d63b41f221a

Barrientos, S., & Smith, S. (2007). Do workers benefit from ethical trade? Assessing codes of labour practice in global production systems. *Third World Q, 28,* 4, 713-729.

Boston Pro. Hockey Ass'n Inc. v. Dallas Cap & E. Mfg., Inc., 360 F. Supp. 459 (N.D. Tex. 1973).

Chitrakorn, K. (2017, September 20). Global sportswear brands making a play for women. *The Business of Fashion*. Retrieved from www.businessoffashion.com/articles/intelligence/how-sportswear-brands-are-making-a-play-for-women

Clothier, A. (2005, September 10). The Chinese footwear industry and its influence on the world trade. *United Nations Industrial Development Organization*. Retrieved from https://leatherpanel.org/sites/default/files/publications-attachments/chineese_footwear_industry.pdf

Commercial revenue by segment of Manchester United from 2012 to 2018 (in million U.S. dollars). (2012). *Statista*. Retrieved from www.statista.com/statistics/383966/manchester-united-commercial-revenue-by-segment

Connolly, M. (2016, May 19). Whether LeBron has a $1B deal or not, Michael Jordan is still the king of Nike. *Forbes*. Retrieved from www.forbes.com/sites/mattconnolly/2016/05/19/despite-lebron-james-1-billion-deal-michael-jordan-still-king-nike/#6246c7139cd0

Decathlon About Us. (n.d.). Retrieved from www.decathlon.co.uk/about-decathlon.html

Dick's Sporting Goods recalls. (2018). Retrieved from www.dickssportinggoods.com/s/recalls

Dick's Sporting Goods settles with Governor's Office of Consumer Protection for $500,000. (2012, May 22). Consumer Protection Division. Georgia Department of Law. Retrieved from http://consumer.georgia.gov/news/press-releases/view/dick-s-sporting-goods-settles-with-governor-s-office-of-consumer-protection-for-500-000

Dick's Sporting Goods vendor code of conduct. (2016, April 1). Retrieved from https://s7d2.scene7.com/is/content/dkscdn/FrontEndDev/DSG/CMS%20Pages/DSG/DSG_0217_Suppliers/DSGVendorCodeOfConduct.pdf

Division for sales agents. (2019). *Code of conduct*. National Sporting Goods Association. Retrieved from www.nsga.org/membership/sales-agents/code-of-ethics

Draper, S. (2018a, October 5). How data breach is inevitable in wearable devices. *Wearable Technologies*. Retrieved from www.wearable-technologies.com/2018/10/how-data-breach-is-inevitable-in-wearable-devices

Draper, S. (2018b, August 9). Pentagon tells soldiers to leave wearable trackers at home when heading to war zones. *Wearable Technologies*. Retrieved from www.wearable-technologies.com/2018/08/pentagon-tells-soldiers-to-leave-wearable-trackers-at-home-when-heading-to-warzones

Dhyani, K. (2018, May 11). Formula 1 announces tie-ups with FanVision and Fanatics. *Inside Sports*. Retrieved from www.insidesport.co/formula-1-announces-tie-ups-fanvision-fanatics-0311052018

Duffy, C. (2018, April 10). More charges filed against former Adidas exec in NCAA corruption scandal. *Portland Business Journal*. Retrieved from www.bizjournals.com/portland/news/2018/04/10/more-charges-filed-against-former-adidas-exec-in.html

Egels-Zanden, N., & Lindholm, H. (2015). Do codes of conduct improve worker rights in supply chains? A study of Fair Wear Foundation. *Journal of Cleaner Production, 107*, 31-40.

Farry, T. (2014, May 31). Players, game makers settle for $40M. *ESPN*. Retrieved from www.espn.com/espn/otl/story/_/id/11010455/college-athletes-reach-40-million-settlement-ea-sports-ncaa-licensing-arm

Fershtman, J. (2017, May 9). Equestrian helmet laws and helmet-related liabilities. Presentation at the Emmett J. Vaughan Agribusiness Conference sponsored by the International Risk Management Institute. Sacramento, California.

FIFA quality programme. (2017). World Federation of the Sporting Goods Industry. Retrieved from www.wfsgi.org/fifa-quality-programme/fifa-quality-programme

Fisher, E., & Mullen, L. (2018, May 14). MLB players receive $125M from union. *Sports Business Daily*. Retrieved from www.sportsbusinessdaily.com/Journal/Issues/2018/05/14/Labor-and-Agents/MLBPA.aspx

Formula One signs merchandise partnership with Puma. (2019, April 4). *Sports Business Journal*. Retrieved from www.sportbusiness.com/news/formula-one-signs-merchandise-partnership-with-puma

Friedman, A. (1995). Protection of sport trademarks. *Loyola of Los Angeles Entertainment Law Review*, 689-716.

Furgiuele, M. (2017, March 16). FIFA awards retail and licensing contract for World Cup 2018. Retrieved from https://en.calcioefinanza.com/2017/05/16/fifa-awards-retail-licensing-contract-world-cup-2018

Global business guide Indonesia. (2017). Retrieved from www.gbgindonesia.com/en/manufacturing/article/2017/indonesia_s_sportswear_industry_strong_growth_from_exports_and_domestic_sales_11710.php

Government advocacy. (2019). National Sporting Goods Association. Retrieved from www.nsga.org/advocacy/legislative-advocacy

Griffin, C. (2017, January/February). Bringing it on home. Top trends in sport licensing. *Sports Insights*.

Grullon, G., Larkin, Y., & Michaely, R. (2017). Are US industries becoming more concentrated? [Working paper]. Retrieved from https://pdfs.semanticscholar.org/138f/249c43bfec315227a242b305b9764d57a0af.pdf

Harwell, D. (2015, August 19). Under Armour is suing pretty much every company using the name 'Armor'. *The Washington Post*. Retrieved from www.washingtonpost.com/news/business/wp/2015/08/19/under-armour-is-suing-pretty-much-every-company-using-the-name-armor/?noredirect=on&utm_term=.c8bcb229e4e6

Heitner, D. (2014, June 17). Sports licensing soars to $698 million in royalty revenue. *Forbes*. Retrieved from www.forbes.com/sites/darrenheitner/2014/06/17/sports-licensing-soars-to-698-million-in-royalty-revenue/#61dcbb48756b

Hilco Steambank. (2016, June). The Sports Authority, Inc. intellectual property assets. Retrieved from www.hilcoglobal.com/docs/librariesprovider10/default-document-library/sportsauthority_teaser.pdf?sfvrsn=2

Hoovers. (n.d.). Retrieved from www.hoovers.com/company-information/cs/company-profile.rawlings_sporting_goods_company_inc.ee6e0b917d7e3565.html

How does the USOPC protect its intellectual property? (2019). *US Olympic and Paralympic Brand Usage Guidelines*. United States Olympic & Paralympic Committee. Retrieved from www.teamusa.org/brand-usage-guidelines

Irwin, R., Sutton, W., & McCarthy, L. (2008). *Sport promotion and sales management*. Champaign, IL: Human Kinetics.

Joseph, A. (2019, April 7.) The Big Baller site appears to be shut down. *USA Today*. Retrieved from https://ftw.usatoday.com/2019/04/big-baller-brand-lavar-ball-site-shut-down-lonzo-nba-alan-foster

Kahn, R. (2004). May the best merchandise win: The law of non-trademark uses of sports logos. *Marquette Sports Law Review, 14*(2), 283-317.

Kaminsky, M. (2018, January 30). *Super Bowl legal blitz: Inside the NFL's legendary trademark defense*. Retrieved from www.forbes.com/sites/michellefabio/2018/01/30/inside-the-nfls-legendary-trademark-defense/#778448e63293

Kass, A. (2019, January 31). Court: counterfeit NFL gear, tickets can be seized ahead of Super Bowl. *AJC*. Retrieved from www.ajc.com/news/local-govt--politics/court-counterfeit-nfl-gear-tickets-can-seized-ahead-super-bowl/RAHDO5QWojNIDE5CbVIBeJ

Key dates in the history of women in the Olympic movement. (n.d.). Retrieved from www.olympic.org/women-in-sport/background/key-dates

Kulczycki, W., Mikas, S., & Koenigstorfer, J. (2017). Where to engage in CSR? The influence of social cause proximity on attitude toward small-sized (vs large-sized) sporting goods retailers. *Sport, Business and Management: An International Journal, 7*(5), 497-514.

Lanham Act of 1946, Pub.L. 79–489, 60 Stat. 427, enacted July 5, 1946, codified at 15 U.S.C. § 1051.

Lefton, T., & Fischer, B. (2019, March 4). LA28-USOC joint venture snags Nike as first partner. *Sports Business Journal*. Retrieved from www.sportsbusinessdaily.com/Journal/Issues/2019/03/04/Olympics/LA28-Nike.aspx

Leitch, W. (2018, October 23). College basketball is literally on trial right now. But its victims are the ones being prosecuted. *NYMag*. Retrieved from http://nymag.com/intelligencer/2018/10/the-ncaa-basketball-and-adidas-pay-for-play-scandal-and-the-nba.html

Leung, D. (2017, February 2). NBA teams banned from using wearables data in contract negotiations, player transactions. *Sports Illustrated*. Retrieved from www.si.com/tech-media/2017/02/02/nba-data-analytics-new-cba-wearable-device

Licensing pre-qualification terms and conditions. (n.d.). National Football League. Retrieved from www.nfl.info/nflconsprod/welcome/cpagreement.htm

List of NHL sports licenses. (2012, March 12). Retrieved from https://licensedsports.blogspot.com/2012/03/list-of-nhl-licensees.html

Lu, A. (2012, November 1). NBA star Francisco Garcia settles exercise ball lawsuit. Retrieved from https://blogs.findlaw.com/injured/2012/11/nba-star-francisco-garcia-settles-exercise-ball-lawsuit.html

Mahoney, S. (2018, July 17). Reebok cheers women on in new #BeMoreHuman ads. Retrieved from www.mediapost.com/publications/article/322338/reebok-cheers-women-on-in-new-bemorehuman-ads.html?edition=110055

Marketline. (2016, July). *Global sports equipment*. Retrieved from Marketline Report Store.

Marrone, D. (n.d.). *Ducks Unlimited trademarks*. Retrieved from www.ducks.org/get-involved/corporate-partners-products/official-du-products-and-services/ducks-unlimited-trademarks

Masteralexis, L., Barr, C., & Hums, M. (2004). Principles and practice of sport management. In S.R. Rosner & K.L. Shropshire (Eds.), *The business of sports*. Burlington, MA: Jones and Bartlett Publishers.

McCann, N. (2019, March 25). High court passes on Nike 'Jumpman' logo fight. Retrieved from www.courthousenews.com/high-court-passes-on-nike-jumpman-logo-fight

Meyersohn, N. (2019, March 14). Dick's Sporting Goods removes guns and ammo from 125 stores. Retrieved from www.cnn.com/2019/03/14/investing/dicks-sporting-goods-guns/index.html

Mihoces, G. (2013, February 23). Under Armour suing Nike over advertising slogan. *USA Today*. Retrieved from www.usatoday.com/story/sports/2013/02/22/under-armour-suing-nike-i-will-advertising/1938605

Mullin, B., Hardy, S., & Sutton, W. (2007). *Sport marketing*. Champaign, IL: Human Kinetics.

MyGolfSpy. (2009, July 16). 10 ways (not) to buy fake gold clubs on eBay! Retrieved from https://mygolfspy.com/fake-counterfeit-golf-clubs

Nike code of conduct. (2017, September). Retrieved from https://sbi-stg-s3-media-bucket.s3.amazonaws.com/wp-content/uploads/2018/05/14214943/Nike_Code_of_Conduct_2017_English.pdf

Nike waffle trainer. (n.d.). Retrieved from https://americanhistory.si.edu/collections/search/object/nmah_1413776

Nisen, M. (2013, May 9). How Nike solved its sweatshop problem. *Business Insider*. Retrieved from www.businessinsider.com/how-nike-solved-its-sweatshop-problem-2013-5

NSGA management conference & team dealer harassment policy. (n.d.). National Sporting Goods Association. Retrieved from www.nsga.org/globalassets/2018-management-conference/nsga-mctds-code-of-conduct---11.10.2017.pdf

O'Bannon v. National Collegiate Athletic Association. (2014). United States District Court for the Northern District of California. No. C 09-3329 CW.

Ocean Reef. (2019, April 2). Ocean Reef safety recall of Neptune Space integrated diving masks. [Recall letter]. Retrieved from https://oceanreefgroup.com/wp-content/uploads/2019/04/Recall-Letter.pdf

Official site of the 2019 Masters Tournament. (2019). Retrieved from www.masters.com/en_US/info/copyright/index.html

Pai, A. (2014, August 12). Athos raises $12.2M for health sensing clothing. Retrieved from www.mobihealth-news.com/35705/athos-raises-12-2m-for-health-sensing-clothing

Patents assigned to Fitbit, Inc. (n.d.). Retrieved from https://patents.justia.com/assignee/fitbit-inc

Petersen, E. (2012). Self-regulation: Managing the business environment through compliance. *Journal of Business Administration* online. Retrieved from https://www.atu.edu/jbao/spring2012/SELF_REGULATION.pdf

Powell, B., & Skarbek, D. (2006, March 1). Sweatshops and third world living standards: Are the jobs worth the sweat? *Journal of Labor Research, 27*(2), 263-274.

PRNewswire. (2016a, November 8). Licensed sports merchandise market - Global industry analysis, size, share, growth, trends, and forecast 2016–2024. London. Retrieved from www.prnewswire.com/news-releases/licensed-sports-merchandise-market--global-industry-analysis-size-share-growth-trends-and-forecast-2016---2024-300375800.html

PRNewswire. (2016b, October 20). Licensed sports merchandise market to reach US$48.17 billion by 2024—A new research report by Transparency Market Research. Retrieved from www.prnewswire.com/news-releases/licensed-sports-merchandise-market-to-reach-us4817-billion-by-2024---a-new-research-report-by-transparency-market-research-597749011.html

Reuters. (2019, March 25). Nike fined 12.5m euros for blocking United, Barcelona merchandise sales in Europe. Retrieved from http://global.espn.com/football/manchester-united/story/3808341/nike-fined-125m-euros-for-blocking-united-and-barcelona-merchandise-sales-in-europe

Rich, J. (2016, February 2). Consumer protection for the sports and fitness industry. Federal Trade Commission. Remarks to the Sports and Fitness Industry Association. Retrieved from https://www.ftc.gov/system/files/documents/public_statements/914483/160202consumerprosports.pdf

Roberts, D. (2017, June 23). Adidas has nearly doubled its US sneaker market share—at Nike's expense. Retrieved from https://finance.yahoo.com/news/adidas-nearly-doubled-us-sneaker-market-share-nikes-expense-153106743.html

Roggie, A. (2019, February 22). CSR at its best. How top brands are stepping up. Retrieved from www.adlibbing.org/2019/02/11/csr-at-its-best-how-top-brands-are-stepping-up

Rosner, S., & Shapiro, R. (2011). *The business of sports* (2nd ed.). Burlington, MA: Jones & Bartlett.

Rovell, D. (2015, December 8). LeBron James signs lifetime Nike deal. *ESPN*. Retrieved from www.espn.com/nba/story/_/id/14314807/lebron-james-signs-life-deal-nike

Rule changes by national sports organizations. (2018, October 25). National Sporting Goods Association. Retrieved from www.nsga.org/news/news-releases/industry-news-archives/national-organization-rule-changes/

Schupak, A. (2018, April). Golf is the No. 1 U.S. sport... for patents. National Golf Foundation. Retrieved from https://www.thengfq.com/2018/04/golf-is-the-no-1-u-s-sport-for-patents/

SFIA overview. (2019). Sport & Fitness Industry Association. Who we are. Retrieved from www.sfia.org/about/overview

Sharp, L., Moorman, A., & Claussen, C. (2017). *Sport law: A managerial approach* (3rd ed.). Oxfordshire, England: Taylor & Francis.

Smith, M. (2012, March 26). Champions: Bill Battle, licensing icon. *Sports Business Journal*. Retrieved from www.sportsbusinessdaily.com/Journal/Issues/2012/03/26/Champions/Battle.aspx

Smith, M. (2016, March 25). PGA Tour moves licensing business. *Sports Business Daily*. Retrieved from www.sportsbusinessdaily.com/Journal/Issues/2016/01/25/Marketing-and-Sponsorship/PGAT-Fermata.aspx

Spoo, R. (2012). Three myths for aging copyrights: Tithonus, Dorian Gray, Ulysses. *Cardozo Arts & Entertainment Law Journal, 31*(1), 77-112.

Sporting goods market: Global demand analysis & opportunity outlook 2023. (2019, May). Report ID 214. Retrieved from www.researchnester.com/reports/sporting-goods-market-global-demand-analysis-opportunity-outlook-2023/214

Sport Market Analytics. (n.d.). Retrieved from http://sportsmarketanalytics.com.eu1.proxy.openathens.net/research.aspx?subrid=177

Stachura, M. (2016, March 3). What you need to know about counterfeit golf clubs. *Golf Digest*. Retrieved from www.golfdigest.com/story/what-you-need-to-know-about-counterfeit-golf-clubs

Statista. (2018). Sporting goods industry—statistics and facts. Excerpt from *Sporting goods market in the United States*. Retrieved from www.statista.com/topics/961/sporting-goods

Sustainability Accounting Standards Board. (2015, September). Toys and sporting goods accountability standards. Consumption II Sector.

Thomas, L. (2019, April 17). Nike's fix for boosting sales at home—women. *CNBC*. Retrieved from www.cnbc.com/2019/04/16/nikes-fix-for-boosting-sales-at-home-women.html

Tracy, M. (2016, September 9). With wearable tech deals, new player data is up for grabs. *The New York Times*. Retrieved from www.nytimes.com/2016/09/11/sports/ncaafootball/wearable-technology-nike-privacy-college-football.html

Turner, B., & Miloch, K. (2017). Marketing for sport business success (2nd ed.). Dubuque, IA: Kendall Hunt Publishing.

van Schaik, J.W. (2019, March 5). *Decathlon's sales up in 2018 but not like in previous years*. Retrieved from www.bike-eu.com/home/nieuws/2019/03/decathlons-sales-up-in-2018-but-not-like-in-previous-years-10135440?vakmedianet-approve-cookies=1&_ga=2.199861550.1803665364.1559675569-46831331.1559675569

Weisheng, C., Kwang-yong, L., & Doyeon, W. (2014). Consumer behavior toward counterfeit sporting goods. *Social Behavior and Personality, 42*(4), 615-624.

Working conditions. (2016, January). *WSFGI code of conduct guiding principles*. World Federation of the Sporting Goods Industry. Retrieved from https://www.wfsgi.org/sites/default/files/inline-files/WFSGI%20Code%20of%20Conduct%202016.pdf

Yahoo! Finance NKE. (n.d.). Retrieved from https://finance.yahoo.com/quote/NKE/financials?p=NKE

Yahoo! Finance UA. (n.d.). Retrieved from https://finance.yahoo.com/quote/ua/financials?p=ua

Zakrzewski, L., & Smith, C. (2018, December 1). Private investment into sport—what governing bodies need to know. Law in sports. Retrieved from www.lawinsport.com/topics/articles/item/private-investment-into-sport-what-governing-bodies-need-to-know

Chapter 11

Adler, B. (2007, June 14). The case against golf. *The Guardian*. Retrieved from www.theguardian.com/commentisfree/2007/jun/14/thecaseagainstgolf

Arai, S., & Pedlar, A. (2003). Moving beyond individualism in leisure theory: A critical analysis of concepts of community and social engagement. *Leisure Studies, 22*, 185-202.

Associated Press. (2003, June 3). Johnson decides to make Masters commercial-free again. *ESPN.com*. Retrieved from www.espn.com/golf/story?id=1562611

Associated Press. (2012, August 21). Augusta adds first woman members. *ESPN.com*. Retrieved from www.espn.com/golf/story/_/id/8284599/augusta-national-admits-condoleezza-rice-darla-moore-first-two-female-members

Blodgett, A.T., Schinke, R.J., Fisher, L.A., George, C.W., Peltier, D., Ritchie, S., & Pickard, P. (2008). From practice to praxis: Community-based strategies for aboriginal youth sport. *Journal of Sport & Social Issues, 32*, 393-414.

Bowers, M.T., & Hunt, T.M. (2011). The President's Council on Physical Fitness and the systematization of children's play in America. *The International Journal of the History of Sport, 28*, 1496-1511.

Bureau of Labor Statistics. (2018, April 13). *Occupational outlook handbook: Fitness trainers and instructors*. Retrieved from www.bls.gov/ooh/personal-care-and-service/fitness-trainers-and-instructors.htm

Card, A.J. (2017). Moving beyond the WHO definition of health: A new perspective for an aging world and the emerging era of value-based care. *World Medical and Health Policy, 9*, 127-137.

Chris Rousses named CEO of 24 Hour Fitness USA, Inc. (2017, May 16). 24 Hour Fitness. Retrieved from www.24hourfitness.com/company/press_room/press_releases/2017/20170516.html

Club Managers Association of America. (2015). Club management: Path to a rewarding future. Alexandria, Virginia. Retrieved from https://www.kopplinandkuebler.com/pdf/student_path_road5.pdf

Coakley, J. (1992). Burnout among adolescent athletes: A personal failure or social problem? *Sociology of Sport Journal, 9*, 271-285.

Council for Responsible Nutrition. (2017, October 19). Dietary supplement usage increases, says new survey. Retrieved from www.crnusa.org/newsroom/dietary-supplement-usage-increases-says-new-survey

De Bosscher, V., Sotiriadou, P., & van Bottenburg, M. (2013). Scrutinizing the sport pyramid metaphor: An examination of the relationship between elite success and mass participation in Flanders. *International Journal of Sport Policy and Politics, 5*, 319-339.

Dietary Supplement Health and Education Act of 1994, Pub. L. 103-417, 108 Stat. 4325, codified as amended in scattered sections of 21 and 42 U.S.C.

Examples of tax-exempt social and recreational clubs. (2019, April 16). Internal Revenue Service. Retrieved from https://www.irs.gov/charities-non-profits/other-non-profits/examples-of-tax-exempt-social-and-recreational-clubs

Findlay, H., Corbett, R., & Lech, D. (2003). *A guide to employment contracts for coaches*. Brock University Center for Sport and Law. Retrieved from http://www.swimontario.com/userfiles/file/Club%20Services/AGM/2009/Presentations/Corbett/employmentcontractsforcoaches.pdf

Gillard, A., & Witt, P. (2008). Recruitment and retention in youth programs. *Journal of Park and Recreation Administration, 26*(2), 177-188.

Hanstad, D.V., & Skille, E.Å. (2010). Does elite sport develop mass sport? A Norwegian case study. *Scandinavian Sport Studies Forum, 1*, 51-68.

IBIS World. (2018, March). *Golf courses and country clubs in the US*. IBIS World industry market research report. Retrieved from www.ibisworld.com/industry-trends/market-research-reports/arts-entertainment-recreation/golf-courses-country-clubs.html

IBIS World. (2019). *Golf courses and country club industry in the US*. IBIS World industry market research report. Retrieved from www.ibisworld.com/industry-trends/

market-research-reports/arts-entertainment-recreation/golf-courses-country-clubs.html

International Health Conference. (1946). *Constitution of the World Health Organization*. Retrieved from http://apps.who.int/gb/bd/PDF/bd47/EN/constitution-en.pdf

Jolly-Ryan, J. (2006). Teed off about private club discrimination on the taxpayers' dime: Tax exemptions and other government privileges to discriminatory private clubs. SSRN. Retrieved from https://papers.ssrn.com/sol3/papers.cfm?abstract_id=894335

Kaiser, J. (2018, March 22). Final 2018 budget bill eases biomedical researchers' policy worries. *Science*. Retrieved from www.sciencemag.org/news/2018/03/final-2018-budget-bill-eases-biomedical-researchers-policy-worries

Kay, T. (2000). Sporting excellence: A family affair? *European Physical Education Review, 6,* 151-169.

Kirk, D. (2005). Physical education, youth sport and lifelong participation: The importance of early learning experiences. *European Physical Education Review, 11,* 239-255.

Koivula, N. (1999). Sport participation: Differences in motivation and actual participation due to gender typing. *Journal of Sport Behavior, 22,* 360-380.

Marmot, M. (2002). The influence of income on health: Views of an epidemiologist. *Health Affairs, 21*(2), 31-46.

McDonald, J. (2019, April 6). Golfers break gender barriers at the Augusta National women's amateur championship. *CNBC*. Retrieved from www.cnbc.com/2019/04/05/augusta-national-hosts-inaugural-womens-amateur-championship.html

Mole, B. (2017, January 23). CDC abruptly cancels conference on health effects of climate change. *Ars Technica*. Retrieved from https://arstechnica.com/science/2017/01/self-censoring-fears-swirl-as-cdc-abruptly-nixes-climate-and-health-summit

Morgan, W.P. (2001). Prescription of physical activity: A paradigm shift. *Quest, 53,* 366-382.

National Club Association. (2010, January 11). Club industry trends and economic outlook. Retrieved from www.nationalclub.org/clientuploads/Howe-NCAClubTrendsandEconomicOutlook-1.11.10.pdf

Organizational profile facts and figures. (n.d.). YMCA. Retrieved from www.ymca.net/organizational-profile

Partner companies. (n.d.). Seidler Equity Partners. Retrieved from www.sepfunds.com/Partner-Companies/overview.html

Pickett, K.E., James, O.W., & Wilkinson, R.G. (2006). Income inequality and the prevalence of mental illness: A preliminary international analysis. *Journal of Epidemiology & Community Health, 60,* 646-647.

Rader, B.G. (1977). The quest for subcommunities and the rise of American sport. *American Quarterly, 29,* 355-369.

Rondeau, C. (2019). Let's be friends. Planet Fitness, Inc. Retrieved from https://www.planetfitness.com/franchising/become-a-franchisee

Salgot, M., & Tapias, J.C. (2006). Golf courses: Environmental impacts. *Tourism and Hospitality Research, 6,* 218-226.

Sirak, R. (2015, February 23). Making big bucks, spending big bucks: How the Masters turns a $29 million profit. *Golf Digest*. Retrieved from https://www.golfdigest.com/story/the-masters-finances-ron-sirak

Statement by Hootie Johnson. (2002, July 9). Retrieved from www.golfchannel.com/article/golf-channel-newsroom/statement-hootie-johnson

Stern, M. (2011). Real or rogue charity? Private health clubs vs. the YMCA, 1970-2010. *Business and Economic History On-Line, 9,* 1-17. Retrieved from www.thebhc.org/sites/default/files/stern.pdf

U.S. Department of Health and Human Services. (2017, January 26). Facts & statistics. Retrieved from www.hhs.gov/fitness/resource-center/facts-and-statistics/index.html

U.S. Department of Health and Human Services. (2018). *Physical activity guidelines for Americans* (2nd ed.). Washington, D.C.: U.S. Department of Health and Human Services.

U.S. Department of Health and Human Services and U.S. Department of Agriculture. (2015). *2015-2020 dietary guidelines for Americans* (8th ed.). Washington, D.C.: U.S. Department of Health and Human Services.

U.S. Federal Trade Commission. (2001, April). *Dietary supplements: An advertising guide for industry*. Retrieved from www.ftc.gov/system/files/documents/plain-language/bus09-dietary-supplements-advertising-guide-industry.pdf

U.S. Food and Drug Administration. (2017, November 6). *FDA 101: Dietary supplements*. Retrieved from www.fda.gov/ForConsumers/ConsumerUpdates/ucm050803.htm

Wall, M., & Côté, J. (2007). Development activities that lead to dropout and investment in sport. *Physical Education and Sport Pedagogy, 12,* 77-87.

Weinreb, M. (2018, April 2). Martha Burk, Hootie Johnson, and Augusta National, 15 years later. *The Ringer*. Retrieved from www.theringer.com/2018/4/2/17187212/martha-burk-hootie-johnson-the-masters-15-years-later

Werner, A. (2017, January 30). Personal training: A historically unregulated occupation with change on the horizon. Retrieved from https://s3.amazonaws.com/documents.lexology.com/2975c178-2c19-4831-8b56-7d9451c5cb63.pdf

Wheeler, K., & Nauright, J. (2006). A global perspective on the environmental impact of golf. *Sport in Society: Cultures, Commerce, Media, Politics, 9,* 427-443.

Woolf, S.H., Aron, L., Dubay, L., Simon, S.M., Zimmerman, E., & Luk, K.X. (2015). *How are income and wealth linked to health and longevity?* Washington, D.C.: Urban Institute.

YMCA. (2011). Board leadership and governance best practices. Retrieved from http://www.csaymca.org/uploads/3/4/6/6/3466162/board-leadership-governance-best-practices.pdf

Chapter 12

About Us. (2019). National Sports Marketing Network. Retrieved from https://sportsmarketingnetwork.com/about.shtml

AOC loses full federal court appeal for Telstra I go to Rio advertisements. (2017, December 22). MinsterEllison. Retrieved from www.lexology.com/library/detail.aspx?g=f552ce63-5e5c-45a5-b311-9849db6534b0

Armstrong, G., & Kotler, P. (2017). *Marketing: An introduction* (13th ed.). London, England: Pearson.

Article 1, officers. (n.d.). Sports Marketing Association. *Constitution and bylaws*. Retrieved from https://static1.squarespace.com/static/54358491e4b0e09faedc4a1b/t/55e9a8a5e4b09902ba0abf63/1441376421037/SMA+--+Constitution.pdf

Bartlett, P. (2007). Ambush marketing. *Convergence, 3*, 31.

Board members. (n.d.). National Sports Marketing Network. Retrieved from https://sportsmarketing-network.com/board.shtml

Chadwick, S., & Burton, N. (2011). The evolving sophistication of ambush marketing: A typology of strategies. *Thunderbird International Business Review, 53*(6), 709-719.

College Football Playoff. (n.d.). CFP governance. Retrieved from https://collegefootballplayoff.com/sports/2019/4/3/governance.aspx

Crimson Hexagon. (2014, February 3). Beats by Dre vs Bose. Retrieved from Beats-vs-bose-analyzing-consumer-response-REBRAND_Mar16.pdf

Crompton, J.L. (2004). Sponsorship ambushing in sport. *Managing Leisure, 9*, 1-12.

Curtis, C. (2019, February 21). Nike's stock dropped after Zion Williamson's shoe exploded. Retrieved from https://ftw.usatoday.com/2019/02/nike-stock-zion-williamson-injury

Cushnan, D. (2014, March). Bose replaces Motorola as NFL headset provider - Sports Sponsorship & Sports Supply news - Football North America - SportsPro Media. Retrieved from www.sportspromedia.com/news/bose_replaces_motorola_as_nfls_headset_manufacturer

Dumais, F. (2014, February 1). Top 10 sponsorship ambushes. Retrieved from https://en.elevent.co/blogs/sponsorship/16644081-top-10-sponsorship-ambushes

Dyer, R.F., & Kuehl, P.G. (1978). A longitudinal study of corrective advertising. *Journal of Marketing Research, 15*(1), 39-48.

Fetchko, M., Roy, D.P., and Clow, K.E. (2018). *Sports marketing*. London, England: Routledge.

FIFA v. Nike, Inc., 285 F. Supp. 2d 64 / D.C. Cir. 2003.

Forbes, Inc. (2019). Sports agencies: The list. Retrieved from www.forbes.com/sports-agencies/list/#tab:overall

Friedman, A. (1995, March 1). Protection of sports trademarks. *Loyola Law School of Los Angeles Entertainment Law Review, 15*, 689-715.

Grauschopf, S. (2019, May 21). Sport sweepstakes: Win sports, fitness, and outdoor prizes. *The Balance Everyday*. Retrieved from www.thebalanceeveryday.com/sports-sweepstakes-win-sports-fitness-and-outdoors-prizes-887118

Handley, L. (2018, September 25). Sponsorship spending to hit $66 billion worldwide, but most firms don't know if it really works. Retrieved from www.cnbc.com/2018/09/25/does-sponsorship-work-deals-value-to-reach-66-billion-in-2018.html

Harris County-Houston Sports Authority. (n.d.). About us. Retrieved from www.houstonsports.org/about-houston-sports/

Helm, B. (2019, April 14). How Dr. Dre's headphones company became a billion-dollar business. Retrieved from www.inc.com/audacious-companies/burt-helm/beats.html

Hepburn, M. (n.d.). Timeline: History of the Coca-Cola Company and the Olympic Games. Retrieved from www.coca-cola.co.uk/stories/making-history-with-the-olympic-games

Hill, K. (2016). Ambush marketing: Is it deceitful or a probable strategic tactic in the Olympic Games? *Marquette Sports Law Review, 27*(1), 197-215.

Horner, S.N. (2014). DMCA: Professional sports leagues' answer to protecting their broadcasting rights against illegal streaming. *Marquette Sports Law Review, 24*(2), 435-462.

Horowitz, B. (2013, March 17). March Madness marketers run the ambush route. *USA Today*. Retrieved from www.usatoday.com/story/money/business/2013/03/17/march-madness-final-four-pizza-hut-spam-hooters/1987889

Hums, M., & MacLean, J.C. (2009). *Governance and policy in sport organizations* (2nd ed.). Scottsdale, AZ: Holcomb Hathaway Publishers.

International Olympic Committee. (2015). *Olympic Charter*. Lausanne, Switzerland: International Olympic Committee.

Jackson, E. (2017, June 30). Why ESPN is still well-positioned to keep NFL rights in 2022 and beyond. Retrieved from www.cnbc.com/2017/06/30/espn-is-well-positioned-to-keep-nfl-rights.html

Jago, L., Chalip, L., Brown, G., Mules, T., & Ali, S. (2003). Building events into destination branding: Insights from experts. *Event Management, 8*, 3-14.

Jago, L., Dwyer, L., Lipman, J., Van Lill, D., & Voyster, S. (2010, October). Optimising the potential of mega-events: An overview. *International Journal of Event and Festival Management, 1*(3), 220-237.

Kissimmee Sports Commission. (n.d.). About us. Retrieved from www.experiencekissimmee.com/sports/about-us

Mazodier, M., Quester, P., & Chandon, J.L. (2012). Unmasking the ambushers: Conceptual framework and empirical evidence. *European Journal of Marketing, 46*(1/2), 192-214.

McKelvey, S., & Grady, J. (2008). Sponsorship program protection strategies for special sport events: Are event organizers outmaneuvering ambush marketers? *Journal of Sport Management, 22,* 550-586.

Meenaghan, T. (1998). Ambush marketing: Corporate strategy and consumer reaction. *Psychology & Marketing, 15*(4), 305-322.

Miller, C. (2018, October 26). Clothing wars: Apparel giant Under Armour sends a cease and desist to local business. Retrieved from www.bendsource.com/bend/clothing-wars/Content?oid=8127194

Mission. (n.d.). *Constitution and bylaws.* Sport Marketing Association. Retrieved from https://static1.squarespace.com/static/54358491e4b0e09faedc4a1b/t/55e9a8a5e4b09902ba0abf63/1441376421037/SMA+--+Constitution.pdf

Mohsin. M. (2019, March 7). 10 social media statistics you need to know in 2019. Retrieved from www.oberlo.com/blog/social-media-marketing-statistics

Muller, M. (2015, December 1). The mega-event syndrome. *Journal of American Planning Association,* 6-17.

National Collegiate Athletic Association (NCAA). (2016). *The NCAA's advertising and promotional guidelines.* Indianapolis, IN: National Collegiate Athletics Association.

O'Brien, D., & Chalip, L. (2007). Sport events and strategic leveraging: Pushing towards the triple bottom line. In A. Woodside and D. Martin (Eds.), *Tourism management: Analysis, behavior and strategy* (pp. 318-338). Wallingford, Oxford: CAB International.

Orange Bowl. (n.d.). About the Orange Bowl: Pillars of the South Florida community. Retrieved from www.orangebowl.org/about/whoweare/abouttheorangebowl/

Osborn, D.W. (2019, April 11). Changing the cycle: Peloton removes songs at heart of copyright infringement suit. Retrieved from www.lexology.com/library/detail.aspx?g=97ae3201-e2ea-45d2-98f3-98aabdb9bc08

O'Sullivan, P., & Murphy, P. (1998). Ambush marketing: The ethical issues. *Psychology & Marketing, 15*(4), 349-366.

Paquette, A. (2015, May 14). 3 corporate functions that need to pay attention to Gen Z now. Retrieved from www.mediapost.com/publications/article/249962/3-corporate-functions-that-need-to-pay-attention-t.html

Pathak, S. (2017, February 23). The definitive oral history of the Oreo 'You can still dunk in the dark' Super Bowl tweet. *Digi.com.* Retrieved from https://digiday.com/marketing/oral-history-oreo-tweet

Paule-Koba, A.L. (2015). Bidding and planning for different events. In T.J. Aicher, A.L. Paule-Koba, & B. Newland (Eds.), *Sport facility and event management* (pp. 83-102). Burlington, MA: Jones & Bartlett Publishers.

Pavitt, M. (2019, April 14). Bach tells athletes to begin negotiations with NOCs over Rule 40 restrictions. *Inside the Games.* Retrieved from www.insidethegames.biz/articles/1077966/bach-tells-athletes-to-begin-negotiations-with-nocs-over-rule-40-restrictions

Payne, M. (1998). Ambush marketing: The undeserved advantage. *Psychology & Marketing, 15*(4), 323-331.

Pedersen, P.M., & Thibault, L. (2014). *Contemporary sport management* (5th ed.). Champaign, IL: Human Kinetics.

Pitts, B.G., & Stotlar, D.K. (2007). *Fundamentals of sport marketing* (3rd ed.). Morgantown, WV: Fitness Information Technology.

Placek, C. (2019, February 13). Report: Elk Grove sees 40-to-1 return on bowl game investment. Retrieved from www.dailyherald.com/business/20190213/report-elk-grove-sees-40-to-1-return-on-bowl-game-investment-

Pritchard, M.P., Havitz, M.E., & Howard, D.R. (1999). Analyzing the commitment-loyalty link in service contexts. *Journal of the Academy of Marketing Science, 27*(3), 333.

Prize scams. (2014, April). Federal Trade Commission. Consumer Protection. Retrieved from www.consumer.ftc.gov/articles/0199-prize-scams

Purdum, D. (2017, March 14). 70 million brackets, $10.4 billion in bets expected for March Madness. Retrieved from www.espn.com/chalk/story/_/id/18901384/70-million-brackets-104-billion-bet-ncaa-tournament

Romaniuk, J., & Sharp, B. (2004). Conceptualizing and measuring brand salience, *Marketing Theory, 4*(4), 327-342.

Scassa, T. (2011). Ambush marketing and the right of association: Clamping down on references to that big event with all the athletes in a couple of years. *Journal of Sport Management, 25*(4), 354-370.

Scotts extends partnership with Major League Baseball. (2019, March 21). Scotts MiracleGro. Retrieved from www.globenewswire.com/news-release/2019/03/21/1758826/0/en/Scotts-Extends-Partnership-With-Major-League-Baseball.html

Seelye, K. (2015, July 29). Many Bostonians feel relief as Olympic bid ends, others see a stagnant city. *The New York Times,* p. A-9.

Shani, D., & Sandler, D.M. (1998). Ambush marketing: Is confusion to blame for the flickering of the flame?* *Psychology & Marketing, 15*(4), 367-383.

Shannon, R. (2010, September 27). What is the undeniable mark of a champion? The Wheaties cereal box. Retrieved from https://bleacherreport.com/articles/473954-the-undeniable-mark-of-a-champion-the-wheaties-cereal-box

Sharp, L., Moorman, A., & Claussen, C. (2017). *Sport law: A managerial approach* (3rd ed.). Oxfordshire, England: Taylor & Francis.

SI Staff. (2018, September 19). Ranking the top 10 athletes by endorsement income for 2019. Retrieved from www.si.com/sports-illustrated/2018/ranking-top-10-athletes-endorsement-deals-income

SI Wire. (2014, October 5). NFL players can no longer wear Beats by Dre headphones on camera. Retrieved from www.si.com/extra-mustard/2014/10/05/nfl-players-beats-dre-headphones-banned

Sliffman, A.J. (2011). Unconstitutional hosting of the Super Bowl: Anti-ambush marketing clean zones' violation of the First Amendment. *Marquette Sports Law Review, 22,* 235-255.

Smith, S. (2018, October 16). Spons-O-Meter: NBA enters season with 26 league-level partnerships. *Street 7 Smith Sport Business Journal Daily.* Retrieved from www.sportsbusinessdaily.com/Daily/Issues/2018/10/16/NBA-Season-Preview/Sponsometer.aspx

Stanglin, R. (2014, January 17). Putin: Gays welcome at Olympics, but leave minors at home. *USA Today.* Retrieved from www.usatoday.com/story/news/world/2014/01/17/vladimir-putin-olympics-sochi-gays/4579389

St. Louis Sports Commission. (n.d.). Who we are. Retrieved from https://stlsports.org/about-us

Supovitz, F. (2005) *The sports event management and marketing playbook.* Hoboken, NJ: John Wiley & Sons.

Sweepstakes as a marketing tool: Everyone's a winner. (n.d.). KMT. Retrieved from www.kleinmoynihan.com/sweepstakes-as-marketing-tool-everyones-a-winner

Tiell, B., & Ying, S. (2016, August 17). Preliminary lessons learned: Cultural implications of uncertainty avoidance, perceptions of health and safety concerns, and decisions to attend the 2016 Rio Olympics. *Proceedings of the 8th International Sport Business Symposium in Rio de Janeiro during the XXXI Olympic Games—Olympics and Agenda 2020.* Proceedings edited by Holger Preuss (University of Mainz) in cooperation with Lamartine DaCosta (Rio de Janeiro).

Tough Mudder. (n.d.). Press room: News, photos and everything else you need to know to cover probably the toughest event on the planet. Retrieved from https://toughmudder.com/press-room

Ukman, L. (2015). *IEG's guide to sponsorship: Everything you need to know about sports, arts, event, and entertainment and cause marketing.* Chicago, IL: IEG, LLC.

Welsh, J. (2002). In defense of ambush marketing. *Sponsorship Report, 21*(11), 4-5.

White, L. (2017, May 9). Priciest naming rights deal ever? Retrieved from www.venuesnow.com/priciest-naming-rights-deal-ever

Wilson, D. (2019, March 21). Reese's celebrates No. 3 seeds with three-cup packs. Retrieved from www.miamiherald.com/sports/college/article228234279.html

World Federation Sporting Goods Industry. (2015). *Advertising around the Olympic Games: What you need to know as a sporting goods brand* [PDF document]. Retrieved from www.wfsgi.org/system/files/2017-01/160504Advertising%20Around%20the%20Olympic%20Games%20What%20You%20Need%20to%20Know%20as%20a%20Sporting%20Goods%20Brand.pdf

Chapter 13

Abelson, J. (2009, May 22). Pats plan lottery tie-in after NFL eases stance. *Boston Globe.* Retrieved from http://archive.boston.com/business/articles/2009/05/22/pats_plan_lottery_tie_in_after_nfl_eases_stance/

About the WLA. (2019). World Lotteries Association. Retrieved from www.world-lotteries.org/about-us/about-the-wla

About TXODDS. (2019). TDODDS. Retrieved from https://txodds.net/about

Americans will wager $8.5 billion on March Madness. (2019, March 18). Press release. America Gaming Association. Retrieved from www.americangaming.org/new/americans-will-wager-8-5-billion-on-march-madness/

Argentina sport betting. (2019). Retrieved from www.safestbettingsites.com/international/argentina

Australian Communications and Media Authority. (2018, November 7). Odds and betting ads in live broadcasts—the rules. Retrieved from www.acma.gov.au/theACMA/odds-and-betting-ads-in-live-sport-the-new-rules

Barker, M., & Britz, M. (2000). *Jokers wild. Legalized gambling in the twenty-first century.* Westport, CT: Praeger.

Betting and baseball. (2019, March 7). *Sport Business News.* Retrieved from http://sportsbusinessnews.com/content/betting-and-baseball

Betting on hockey. (2019, March 7). *Sport Business News.* Retrieved from http://sportsbusinessnews.com/content/betting-hockey

Bienvenido [Welcome]. (2019, March 4). Grupo Caliente. Retrieved from www.grupocaliente.com.mx/

Booton, J. (2019, June 5). MLS seeks player tracking in upcoming CBA negotiation. Retrieved from https://www.sporttechie.com/mls-soccer-player-tracking-wearables-data-cba-negotiation/

Breer, A. (2018, May 21). Legal gambling. Political football. *Sports Illustrated,* 16.

Bricknell, S. (2015, February 16). Corruption in Australian sport. *Trends and Controversies, 460.* Canberra: Australian Institute of Criminology.

Bustillos, E. (2018, August 9). Tucked away inside the Mohegan Sun Casino in Uncasville, Conn. is the Mohegan Sun Arena. Retrieved from www.wgbh.org/news/local-news/2018/08/09/the-mohegan-tribe-stands-apart-in-the-world-of-sports-ownership

China Sports Lottery Administration Center. (2011). *Annual report and accounts 2010.* Retrieved from www.lottery.gov.cn/events/2010/Default.aspx

Council of Europe Convention on the Manipulation of Sports Competitions, C.E.T.S. No. 215. Retrieved from www.coe.int/en/web/conventions/full-list/-/conventions/treaty/215

Davies, R. (2017). *Sports in American life: A history* (3rd ed.). Malden, MA: Blackwell Wiley.

Delaware sports betting. (2019, April 12). *Legal Sports Report*. Retrieved from www.legalsportsreport.com/delaware

Del. Code Ann. tit. 29, § 4801 (2019).

Draper, K. (2018, August 1). NBA has gaming partner. First in the U.S. *The New York Times*, p. B-10.

Enforcement Division. (n.d.). Nevada Gaming Control Board and Gaming Commission. Retrieved from https://gaming.nv.gov/index.aspx?page=46

The European Lotteries charter 2012. (2012). European Lotteries. Retrieved from www.european-lotteries.org/sport-charter

The European Lotteries code of conduct on sport betting. (2014, June 4). European Lotteries. Lisbon, Portugal. Retrieved from https://www.european-lotteries.org/document/el-code-conduct-sports-betting

The European Lotteries sports integrity plan. (2013, March). The 7-point program for the benefit and the further development of sport in Europe. European Lotteries. Retrieved from https://www.european-lotteries.org/sports-integrity-action-plan

Explanatory Report to the Council of Europe Convention on the Manipulation of Sports Competitions. (2014). C.E.T.S. No. 215. Retrieved from https://rm.coe.int/CoERMPublicCommonSearchServices/DisplayDCTMContent?documentId=09000016800d383f

FIFA integrity. (n.d.). *Federation Internationale de Football Association*. Retrieved from https://img.fifa.com/image/upload/sflftaz9asa0wajwlcio.pdf

FIFA strengthens global football integrity programme with Sportradar agreement. (2017, February 3). *Sportradar*. Retrieved from https://integrity.sportradar.com/news-archive/news/2017/02/fifa-strengthens-global-football-integrity-programme-sportradar-agreement

Gambling Commission. (2019, May). License conditions and codes of conduct. Great Britain. Retrieved from https://www.gamblingcommission.gov.uk/PDF/LCCP/Licence-conditions-and-codes-of-practice.pdf

The gambling (gaming and betting) control bill. (2016, August). Legal Supplement Part C to the Trinidad and Tobago Gazette, 55, 97. Retrieved from http://www.ttparliament.org/legislations/b2016h10.pdf

Gambling laws in Africa. (2019). Regional differences. Retrieved from www.gamblingsites.org/laws/africa

Gambling laws in Europe—the latest betting legislation changes. (2017, May 15). Retrieved from www.bookmakers.bet/12074/gambling-laws-europe

Glanz, J. (2018, May 24). States are making their case to keep federal regulation out of sports gambling. *The New York Times*, p. B9.

GLMS code of conduct: Embodying integrity. (2018, November). Global Lottery Monitoring System. Retrieved from https://glms-sport.org/wp-content/uploads/2019/03/Code-of-Conduct_FINAL.pdf

GLMS mid-term monitoring report 2018. (2018, July). Global Lottery Monitoring System. Retrieved from https://glms-sport.org/news/glms-mid-term-monitoring-report-2018-3/

Goldstein, J. (2003, November 19). Explosion: 1951 scandals threaten college hoops. *ESPN*. Retrieved from www.espn.com/classic/s/basketball_scandals_explosion.html

Gray, A. (2018, August 1). The history of sports betting legislation in the USA (Part I). *Sports Betting Dime*. Retrieved from www.sportsbettingdime.com/guides/legal/sports-betting-history-part-i/

Gray, A. (2019, January 25). The Vegas era: Major sports betting legislation in the USA (Part II). *Sports Betting Dime*. Retrieved from www.sportsbettingdime.com/guides/legal/sports-betting-history-part-ii/

Hanamizu, K. (2016, December 1). Gaming in Japan: An overview. Retrieved from https://content.next.westlaw.com/Document/I4a7d9db1bd5311e698d-c8b09b4f043e0/View/FullText.html?contextData=(sc.Default)&transitionType=Default&firstPage=true&bhcp=1

History. (n.d.). History Club Tijuana Xoloitzcuintles de Caliente. Retrieved from www.xolos.com.mx/historia.html

The history of the NASPL. (n.d.). North American Association of State and Provincial Lotteries. Retrieved from www.naspl.org/nasplhistory

Holden, J. (2019, March 12). Renewed hope for legal Canada sports betting springs up in Ontario. *Legal Sports Report*. Retrieved from www.legalsportsreport.com/30147/canada-sports-betting-push

Humphreys, B. (2017). An overview of sports betting regulation in the United States. [Working paper]. West Virginia University College of Business and Economics.

International Olympic Committee. (2016, May). *Handbook on protecting sport from competition manipulation*. Interpol-IOC Integrity in Sport Initiative. Retrieved from https://stillmed.olympic.org/media/Document%20Library/OlympicOrg/IOC/What-We-Do/Protecting-Clean-Athletes/Betting/Education-Awareness-raising/Interpol-IOC-Handbook-on-Protecting-Sport-from-Competition-Manipulation.pdf

James, E. (2018, May 17). NCAA supports federal sports wagering regulation. Board allows championships in states that permit sports wagering. *NCAA News*, 1.

The jewels of Caribbean archipelago that offer online sportsbook licenses. (2019, January 25). Retrieved from www.sportsbettingdime.com/guides/legal/caribbean-licensing-regions/

Johnson, R. (2018, May 18). The centuries-old history of how sports betting became illegal in the United States in the first place. *SBNation*. Retrieved from www.sbnation.com/2018/5/18/17353994/sports-betting-illegal-united-states-why

Lapointe, J. (2019, March 18). Expert views: Q&A: Richard McGowan on legal sports betting. SAGE Business Researcher. doi: 10.1177/237455680509.n6

Levinson, M. (2006). A sure bet: Why New Jersey would benefit from legalized sports wagering. *Sports Lawyers Journal, 13*, 143-178.

Li, H., Zhang, J., Mao, L., & Min, S. (2012, January). Assessing corporate social responsibility in China's sports lottery administration and its influence on consumption behavior. *Journal of Gambling Studies, 28*, 515-540.

A look inside the numbers of sports betting in the U.S. and overseas. (2018, April 16). *Street & Smith's Sports Business Journal*. Retrieved from www.sportsbusinessdaily.com/Journal/Issues/2018/04/16/World-Congress-of-Sports/Research.aspx

Maule, T. (2015, May 12). SI vault: Players are not just people: The NFL suspends its "Golden Boy." *Sports Illustrated*. Retrieved from www.si.com/nfl/2015/05/12/si-vault-paul-hornung-alex-karras-pete-rozelle

Meister, A. (2017). Casino city's Indian gaming industry report 2017. Casino City Press.

Mexico sports betting. (n.d.). Retrieved from www.safestbettingsites.com/international/mexico

Mise-Au-Jeu. (n.d.). *Loto Quebec*. Retrieved from https://miseojeu.lotoquebec.com/en/how-to-play/home

Miselem, S. (2018, September 8). Maradona's new club owned by powerful clan with shady ties. *IOL*. Retrieved from www.iol.co.za/sport/soccer/maradonas-new-club-owned-by-powerful-clan-with-shady-ties-16952787

Miss. Code Ann. §75-76-301 (2018).

Mississippi sports betting. (2019, April 12). *Legal Sports Report*. Retrieved from www.legalsportsreport.com/mississippi

Moorman, A. (2010, June 1). Sport lotteries: The professional sports leagues take on the state of Delaware, again! *Sport Marketing Quarterly, 19*, 107-109.

Murphy v. NCAA, 138 S. Ct. 1461 (2018).

National Basketball Association. (2012). *Constitution and by-laws of the National Basketball Association*. Retrieved from http://thesportsesquires.com/wp-content/uploads/2014/01/NBA-Constitution-and-By-Laws.pdf

National Football League. (2006). *Constitution and bylaws of the National Football League*. Retrieved from http://static.nfl.com/static/content//public/static/html/careers/pdf/co_.pdf

NBA announces first betting-data partnership in U.S. with Sporttradar, Genius Sports. (2018, November 28). NBA official release. Retrieved from www.nba.com/article/2018/11/28/nba-sportradar-genius-sports-partnership-official-release

NBA collective bargaining agreement. (2017). National Basketball Players Association. Retrieved from https://nbpa.com/cba

NCAA examining impact of sports wagering. (2018, July 19). National Collegiate Athletic Association. Retrieved from www.ncaa.org/about/resources/media-center/news/ncaa-examining-impact-sports-wagering

NCAA uses technology services to monitor sports wagering. (2018, September 4). *National Collegiate Athletic Association*. Retrieved from www.ncaa.org/about/resources/media-center/news/ncaa-use-technology-services-monitor-sports-wagering

NCAA v. Governor of New Jersey, 730 F. 3d 208 (2013).

NCAA v. Governor of New Jersey, 832 F. 3d 389 (2016).

Nevada sports betting. (2019, March 10). *Legal Sports Report*. Retrieved from www.legalsportsreport.com/nevada

Nev. Admin. Code § 22.120 (2018).

NFL collective bargaining agreement. (2011). *National Football League*. Retrieved from https://nfllabor.files.wordpress.com/2010/01/collective-bargaining-agreement-2011-2020.pdf

The Nielsen Company. (2018). How much do leagues stand to gain from legal sports betting? *Nielsen Sports*. Retrieved from www.americangaming.org/sites/default/files/Nielsen%20Research%20-%20All%204%20Leagues%20FINAL.pdf

N.J. Admin. Code § C.5:12A-10 (2018).

Ofc. Comm. Baseball v. Markell, 579 F.3d 293 (2009).

Olympic movement code on the prevention of the manipulation of competitions. (n.d.). International Olympic Committee. Retrieved from www.olympic.org/prevention-competition-manipulation/regulations-legislation

Ostertag, T. (1992). From Shoeless Joe to Charlie Hustle: Major League Baseball's continuing crusade against sports gambling. *Seton Hall Journal of Sports Law, 2*, 19-49.

Pacifici, A. (2014). Scope and authority of sport league commissioner disciplinary power: Bounty and beyond. *Berkeley Journal of Entertainment and Sport Law, 3*(1), 93-116.

Panorama of the Macolin convention on the manipulation of sports competitions—Macolin convention (CETS No. 215). (2018, October 23). Council of Europe. Retrieved from https://rm.coe.int/panorama-of-the-macolin-convention/16809004c2

Pennsylvania sports betting. (2019, May 28). *Legal Sports Report*. Retrieved from www.legalsportsreport.com/pa

Perry, W., & Swanson, E. (2019, March 21). U.S. split on college vs. pro sport betting. *Charleston Gazette*, A-2.

Popularity of sport betting in Africa. (2019). Retrieved from www.gamblingafrica.com/indepth/online-sports-betting-growing-in-africa.asp

PricewaterhouseCoopers. (2014). Raising the stakes in Africa. Gambling outlook 2014-2018. Retrieved from https://www.pwc.co.za/en/assets/pdf/gambling-outlook-2014.pdf

Professional and Amateur Sports Protection Act, 28 U.S.C. § 3701, et seq.

Pro-Line. (n.d.). Ontario Lottery and Gaming Corporation. Retrieved from www.proline.ca/#proline?faq=show

Repetti, T., & Jung, S. (2014, July 1). Cross-border competition and the recession effect on Atlantic City's gaming volumes. *UNLV Gaming Research and Review Journal, 18*(2), 23-38.

Rhode Island sports betting. (2019, May 23). *Legal Sports Report.* Retrieved from www.legalsportsreport.com/ri

Rodenberg, R. (2015, March 25). The shield stands alone: Why does the NFL hate sports gambling? *Vice.* Retrieved from www.vice.com/en_us/article/53v87a/the-shield-stands-alone-why-does-the-nfl-hate-sports-gambling

Rodenberg, R. (2019, March 11). NCAA pivots to address sports integrity. *ESPN.* Retrieved from www.espn.com/chalk/story/_/id/26229344/how-ncaa-pivoting-address-sports-betting-integrity

Rose, P., & Hill, R. (2000). *Pete Rose: My prison without bars.* Emmaus, PA: Rodale Press.

Rosen, D. (2018, October 29). NHL, MGM Resorts form sports betting partnership. *NHL.com.* Retrieved from www.nhl.com/news/nhl-mgm-resorts-sports-betting-partnership/c-301392322

Schoenfeld, B. (2019, January 29). Will sport betting transform how games are watched or even played? *The New York Times.* Magazine feature.

Schwartz, L. (2003, November 19). Hornung, Karras suspended for betting on NFL. *ESPN.* Retrieved from www.espn.com/classic/s/moment010417hornung-karras-betting.html

Silver, A. (2014, November 14). Legalize sports betting. *The New York Times,* p. A27.

Smiley, B. (2017, November 13). A history of sport betting in the United States. Gambling laws and outlaws. Retrieved from https://sportshandle.com/gambling-laws-legislation-united-states-history/

Smith, G. (1992). Sucker bet or sure thing: A critical analysis of sports lotteries. *Journal of Gambling Studies, 8*(4), 331-349.

Sport betting revenue by state in 2019. (2019). Retrieved from www.thelines.com/betting/revenue

Sports betting in Japan. (2019). Retrieved from www.expatbets.com/japan/sports-betting

Sports betting law in South Africa. (2019). Retrieved from www.bethq.com/how-to-bet/articles/sports-betting-law-in-south-africa

Sports wagering law forces NCAA to remove championships from New Jersey. (2012, October 15). *NCAA News, 2,* 1.

Sports Wagering Market Integrity Act of 2018. S.3793. Congressional Bill 115th Congress. (2018, December 19).

Stadbrooke, S. (2019, January 10). Poland's sports betting turnover jumps 55% in 2018. Retrieved from https://calvinayre.com/2019/01/10/business/poland-sports-betting-turnover-2018/

The state of sports betting in Ghana. (2018, September 12). *Modern Ghana.* Retrieved from www.modernghana.com/sports/881989/the-state-of-sports-betting-in-ghana.html

Super Bowl LIII wagering estimates. (2019, January 28). Retrieved from www.americangaming.org/resources/super-bowl-liii-wagering-estimates

Trinidad and Tobago. (n.d.). *Simon's Online Betting Blog.* Retrieved from https://simonsblogpark.com/onlinegambling/simons-guide-to-gambling-in-trinidad-and-tobago

UK sports betting. (2019). Retrieved from www.onlinegambling.co/uk-bookmakers/

An unlimited number of licenses is the best option for Brazil's sports betting. (2019, May 28). Retrieved from www.yogonet.com/international/noticias/2019/05/23/49894-an-unlimited-number-of-licenses-is-the-best-option-for-brazils-sports-betting

U.S. Congress. (2018, December 19). S.3793 - Sports Wagering Market Integrity Act of 2018. Text. Retrieved from www.congress.gov/bill/115th-congress/senate-bill/3793/text

U.S. Sports Integrity. (2018). Retrieved from https://ussportsintegrity.com/

Vacek, H. (2011). The history of gambling. Center for Christian Ethics, Baylor University. Retrieved from https://www.baylor.edu/content/services/document.php/144593.pdf

Welcome to NASPL. (n.d.). North American Association of State and Provincial Lotteries. Retrieved from www.naspl.org

West Virginia sports betting. (2019, May 23). *Legal Sports Report.* Retrieved from www.legalsportsreport.com/wv

What is GLMS. (2019). Global Monitoring System. Retrieved from www.world-lotteries.org/members/glms

What we do. (n.d.). United Kingdom Gambling Commission. Retrieved from www.gamblingcommission.gov.uk/about/Who-we-are-and-what-we-do/Who-we-are-and-what-we-do.aspx

Which countries allow gambling on sports? Assessing the impact of betting around the world. (2018, May 16). ESPN Staff. *ESPN.* Retrieved from www.espn.com/espn/story/_/id/23518003/which-countries-allow-gambling-sports-assessing-impact-betting-world

World casino directory. (2019). Retrieved www.worldcasinodirectory.com

World Lottery Association bylaws. (2018, November 21). World Lottery Association. Retrieved from https://www.world-lotteries.org/about-us/wla-by-laws

World Lottery Association code of conduct. (2016, November). World Lottery Association. Retrieved from https://www.world-lotteries.org/images/documents/code-of-conduct/WLA_Code_of_Conduct_en_09-17.pdf

Chapter 14

About the British Esports Association. (2018). Retrieved from www.britishesports.org/about-us.html

About Worlds 2018 infographics viewership. (2018). Esc.watch. Retrieved from https://esc.watch/tournaments/lol/worlds-2018

AESF confirms 2018 Asian Games esports events. (2018, May 15). Press release, Asian Electronic Sports Federation Limited.

American Bar Association. (2016, December 15). The eSports explosion: Legal challenges and opportunities. Retrieved from www.americanbar.org/publications/landslide/2016-17/november-december/the_esports_explosion_legal_challenges_and_opportunities/

Andrews, M. (2018, July 11). NHL has 'no plans' to follow NBA 2K esports model. *SP Sports Series*. Retrieved from www.sportspromedia.com/news/nhl-esports-world-championships-nba-2k-plans

Anon. (n.d.). *History of eSports*. Retrieved from https://esportsforgamers.weebly.com/history-of-esports.html

Associated Press. (2019, March 6). Warriors draft first female player into NBA 2K esports league. Retrieved from www.nba.com/article/2019/03/06/warriors-draft-first-woman-nba-2k-league

Blum, B. (2017, October 23). The NCAA and esports don't mix—but soon, they might have to. Retrieved from www.espn.com/college-sports/story/_/id/21121852/the-ncaa-esports-mix-soon-to

Burk, D. (2013). Owning esports: Proprietary rights in professional computer gaming. *University of Pennsylvania Law Review, 161*, 1535-1578.

Carle, C. (2010, March 31). *Street Fighter. The complete history*. San Francisco, CA: Chronicle Books.

Chalk, A. (2014, October 31). Korean esports association proposes minimum salaries for pro gamers. *PC Gamer*. Retrieved from www.pcgamer.com/korean-e-sports-association-proposes-minimum-salaries-for-pro-gamers/

Chao, L. (2017). You must construct additional pylons: Building a better framework for esports governance. *Fordham Law Review, 86*(2), 15, 737-765.

Chmielewski, D. (2014). *Sorry, Twitch: ESPN's Skipper Says eSports "Not a Sport."* Retrieved from www.recode.net/2014/9/4/11630572/sorry-twitch-espns-skipper-says-esports-not-a-sport

Coakley, J. (2001). *Sport in Society: Issues and controversies*. New York: McGraw Hill.

Coogan, K. (2018). Let's play: A walk through a quarter-century-old copyright precedent applied to modern-day video games. *Fordham Intellectual Property, Media, and Entertainment Law Journal, 28*(2, 4), 381-419.

Definition of terms. (n.d.). *NCAA emerging sports for women program process guide*. Indianapolis, IN: National Collegiate Athletic Association.

Deloitte Insights. (2018). Esports graduates to the big leagues. Deloitte Center for Technology, Media, and Telecommunications.

DOSB closes before esports. (2018, October 29). Press release. Esports-Bund Deutschland. Berlin.

Esports constitution and bylaws. (2016, September 27). National Association of Collegiate eSports. Retrieved from http://nacesports.org/wp-content/uploads/2017/02/NAC-eSports-Constitution-Bylaws-9-29-2016-1-1.pdf

Esports in high school. (2018). National Federation of State High School Associations. Retrieved from www.nfhs.org/sports-resource-content/esports

Federation office. (n.d.). North American Scholastic Esports Federation. Retrieved from www.esportsfed.org/about/federation-office/

Fisher, M. (2018, November 19). Final Four Nite? NCAA explores move to sponsor esports. Retrieved from https://esportsobserver.com/final-four-nite-ncaa-explores-move-sponsor-esports/

Fogel, E. (2019, February 27). HSEL spring majors has largest prizing in high school esports history. Retrieved from https://variety.com/2019/gaming/news/hsel-spring-majors-2019-1203151045/

Funk, D., Pizzo, A., & Baker, B. (2018). eSport management: Embracing eSport education and research opportunities. *Sport Management Review, 21*, 7-31.

Garren, P. (2017, September 20). Asian esports federation elects new president with ties to Hong Kong Olympic committee. *Esports Observer*. Retrieved from https://esportsobserver.com/asian-esports-federation-new-president/

Gaudiosi, J. (2015, October 28). Global esports revenues to surpass $1.9 billion by 2018. *Fortune*. Retrieved from http://fortune.com/2015/10/28/global-esports-revenues-nearing-2-billion/

Good, O. (2012). Today is the 40th anniversary of the world's first known video gaming tournament. Kotaku.com. Retrieved from https://kotaku.com/5953371/today-is-the-40th-anniversary-of-the-worlds-first-known-video-gaming-tournament

Green, C., & Bavelier, D. (2015). Action video game training for cognitive enhancement. *Current Opinion in Behavioral Sciences, 4*, 103-108.

Hallmen, K., & Geil, T. (2018). eSports—competitive sports or recreational activity? *Sport Management Review, 21*, 14-20.

Hamari, J., & Sjöblom, M. (2017). What is eSports and why do people watch it? *Internet Research, 27*(2), 211-232.

Heitner, D. (2018, July 25). Match-fixing remains a threat to esports community. Retrieved from www.forbes.com/sites/darrenheitner/2018/07/25/match-fixing-remains-a-serious-or-moderate-threat-to-esports-community/#77bf81b765ea

Higgins, C. (2016, July 7). Does the ESIC have the teeth to enforce esports integrity? Retrieved from www.pcgamer.com/does-esic-have-the-teeth-to-enforce-esports-integrity/

High school esports. (2018). Handbook. Version 2018.10.24.

Holden, J., & Echrich, S. (2017, October). Esports, skins betting, and wire fraud vulnerability. *Gaming Law Review*, 566-578.

Holden, J., Kaburakis, A., & Rodenberg, R. (2017). The future is now: Esports policy considerations and potential litigation. *Journal of Legal Aspects of Sport, 27*, 46-78.

Holden, J., Rodenberg, R., & Kaburakis, A. (2017). Esports corruption: gambling, doping, and global governance. *Maryland Journal of International Law, 32*(1), 10, 236-273.

Hollist, K.E. (2015). Time to be grown-ups about video gaming: The rising eSports industry and the need for regulation. *Arizona Law Review, 57*, 823-847.

Horvath, V. (2013, November 11). International eSports Federation overview. Retrieved from www.crwflags.com/fotw/flags/int@iesf.html

Ifrah Law. (2018). The Ifrah guide to esports law: The definitive guide to iGaming in the United States. Retrieved from https://kisacoresearch.com/sites/default/files/documents/esports-download_ifrah.pdf

International e-Sports Federation. (2017, October 11). Statutes. Retrieved from https://www.ie-sf.org/images/9j6q2plki25i/1Fjm3fEACgag0oEuOMGGOQ/96e69683abe60fa6b27b20bd42ad0d27/IeSF_Statutes__As_of_Oct_08_2016_.pdf

IOC News. (2017, October 27). Communique at the Olympic summit. Retrieved from www.olympic.org/news/communique-of-the-olympic-summit

IOC News. (2018, July 23). International Olympic Committee. Olympic movement, esports, and gaming communities meet at the esports forum. Retrieved from www.olympic.org/news/olympic-movement-esports-and-gaming-communities-meet-at-the-esports-forum

Ionica, G. (2017, May 13). French government pass legislation to regulate esports player contracts. Retrieved from https://esportsinsider.com/2017/05/5659/

Is golf a sport? (2013, December 18). *ProCon.org*. Retrieved from http://golf.procon.org/

Kim, E. (2014, August 25). Amazon buys twitch for $970 million in cash. *Business Insider*. Retrieved from www.businessinsider.com/amazon-buys-twitch-2014-8

Lafayette, J. (2018, February 8). Out-of-home count adds 12M Super Bowl viewers. Broadcasting & cable. Retrieved from www.broadcastingcable.com/news/out-home-count-adds-12m-super-bowl-viewers-171669

Lanier, L. (2018, July 23). Esports could be in the Olympics by 2024. *Variety*. Retrieved from https://variety.com/2018/gaming/news/esports-olympics-2024-1202880818/

Li, R. (2016). *Good luck have fun: The rise of eSports*. New York, NY: Skyhorse Publishing.

McGlaun, S. (2011). CRT amusement device from 1947 was world's first video game. Technabob.com. Available at https://technabob.com/blog/2011/05/24/crt-amusement-device-first-video-game

McTee, M. (2014). E-sports: More than just a fad. *Oklahoma Journal of Law and Technology, 10*(1). Retrieved from https://digitalcommons.law.ou.edu/okjolt/vol10/iss1/3

Member nations. (n.d.). International eSports Federation. Retrieved from www.ie-sf.org/about/#member-nations

Members. (n.d.). Global Association of Sport Federations. Retrieved from https://gaisf.sport/members/#

Members and supporters. (n.d.). Esports Integrity Commission. Retrieved from www.esportsintegrity.com/

Morgan, L. (2019, February 25). Liam Morgan: esports is coming to the Olympics after all as Paris 2024 reveal ideas to improve fan engagement. Retrieved from www.insidethegames.biz/articles/1075990/liam-morgan-esports-is-coming-to-the-olympics-after-all-as-paris-2024-reveal-ideas-to-improve-fan-engagement

Mueller, S. (2015, August 12). eSports drug testing update: ESL announces list of banned substances including Adderall, cocaine, pot, steroids and more. *International Business Times*. Retrieved from www.ibtimes.com/esports-drug-testing-update-esl-announces-list-banned-substances-including-adderall-2050245

Needleman, S. (2016, October 6). Wagering with video-game loot draws regulatory scrutiny. *The Wall Street Journal*, p. A1.

New Zoo. (2018). Free 2018 esports market report. Electronic Sport League. Retrieved from https://asociacionempresarialesports.es/wp-content/uploads/newzoo_2018_global_esports_market_report_excerpt.pdf

Nordmark, M. (2018, March 16). Korean Brood War player arrested for match-fixing. Retrieved from https://dotesports.com/starcraft/news/korean-brood-war-rattled-match-fixing-21936

O'Brien, C. (2016, May 3). French government announces plans to legalize and regulate esports industry. *VentureBeat*. Retrieved from https://venturebeat.com/2016/05/03/french-government-announces-plans-to-legalize-and-regulate-esports-industry/

Polacek, S. (2016, April 18). International e-sports federation to apply to be recognized as Olympic sport. *Bleacher Report*. Retrieved from https://bleacherreport.com/articles/2633871-international-e-sports-federation-to-apply-to-be-recognized-as-olympic-sport

Poole, S. (2000). *Trigger happy*. New York: Arcade Publications.

Presentation of the France Esports Association. (n.d.). Retrieved from www.france-esports.org/presentation/

Principles. (n.d.). Esports Integrity Coalition. Retrieved from www.esportsintegrity.com/principles/

Professional esports association launches. (2016, September 8). News. Complexity. Retrieved from www.complexitygaming.com/articles/news/press/4715/professional-esports-association-pea-launches

Ptascynski, J. (2018, January). Esports disputes: Choosing your battleground. *Bird & Bird*. Retrieved from www.twobirds.com/en/news/articles/2018/global/esports-disputes-choosing-your-battleground

Pugatschew, R. (2018, January 22). 13 Overwatch cheaters arrested in South Korea, face jail time. Retrieved from www.nerdmuch.com/games/153331/13-overwatch-hackers-arrested-south-korea/

Roberts, D. (2018, August 22). ESPN says esports is not a fad. *Finance.yahoo.com*. Retrieved from https://finance.yahoo.com/news/espn-says-esports-not-fad-124537864.html

Rodriguez, H., Haag, M., Abner, S., Johnson, W., Glassel, A., Musselman, R., & Wyatt, R. (2016). *The making of eSports champions*. New York, NY: HarperCollins Publishers.

Rosser, J.C., Lynch, P.J., Cuddihy, L., Gentile, D.A., Klonsky, J., & Merrell, R. (2007). The impact of video games on training surgeons in the 21st century. *Archives of Surgery, 142*(2), 181-186.

Schwartz, S. (2018, May 30). Gamers are the new high school athletes: The rise of esports. *Education Week, 37*(33), 19.

Season guide to fall 2018–spring 2019. (2018). College star league. Rules. Retrieved from www.cstarleague.com/lol/rules

Segerra, L. (2019, March 22). Why the Olympic Games are steering clear of e-sports. *Fortune*. Retrieved from https://fortune.com/2019/03/22/esports-olympic-future/

Sheff, D. (2011). *Game over: How Nintendo conquered the world*. New York: Vintage.

Space invaders revel at New York Super Bowl. (2015, June 22). Playing in the world game. 1980 – National "Space Invaders" championship. Retrieved from https://playingintheworldgame.com/2015/06/22/1980-national-space-invaders-championship

Sperdlow, A., & Tangle, U. (2018, September 2). Legalized gambling may have implications for esports. Retrieved from https://venturebeat.com/2018/09/02/legalized-gambling-could-have-major-implications-for-esports

Steinbach, P. (2017, June). Leveraging the eSports popularity boom. *Athletic Business*, 158-160.

Strege, J. (2012, May 29). Is golf a sport? And the answer is . . . it depends. *Golf Digest*. Retrieved from www.golfdigest.com/story/is-golf-a-sport-and-the-answer-isit-depends

Stroud, L.C., Amonette, W.E., & Dupler, T.L. (2010). Metabolic responses of upper-body accelerometer-controlled video games in adults. *Applied Physiology, Nutrition & Metabolism, 35*(5), 643-649. doi:10.1139/H10-058

Stubbs, M. (2016, November 3). WESA introduces arbitration court for eSports. Retrieved from www.mcvuk.com/business/wesa-introduces-arbitration-court-for-esports

Student eligibility. (n.d.). North American esports Federation. Retrieved from www.esportsfed.org/clubs/season-2

Thiborg, J. (2009). *Esports and governing bodies*. Paper presented at the Linköping Electronic Conference in Kultur-Natur, Norrköping Sweden.

2018 fall registration packages. (2018). Retrieved from www.highschoolesportsleague.com/pricing/

Twin Galaxies. (n.d.). *Revolvy*. Retrieved from www.revolvy.com/page/Twin-Galaxies

U.S. Citizenship and Immigration Services. (n.d.). P-1A internationally recognized athlete. Retrieved from www.uscis.gov/working-united-states/temporary-workers/p-1a-internationally-recognized-athlete

Vansyngel, S., Velpry, A., & Besombes, N. (2018, May 21). French esports institutionalization. *Proceedings of the GamiFin Conference*. Pori, Finland, 123-136.

Vincent, B. (2016, September 8). The Professional eSports Association officially launches in 2017. Retrieved from www.engadget.com/2016/09/08/pea-launches-2017-esports/

Wagner, M. (2006). On the scientific relevance of eSports. In *International conference on internet computing*, 437-442. Retrieved from http://citeseerx.ist.psu.edu/viewdoc/download?doi=10.1.1.84.82&rep=rep1&type=pdf

Wang, T. (2018). Understanding esports from the perspective of team dynamics. *The Sport Journal*. Retrieved from http://thesportjournal.org/article/understanding-esports-from-the-perspective-of-team-dynamics

WESA founded. (2016, May 13). Press release, World Esports Association. Retrieved from www.wesa.gg/2016/05/13/world-esports-association-wesa-founded/

WESA structure. (n.d.). Executive board. World Esports Association. Retrieved from www.wesa.gg/structure/

What we do. (n.d.). Esports Integrity Coalition. Retrieved from www.esportsintegrity.com/about-us/what-we-do/

World Esports Association. (2016, August 17). *Arbitration rules.*

Wolmorans, K. (2017, November 27). Arrest warrant issued for former Korea esports association president. Retrieved from www.criticalhit.net/gaming/arrest-warrant-issued-former-korea-esports-association-president

Youngmisuk, O., & Wolf, J. (2018, April 3). How Adam Silver has made his mark on esports in North America. *ESPN.* Retrieved from www.espn.com/esports/story/_/id/23006808/how-adam-silver-made-mark-esports-north-america

Case Study Abstracts

Aspen Institute. (2016). Should the Olympics move back to Athens? Bob Costas' take. Retrieved June 27, 2016, from https://www.youtube.com/watch?v=2lnZvITa5to

Baade, R.A., & Matheson, V.A. (2016). Going for the gold: The economics of the Olympics. *The Journal of Economic Perspectives, 30*(2), 201–218. Retrieved from http://proxy.ussa.edu:2069/10.1257/jep.30.2.201

Bragg, T. (2018, January). Sex tourism in Pattaya: Is the party over? Retrieved from https://asiancorrespondent.com/2018/01/sex-tourism-pattaya-party

Friedman, U. (2016). What if the Olympics were always held in the same city? *The Atlantic.* Retrieved from www.theatlantic.com/international/archive/2016/08/rio-olympics-permanent-host/494264

Harley-Jesson, K. (2017). Our sport is called "SYNCHRONIZED SWIMMING!" Change.org. Retrieved from www.change.org/p/federation-internationale-de-natation-fina-our-sport-is-called-synchronized-swimming

Hyde, M. (2016, Aug. 17). Blame it on the IOC: Its profiteering Olympics has never looked more exploitative. *The Guardian.* Retrieved October 1, 2017, from www.theguardian.com/sport/blog/2016/aug/17/ioc-olympics-profiteering-rio-empty-seats

International Weightlifting Federation 2017 Anti-Doping Policy. (2017, June 15). International Weightlifting Federation. Budapest, Hungary.

Morgan, L. (2019a, June 11). Exclusive: AIBA warned it is on verge of collapse without radical reform as attacks on interim president intensify. *Inside the Games.* Retrieved from www.insidethegames.biz/articles/1080470/exclusive-aiba-warned-it-is-on-verge-of-collapse-without-radical-reform-as-attacks-on-interim-president-intensify

Nair, R. (2019, March 8). Weightlifting: Thailand to host world championships despite voluntary ban. *Reuters.* Retrieved from www.reuters.com/article/us-weightlifting-doping-thailand/weightlifting-thailand-to-host-world-championships-despite-voluntary-ban-idUSKCN1QP155

Patrick, D. (2017, Sept. 9). L.A. Mayor Eric Garcetti: Olympics having a regular rotation of host cities makes sense. *YouTube.* Retrieved from www.youtube.com/watch?v=5F9QPCAK-e4

Wichasin, P., & Wannasuth, S. (2018). Encouraging Thailand as a quality adventurous sport tourism destination for high value tourists for the sustainable competitive advantages. Unpublished paper. Ministry of Tourism & Sport and the Sport authority of Thailand.

Worstall, T. (2016, Aug. 7). Time for a permanent home for the Olympics before it bankrupts another city. *Forbes.* Retrieved October 1, 2017, from www.forbes.com/sites/timworstall/2016/08/07/time-for-a-permanent-home-for-the-olympics-before-it-bankrupts-another-city/#41db971a134f

Index

Note: The italicized *f* and *t* following page numbers refer to figures and tables, respectively.

About the Authors

Bonnie Tiell

Bonnie Tiell, EdD, is a professor of sport management at Tiffin University (TU). She has served as the faculty's NCAA athletic representative, dean of graduate studies, and MBA chair. Prior to her faculty appointment, she served as an administrator and an assistant athletic director. She is a member of the TU Hall of Fame in recognition of her extensive accolades for coaching volleyball, softball, and tennis.

Tiell also serves as a nonresident faculty member for the United States Sports Academy as an instructor in their doctoral program. She routinely travels abroad to instruct in the academy's international sport administration certificate programs. On behalf of the academy and select sport ministries, she has extensive experience working with executives, military leaders, elite coaches, and administrators representing international and national sport federations and associations.

Widely recognized for her contributions to intercollegiate athletic administration and global sport governance, Tiell is the founder and codirector of the Academic Experience with Olympians, a program initiated in Athens, Greece, in 2004 that offers students from around the world the opportunity for on-site study of the organization, supervision, and management of international sport venues and elite competition in an Olympic host city. She is also cofounder of the Women's Leadership Symposium in Intercollegiate Athletics, a program partially financed and now administrated by the NCAA and Women Leaders in College Sports.

Tiell holds a bachelor's degree in physical education from Troy University, a master's degree in sport administration from the University of North Carolina at Chapel Hill, and a doctorate of education in sport management from the United States Sports Academy (USSA). She writes a monthly column for the *Advertiser-Tribune* that focuses on economic, global, and social issues in sport, and she is also the author of the textbook *Human Resources in Sports: A Managerial Approach*.

Kutztown University of Pennsylvania

Kerri Cebula, JD, is an associate professor of sport management at Kutztown University of Pennsylvania. She holds a juris doctorate from Marquette University Law School (MULS), where she also earned the certificate in sports law from the National Sports Law Institute (NSLI). While at MULS, she was a member of the Marquette Sports Law Review and served as a research assistant to Professor Paul Anderson, the director of the NSLI. She also holds a bachelor's degree in political science and justice from American University. She has presented at the conferences of the College Sport Research Institute, the Sport Marketing Association, the Sport and Recreation Law Association, and the European Association of Sport Management. She has been published in the *Journal of Brand Strategy*, *Journal of NCAA Compliance*, and *Concussion Litigation Alert*. Her work also appears in the *Handbook of International Sport Business* and *Sports Leadership: A Concise Reference Guide*.

Prior to coming to Kutztown, Kerri worked as a compliance officer in the athletic departments of Villanova University and the University of Delaware.

About the Contributors

Steve Borawski is an instructor of psychology in the School of Criminal Justice and Social Sciences at Tiffin University, where he was instrumental in developing the esports studies minor. Borawski previously worked in the Cognitive Developmental Neuroscience lab at Boston University's School of Medicine, where his focus was autism research. Borawski previously taught psychology at Bay State College and Anne Arundel Community College, where he served as a full-time faculty member. He received a master's degree from Bowling Green State University with a specialization in cognitive neuroscience.

Shonna Brown is the associate commissioner for business affairs and chief financial officer at Conference USA. Brown previously served as deputy commissioner for the America East Conference, associate commissioner/SWA at the Mid-American Conference, and compliance assistant for the Patriot League. She also served three years as the assistant director of championships at the NCAA and one year as assistant director for corporate partnerships and special events for the Miami Dolphins and Hard Rock Cafe. Brown has a master's degree in sport administration from St. Thomas University and a bachelor of science degree in sport administration from the University of Southern Mississippi. Brown is also a member of Alpha Kappa Alpha Sorority.

Stephen L. Butler, PhD, is the director of the Language Training Detachment at the United States Air Force Special Operations School. Prior to his current post, Butler served as the dean of academic affairs at the United States Sports Academy. Butler also served as site director for Troy University's satellite campus in Augusta, Georgia; director of the Fort Benning campus for Columbus State University; and assistant director for the Office of Teaching, Learning, and Assessment at Auburn University's Harrison School of Pharmacy, where he received his doctorate in administration of curriculum and instruction.

Galen Clavio, PhD, is an associate professor in the Media School at Indiana University, with a scholarly focus on sports media. He also serves as the director of the university's National Sports Journalism Center and is the head of the university's sports media program, which is one of the largest sports media programs in the United States. He has authored over 50 peer-reviewed articles on sport communication, focusing on social media, broadcasting, and journalism. Prior to entering academia, Clavio served as a play-by-play broadcaster, sports reporter, and public relations director for a variety of sport teams and journalistic outlets. Clavio maintains an active professional agenda as a podcaster, serving as cohost of the Indiana University athletics–focused show *CrimsonCast*, and as the producer and engineer for a variety of podcasts focusing on sports media, higher education, and early childhood education.

Dexter Davis, EdD, is an associate professor of sport management and the sport business program coordinator for the University of Tennessee at Martin College of Business and Global Affairs. He also serves as a nonresident faculty member for the United States Sports Academy. Prior to joining the University of Tennessee at Martin faculty in 2013, Davis served as a visiting professor of sport management at York College of Pennsylvania. He is also a former faculty member at Niagara University and Alfred State College, both located in New York. He has coordinated student volunteer services with On Location Experiences at the Super Bowl, GolfWeek Amateur Tour National Championship, and MLB spring training. Davis earned a bachelor of science degree in physical education from Houghton College, a master of science degree in athletic administration from Canisius College, and a doctor of education degree from the United States Sports Academy.

Chloe Goodlive, JD, is an associate attorney at Ward Law Office in Tiffin, Ohio, and formerly worked in the editorial operations department for CAS, an information technology firm in Columbus, Ohio. She received her juris doctorate from The Ohio State University's Moritz College of Law, specializing in intellectual property law.

Scott R. Jedlicka, PhD, is an assistant professor of sport management at Washington State University, where he teaches courses in sport governance, sport in popular culture, and sport ethics. Jedlicka's research examines issues of sport governance and policy in historical contexts. He completed his doctoral studies in sport management at the University of Texas at Austin.

Daniel Kane is an instructor in the tourism and hospitality department at CUNY Kingsborough Community College and also teaches at CUNY

School of Professional Studies. In addition to teaching, Mr. Kane has held the roles of director of resources for educational and employment opportunities at CUNY Kingsborough Community College and events coordinator and pedagogy support for CUNY Institute for Virtual Enterprise. Prior to his career in higher education, he worked in the financial industry for Independence Community Bank and J.P. Morgan Chase. Mr. Kane is also a doctoral student at the United States Sports Academy.

Michael Kidd, PhD, is the Information Technology Program Director at Baker College in Michigan and was formerly an assistant professor of information technology (IT) for Tiffin University, where he served as chair of the bachelor of science IT program and a member of the coaching staff for the esports team. Prior to joining Tiffin University, Kidd spent 15 years building a career in network administration and cyber security, with a focus on enterprise intrusion defense and counter-hacking. Kidd started his career in the U.S. Army as a network support specialist for the U.S. Pacific Command under Admiral Blair from 1999 to 2002. In the gaming world, Kidd was a founding member of the largest and most active *City of Heroes* guild until the games were shut down in 2012. Kidd has been an active member in the esports sector since the late 1990s when he actively participated in *StarCraft* tournaments.

Morgan Fuller Kolsrud is a sports event and volunteer management professional and a member of the 2012 U.S. Olympic Synchronized Swimming Training Squad. Morgan serves as the USOPC Athletes' Advisory Council representative for synchronized swimming and is on the USA Synchro Board of Directors. She currently serves as the head of client success (USA) for Rosterfy, a global event workforce management system. Morgan has extensive event experience, including the 2019 College Football Playoff National Championship, the 2018 Rugby World Cup Sevens, the 2017 and 2015 World University Games, and Super Bowl 50, and she led projects for the 2018 Olympic Winter Games as a contractor for the United States Olympic & Paralympic Committee. Morgan holds a master of arts degree in sport management from the University of San Francisco and a bachelor of arts degree in psychology from Stanford University, where she was a member of the national championship–winning synchronized swimming team.

Justin B. Kozubal is an executive professor and doctoral student in the sport management program at Troy University, where his research focuses on risk management and legal issues in sport. Prior to his transition to academia, Justin spent 25 years

as a sport business practitioner, holding marketing roles with professional sport teams and leagues. He earned his bachelor of science degree in communications at Ball State University and his master of sport administration degree from Ohio University.

Mark S. Nagel, EdD, is a professor of sport and entertainment management in the College of Hospitality, Retail, and Sport Management at the University of South Carolina. He is also the 2016 recipient of the Distinguished Educator Award from the North American Society for Sport Management (NASSM). Prior to joining the faculty at the University of South Carolina, Nagel was the director of the graduate sport management program at Georgia State University and a sport management professor at the University of West Georgia and San Jose State University. He currently serves as an adjunct faculty member at the IE Business School in Madrid, the University of San Francisco, and St. Mary's College of California. Nagel has coauthored eight textbooks. He has served as treasurer for NASSM and the Sport and Recreation Law Association. He has also served as the associate director of the College Sport Research Institute since its creation in 2006. Nagel earned his doctorate from the University of Northern Colorado.

Michael A. Odio, PhD, is an assistant professor in the University of Cincinnati sport administration program and holds a doctorate in sport management from the University of Florida. He teaches courses in sport sales, strategic management, human resources, and experiential learning. Prior to joining the University of Cincinnati, Odio was a program director for the sport and business administration graduate program at the University of Houston.

Daniel A. Rascher, PhD, is a professor and the director of academic programs for the sport management program at the University of San Francisco, where he has taught sports economics and finance as well as business research methods. As president of SportsEconomics and a partner at OSKR, his clients have included organizations involved in professional sports (football, baseball, basketball, hockey, soccer, golf, auto racing, boxing, and mixed martial arts), college sports, endurance sports, sports media, sporting goods, local sport commissions, and various government agencies. Rascher has served on the editorial boards of *Case Studies in Sport Management, Journal of Sport Management, Sport Management Review, International Journal of Sport Finance, International Journal of Sport Management and Marketing,* and *Journal of Quantitative Analysis in Sports.* He has previously taught at Northwestern University, the University of Massachusetts, and the

Instituto de Empresa Business School in Madrid. He has been named a research fellow of the North American Society for Sport Management and also received the Applied Sport Management Association's Lifetime Achievement Award. He is co-owner of the Kansas City Comments indoor soccer team. Rascher earned a doctorate of economics from the University of California at Berkeley.

Jonathan Rosenberg is the director of the sport management and an instructor of business and economics at the College of Mount Saint Vincent in Riverdale, New York. Rosenberg also served as chair of the 2018 Sport and Society: Exploration and Discovery in the 21st Century Conference. Rosenberg previously served as assistant director and adjunct instructor at New York University. He also spent five years as the community outreach coordinator for the New York Mets (MLB). Rosenberg is a doctoral student at the United States Sports Academy.

Cory Schierberl, EdD, CSCS, TSAC-F, is certified by the National Strength and Conditioning Association as a strength and conditioning specialist and a tactical strength and conditioning facilitator. He is the head strength and conditioning coach for the Red Storm women's basketball and softball teams and the University of Rio Grande softball and basketball teams. He was previously employed as the athletic performance director at Force 10 Performance, the official training center of the Seattle Storm (WNBA). He is currently an instructor in the sports and exercise studies department at the University of Rio Grande.

David W. Walsh, PhD, is a clinical assistant professor of sport administration and the director of internships at the University of Houston. He has 14 years of practical experience in the sport industry, with 9 years spent with the marketing and sponsorship departments for the San Antonio Spurs (NBA). Walsh earned his doctorate in sport management from the University of Texas at Austin.

Kelley Walton, JD, is the director of Ohio University's online master of athletic administration program. She is an attorney, professor, and consultant with over 10 years of legal and human resources experience. Kelley worked for the Columbus Blue Jackets (NHL) for its first 10 years of existence, including roles in the legal department and as the director of human resources, where she oversaw the employment of more than 150 full-time and 300 part-time employees. She received a bachelor's degree from Eastern Michigan University and a juris doctorate from Capital University Law School.

Sinsupa Wannasuth (Dr. Mink), PhD, is a professor of customer service and management at Suan Dusit University in Bangkok, Thailand. She is a world-class sailor and a former member of the Thai national sailing team. In addition to teaching, she serves as a consultant for the Thailand Triathlon Federation and the International Committee of the Asian Triathlon Committee.

Jacob M. Ward, JD, is a registered patent attorney and founder of Ward Law Office in Tiffin, Ohio. He is also registered as a nonresident patent agent in Canada and is the author of *Anticipate This! Patent and Trademark Law Blog.* He serves as an adjunct professor for the University of Toledo College of Law and previously taught in the Tiffin University MBA program. He received his juris doctorate with a certificate concentration in intellectual property law from the University of Toledo.

Noemi Zaharia, OLY, a two-time Olympic swimmer (1988 and 1992) with two Olympic medals, represented Romania at all world competitions. She is also the winner of multiple NCAA titles. She currently serves as director of the Aquatic and Fitness Center at Miami Dade College. She is also an adjunct professor of sport management and exercise science at Florida International University and is a doctoral candidate in education of sport management and leadership, with a specialization in coaching, at the United States Sports Academy.

Valentin Cristian Zaharia, OLY, is a 1992 Olympian and World Championship bronze medalist in team handball. He was a national champion and MVP as a professional handball player in Romania, Sweden, France, and Germany. As the head coach of the U.S. men's national team, he won the bronze medal at the Pan Am Games in 2003. Zaharia is an adjunct professor at Florida International University, teaching business courses as part of the sport management degree. He also teaches business courses at Miami Dade College. He holds an MBA from Western Governor's University and a baccalaureate degree in business from Miami Dade College.

Matthew Zimmerman, PhD, is an assistant professor of sport studies in the department of kinesiology at Mississippi State University. Zimmerman previously served as an assistant professor of public relations at Auburn University and as an instructor at Indiana University and Ball State University. He was previously a freelance journalist for *Major League Soccer* magazine and a sports journalist at the *Press-Telegram* (Long Beach) as well as an editorial assistant for the *Daily Breeze* (South Bay). A former Carnegie Fellow with the ABC investigative unit in New York City, Zimmerman earned his doctorate degree in sport management from Indiana University.